The Encyclopaedia Africana

DICTIONARY
OF
AFRICAN
BIOGRAPHY

The *Dictionary of African Biography* is a new 20-volume work of major significance. It is written under the direction of the Secretariat of the *Encylopaedia Africana* Project in Accra, Ghana, directed by Dr. L.H. Ofosu-Appiah. It represents the first tangible outcome of the dream of an African encyclopedia conceived in 1909 by the late Dr. W.E.B. Du Bois, the first Director of the Project.

A total of 137 Sierra Leone and 102 Zaire biographies (living persons not included) by some 40 contributors comprise the second volume of this epoch-making work, which forms a historic landmark in cultural understanding between African and America.

Spanning the centuries, the Dictionary assembles the biographies of African emperors and empresses, kings, queens, statesmen, religious leaders, soldiers, adventurers, politicians, writers, lawyers, merchants, and others who, down the centuries, have influenced the course of events—many of them overlooked by Western literature, but all of special significance.

Each national series of biographies is arranged alphabetically, and is preceded by a special historical introduction, written by a leading national scholar. Each series is also accompanied by a glossary of unfamiliar terms. The articles are cross-referenced, and articles are followed by bibliographies. Each volume is illustrated with pictures and maps and is fully indexed.

DICTIONARY
OF
AFRICAN
BIOGRAPHY

SYMBOL OF WISDOM

This design was drawn for *Encyclopaedia Africana* by the late Kofi Antubam, the Ghanaian artist. The scroll bears traditional Akan symbols, signifying wisdom and applied knowledge. The meaning is expressed by the words *Mate-Masi* ("I have heard and kept"); the maxim: in the depths of knowledge is wisdom.

The Encyclopaedia Africana

DICTIONARY

OF

AFRICAN

BIOGRAPHY

(IN 20 VOLUMES)

VOLUME TWO

SIERRA LEONE—ZAIRE

REFERENCE PUBLICATIONS INC.
218 ST. CLAIR RIVER DRIVE, ALGONAC, MICHIGAN 48001

The Encyclopaedia Africana
DICTIONARY OF AFRICAN BIOGRAPHY

Library of Congress Cataloging in Publication Data

Main entry under title:

Dictionary of African biography.

(The Encyclopaedia Africana)
"Editor-in-chief: L.H. Ofosu-Appiah."
Vol. 2 published in Algonac, Mich.
Includes bibliographical references and indexes.
1. Africa-Biography. I. Ofosu-Appiah, L.H.
II. Series.

DT18.D55   920'.06   76-17954
ISBN 0-917256-01-8 (v.1)

Printed in the United States of America

Library of Congress Catalog Card Number: 76-17954

International Standard Book Number: 0-917256-06-9

THE COUNTRIES OF AFRICA

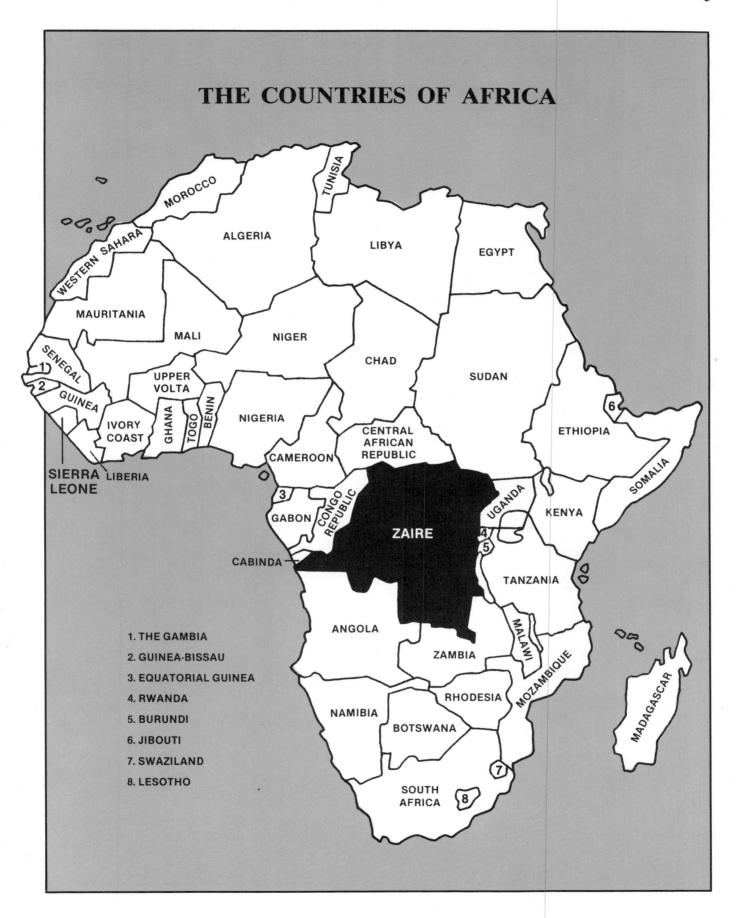

1. THE GAMBIA
2. GUINEA-BISSAU
3. EQUATORIAL GUINEA
4. RWANDA
5. BURUNDI
6. JIBOUTI
7. SWAZILAND
8. LESOTHO

The *ENCYCLOPAEDIA AFRICANA*

DICTIONARY OF AFRICAN BIOGRAPHY

DIRECTOR

L.H. OFOSU-APPIAH

National Chairman for Sierra Leone	Dr. Eldred Jones
National Editor for Sierra Leone	Dr. Arthur Abraham
Deputy National Editor for Sierra Leone	Dr. C. Magbaily Fyle
National Chairman for Zaire	Dr. Ndaywel è Nziem

Editorial Staff

J.O. Vanderpuye	Senior Research Officer
Grace Bansa	German Language Research Officer
E.T. Ashong	Administrative Secretary
Gladys K. Kotie	Secretary

REFERENCE PUBLICATIONS, INC.

Encyclopaedia Africana

DICTIONARY OF AFRICAN BIOGRAPHY Project

L.H. Ofosu-Appiah	*Editor-in-Chief*
Keith Irvine	*General Editor*
John Somers	*Business Manager*
Una Flett	*Sierra Leone Biography Editor*
John C. Yoder	*Zaire Biography Editor*
Edward S. Ayensu Hans Panofsky Ivor Wilks	*Consultants*
Michael Culhane Barbara LePoer	*Picture Research*
Jane Gramer Leona Schunck	*Production*

ACKNOWLEDGEMENTS

Acknowledgements are due to the many persons who have been engaged in the various aspects of writing, editing, and production of this volume, or who have helped in other ways.

Particular thanks are due to Monsignor Tshibang-Tsitsiku, Rector of the National University of Zaire, who made it possible for the Director of the *Encyclopaedia Africana* Project to visit the University of Zaire in 1974, in order to discuss the work with the Zaire National Committee. In consequence, the National Chairman for Zaire, Dr. Ndaywel è Nziem, arranged for the writing of the articles, thus making Zaire the first French-speaking state to be included in a volume of the *Dictionary of African Biography.*

Acknowledgements are also made to the Sierra Leone National Chairman, Dr. Eldred Jones, as well as to Dr. Arthur Abraham, the National Editor for Sierra Leone, whose energy and despatch made possible the completion of the Sierra Leone articles at an early date, together with the dedicated assistance of Dr. C. Magbaily Fyle.

Data for the Concise Guide to Sierra Leone Names and Terms was also provided by Dr. Abraham and Dr. Magbaily Fyle.

Thanks are also due to Yogolelo Tambwe ya Kasimba, for providing data for the Concise Guide to Zaire Names and Terms.

We cannot hope to mention all those who have helped the project forward in various ways, and can only hope that these friends of the Project will forgive us sins of omission. We wish, however among others, to express our gratitude to Rosalind Cole of London, Professor Christopher Fyfe of the Centre for African Studies, Edinburgh University, Scotland, Donald Holsinger of Evanston, Illinois, Jeff Hoover of Washington D.C., Hans Panofsky, Dan Britz, and Mette Shayne of Northwestern University's Africana Library, and Herbert F. Weiss, of Columbia University's Central Africa Project.

CONTRIBUTORS

Arthur Abraham
Division of Social Science, Cuttington University College, Liberia; formerly with History Department, Fourah Bay College, University of Sierra Leone. Author, *Topics in Sierra Leone History* (1976), and *Mende Government and Politics Under Colonial Rule* (1978).
BANGURA, J.A.; BENKA-COKER, S.A.; BUREH, BAI; CAULKER, R.C.B.; CAULKER, T.N.; EASMON, J.F.; EZZIDIO, J.; FAWUNDU, F.; GBANKA; GBANYA LANGO; GULAMA; HORTON, J.A.B. (with C. Magbaily Fyle); HUGHES, W.H.; HUMONYA, MADAM; KABBA SEI; KAI LONDO; KAI SAMBA I; KAI TONGI; KAYAMBA; KISIMI KAMARA; KOGBANDI VANGAHUN; KAPANA LEWIS (with Christopher H. Fyfe); KPOWAMƆ-ei-NƆPƆ; LAMBOI; MAKAVORAY; MANA SIAKA; MANNAH-KPAKA, J.; MARGAI, M.A.S.; MATTURI; MENDEGLA; MOMO JA; MOMO KAI KAI; NDAWA; NJIAMUNDOHUN; NYAGUA; OMARU; POREKERE (with C. Magbaily Fyle); PORTER, A.T.; RAYMOND, W.; SENGBE PIEH; SHORUNKEH-SAWYERR, A.J.; SORI KESSEBEH; TOM KEBBIE SMITH; TUCKER, N.; VA FORAY SASSABLA; WILBERFORCE, D.F.; YOKO, MADAM

Bekimi Bonzeke
Lubumbashi Campus, Université Nationale du Zaire.
MPAGNI

Belepe Bope Mabintch
Lubumbashi Campus, Université Nationale du Zaire.
MISHA miSHYAANG MATUUM; SHYAAM aMBUL aNGOONG (with Ndaywel è Nziem).

Dimandja Luhaka
Lubumbashi Campus, Université Nationale du Zaire.
LUPUNGU; NGONGO LUHAKA; WEMBO NYAMA

Dorothy H. Cummings
Curator, Sierra Leone National Museum
EASMON, M.C.F.

Gustav K. Deveneaux
History Department, Fourah Bay College, University of Sierra Leone.
BOKARI, BOKARI BOMBOLAI (with Cyril P. Foray); DOUGAN, R.; FADUMA, O.; MANKAH, J.; MOMOH SANKOH; MORIBA KINDO BANGURA; SATTAN LAHAI

Elagna Ivari
Lubumbashi Campus, Université Nationale du Zaire.
MABERA, B.(with Ndaywel è Nziem).

Cyril P. Foray
History Department, Fourah Bay College, University of Sierra Leone. Author, *Historical Dictionary of Sierra Leone* (1977).
AKAR, J.J.; BOKARI BOMBOLAI (with Gustav K. Deveneaux); BRESSILAC, M. DE MARION; CARDEW, F.; CLARKSON, J.; FORNA, MOHAMED S.; LANSANA, D.; NEMGBANA, J.F.; RAINY, W.; ROGERS-WRIGHT, C.B.; TAQI, I.B.; TOM II, "KING"; WALLACE-JOHNSON, I.T.A.

Christopher H. Fyfe
Centre of African Studies, University of Edinburgh. Author, *A History of Sierra Leone* (1962), and *Sierra Leone Inheritance* (1964).
FARMA TAMI; GOMBU SMART (KOKO); KPANA LEWIS (with Arthur Abraham); McCARTHY, C.; MACFOY, S.B.A.; NEMGBANA; PETERS, T.; ROGERS, Z.; SIBTHORPE, A.B.C.

C. Magbaily Fyle
History Department, Fourah Bay College, University of Sierra Leone, and Acting Director, Institute of African Studies, University of Sierra Leone. Author, *Almamy Suluku of Biriwa Limba,* (in press).
BA FODAY MANSARAY; BALANSAMA MARA; BAMBAFARA; BALALI; BOSTON, H.J.L.; DUSU SORI; FODAY TARAWALY; FOMGBOE; HEDDLE, C.; HORTON, J.A.B. (with Arthur Abraham); ISA; KARIMU; KEMOKO BALALI; MACAULEY, J.; MANSA KAMA; MARLAY BOKARI; McCORMACK, J.; POREKERE (with Arthur Abraham); SEWA; SMART, C.; SORI SESAY; SULUKU; SAMURA; SUMAN; THOMAS, J.; TOKBA ASANA SAMURA

Hangi Shamamba
Lubumbashi Campus, Université Nationale du Zaire.
(with Yogolelo Tambwe ya Kasimba)
BUSHIRI, L.

Hargreaves, John D.
History Department, University of Aberdeen. Author, *A Life of Sir Samuel Lewis* (1958), and *Prelude to the Partition of West Africa* (1963).
LEWIS, S.

Clifton J. Johnson
Director, Amistad Research Center, Dillard University, New Orleans.
ROOT, B.; TUCKER, T.D.

Eldred D. Jones
Principal, Fourah Bay College, University of Sierra Leone. Author, *Othello's Countrymen* (1965), and *The Writings of Wole Soyinka* (1973).
BALLANTA-TAYLOR, N.J.G.

Pilipili Kagabo
Lubumbashi Campus, Université Nationale du Zaire.
MAKOMBI

Martin H.Y. Kaniki
History Department, University of Tanzania. Co-author, *A Handbook for Teachers*.
HAIDARA KONTORFILLI

K. Khang Zubal, Nk. K.
Lubumbashi Campus, Université Nationale du Zaire.
LUMUMBA, P.E.

Akiwande J. Lasite
Vice-Principal, Sierra Leone Grammar School.
LAWSON. T.G.; PARKES, J.C.E.

Lohaka Omana
NGONGO LETETA (with Tshund'olela Epanya Shamololo).

Lukengu Tshipanda wa Mukenyi
MUKENGE a TUNSELE (with Mumbanza mwa Bawele na Nyabakombi Ensobato).

Lumenga-Neso Kiobe
THYS, A.

Malengu Mubaya
Lubumbashi Campus, Université Nationale du Zaire.
KALALA KAFUMBE

Atiwiya Masikita
Lubumbashi Campus, Université Nationale du Zaire.
MANDRADELE TANZI

Mbasami Mbambi
Institut Supérieur Pedagogique, Kinshasa
SIMS, A.

Mfiri Mapasa
Lubumbashi Campus, Université Nationale du Zaire.
NGANKABI

Mumbanza mwa Bawele na Nyabakombi Ensobato
Lubumbashi Campus, Université Nationale du Zaire.
BADJOKO, J.; BOLANGWA; EBEYA; EDJUMBU; ENSALA; ESEKO; IBAKA; IKENGE; KOLA NGBANI; LELEKA; MALANGA; MOTENGO; MUKENGE A TUNSELE (with Lukengu Tshipanda wa Mukenyi); MUMBENDU; MUMPEMA; MUNGEMBE; MWANANDUNGU; NGALIEMA; NGEMBA; NYAIYONGWA; SEMOPA BAVON

Muteba Kabemba Nsuya
Lubumbashi Campus, Université Nationale du Zaire.
KASONGO KINIAMA; LUMPUNGU: TSHOMBE, M.

Ndaywel è Nziem
Lubumbashi Campus, Université Nationale du Zaire.
ALAVER, R.; BUKASA, L.; BUSIMBA; HENRIQUE; IYONKUM MARCEL; KALALA ILUNGA; KASHAMA N.; LANKWAN, A.; MABERA, B. (with Elagna Ivari); MAKANDA KABOBI; MANUEL, DOM; MBIDI KILUWE; NGONSO, S; NKONGOLO; NSAKU NE VENDA; SHYAAM aMBUL aNGOONG; TARA, P.

N'Dua Solol Kanampumb
Lubumbashi Campus, Université Nationale du Zaire.
CHIBIND YIRUNG; KASONGO NYEMBO I; MUSHID a NAMBING; NAWEJ a DITEND; RUWEJ a NKOND

Dominic Ofori
Library, House of Representatives, Freetown, Sierra Leone.
CAULKER, S.B.; CUMMINGS, E.H.T.; WRIGHT, E.J.

L.H.Ofosu-Appiah
Director, Secretariat, *Encyclopaedia Africana* Project. Author, *The Life and Times of Dr. J.B. Danquah*, (1974), and other works.
RYCKMANS, P.M.J.

Ruduri Kwezi
Lubumbashi Campus, Université Nationale du Zaire.
(with Ruriho Munanira) KAJIGA BALIHUTA

Ruriho Munanira
Lubumbashi Campus, Université Nationale du Zaire.
KAJIGA BALIHUTA (with Ruduri Kwezi).

Sabakinu Kivilu
Lubumbashi Campus, Université Nationale du Zaire.
DISENGOMOKA; KASA-VUBU, J.; KIMBANGU, S.; KINZONZI, A.; MAKITU; MANTANTU DUNDULU

Sikitele Gize a Sumbula
Lubumbashi Campus, Université Nationale du Zaire.
GANDANDA GIBANDA; KALAU, L.; KIKOSO GIBANDA MAFU; KIMBAMBA; KINGWENGWE KIFOFO; KOMBO KIBOKO; MAI MUNENE; MALANGI a PHUMBA; MATEMU a KELENGE; MBUNDU a GAMONI; MIGWA KASANZA; MU-LELE, P.; MUYANGALA; MWATHA KOMBANA; MWENE PUTU KASONGO

David H. Thomas
Classics Department, Fourah Bay College, University of Sierra Leone.
JONES. E.N.

Tshibangu Kabet Musas
Lubumbashi Campus, Université Nationale du Zaire.
KABEY a MWANB (with John C. Yoder); KAN-YIMBU NEWEJ MPEMB; KAPEND TSHOMB; KIMBA, E.; KIWELE, J.; LUKWESA ILUNGA; M'SIRI NGELENGWA; MUTAND YEMBIYEMB; NGAND a BILOND.

Tshund'olela Epanya Shamololo
Lubumbashi Campus, Université Nationale du Zaire.
MOPOIE BANGEZEGINO; NABIEMBALI; NGON-GO LETETA (with Lohaka Omana); ONEMA, MAMA

Tsimba Mabiala
Lubumbashi Campus, Université Nationale du Zaire.
KIMPA VITA; LUKENI; MPANZU a NZINGA; MVEMBA NZINGA; NKANGA LUKENI; NZINGA MPUDI; VITA NKANGA

E. Amadu Turay
History Department, Fourah Bay College, University of Sierra Leone.
BRIMA; DURA I; HAZELEY, P.P.; JOHNSON, P; KANFORI; KNIGHT, C.; KONKO GBAKU; MAY, J.C.; MORLAI LIMBA, PA; RASSIN, ALIMAMY; SARA BAYO; WURIE, A.; YUSUFU, BOMBO LAHAI

Akintola J.G. Wyse
Department of History, Fourah Bay College, University of Sierra Leone.
ABAYOMI-COLE, J.A.; BANKOLE-BRIGHT, H. C.; BARLATT, S.J.S.; BUNJIE, A.; JOHNSON, O.A.; MILLER, F.A.; SHORUNKEH-SAWYERR, J.C.; THOMAS, S.B.; TUBOKU-METZGER, A.E.

John C. Yoder
Social Science Department, North Park College, Chicago. Formerly collected oral histories for the Université Nationale du Zaire.
KABEY a MWANB (with Tshibangu Kabet Musas).

Yogolelo Tambwe ya Kasimba
Lubumbashi Campus, Université National du Zaire.
BUSHIRI (with Hangi Shamamba); LONGANGI; MOPIPI MULONGEKI; MOPIPI MUTIMANA

TABLE OF CONTENTS

Map of Africa...5
Contributors..7

SIERRA LEONE
Sierra Leone: An Historical Introduction by Arthur Abraham and C. Magbaily Fyle.....17
ABAYOMI-COLE, J.A., by Akintola J.G. Wyse......................................35
AKAR, J.J., by Cyril P. Foray...36
BA FODAY MANSARAY, by C. Magbaily Fyle..37
BALANSAMA MARA, by C. Magbaily Fyle...38
BALLANTA-TAYLOR, N.J.G., by Eldred D. Jones...................................38
BAMBAFARA, by C. Magbaily Fyle..39
BANGURA, J.A., by Arthur Abraham..40
BANKOLE-BRIGHT, H.C., by Akintola J.G. Wyse...................................40
BARLATT, S.J.S., by Akintola J.G. Wyse..42
BENKA-COKER, S., by Arthur Abraham..43
BEOKU-BETTS, E.S., by Josephine A. Beoku-Betts...............................43
BALALI, by C. Magbaily Fyle...45
BOKARI, by Gustav K. Deveneaux..46
BOKARI BOMBOLAI, by Gustav K. Deveneaux and Cyril P. Foray....................47
BOSTON, H.J. LIGHTFOOT, by C. Magbaily Fyle...................................48
BRESSILAC, M. DE MARION, by Cyril P. Foray....................................48
BRIMA, by E. Amadu Turay..49
BUNGIE, ALIMAMY, by Akintola J.G. Wyse..50
BUREH, BAI, by Arthur Abraham...50
CARDEW, F., by Cyril P. Foray...52
CAULKER, R.C.B., by Arthur Abraham..54
CAULKER, S.B., by Dominic Ofori...55
CAULKER, T.N., by Arthur Abraham..56
    CINQUE, J. See Sengbe Pieh
CLARKSON, J., by Cyril P. Foray...56
    COLE, J.F. See Gulama, J.
CUMMINGS, E.H.T., by Dominic Ofori..58
DALLA MODU, by Victor Bong Amaazee..58
    DAVIES, W. J. See Faduma, O.
DOUGAN, R., by Gustav K. Deveneaux..60
DURA I, by E.Amadu Turay..60
DUSU SORI, by C. Magbaily Fyle..61
EASMON, J.F., by Arthur Abraham...62
EASMON, M.C.F., by Dorothy H. Cummings..63
EZZIDIO, J., by Arthur Abraham..64
FADUMA, O., by Gustav K. Deveneaux..65
FARMA TAMI, by Christopher Fyfe...66
FAWUNDU, F., by Arthur Abraham..67
FODAY TARAWALY, by C. Magbaily Fyle...68
FOMGBOE, by C. Magbaily Fyle..68
    FORAY KALLON. See Va Foray Sassabla
FORNA, MOHAMED S., by Cyril P. Foray..69
GBANKA, by Arthur Abraham...70
GBANYA LANGO, by Arthur Abraham...70
GOMBU SMART, by Christopher Fyfe..71
GULAMA, J., by Arthur Abraham...72
HAIDARA KONTORFILLI, by M.H.Y. Kaniki...73
HAZELEY, P.P., by E. Amadu Turay..74
HEDDLE, C., by C. Magbaily Fyle...75
HORTON, J.A.B., by C. Magbaily Fyle and Arthur Abraham........................76
HUGHES, W., by Arthur Abraham...79
HUMONYA, MADAM, by Arthur Abraham...79
ISA, by C. Magbaily Fyle..81
JOHNSON, O.A., by Akintola J.G. Wyse..82
JOHNSON, P., by E. Amadu Turay..82
JONES, E.N., by D.H. Thomas...83
KABBA SEI, by Arthur Abraham..85

KAI LONDO, by Arthur Abraham..86
KAI SAMBA I, by Arthur Abraham..88
KAI TONGI, by Arthur Abraham..90
KANFORI, by E. Amadu Turay..92
KARIMU, by C. Magbaily Fyle...92
KAYAMBA, by Arthur Abraham..93
   KEBELAI. *See* Bai Bureh
KEMOKO BILALI, by C. Magbaily Fyle......................................94
KISIMI KAMARA, by Arthur Abraham..95
KNIGHT, C., by E. Amadu Turay...95
KOGBANDI VANGAHUN, by Arthur Abraham....................................96
   KOKELLY, PA. *See* Tom II, ''King''
   KOKO. *See* Gombu Smart
KONKO GBAKU, by E. Amadu Turay..97
KPANA LEWIS, by Arthur Abraham and Christopher Fyfe.....................98
KPOWAMO-ei-NEPO, by Arthur Abraham......................................99
LAMBOI, by Arthur Abraham..100
   LAMINAH SANKOH. *See* Jones, E.N.
LANSANA, D., by Cyril P. Foray...100
LAWSON, T.G., by Akiwande J. Lasite....................................101
LEWIS, S., by John D. Hargreaves.......................................102
MacCARTHY, C., by Christopher Fyfe.....................................104
MACAULEY, J., by C. Magbaily Fyle......................................105
MACFOY, S.B.A., by Christopher Fyfe....................................106
MAKAVORAY, by Arthur Abraham...107
MANA SIAKA, by Arthur Abraham..108
MANKAH, J., by Gustav K. Deveneaux.....................................109
MANNAH-KPAKA, J., by Arthur Abraham....................................109
MANSA KAMA, by C. Magbaily Fyle..110
MARGAI, M.A.S., by Arthur Abraham......................................111
MARLAY BOKARI, by C. Magbaily Fyle.....................................113
MATTURI, by Arthur Abraham...113
MAY, J.C., by E. Amadu Turay...114
McCORMACK, J., by C. Magbaily Fyle.....................................115
MENDEGLA, by Arthur Abraham..117
MILLER, F.A., by Akintola J.G. Wyse....................................117
MOMOH SANKOH, by Gustav K. Deveneaux...................................118
MOMO JA, by Arthur Abraham...120
MOMO KAI KAI, by Arthur Abraham..121
MORIBA KINDO BANGURA, by Gustav K. Deveneaux...........................122
   MORI LAMINA. *See* Bilali
MORLAI LIMBA, PA, by E. Amadu Turay....................................123
   NAIMBANA. *See* Nemgbana,
NAIMBANA, J.F. *See* Nemgbana, J.F.
NDAWA, by Arthur Abraham...124
NEMGBANA, by Christopher Fyfe..125
NEMGBANA, J.F., by C.P. Foray..125
NJIAKUNDOHUN, by Arthur Abraham..126
NYAGUA, by Arthur Abraham..127
OMARU, by Arthur Abraham...128
PARKES, J.C.E., by Akiwande J. Lasite..................................129
PETERS, T., by Christopher Fyfe..131
POREKERE, by C. Magbaily Fyle and Arthur Abraham.......................132
PORTER, A.T., by Arthur Abraham..132
RAINY, W., by Cyril P. Foray...133
RASSIN, ALIMAMY, by E. Amadu Turay.....................................134
RAYMOND, W., by Arthur Abraham...135
ROGERS, Z., by Christopher Fyfe..137
ROGERS-WRIGHT, C.B., by Cyril P. Foray.................................137
ROOT, B., by Clifton H. Johnson..138
SAMURA, by C. Magbaily Fyle..138
SARA BAYO, by E. Amadu Turay...139
   SASSABLA, VA FORAY. *See* Va Foray Sassabla
SATTAN LAHAI, by Gustav K. Deveneaux...................................140
SENGBE PIEH, by Arthur Abraham...141
SEWA, by C. Magbaily Fyle..144

SHORUNKEH-SAWYERR, A.J., by Arthur Abraham..145
SHORUNKEH-SAWYERR, J.C., by Akintola J.G. Wyse...146
SIBTHORPE, A.B.C., by Christopher Fyfe...147
SMART, C., by C. Magbaily Fyle...148
SORI KESSEBEH, by Arthur Abraham...148
SORI SESAY, ALMAMY, by C. Magbaily Fyle..149
SULUKU, ALMAMY, by C. Magbaily Fyle..150
SUMAN, ALMAMY, by C. Magbaily Fyle...152
TAQI, I.B., by Cyril P. Foray..152
THOMAS, J. "MALAMAH," by C. Magbaily Fyle..152
THOMAS, S.B., by Akintola J.G. Wyse..154
TOKBA ASANA SAMURA, by C. Magbaily Fyle..154
TOM II, "KING," by Cyril P. Foray..155
TOM KEBBIE SMITH, by Arthur Abraham..155
TUBOKU-METZGER, A.E., by Akintola J.G. Wyse..156
TUCKER, N., by Arthur Abraham..157
TUCKER, T. DeSALIERE, by Clifton H. Johnson...157
VA FORAY SASSABLA, by Arthur Abraham...158
WALLACE-JOHNSON, I.T.A., by Cyril P. Foray...159
WILBERFORCE, D.F., by Arthur Abraham...161
WRIGHT, E.J., by Dominic Ofori...162
WURIE, A. by E. Amadu Turay..163
YOKO, MADAM, by Arthur Abraham...164
YUSUFU, by E. Amadu Turay..166

Concise Guide to Sierra Leone Names and Terms...168
Sierra Leone Maps...175

ZAIRE

Zaire: An Historical Introduction by Ndaywel è Nziem...................................179
AFONSO I. *See* Mvemba Nzinga
ALAVER, R., by Ndaywel è Nziem..189
ANTONIO I. *See* Vita Nkanga
BADJOKO, J., by Mumbanza mwa Bawele na Nyabakombi Ensobato..............................190
BEATRIZ, DONA. *See* Kimpa Vita
BOLANGWA, by Mumbanza mwa Bawele na Nyabakombi Ensobato.................................191
BUKASA, L., by Ndaywel è Nziem..192
BUSHIRI, by Yogolelo Tambwe ya Kasimba and Hangi Shamamba..............................193
BUSIMBA, by Ndaywel è Nziem...195
CHIBIND YIRUNG, by N'Dua Solol Kanampumb..196
DIOGO I. *See* Nzinga Mpudi
DISENGOMOKA, E.A., by Sabakina Kivilu...197
EBEYA, by Mumbanza mwa Bawele na Nyabakombi Ensobato....................................198
EDJUMBU, by Mumbanza mwa Bawele na Nyabakombi Ensobato..................................198
ENSALA, by Mumbanza mwa Bawele na Nyabakombi Ensobato...................................201
ESEKO, by Mumbanza mwa Bawele na Nyabakombi Ebsobato....................................201
GANDANDA GIBANDA, by Sikitele Gize a Sumbula..202
GARCIA II. *See* Nkanga Lukeni
HENRIQUE, by Ndaywel è Nziem..204
IBAKA, by Mumbanza mwa Bawele na Nyabakombi Ensobato....................................204
IKENGE, by Mumbanza mwa Bawele na Nyabakombi Ensobato...................................206
ILUNGA MBILI. *See* Mbidi Kiluwe
IYONKUM MARCEL, by Ndaywel è Nziem..208
KABEY a MWANB, by Tshibangu Kabet Musas and John C. Yoder..............................209
KAJIGA BALIHUTA, by Ruduri Kwezi and Ruriho Munanira...................................210
KALALA ILUNGA, by Ndaywel è Nziem...211
KALALA KAFUMBE, by Malengu Mubaya...212
KALAMBA. *See* Mukenge a Tunsele
KALAU, L., by Sikitele Gize a Sumbula...213
KANYIMBU NEWEJ MPEMB, by Tshibangu Kabet Musas...214
KAPEND TSHOMB, J., by Tshibangu Kabet Musas..215
KASA-VUBU, J., by Sabakinu Kivilu...216

KASHAMA, N., by Ndaywel è Nziem..220
KASONGO KINIAMA, by Muteba Kabemba..220
KASONGO NYEMBO I, by N'Dua Solol Kanampumb..................................222
KIKOSO GIBANDA MAFU, by Sikitele Gize a Sumbula.............................223
KIMBA, E., by Tshibangu Kabet Musas...224
KIMBAMBA, by Sikitele Gize a Sumbula..226
KIMBANGU, S., by Sabakitu Kivilu..227
KIMPA VITA, by Tsimba Mabiala...229
KINGWENGWE KIFOFO, by Sikitele Gize a Sumbula...............................230
KINZONZI, A., by Sabakinu Kivilu..231
KIWELE, J., by Tshibangu Kabet Musas..232
KOLA NGBANDI, by Mumbanza mwa Bawele na Nyabakombɪ Ensobato..................233
KOMBO KIBOKO, by Sikitele Gize a Sumbula....................................233
LANKWAN, A., by Ndaywel è Nziem...234
LELEKA, by Mumbanza mwa Bawele na Nyabakombi Ensobato.......................234
LONGANGI, by Yogolelo Tambwe ya Kasimba.....................................236
LUKENI, by Tsimba Mabiala...237
LUKWESA ILUNGA, by Tshibangu Kabet Musas....................................238
LUMPUNGU, by Mutaba Kabemba Nsuya...240
LUMUMBA, P.E., by K. Khang Zubal, Nk. K.....................................242
LUPUNGU, by Dimandja Luhaka...247
MABERA BENOIT, by Ndaywel è Nziem and Elagna Ivari..........................248
MAI MUNENE, by Sikitele Gize a Sumbula......................................249
MAKANDA KOBOBI, by Ndaywel è Nziem..250
MAKITU, by Sabakinu Kivilu..251
MAKOMBE, by Pilipili Kagabo...252
MALANGA, by Mumbanza mwa Bawele na Nyabakombi Ensobato......................253
MALANGI a PHUMBA by Sikitele Gize a Sumbula.................................254
MANDRADELE TANZI, by Atiwiya Masikita.......................................255
MATANTU DUNDULU, by Sabakinu Kivilu...256
MANUEL DOM, by Ndaywel è Nziem..257
MATEMU a KELENGE, by Sikitele Gize a Sumbula................................258
MBIDI KILUWE, by Ndaywel è Nziem..259
MBUNDU a GAMONI, by Sikitele Gize a Sumbula.................................259
MIGWA KASANZA, by Sikitele Gize a Sumbula...................................261
MISHA MISHYAANG MATUUM, by Belope Bope Mabintch.............................261
MOPIPI MULONGEKI, by Yogolelo Tambwe ya Kisimba.............................262
MOPIPI MUTIMANA, by Yogolelo Tambwe ya Kasimba..............................264
MOPOIE BANGEZEGINO, by Tshund'olela Epanya Shamololo........................265
MOTENGO, by Mumbanza mwa Bawele na Nyabakombi Ensobato......................265
MPAGNI, by Bekimi Bonzeke...266
MPANZU a NZINGA, by Tsimba Mabiala..267
M'SIRI NGELENGWA, by Tshibangu Kabet Musas..................................268
MUKENGE a TUNSELE, by Lukengu Tshipanda wa Mukenyi and Mumbanza mwa Bawele na
    Nyabakombi Ensobato...270
MULELE P., by Sikitele Gize a Sumbula.......................................272
MUMBENDU, by Mumbanza mwa Bawele na Nyabakombi Ensobato.....................274
MUMPEMA, by Mumbanza mwa Bawele na Nyabakombi Ensobato......................275
    MUNDELE FUNJI. *See* Matemu a Kelenge
MUNGEMBE, by Mumbanza mwa Bawele na Nyabakombi Ensobato.....................276
MUSHID a NAMBING, by N'Dua Solol Kanampumb..................................277
MUTAND YEMBIYEMB by Tshibangu Kabet Musas...................................278
MUYANGALA, by Sikitele Gize a Sumbula.......................................279
MVEMBA NZINGA, by Tsimba Mabiala..280
MWANANDUNGU, by Mumbanza mwa Bawele na Nyabakombi Ensobato..................281
    MWANZA KASONGO. *See* Ngongo Leteta
MWATHA KOMBANA, by Sikitele Gize a Sumbula..................................282
MWENE PUTU KASONGO, by Sikitele Gize a Sumbula..............................283
NABIEMBALI, by Tshund'olela Epanya Shamololo................................285
NAWEJ a DITEND, by N'Dua Solol Kanampumb....................................286
NGALIEMA, by Mumbanza mwa Bawele na Nyabakombi Ensobato.....................287
NGAND a BILOND, by Tshibangu Kabet Musas....................................288
NGANKABI, by Mifiri Mapesa..289
NGEMBA, by Mumbanza mwa Bawele na Nyabakombi Ensobato.......................290
NGONGO LETETA, by Tshund'olela Epanya Shamololo and Lohaka Omana............292
NGONGO LUHAKA, by Dimandja Luhaka...294

NGONSO, S. by Ndaywel è Nziem...295
NKANGA LUKENI, by Tsimba Mabiala.......................................295
NKONGOLO, by Ndaywel è Nziem...297
   NLEMVO. *See* Mantantu Dundulu
NSAKA ne VUNDA, by Ndaywel è Nziem.....................................297
NYAIYONGWA, by Mumbanza mwa Bawele na Nyabakombi Ensobato............298
NZINGA MPUDI, by Tsimba Mabiala..299
ONEMA, MAMA, by Tshund'olela Epanya Shamololo..........................300
RUWEJ a NKOND, by N'Dua Solol Kanampumb.................................300
RYCKMANS, P.M.J., by L.H. Ofosu-Appiah....................................301
SEMOPA BAVON, by Mumbanza mwa Bawele na Nyabakombi Ensobato...........303
SHYAAM aMBUL aNGOONG, by Belepe Bope Mabintch and Ndaywel è Nziem......304
SIMS, A., by Mbasami Mbambi...305
TARA PLACIDE, by Ndaywel è Nziem...306
THYS, A., by Lumenga-Neso Kiobe...307
TSHOMBE, M., by Muteba Kabemba Nsuya......................................309
VITA NKANGA, by Tsimba Mabiala...312
WEMBO NYAMA, by Dimandja Luhaka..313

Concise Guide to Zaire Names and Terms....................................315
Zairian Geographic Names..328
Chronologies of the Kings of Kongo and the Ant Yav (rulers) of Lunda......329
Zaire Maps..330
Index...334

SIERRA LEONE — AN HISTORICAL INTRODUCTION

Arthur Abraham and C. Magbaily Fyle

Sierra Leone is a small country, roughly circular in shape, and occupying the southwest coast of West Africa between 6° 55' and 10° N latitude, and 10° 16' to 13° 8' W. It is 27,925 sq mi (72,326 sq km) in area, with a coastline extending for 212 mi (339 km) along the Atlantic Ocean. Sierra Leone is bordered on the north and northeast by the Republic of Guinea, while Liberia spans its southeastern boundary.

In relief, Sierra Leone is varied, especially for its small size. Entering the Sierra Leone harbor from outside, the mountainous peninsula would suggest to the observer that the entire country is extremely rugged. But immediately behind the hilly peninsula is a low coastal plain extending for a considerable distance, but rising sharply northeastwards into the Loma Mountains. The highest peak of these mountains, the Bintumane, is 6,390 ft (1,948 m) in height, being the highest mountain in West Africa west of the Cameroons. The plains are dotted with isolated hills and are strewn with swamps, which are found in shallow valleys and depressions.

Climatically, Sierra Leone falls within the tropical region. There are two seasons—the rainy season from May to October, and the rest of the year, which constitutes the dry season. The rainy season enjoys a mean annual rainfall of more than 80 inches (203 cm), while temperatures of about 80°F (27°C) are experienced throughout the year, but rising to about 95°F (45°C) in the dry season. The latter season also includes the harmattan period—December and January—when cold dry winds from the Sahara bring temperatures to as low as 55°F (13°C), especially in the north. There is, however, a high humidity of about 70 percent average throughout the year.

Three main types of vegetation can be distinguished in Sierra Leone. The most typical vegetation of the coast is mangrove swamp, now being extensively cleared for cultivation. Similar clearings have been made in the once-dense rain forest of the wetter South, though some preservation now occurs in, for example, the Gola forest, in the southeastern hill country near the Liberian frontier. Moving northwards towards drier areas, one encounters savanna grassland, interspersed with farm "bush" country, where much cattle keeping is done.

CONNOTATIONS OF "SIERRA LEONE"

Historically, the term Sierra Leone bears different connotations in the minds of many. The present political boundaries of Sierra Leone, like those of all African countries, are a product of European imperialism. In the 15th century Sierra Leone was the name given to the mountainous peninsula by the Portuguese who are said to have been the first Europeans to land here. After the establishment of a British colony in this peninsula in the late 18th century, the name Sierra Leone came to refer to that colony. Up until the late 19th century, the colony was gradually extended by treaties purporting to cede certain adjacent areas and islands to the British. These areas included the Sherbro, parts of Koya country, Bunce, Banana and Tasso Islands, and the estuary of the Rokel River. The Sierra Leone of today came to include what was referred to in the 19th century as the hinterland, or the interior of the colony. This hinterland spilled over present-day boundaries to include places like Futa Jallon and Melacourie—areas where the British continued to exert considerable influence until the 1890s. The boundaries were demarcated by agreements between the governments of Britain, France, and Liberia, beginning in 1895. The present boundaries were finally ratified in 1917.

MIGRATION AND SETTLEMENT

This geographical area of present-day Sierra Leone, before the foundation of the colony, included a number of ethnic groups widely dispersed over its mountains and plains, Among the oldest inhabitants of the coastal area are the Bullom, together with other ethno-linguistically related West Atlantic groups, such as the Gola in the south, the Kissi in the east, the Baga and Nalou in the northeast. The traditions of the Temne, another early group (though apparently not so long established as the others named), indicate that they came from Futa Jallon, the mountainous region in what is now Guinea, having been driven from there by warlike neighbors. They gradually spread southwards from the Scarcies valley, coming to live beside the coastal Baga.

A reorganization of these coastal groups occurred due to the invasion of a Mande-speaking people called the Mani, in the middle of the 16th century, which also gave rise to the largest ethnic group in Sierra Leone, the Mende. The Mani were a Mandinka group emanating from the Mali Empire, whose leader, a queen named Masarico, is said to have been exiled by the *Mansa* (king) of Mali. Masarico led her followers first southwards, then westwards until they finally made a base in the Cape Mount area of Liberia by the 1540s. From this area, their armies were sent out to subjugate most parts of the present-day Sierra Leone hinterland, thereby creating sub-kingdoms owing allegiance to the parent one. Often if the sub-kingdoms failed to recognize their obligation to the headquarters at Cape Mount, a further invasion was sent against such entities. Thus successive waves of Mani invasions, sometimes 20 years apart, led to further settlement and often the creation of a new ethnic group.

The Temne

Temne traditions speak of Farma Tami (*q.v.*), who came from the east, as having been the one who first organized them as an important political group. Farma has been identified as a 16th-century Mani king of this area of Temne country. He brought a number of coastal groups, probably as well as some others, such as the Loko and Limba, together in a loose political structure generally known as the Sapi Confederacy of which he became king. This polity had a formalized structural hierarchy which survived Farma. When he died, he was buried at Robaga (the name suggesting Temne settlement in Baga country—the prefix "ro" in Temne meaning "at"). This became the burial place of all kings of Koya who now took the title of Bai Farma—the Temne kingly title of "Bai" being added to Farma's name.

The Loko

When during his lifetime Farma became too independent of the Cape Mount base, another Mani invasion was sent against him. The effect of the settlement of the Mandinka elements of this invasion on the West Atlantic groups neighboring the Temne is said to have given rise to the Loko. Farma's invading groups had been assimilated by the Temne. But the Mandinka element of this second invasion predominated over the West Atlantic to give rise to the Loko group which has a language very similar to Mende. The Loko are still remembered today by the Gbandi of Liberia, a Mande group, as their brothers who went west.

The Sherbro

A southern Bullom group called the Sherbro apparently came to be so called because of a Mani king, Sherabola, who lived on Sherbro Island in the 18th century. The contact with the Mande element gave rise to the Sherbro language, slightly different from that of the Bullom. The territory was originally referred to as Sherbro to differentiate it from the northern Bullom area, but over time has come to denote the people themselves.

An ivory salt cellar with a lid, which was carved by Bullom craftsmen to Portuguese specifications.

The Mende

The largest ethnic group to emerge from the Mani invasion in the Cape Mount area was the Mende, another product of a mixture of Mani with a West Atlantic Bullom/Gola substratum. It was only in the 18th century that the Mende began moving west of the Sewa River, in south Sierra Leone, in small invading bands. The first dynamic move of the Mende into the Sierra Leone hinterland proper apparently occurred by the early 19th century. It is identified with the Kpaa-Mende (a subgroup), who pressed the original inhabitants, the Banta, southwards to form the Mendenized state of Bumpe (usually referred to as Banta).

Taken in all, then, the Mani invasions, though they had some deleterious effects on the original people—such as, for example, the disappearance of certain skills, such as ivory carving among the Bullom—gave a more variegated picture to the ethnic scene. They also had some useful social and economic effects by stimulating better metal working and probably cloth weaving.

The Limba

The other streams of migration came into the Sierra Leone hinterland more directly from the north. The Limba are another old group in Sierra Leone having been, it appears, around the Wara Wara hills since at least the 8th century. They may originally have come from the Futa Jallon mountains, which area was indeed a point of dispersal of various ethnic groups towards the Atlantic coast. From the Wara Wara hills, the Limba spread southwards and westwards to occupy areas of Temne and Loko country.

The Soso

The Limba were later affected culturally by other incoming groups. The more northwesterly, which became the Sela Limba and Tonko Limba, were invaded by the Soso (Susu), another Mande group found in the extreme northwest of Sierra Leone. The Soso identify themselves in their traditions with the 13th-century Soso empire of Sumanguru in the western Sudan. They claim to have moved towards the Atlantic coast through Futa Jallon after the breakup of Sumanguru's empire. The Soso, who are found more predominantly in the coastal areas of the Republic of Guinea, settled also among the Temne and this has created a particular Soso strain among the Temne of the present-day Kambia and Port Loko districts. In fact, the Soso virtually assumed control of the Temne around Port Loko in the 18th century until they were ousted by the Temne in 1816.

The Koranko

Newer Mande-influenced clans emerged among other Limba sub groups like the Wara Wara and Biriwa. This time they were affected by Mandinka elements from Mali, most likely the Koranko. This latter group, a branch of the Mandinka, (their languages being inter-intelligible), settled by the 15th century east of the Upper Niger, in Sankaran country in the present-day Republic of Guinea. From there Koranko elements started entering Sierra Leone, the major migration being led by Mansa Morifing of the Mara clan but involving also Koroma and Kagbo Koranko clans. The major thrust of the Kagbo clan by the early 16th century, led by Mansa Kama (q.v.), moved deeply into the Sierra Leone hinterland, probably reaching the Atlantic coast. This brought strong Koranko connections with more southerly peoples like the Temne who were spreading eastwards. In due course, Mansa Kama died and was buried at Rowala in what is today Temne country. The eastern Temne today retain a markedly strong Koranko cultural influence. It was perhaps smaller movements of Koranko clans that gave rise to the Konte, Mara, and Mansaray clans of the Wara Wara and Biriwa Limba.

Yalunka, Kono, and Vai

Towards the extreme northeast, the Yalunka, a Mande group, fanned out of Futa Jallon to form disparate settlements, later receiving other Mandinka elements by the 17th century and, in conflict with the Fula of Futa Jallon, formed a strong state called Solimana by the late 18th century. There were other Mande movements like the Kono/Vai group which is said to have entered the Sierra Leone hinterland from the north before the 15th century. Kono and Vai are mutually intelligible languages, and both groups are said to have originally been a single entity. In the area of present day Kono country, the group is said to have split up, the one remaining behind being told "Mu-kon" by the moving group, meaning "wait here." So the Kono got their name. The moving group, the Vai, reached the Atlantic coast where the Portuguese met them in the mid-15th century. The Portuguese called their country Gallinas (Gallina meaning hen), because of a preponderance of chicken in what became Vai country.

EUROPEAN CONTACTS: THE FOUNDING OF THE SIERRA LEONE COLONY

While all these developments were taking place in the interior, Europeans were establishing links with the peninsula which eventually culminated in the establishment of the Colony of Sierra Leone in 1787.

Portuguese explorers were stopping at the peninsula as early as the middle of the 15th century and the estuary of the Sierra Leone (Rokel) River quickly became known as a fine natural harbor and a place for obtaining fresh water.

More regular contacts were established through trade, with gold, ivory, and more especially slaves being exchanged by the local inhabitants for European manufactured goods. Between 1482 and 1495, the Portuguese built a fort on the site of modern Freetown where their traders settled. Some Portuguese then went inland and took African wives. The offspring of such unions came to constitute a privileged group of traders and factors. Attempts were also made by the Portuguese to convert the Africans to Christianity. Father Balthazar Barreira of the Roman Catholic Jesuit order came to Sierra Leone in 1605. He was well received and allowed to build a church near Kru Bay, in the vicinity of modern Freetown. His attempts to convert the Soso were, however, a complete failure and he left disappointed in 1610. Subsequent attempts throughout the 17th century similarly met with failure. By the end of the century, regular mission work had been given up completely.

Trade contacts, chiefly in slaves, continued

An old print showing the Province of Freedom. The inscription reads: "A view of Sierra Leone River, from St. George's Hill, where the Free Black settlement was made in the year 1787."

however, and from the 17th century the British took the lead. They built trading depots (called factories, because they were managed by factors, or commercial agents), which were strongly fortified. Rent was paid to local rulers for these forts or factories. The English crown granted monopolies to merchants to maximize profits and reduce smuggling. Thus a number of British companies, such as the Royal African Company and the Royal Adventurers of England Trading to Africa, received charters and traded on the Sierra Leone coast with varying degrees of fortune. Employees of these companies as well as other big English traders married African women, often daughters of rulers or powerful men, and their descendants often claimed and won rights to rule. Thus there came into existence some of the best known coastal families of Sierra Leone today, such as the Caulkers, the Tuckers, the Rogers (Kpakas), and others.

The Founding of the Sierra Leone Colony

But the major impact of British links with the coast was to be the birth of the Sierra Leone Colony. The activities of a few individuals in England, such as the philanthropist Granville Sharp (1735-1813), led to the much talked of Mansfield Judgement of 1772, emphasizing that the state of slavery was not recognized in English law. This at once released a number of slaves in England who began to constitute a social problem. A group of humanitarians in England, including Sharp and the politician William Wil-

berforce (1759-1833), formed an anti-slavery movement to try and find a home in Africa for these freed slaves. But to imagine that humanitarianism alone was responsible for creating the conditions that led to the founding of the Colony of Sierra Leone would be a distortion of history. The greatest slavers in the previous two centuries, the British, were suffering declining economic fortunes in the later 18th century, particularly as competition from the French sugar islands, especially San Domingo (now Haiti and the Dominican Republic), became more severe. The "West India Interest," a powerful group based on slave-operated plantations in the West Indies and North America, which was reputed to be able to bring down a government in Whitehall if it decided to vote against it, began to relax its attitude toward slavery and the slave trade. Absentee landlordism, bad management, soil exhaustion, and many other factors had increased production costs and reduced profits considerably. Consequently the price of sugar from Jamaica, the British sugar island, rose proportionately. The French islands, on the other hand, were producing cheaper sugar, and an inchoate industrial Britain preferred to buy its food at the cheapest price. The West India Interest did not oppose the proposals of the humanitarians to repatriate the ex-slaves, although they consistently voted against the British abolition of the slave trade. On the suggestion of Dr. Henry Smeathman (17?-1786), a botanist who had visited Sierra Leone, the British government selected the Sierra Leone Peninsula. Thus in 1787 the first batch was repatriated, together with some white women, and settled on a piece of land obtained from the Temne rulers of the peninsula.

This was initially not a British colony. It was a self-governing entity called the Province of Freedom equipped with an idealistic constitution drafted by Granville Sharp and with a government run by the settlers themselves. But this first settlement failed and was abandoned in 1789 largely because of the hostile environment and hostile neighbors. Sharp persisted in his efforts to rehabilitate these former slaves. Consequently, shortly afterwards the Sierra Leone Company was chartered to finance the settlement, under the direction of a banker, Henry Thornton. A number of slaves who had been freed in Nova Scotia as a reward for their loyalty to the British during the American War of Independence (1776-83), were now transported to Sierra Leone to join some of the original settlers. The company took over the administration of the settlement and in 1792 appointed Lt. John Clarkson (*q.v.*) as the first governor.

In 1800, another group known as the Maroons, from Jamaica, joined the two other groups, thus swelling the population. In origin, the Maroons were mostly from Asante (Ashanti) in what is now Ghana. In Jamaica, they had escaped into the mountains, become marooned there, and had then constantly harassed the Jamaican administration. They arrived in Sierra Leone at a particularly auspicious moment for the company which was faced with a rebellion of Nova Scotians arising from accumulated grievances over land allotments, quit-rents, and other matters. The Maroons readily assisted the company to suppress the revolt.

In 1808, the British government took over the settlement as a Crown Colony. Almost from the beginning, the company had been in financial straits, as most attempts to increase revenue, for example by growing cash crops, had failed. Its request to the British government to take over the administration was accepted because, with the abolition of the slave trade imminent, the British needed a West African naval base. This base was to become the home port of the naval squadrons assigned to arrest slave ships, as well as the seat of an Admiralty court to try the slavers who were caught. When the Abolition Bill was being passed in the British Parliament in 1807, the West India Interest, whose profit had been reduced to zero, voted in favor. The Admiralty Court in Sierra Leone was transformed into a Court of Mixed Commission when Britain got other nations similarly to proscribe the slave trade. In this way the court was able to try all nationals whose countries had anti-slave-trade treaties with Britain.

The village of Bathurst in the mountains south of Free-town in the earlier 19th century. Named for the 3rd Earl of Bathurst (British secretary of state for war and the colonies from 1812-27, who was intimately involved in the abolition of the slave trade), Bathurst gave its name to the neighboring village of Leopold, with which it was amalgamated in 1825.

The Recaptives

The British squadron patrolled the whole West African coast, and brought offending ships to Freetown, as the capital of Sierra Leone had been named in 1792. In Freetown, after adjudication, the captives were set free. These people—first captured and enslaved, then recaptured on the high seas and subsequently freed—were known as Recaptives or Liberated Africans. They added a new element in the population to that of the original westernized settlers. Many of the Recaptives were of Yoruba origin. But there were others from the Congo and elsewhere, and even some Kissi Recaptives from Sierra Leone itself. These were settled in places surrounding the colony which often bore the names of their areas of origin. Eventually thousands of Recaptives—more than 40,000 by 1850—swelled the colony's population. Many villages were founded, where Recaptives usually practiced their original modes of living.

Largely through thrift and industry, many of the Recaptives broke into the snobbish and hitherto exclusive domain of the settlers of Freetown. They became wealthy through trade, bought property in Freetown, intermarried with the settlers, became Christians and assumed some western habits. By the second half of the 19th century, this breaking into the preserve of the settlers had ushered in a fusion of the two groups—Recaptives and Settlers—to give rise to the Krios (Creoles). Krio culture became a fusion of the indigenous customs of the Recaptives—mainly

Yoruba—and westernized habits of the settlers, coupled with missionary and Victorian values brought in through the colonial experience.

DEVELOPMENTS IN THE INTERIOR: THE 18th AND 19th CENTURIES

Meanwhile developments in the interior were leading towards the consolidation of some relatively extensive polities as well as intricate commercial networks. This was to have considerable implications for relations between the hinterland and the Sierra Leone Colony, and indeed was later to result in the establishment of colonial rule over the rest of what is today Sierra Leone.

Political Organization

The creation of the Yalunka state of Solimana in the late 18th century has already been mentioned. The state was centered around the capital, Falaba. The manga (ruler) ruled the state and initially also the capital, aided by an assembly of elders. Various Yalunka khoris (countries) which constituted the state, were ruled in all internal matters by their own tamangana (town rulers). Various rights of appeal, inter-khori relations, declarations of war and similar questions, were, however, subject to the authority of the ruler. Large areas of Koranko country were also part of Solimana, but only insofar as Solimana could exercise a dominant influence and obtain regular tribute. The state of Solimana lasted until 1884, when it was destroyed by the forces of the Mandinka warrior, Samori Touré.

Many precolonial states of varying sizes in the Sierra Leone hinterland were organized along similar lines. Another strong and extensive state ruled by Almamy Suluku (q.v.), existed among the Limba of Biriwa in the second half of the 19th century. By the mid-19th century the Koranko had relatively smaller polities, but these were linked in a kind of psycho-political chain with Morifindugu, which had apparently been their point of dispersal into the Sierra Leone hinterland. Though the ruler of Morifindugu—who, in the second half of the 19th century was Marlay Bokari (q.v.)—did not rule these other Koranko states, the latter often resorted to Morifindugu in times of difficulty.

By the later 19th century, state organization among the Mende followed one or the other of two patterns. One type was based on the personality of the ruler, and included such states as those under Kai Londo (q.v.) of Luawa, Nyagua (q.v.) of Panguma, Mendegla of Joru (q.v.), and Makavoray of Tikonko (q.v.). These tended to be amorphous, and territory could be added to or taken away from them depending

One of the few remaining examples of the thatched cottages built in Freetown by the early settlers.

on the forcefulness of the king. The other type had relatively fixed territorial limits and existed as it was despite the activities of the ruler, who was more or less a primus inter pares ("first among equals"). Rulers in the latter type of state—a category which included Sherbro, Gallinas, Bumpe, and Kpaa-Mende—did not assume the dominant position held by rulers in the amorphous states. In all states, however, walled towns with open fakais (farm settlements) were grouped into countries, and a number of these later constituted the state. The Sherbro was a strong state in the 18th century, ruled by the Bai Sherbro (king), who lived on the Sherbro Island. But by the close of the 19th century it had become a Mendenized and declining polity whose provincial rulers were virtually independent of the Bai, although they still paid homage to him.

Succession to high office was basically similar in both types of state, though slight variations existed. It was generally based on a demonstration of some outstanding quality, usually leadership in war, but a successful moriman (charm-maker priest) could become a ruler. Among the Mende this did not mean that rulers came from a "ruling family," except that members of certain families had more opportunities to demonstrate the necessary prowess. In some other areas, in the territories of the Koranko and Limba, candidates for high office had to demonstrate such qualities, but usually also had to belong to a ruling family.

Internal Commercial Organization and Interior Wars

Many of these polities were linked with each other by commercial needs. Internal modes of exchange involved the use of commodities produced locally as well as from distant states or towns. Labor was exchanged for goods, as was expertise. Travelling

Goods traveled long distances over the trade routes of the interior. Here, where a route runs over a river, it was spanned by a hammock bridge.

Yalunka blacksmiths visited Koranko country on contract. Later, Koranko smiths made similar visits to Mende country. Manufactured goods, such as country cloth, soap, or hoes, were traded extensively. Certain goods were traded over long distances, passing through a number of states. These included gold, cattle, and cotton. Gold was traded from Bouré in the upper Niger to various areas of the Sierra Leone hinterland. Cotton from Sankaran, now across the frontier in central Guinea, found its way to Limba country where it was exchanged for cattle from Futa Jallon. Kono cloth was valued as far away as the state of Biriwa Limba, ruled by Almamy Suluku, while Sankaran cloth was famed in distant Freetown. International markets to handle the trade also developed in the interior. In the 19th century, there were, for instance, such markets at Katimbo in Biriwa Limba, at Koindu in Kissi country, at Falaba in Solimana, and at other places. Indigenous currency systems emerged as well, for example in the Kissi/Mende areas.

Wars in the interior did not often affect this trade, despite the strong belief to the contrary of the colonial administration in Sierra Leone. Centers of strong political authority became areas of protection for trade routes. Wars were sometimes fought, as among the Temne in the late 18th and 19th centuries, for the control of important trading areas such as the headwaters of navigable rivers. Sometimes rulers in the interior, such as Sattan Lahai (q.v.) in Kambia, on the Great Scarcies River in the northwest, deliberately blocked trade routes for political reasons.

But this did not always stop the trade, nor, often, did political wars. Stoppages were often temporary, and alternative routes were quickly developed in areas where a continuous stoppage occurred. In 1877, for instance, the Limba of Yagala destroyed the way station at Kabala on the important Falaba-Bumban-Port Loko trade route. The ruler of Kabala, Boltamba, quickly teamed up with Suluku of Biriwa Limba to found another route. What often created the alarm was that those at one end of a particular route, for example the Krio traders at Kambia, who were affected by Sattan Lahai's activities, made a major issue of the matter. The economic difficulties of the 1870s and 1880s were quickly blamed on the interior wars, and not on the world trade depression which prevailed at that time. In fact, the volume of exported produce increased in these periods, although the value declined. In 1875, a war waged by Mende professional warriors spilled over into "British Sherbro." Governor Sir Samuel Rowe (term of office 1885-88) determined to teach the Mende a lesson for violating "British territory." He led an expedition to the Bagru region in Sherbro country, entered into an agreement with the Mende never to hire out warriors, and fined them 10,000 bushels of rice (because, he said, "the country is one immense rice farm").

Relations with the Interior

It was primarily the trade from the interior that led to the development of relations between the Colony and the hinterland beyond it. By the early 19th century, it had become evident to the colonial administration in Sierra Leone, as well as to its inhabitants, the trade with the interior was the key factor in the colony's economy. The authorities therefore began to promote this trade. In Freetown, a newspaper, *The Royal Gazette and Sierra Leone Advertiser,* was founded in 1808, and gave much of its space to reporting situations in the interior, which were felt to affect trade. It also paid attention to areas where gold and other commodities were plentiful. Traders coming from the far interior were well treated by the authorities, and their visits widely publicized.

The administration also tried hard to promote good relations with rulers in the interior. Expeditions, or missions, headed by Europeans, were successively sent inland primarily to discover commercial possibilities and to meet the rulers from those areas from which much of the trade came. In 1822 the Scottish explorer, Gordon Laing (1793-1826) went as far as Falaba; Cooper Thompson (?-1843), a Church Missionary Society linguist, went to Timbo, the capital of Futa Jallon, in 1841. Winwood Reade (1838-75), traveller and author, reached Bouré, on the headwaters of the Niger in what is now Mali, in 1870; William Budge was sent to the Kpaa-Mende in 1879. Numerous other missions headed by Africans were also sent, like those of the educationist Edward Blyden (1832-1912) to Falaba (1872) and to Timbo (1873).

Apart from missions to the interior, the interests of the Sierra Leone authorities consistently accompanied those of its subjects (as the Africans in Sierra Leone were regarded) into the hinterland. By the mid-19th century, many Krio traders from Freetown had settled on the headwaters of rivers at the farthest navigable points—such as Port Loko, on the Port Loko Creek, Kambia, on the Great Scarcies River, Mofwe, on the Bum River, and Senehun, on the Bumpe River, which thus became centers of small Krio trading communities. Here much of the trade in gold, ivory, hides, palm kernels, and other products, was handled before being sent to Freetown or Bonthe for shipment to Europe. In Kambia, by the 1880s, the Krio traders had elected themselves a "king of the Creoles" in the person of an influential trader, Thomas Johnson.

The direct involvement of the British from Sierra

View of a street in Freetown, as it appeared in about the 1860s.

Leone in these inland areas was motivated partly by a wish to protect British subjects, but more by the desire to mediate in or forcibly put down any conflict between the local inhabitants which was felt to be inimical to trade. The Krios habitually capitalized on this, and reported the least disturbance which affected them, often in the form of lengthy memoranda to Freetown or to metropolitan chambers of commerce, of which many Krios were members. The disturbances at Kambia in the 1850s between Bilali (*q.v.*) of Tonko Limba and the Soso alliance, spearheaded by Sattan Lahai, and the so-called Yoni disturbances of 1887-88, are cases in point.

British involvement often led to the signing of treaties with the local rulers and the exchange of presents. Treaties, for instance, were signed with the rulers of the Sherbro, with those of Morea country (around the Melacourie River in what is now Guinea), with the Temne, who had ruled Port Loko since 1836, and with Futa Jallon in 1873. Most of these early treaties, that is those before the 1880s, were meant to prevent the local rulers making wars which were thought to affect trade adversely. British subjects who had settled in the territories of these rulers were to be protected. Sometimes by these treaties the British government, as represented in Sierra Leone, was given the right to adjudicate in disputes between indigenous rulers. Territories in which the British had such treaties were often described as being under British 'infuence.'

By the later 19th century, a department had been set up in Freetown to handle relations with the interior. Initially, it was a one-man department under T.G. Lawson (*q.v.*) who was appointed "Native Interpreter and Government Messenger" in 1852. Lawson took charge of the traders coming from the hinterland and reported to the Colonial Secretary all information received about developments in the interior. He also accompanied expeditions to the interior to sign treaties or settle disturbances. In 1888, after Lawson retired, the department, reconstituted first into the Aborigines

Fourah Bay College in earlier days.

Department, then as the Department of Native Affairs in 1891, was headed by J.C.E. Parkes (*q.v.*) who had been working with Lawson. Overland messengers, and an Arabic writer and his assistant, were all incorporated in the enlarged department.

POLITICAL AND SOCIAL DEVELOPMENT IN THE COLONY

The Krios, who were directly or indirectly involved in these maneuvers by the Administration, were becoming more vocal as the century wore on. They were becoming increasingly educated and affluent, and were increasingly able to participate in the business of the Sierra Leone establishment.

In 1848 the Church Missionary Society (C.M.S.) Grammar School was opened, and its counterpart for girls (later to be renamed the Annie Walsh Memorial School), in 1849. Krios, a few sons of chiefs in the interior, and Africans from other parts of British West Africa, increasingly gained secondary and, later, college education in Freetown. Earlier, the C.M.S. had set up an institution to train local teachers and missionaries at Fourah Bay in 1827. As the years went by, this college was enlarged in scope and began to offer degrees after becoming affiliated to the University of Durham in England in 1876. The more affluent, however, sent their children to Britain, often to pursue courses that were not available at Fourah Bay, such as medicine and law.

Thus many young Krio doctors, lawyers, and clergymen became eminent not only in Sierra Leone society but along the West African coast as well. The first African to become a bishop was Adjai Crowther (1809-91), the first student of Fourah Bay. The first two Krio doctors—Africanus Horton (*q.v.*) and William Broughton Davies—qualified in 1859. The first African to be knighted in England was the distinguished Krio barrister, Sir Samuel Lewis (*q.v.*).

Thus, prospering in trade and obtaining education, the Krios became more and more articulate, making their views heard in petitions, in addresses, and in their own newspapers, such as the *New Era* in the 1830s, as well as in the *Sierra Leone Times*. But they had no control over policy under Crown Colony rule. Before the 1860s, the Colony was ruled by the "Governor in Council"—the Council in effect being comprised largely of senior European officials, such as the Chief Justice, the Officer Commanding the Troops, and the Colonial Secretary. Laws for the Colony were made by this body, but the governor could if he so decided ignore his council and override its decisions.

In 1863 the British government granted a new constitution to the Colony, due in part to press agitation, particularly that of the *New Era*. The Governor's Council was abolished and in its place an Executive Council and a Legislative Council were established. The former was virtually a replica of the old Governor's Council. The Legislative Council had provision for only two unofficial members, who were appointed by the governor. Initially, the only Krio representative appointed by the governor was Charles Heddle (*q.v.*). The governor then asked the business community to elect one representative. John Ezzidio (*q.v.*), an African, defeated John Levi, a European. The Secretary of State for the Colonies then advised the governor that the post was meant to be filled by his appointee, and that in the future he should appoint a representative, and not have him elected. The elective principle thus disappeared for the next six decades. Though the Legislative Council made laws, these had to be ratified in Britain and could be set aside if the British so desired. Thus the Krios were politically powerless in the Colony. They were furthermore to lose what economic and social power they had as the 19th century ended. For the British, due to the

Fourah Bay College at Mount Aureol, as it appeared in the 1970s.

prevailing doctrine of Social Darwinism (a popular theory of that age, which held that life was a struggle for existence in which the fittest survived), changed their former policy of encouraging Africans to take over administration. In consequence, Africans were no longer appointed to important positions. No African doctor, for example, was allowed to be senior to a European counterpart, even if he was more qualified. With the advent of big European firms and, later, of Lebanese businessmen, to whom concessions were granted, the Krios found themselves unable to compete, and their economic strength declined.

THE SAMORIAN ERA

Developments in the north of Sierra Leone were to coincide with the era of European imperial expansion and would contribute to the establishment of a protectorate by the British over the rest of Sierra Leone in 1896. By the 1870s, Samori Touré (1830-1900), a great Mandinka warrior and leader, was establishing an empire around Konya country, in what is now the Republic of Guinea. Samori received the bulk of his arms supply from Sierra Leone through long distance trade across the hinterland. By 1822, he had decided to bring certain areas of this hinterland under his hegemony so as to have control of the trade routes. He therefore sent one of his generals, 'Nfa Ali, to subdue these areas.

The attack on what is today the Sierra Leone hinterland began early in 1884. By September the Yalunka state of Solimana had been destroyed by the Sofa, Samori's warriors. Limba country, including Almamy Suluku's state of Biriwa Limba, was subdued before the year was out. Also conquered were large sections of Koranko country.

The governor of Sierra Leone wrote a letter to Samori during the siege of Falaba, the capital of Solimana, indicating that "Falaba and the countries below it, (meaning the Sierra Leone hinterland), are on friendly terms with this (Sierra Leone) government," and that it would be unfortunate if Samori took Falaba. But this did not deter the Sofa. Samori, however, wanting to please Sierra Leone, the source of his arms, promised the governor that he would rebuild Falaba. He kept his promise, and similar sentiments made it possible for a British officer, Major Morton Festing, to succeed in ridding Suluku's state of Biriwa Limba of the Sofa forces of occupation in 1888.

But by 1890, a revolt in Samori's empire led him to send his Sofa out again to reconquer large sections of the Sierra Leone hinterland. One of his lieutenants, Foday Benia Porekere (q.v.), attacked the eastern portions of the Sierra Leone hinterland in 1893. After assisting rebellious groups in the state of Kai Londo

The Sofa, warriors of Samori Touré, the great Mandinka warrior leader, posed a challenge to the European powers in the later years of the 19th century. This picture shows a mounted Sofa warrior.

(q.v.), Porekere moved to Kono where Kai Londo re-established his authority. He took a number of towns belonging to Nyagua, and then threatened to over-run Konike Temne (in central Sierra Leone, near the headwaters of the Taia, known in Sherbro country as the Jong River) so as to control an alternative route to Freetown. Nyagua, in treaty relations with the British, reported the attack on his territory. Porekere was warned by the British administration to desist from his threatened attack on Konike. Meantime, the French were attacking him from the rear while the British joined Nyagua to attack him from the front. As a result of misinformation, the British and French ended up fighting each other, each party thinking the other to be the Sofa. Both commanders were killed. Then Porekere advanced to Bagbema on the Sewa River, ready to pounce on Tungea, near Panguma. There he was attacked by the British force and killed by a chance shot. Thus the Sofa threat was warded off.

THE PRELUDE TO THE COLONIAL OCCUPATION

By this time, however, British interest in the hinterland had developed beyond that in trade alone. This was the period usually described as the "Scramble for Africa." Britain did not want to be over-reached by the other European power in this area, France. The French had been active from their base in Senegal and had signed a few treaties in the area of the Northern Rivers—i.e. the Melacourie, Bereira, Rio Pongas, and Rio Nunez, all in what is now the Republic of Guinea. Unlike the British treaties, some of the French agreements were claimed to be treaties of "suzerainty and protection." British and French interests in this area of the northern Sierra Leone hinterland were thus bound to come into conflict.

The two powers therefore consulted in 1882, and drew up a convention to impose a boundary between the Scarcies and Melacourie rivers, demarcating their areas of interest. This was the beginning of a series of boundary delimitation agreements between European powers which were to determine the present boundaries of African states.

Though the French depended on treaties signed with the indigenous rulers as a basis for claims to territory, a great portion of the hinterland was claimed by them "by right of conquest." The French had driven the Sofa out of this area, so they claimed that it had become theirs. If the French could have occupied all

Disturbances were frequent in the interior in the final years of the 19th century. This picture shows a Mende warfence, built to discourage attack.

the areas they claimed, the Sierra Leone hinterland would have been lost to the British, and the Colony itself would have been hemmed in, thus losing its trade, profits, and revenue.

The British therefore proceeded to sign more treaties on which they relied to counter French influence. They had begun to fear that local rulers would cede their territories to France, and therefore in 1888 produced a "standard treaty" containing a special clause that no ruler was to cede his territory to any other foreign power "except through and with the consent of the Government of Her Majesty." This clause made its first appearance in a temporary treaty signed by Major Festing with Almamy Suluku of Biriwa Limba in February 1888. Two British commissioners were appointed in 1889 to tour the hinterland and sign these treaties. G.H. Garrett was to sign treaties in the north while T.J. Alldridge was to do so in the south. There was no protectorate or protection clause in these treaties.

In 1890 the Sierra Leone Frontier Police Force was inaugurated. Its duties were supposed to be only those of a "frontier Force." These included guarding the frontier road which Governor Sir James Hay (term of office 1888-91) had encouraged local rulers to construct. This road ran parallel to the coast, from Kambia in the northwest to Sulima in the south, approximately marking the boundary between the colony and its hinterland. Its construction was intended to stop the passage of large slave caravans, prevent local wars, and protect British subjects, such as Krio traders. But before long the force won notoriety for petty tyranny. An avalanche of complaints kept bombarding the governor's office, drawing attention to a paradoxical situation in which the ostensible protectors of the people had become their oppressors. Although not supposed to interfere with local customs, members of the force meddled frivolously in local affairs. They maltreated and disrespected kings and chiefs in the presence of their subjects. Even Governor Sir Frederic Cardew (term of office 1894-1900), who was often prone to side with them, admitted their brutalizations and misconduct, dismissing a number of them in 1895.

Apart from the restrictive clause about cession of territory, these 'standard treaties' were still treaties of peace, amity, and commerce. Many of the local rulers regarded these treaties as allying them with the British. Especially in the north, where the Sofa presence was still imminent, the rulers were looking for allies against the Sofa enemy. In fact, when the French were engaged in fighting the Sofa while the British appeared cool about participating in the struggle, some rulers, such as Bambafara of Nieni (q.v.), told British emissaries that they would move their allegiance to the French if the British would not help them. In 1890, Garrett reported to the governor that many rulers of Sankaran, Solimana, and Koranko countries had signed treaties offering their countries to the British "on condition they be protected against the Sofas." The ruler of Kaliere in the former Solimana state had signed a treaty with the British in 1890. When his son, Isa (q.v.), succeeded him in the same year, he fell out with the Sofa, whom he had been supporting. The British refused to help him when the Sofa attacked his town, so he returned the treaty and went to the French with presents to seek help.

THE PROTECTORATE AND THE NATIONAL LIBERATION STRUGGLE

But the pace of imperial expansion moved quicker. Soon any attempts to parley with the indigenous rulers were abandoned. The original agreements between the European powers on the one hand, and treaties with the local rulers, concluded during the 1880s and early 1890s, on the other, were likewise now abandoned. The British had fraudulently claimed these treaties of friendship to be treaties of protection.

But by the mid-1890s, the British no longer bothered to sign treaties with distant areas with which by then they had become familiar. In January 1895, Britain and France signed a new agreement delimiting their spheres of influence. When local rulers in the north questioned the British as to which side they were to consider themselves to belong, the governor urged them "to await patiently the settlement of the boundary question." Their views no longer counted.

The Anglo-French agreement of 1895 fixed the eastern boundary at 14° W longitude. This made Sierra Leone's eastern boundary a straight line which cut Kai Londo's state into two, with one half, including the capital, Kailahun, in Liberian territory. Despite appeals from the governor to ease the hardship consequently imposed on Kai Londo's successor, Fa Bundeh, the Colonial Office paid little attention to the matter. The Liberian government sent a customs official to Kailahun in 1907, but he was ejected soon after. In 1911, an agreement was made granting the "Kailahun Salient" to Sierra Leone in return for a slice of Gola territory to the south. This agreement was finally ratified in 1917, giving Sierra Leone its present boundaries.

The boundary demarcation was therefore a matter of convenience only to the European colonial states, which ignored African interests. Limba traditions claim that the boundary ran through one Limba house in Wara Wara country; the front verandah formed part of French Guinea, while the back room was in Sierra Leone!

When Governor Cardew took charge of the Colony in 1894, he lost no time in requesting the Colonial Office to approve his plans for the declaration of a protectorate over the British sphere of influence. He made two tours into the hinterland in 1894 and 1895 to promote his protectorate idea and to familiarize himself with the area. Apparently, he made little mention of his proposed house tax which was expected to pay for the protectorate administration. In 1896, the Protectorate Ordinance was passed although its provisions were not properly explained to the people.

The Protectorate was divided into five administrative divisions—the Karene, Ronietta, Bandajuma, Panguma, and Koinadugu districts. Each of these was under the control of a district commissioner. A new hierarchy of courts was constituted, and many legal matters, which the local rulers had previously settled, were removed from their jurisdiction. These measures were introduced at a time when the rulers were still recovering from their vexations with the Frontier Police. To further complicate matters, the British imposed a house tax, which was rightly interpreted in customary law to mean that the people did not own their houses and the rulers did not own the country. Lengthy petitions were written and several delegations were sent to the governor to state a host of grievances. In every instance the house tax in particular was abhorred.

The governor dismissed these petitions, and informed the rulers that two districts—Panguma in the east and Koinadugu in the northeast—because of their distance from European contacts were not to pay tax in the first instance. The remaining three were to pay beginning in 1898. Governor Cardew appointed Frontier Police officers to act as district commissioners and to begin collecting the tax promptly. The collectors, however, encountered a general reluctance to pay. The Frontier Police therefore used methods that were to provide the spark necessary to light the powder keg of revolution. When Captain Wilfred S. Sharpe, the district commissioner of Karene, northeast of Port Loko, attempted to collect the tax by force, deposing chiefs and sentencing those who would not pay, he made the fatal mistake of firing at people supposed to be supporters of Bai Bureh (q.v.), the ruler of Kasse, north of Port Loko, who was believed to be the brain behind the resistance.

The so-called Hut Tax War had begun. Bai Bureh's almost legendary fame spread far beyond the imaginable confines of the areas immediately under his influence. He thus became the center of the so-called Temne resistance.

While British troops were engaged in fighting Bai Bureh in the north, in April 1898 there occurred a sudden, spontaneous, and unexpected outburst of resistance in the Mende areas to the south, directed against all European or colonial establishments or persons. Missionaries, traders, colonial officials, and others, were plundered and massacred. Thomas Neale Caulker (q.v.), chief of Shenge, a small port on the coast opposite the Plantain Islands, who asked his people to pay, was murdered by his own family. Madam Yoko (q.v.), and Nancy Tucker (q.v.), who promised to pay, barely escaped with their lives. Few escaped. Because of the nature of this revolt, it petered out before long, there being no clear leader. But Bai Bureh conducted a highly-organized guerrilla war which engaged British troops for ten months.

After the rainy season, the British, with the aid of a few African collaborators, formed 'flying columns' and took the offensive, shelling ruthlessly, and destroying crops ready for harvest. The supposed ringleaders, Bai Bureh, Nyagua, and Bai (Beh) Sherbro, were arrested. A commission of enquiry was set up. But, there being no evidence against them to warrant a conviction, the three were exiled to the Gold Coast in July, 1899. Many other people were tried for murder in the Mende areas, however, and were hanged.

THE ESTABLISHMENT OF COLONIAL RULE

After the resistance of 1898, the British became more concerned about consolidating their rule. Until the end of World War I, the large pre-colonial states in what is now Sierra Leone were broken up, and subordinate rulers, styled paramount chiefs, accepted on the same footing as their former overlords or kings. Chiefdoms replaced states, and their number increased with bewildering rapidity, reaching a total of 217 by 1924.

Moreover, after those who had fought the British had been exiled or hanged, puppets, including women, were put forward and also recognized as paramount chiefs. The source of legitimacy to traditional authority was transferred to the British administration. Any paramount chief whose conduct was supposed to be detrimental to British interests was promptly deposed. The British were now in full control, and the people settled down to a helpless acceptance of alien rule.

SOCIO-ECONOMIC TRENDS

The first few decades of colonial rule were characterized by a colonial preoccupation with law and order. No proposals likely to disturb the *pax Britannica* by uprooting people from their natural avocations were approved. Until the 1930s, it was a period of colonial consolidation.

In 1906, a school was opened at Bo, 177 km (110 mi) east-southeast of Freetown, for the "sons and nominees of chiefs." The main purpose was to familiarize the pupils with European ways without alienating them from their traditional culture. They were expected to become model colonial chiefs. Emphasis was put on the dignity of labor. None of the graduates was to be employed in any official establishment. By 1916, however, several factors had combined to make this policy unrealistic. A negligible number had succeeded to paramount chiefships, but those who did were far from model chiefs. In addition, the presence of educated elements in chiefdoms that were excluded from the corridors of power was thought to be dangerous to peace and order. Consequently, Bo School graduates began to be employed in the lower rungs of the colonial service as agricultural instructors, surveyors, and clerks.

As early as 1894, Governor Cardew, impressed by the quantity of the natural produce of the country, had proposed a railway running eastwards across the country, into the hinterland. Its construction began in 1896. By 1906 it had reached Balima, where it marked time for two years before reaching what was to be its terminus, Pendembu, 463 km (227 mi) away

The building of a government railway, running eastwards across the country, stimulated the export of palm products, but did not achieve other hoped-for results. This picture shows Bauya Junction in 1925.

from Freetown, in 1908. A branch line, completed in 1915, was also constructed from Bauya, 80 km (50 mi) east-southeast of Freetown, to Makeni in the northern province.

Before the mining boom of the 1930s, the railway represented the only capital investment project in Sierra Leone. Not oriented towards production, it was intended to serve a pre-existing extractive industry, which produced palm oil and kernels. No new varieties were introduced, no large-scale plantations were undertaken, and above all no new technologies were encouraged. In the event, the export of palm products doubled within a few years of the building of the railway, but failed to have a magic-wand effect upon the Sierra Leonean economy. The railway itself was declared a liability in the 1940s, and was eventually phased out in the late 1960s.

About the turn of the century, Levantines, incorrectly described as Syrians but in actuality Lebanese, began to arrive in Sierra Leone. With little or no money, they seized every opportunity to trade and make profits as the recaptives had done before them. They did not fear or hesitate to move to remote hinterland areas and to open shops there, advancing goods to the local inhabitants in return for produce, after they themselves had obtained the goods from large European firms operating in the country. Before long, many had become fairly prosperous but earned the displeasure of local middlemen, whom they were gradually displacing. Then, in 1919, a food shortage, especially of rice, occurred. Suspected of hoarding the staple food, the establishments of the Lebanese, who had shops in at least 24 towns, were raided and looted in the so-called "anti-Syrian riots," until the colonial administration intervened to protect them from further molestation.

By the 1920s, it had become clear that the railway would not solve the increasing financial problems of

Sierra Leone, as the export of produce had stagnated instead of spiralling, due to lack of feeder roads. A program for the construction of feeder roads gained momentum in the same decade. The Lebanese were among the earliest truck (lorry) owners.

Income, however, did not increase as fast as was expected. The establishment, worried over a stagnant colonial revenue at a time when increasing new demands for expenditure were being made, began prospecting for minerals in 1926. At the same time, much encouragement was given to the development of cash crops, such as coffee and cocoa.

Many minerals were discovered, the most important being iron in Marampa, 35 km (22 mi) east-south-east of Port Loko, gold in the Pampana river basin in the northern province, and, in 1930, diamonds in the Sewa river basin. Other minerals such as platinum and chromite did not prove to be of sufficient economic interest. Their production fell quickly and stopped altogether within a few years.

A few European firms immediately undertook to mine while Africans also formed syndicates and began operations. The Lebanese, too, did not let this opportunity slip by. Gold mining needed little technical knowledge, and enjoyed a short-lived boom during the 1930s. Production reached a peak in 1936, but thereafter gradually declined. By the 1940s, gold mining had been virtually abandoned.

Iron ore proved more promising, since smuggling of the ore was impossible. Having obtained a 99-year concession lease, the Sierra Leone Development Company (Delco) was formed to exploit the ore, constructing a 83 km (52 mi) railway from Marampa to Pepel, at the mouth of the Sierra Leone River, where a jetty was built to export the ore. Regular shipments amounting to 24,000 tons began in 1933 and had risen dramatically to about 3,000,000 tons a year when the company went bankrupt and closed in 1975.

Diamonds were discovered in Kono in 1930, but mining did not begin until 1932, after the Consolidated African Selection Trust (CAST) had obtained a license. In 1934, "sole and exclusive right" to exploit the diamonds for 99 years was granted to the Sierra Leone Selection Trust (SLST), a subsidiary of CAST. Diamond mining expanded more dramatically than that of any other mineral. The illicit mining that was also carried on made it difficult, however, to compile accurate production statistics.

Nevertheless, the advent of mining had major consequences for the economy as a whole. The search for alternative revenue, which had led to prospecting in the first place, was vindicated. As mining contribution to colonial revenue increased from the 1930s onwards, especially during the Great Depression of that decade, so did the traditional customs revenue

drop proportionately. Mining also offered job opportunities, employing more than 16,000 in 1939, and paying better wages than in most other jobs. Consequently, not only did the colonial administration cease to be the principal employer of labor, but new employment centers arose in the Protectorate as well as in Freetown.

Agriculture was not adversely affected by mining activities, as agricultural production figures show a remarkable consistency. Without being revolutionized, agriculture found new markets for its products. Certainly mining destroyed the soil where actual digging was done, but the effect was to be felt later. A boom in trading also occurred and a new class of petty traders arose to supply the consumer goods demanded by mine workers. Sierra Leone remained a supplier of raw materials to the metropolitan countries. Nothing was processed in the country itself, and all manufactured goods still had to be imported. Of importance, however, was the fact that the rise of mining led to a change in the composition of exports, by contributing to the relative decline in the value of agricultural exports, thus changing the pattern of one-and-a-half centuries of economic history. But, in the mid-1970s, agriculture

Diamond mining began in Sierra Leone in 1932. Here workers are seen digging for diamonds.

still remained the main source of cash income for the ordinary people.

Important developments took place in the 1950s. Trade unionism became fashionable as a direct consequence of mining. But diamonds had become the quickest way of making money. Thus smuggling increased on an unprecedented scale, particularly as mining spread from Kono to the Kenema and Bo districts in 1954. The 'Diamond Rush' was at its height. The self-governing administration of the day tried to stop the loss of revenue caused through smuggling by suppressing illegal diggers by force. It failed. It thus accepted their presence as an accomplished fact and legalized private diamond mining by issuing licences. Pressure mounted in the 1960s to nationalize a "foreign company" which since 1950 had been contributing an average of two-thirds to the national revenue of Sierra Leone. Nationalization took place in 1971, with the Sierra Leone government taking 51 percent of the company's shares.

As independence began to approach in the late 1950s, economic planners became obsessed with such questions as import-substitution, industrialization, and a full diversification of the economy. The results, however, were disheartening. A number of industries failed and had to shut down because of inept management, shortages of raw materials which had to be imported, high production costs, or other reasons. Those industries which survived did so because they enjoyed a monopoly or relied on "protection measures." The consequence was that average consumers paid more for locally produced goods than they would have done for imported ones.

The socio-economic trends of the 20th century hardly justify any talk of development or progress. By the mid-1970s, Sierra Leone was still an exporter of raw materials, and an importer of manufactured goods, with the value of imports always exceeding that of exports. Economic "development" on the whole was extractive rather than "productive." A new dimension was added in the 1960s and 1970s by world inflation and frequent shortages of the country's staple food, rice—developments which combined to make life unpleasant for ordinary people. The Sierra Leone Produce Marketing Board, created to stabilize prices, did not always favor the farmer. While the Board undertook to develop plantations, especially of palm oil, some of the machines provided were idle some of the time because of lack of raw materials. Agricultural development had failed to take place as planned, and ill-advised attempts to modernize agriculture, for example by the large-scale provision of tractors, proved expensive failures. Economic hopes were therefore placed in the discovery of more minerals, and in the identification and introduction of better conceived agricultural projects.

POLITICAL CHANGES

The constitution of 1863 was still in force when it was superseded by the Slater Constitution (named for Sir Ransford Slater, governor from 1922-27) in 1924. After World War I, the National Congress of British West Africa was formed in 1920, to present African grievances to the imperial government. It demanded, among other things, the abolition of racial discrimination in the public service, the granting of power and responsibility to Africans, and the creation of the West African university. Nothing specific resulted, but Governor Slater nevertheless decided to make some concessions to the Africans in a new constitution. The unofficial membership of the Legislative Council was increased from four to ten, seven being appointed by the governor, and three being elected to represent the Colony. Of the seven appointed, three had to be paramount chiefs to represent Protectorate interests. Thus the Slater Constitution allowed the elective principle, denied in 1863, and for the first time provided for the representation of the Protectorate on the Council, which had been enacting laws for it since 1896. But the governor had only to make a token concession. For he remained convinced that official control over policy must remain.

Up to 1937, the Protectorate had been administered on the basis of a kind of quieta non movere ("let sleeping dogs lie") policy. With the rise of mining and labor movements, it was however discovered that chiefdom administration as it then existed was unsuitable for "development." Thus J.S. Fenton was sent to Nigeria to study the system of Native Administration there, and on the basis of his report, a similar system was adopted in Sierra Leone. Paramount chiefs had to give up their traditional revenues in exchange for a fixed salary, chiefdom courts had to have a regular composition, and treasuries were established to keep revenue to be used for salaries and "development projects." There was, however, no haste to introduce these measures. Chiefdoms that so wished would adopt the new Native Administration, but none was forced to accept it. Tiny chiefdoms were encouraged to amalgamate to make the project meaningful. The introduction of Native Administrations thus proceeded slowly. At the time of independence in 1961, not all chiefdoms had Native Administrations.

World War II ushered in many changes favorable to African demands for self-government. But national self-determination, accepted as a principle for the political rehabilitation of Europe, was denied by Britain to her African colonies, including Sierra Leone. Both the Soviet Union and the United States, however, put continuous pressure on Britain to move towards such self-determination. The electoral victory of the British Labour Party in 1945, shortly before the end of World War II, also increased the prospects for advancement of African interests. The principle of eventual independence for African colonies was gradually accepted, and the Colonial Development and Welfare Acts (1940-45) were passed in Britain in order to facilitate the process by granting socio-economic assistance to African territories.

In 1946, a Protectorate Assembly was established, and district councils were introduced. Each district council was to represent its own district, all paramount chiefs being members automatically. The district councils were to obtain an imprest (advance of funds) on the chiefdom local tax to carry out development projects within the district. They were also to elect members to the Protectorate Assembly which was to discuss matters concerning Protectorate welfare as well as matters referred to it by the governor in council.

Governor Hubert Stevenson (term of office 1941-48) introduced a new constitution in 1947 which gave a majority to elected members in the Legislative Council, and allowed Protectorate Africans greater participation in the management of the affairs of the country. Because of opposition from entrenched Krio interests, which became united in the National Council of Sierra Leone (N.C.) to oppose the provisions of the constitution on the unreasonable grounds that the Protectorate and its inhabitants were foreign, the constitution was not passed until 1951. By then Protectorate interests too had crystallized into the Sierra Leone People's Party (S.L.P.P.) under the leadership of Dr. M.A.S. (later Sir Milton) Margai (*q.v.*). Indirect elections were held, and after much political maneuvering, the S.L.P.P. emerged with 15 seats, while the N.C. obtained 5 out of an unofficial membership of 21 in the Legislative Council. The governor, Sir Beresford Stooke (in office 1948-53) therefore asked Dr. Margai to nominate six from his party to sit on the Executive Council. Dr. Margai himself became chief minister.

Elections were due in 1957. But before this, in 1955, there were serious riots in Freetown and in many parts of the Northern Province. These came to be called anti-chief riots, since they were mainly directed against oppression by chiefs. As part of the preparations for the elections, however, following the recommendations of an electoral reform commission headed by Sir Keith Lucas, a number of reforms were introduced. The Protectorate Assembly was abolished. The Legislative Council (renamed the House of Representatives) was given a membership of 57, including 12 paramount chiefs, each representing a district. In addition, the chief minister became premier. Direct elections were then held for the first time, and the S.L.P.P. won 44 seats. In the meantime, a number of mushroom parties had emerged. But the official opposition was the United People's Party (U.P.P.), led by C.B. Rogers-Wright, a lawyer who was later to be disbarred for professional misconduct.

In 1958, the S.L.P.P. split because of differences between Dr. Margai and his younger brother, Albert, a lawyer with radical inclinations, who was supported by Siaka Stevens, the leading trade unionist of the time. The new splinter group formed the People's National Party (P.N.P.). All parties agreed, however, to form a United National Front to negotiate for independence. At the constitutional conference in London in May 1960, it was agreed that April 27, 1961 would be the date for regaining independence. But Siaka Stevens announced himself unable to sign the constitutional document, due in part to differences with Albert Margai. Therefore the P.N.P. split, and what began as an "elections-before-independence" movement (known as the Stevens faction) was officially transformed into the All People's Congress (A.P.C.) party, drawing much of its support from discontented urban groups and Northern elements.

The A.P.C. was quite popular and within two months of its formation won the elections to the Freetown City Council. The S.L.P.P. won the general election held in 1962, but the A.P.C. had emerged meanwhile as the strongest opposition party. The A.P.C. won even more support when Sir Milton died in 1964, and was succeeded by his brother Albert. A number of influential S.L.P.P. members declared for the A.P.C. By 1966 the S.L.P.P. had become unpopular following the declaration of the intention of Sir Albert to introduce a one-party system as well as a republican constitution, when the country was

I.T.A. Wallace-Johnson campaigning for the All People's Congress (A.P.C.) in the 1962 general election.

Sir Milton Margai campaigning for the Sierra Leone People's Party (S.L.P.P.) in the 1962 general election.

suffering from economic difficulties and food shortages. After bitter opposition from the A.P.C., intellectuals, and others, Sir Albert declared that he had dropped both issues, but not before the republican bill designed to introduce a non-executive presidency had passed the house. Sir Albert also announced that he had discovered a plot against the government led by Col. John Bangura (*q.v.*), who was then sent overseas to a diplomatic post in the United States.

In these circumstances, Sir Albert called general elections in April 1967. After a close contest, the official figures announced were S.L.P.P., 32; A.P.C., 32; and Independents, 2. But the governor-general, using his constitutional powers, decided that the A.P.C. had won the election, and swore in Siaka Stevens as prime minister. The military then intervened, the force commander, Brigadier David Lansana (*q.v.*), announcing that no party had had a majority. The following day, his senior officers arrested Lansana, sent him off to a diplomatic post, and created a National Reformation Council (N.R.C.) under Col. Andrew Juxon-Smith. The N.R.C. then set up a commission of enquiry into the conduct of the 1967 general elections, which concluded that the A.P.C. had won. Exactly a year after it had come into existence, the N.R.C. was overthrown by a revolt of non-commissioned officers, and John Bangura was recalled from abroad to head the army. He pledged to return the country to civilian rule, which he did within a week. Siaka Stevens was again sworn in as prime minister, but this time as prime minister of a national government which included S.L.P.P. ministers. After some time, however, the S.L.P.P. members thought that they would be better off if they constituted themselves into an official opposition. This was because there had been clashes with the A.P.C., particularly after mass arrests of S.L.P.P. supporters

had taken place in late 1968, and faction fights had occurred in several places. Thus within a year, an all-A.P.C. government had been constituted.

In 1970, two former cabinet ministers resigned their party membership and joined other younger elements to form a new party, the United Democratic Party (U.D.P.) under the leadership of Dr. John Karefa Smart. Karefa Smart had once been a minister under Sir Milton Margai, but had resigned and joined the A.P.C. when Albert Margai took over. The U.D.P. accused the A.P.C. leadership of authoritarian tendencies. Violent clashes occurred between the U.D.P. and A.P.C. supporters. The government then arrested the U.D.P. leaders and proscribed the party itself.

Shortly after, there was an attempted coup by Brigadier John Bangura who had become the force commander. The coup was, however, unsuccessful. Tried and found guilty by a court martial, Bangura and others were executed.

The next political development was the emergence of a movement towards the declaration of a republic. It was argued that it was colonialist for the Queen of England to be head of state. To cast off this "last vestige of colonialism," a republic should be established. Since this implied a change in the constitution, the republican bill had to be introduced and passed in two successive parliaments with a two-thirds majority, a general election having been held in between. With slight modifications, the republican bill passed by Albert Margai in 1966 was re-introduced and passed. Sierra Leone thus became a republic in April 1971 with the chief justice, C.O.E. Cole, as ceremonial president.

Two days later, an amendment was adopted creating an executive presidency, with Siaka Stevens as the first executive president of Sierra Leone.

Elections were due to be held in 1973, and on nomination day the A.P.C. won 46 out of 97 seats unopposed. The S.L.P.P. charged that thugs broke into nomination centers and destroyed their papers, preventing them from entering nomination centers at all in 6 districts out of 12. The S.L.P.P. then withdrew from the general elections altogether on grounds that they were in physical danger if they contested them, while those who had succeeded in having themselves nominated withdrew their nominations. In addition, the S.L.P.P. stated there was no point in contesting an election when half the seats had already been won by the government. In July 1974, a plot to overthrow the government was uncovered involving ex-Minister Dr. Forna and 14 others. Found guilty, they were executed in July 1975.

Thus from 1973 to 1977, there was no official opposition in parliament, until events early in the year precipitated general elections, which would normally have been held in 1978. As chancellor of the University of Sierra Leone, President Stevens was conferring degrees on graduates when students staged a demonstration and disrupted the proceedings. The students made a number of demands, including, among other things, the holding of free and fair elections. Parliament was dissolved, and elections announced. On nomination day in April, the A.P.C. obtained unopposed all the seats in four Northern districts, and one Southern district. The S.L.P.P. charged that it had been prevented from nominating its candidates by A.P.C. stalwarts. Nominations in Bo district, where eight seats were in contest, were postponed, to be held later, with the A.P.C. winning all unopposed. In areas where the S.L.P.P. was able to nominate candidates, however, it won 15 seats. It then constituted the official opposition in the Sierra Leone Parliament.

———————————————

ABAYOMI-COLE, J.A.

John Augustus Abayomi-Cole (1848-July 1943) was a talented and versatile Krio (Creole) who, in the course of his long career, made his mark as priest, politician, author, agriculturist, herbalist, and administrator.

He was born at Ilorin in Nigeria, of Sierra Leone stock, in 1848. He received his schooling in Sierra Leone, first under A.B.C. Sibthorpe (*q.v.*) at Hastings, and then at Freetown's C.M.S. Grammar School. He was later employed by the United Brethren Church (U.B.C.) at Shenge, in the Bonthe district. While with the mission, he went to the United States, where he was ordained priest in the American Wesleyan Methodist Church. While in the States, he gave a series of lectures. One of these was his *Revelation of the Secret Orders of Western Africa: Including an Explanation of the Beliefs and Customs of African Heathenism*, which was published by the United Brethren Publishing House of Dayton, Ohio. It is a well-written book, but some of his arguments are inconsistent, and reveal that he had not yet come to terms with the worth and usefulness of African ritualistic societies. It seems, however, that this work opened his eyes to a different world, and gave him an absorbing interest in the cosmos. From this time on he began to delve into esoterism in general, and various secret societies, including freemasonry, in particular.

Upon returning to Sierra Leone, he took over superintendence of the Maroon Chapel in 1887. By 1893, however, after differences with his congregation, he removed for a time to "Beulah Hills," on the way to Leicester, near Freetown, where he farmed ginger, a crop that was then in demand in England.

In the years that followed, while continuing his intellectual activities, he founded his own church, practiced herbal medicine, and engaged in practical farming and small-scale industrial activities, as well as in politics.

He became a Cabbalist, and fashioned his own brand of religion. In May 1905 he established an African church, the Gospel Mission Hall, where various ethnic groups congregated to worship. His piety appears to have amused a number of sceptics—he was known to some as "Jesus-passing-by." But his religious activities nevertheless filled a need, as is witnessed by the number of adherents, including solid citizens such as A.J. Shorunkeh-Sawyerr (*q.v.*) and J.C. Shorunkeh-Sawyerr (*q.v.*), who flocked to his church.

As a herbalist, he was affiliated with the National Association of Medical Herbalists in Great Britain. Gleanings from his *Revelation* indicate that he was

very interested in the useful medicines of the secret societies. He consequently made a life-long study of remedial and medical herbs whose healing properties he employed to aid the sick. His literacy and interest in science gave him knowledge that he combined with the lore of traditional medicine to produce effective antidotes against rheumatic pains, skin troubles, nervous ailments, mental derangements, and other ills. He is even credited with having given two blind men their sight!

He contributed regularly to the *Sierra Leone Weekly News*, a leading West African newspaper, and also wrote a news summary in Arabic that was published in *Saturday Ho*, a magazine-like publication that appeared from 1891-96. (He was known to be sympathetic to Islam, and it was said that his father was an imam, i.e. the spiritual head of an Islamic community.) In effect, he was eclectic in his approach. He was capable of discussing Christian theology with the foremost prelate, while also treating the rituals and beliefs of esoteric societies with the same knowledgeable ease. One of his intellectual excursions in this vein was a paper entitled the "Philosophy of Paganism," which he wrote in 1904.

He also wrote a Mende grammar. Abstract ideas did not, however, consign him to an "ivory tower" existence. He was a practical man, very much of this world despite his rapport with the "other world."

His practical capabilities included a proficiency at distilling spirits (for which he was chased out of Sierra Leone in 1911), at manufacturing sugar from molasses, at making soap, and at extracting various foods from corn. He also ventured into the palm oil trade, as well as into growing such cash crops as cocoa, cassava, yams, corn, and vegetables. To some, his schemes appeared too grandiose, yet if the government of the day had given them support, some success might have been achieved, particularly in diversifying the staple food of Sierra Leone, which was one of his aims. His belief in the importance of the soil was hammered home in numerous tracts on agricultural science. In his later years, he showed unbounded enthusiasm in founding the Agricultural Society (1922). Earlier, in about 1909, he had also founded the Sierra Leone Farmers Association, of which he was president.

In the earlier stages of his political career, he inspired the establishment of some pressure groups. One of these was the Public Committee Against the Introduction of the Criminal Code (1918), at a time when it was feared that the code would give too much power to district commissioners. Another such group was the Sierra Leone National Defence Fund (1908), set up to defend Sierra Leoneans against the racial arrogance of the colonial establishment. His views on political matters were original and well-argued. For a short while, from about 1911 to 1914, he became the Liberian Commissioner for the Interior (Native Affairs). Documents covering this period stored in the Public Records Office in London are full of complaints by the British authorities about his activities as a Travelling Commissioner, especially during the period of border difficulties between Sierra Leone and Liberia. But 1911 did not represent his first contact with Liberia. As early as 1886 he had been invited to Liberia by the Hon. C.T.O. King, father of C.D.B. King who was in office as Liberian president in 1926. In 1914 he was decorated with the insignia of Knight Commander of the Liberian Order of African Redemption for his diplomatic services and for his ministrations to the sick. Later, in 1926, he was also to be awarded an honorary doctorate by the College of Liberia.

His name is to be found associated with almost all the major political movements of his day. After World War I, he was a key figure in the local activities of the National Congress of British West Africa, founded in Accra, in what was then the Gold Coast, in 1920, and which held its second meeting in Freetown in 1923.

Like another activist, J.C. Shorunkeh-Sawyerr, Abayomi-Cole did not enter the Legislative Council. Although he was considered for nomination in 1921, being a man of "outstanding influence and undoubted ability," he was passed over because he was "eccentric in his views," was 71 years old, and was "not a lawyer."

One of the most striking facts about Abayomi-Cole was his remarkable versatility. Many talents were packed into the little bundle of a man who was described in a pen portrait in 1926 as a nondescript person, but with depth of character, who looked only 30 or 40 years old when he was in his 74th year.

Sierra Leone lost an original thinker when Abayomi-Cole died in July 1943.

AKINTOLA J.G. WYSE

BIBLIOGRAPHY: J. Abayomi-Cole, *Revelation of the Secret Orders of Western Africa: Including an Explanation of the Beliefs and Customs of African Heathenism*, Dayton, Ohio, 1886, *The Interior of Sierra Leone. What Can It Teach Us ?*, Dayton, Ohio, 1887, *Astrological Geomancy in Africa*, London 1898, *Hala Goloi Mende Yiahu. First Book in the Mende Language*, pamphlet, London, 1900, "Trees, Herbs, and Roots in West Africa," *Journal of the Royal Society of Arts*, September 22, 1906; Christopher Fyfe, *A History of Sierra Leone*, London 1962; Leo Spitzer, *The Creoles of Sierra Leone,* Ile Ife, 1975; "Pen Portrait of Dr. Abayomi Cole," in *African World Supplement,* June, 1926.

AKAR, J.J.

John Joseph Akar (May 20, 1927-June 23, 1975) was a broadcaster, short-story writer, actor, playwright, journalist and, finally diplomat.

He was born at Rotifunk, 64 km (40 mi) east-southeast of Freetown. His father, Joseph Philip Akar, was a Franco-Lebanese, born in Rufisque, Senegal, who had eventually settled in Sierra Leone. His mother, Madam Dankay Mansaray, is a Sierra Leonean of the Mandinka tribe.

John Joseph had a varied educational career, attending the Evangelical United Brethren Day School at Rotifunk, the Albert Academy in Freetown, and, in the United States, Otterbein College in Ohio (1947-49), and the University of California at Berkeley (1949-51). He also attended the London School of Economics.

In 1954 his unpublished play, *Valley Without Echo,* was produced in Europe by the British Council. His second play, *Cry Tamba,* was published in *West African Review* in the same year.

In 1957, Akar was appointed head of programs in the Sierra Leone Broadcasting Service, becoming Director of Broadcasting from 1960-66. In 1961, at the time Sierra Leone gained its independence, he composed the national anthem. In order to help gain greater

cultural recognition for Sierra Leone, he organized the National Dance Troupe, of which he was director from 1961-66, which he led in many successful performances around the world. In 1964 the troupe was acclaimed as the "best dance ensemble" at the New York World's Fair.

In 1969 he was appointed Sierra Leone ambassador to the United States. Because of his disagreement with the Sierra Leone government over the declaration of a republic, he quit his post in April 1971, taking a position for a time as assistant to the president of the University of California at Berkeley.

He then went to Jamaica, where he became a staff member of the *Gleaner,* where he wrote a regular column entitled "Man on the Move." He died of a heart attack in Jamaica in 1975.

CYRIL P. FORAY

BIBLIOGRAPHY: J. Akar, "Cry Tamba," *West African Review,* July, 1954, "The Arts in Sierra Leone," *African Forum* I:2, Fall 1965, pp. 87-91.

BA FODAY MANSARAY

Ba Foday Mansaray (circa 1750s-1818) was a Limba leader who founded a state in Wara Wara district, based on Bafodea (Bafodaya), a capital named after him.

He appears to have been born about the middle of the 18th century. His father was Papay Ndayin, who had led migrants of the Mansaray clan (a Mandinka group) from the north into Wara Wara Limba country, in the present Koinadugu district, earlier in the century. After Ndayin had settled at Kayinbon, a town belonging to the Kamara, a Limba clan, he was given the daughter of Temeta, the Kayinbon chief, as his wife. Her name was Binti, and she became Ba Foday's mother. Thus Ba Foday was born of a Mansaray and Kamara union.

Upon the death of Ndayin, Ba Foday became ruler of Kayinbon himself—a development that signified the assumption of Mansaray (Mandinka) in place of Limba rulership over Kayinbon. Ba Foday then convinced his Mansaray and Limba kinsmen to move away from Kayinbon, which was in a hilly district, and to establish a new town in a well-watered valley. Participating family units, whether Kamara, Mansaray, or Konte (another Mandinka group) from about 15 neighboring Wara Wara Limba towns and villages built houses for themselves in the new town. The town, ruled by Ba Foday, was named Ba Fodaya (today called Bafodea) after him, and became the capital of the towns and villages which had participated in its construction.

Ba Foday, from this new base, then consolidated his rule, and expanded it to include what is now the Wara Wara Yagala chiefdom of Kamuke, as well as large sections of what is now the Kasunko chiefdom. By the end of the 18th century, Ba Foday was himself appointing the heads of the towns under his control, although these appointees continued to be selected from among the towns' ruling families.

During the time of his rule, Ba Foday successfully resisted attempts by the Fula of Futa Jallon (the mountainous district in what is now the Republic of Guinea) to subdue Wara Wara country. Earlier, the Fula had successfully launched a jihad (holy war waged on behalf of Islam) in Futa Jallon in 1727-28, and subsequently envisaged extending the jihad to neighboring countries. By the second decade of the 19th century, however, Ba Foday had repelled the Fula army from his Kamuke province. But the exertions called forth by the war took their toll, and Ba Foday died soon after, probably about 1818.

Though Wara Wara country, centered on the town of Bafodea, temporarily passed under the control of Futa Jallon soon after Ba Foday's death, this great Limba leader had nevertheless succeeded in consolidating a polity which was to survive into the colonial period, when it was split up into a number of chiefdoms. He also secured the rulership of this state for his descendants.

C. MAGBAILY FYLE

BIBLIOGRAPHY: C. Magbaily Fyle, "The Kabala

Complex: Koranko-Limba Relationships in Nineteenth and Twentieth Century Sierra Leone," in A. Abraham, *Topics in Sierra Leone History*, Freetown, 1976.

BALANSAMA MARA

Balansama Mara (mid-18th century?-1830s?) was a ruler of Barawa, a Koranko chiefdom in what is now part of the Nieni chiefdom in the Koinadugu district of northeastern Sierra Leone. He promoted trade with neighboring states, as well as with Freetown.

In contemporary tradition, he is referred to as Maran Balansama. The name Balansama is common among the Koranko, and is particularly associated with rulers of the Koranko Mara clan, to which he belonged. At the turn of the last century, for instance, a Balansama Mara ruled the Koranko chiefdom of Sengbe in what is now Koinadugu District. In the 1970s this same chiefdom had yet another Balansama Mara as paramount chief.

Balansama Mara was born probably about the middle of the 18th century, and was the son of Mansa Sewa of the Koranko of Barawa. By the end of that century, Balansama appears to have succeeded his father as ruler of Barawa, and having his capital at Kulakonka. He also ruled over the domain of the Koranko of the Koroma clan, then centered at Kamarow, now an abandoned site in the Koranko chiefdom of Diang, in the Koinadugu district.

Alexander Gordon Laing (1793-1826), a British traveler who is believed to have been the first European to have visited Tombouctou, visited Kulakonka in 1822, and gave the following description of Balansama and his domain:

The capital of North Western Koranko is Kulakonko, where Balansama, the present king, resides; he is a man of considerable influence and property and is the most powerful chief between his country and Sierra Leone; his authority extends as far as the banks of the Niger and his capital is visited by the nations of Sangara (Sankaran) for the purposes of trade.

It appears that in the 18th century Balansama's father, Sewa, had joined with the Yalunka of the state of Solimana to oppose the jihad (holy war waged in the name of Islam) launched by the Fula of Futa Jallon. This gave the Solima, the people of Solimana, a dominant influence over the Barawa. Later, when Balansama had consolidated his authority in Barawa, he apparently tried to end Solima influence. In consequence, a Solima force attacked Kamarow, then an important town in Balansama's domain. This led to much conflict between Balansama and the manga (ruler) Sori Wuleng of the Solima.

The counter-influence exerted by the Solima did not, however, effectively diminish Balansama's authority, as Laing attests. Balansama placed his sons as rulers of the major towns in his domain. One son, named Kalu, became headman of Kulakonka. By the 1820s, large trading caravans were being organized in Balansama's territory to travel to Freetown. Numerous other trade caravans from Sankaran country (a region on the headwaters of the Niger River, south of Kankan, in what is now the Republic of Guinea) traded with Kulakonka, or passed through that town en route to Freetown. Balansama appears to have assured the safety of the trade route through Barawa, and in return levied tolls that gave him wealth and consequent influence.

Balansama's death probably occurred in the 1830s. He was succeeded by his son Damatibolo.

C. MAGBAILY FYLE

BIBLIOGRAPHY: A.G. Laing, *Travels in Timannee, Kooranko and Soolima Countries in Western Africa*, London, 1825; C. Magbaily Fyle, "Solimana and its Neighbours," Ph.D. dissertation, Northwestern University, Evanston, Illinois, 1976.

BALLANTA-TAYLOR, N.J.G.

Professor Nicholas Julius George Ballanta-Taylor (1893-1962) was a musicologist, organist, and composer.

He was born in Freetown, and educated at the local Church Missionary Society (C.M.S.) Grammar School, and at Fourah Bay College.

While in government service in the Gambia in 1914, he observed that a Bambara flutist produced a note between B—natural and B—flat, a note which he could not match on his harmonium. This prompted a search into the nature of African music which took him to many parts of West and Central Africa, America, and Europe. In 1921, in the United States, he studied the affinity between Black American and African music. Aided by funds from George Peabody, Ballanta studied piano with John Orth, and composition under Yacehia of the Boston Conservatory. He graduated from the Institute of Musical Art in 1924.

From 1924 to 1926, he toured Africa collecting specimens of musical forms. On a Guggenheim award, he did theoretical work on musical scales in Germany, and carried out more field work in 1926-27. His completed manuscript, "The Aesthetics of African Music," which included 350 musical examples, is a unique document in this field.

Returning to Sierra Leone in 1933, he taught music, played the organ, and wrote and produced three operas—"Afiwa," "Boima," and "Effuah"—as well as a concert overture.

Because he worked at a time when little was known about African music, his original research was only fully appreciated after his death. The publication of his manuscript will place him among Africa's great pioneers in the musical field.

ELDRED D. JONES

BAMBAFARA

Bambafara (circa 1830s-July 7, 1921) was the ruler from the 1870s to 1921 of Nieni, today a chiefdom in the Koinadugu District in northeastern Sierra Leone. In the 1890s, he resisted the territorial expansion of Samori Touré (1830-1900), the famous Mandinka warrior whose power at one time extended from Futa Jallon to Upper Volta.

Popularly known as "Bambafara of Nieni," he was the son of Yirimusukali of the Koroma clan of the Koranko, who was the ruler of Nieni before him. He was born at Yifin, which was the chief town in the Nieni country. Much of Lower Koranko (which was south of the Seli, or Rokel, River) as well as parts of Konike Temne country had by this time apparently come under the rule of his father. In consequence, Bambafara grew up secure in the knowledge that he was the son of an important mansa (ruler).

By the 1850s, war had developed between the Koranko of Nieni, led by Yirimusukeli, and the Biriwa Limba, led by their kurugba (military leader) Suluka (q.v.). After six years of fighting, Nieni was overcome, and young Bambafara was captured. He was taken as a prisoner to Bumban, the capital of Biriwa Limba. He apparently spent a number of years at Bumban, where he was accorded the treatment due to one of noble birth, and continued to be trained in the warrior tradition. By the 1870s, he had been released, after some of his Koranko brethren had traveled to Bumban bearing presents to petition Suluku (who had become gbaku, or ruler, of Biriwa) to let him return home again.

Upon his release, Bambafara became ruler of Nieni. He first consolidated his rule over the state he inherited from his father, which was of considerable extent. In the neighboring Kaliang country of the Thoronka Koranko, (in the western part of what is now the Nieni chiefdom) to which his authority extended, he installed as sub-ruler one of his lieutenants, Sayo Demba, himself a Thoronka and a great warrior. Bambafara also exerted some control or influence over the Kono of Sando (a pre-colonial state) and the Koranko of Sambaia (now in Tonkolili District), as well as over the territory of Wuli, in the northern section of what is now Nieni, where another of his lieutenants, Banda Karifa, ruled. As ruler of this extensive area, he was renowned for the help he gave his subjects, which earned him the name of konkifaga, or hunger killer.

By 1890, the political and military expansion of the Mandinka warrior Samori Touré had reached Nieni. Bambafara resisted Samori, but lost his able general, Sayo Demba, in the fighting. He nevertheless successfully defended Nieni itself against the Sofa, as Samori's warriors were called. It is recorded in Koranko tradition that he won some important battles against the Sofa north of the Loma Mountains of northeast Sierra Leone. In this he was aided by his lieutenant Banda Karifa of Wuli. But the overwhelming force of the Sofa led him to move his capital from Yifin (probably destroyed by the attacking forces) to Kintibalia. Here, on one of the peaks of the Loma ranges, many of the Kono of Sando rallied to him to seek his protection. At Kintibalia, in 1893, he met with Captain E.A.W. Lendy of the Sierra Leone Frontier Police who was on a mission against the Sofa. (In December of the same year, Lendy was shot dead by mistake, when British and French forces clashed, each being under the erroneous impression that they were fighting Samori.)

By the time the Sofa threat had lessened, the British were moving in to establish a protectorate over the Sierra Leone hinterland. Early in 1895 the British convinced Bambafara to move his capital from the impregnable Kintibalia to a newly-built town named Kruto, about 6 km (4 mi) away. Bambafara was initially recognized by the British as paramount chief of Nieni, Kaliang, Wuli, and Sambaia—the areas over which he had ruled before the Sofa invasion.

By 1899, however, his territory had been reduced. His former lieutenant, Banda Karifa, was made paramount chief of Wuli, after which other paramount chiefs were appointed to rule Sambaia and Kaliang. Bambafara, however, who continued to rule as paramount chief of Nieni, remained much respected by these chiefs. His authority was habitually invoked by the British colonial administration in the settlement of disputes in many neighboring Koranko and Temne chiefdoms. He died, a grand old man, in 1921.

C. MAGBAILY FYLE

BIBLIOGRAPHY: E.F. Sayers, "Notes on the Clan or Family Names Common in the Area of Temne Speaking Peoples," *Sierra Leone Studies*, December 1927; C. Magbaily Fyle, "Almamy Suluku of Sierra Leone," (forthcoming).

BANGURA, J.A.

John Amadu Bangura (March 8, 1930-June 29, 1971) was a career officer in the Sierra Leone armed forces. He briefly headed an interim government in 1968, and was executed in 1971 after unsuccessfully attempting to overthrow the Sierra Leone government.

He was born of Loko parentage, at Kalangba, in the Bombali district of the Northern province. He received his primary school education at Binkolo, and later at the American Wesleyan Methodist School in Rogbane, both of which were also in the Bombali district. He then attended Koyeima Central School, and then attended the Bo Government School. He finished his schooling in 1949.

He joined the army as a private in 1950. He attended military courses in what is now Ghana and Nigeria, gaining the distinction of graduating first in the platoon commander's course in Ghana, organized for warrant officers and senior non-commissioned officers. After showing much talent and promise, he was sent to the British Military Academy at Sandhurst in England, where he received officer cadet training. After graduating, he was transferred to Mons Officers' Cadet School at Eaton Hall, Chester, England, in 1952. In August 1954, he graduated with the rank of second lieutenant.

Returning home in 1955, Bangura was appointed platoon commander of 'A' Rifle Company in the 1st Battalion of the Royal Sierra Leone Regiment, rising to the rank of captain in 1958. When the United Nations sent a peacekeeping force to the Congo (now Zaire) in the early 1960s, Bangura served there in 1963 with the first United Nations Emergency Force (U.N.E.F.). On his return, he was promoted major, and in 1964 became lieutenant-colonel and commander of the 1st Battalion. In 1966 he became a colonel.

Shortly before the 1967 general elections, Bangura was arrested and detained on charges of mutiny. He was, however, released before long, and appointed counsellor and head of chancery at the Sierra Leone Embassy in Washington. When, during the political crisis following the 1967 general elections, the military seized power, Bangura unceremoniously abandoned his diplomatic appointment, and proceeded to the Republic of Guinea in an effort to overthrow the military government of the National Reformation Council (N.R.C.) in Sierra Leone.

In April 1968, however, the N.R.C. was overthrown by a revolt of non-commissioned officers. Bangura was immediately recalled to become chairman of the National Interim Council which, for a brief period, was the effective government of the country. Bangura, upon assuming leadership, promised to return the country to civilian rule within a week. He kept his promise, and ensured the return of Siaka Stevens as prime minister. After this, Bangura, who resumed his command of the 1st Battalion, also became commander of the Royal Sierra Leone Military Forces. In May 1969, he was promoted brigadier and, in the 1970 New Year's Honours Awards, received the decoration of Commander of the British Empire (C.B.E.), Military Division.

In March 1971, Brigadier Bangura was arrested with other senior officers on charges of mutiny and treason, in attempting to overthrow the government he had been instrumental in returning to power, by unlawful means. Convicted and sentenced to death, he was hanged, together with three other senior officers, at Pademba Road prisons the same year.

ARTHUR ABRAHAM

BIBLIOGRAPHY: C.P. Foray, *Historical Dictionary of Sierra Leone*, Metuchen, New Jersey, and London, 1977; *Sierra Leone Year Book*, Freetown, 1971.

BANKOLE-BRIGHT, H.C.

Dr. Herbert Christian Bankole-Bright (August 23, 1883-December 12, 1958), whose political career spanned four decades, from the 1920s to the 1950s, was one of the most controversial, enigmatic, and misunderstood politicians of pre-independence Sierra Leone.

He was born at Okrika, a Delta state in Nigeria, east of the mouth of the Niger. His father, Jacob Galba-Bright, a "diplomatic agent" in the service of the Royal Niger Company, took his family back home to Freetown upon his retirement. Galba-Bright then set up a thriving commercial business in Freetown, and used his wealth to educate his children.

After attending the Methodist (then Wesleyan) Boys' School in Freetown, Bankole-Bright went to study medicine at Edinburgh, in Scotland. In 1910 he qualified as a medical doctor, and returned to Sierra Leone. In 1911 he married Adda Bishop whose father, the Hon. T. Colenso Bishop, an affluent merchant, was mayor of Freetown at the time of his death in 1898. They had four children.

By the 1920s, in addition to running a nursing home, Bankole-Bright had become a leader of the more progressive faction in local politics. His political views found expression through his newspapers, the *Aurora* (1918-circa 1925) and the *Evening Despatch,* (founded in the 1950s) notable for their extremism, and through his membership in the Legislative Council.

The 1924 Constitution had given him the opportunity to enter the Legislative Council as an elected member. Gifted in oratory, Bright, and his fellow elected member, E.S. Beoku-Betts (*q.v.*), dominated local politics for the next 12 years, agitating on issues associated with the activities of I.T.A. Wallace-Johnson (q.v.) and his West African Youth League. In addition to pressing for the repeal of the Assessor's Ordinance (which provided for trial by three Assessors, nominated by the government, rather than by a jury, in some criminal cases involving government employees), they also urged the establishment of a West African Court of Appeal, workmen's compensation, the extension of the franchise, the introduction of an unofficial majority in the Legislative Council, better pay and the abolition of discrimination against African staff.

Bright's championship of the dignity and rights of the Sierra Leonean often placed him in opposition to the colonial administration. But, paradoxically, he remained a loyal British subject, and was a member of the Royal Colonial Institute. He believed in constitutionalism, however intemperate his language at times. This belief, and his affirmation of "organic connections with the British Crown," were shared by leading contemporaries in West African politics, who maintained contact with one another across territorial boundaries. Bright, like his other contemporaries, supported the National Congress of British West Africa, a pan-West-African movement which had been inaugurated in Accra, in what was then the Gold Coast, in 1920. Bright himself was secretary-general of the delegation which the Congress sent to London in 1920 in an unsuccessful bid to meet with Lord Milner, British Secretary of State for the Colonies from 1918-

21. He remained, however, an active Congress politician to the end. The National Congress of West Africa grew less effective after the death of its founder, J.E. Casely Hayford (1866-1930) of the Gold Coast. But the ideals of the Congress had been embodied in the West African Student's Union, which was founded in London in August 1925 through Bright's efforts, and which carried on agitation for independence throughout the 1930s and 1940s. Such was the impact of Bright on local and regional politics that by the 1930s his prominence was generally recognized. One source described him as "the best politician in Freetown," while an admiring but critical pen-portrait written in 1933 stated that: "Were West Africa a republic, he would be a fit candidate for the presidency."

But by the late 1930s, Bright had "mellowed." Some British officials, who would have liked to see Bright in jail, noted his declining popularity and effectiveness with glee. The decline was due to a number of causes, some of them domestic. More importantly, contemporary developments required a more "populist" approach to politics than the sedate stance of Congress. In addition, Bright had supported unpopular government measures, such as the Three Bills of 1939. These bills, connected with undesirable literature, with sedition, and with expulsion, were passed by the colonial administration to neutralize the activities of the West African Youth League formed by Wallace-Johnson. Bright's attitude on the Three Bills so angered his constituents that he was the subject of a vote of no confidence. He was dismissed as vice-president of the local National Congress, and resigned his seat in the Legislative Council. For the following 11 years he was to remain outside the Legislative Council.

When Bright returned to the Council in 1951, the experience was less than rewarding. The memory of his positive contributions in earlier days was dimmed by his role in opposing the political influence of the peoples of what was then the Protectorate, which they had gained under the provisions of the Stevenson Constitution of 1947. He conducted these activities in his capacity as leader of the National Council of Sierra Leone, which represented the Krio (Creole) party.

Though he opposed the predominance of the Protectorate in politics, he actively sought the interests of the Protectorate in the Legislative Council. For instance, he championed the case of A.T. Summer, the Mende linguist, who sought a better salary, and also agitated for the employment of Dr. M.A.S. Margai (q.v.), the first Protectorate-born doctor, later to become Sierra Leone's first prime minister.

Bright's overbearing manner and his great pride in his family status often made him arrogant, conceited, and sometimes unscrupulous. It was therefore often difficult for the colonial administration, or the succeeding African government, to appreciate his finer points. His highest official title in Sierra Leone was Leader of the Opposition, and he was granted the title of "Honorable" for life. This last honor, however, came too late to mean anything to him. He was never given a decoration or an honor by the British Crown.

His other characteristics were his remarkable forthrightness and bluntness, acknowledged by friends and enemies alike, as well as his devotion to his church and his people. He was a trustee of his church, the Gibraltar Methodist, and used to organize activities for schoolchildren in his home village of Wellington.

Opinions on Bankole-Bright will continue to differ, but when he died in 1958, broken in spirit, Sir Milton Margai, prime minister of a non-self-governing Sierra Leone, described his death as the end of an epoch:

> The grand old man of politics was a stalwart pioneer in a field which held very little rewards... His contributions to West African nationalism, to the political consciousness and activity of Sierra Leone, to the general cause of freedom and justice, are too numerous to mention... History and those who write history will make a spacious room to record (his) life and achievements.

AKINTOLA J.G. WYSE

BIBLIOGRAPHY: Michael Crowder, "An African Aristocracy," *The Geographical Magazine,* August, 1958; W.H. Fitzjohn, *Ambassador of Christ and Caesar*, Ibadan, 1975; J.D. Hargreaves, "Western Democracy and African Society," *International Affairs,* 3, 1955; C. Kessie, "Pen Portrait of the Hon. Dr. H.C. Bankole-Bright, M.L.C.," *West African Students Union,* March, 1934; Martin Kilson, *Political Change in a West African State*, Cambridge, Massachusetts, 1966; W.S. Marcus-Jones, "The Protection of Fundamental Rights and Freedoms of the Individual in Sierra Leone," unpublished thesis, Yale, n.d.; G. Padmore, "Democratic Advance in Sierra Leone," *The Crisis,* March, 1954; Leo Spitzer, *The Creoles of Sierra Leone,* Ile-Ife, 1975.

BARLATT, S.J.S.

Samuel Josiah Sigismund Barlatt (1867-September 7 or 8, 1940) was Mayor of Freetown from 1918-20, during which time he played a moderating role during various troubles which occurred in the years immediately following World War I.

He was born in Freetown, and was the eldest son of

C.J.G. Barlatt, a former mayor of Freetown (1901). Young Barlatt was educated at the Church Missionary Society (C.M.S.) Grammar School and, later, at Fourah Bay College, then affiliated with the University of Durham, where he gained a Bachelor of Arts degree, and a licentiate in theology. In 1906 he worked for some time as chief clerk for the Royal Garrison Artillery's brigade office at Tower Hill, in Freetown, before leaving for Britain to study law. In 1909 he was called to the Bar at Gray's Inn in London, and received the degree of M.A. from Durham University. He returned home in 1910 to set up a successful law practice.

His proficiency was appreciated by the government, and on several occasions he acted as police magistrate. A brilliant and witty counsel, his erudition was impeccable, and his delivery first class. With such qualities, and his family connections, he was elected Mayor of Freetown in November 1918 remaining in office until 1920 (i.e. for two terms). He did yeoman service as mayor during the troubled years of 1918 and 1919. During the influenza epidemic of 1918, for example, the Mayor could be seen with his sleeves rolled up tending to the sick and the dead.

As Mayor, Barlatt was instrumental in promoting peace in times of trouble, especially during the anti-Syrian riot of 1919. On that occasion, his moderating influence and solicitous help to the Lebanese (mistakenly called Syrians in Sierra Leone) helped to bring peace more quickly and easily at a time when the atmosphere was taut with racial strife between Krios (Creoles) and white officials. Indeed, Barlatt himself suffered insult from a white army officer who assaulted him.

Following the 1919 strike, the colonial administration established the Parodi Commission, with Barlatt as a member, to investigate the event. The commission placed responsibility for the strike on the City Council and imposed on it a fine of £36,000. At Barlatt's special plea, however, the administration was induced to reduce the amount.

Another labor dispute in which he played a key role was the Elder Dempster Lines' seamen's strike of 1920. He persuaded the men to return to work, and in appreciation of his services, Elder Dempster gave him a silver service.

While Barlatt was a man of peace and moderation, he was perhaps too conservative for many of his contemporaries. He hurt his reputation when he argued against the name "Sierra Leone Native Defence Fund." The fund had been established to give aid and to defend Sierra Leoneans against heavy-handed acts of the government. But according to Barlatt, the word "defence" gave the impression of an antagonism to the colonial government, and suggested a conflict of interest between the government and the people.

Nevertheless, he did participate in the activities of the National Congress of British West Africa, and often addressed political meetings. Like his contemporaries, he was a serious churchman. He was a member of the Fourah Bay College Council, and a prominent member of the Native Pastorate Church. He was also a student of the classics.

Though he was at one time considered for nomination to the Legislative Council, because of his "influence over the uneducated classes," he never served on it.

AKINTOLA J.G. WYSE

BIBLIOGRAPHY: Allister Macmillan (ed.), *The Red Book of West Africa*, London, 1920; *Sierra Leone Weekly News*, Freetown.

BENKA-COKER, S.A.

Sir Salako Ambrosius Benka-Coker (June 16, 1900-December 7, 1965) was the first Sierra Leonean to become Chief Justice, serving from 1960 to 1963.

The son of Ambrose Benka-Coker, a civil servant who had worked in Nigeria, Salako was educated first at the Church Missionary Society (C.M.S.) Grammar School. He entered Fourah Bay College (then affiliated with the University of Durham) in 1916, and took his B.A. there in 1918. He then taught school for a year, after which he worked as a mercantile clerk for two years, from 1919-21. He then went to England, where he read law in London, and was called to the Bar of the Middle Temple in January 1926.

He went to the Gambia in the same year and engaged in private practice in Bathurst (now Banjul). From 1926-35, the year in which he left the Gambia to return to Sierra Leone, he was the Commissioner for the Boy Scouts of the Gambia, and in 1929 took the Gambia contingent of Scouts to the World Jamboree of Scouts held in Birkenhead, England. In 1932 he married Hannah Luke.

In Sierra Leone, he continued to practice from 1935-43, when he was appointed Crown Counsel, a post he held for ten years. He became Solicitor-General in 1953, and acting Attorney-General for some months in 1954-55, and again in 1956. In 1957 he became an acting puisne judge, holding the post substantively in 1958. He was also vice-chairman of the Sierra Leone Sports Council from 1956-58, and became its chairman, as well as chairman of the Sierra Leone Football Association, in 1961.

He became acting Chief Justice in 1959, and was appointed substantive Chief Justice in 1960. In 1961 he was knighted, and in 1962 he received the honorary degree of doctor of civil law from Durham University.

During his term as Chief Justice, Sir Salako acted as Governor-General on four occasions. He died in 1966 after a distinguished legal career.

ARTHUR ABRAHAM

BIBLIOGRAPHY: Cyril P. Foray, *Historical Dictionary of Sierra Leone*, Metuchen, New Jersey, and London, 1977; *Sierra Leone Year Book*, Freetown, 1965.

BEOKU-BETTS, E.S.

Ernest Samuel Beoku-Betts (March 15, 1895-September 23, 1957) was one of the most outstanding Krio (Creole) liberals of his time. As one of the first three Africans to be elected to the Legislative Council of Sierra Leone in 1924, he served as first urban member until 1927, when he became its vice-president. He was the first Sierra Leonean to attain this post. Both he and H.C. Bankole-Bright (*q.v.*)—the "double Bs" as they were often called—dominated the politics of the Legislative Council in the 1920s and 1930s. They were gadflies to the colonial administration.

Born in Freetown, Ernest was one of the five children of C.W. Betts, an enterprising and successful Krio hardware merchant. Betts was noted for selling almost anything in the trade from 'pin to anchor,' as someone fondly commented. As sole agent for the celebrated Singer Sewing Machine company, and as the owner of five hardware stores in Freetown, Ernest's father wielded considerable influence within the local community.

Beoku-Betts was educated at the Leopold Educational Institute (a secondary school), and later graduated with a B.A. from Fourah Bay College, Freetown. In 1914 he went to England to study law. He obtained his B.C.L. (Bachelor of Civil Law) and M.A. degrees from Durham in 1915, and his L.L.B. (Bachelor of Laws), with honors, from London, and was called to the Bar at the Middle Temple in London in 1917.

On his return home, he went into private practice for a few months with H.J.L. Boston (*q.v.*), a well-known Freetown barrister. He then began his own practice, which flourished, as there were then few competent African lawyers.

He was inspired by nationalist sentiments and, after his returned home, altered his family name—which had previously been simply "Betts"—by prefixing it with "Beoku," an abbreviation of the name of the town of Abeokuta, in Nigeria, where his father's family had originated. Outspoken and intelligent, he took to politics. In 1919 he became a member of the Freetown City Council, on which he served until 1926. This was at a time when the African intelligentsia suffered much discrimination at the hands of the colonial establishment. Qualified African barristers were not employed in the judiciary, while no African doctor was to be senior to a European, however qualified or experienced he might be. Lebanese traders were also being given preferential treatment at the expense of the well-established Krio merchants, who consequently suffered irreparable economic loss. Moreover, until 1924 Africans were not allowed elected representation in the colony's Legislative Council.

Such disabilities forced people like Beoku-Betts to become actively involved not only in local politics but also in the activities of the National Congress of British West Africa (N.C.B.W.A.), the pan-West-African movement that was founded in Accra, in what was then the Gold Coast, in 1920.

The 1924 constitution, which increased the unofficial membership of the Legislative Council to 10, made provision for only 3 members to be elected to represent colony interests. Beoku-Betts was among the first members to be elected. He also served as Mayor of Freetown from 1925-26. Although his western education and social background had conditioned him not to be totally opposed to the colonial presence in Africa, yet he often criticized and condemned the inequitable way in which Africans, particularly those

with a western education, were being treated by the colonial establishment. Both he and Bankole-Bright, as well as other West Africans of similar social standing, demanded justice and fair play for Africans, and the "two Bs" worked almost as partners in the Legislative Council.

Most of the issues raised by Beoku-Betts were wide-ranging and often controversial. He often focussed on critical questions which sought not only to end discrimination against Africans in the colonial service, but also to improve their conditions of service in general. He constantly embarrassed the colonial establishment by asking questions concerning vacancies in the colonial service which could adequately be filled by qualified Africans. He was particularly interested in the protection of the rights and the improvement of the conditions of railway workers. He openly supported the railway strike of 1926, which earned him severe castigation in the official dispatch of Governor Sir Ransford Slater (term of office 1922-27) to the Secretary of State for the Colonies. He also strongly criticized the increasing presence in Sierra Leone of Lebanese traders, who were prospering at the expense of the local business community. In the Legislative Council he supported motions which sought to protect the underdog, particularly chiefs, who were often made to look undignified in the eyes of their subjects. He even sought the welfare of prisoners.

In 1937, he was invited to represent Sierra Leone at the coronation of King George VI of the United Kingdom. In that same year he resigned from active participation in politics to become the first Sierra Leonean police magistrate. This caused some dissension between him and his political ally, Bankole-Bright. But in spite of this, and also in spite of the fact that he stood to lose financially, for his legal practice was then flourishing, he accepted the appointment. This was because he felt it his personal duty to prove that an African was just as capable as any European of holding such a responsible position. Indeed, soon after his appointment other Sierra Leoneans began to be appointed to the Bench.

In 1945, he became a puisne judge, and, in the following year, a judge of the West African Court of Appeal. He again came to the fore by playing a crucial role in the settlement of the traumatic general strike, and the accompanying disturbances, which occurred in 1955.

Privately and publicly, he brought together the disaffected workers led by Marcus Grant on the one hand, and members of the government under the Chief Minister, Sir Milton Margai (q.v.), with Siaka Stevens as his Minister of Labour, on the other. It was through his tireless endeavors that a compromise was effected, and the disputes finally settled.

Apart from his political activities, Beoku-Betts was a keen all-rounder in sports, playing cricket, soccer, and tennis. For many years till his death he served as president of the Sierra Leone Football and Cricket Associations.

For his distinguished service he was awarded a knighthood by Queen Elizabeth II in 1957, becoming the second Sierra Leonean to be so honored. He died later that year in Freetown.

JOSEPHINE A. BEOKU-BETTS

BIBLIOGRAPHY: Akintola J.G. Wyse, "Research Notes on Dr. Bankole-Bright (1883-1958); his life to 1939," *Africana Research Bulletin,* October, 1974; *Daily Mail Year Book 1925; Legislative Council Debates,* Freetown, 1924, 1925, 1926, 1927.

BILALI

Bilali (circa 1810-1880s) also known as Mori Lamina, was the ruler of Tonko Limba. He was born to servile status among the Soso, but subsequently became an independent ruler in Limba country.

He was the son of a Koranko slave woman, and of Mori Shaka, one of the Soso rulers of Kukuna, in what is now the Kambia district. Because his father did not publicly acknowledge him as his son, Bilali retained his servile status. But his father had him brought up in the warrior tradition, and he became a great warrior, feared by the neighboring Tonko Limba. When Mori Shaka died, he left the knowledge of the use of his war charms with Bilali, even though he had many other sons.

As Shaka had left many debts, his other sons proposed to pay them off by selling off some of the 200 slaves Shaka had left behind. The head slaves, of whom Bilali was one, told the creditors that they were willing to work off the debt by farming and by trading with canoes. But the creditors drove them away, scorning any settlement with slaves. Apparently jealous of Bilali's prowess, his brothers attempted to pay off part of the debt by selling some of the slaves, including Bilali's two sons. Bilali and the other head slaves redeemed those sold. Later Bilali also redeemed his sister and some of his other children, who had also been sold by his brothers.

By this time Bilali had decided that he had to escape from Kukuna. Together with the slaves supporting him, he fled from Kukuna in 1836, after negotiating for protection with the ruler of Tonko Limba. His brothers pursued him, but he defeated them in combat. He then marched on in triumph to Tonko Limba, where he built a town called Kolunkuray on land given him by the Bombo Lahai, ruler of Tonko Limba.

Kolunkuray was located on the border between Kukuna and Tonko Limba. Later, Bilali expanded the area of his authority by building more towns. Laminaya became his chief town.

From the time of his escape in 1836 onwards, Bilali's brothers, who later became the rulers of Kukuna, never gave up the idea of recapturing him. They formed several coalitions for this purpose, which included the Soso of the Morea state centered on Forecaria, as well as the Soso of Kambia under Sattan Lahai (q.v.). But, aided by the Tonko Limba, Bilali successfully resisted their attacks. In the event, the constant campaigning eventually reduced the ruler of Kukuna to poverty, while Bilali continued to thrive, as more and more slaves rallied to his cause. By the 1870s, he had entered into diplomatic relations with neighboring Koranko and Loko rulers, in order to strengthen his power. He was, by this time, regarded as an important independent ruler in his own right. He was also one of the rulers who accorded protection to the trade caravans which travelled to Sierra Leone Colony from the interior.

Bilali apparently died in the 1880s, having for half a century successfully maintained his own freedom and independence, despite his original status.

C. MAGBAILY FYLE

BIBLIOGRAPHY: Christopher Fyfe, *A History of Sierra Leone,* London, 1962; C. Magbaily Fyle, "The Idea of Slavery in Nineteenth Century Sierra Leone and the Career of Bilali," *Journal of the Historical Society of Sierra Leone*, Vol. II, No. 1, January, 1978.

BOKARI

Almamy Kandeh Bokari (18?-1880s?) was ruler of the Soso state of Morea, today divided between the Republic of Guinea and Sierra Leone. He was one of the most powerful political personalities in the northern Sierra Leone area during the latter half of the 19th century. From the 1850s to the 1880s he figured prominantly in political disputes, not only between rival African parties, but also between the British and the French. His activities and alliances show him to have been astute under extremely complicated, fluctuating, and dangerous circumstances.

The Morea country, of which Forecaria was the capital, was situated in the Melacourie river basin. The Melacourie, as well as the Scarcies, and other rivers in the region, being at that time important trade arteries, were the scene of intense power conflicts not only between rival African states and claimants to authority, but also between European and African merchants.

In 1865, Alimamy Foday Wise, the ruler of Morea, died, leaving the succession unclear. Bokari and his cousin, Maligi Gbele, vied for the succession. The resulting power struggle threatened to disrupt trade, which displeased French and British interests in the area. Initially, despite Bokari's hiring of Temne mercenaries to fight in his cause, of whom Kebelai, popularly known as Bai Bureh (*q.v.*) was foremost,

Maligi Gbele won, and his position was confirmed by a treaty with the French. The French had sent a gunboat to overawe Bokari, and to extract reparation from him for the losses of certain French traders. In return, the French gained from Morea port facilities at Gbinti, on the mouth of the Melacourie. This gave them an advantage over the British trading in the area. (The British also had sent a gunboat in about 1865/66, and Bokari was "crowned" in their presence).

In 1866, however, Bokari succeeded in having Maligi beheaded, and in making himself ruler of Morea, with authority over Gbinti. The French, in

their own interests, recognized him immediately, and signed a treaty with him similar to the one they had signed with Maligi.

While the British, based in Freetown, did not like such French predominance, the authorities in London cautioned restraint. In 1869, therefore, Britain also extended recognition to Bokari.

As French influence continued to expand in the region, Bokari appears to have become disenchanted with the French. He then embarked on a policy of playing off one European power against the other, in order to enhance his position. In this he displayed political astuteness, as also did other African leaders, such as Samori Touré, the famous Mandinka warrior, at this time.

In 1877, Bokari complained of French pressure on him, and sought British friendship. The governor of Sierra Leone, Sir Samuel Rowe (terms of office 1877-80 and 1885-88), accepted his overtures and visited him. Undeterred, the French continued to press their claims, and occupied Samu, the territory between the Melacourie and Scarcies Rivers, as well as the island of Matacong, off the coast, in 1879. To counter French claims, Rowe signed a treaty with the Kaloun Baga, north of Morea. In order to avert a conflict with the French, however, the British Colonial Office disavowed the treaty.

Probably partly at French instigation, and partly because of Bokari's growing political weakness—probably resulting from old age and internal opposition, as well as French harassment—his position was threatened when fighting broke out at Maligia, a town on the Melacourie River upstream from Gbinti, in 1880. Bokari fled southeast into exile in Kambia, on the Great Scarcies River, as his nephew Foday Tarawaly, namesake of the famous Islamic scholar (*q.v.*) from the same area, who had massive Soso support, took the offensive. Foday Tarawaly also received active backing from the French. Bokari does not appear to have recovered from this setback, and his fortunes thereafter declined.

GUSTAV K. DEVENEAUX

BIBLIOGRAPHY: H.A. Gailey, "European Rivalry and Diplomacy in the Millacourie, 1879-1882, *Sierra Leone Studies*, December, 1961; Christopher Fyfe, *A History of Sierra Leone*, London, 1962; John D. Hargreaves, *Prelude to the Partition of West Africa*, London, 1966; C. Newbury and A.S. Kanya-Forstner, "French Policy and the Origins of the Scramble for West Africa," *Journal of African History,* X, 1969; Gustav K. Deveneaux, "The Political and Social Impact of the Colony in Northern Sierra Leone," unpublished Ph.D. dissertation, Boston University, 1973.

BOKARI BOMBOLAI

Bokari Bombolai (18?-circa 1898) was Bai Kompa (ruler) of Koya, the Temne chiefdom to the east of Freetown, from 1890-98. He also added the name of William Rowe (governor of Sierra Leone from 1877-80 and from 1885-88) to his own.

His date of birth is unknown, but in 1857, in his younger days, he served a prison sentence for kidnapping. By the 1870s, when he came into prominence in Koya politics, he must already have been a mature man. He was probably partially of Fula ancestry, or else had married someone closely connected with the Fula Bundu family who ruled Foredugu, a Koya town. This speculation is based on the fact that the Bundu were among his strongest allies in his struggle to rule Koya. The influence of the Fula Bundu was significant not only religiously (they were Muslim) and commercially with respect to other Fula clans, but was also important because of their links with the Temne in the Rokel river region. In the late 1870s, Bokari Bombolai assisted Governor William Rowe on his tour of the hinterland, and added the governor's name to his own because he admired him.

The Koya kingship had been vacant since 1872, and the two aspirants to the succession were William Lawson, son of T.G. Lawson (q.v.), an influential government interpreter, and Bokari Bombolai, who was supported by the Bundu and their allies.

Koya, situated between Freetown and the northern interior, was the meeting place of several ethnic groups, including the original inhabitants, the Koya, now few in number, the Temne, the Fula, the Mende, the Kossoh, and a number of Liberated African settlers. The British in Freetown had long wished to annexe Koya, which was for them a frontier province into which warfare from the interior occasionally spilled over, creating instability on the borders of the Colony. At this juncture, the rivalry between the two claimants was exacerbated by fighting between the Temne and Loko which broke out in the east, while further fighting in the north between the Temne Marampa and Yoni clans also occurred. At one moment, Bokari Bombolai was arrested again by the British, and imprisoned for a while. Eventually, however, in 1888, the British, after years of attempting to end the fighting in the north, sent in a force of Frontier Police and ended the struggle. At about the same time, T.G. Lawson retired from government service, thereby weakening the claim of his son to the rulership of Koya.

Following these events, and in order to promote political and economic stability, the British recognized Bombolai as ruler of Koya in 1890. He was crowned Bai Kompa at a ceremony attended by Governor Sir James Hay (term of office 1888-91), and J.C.E. Parkes, successor to T.G. Lawson as government interpreter. Thereafter, conditions in Koya remained stable, to the satisfaction of the British.

When the hut tax was levied in Ronietta, further inland, Bokari Bombolai was one of the chiefs accused of resisting the tax. Captain H.G. Warren, the assistant inspector at Kwelu, headquarters of Ronietta, was sent to arrest him for inciting resistance and intimidating loyal chiefs. Bokari Bombolai thereupon moved to Romangi, one of his villages, where Warren, after trying to remove him forcibly, had doubts about the legality of his action, since he was unsure whether Romangi was in the Colony or the Protectorate. He therefore let Bokari Bombolai go. Bokari Bombolai thereupon complained to Governor Sir Frederic Cardew (term of office 1894-1900) about Warren's conduct towards him, but was told to comply with orders, collect the tax, and report to Captain Samuel Moore at Kwelu.

When he failed to report to Moore, Bokari Bombolai was accused by a Loko chief, Charles Smart of Mahera, of organizing resistance and of being in league with Bai Bureh (q.v.) of Kasseh. Early in March 1898, Moore, with a force of 40 Frontier Police, and helped by Smart, set out in search of Bokari Bombolai. The force burnt villages and killed several of his subjects, but failed to capture him, returning to Kwelu disappointed. Eventually Bokari Bombolai sent a tax payment of £30 from his hide-out. He was, nevertheless, deposed, and was replaced as ruler of Koya by Fula Mansa Gbanka (q.v.). He died shortly after the 1898 uprising was suppressed.

GUSTAV K. DEVENEAUX and CYRIL P. FORAY

BIBLIOGRAPHY: Gustav K. Deveneaux, ''A Turbulent Frontier: Aspects of Relations Between the Colony of Sierra Leone and Koya: 1787 to 1890,'' *Journal of the Historical Society of Nigeria*, 2, 1970, ''The Political and Social Impact of the Colony in Northern Sierra Leone,'' unpublished Ph.D. dissertation, Boston University, 1973; V.R. Dorjahn, ''A Brief History of the Temne of Yonni,'' *Sierra Leone Studies*, December, 1960; Christopher Fyfe, *A History of Sierra Leone*, London, 1962; J.M. Harris, *Annexations of Sierra Leone and Their Influence on British Trade with West Africa*, London, 1883; E. Ade Ijagbemi, ''History of the Temne in the Nineteenth Century,'' unpublished Ph.D. thesis, Edinburgh University, 1968; D. Skinner, ''Islam in Sierra Leone During the Nineteenth Century,'' unpublished Ph.D. dissertation, University of California, Berkeley, 1971.

BOSTON, H.J.L.

Henry Josiah Lightfoot Boston (August 19, 1898-January 11, 1969), after a distinguished legal career, became the first Sierra Leonean to become governor-general, a position he held from 1962 to 1967.

He was born in Bullom, in the Port Loko district, a son of the Rev. N.H. and Lauretta Boston. His family background predisposed him to educational achievement, for his father had been one of the first graduates of Fourah Bay College in 1879, after the college had become affiliated with the University of Durham in England.

Young Henry attended the Cathedral Boys Primary School in Freetown, and, later, the Church Missionary Society (C.M.S.) Grammar School, the oldest secondary school in West Africa. He graduated from Fourah Bay with an M.A. degree in 1920. He then entered the colonial civil service in Sierra Leone, working in the Secretariat and the Treasury. Studying privately, he passed the London University intermediate law examination in 1922, and left in the same year to continue his legal studies at Lincoln's Inn in England. In 1924 he gained first class honors in the final examinations of the Council of Legal Education. In 1925 he obtained Bachelor of Laws (LL.B.) and Bachelor of Civil Laws (B.C.L.) degrees, both from Durham University. He was also awarded the Barstow scholarship in 1926, returning home to Sierra Leone the same year.

In Freetown, he entered private practice as a barrister and solicitor, and was city solicitor from 1926-27. In 1935 he was appointed justice of the peace, and in 1946 he became a police magistrate. He became registrar-general of the Supreme Court in 1954, and a senior police magistrate in 1955. During the period from 1945-57, he acted on many occasions as a judge of the Supreme Court. When constitutional changes occurred in Sierra Leone, he was appointed Speaker of the newly constituted House of Representatives in 1957.

In 1962 he became governor-general of Sierra Leone, and in November of the same year knighted by the Queen of England. During the 1967 general elections, the leading political parties—the Sierra Leone People's Party (S.L.P.P.) and the All People's Congress (A.P.C.)—emerged as close rivals. The onus rested on the governor-general to choose a new prime minister. Sir Henry, after examining the situation, chose Siaka Stevens, the former Leader of the Opposition.

Soon afterwards the commander of the Armed Forces, Brigadier David Lansana (q.v.), announced a military take-over of the government, and put both the governor-general and Prime Minister Siaka Stevens

under house arrest. A military government soon followed, remaining in power for a year, during which time Sir Henry was kept under constant surveillance. His health, which was not good during his later years, was further affected during this difficult period.

In April 1968 he went to London for his health, and died there the following January. He was buried in state in Freetown.

C. MAGBAILY FYLE

BIBLIOGRAPHY: Cyril P. Foray, *Historical Dictionary of Sierra Leone*, Metuchen, New Jersey, and London, 1977; Christopher Fyfe, *Sierra Leone Inheritance*, London, 1964; *Sierra Leone Year Book*, Freetown, 1963.

BRESSILAC, M. DE MARION

Melchoir de Marion Bressilac (1813-June 25, 1859), was the first Catholic bishop of Sierra Leone, and the founder of the Society of African Missions (S.M.A.).

Marion de Bressilac served as a missionary in India from 1842-54. In 1854 he was consecrated bishop of a diocese in Madras, India, but resigned this see in 1855 to avoid an open conflict with his European confrères over his policy of Indianization of the local clergy. Returning to Rome, he volunteered to serve as a simple missionary in Africa, but instead the Vatican authorized him to found "a society of priests for the evangelization of Africa." This later resulted in the establishment of the Society of African Missions, inaugurated in Lyons, France, on December 8, 1856. Meanwhile, the "Vicariate Apostolic of Sierra Leone" had been set up on April 13, 1856, and Marion de Bressilac was named as its bishop in June.

At that time, Sierra Leone was part of the vast "Mission of Two Guineas," entrusted to the Congregation of the Holy Ghost with headquarters in Dakar, Senegal, with ill-defined limits along the coast south of Gabon, and with no fixed limit inland to the west. An advance S.M.A. party of two priests and a lay helper sailed from Marseilles, France, and arrived in Freetown on January 12, 1859. Despite the alarm of British Protestant groups at the arrival of French Catholics in the country, the governor of Sierra Leone, Col. S.J. Hill (term of office 1854-62) promised the S.M.A. the "same protection as he gave to other religious bodies."

In March 1859, Monsignor Marion de Bressilac sailed from Brest, France, with a priest and a lay brother. After visiting Dakar en route, the three arrived in Freetown on May 14. The city was then experiencing the worst yellow fever epidemic it had known for more than 25 years. The captain of the ship tried to convince the bishop and his companions not to go ashore, but Marion de Bressilac insisted on landing, in order, he said, "to share the misfortune of his children."

The S.M.A. missionaries then began to plan visits into the interior. By June 13, 1859, however, three of the S.M.A. missionaries had died of yellow fever. The bishop himself died on June 25, and was buried the next morning. The other S.M.A. missionary died on June 28, leaving only a lay helper, who returned to France.

After this, the S.M.A. transferred its African headquarters to Dahomey. Bishop Marion de Bressilac's work was not, however, in vain. In 1959, on the centenary of his death, his spiritual successors in West Africa had charge of 5 archdioceses, 13 dioceses, 1 vicariate, and 2 prefectures apostolic, while 150 African priests and 3 African bishops shared the apostolate with 800 other members of the S.M.A. Marion de Bressilac's "grasp of the absolute need of indigenous clergy," it has been written, "was taken over into the Society of African Missions and remained a cornerstone of all its future policy."

CYRIL P. FORAY

BIBLIOGRAPHY: Christopher Fyfe, *A History of Sierra Leone,* London, 1962; Holy Ghost Fathers, *Centenary Souvenir of the Holy Ghost Fathers in Sierra Leone,* Freetown, 1964; H.M. Joko-Smart, "The Contribution of the Holy Ghost Fathers to Education in Sierra Leone, 1864-1967," unpublished dissertation, Fourah Bay College-University of Durham, 1958.

BRIMA

Bombo Lahai Brima (19?-August 17, 1975), or Bombolai Brima, was chief of Tonko Limba in the Northern Province from 1952-75. In 1955, following some disaffection, he moved the administrative center of Tonko Limba from Kabubuya to Kanumeya.

He was the son of Bombo Lahai Konko Gbanku (*q.v.*) and Binti Kayako. His father ruled Tonko Limba from about 1884 to 1911. His mother was later married to Bombo Lahai Yusufu (*q.v.*), in whose household Brima was brought up. Bombo Lahai Yusufu ruled Tonko Limba from 1922 to 1931, when he was deposed.

On his election in 1952, Brima became the seventh recorded paramount chief of Tonko Limba. His main opponent was Sori Bangura of the Kabubuya ruling house. (The Kabubuya ruling house, together with three other ruling houses had the right to nominate successors to rule Tonko Limba chiefdom.)

Three years after his election, there were anti-chief riots in many parts of the Northern Province. Though his chiefdom was not directly affected, Brima himself suffered some inconvenience. A group of dissidents purporting to represent a large section of the chiefdom made a series of allegations against him. The charges made ranged from the imposition of extortionate fines to the pursuing of a political vendetta against his opponents.

As commissions of inquiry into the conduct of other chiefs were being appointed in neighboring chiefdoms, the dissidents petitioned that a similar inquiry be instituted into Brima's conduct. Failing to secure official approval for this action, however, some of the petitioners razed to the ground houses inhabited by members of Brima's family. Convinced that Kabubuya, the headquarters of the chiefdom, was hostile territory, Brima established a new headquarters at Kanumeya, a town then inhabited by Mandinka blacksmiths who had immigrated to Tonko Limba mostly from neighboring chiefdoms.

In the years immediately following Sierra Leone's independence in 1961, Brima gave his political loyalty to the Sierra Leone People's Party (S.L.P.P.), whose support was largely based on the influence of chiefs and other traditional authorities. But when the All People's Congress (A.P.C.) was founded in 1960, Brima again found himself at odds with his subjects, who saw the new party as a largely Limba organization which deserved their support. The differences became aggravated when Brima, on instructions from the government, banned meetings planned by the A.P.C. Despite this harassment, the A.P.C. won the Kambia East seat in the general elections held in 1962, and won it again in 1967.

When the A.P.C. came to power in 1968, Brima and many of his opponents became reconciled. Nevertheless, he never returned to Kabubuya, his former administrative center.

An ardent Muslim, Brima offered his Friday prayers regularly. He made the pilgrimage to Mecca, thus securing the title "Al-Hajj." Though he had no formal schooling, he had no difficulty in dealing with official correspondence. He died in 1975, after 23 years in office.

E. AMADU TURAY

BIBLIOGRAPHY: J.R. Cartwright, *Politics in Sierra Leone 1947-1967*, Toronto, 1970; H. Cox, *Report of Commission of Inquiry into Disturbances in the Provinces, November 1955 to March 1956*, London, 1956; V.R. Dorjahn and A.S. Tholley, "A Provisional

History of the Limba with Special Reference to Tonko Limba Chiefdom.'' *Sierra Leone Studies*, December, 1959; R. Finnegan, *A Survey of the Limba People of Northern Sierra Leone*, London, 1965; R. Finnegan and D. Murray, in M. Crowder and O. Ikime (eds.), *West African Chiefs*, Ile-Ife, 1970.

BUNGIE, ALIMAMY

Alimamy Bungie (December 3, 1870-August 20, 1935) was a colorful Krio (Creole) personality who was prominent in Freetown during the earlier decades of the 20th century. He was originally known as William Rainy Lumpkin.

Bungie did not come from a poor family, and began life as an apprentice to a master carpenter. His grandfather was the Honourable Henry Lumpkin, an Aku (Yoruba) recaptive, who became an influential businessman and was the first nominated African member of the Sierra Leone Legislative Council. He gave the name of William Rainy to his grandson, who in turn changed it to Alimamy Bungie. Bungie's father was a money-lender whose legal knowledge was good enough to enable him to practice as a quasi-barrister, though he had not been called to the Bar.

Young Rainy attended St. John's Maroon School and the Government Model School. He left school early, and was apprenticed to Tillotson Shaw, who ran a flourishing joinery shop and undertaking business on Kissy Road in Freetown. Bungie proved himself hardworking. Subsequently he went to try his luck in Sherbro country, where he worked with a brass band, and obtained experience in newspaper work. In search of adventure, he went to the Congo (now Zaire), at that time a land of opportunity for many Krios. He was away in the Congo for a number of years, and returned home in 1905.

Upon his return to Freetown, he set up a carpenter's shop in Kissy Street. Soon his diligence marked him out as a successful man, while his latent flamboyance, which became manifest, also proved an asset. He was generous by nature, and his annual invitations to an Awujoh, or feast, at the Recreation Grounds were much sought after. His advertisements were humorous. He made excellent coffins for the poor, no less than for the rich, and if his clientele was short of money, he would advance credit. During the influenza epidemic of 1918, he supplied some coffins free to needy bereaved families.

Bungie had a penchant for the dramatic. When the Prince of Wales visited Freetown in 1925, no provision was made for individuals to welcome the royal visitor. Bungie, an enthusiastic supporter of the royal family, had sent a congratulatory cablegram to the Prince in England, and had asked the governor, Sir Ransford

Slater, (term of office 1922-27), if the royal procession would stop at his store so that he could pay his respects to ''King Pikin'' (the ''Little King''). The request was refused. Undaunted, Bungie painted the exterior of his house completely black, and made his own preparations. At the moment when the royal procession reached his shop, his hired band played ''God Save the King,'' obliging it to come to a stop. Bungie had won recognition as an important citizen.

Graham Greene, the English novelist used the example of Bungie to ridicule Krio society. In *Journey Without Maps* (1935) he wrote: ''A few Creoles make money out of their prefects by deliberately playing the inferior, the lower boy: R. Lumpkin, alias Bungie, is the most famous example. He has become a character. Tourists are taken to see his shop.'' Greene also reproduced one of Bungie's melodramatic advertisments in his book.

He liked his pleasures and jokes, and wanted others to be happy. He maintained two country homes, at Hastings and at Brookfields, both near Freetown, which were respectively christened ''Refreshing Bungalow'' and ''Awujoh Grounds.'' On one occasion however, his boisterous habits led to his arrest for causing a breach of the peace. The governor, however, reported to London that Bungie meant no harm, and liked only to enjoy himself.

His humor, generosity, good nature, and cheerfulness made him widely known in Freetown society. He had little formal education, and was not actively interested in politics, although he numbered the leading politicians of his day among his friends, and contributed to the coffers of the National Congress of British West Africa. He was born an Anglican, but later became converted to Roman Catholicism. He was a devoted husband, but had no children.

On his death, his funeral was conducted with considerable pomp, and the cortege had a police escort. A life-sized painting of him was placed in Wilberforce Memorial Hall in Freetown the following year.

AKINTOLA J.G. WYSE

BIBLIOGRAPHY: Graham Greene, *Journey Without Maps*, London, 1935; Christopher Fyfe, *A History of Sierra Leone*, London, 1962; Leo Spitzer, *The Creoles of Sierra Leone*, Ile-Ife, 1975.

BUREH, BAI

Bai Bureh of Kasseh (circa 1840s?-circa 1908), originally called Kebelai, was the resilient general and military strategist who led the 1898 Temne uprising against the British.

He was born at Rothkeni, near Makeni, in the northern province of Sierra Leone. His father was a Loko war-chief. He himself was sent to Gbendembu Gowahun, a training school for warriors, where he was nicknamed "Kebalai," literally "one whose basket is never full," i.e. one who killed many enemies. Before he became a political figure, he gained recognition as a warrior of no mean standing.

In about 1865 he was called in to Soso territory to help Almamy Kandeh Bokari (*q.v.*) in his conflict with his nephew, Maligi Gbele, over the chieftainship of Morea. Kebalai won extraordinary military success, and within three years had vanquished the enemy. But Bokari himself was not popular with the Soso, so that after a time the struggle was renewed. The resultant disturbances took on a complex character, continuing spasmodically for nearly three decades, with the British colonial administration in Freetown vainly trying to keep the peace "in order to facilitate trade."

In the 1880s, thanks to his military prowess, Kebelai was installed in the chiefship of Kasseh, a small territory on the left bank of the Scarcies River, which had been receiving a British stipend since 1871. At this time he was given the title of Bai Bureh, by which he was subsequently to be known. In his new position, he rapidly gained predominance over the other chiefs in the area.

In 1890, war broke out in Sanda country between the Soso, supported by Bai Bureh, and the Limba. The following year the British, who were backing the Soso against the Limba, sent a travelling commissioner, G.H. Garrett, to conclude peace with the Limba. On his return journey, Garrett met with Bai Bureh, who resented the fact that peace had been made in his absence. He therefore declared his intention of continuing the war. Arrested for his defiance by Garrett, Bai Bureh succeeded in escaping from British custody.

Subsequent events were to show that **Bai Bureh** was not permanently hostile to the British administration. At this time disturbances were continuing in the Scarcies region, and the leading figure, Karimu of Samaya (*q.v.*), was reported to have camped at Tambi. The British sent an expedition to attack this town in 1892. Suffering reverses, and fearing the humiliation of having to send for regular troops, the administration requested Bai Bureh's assistance in capturing Tambi, which he helped them to do.

In 1895, however, he received rough justice at the hands of the British administration. The French had complained that a Soso Bena chief, Surakata, had led incursions into the French sphere of influence, aided by Bai Bureh's warriors. Governor Frederic

Cardew (*q.v.*), indignant because "the matter compromised our international relations with a friendly power," determined to put a stop to all Bai Bureh's warlike activities.

A small British force was sent to arrest him, but failed to accomplish its mission. Subsequently, Bai Bureh, after having been given safe conduct, met Governor Cardew at Port Loko in June. Cardew ordered him to surrender 50 guns to compensate for his "offences" of assisting Surakata, and of offering armed resistance to the police. The warrior, not willing to provoke an incident, paid the fine promptly. Despite this, Bai Bureh was given a bad record by the British, who charged him with being "recalcitrant," and with failing to acknowledge British authority.

In 1896 the British Protectorate was proclaimed, and in 1898 a house tax was imposed. Apathy thereupon gave way to resistance, as the British tried to enforce new and unwelcome laws. Governor Cardew, however, was impervious to all entreaties, and proceeded to try to collect the new tax on schedule. The people, however, decided not to pay. In Port Loko, the district commissioner, Capt. Wilfred Sharpe, deposed the chief and installed a puppet who had no legitimate claim. Sharpe's nominee, Sori Bunki, spread false rumors intended to foment a conflict. Without examining the validity of these rumors, Sharpe convinced Cardew that Bai Bureh had to be arrested and deposed before the tax could be collected.

Three parties sent to arrest Bai Bureh failed in their missions. The last one opened fire in Romani, one of Bai Bureh's towns, and the people retaliated. The British administration had precipitated the resistance war of 1898. After its outbreak, in February, Bai Bureh pursued a well-organized guerrilla war that kept British troops engaged until November, when he surrendered.

Cardew proposed that he be tried for treason, but the British crown law officers ruled that the Protectorate was 'foreign,' so that he owed no allegiance to Queen Victoria, and therefore could not commit treason. He was therefore detained by ordinance. It was proposed to release him later, but when it was suspected that he was sending messages to his people telling them that he was going to return, the administration feared that the precarious Pax Britannia might be endangered.

On July 30, 1899, Bai Bureh was banished to the Gold Coast (now Ghana). He returned in 1905, and in the following year was reinstated as chief of Kasseh. He died in about 1908.

ARTHUR ABRAHAM

BIBLIOGRAPHY: D.W. Scotland, "Notes on Bai Bureh of 1898 Fame," *Sierra Leone Studies*, December 1955; E. Hirst and I. Kamara, *Benga,* (a historical novel), London, 1957; Christopher Fyfe, *A History of Sierra Leone,* London, 1962; Arthur Abraham, "Bai Bureh, the British and the Hut Tax War," *International Journal of African Historical Studies,* VII, 1, 1974.

CARDEW, F.

Sir Frederic Cardew (1839-July 6, 1921) was governor of Sierra Leone from 1894-1900. During his energetic governorship, a Protectorate was declared over the British sphere of influence in the interior, and construction of the first railroad in British West Africa —the Sierra Leone Railway—was begun. But he became alienated from most Sierra Leoneans, and introduced a policy progressively excluding Krios (Creoles) from senior government posts.

In 1858 Cardew had joined the Indian Army as an ensign in the 50th Bengal Native Infantry. He was in the Indian Army for 20 years, serving in the North West Frontier campaign of 1868, as well as in China. Promoted colonel in 1887, he then spent five years in South Africa, serving in the Zulu and Transvaal campaigns of 1879-81. He was resident commissioner in Zululand from 1890-94.

On March 14, 1894, he arrived in Freetown as interim governor. In May he was awarded the Order of St. Michael and St. George (C.M.G.), and on December 3 was appointed governor. He was later to be knighted in June 1897.

Cardew was 55 years old upon his arrival in Sierra Leone. His health was excellent, and he neither smoked nor drank. He quickly demonstrated his energy by making three tours of the hinterland. The first took him through Mende country to Panguma in the east, then northwards to Falaba, returning by the Scarcies. En route, he visited Waima, where he made arrangements for the upkeep of the graves of British soldiers killed in a clash with the French in a tragic mishap which had occurred in the previous year, 1893. His second tour, in 1895, took him eastwards to Kailahun near the Liberian border, then across the entire territory, through Kono, Koranko, Limba, Loko, and Temne country—to Kambia, near the border of what was then French Guinea to the northwest, and back to Freetown by way of the Great Scarcies. His third tour, undertaken in 1896, took him along the Rokel River northeastwards to the region of the Niger sources, then southwards along the Anglo-Liberian frontier, and then back to Freetown by way of Bonthe on the coast.

Cardew's aim, in these tours, was to prepare for the proclamation of a Protectorate over what was at that time the British sphere of influence in the hinterland. This implied not only making administrative preparations, but also reaching agreements on exact

boundaries with the French (with respect to French Guinea), and with the Liberians. By 1896, agreement had been reached with the French on the Guinea boundary. Rough agreement had previously been reached with the Liberians, in 1886, but as Monrovia's control over the hinterland was uneasy at that time, the Liberian government was unwilling to negotiate an exact boundary line. In practice, however, the Liberians permitted Cardew to ignore the boundary for the purposes of stopping wars which might spread into Sierra Leone.

Cardew also claimed to have found vestiges of slavery in the interior. The prospect of slavery being eliminated from the proposed Protectorate discouraged some criticisms of the move that might otherwise have been made.

A British Protectorate over the interior was therefore proclaimed on August 31, 1896. While some of the chiefs in the Protectorate had concluded treaties of cession or of friendship with the British, or received British stipends, some were not consulted, or did not understand the implications. The term "Protectorate" remained ill-defined in Sierra Leone, no less than in Europe, and in practice could be interpreted by the British to mean what they chose.

Cardew also initiated, with the support of Joseph Chamberlain, Colonial Secretary from 1895-1903, the construction of the first stage of the Sierra Leone Railway. It ran southeast, from Freetown harbor to Songo Town, and work began in 1896. The railroad was planned to run through Mende country, and was eventually extended to Pendembu, near the Liberian border.

The Protectorate was divided into five districts, a district commissioner being appointed to administer each. Cardew proposed to defray the costs of administration and of policing the frontiers by imposing a tax on houses, graduated on the number of rooms in each house. The house tax—subsequently to be known by its critics as the Hut Tax—was to become effective on January 1, 1898. The chiefs were entrusted with collecting the tax in their chiefdoms, and the district commissioners, in turn, were to collect from the chiefs.

Opposition to the new tax was widespread, either on grounds that it was too high, or else that the chiefs and people did not recognize British sovereignty. The British Colonial Office also had some misgivings as to the advisability of its imposition at that time. By the end of 1897, however, Cardew, taking some of the criticisms into account, modified the original proposals by imposing a flat rate of five shillings per dwelling, and by exempting two of the remoter districts, Panguma and Koinadugu. But when the Frontier Police were sent to collect the tax by force,

the protests quickly became widespread, developing into open uprisings over large areas. In Mende country, the uprising took an anti-Western turn. Not only Frontier Police were attacked, but European missionaries and traders, and many Krios, themselves a Westernizing influence, were massacred. Eventually, by the end of 1898, the uprising was quelled by force, with 96 of its leaders being hanged. In addition, three prominent chiefs—Bai Bureh (q.v.), Bai Sherbro, and Nyagua (q.v.) were exiled to the Gold Coast (now Ghana).

Sir David Chalmers, a royal commissioner, arrived in Sierra Leone from London to investigate. He ascribed the uprising to the Hut Tax, and made a number of recommendations, including a review of the powers of the district commissioners. His conclusions were contested by Cardew. In the event, the Colonial Office supported Cardew, rejecting Chalmers' more extreme recommendations.

Upon his arrival in the colony, Cardew had at first enjoyed good relations with Sir Samuel Lewis (q.v.), the famous lawyer, who was the leading Krio personality in Freetown, and had recommended him for his knighthood. But following a series of scandals involving Krios in government office, Cardew became antagonistic to Krios in general, and his relations with Lewis also deteriorated. When Lewis undertook to become the advocate for African petitioners in a land dispute at a village named Mokassi, thereby challenging the government, Cardew became resentful, and the two men clashed repeatedly in the Legislative Council.

In June 1898, at Cardew's prompting, an ordinance was passed which encroached upon jury rights in noncapital cases, giving discretionary powers to judges when, in the opinion of the judge, a gross miscarriage of justice had occurred.

This development, no less than others, was a setback to the Krios, whose prestige in the hinterland had also been affected by the Mende attacks upon them in the same year. Furthermore, angered by his legal battles with Lewis, and disenchanted with the misconduct of certain Krios, including the postmaster, Cardew made the assertion that no Krio was fit to be head of a government department. He also referred to Krios in offensive terms. It was at this time that he initiated a policy that was increasingly to result in the exclusion of Krios from senior governmental posts, and of their progressive replacement by European officers. In 1892, two years before Cardew was governor, Krios had held almost 50 percent of the senior governmental positions in the Colony. Some years later, by 1912, however, the proportion was down to 15 percent, and it was to drop still further in later years.

Among other things, Cardew sought to promote agriculture by establishing a botanical station (the precursor of the present Ministry of Agriculture and Natural Resources), by offering incentives to produce better crops and livestock, and by introducing agricultural subsidies on a small scale.

Cardew's governorship was a milestone in the development of Sierra Leone, both because of the proclamation of the Protectorate over the hinterland, and because of the economic expansion that occurred at that time, symbolized by the coming of the railway. He was temperate, and religious, and had the directness of a soldier. But he believed in rapid solutions to complex problems, and had little time for what he saw as legal niceties. Once he had taken a decision, he showed intolerance of other viewpoints. He soon became alienated from most Sierra Leoneans, and his ethnocentrism did not enhance good race relations in the colony. The strain of office also seems to have told upon his health. Whereas upon his arrival in 1894 he enjoyed full health and vigor, three years later, in 1897, he was suffering from neuralgia, insomnia, and shingles. His wife was active in social work in Freetown.

After his Sierra Leone service ended, he retired into private life until his death on July 6, 1921.

CYRIL P. FORAY

BIBLIOGRAPHY: J.J. Crooks, *A History of the Colony of Sierra Leone, Western Africa,* 2nd ed., Dublin, 1903, reprinted, London, 1972; Cyril P. Foray, *Historical Dictionary of Sierra Leone,* Metuchen, New Jersey, and London, 1977; Christopher Fyfe, *A History of Sierra Leone,* London, 1962,(ed) *Sierra Leone Inheritance,* London, 1964; J.D. Hargreaves, "The Establishment of the Sierra Leone Protectorate and the Insurrection of 1898," *Cambridge Historical Journal,* XII, 1956, *A Life of Sir Samuel Lewis,* London, 1958; A.T. Porter, *Creoledom,* London, 1953.

CAULKER, R.C.B.

Richard Canray Ba Caulker (18?-1901) was ruler of the Bumpe chiefdom, in Sherbro territory, about 64 km (40 mi) southeast of Freetown, from 1864-88, and from 1895-98.

He was a member of the Caulker family, long prominent in Sherbro territory, which also ruled over another chiefdom from Shenge, further south. He was educated at the Church Missionary Society (C.M.S.) grammar school at Freetown at the expense of the colonial administration. He succeeded his uncle, Theophilus Caulker (ruled 1857-64) as ruler of Bumpe on the latter's death in 1864.

He was a friend of Gbenjei, ruler of the Kpaa-Mende (the western branch of the Mende), and married one of Gbenjei's daughters, Yogbo. When she left home to join Caulker, she brought with her her brother Bagi. Upon graduating from the Sande and Poro secret societies respectively—i.e. upon reaching puberty—Yogbo took the name of Bora, and Bagi took the name of Kong. The territory around Senehun came to be called Kongbora, which name it retains to this day.

Bora was a dutiful wife, but had no children. Richard Caulker decided to compensate her by building for her and her brother a new town, not far from Rotifunk. Originally called Mobagi, the name of the town was changed to Senehun as it expanded. Other towns founded in the neighborhood by Kpaa-Mende warriors were annexed to Senehun, thus increasing the territory of the Kpaa-Mende state in the region.

In 1875, the so-called Kinigbo war occurred in Caulker territory. George Stephen Caulker II, who ruled a chiefdom from Shenge, on the coast opposite the Plantain Islands, quarreled with his cousin and deputy, John Caulker. After being attacked by George, John hired Mende warriors, led by Kinigbo and Vana, who devastated the Shenge chiefdom. The acting governor of Sierra Leone, Samuel Rowe, (later to serve as governor from 1877-80 and from 1885-88), led two punitive expeditions against the Mende in 1875, and had the three ringleaders—John Caulker, Kinigbo, and Vana—sent to Freetown for trial. Found guilty of murdering a policeman in British territory, they were hanged at Bendu, opposite Sherbro Island.

To profit from his victory, Rowe called a large meeting of chiefs at Senehun, in the course of which he made an agreement with the two Caulker rulers, George Stephen, and Richard Canray Ba. By the terms of this compact, they agreed to grant the Colony the right to collect customs duties in their territories, and to submit disputes to the governor for arbitration.

On December 19, 1881, Richard, like the other Caulkers, acknowledged the validity of the the Turner Treaty of September 24, 1825, thus bringing the Caulker chiefdoms under the British crown. This treaty, originally concluded with the chiefs of Sherbro country, including the Caulkers, by Governor Sir Charles Turner (term of office 1825-26), had ceded the Sherbro territories to Sierra Leone Colony. It had, however, not been ratified by the British Colonial Office, as the British were then seeking to avoid any extension of their responsibilities. Now, however, in 1881, Rowe was reviving and confirming the treaty.

Although the chiefs had agreed to submit disputes to the British, another Caulker family feud turned into open warfare in 1888. Serious disturbances occurred as two Caulkers, William and Thomas Kugba, again brought in Mende warriors, this time against Thomas Neale Caulker (q.v.), ruler of Shenge. But William and Thomas Kugba Caulker were taken captive by the British, and were hanged for murder. Richard Canray Ba was suspected of complicity in the disturbances, but could not be convicted. Instead, he and three other supporters of William were sent into exile in the Gambia.

After seven years of exile, Richard returned in 1895, and was reinstated as chief of Bumpe. When the Protectorate was proclaimed in 1896, and the Hut Tax imposed, Richard was at first inclined to ask his people not to pay. He then changed his mind, however, and paid £10. But Governor Sir Frederic Cardew (q.v), who was in office from 1894-1900, was suspicious of him, and had him deposed. He was imprisoned at Kwelu, inland from Bumpe. His successor was his cousin, James Canray Ba Caulker, who had already been made a paramount chief in 1889.

ARTHUR ABRAHAM

BIBLIOGRAPHY: Arthur Abraham, *Mende Government and Politics Under Colonial Rule*, Freetown, 1978; Christopher Fyfe, *A History of Sierra Leone*, London, 1962.

CAULKER, S.B.

The Rev. Solmon Brooks Caulker (February 25, 1911-August 29, 1960) was a well-known broadcaster who became vice-principal of Fourah Bay College.

He was born in the village of Mambo, in Kagboro chiefdom, Moyamba district, Southern Province. The son of George Augustus Caulker, he was the fifth in a family of 12. He was educated at two Evangelical United Brethren (E.U.B.) schools—the Shenge primary school, and the Albert Academy in Freetown.

From 1932 to 1934 he was an assistant teacher in Bonthe on Sherbro Island, and then taught at the Albert Academy from 1934-37. In 1937 he travelled to the United States, where he attended Lebanon Valley College, Annville, Pennsylvania, where he obtained his B.A. in 1941. He then studied at Bonebrake Theological Seminary, Dayton, Ohio, where he graduated as Bachelor of Divinity in 1944. He also read philosophy and religion at the University of Chicago from 1944-45.

Caulker returned home on June 1, 1946, together with his wife, the former Olive Selby, an Afro-American from Nashville, Tennessee. He joined the staff of Fourah Bay College as a lecturer in philosophy. He was a witty conversationalist with a sense of humor, and became a well-known broadcaster, conducting the popular weekly program "Radio Forum." He was also a minister in the E.U.B.

church, and associate pastor of King Memorial Church in Freetown.

At Fourah Bay, where he was popularly known as "S.B.," or "Show Boy," he showed interest in the welfare of the students. In 1958 he became vice-principal of the college.

In 1960 he attended the International Conference on Science in the Advancement of New States at Rehovoth, Israel, where he stressed the importance of taking steps to reduce child mortality.

On August 29, 1960, he was killed in a tragic plane crash at Dakar, Senegal.

DOMINIC OFORI

BIBLIOGRAPHY: *The Sierra Leone Daily Mail,* August 30, 1960; private papers of the late Rev. S.B. Caulker; News Bulletin, Independence Series, Ministry of Information, Sierra Leone, 1960-61; personal file of S.B. Caulker, Fourah Bay College.

CAULKER, T.N.

Thomas Neale Caulker (18?-late April or May, 1898), one of the famous Caulker family which was prominent in the Sherbro region, was ruler of the Caulker chiefdom based on Shenge from 1881-98. He was one of the only three chiefs in southern Sierra Leone to side openly with the British at the time of the Hut Tax War of 1898. The other two chiefs were Nancy Tucker (*q.v.*), and Madam Yoko (*q.v.*).

In 1881 the incumbent ruler of the Shenge chiefdom, George Stephen Caulker II, had died. In December of the same year, the Turner Treaty of 1825, which had placed Sherbro territory under the British crown, but which had not been ratified at the time, was recognized as valid. Governor Arthur Edward Havelock (term of office 1881-84), who was then engaged in bringing the entire coastline of Sierra Leone under British fiscal jurisdiction, recognized Thomas Neale Caulker, the half-brother by a slave woman of the late chief, as regent chief. This was resented by William Caulker, who aspired to the chiefdom himself. Publicly, however, William and Thomas both agreed to settle all their differences, although they secretly remained bitter enemies.

In 1883, Thomas accused William of abbetting a robbery, and had him sent to Freetown for trial. He was, however, acquitted. William returned home, bent on revenge. He found that Thomas, who was showing himself ruthless and oppressive, was hated by many of his sub-chiefs, and saw an opportunity in their discontent.

Obtaining the support of his elder brother, Thomas Kugba, he hired Mende mercenaries to help him, on the pretext that he was fighting a private enemy. These warriors attacked Shenge, and were only narrowly beaten back. The British sent police and a naval cruiser to restore peace, and William and Thomas Kugba Caulker were both taken prisoner. They were taken to Freetown and tried for murder. Found guilty, the two brothers were publicly hanged at Shenge.

Thomas thus retained his position, and remained loyal to the colonial administration. In 1896, Governor Sir Frederic Cardew (*q.v.*), in office from 1894-1900, visited Shenge to explain the Hut Tax. Advised by his family to refuse to pay, Thomas nevertheless determined to prove his fidelity to the administration. In 1898, Frontier Police were sent to assist him collect the tax. The police went through the chiefdom, demanding instant payment. Those who refused were tied up until they paid, or their houses were burnt. Tax was even exacted from exempt villages. Altogether £300 was collected, but at the price of creating bitter resentment. The people came to see Thomas Neale Caulker as a usurper, and to consider the hanged William as a martyr.

When the Hut Tax war broke out at the end of April 1898, and massacres of those associated with Freetown began in Sherbro country, an attempt was made to persuade Thomas Neale to escape to the Plantain Islands. This, however, he declined to do. He was captured by his cousin Francis, and put to death.

ARTHUR ABRAHAM

BIBLIOGRAPHY: Arthur Abraham, *Mende Government and Politics Under Colonial Rule,* Freetown, 1978; G.M. Domingo, "The Caulker Manuscript," *Sierra Leone Studies,* October, 1920; Christopher Fyfe, *A History of Sierra Leone,* London, 1962.

CINQUE, J. See SENGBE PIEH

CLARKSON, J.

Lieutenant John Clarkson (1763-1828) brought more than 1,100 North American freedmen from Nova Scotia to Sierra Leone, and became first governor of the Sierra Leone settlement. Freetown was founded during his governorship.

He was the younger brother of Thomas Clarkson (1760-1846), the English abolitionist. He served in the British Royal Navy, which he had joined at the age of 11, and was promoted lieutenant. But his experiences in the West Indies led him to leave the Navy, as he had come to question the morality of war.

He became keenly interested in the plans of the English abolitionist Granville Sharp (1735-1813) to send freed slaves from North America back to Africa. These former slaves, mostly from Virginia and South

Carolina, who had sided with the British during the American War of Independence (1776-83), had after the war sought refuge in Nova Scotia, where they suffered from the severe climate and harsh labor conditions. In August 1791, Clarkson offered the Sierra Leone Company, which sponsored the "Province of Freedom," as the settlement was then called, his services to bring the Nova Scotia freedmen over to Sierra Leone. His offer was accepted.

He arrived in Halifax, Nova Scotia, in October 1791, and quickly obtained the trust of the freedmen, offering them free land in Africa. At the expense of the British Treasury, 15 ships were chartered. Clarkson, with his naval experience, oversaw their fitting out. On January 15, 1792, the ships set sail, with Clarkson in command, carrying 1,190 freedmen. He was ill with fatigue when they left Halifax, and developed fever during the voyage.

The ships arrived severally about six weeks later, 67 of the "Nova Scotians" (as the freedmen came to be called) having died en route. Clarkson's ship arrived on March 7. He found the colony ruled by a council consisting of "eight gentlemen, invested with great power, each of them acting for himself." Their administration was divided and incompetent. The company directors, writing from London, asked him to remain in Sierra Leone as Superintendent of the colony, and he agreed, taking the oath of office on March 10. His authority was not, however, recognized by the councillors, who were making free with the company's supplies, and he sent a fast schooner to England, asking for full powers to govern. The company thereupon appointed him governor, and disbanded the council.

Clarkson proceeded to negotiate with the local chiefs, paying one of them a second time for land already bought, in order to avoid trouble. He also incorporated the European settlers at nearby Granville Town into the company's colony, thereby effectively founding Freetown (as the settlement was named). He supervised the clearing of land, and the laying out of streets, which he named after the company's directors. When he left to make the visit to England that his health demanded, he had the support of the Nova Scotians, and had established good relations between Freetown and the local chiefs. Before leaving, he began the distribution of allotments promised to the Nova Scotians. He took leave of the settlers with a long public prayer, still venerated in Freetown as "Clarkson's Prayer." He sailed for England on December 30, 1792.

The company directors in London gave him a friendly reception, declaring he had saved the colony. But when Clarkson criticized them for parsimony and incompetence, they charged him with exceeding his instructions, and withholding information from them. In April 1793, as he was about to leave London for Norfolk to be married, he was dismissed. Shocked, he nevertheless made no public protest in order not to give ammunition to the settlement's enemies.

He settled down in England, becoming a banker in East Anglia. He later helped found the Society for the Promotion of Universal Peace.

CYRIL P. FORAY

BIBLIOGRAPHY: John Clarkson, *The Substance of a Letter Addressed to a Clergyman of the Established Church on the Subject of War,* York, 1827; A.M. Falkonbridge, *Two Voyages to Sierra Leone during the Years 1791-2-3,* London, 1794, reprinted, London 1967; Christopher Fyfe, *A History of Sierra Leone,* London, 1962; Claude George (Esu Biyi), *The Rise of British West Africa,* London, 1903, reprinted, London, 1968; E.L. Griggs, *Thomas Clarkson,* London, 1936; E.G. Ingham, *Sierra Leone After a Hundred Years,* London, 1894, reprinted, London, 1968; E.C.T. Lascelles, *Granville Sharp and the Freedom of Slaves in England,* London, 1928, reprinted, Detroit, 1969; A.B.C. Sibthorpe, *The History of Sierra Leone,* 2nd ed., London, 1881, reprinted, London, 1970.

COLE, J.F. See GULAMA, JULIUS

CUMMINGS, E.H.T.

Dr. Eustace Henry Taylor Cummings (December 7, 1890-June 16, 1967), a distinguished doctor and educationist, was Mayor of Freetown from 1948-54.

He was the son of a leading Krio (Creole) merchant, the Hon. Emmanuel Henry Cummings, M.B.E. (Member of the British Empire), who was thrice Mayor of Freetown (1915, 1917-18, and 1921-22). Eustace was educated at the Wesleyan Boys' School (now Methodist Boys' High School), and from 1909-11 studied at Fourah Bay College. He then went to Britain, where he became the first African to qualify as a doctor at the University of Liverpool. His medical qualifications were extensive, and were unique for an African at that time. From 1919-20 he was resident medical officer at the Lozelles General Dispensary in Birmingham, before returning to Sierra Leone in 1920 to join the medical service.

Attached to the sanitation department, he made an extensive tour of the Protectorate. In 1936 he was appointed medical officer at Kissy, a suburb of Freetown. Several Europeans on the medical staff resigned rather than be subordinate to an African doctor, but Cummings was unimpressed. For years he worked to improve the insanitary condition of Freetown, advocating a proper drainage system and better venti-

lation in houses. By the time of his retirement in 1947 he was senior medical officer. (He was later to return for another two years service from 1955-57).

In 1943 he had been a member of the Elliot Commission on Higher Education in West Africa, established by the British government. The commission's recommendations resulted in the establishment of the university colleges of Ibadan and of the Gold Coast. Dr. Cummings himself advocated that Fourah Bay College be retained as a college of Durham University, and be allowed to develop into an autonomous university, as subsequently happened.

In 1948 he became Mayor of Freetown, serving until 1954, and making contributions to both education and public affairs during his term of office as well as later on. Thanks to his representations, the Freetown City Council established the Interim Municipal School (now Regent Square Municipal School), and the colonial government built two new schools in Freetown. From 1950-53, he was also president of the Fourah Bay College Council, being the first African to hold this position. Subsequently, in 1960, he was awarded the honorary degree of doctor of civil law by Durham University for his services. In the same year he was awarded the decoration of C.B.E. (Commander, Order of the British Empire).

Dr. Cummings was an active member of the Methodist Church, and was also interested in tennis, football, and cricket. He died at the age of 77.

DOMINIC OFORI

BIBLIOGRAPHY: *West Africa,* July 1, 1967; Freetown City Council papers; private papers of Dr. E.H. Taylor Cummings.

DALLA MODU

Dalla Modu (circa 1770-1841) was for many years an intermediary between the British in Freetown and the chiefs of the hinterland, coming to wield great influence with both. In 1836 he was recognized as regent of Loko Masama, a chiefdom between the Bullom Shore, north of Freetown, and the Small Scarcies River. In 1837 he became chief of Rokon.

He was the son of Fenda Modu, an important Soso who was the virtual ruler of Wonkafong, near Conakry in what is now Guinea. In 1794, Fenda Modu, bringing Dalla Modu with him, visited Freetown to establish trade links. On May 18, 1795, Dalla Modu and 50 followers decided to settle in the Colony to trade. The government welcomed them, as it wished to trade with the interior. In Freetown, Dalla Modu learned English and also studied the Colony's currency and its system of weights and measures. He thus became eminently well equipped to play the role of political and economic intermediary. He and his followers lived in a settlement adjoining Freetown to the west, just outside the defensive wall.

In 1800 the Nova Scotian immigrants in the Colony staged an uprising, with the support of Soso and Mandinka chiefs. In 1802, Dalla Modu, with the help of Betsy Heard, the ruler of Bereira in what is now Guinea, helped to end the uprising. They persuaded the Soso and Mandinka chiefs to withdraw their support from the Nova Scotians, and to hand the leader of the uprising, Nathaniel Wansey, and two others, over to the British.

In 1806, Dalla Modu was charged by the British with slave trading. At the hearing he appeared not in the European clothes that he usually wore, but in Muslim dress. This was seen by the British authorities as a sign of his defiance. Expelled from the Colony, he and his men joined his grandfather-in-law, the Bai Sherbro, at Medina on the Bullom Shore, north of the Rokel (Sierra Leone River). Here he continued to act as a broker between the Colony and the chiefs of the interior, to the advantage of both the British and himself.

In the years that followed he consolidated his position on the Bullom shore. The wealth that he acquired as a broker enabled him to protect and foster the expansion of the Soso community. He consolidated his power by marrying relatives of local rulers.

He claimed part ownership of the Islands of Los, off the coast opposite Conakry, and in 1818 he persuaded other chiefs to join him in ceding them to the British crown. He did this to help Governor Sir Charles MacCarthy (term of office 1814-24), who sought authority over the islands to stop British traders there from using the islands to smuggle goods into the Colony, thereby evading customs dues. In return for this service he received an annual payment of 500 bars of iron from the British, which they were still paying him in 1826.

Later, in 1825, he acted to ensure that Matacong Island, off the coast of what is now Guinea, was also ceded to the British. He did this to prevent business rivals from using it as a cattle depot, thereby jeopardising the army meat contract held by Dalla Modu's business associate, Kenneth Macaulay, who was acting governor for a short time in 1826.

He maintained his contacts with the Freetown trading community, and in 1824 became the agent of Macaulay and Babington, a timber firm. He employed his slaves to fell trees and bring the timber to river banks for loading. He received £1,000 as partial payment for the 1826 season alone.

Traders coming from the interior via Port Loko used his house as the last stop before reaching the Colony. It was there that they received information on the best prices and places to sell their goods in Freetown. Dalla Modu sometimes directed them to particular merchants, or sent people to accompany them into the Colony.

Chiefs in the interior also used him to send messages to the governor. In November 1832, for example, Alimamy Bokari of Timbo in Futa Jallon assured the governor, through Dalla Modu, of his willingness to cooperate in maintaining peace along the trade routes. In 1833, Lt. Governor Octavius Temple (term of office 1833-34) saw Dalla Modu's role as beneficial to all parties, and sent him gifts in appreciation. Further benefits accrued to him in 1834 when many gold merchants from the interior came to the Colony, bringing him wealth in broker's fees.

In 1833 a Mandinka resident of Freetown was hanged for kidnapping. He had been a tenant of Dalla Modu, who therefore had to pay compensation to the Mandinka's relatives, and also found himself accused of abetting slave trading.

But in 1835, he again proved his value to the British. A rebellion by Sesay Bety of North Rokel disrupted trade and placed British subjects and their property in danger. Accompanied by an officer from the Colony, Dalla Modu undertook a mission of arbitration, which resulted in a truce.

Lt. Governor Henry Dundas Campbell (term of office 1835-37) visited him, and was struck by his intelligence as well as by the style in which he lived. The two men cooperated to end the Temne-Loko war then in progress. In April 1836, Dalla Modu organized a gathering of the leading Temne and Loko chiefs at Magbele on the Rokel River. Campbell arrived, and a peace treaty was signed. Dalla Modu was then recognized as regent of Loko Masama—a position he had held since 1829. He then crowned a sub-chief named Pa Charly as Bai Maro (ruler) of Loko Masama. He himself stayed on at Magbele as Campbell's agent, with powers which made him dominant in the Rokel region.

Campbell, however, had difficulty in having the treaty confirmed by his superiors, as one clause provided for the return of runaway slaves to the chiefs. Campbell therefore had to negotiate a new treaty. Dalla Modu continued to help him, and also used his followers, armed with muskets, to help Freetown traders to collect their debts.

Campbell's successor, Governor Richard Doherty (term of office 1837-40), followed a different policy, however, and found Dalla Modu uncooperative. Not until 1841, when Governor Sir John Jeremie (term of office 1840-41) reaffirmed Campbell's treaty, and made payments to the chiefs—Dalla Modu receiving £341—was cooperation restored. In July of the same year, at the behest of the governor, he secured the release of "liberated" Africans, who were British subjects, from the hands of Temne and Loko chiefs.

Dalla Modu's funeral was attended by many chiefs, as well as by Europeans from the Colony. During the celebrations more than 80 cows were killed and eaten. One of his sons, Amara Modu, succeeded him.

VICTOR BONG AMAAZEE

BIBLIOGRAPHY: Christopher Fyfe. *A History of Sierra Leone,* London, 1962; Victor Bong Amaazee, "The Relations Between the Colony of Sierra Leone and its Northern Hinterland in the Nineteenth Century," unpublished thesis, University of Sierra Leone, 1974.

DAVIES, W.J. See FADUMA, O.

DOUGAN, R.

Robert Dougan (circa 1800-1871), an Afro-West-Indian, was acting governor of Sierra Leone from 1854-55. He was dismissed after a military expedition he had sent out without authority met with an unprecedented disaster.

Dougan, who was probably born in the West Indies, came to Freetown in 1822, and joined the trading firm of Macaulay and Babington. In the absence of one of the principals, Kenneth Macaulay (acting governor from March to July 1826), he acted as his agent. He bought property and settled down. His first wife, a European, died, and he married Ann Leigh, daughter of a British slave trader and his Nova Scotian wife. He subsequently established himself as a major legal practitioner in Freetown. In 1853 he became a Queen's advocate.

When Governor Arthur E. Kennedy (terms of office 1852-54 and 1868-72) left Sierra Leone in 1854, Dougan was appointed acting governor—the third Afro-West-Indian to hold the post. At that time, some of the chiefs in the Northern Rivers area were complaining of interference by the Sierra Leone government with the institution of slavery. In November 1854, to exert pressure, a chief of Maligia, on the Melacourie River in what is now Guinea, who was named More Mina Lahai, closed the Melacourie River to European traders, and ordered their expulsion within 10 days.

Dougan reacted impetuously and without consulting his council. He sent the sloop *Premetheus* to Maligia, where it was later joined by two more vessels, the *Dover* and the *Britomert,* with the demand that Lahai pay reparations. Lahai agreed to pay £2,060 within three months, and Dougan, confident that it would be paid, had the ships withdrawn. Meanwhile he received

a report, that later proved untrue, that his own brother had been enslaved by a chief on the Rio Nunez, also in what is now Guinea, and again sent a gunboat.

By May 1855, Lahai had still not paid reparations, and Dougan lost patience. Again without consulting his council, he sent his secretary, Eugene Dillett, also an Afro-West Indian, together with another naval gunboat, H.M.S. *Teazer.* When Lahai did not pay forthwith, Dillett obtained 200 soldiers from the West India regiments stationed in Sierra Leone, and attacked Maligia. The troops landed to burn houses, but were surprised, and fled to the single boat which had landed them. The boat capsized, and 77 soldiers were killed, drowned, or captured. The British had never known such a military reverse since arriving in Sierra Leone.

An investigation was held, and revealed that Dillett had mishandled matters, for which he was reprimanded. It was, however, Dougan who bore the major share of the blame for having acted without consulting either London or his council. He was dismissed, and also removed with disgrace from his position as Queen's advocate. A.B.C. Sibthorpe (q.v.) later wrote that he was "of ambitious character, rash, of small discretion and of little wit."

In his later years he continued to practice law in Freetown, and received a pension.

GUSTAV K. DEVENEAUX

BIBLIOGRAPHY: Christopher Fyfe, *A History of Sierra Leone,* London, 1962; A.B.C. Sibthorpe, *A History of Sierra Leone,* London, 1962; Gustav K. Deveneaux, "The Political and Social Impact of the Colony In Northern Sierra Leone 1821-96," unpublished thesis, Boston University, 1975.

DURA I

Alimamy Dura I (later 19th century-September 14, 1946) was paramount chief of Safroko Limba, a former chiefdom under the Biriwa Limba in northern Sierra Leone. Ruling from 1916-46, he overcame disaffection at the outset of his rule, after which he encouraged education and agriculture.

When Suluku (q.v.) of Biriwa Limba died in 1906, Safroko, which had been under the influence of this powerful ruler, became an autonomous chiefdom. Dura's father, Alimamy Omaru, was appointed its first paramount chief in 1907. Though there was some unrest during Omaru's rule, it was not as serious as the disaffection which erupted when Dura was appointed to succeed his father on a year's probation in 1916.

Three important people in Safroko Limba were implacably opposed to Dura's election. One of these was a former court messenger named Sorie Limba, who claimed the chiefship on the ground that he had played a significant role in securing autonomy for the chiefdom. The second, Lamina Suntu, said that Omaru had promised him the chiefship on his death bed, and threatened to put the chiefdom under a potent curse if he did not receive it. The third man, Diko, was the chief of a section called Kamasele.

Although the colonial administration confirmed Dura's appointment, the malcontents did not abandon their opposition. Section chief Diko refused to pay his tax, and gave up his resistance only after he was put under arrest. Sorie Limba, by means of a powerful "swear," put the chiefdom under a heavy curse, and only refrained from further hostile acts when he was sentenced to six months' imprisonment. But Lamina Suntu's opposition was the most determined, and continued long after Dura's confirmation. At one stage, in December 1917, he marched on Kabinkolo, the chiefdom's headquarters, with about 100 followers armed with sticks. For this act, he was banished to Makeni, a short distance to the southwest of Kabinkolo.

Despite these circumstances, Dura showed remarkable forbearance, although he reported every incident of insubordination in scrupulous detail to the colonial authorities. The colonial administration gave him moral support, while neighboring paramount chiefs, such as Pompoli of Biriwa Limba, offered friendly advice.

But external forces increased Dura's troubles. In January 1918, Bayo Yembe, the paramount chief of Kalantuba chiefdom, to the northeast, invaded Safroko Limba in an attempt to secure control of two sections of Dura's chiefdom. He was accompanied by an "army" of about 400 men, many of them carrying guns. Despite this extreme provocation, Dura remained calm.

The colonial authorities instituted an enquiry into Bayo Yembe's conduct. Though banishing him was considered, it was eventually decided—on account of his old age and his record of proven loyalty to the administration—that he should only be ordered to make financial amends to Dura. It also transpired that the old chief had been the tool of two disaffected Safroko section chiefs, who were each given short prison terms.

Having triumphed over his antagonists, Dura urged his people to rebuild roads and cultivate rice. He also encouraged them to seek education in the local schools established by the American Wesleyan Mission. As a result of his encouragement, many farmers began to cultivate oil palm in addition to rice.

He died in 1946, and was succeeded the following year by his son, Alimamy Dura II.

E. AMADU TURAY

BIBLIOGRAPHY: N.C. Hollins, "Précis of Events in the Safroko Limba Chiefdom," *Sierra Leone Studies*, July, 1925; *Sierra Leone Gazette*, October 3, 1946; R. Finnegan, *Survey of the Limba People of Northern Sierra Leone*, London, 1965; M.R. Lipschutz, "North-East Sierra Leone After 1884: Reactions to the Samorian Invasions and British Colonialism," unpublished Ph.D. dissertation, University of California at Los Angeles, 1973; Emily-Ann Langworthy, "The Establishment of British Rule in the Sierra Leone Protectorate, 1896-1924," unpublished Ph.D dissertation, University of Edinburgh, 1974.

DUSU SORI

Dusu Sori (circa 1840-circa March 15 or 16, 1940), was ruler of the Dembelia-Musaia chiefdom in northeastern Sierra Leone from about 1881 to 1940, except for a short interval in the mid-1880s.

He belonged to the Jawara clan, the predominant Yalunka clan in what is now the Dembelia Musaia chiefdom in the Koinadugu district. He was born probably about the 1840s in Musaia, the chief town of Dembelia country, then part of the Solima Yalunka state. He was the son of Ba Hamadi, the second ruler of Dembelia country. His mother, Dusu, was a Koranko, for Musaia was originally Koranko country before the Jawara Yalunka came there to settle in the 18th century. Dusu Sori became ruler of Musaia in about 1881.

When the Sofa (warriors) of Samori Touré (1830-1900), the great Mandinka warrior and leader from what is now the Republic of Guinea, took the Solima state in 1884, Dusu Sori was deposed. Another ruler, Hamadu, was installed in his place. But Hamadu disappeared in 1888—whether he was executed or fled is uncertain—and Dusu Sori was reinstated. Under Dusu Sori, Musaia became a rallying point for all Yalunka who had formerly belonged to the Solima state, as Falaba, their former capital, had been destroyed by the Sofa.

As the British moved in to establish a Protectorate over the Sierra Leone hinterland in the 1890s, Dusu Sori became a spokesman for the other Yalunka rulers in the area, dealing with the British about their appointments of paramount chiefs. From this advantageous standpoint, he was able to expand his own power. He included the Limba town of Largo and parts of the neighboring Folosaba Yalunka country within the area he claimed as being under his jurisdiction. The British confirmed his claims and made him paramount chief of the enlarged Dembelia Musaia chiefdom. This caused much dissatisfaction among the Folosaba and Wara Wara Limba people to whom Largo had belonged. But Dusu Sori, secure in the backing of the colonial administration, continued to exercise authority undisturbed.

He was one of the few paramount chiefs of the Protectorate who was able to rule for a very long time. On his death in 1940, he was described by the British district commissioner of Koinadugu as "the doyen of "Protectorate chiefs." He is still remembered in the traditions of the Musaia people as one of their greatest rulers.

C. MAGBAILY FYLE

BIBLIOGRAPHY: C. Magbaily Fyle, "Solimana and Its Neighbors," unpublished Ph.D. dissertation, Northwestern University, Evanston, 1976.

EASMON, J.F.

Dr. John Farrell Easmon (June 30, 1856-June 9, 1900), was a distinguished Sierra Leonean doctor who was chief medical officer of the Gold Coast from 1893-97.

He was the son of Walter Richard Easmon, whose parents were probably members of the contingent of freedmen from Nova Scotia who landed in Freetown in 1792. John's mother was Mary Ann McCormack, daughter of an adventurous Irish trader, John McCormack (q.v.), who came to West Africa in 1812.

He was educated in Freetown at a Roman Catholic primary school, and then at the Church Missionary Society (C.M.S.) Grammar School. He then entered the Colonial Hospital in Freetown as a learner dispenser and nurse, hoping eventually to become a doctor. His father, who spent his life trading at Forecaria in the Northern Rivers area in what is now the Republic of Guinea, had lost his fortune when the French advance was resisted by the Soso, so he could not afford to pay for the education he had wanted to give his children. But his maternal grandfather, John McCormack, left him money on his death, enabling John Farrell Easmon to study in Europe.

He went to England in 1876, and entered University College Hospital in London, where he qualified as a medical doctor in 1879, winning the Liston clinical medal for surgery, and other prizes. After a brief spell of service in Ireland, he went to Brussels, Belgium, where he obtained another medical degree with distinction.

He returned to Freetown in 1880. The following year he was appointed as assistant colonial surgeon in Accra. He took his work seriously, and did much research on black water fever, the results of which were published in 1886. According to one authority, "his work on black water fever was the first original contribution made by an African doctor to European medical science."

On eight occasions he acted as chief medical officer in the Gold Coast. In 1893 he was appointed chief medical officer, a post he had failed to obtain in Sierra Leone.

When Sir William Maxwell became governor of the Gold Coast (term of office 1895-97), he opposed an African heading the medical department, and advised the Colonial Office against such appointments. Opposition also came from another quarter. In 1894, Dr. B.W. Quartey Papafio, a Gold Coast medical officer, petitioned the British Secretary of State for the Colonies against Easmon's appointment, on the grounds that Easmon was not a Gold Coaster, and that Papafio himself deserved the position. The *Gold Coast Chronicle*, partly owned by Dr. Papafio, published an article attacking Easmon on June 23, 1894. This dispute led the Sierra Leoneans in Accra to found a paper, *The Gold Coast Independent*, that was published from 1895-98. Governor Maxwell used Easmon's connection with the *Gold Coast Independent*, and the fact that he was carrying on private practice, which was against regulations, to suspend him from his post. But Dr. Quartey Papafio did not get the appointment.

When Easmon went on leave to London in 1897, he defended himself before the Secretary of State for the Colonies. The Secretary was apparently quite satisfied, and asked Easmon to return to his post in Accra. But in his absence Governor Maxwell had appointed Easmon's deputy, a European, as chief medical officer. On Easmon's return, he was asked to proceed to Kumase. He refused, and instead moved to Cape Coast, where he set up in private practice, after which Cape Coast merchants offered him a retainer fee of

£1,000 a year. He died of pneumonia at Cape Coast in 1900, after a three-day illness.

ARTHUR ABRAHAM

BIBLIOGRAPHY: M.C.F. Easmon, "A Nova Scotian Family," in *Eminent Sierra Leoneans in the Nineteenth Century,* Freetown, 1961; Christopher Fyfe, *A History of Sierra Leone,* London, 1962; David Kimble, *A Political History of Ghana 1850-1928,* London, 1963.

EASMON, M.C.F.

Dr. McCormack Charles Farrell Easmon (April 11, 1890-April 30, 1972) was a medical officer who for many years combated racial discrimination in the Sierra Leone medical services. Prominent in Sierra Leone's public life, he played a major role in founding the Sierra Leone National Museum, of which he was the first curator.

The son of Dr. John Farrell Easmon (*q.v.*) and his wife Annette Kathleen, he was born in Accra, in the Gold Coast (now Ghana), a country in which his father was then working. At the time of his father's death in 1900, "M.C.F." (as he was later to be affectionately called) was only 10 years old. From this time on his mother and his three aunts helped to shape his career.

He had begun his education at a school run by one of his aunts, Miss Emma Smith, with the help of another aunt, Mrs. Casely Hayford, wife of J.E. Casely Hayford, (1866-1930), founder of the National Congress of British West Africa. Later he studied at the Church Missionary Society (C.M.S.) Grammar School in Freetown. He was then sent to England where he attended St. Paul's Preparatory School, Colet Court, London, from 1901-03, and studied at Epsom College in Surrey from 1903-07.

Winning two scholarships, he entered the Medical School of St. Mary's Hospital in London in 1907, graduating in medicine and surgery in 1912. In 1913 he passed the examination of the London School of Tropical Medicine.

He returned to Sierra Leone in 1913, but was refused a post in what was then called the West African medical service because he was of West African origin. At that time the regulations were that candidates should be of pure European descent. There were thus two categories of doctors—those in the "colonial" and those in the "local" service. Relegated to the second category, he was appointed Country Hospital Native Medical Officer. Meanwhile, because of his persistent efforts to change constitutionally the conditions of service of African doctors, he was nicknamed the "Yellow Peril" by European officials.

During World War I he enlisted in the army, and served as a medical officer in the Cameroons. After the war, he once more went to England for post-graduate studies, and in 1925 was awarded a medical degree in obstetrics and gyneacology by London University.

Returning home, he then served most of his working life in what was then the Protectorate. He was posted to many different stations, and received a deep insight into, and developed a great admiration for, traditional life and culture. This enabled him to write many publications of a cultural and historical nature, the best known being *The Sierra Leone Country Cloths*, which he wrote for the Sierra Leone section of the British Empire Exhibition of 1924. He also published articles on medical subjects.

Meanwhile, in association with his colleagues in the "local" service, he continued the fight against discrimination. His efforts over the years from 1912 to 1946 largely contributed towards the colonial administration's final decision to unify the "colonial" and "local" services, after which all doctors were called "Medical Officers" irrespective of their racial origin. He retired in 1945, but was re-employed as a temporary medical officer in 1949, and in 1954 was awarded the Order of the British Empire (O.B.E.) for meritorious service.

His public life was a varied one. He was keenly interested in education, and served on various educational bodies. Being of Maroon descent, in 1947 he became chairman of the Nova Scotian and Maroons Descendants' Association. He was also a member of a number of social and professional clubs. He was a member and then chairman of the Mining Wages Board in 1947, and chairman of the Maritime and Waterfront Wages Board in 1948. He became the local secretary of the Royal Society for Tropical Medicine and Hygiene in 1956. He also served as the first director of the Bank of Sierra Leone from 1963-67.

Because of his keen interest and active participation in the Monuments and Relics Commission, which was founded in 1947, and of which he was chairman, he was given another nickname—"Ancient Easmon." He was a member of the Sierra Leone Society, and also of its sub-committee, which founded the Sierra Leone National Museum. The museum was opened on December 10, 1958, with Dr. Easmon as its first curator. Through his efforts, some 20 national monuments were declared and developed.

He was also a keen historian, and contributed regularly to *Sierra Leone Studies* and other journals and magazines. He gave a series of broadcast talks entitled "Sierra Leone in Retrospect," which dealt with such topics as the Maroons, Old Freetown buildings, and Freetown street names.

In 1969, he went to England for a holiday, and fell ill. His health problems persisted, and he never again returned to Sierra Leone. He died in 1972, and was buried in England.

DOROTHY A. CUMMINGS

BIBLIOGRAPHY: M.C.F. Easmon, *The Sierra Leone Country Cloths*, London, 1924, "Helminthiasis in the Sierra Leone Protectorate," *Journal of Tropical Medicine and Hygiene*, November 15, 1924, "Conditions of Medical Work in a West African Bush Station," *Journal of Tropical Medicine and Hygiene*, March 16, 1925, "The Massaquoi Crown," *Sierra Leone Studies, (SLS)*, September, 1939, "The Departure of Governor Kennedy from Freetown in 1854," *SLS*, June 1956, "Sierra Leone Doctors," *SLS*, June, 1956, "Paramount Chief Bai Kurr, M.B.E., M.L.C.," *SLS*, June, 1957, "Freetown in 1856," *SLS*, December, 1957, "Madam Yoko: Ruler of the Mendi Confederacy," *SLS*, December, 1958, "Paul Cuffee," *SLS*, December, 1959, "Sierra Leone and Nigeria," *West African Review*, October, 1960, "Development of Freetown," *The Times*, Sierra Leone Supplement, April 27, 1961, *Museum*, Freetown, 1961, "Notes on the Growth of Medical Services in Sierra Leone," *Health Week Handbook*, 1961, "Sierra Leone's Connection with Royalty," *SLS*, June, 1962, "Bunce Island Where History Sleeps," *Selection* (Magazine of the Sierra Leone Selection Trust), October, 1964, "A Note on the Waiima Incident," *SLS*, January, 1966.

EZZIDIO, J.

John Ezzidio (circa 1810-October 1872) was a recaptive from Nupe, in what is now Nigeria, who became the first African to sit on the Sierra Leone Legislative Council, on which he served from 1863-71.

Born in Nupe, he was kidnapped as a child and taken south to Yoruba country. Then in his teens, he was sold as a slave to be resold in Brazil. The ship carrying him was captured by the British Royal Navy's Africa squadron in 1827, brought to Freetown, and the captives released. Ezzidio was apprenticed to a French shopkeeper, Jean Billaud, and quickly took to business. Billaud called him "Isadore," a name which over the years became transformed to "John Ezzidio." When Billaud died, Ezzidio worked for two other European firms. Within a decade of his recapture, he had saved enough to establish his own business. He bought a plot of land in 1839, and a house in 1841.

In addition to this prosperous business career,

Ezzidio played an even more important role in politics. In 1844 he was appointed alderman on the Freetown Town Council, and the following year became Mayor.

In 1835, he had joined the Wesleyan Methodist Society. Being active in church affairs, he became class-leader and a local preacher. The general superintendent of the Wesleyan Mission, the Rev. Thomas Dove, was so impressed by Ezzidio's qualities that in 1842 he took him to visit England, where he introduced him to wholesale firms. This enabled Ezzidio to place his orders direct, instead of through middlemen. By 1850 he was importing a variety of European merchandise valued at from £3,000 to £4,000 annually. In 1859, together with other recaptives, he became one of the founders of the National Society of the Liberated Africans and Their Descendants. In the same year he revisited England.

In 1863 constitutional change resulted in the establishment of the Sierra Leone Legislative Council, to which Ezzidio was elected as an unofficial member by the Sierra Leone mercantile community, having defeated a European rival candidate, John Levi. He thus became the first African to serve on the Council, and was invested with the title of "Honourable." After the event, however, the British decided that the elective principle was potentially dangerous to the colonial status quo, and it was disallowed for the future until 1924. Governors were therefore instructed to appoint all members. Thus for more than half a century Ezzidio was to be the first and last *elected* member of the Legislative Council.

As a prominent Sierra Leonean, he was also, over the years, signatory to a number of petitions to the British authorities in London on various administrative matters. In 1847, for example, he was one of those who petitioned the British Secretary of State for Colonies to remove Governor Norman William Macdonald (term of office 1846-52).

Ezzidio remained an active churchman, and contributed generously to church funds. When Dove left in 1863, he took over supervision of the Wesleyan Mission for a time, but requested that another general superintendent be sent out from England. The new superintendent was the Rev. Benjamin Tregaskis, a man of authoritarian tendencies. A split occurred between them which damaged relations to such an extent that the building of Wesley Church, which Ezzidio had done so much to begin, remained unfinished at the time of his death. Shortly before the arrival of Tregaskis, the Church Missionary Society (C.M.S.), which was initiating a policy of "decolonization," had substituted a Native Pastorate Church for the previous one in 1861. Twice, in 1863 and 1867, Ezzidio voted in the Legislative Council for an annual grant to this C.M.S. church. Tregaskis, because of his doctoral orientation, was annoyed, and set about turning Ezzidio's friends against him. To crown it all, Ezzidio lost £3,000 in his business. These misfortunes combined to make him ill. He recovered and travelled to England again in 1870, but returned home ill again. His health remained precarious, but he managed to attend Legislative Council debates, voting in 1871 for the 1872 estimates, including a grant to the Native Pastorate Church. But in December 1871 he became permanently ill, and gave up public business. He was confined to his house, where he died in October 1872.

ARTHUR ABRAHAM

BIBLIOGRAPHY: Christopher Fyfe, "The Life and Times of John Ezzidio," *Sierra Leone Studies,* June, 1955; John Peterson, *The Province of Freedom,* London, 1969.

FADUMA, O.

Orishatukeh Faduma (1860-January 12, 1946), also known as William James Davies, a recaptive of Nigerian descent, had a long and distinguished career both in Sierra Leone and in the United States as an educationist and Christian minister.

He was born in British Guiana (now Guyana), and was the son of John and Omolofi Faduma, who were freed African slaves from Yoruba country in what is now Nigeria. Faduma and his parents were "repatriated" to Freetown, when he was probably aged seven or eight. He was baptised a Christian on arrival in the Colony. In keeping with missionary attitudes, which then regarded African names as "heathenish," he was given the name of William James Davies, by which he was known until 1887. Like the children of other recaptives, he received his education to secondary school level at the Methodist Boys' High School.

He then attended Wesleyan (now Queens) College, Taunton, England, from 1882-83, after winning first place in a competitive scholarship. Later, he attended London University, where he became the first Sierra Leonean to obtain a bachelor of arts degree there. He then returned to Sierra Leone, where he was employed as senior master at his former high school.

In 1891, however, he went to the United States to continue his education. He obtained a degree from Yale Divinity School in 1895, and won $400 for postgraduate study of the philosophy of religion.

After completing his studies at Yale, he remained in the United States. At some time between 1891 and 1895, Faduma had become affiliated with the American Missionary Association, whose major focus was the evangelization of Afro-Americans and Africans. During this period, he also became more closely associated with the African Methodist Episcopal (A.M.E.) Church, the first separate religious denomination for black Americans, and was most likely ordained a minister, since thereafter he was referred to as pastor.

From 1895-1914, he was principal and pastor-in-charge of Peabody Academy, Troy, North Carolina. This institution had been established in 1880 under the sponsorship of the American Missionary Association, for the education of black Americans. In the early 1900s it had four teachers, apart from the principal, one of whom was Faduma's Afro-American wife, Mrs. Henrietta Faduma.

He returned to Sierra Leone, and from 1916-18 was principal of the United Methodist Collegiate School in Freetown. From 1918-23, he served as an inspector of schools in the Colony (now the Western area), and as officer-in-charge of the Model School, where he was also an instructor. The Model School generally prepared those students for entry into the job market who had failed entrance examinations for secondary school.

He returned to the United States in 1924, and continued teaching in North Carolina until 1939, serving as assistant principal and instructor in Latin, ancient and modern history, and English literature, at Lincoln Academy, King's Mount. Upon retirement, Faduma took another assignment at Virginia Theological Seminary and College, Lynchburg, Virginia, where he taught Latin, Greek, French, and African history until his death at High Point, North Carolina, in January, 1946.

Orishatukeh Fadumah's life, however, ranged beyond teaching. He was greatly influenced by the contemporary trends not only in Sierra Leone, but also elsewhere in Africa, as well as in the United States. Thus soon after his return from England in 1887, he joined with other public-spirited members of the Freetown community, including the distinguished pan-African patriot, Dr. Edward Blyden, and A.E. Toboku-Metzger (*q.v.*), also one of the earliest Sierra Leone graduates, to form what was known as the Dress Reform Society. The aim of this society was to foster the wearing of African robes more suited to the African climate than the Victorian mode of European dress.

It was at this time, also, that Faduma, as mentioned above, dropped his English names, William James Davies, and instead adopted the names Orishatukeh Faduma, derived from the Yoruba deity, Orisha, and from his father's name, Faduma.

Later, Professor Faduma, as he was commonly known, continued to display both political awareness and breadth of vision. In 1923, when the second meeting of the National Congress of British West Africa was held in Freetown, Faduma was one of the participating delegates.

In the United States, Faduma was also active in public service. In 1892, he served on the Advisory Council on African Ethnology at the World's Exposition in Chicago. In 1894 he represented Yale as delegate to the Inter-Seminary Missionary Alliance meeting held in Rochester, New York, and contributed a paper on "Industrial Missions in Africa." In 1895, he attended a missionary congress in Atlanta, Georgia, where he presented two papers, one on Yoruba religion and the other on missionary work in Africa. It was at this time that the Cotton States Exposition was being held in Atlanta, at which, in September, Booker T. Washington, the leading spokesman for black Americans at that time, made his landmark "Atlanta Compromise" speech, suggesting that blacks stop agitating for political and social rights in return for economic opportunity. The missionary congress was probably affiliated with the exposition.

Faduma became a member of the American Negro Academy, a forum based in New York, which had been established in 1904 by leading Afro-American intellectuals for expressing their views on important issues affecting blacks. He was the only African to address the Academy, taking as his subject "The Defects of the Negro Church."

In September 1895, after his appointment to the Peabody Academy, he married one of the teachers there, Henrietta Adams. They had two children—one, born in 1902, named Omojowu (a Yoruba name), and the other, born in 1922, called Du Bois (presumably after the famous black scholar and civil rights activist, W.E.B. Du Bois).

In addition to public speaking and writing, Faduma also wrote poetry. In one poem, "A Ballad on Egbaland," he revealed that by descent he was an Egba from Yorubaland. In another, "In Memoriam: The Centenary of Sierra Leone," he saw Sierra Leone as a symbol for the whole of Africa, and exhibited both nationalist and pan-Africanist sentiments.

The speeches, writings, and activities of the long life of Faduma reveal that he was endowed with keen wit, possessed tremendous energy, and had a passion for involvement in political and social issues. His prime avocation was education. He was also a devoted Christian. But early in his career he saw the gap that often exists between professed and practised Christianity, as well as the contradictions regarding race, and the contempt for black and African values, that are sometimes to be found within the Christian ministry. He sought to combat these evils.

Professor Faduma's experiences in the United States particularly sharpened his consciousness of race. Living in America at the height of "Jim Crowism," he had to develop emotional mechanisms of accommodation to racial and legal segregation. Not only by his work, however, but also by his thoughts and writings, he inveighed against discrimination and sought to elevate the black man. He was nevertheless temperate, and not given to bitter attacks but to caustic wit.

GUSTAV K. DEVENEAUX

BIBLIOGRAPHY: Charles Alexander, *One Hundred Distinguished Leaders,* Atlanta, 1899; Orishatukeh Faduma, "A Ballad on Egbaland," *The AME Church Review,* Vol. VI, No. 1, July, 1888, "In Memoriam: The Centenary of Sierra Leone," *The AME Church Review*, Vol. VI, No. 2, October, 1889, "Thoughts for the Times, or the New Theology," *The AME Church Review*, Vol. VII, No. 2, October, 1890, "Africa or the Dark Continent," *The AME Church Review,* Vol. IX, No. 1, July, 1892, "Religious Beliefs of the Yoruba People in West Africa," and "Success and Drawbacks of Missionary Work in Africa by an Eye-Witness," in *Africa and the American Negro,* Prof. J.W.E. Bowen (ed.), 1896, reprinted Miami, Florida, 1969, "The Defects of the Negro Church," Occasional Paper No. 8. 1904, reprinted in *The American Negro,* New York, 1969, "Africa the Unknown," *The Mission Herald,* No. 43, November-December 1939, "An African Background: My Pagan Origin and Inheritance, *The Mission Herald,* No. 44, September-October, 1940, *Who is Who in Colored America,* New York, 1940; William H. Ferris, *The African Abroad, or His Evolution in Western Civilization,* New Haven, 1913, reprinted New York, 1968.

FARMA TAMI

Farma Tami, a folk hero, who lived at an uncertain date, is traditionally believed to have established the Temne of Sierra Leone as an important political group.

Temne oral traditions record Bai (king) Farma Tami as the leader who organized them politically into powerful kingdoms. He probably was not a Temne himself, but must have migrated to the coast from one of the Mande-speaking countries inland.

It is uncertain at what period he lived. A tradition recorded in the 1860s by the Rev. C.F. Schlenker, a German missionary, says it was 300 generations ago. But the same tradition goes on to describe him as killing white men, though they did not reach Sierra Leone until the 15th century, if the possibility of visits in antiquity is discounted. Tradition also described him as fighting the Maroons of the Sierra Leone Colony, who only arrived in 1800. Sixteenth-century accounts mention a King Farma, a leader of the

"Manes" people, ruling the country northeast of the Sierra Leone estuary. So he may have been a leader in the 16th century invasion of the coast by the inland "Manes"—probably the ancestors of the modern Vai people.

In spite of these uncertainties, he is looked upon by the Temne as their founder. The name Bai Farma, which is written "Farama" by Europeans, survived as a Temne royal title. Robaga, in the Sierra Leone estuary, where he lived, became a holy place for the Temne, and is still regarded as such today. Whatever doubts historians may have about the details of his life, his story seems to be a valid myth of Mande rule over the Temne. In Ijagbemi's words, "the legend of Bai Farma Tami—an account of the origin of a "Mande" ruling family over the Temne—if not true in fact, is most likely true to type."

CHRISTOPHER FYFE

BIBLIOGRAPHY: M. McCulloch, *The Peoples of Sierra Leone Protectorate*, Ethnographic Survey of Africa: Western Africa, London, 1950; C.F. Schlenker, *A Collection of Temne Traditions, as Fables and Proverbs, with an English translation*, London, 1861, *Grammar of the Temne Language*, London, 1864; E. Ijagbemi, "A History of the Temne in the 19th Century," unpublished doctoral thesis, University of Edinburgh, 1968.

FAWUNDU, F.

Francis Fawundu (18?-circa 1920) was ruler of Mano Gbonjeima, a chiefdom near the coast in southern Sierra Leone, from 1893-98, and from 1899-1914.

He was the son of Sengbe Fawundu, who was chief of Mano before him. Francis himself was educated at one of the Mende mission schools in the Sherbro, but returned to Mano and took up trading. Mano itself is strategically located on the shore of Lake Kasseh, which is linked with the Sherbro country by the Kittam River. Combining his educational advantages and the trading opportunities offered by the location of Mano, Fawundu became a wealthy man within a comparatively short time.

In January 1892, Sengbe Fawundu died. The previous year, he had signed a treaty with T.J. Alldridge, the British travelling commissioner, receiving by its terms a stipend of £5 a year. In January 1893, Francis Fawundu was elected to succeed his father, and in 1894 he was formally recognized by Governor Sir Frederic Cardew (term of office 1894-1900).

In 1896 the British promulgated the Protectorate ordinance, placing the hinterland under British juris-diction. Having been authorized to do so by Chief Momo Kai Kai (*q.v.*), Fawundu addressed Governor Cardew on the subject, saying that the ordinance entirely set aside the sovereign rights of the rulers of the territories affected.

In 1897, Fawundu was a leading member of a deputation of chiefs that went to see Cardew to plead against the payment of the house tax which had just been imposed. Cardew told the chiefs to return to their homes and pay the tax. Fawundu, however, stayed on in Freetown, and informed J.C.E. Parkes, the British Secretary for Native Affairs, that "in his foreign relations" he would rather deal officially with Cardew. He added that he preferred dealing with Cardew in writing, as he found the circumstances in which the British had placed his country, his subjects, and himself "very very painful and distressing to my mind."

Upon receiving Fawundu's letter, Cardew instructed Parkes to inform the chief that his letter was "disrespectful and insubordinate," and that his assertion of independence was inadmissible. Particularly irritating to Cardew was Fawundu's signing himself as 'King of Manoh,' thus, said the governor, "arrogating" to himself the position of an independent power. Fawundu was told to apologize for the "disrespectful and disloyal tone" of his letter, and further directed to leave Freetown and "return to your own country within 24 hours."

Fawundu argued logically that there was no inconsistency in signing himself 'King of Mano,' for his father before him had been addressed by that title by the British, and now he had succeeded his father. He also stated that he never knew before that day that he was a British subject. Cardew considered the "attitude" of the letter "impertinent," and declined to accept it as an apology

On Janury 20, 1898, therefore, Fawundu was deposed as chief of Mano, subject to the approval of the British Secretary of State for the Colonies. The action was taken on the grounds that he had "repudiated being a British subject." Cardew convinced the British Colonial Office that it was necessary to make a "severe example" of Fawundu as a "deterrent to others" at that particular time, since most chiefs were then in opposition to the house tax. The British Secretary of State for the colonies later approved Cardew's action. As, however, the Colonial Office was unsure of the legality of its position, the proviso was added that Fawundu might be reinstated if he submitted to British authority.

Shortly after this, the Hut Tax War of 1898 broke out. It was suspected that Fawundu was using his influence in Freetown to induce the Mende to rebel against the British. He was therefore immediately arrested and jailed. Boakei Mina, "who has always remained a loyal chief," was appointed to take charge of Fawundu's chiefdom during his internment.

In November 1898, Fawundu was released and allowed to return to his home. He was reinstated as paramount chief of Mano Sakrim on January 6, 1899, "after publicly submitting" to Cardew's authority. As a wealthy trader, he spent much time thereafter trying to improve conditions so that commerce might thrive in his chiefdom.

By 1914 Fawundu had become very old and drank too much. He was regarded as "having been a constant thorn in the side of the British government." He was exiled from Northern Sherbro district to another part of Sierra Leone the same year, and died probably not long afterward.

ARTHUR ABRAHAM

BIBLIOGRAPHY: Arthur Abraham, *Mende Government and Politics Under Colonial Rule*, Freetown, 1978; Christopher Fyfe, *A History of Sierra Leone*, London, 1962; "Records of Paramount Chiefs," Sierra Leone Government Archives, 1899.

FODAY TARAWALY

Foday Tarawaly (circa 1780s-1880s), chief of Gbile (Billeh), a town on the Great Scarcies River, opposite Kambia, in northern Sierra Leone, was an Islamic scholar, who founded a center of Koranic learning which flourished from the middle of the 19th century until 1875.

He was born in the Morea Soso country in the Northern Rivers region in what is now the Republic of Guinea. As a youth, he received his Islamic education in Morea, and his erudition won him a reputation as a respected scholar.

About the 1820s, he left Morea with his elder brother, Brima Kondito, and traveled towards Dixing in the Kambia district of northwestern Sierra Leone. There they became subject to the Soso Sankoh family, which controlled the Great Scarcies river ports north of Kambia. The Sankoh gave Brima Kondito the village (as it then was) of Gbile. As Brima Kondito wished to travel further south into Temne country, however, he left Foday Tarawaly to rule Gbile.

At Gbile, Foday Tarawaly founded a center of Koranic learning which quickly grew in size. His erudition and piety earned him the designation of "High Priest of the Morea." By the mid-19th century, the center had become an institution which astonished observers. Edward Wilmot Blyden visited the institution in January 1872, and described Foday Tarawaly, the rector, and his activities in the following terms:

> Opposite Kambia, on the northern bank of the Great Scarcies, is the Mohammedan town of Billeh, whose presiding genius, Fode Tarawally, enjoys great literary celebrity. Billeh is a sort of university town, devoted altogether to the cultivation of Mohammedan learning. On the 12th of January I visited it and made a small present to the literary chieftain. I found him... reading a manuscript... He received me with an easy grace and dignity and had all the gravity and reserve of a teacher. He addressed me occasionally in Arabic... He not only seemed at home in the dogmas of his faith, but he discussed instructively some of the most important subjects of human inquiry, and quoted, in support of his views, the opinions of leading Arabic writers. He spoke in high terms of Beidhwai and Jelaladdin as commentators on the Koran.

By this time, the center had "several hundred young men" as students, and also held classes for women. Three of Foday Tarawaly's sons had graduated to become instructors in the university.

Disaster, however, struck the institution in 1875, when the Temne of Dixing drove Foday Tarawaly from Gbile and dispersed his students. In 1876 he was reported as having no center of his own, although he was still considered significant enough to be included in a listing of chieftains in northern Sierra Leone. But Foday Tarawaly was by now about 90 years old, and must have died shortly thereafter.

C. MAGBAILY FYLE

BIBLIOGRAPHY: E.W. Blyden, "Report on an Expedition to Falaba," *Proceedings of the Royal Geographical Society*, Vol.V, No. 17, 1872-73; "Information Regarding the Different Districts and Tribes of Sierra Leone and its Vicinity," Public Record Office, Colonial Office, 879/15/332.

FOMGBOE

Fomgboe (who lived in the mid- and later 19th century), a Loko leader, was the ruler of Tembu, a town in Lower Loko country, to the northeast of Freetown. He acquired a following and became influential in Lower Loko affairs from the 1870s to 1894, when he was imprisoned by the British.

He appears to have been born of relatively insignificant parentage in Lower Loko country in the earlier half of the 19th century. As a young man he travelled to seek his fortune in Sierra Leone Colony, where he worked for some years as a groom in Freetown. On his return to his country, his Freetown experience and his own personal qualities of leadership gained him popularity. By the 1870s he had acquired a sizeable following, and had founded, or become ruler of, the thriving town of Tembu.

He became powerful enough to influence affairs in Lower Loko, then under the rule of Kiha of Gbendembu, but ultimately, if somewhat nominally, subject to Alimamy Samura of Bonko in Sanda (Upper Loko).

By 1887 Fomgboe had gained further prominence as a result of the conflict between Karimu (*q.v.*) of Samaya and the Tonko Limba. Apparently assisting the Tonko Limba against Karimu, Fomgboe became seen by Karimu as one of his chief enemies. Karimu attacked Tembu, Fomgboe's town, without success. Fomgboe then became a leading figure in a coalition against Karimu which included Bai Bureh (*q.v.*) of Kasseh, Brima Sanda of Sanda Loko, and Bombo Lahai (*q.v.*) of Tonko Limba.

At the end of 1890, Fomgboe complained to the British colonial administration that he could not capture Karimu's stronghold at Laminaya because Karimu was receiving aid. By 1891, however, the British had forced Karimu further north, out of Fomgboe's reach.

The activities of Fomgboe in the Karimu affair apparently incurred the displeasure of his nominal overlord, Samura. Fomgboe had apparently passed through Samura's territory to fight against Karimu, and had drawn Brima Sanda, who was subject to Samura, into the struggle. Samura consequently became hostile to Fomgboe. Details of the initial stage of the ensuing conflict are unknown. Fomgboe took up arms against Samura, claiming that the Sanda Loko people under Samura's leadership had "spoilt his country." In the conflict he was not supported by Korba, ruler of Lower Loko, although he was joined by Bonney (Maaju Turay), the Mandinka ruler of Madina, and Dambia, another Lower Loko chief. Fomgboe also sought the help of Biriwa Limba, but without success.

Fomgboe and Bonney together attacked Sanda Loko in 1892, but were repelled. It is said that Dambia betrayed Fomgboe by informing the Sanda Loko of the impending attack. When Fomgboe's forces fell back on Dambia's town, supposing it to be friendly, Dambia's people attacked them. Bonney was killed, and several captives taken.

In practicing this deception, Dambia was remaining loyal to his overlord, Korba. The Sanda Loko, however, continued to believe that all Lower Loko was supporting Fomgboe. Korba therefore had to ask the governor of Sierra Leone to mediate with Samura in order to re-establish good relations with Samura.

Failing to get help from Lower Loko against the Sanda, Fomgboe then enlisted the support of two Temne leaders—Susa, a warrior, and Abdul Lahai Kaloko of Rokrifie, a chief. But by now Fomgboe was also opposed by the Lower Loko, who resented his disruption of their relationship with Samura. When Fomgboe's combined forces attacked Tonkapa, a Loko town, they were beaten off with losses.

These events occurred in about 1894, at the time when the British were establishing control over the Sierra Leone hinterland. The British offered a £20 reward for the capture of Fomgboe, and sent a detachment to destroy his headquarters at Tembu. They then pursued him into Sela Limba country, where he had set up new headquarters at Kamakuya. The British then burnt Kamakuya, but Fomgboe escaped.

He was finally captured in July 1894 in Tonko Limba as a result of information given by Bomboh Lahai. He was then imprisoned in Freetown, and was later deported to the Gambia. Nothing was heard of him thereafter.

C. MAGBAILY FYLE

BIBLIOGRAPHY: C. Magbaily Fyle, "Apropos of Loko History: The Career of Fomgboe of Lower Loko," *Africana Research Bulletin*, VII, 3, 1976.

FORAY KALLON. See VA FORAY SASSABLA

FORNA, MOHAMED S.

Dr. Mohamed Sorie Forna (November 25, 1935-July 19, 1975), a medical doctor who became a politician, was Minister of Finance from 1968-70, and was executed for treason in 1975.

Born in the Tonkolili district in central Sierra Leone, he attended the Evangelical United Brethren (E.U.B.) School at Moyamba, and then the Bo Government Secondary School. He then went to the United Kingdom, where in 1962 he qualified as a medical doctor at Aberdeen University in Scotland. He returned to Sierra Leone in 1966, becoming a medical officer in the army, with the rank of captain, before entering private practice.

In 1967 he won a seat in Parliament as member for Tonkolili West constituency, on an All People's Congress (A.P.C.) ticket. When the military intervened after the elections, the National Reformation Council (N.R.C.) detained him from July to November of the same year.

When in 1968 an army revolt overthrew the N.R.C., returning the country to civilian rule within a week, he was appointed Minister of Finance in the A.P.C. government of Siaka Stevens. In September 1970, he resigned his cabinet post as well as his membership in the A.P.C. to join the newly-formed United Democratic Party (U.D.P.). He was detained under emergency regulations, and his parliamentary seat was subsequently declared vacant.

In 1973 he was freed from prison, and went into business. But in July 1974, together with 14 others, he was arrested and charged with treason. Found guilty, he was executed at Pademba Road Prisons, Freetown, in July 1975.

CYRIL P. FORAY

BIBLIOGRAPHY: Cyril P. Foray, *Historical Dictionary of Sierra Leone*, Metuchen, N.J., and London, 1977.

GBANKA

Gbanka (18?-May 1898) was Fula Mansa of Yoni Temne, a chiefdom about 112 km (70 mi) due east of Freetown. He opposed the British in the Yoni campaign of 1886-87, and was subsequently banished by them for seven years. On returning to power in 1895, he cooperated with the British, but was killed in the Hut Tax War of 1898.

The original holder of the title of Fula Mansa was a Muslim Fula who settled in Yoni Temne country in the 18th century. He became powerful by slave-dealing, and by marrying into most of the neighboring families, after which he took the title of Fula Mansa. This title was held by successors, who ruled a part of Yoni Temne country.

Gbanka, the last Fula Mansa of Yoni Temne in the 19th century, was prominent in the so-called Yoni disturbances of 1886-87. After vainly trying to make peace, the British decided to send an expedition against the Yoni, who had captured towns and people belonging to their loyal ally, Madam Yoko (*q.v.*). The British War Office sent Sir Francis de Winton to lead the expedition. Supported by more than 700 "irregulars"—opponents of the Yoni—de Winton attacked. His forces stormed the Yoni stronghold of Robari, and advanced on Ronietta, where there was some resistance. The whole campaign was over within a month.

Gbanka, the Fula Mansa, was one of the six leaders opposing the British who de Winton recommended should be exiled to Elmina on the Gold Coast (now Ghana), because their return "might only lead to fresh disorder and trouble." After seven years of banishment, the Fula Mansa returned on the eve of the proclamation of the Protectorate in 1895.

Convinced of the futility of resisting British power, he raised little or no objections to the ordinance establishing the Protectorate. On the contrary, he was active in promoting British interests.

When the time came to collect the house tax imposed in the Protectorate, early in 1898, the acting district commissioner of Ronietta, Dr. T. Hood reported to Governor Sir Frederic Cardew (*q.v.*) that there was general apathy towards payment of the tax. Cardew reacted characteristically. He relieved Hood

of his duties, sending in his place Capt. Samuel Moore of the Frontier Police Force. Moore called a meeting of chiefs at Kwelu, where the Frontier Police barracks were located, and there the Fula Mansa betrayed his colleagues. He secretly informed Moore that the chiefs had taken a strong oath to resist payment of the tax. Solely on the Fula Mansa's testimony, Moore immediately arrested ten chiefs.

Meanwhile the district commissioner of Karene district, northeast of Port Loko, Captain Wilfred S. Sharpe, had been brutalizing certain people to induce them to pay the tax. The Fula Mansa again acted as an informant against the chiefs who had decided not to pay. In consequence, Bai Sherbro, ruler of one section of the Yoni Temne, was accused of instigating the other chiefs not to pay. He was sentenced to 12 months imprisonment, and the Fula Mansa was appointed to take charge of his territory.

After the outbreak of the Hut Tax War in 1898, the British organized a campaign to suppress the insurrection after the rainy season. Their strategy was to form five "flying columns," and to seize the offensive. The Fula Mansa contributed more than 1,000 warriors, characterized by the British as "friendlies," and placed himself at their head. But at Gbonjeima, near Moyamba, south of Yoni, he was killed as he attempted to lead the movement to overrun the town.

ARTHUR ABRAHAM

BIBLIOGRAPHY: Arthur Abraham, *Topics in Sierra Leone History*, Freetown, 1976, *Mende Government and Politics Under Colonial Rule,* Freetown, 1978; Cyril P. Foray, *Historical Dictionary of Sierra Leone*, Metuchen, N.J., and London, 1977; Christopher Fyfe, *A History of Sierra Leone*, London, 1962.

GBANYA LANGO

Gbanya Longo (18?-1878) was the last great ruler of the Kpaa-Mende (the western branch of the Mende, in south central Sierra Leone) in the pre-colonial period. He distinguished himself in the third quarter of the 19th century as an outstanding organizer of professional warriors.

By the 1850s he had already gained prominence in warfare and had carried out many campaigns on behalf of Gbenjei, his uncle, who was then the ruler. In accordance with Mende law, on the death of Gbenjei, he took one of his late uncle's widows, Yoko (*q.v.*), as his wife. She in turn was to succeed to the rulership of the Kpaa-Mende when Gbanya died in 1878.

From 1860 onwards, Gbanya was described officially as a "friendly ally with the Government."

In 1861 he was asked to come to the assistance of Col. Sir Stephen John Hill, governor from 1854-62, who had annexed part of Koya Temne (a chiefdom east of Freetown) to the Colony in order to stop Temne attacks on peaceful traders. When a Loko (a Mande group in northwest Sierra Leone) trader under British protection reported being molested by the Temne, Hill "bought war" from Gbanya, who led several hundred Mende to defeat the Temne.

His help was again asked in 1873, when Garnet Joseph Wolseley (1833-1913), (later Lord Garnet Wolseley), commander-in-chief of the colony, engaged in war against the Asante (Ashanti) of what is now Ghana, ostensibly to check an invasion of the British Gold Coast protectorate. A Mende contingent was raised—125 from Waterloo, 27 km (17 mi) southeast of Freetown, and 35 sent by Gbanya from Taiama on the Tai (Jong) River, once the capital of the Kpaa-Mende. Gbanya's force was led by his son, Kong Gbanya.

Gbanya had meanwhile moved his administrative capital from Taiama further east to Senehun. Technically speaking, Senehun was in Sherbro country, but the territory had been given to the Kpaa-Mende by R.C.B. Caulker (q.v.), in return for a wife, several years earlier. A Krio (Creole) trading center on the Bumpe River, Senehun provided a waterside point to which tradesmen from the interior came to exchange their produce for European merchandise. (It remained the capital of Kpaa-Mende until 1902, when it was moved to Moyamba.)

In 1875, Gbanya became implicated in a serious dispute which arose between Chief George Stephen Caulker of Shenge (a chiefdom on the coast opposite the Plantain Islands), and his speaker (deputy) and cousin, John. John hired Kpaa-Mende mercenaries to fight for him under his chief associates, Kinigbo and Vana, in a war which became known as the Kinigbo war. Ignoring the so-called British frontier, Gbanya's mercenaries swooped into Bagru country (a Sherbro chiefdom in southern Sierra Leone) in a campaign of plunder and destruction.

Samuel Rowe, acting governor (who was later to serve as governor from 1877-80 and from 1885-88), held Gbanya responsible for allowing his warriors to take part in the war, and sent the commandant of Bonthe, Darnell Davis, on a punitive expedition which was beaten off. Rowe himself then took to the field with a force of regulars, police, and Kru laborers (migrant workers from Liberia), using for the first time colonial force in Bagru and Kpaa-Mende.

Rowe used typically high-handed methods; he had Gbanya flogged when he came to protest his innocence of the raid. He also burned towns whose people he suspected of being accomplices in the raid. He then summoned a meeting of chiefs at Senehun where an agreement was signed in which rulers were under threat of losing their jurisdiction if they did not honor the terms, one of which was that all disputes must be submitted to the governor. The Mende raiders were fined 10,000 bushels of rice. The ring-leaders, John Caulker, Kinigbo, and Vana, were found guilty of murdering a policeman on British territory, and were hanged at Bendu, opposite Sherbro Island.

Gbanya was nonetheless still considered one of the greatest allies of the British, though he was neither in treaty with them, nor received a stipend from them. Lord Kimberley, British Secretary of State for the Colonies from 1871-74, noted that: "Gbanya has been long distinguished for his friendly disposition to this Government." Before his death in July 1878, Gbanya gave permission for the opening of a Church of God mission at Senehun.

ARTHUR ABRAHAM

BIBLIOGRAPHY: Arthur Abraham. *Mende Government and Politics Under Colonial Rule,* Freetown, 1978; Christopher Fyfe, *A History of Sierra Leone,* London, 1962.

GOMBU SMART

Gombu Smart or Koko (18th-early 19th centuries) was an ex-slave who became a powerful chief, ruling at Rokon near the Rokel (Sierra Leone) River in the Sierra Leone colony towards the end of the 18th century.

A Loko from Kalangba, in what is now Bombali district, he accidentally killed his brother as a boy, and fled from home. He was eventually sold as a slave at Bence (today called Bunce) Island a British trading post on the Rokel River, where he showed such intelligence (hence his nickname 'Smart') that he was kept as an employee instead of being sold. Sent inland as a slave-buying agent, he bought up many of his own Loko countrymen, but retained them as followers, soon to become powerful enough to make himself independent of his European employers.

He joined the Wunde Society (a Kapaa-Mende secret society), which specialized in military training, and took the name "Gombu," meaning "fire." When civil war broke out among the Rokel Temne he was called to help, and was ultimately rewarded by the Temne by being allowed to settle with his people at Rokon in Masimera state, on the Rokel River, where he built a large, well laid out town.

When the Sierra Leone Company established itself on the Sierra Leone peninsula in 1791 Smart made friends with its European employees. Several of them visited Rokon, and he allowed Christian missionaries to settle there, though they left without accomplishing anything. He also supported the Sierra Leone Company in its wars against the Koya Temne under "King" Tom II (*q.v.*) in 1801-2. He was still alive in 1806 when he was visited by Joseph Corry, an employee of a trading firm on Bence Island, who mentioned Smart in his *Observations* (a book on the Sierra Leone coast published in 1807), but was dead by the 1820s.

CHRISTOPHER FYFE

BIBLIOGRAPHY: Joseph Corry, *Observations upon the Windward Coast of Africa*, London, 1807; Christopher Fyfe, *A History of Sierra Leone*, London, 1962.

GULAMA, J.

Julius Gulama (1893-March 8, 1951) was a paramount chief of Kaiyimba in Moyamba district who played a prominent part in developing education and political awareness among the people of the Protectorate, in the last decade before independence. He was one of the main forces behind the formation of the Sierra Leone People's Party in 1951.

Born in 1893, he was originally known as Julius Foday Cole. His father was a Mende, Momoh Gulama, the sub-chief of Moyamba, and his mother was a Temne from Masimera in the Port Loko district of the Northern Province. Julius attended the Evangelical United Brethren School at Rotifunk in Moyamba district and later went to the Albert Academy in Freetown. On completing his schooling, he returned to Moyamba to teach at the dayschool which later became the Harford Girls' School. In 1912, he joined the Railway Department as a ticket examiner (as ticket collectors are known in Sierra Leone) working there until 1914, when during World War I he was enlisted as a carrier clerk in the Cameroons campaign. After demobilization in 1918 he worked first in the Medical Department as a vaccinator, and later as store clerk in the firm of Paterson, Zochonis & Co. when it opened a branch in Moyamba.

By the time of his election as paramount chief in 1928, Julius Gulama was already a popular and well-known figure. Within his own chiefdom he instituted various reforms in the system of tribute to be paid by his people. Attempts to regularize the payment of tribute by subjects to their chiefs had been embodied in a Protectorate Native Law Ordinance as early as 1905, but had met with opposition over the clause relating to commutation of labor for a fixed payment of tithe. After experiments in two chiefdoms, reported to be successful, the Colonial Office decreed that commutation policy should be a discretionary matter left to individual chiefs and their subjects. In 1934,

Julius agreed with his people to abolish the existing ad hoc system of tribute and replace it by a fixed tribute, as well as a fixed amount of labor for public works. Other reforms included prohibitions against public gambling and the polluting of streams.

A staunch supporter of the war effort, when World War II broke out Julius was active in raising volunteers among the citizens of Moyamba, as well as engaging in fund-raising activities.

A man of progressive ideas, he was instrumental, along with Dr. M.A.S. Margai (*q.v.*) in organizing regular conferences of chiefs to discuss matters of common concern and to submit recommendations to the colonial administration. This movement which began in Moyamba district, quickly spread to other districts, and formed the basis for the district councils and Protectorate Assembly, set up by statute in 1946.

His efforts were not only directed towards administrative reform but to the consolidation of the various political factions in the Protectorate. He initiated moves that resulted in the formation of the Protectorate Education Progress Union, (P.E.P.U.), a body which aimed, through the provision of scholarships for Protectorate youths of promise, to raise educational standards and to lessen the wide gap between Protectorate and Colony in this respect. He was also the honorary president and only paramount chief member of the Sierra Leone Organization Society (S.O.S.), a political pressure group founded in 1946 to give voice to the aspirations of the Protectorate educated élite.

During the debates between Colony and Protectorate over the implementation of the constitutional changes proposed in 1947 by Governor Sir Hubert Stevenson (1941-48), the S.O.S. took a strongly critical line against the continuing preeminence of traditional leaders, the paramount chiefs, as Protectorate representatives to the proposed Legislative Council. Due to the influence of Chief Gulama and Dr. Margai, this anti-chief stance was modified and the S.O.S. merged with other political groups (the P.E.P.U. and the People's National Party) to form the Sierra Leone People's Party in 1951.

Julius Gulama did not live to witness the march towards independence under the party which he had done so much to shape. He died on March 8, 1951.

ARTHUR ABRAHAM

BIBLIOGRAPHY: Cyril P. Foray, *Historical Dictionary of Sierra Leone,* Metuchen, New Jersey and London, 1977; B.H.A. Ranson, *A Sociological Study of Moyamba Town,* Zaire, 1968; B. Timothy, "The Architects of Sierra Leone's Independence," *The Sierra Leonean,* No. 7, March, 1961.

HAIDARA, K.

Kontorfilli Haidara (1890?-February 16, 1931) was a Soso Muslim (a Mande speaking group spreading across northwest Sierra Leone and Guinea) who had a short and dramatic career in Sierra Leone as a radical religious leader of Islamic reform. He posed a dangerous threat to the colonial administration at a time of serious economic crisis by openly defying its rule and combining his religious radicalism with political resistance. This led eventually to the Haidara War of 1931—an armed confrontation with the government troops sent to arrest him, during which he killed the commanding officer, and was himself killed.

Haidara entered Sierra Leone from the then French colony of Guinea as a "missionary" in May 1930. It is not known when exactly he was born, but judging from the estimates of contemporary observers he would appear to have been between 30 and 45 when he arrived. After initial wanderings in the northwestern part of the country, he settled at Bubuya in the Kambia district from where he disseminated his religious teaching. His second name, "Kontorfilli"—a descriptive name that comes after his real name—is a nickname, meaning "unsteady" in the Soso language.

By October 1930, less than six months after his arrival, Haidara's influence was already strong and he had attracted a considerable following. His religious fanaticism, healing power and ability to perform miracles drew people of all kinds from Sierra Leone and Guinea who would travel long distances to hear him preach or to receive medical treatment. Towards the end of 1930 he intensified his campaign of radical missionary activity, preaching the necessity for religious reform. On January 2, 1931, he wrote to the district commissioner in Kambia, threatening to kill all those who would not adhere to Islam and practice the true faith.

The colonial administration, reacting with a mixture of fury and confusion, took no chances. Haidara was charged with subversion and served with an expulsion order on February 9, 1931. He ignored the order. The following day, on February 10, 1931, he wrote an open letter to the people of Kambia, in present-day Kambia district, telling them that Bai Inga, the paramount chief of Mange Bure chiefdom, in Port Loko district, had fallen (i.e. lost his political powers), and that nobody should fear a European, either French or British. Furthermore, he urged them not to pay the hated house tax (*see* Historical Introduction). It was at about this time that Haidara declared himself Alimamy—a title, usually that of a sub-chief, found among the Temne and neighboring groups influenced by Islam. (This was also the title adopted by Samori Touré, the great Mandinka leader of anti-imperialist resistance in Upper Guinea.)

It was now clear to the administration that Haidara was openly challenging the foundations of colonialism, and would not leave Sierra Leone unless forced to do so. Accordingly, on February 16, 1931, troops of the Royal West African Frontier Force were dispatched from Kambia to arrest him at Bubuya. Haidara, encouraged by the size of his following, refused to submit to a humiliating arrest. Armed with swords and machetes, he and some of his followers went out to meet the advancing troops. In the ensuing fight, which lasted only a few minutes, Haidara and four of his followers were killed, but not before he had killed the commanding British officer, Capt. H.J. Holmes. Thus ended Hiadara and his movement. Nothing remained to be done except to disperse the crowds at Bubuya.

Haidara's short rise to influence has earned its place in history due to factors other than his own religious-inspired leadership. Had it not coincided with the worst economic depression the colonial administration had so far experienced, his activities might not have been taken so seriously, and bloodshed would have been avoided. With the example of the Gold Coast cocoa hold-up (boycott) of late 1930 and early 1931 before them, however, the administration had reason to panic at the possibility of a similar hold-up in Sierra Leone. Yet although the administration detected "seeds of discontent" in the depression, Haidara's area suffered no special hardships; neither did he exploit the situation to promote his religious and political interests. From the evidence at present available, it would be misleading to speak of him as a manipulator of rural discontent.

Nevertheless, his movement, based on Islamic revivalism, reminded both British and French of events during the partitioning of Africa a few decades earlier, when organized resistance had occurred in different parts of the continent. For months after Haidara's death, the French in Conakry, the capital of Guinea, and the British in Freetown, continued to exchange information about the political situation in the border regions, and succeeded in restoring calm within a short time.

In spite of the political implications of his teaching, it should be emphasized that Haidara rose and died as a religious leader. Like Usman dan Fodio (1754-1817), the revolutionary reformer and mystic who founded a militant Muslim state in what is now northern Nigeria, as well as some others in the 19th century, he was out to reform Islam. Only after he discovered that the government of "infidels" (according to the Koran) would not allow him to carry out his mission did he declare himself both a religious and a political leader. Significantly, in Islam the division between the two is almost non-existent. Unfortunately Haidara did not live long enough to make his movement an effective political weapon.

M.H.Y. KANIKI

BIBLIOGRAPHY: C.E. Cookson, "The Idara's Rebellion," *Sierra Leone Studies,* June, 1955; M. Crowder, *West Africa Under Colonial Rule,* London, 1968; B.M. Jusu, "The Haidara Rebellion of 1931," *Sierra Leone Studies,* December, 1954; M.H.Y. Kaniki, "The Idara Rebellion of 1931: A Reappraisal," *Journal of the Historical Society of Sierra Leone,* Vol. I, 1977; M. Kilson, *Political Change in a West African State,* Cambridge, Massachussetts,

HAZELEY, P.P.

Peter Philip Hazeley (March 2, 1862-November 18, 1942) was a Wesleyan Methodist missionary who headed the mission station at Tonko Limba for many years. Known as the "Apostle to the Limba," he wrote a Wesleyan catechism in Limba, and did much to promote teaching in that language.

A Krio (Creole), he was born and attended school in Freetown. He attended the Ebenezer Wesleyan Day School, and, later, from 1875-78, the Wesleyan Boys' School. He was a student at the Theological Institution from April to December 1884, and also attended lectures at Fourah Bay College.

He became a local preacher in 1881, holding the position until 1884, when he was appointed catechist to the Methodist station in Tonko Limba, where, with intermissions, he was to spend the better part of his career. In 1889 he went to Richmond College at Cape Coast, in what is now Ghana, for a year. Upon his return in 1890, he was again appointed to the Limba mission. He was ordained in February 1895, together with his life-long colleague at the Limba mission, Philip Johnson (*q.v.*).

During the first decade of its existence, the Tonko Limba mission underwent a series of crises. In 1890 it lost its leader, James Booth, a pioneer English missionary who repudiated his calling and turned trader, after which Hazeley took control. But continuing conflict between the Limba and their Soso neighbors hampered him in his duties, and he was obliged to retire to Freetown in 1891. He then served on the Wesleyan mission circuit there until peace was restored in Tonko Limba late in 1892.

The imposition of the British Protectorate in 1896 put an end to the protracted fighting between the Soso and the Limba, and the mission, resuming operations under Hazeley, entered a period of prosperity. He ran both a day and a night school, aware that many children spent the day working on the farms. But his efforts were made more difficult by the violent activities of the Human Leopard Society (Kopwno-ei-Nepo), which were rife until they were suppressed in 1898. Under cover of darkness members of this association, disguised as leopards, would attack political enemies or unsuspecting passers-by, killing them and removing parts of their bodies for the concoction of powerful medicine.

During his long stay in Tonko, Hazeley seems to have become arrogant and high-handed, particularly with regard to possible successors. Treating the mission as his particular preserve, he discouraged the efforts of one of the earliest Limba converts, James Lahai Booth, who would have served as a better spokesman for indigenous interests. But Hazeley became increasingly intolerant of any attempt to scrutinize his conduct to affairs. Although he emerged triumphant in the tussle with his subordinates, he was censured by fellow clergymen at annual Synod meetings in Freetown. As reports of conflicts in his circuit reached the capital, he was asked to relinquish control of the mission. At first he refused, but finally he gave in and moved to Freetown in 1907, allegedly removing the mission records.

He remained active however, working in the York, Bonthe, Waterloo, Hastings, and Freetown (Zion) mission circuits after his departure from Tonko Limba.

He had become an authority on the Limba language, having some years earlier produced a Wesleyan catechism in the vernacular. He had also served on the Limba section of the Board of Examiners for Vernacular Studies, established in 1902 following the decision by the Sierra Leone Methodist Mission that ordination of new ministers would depend on their knowledge of a native language.

As late as the 1930s, he was still teaching at the Wesleyan City Mission School in Freetown—an educational establishment founded in the 19th century when energetic attempts were made to convert the large numbers of people moving from the interior to the city. Though enfeebled by age, Hazeley gave Limba lessons to children attending the school. He was also secretary of the Limba Literature Committee, which in 1936 issued two booklets in Limba for the school pupils.

He died in Freetown on November 18, 1942.

E. AMADU TURAY

BIBLIOGRAPHY: Christopher Fyfe, *A History of Sierra Leone*, London, 1962; P.P. Hazeley, *Gnatagpa Gna Ka Tontinginua In Gna Ka Nia Gna Ka Bia Bi Dorma Na Weslen Mesodising* ("The Papers that Ask Questions and Give Answers About the Activities of the People called the Wesleyan Methodists"), London, 1903, *Limba Mission Jubilee Sermon*, n.d., circa 1930; C. Marke, *Origin of Wesleyan Methodism in Sierra Leone,* London, 1913.

HEDDLE, C.

Charles Heddle (1812-187?) was an outstanding businessman who pioneered the export trade in peanuts (groundnuts) from Sierra Leone , and became in time the most prosperous merchant in the Colony. He commanded general respect and was entrusted by the governor to negotiate with local chiefs in order to safeguard British trade from French encroachments. A prominent and active public figure, he was appointed first to the Governor's Council and later to the Legislative Council which replaced it. He was also largely instrumental in establishing a mail packet service between Britain and Freetown.

Born in Freetown in 1812, Heddle was the son of a British army doctor, from the Orkney Islands and an African mother. As a child he visited the Orkneys. After his education (possibly in Britain like his brothers) he went into business, first at Bathurst in the Gambia in 1834 and a few years later in Freetown, where his European ancestry stood him in good stead in official circles. He was in partnership for a while with J.P. Pellegrin, a merchant from Senegal, and by 1840 had established his own firm of Heddle & Co.

It was Heddle who opened up the peanut (groundnut) trade. Peanuts, together with timber, were among the earliest exports from Sierra Leone Colony. In 1837, £13 worth of peanuts was exported, largely by his firm, and shortly after he went into business on a grand scale. He bought up factories from the timber trader, John McCormack, at strategic points on Kikonke Island at the mouth of the Scarcies River, and at Ghinti on the Melacourie River, in what is now Guinea. From these points he could tap the peanut production of the interior.

By the mid-1840s, he already owned half a dozen ships transporting peanuts and timber to Freetown, and by 1850 had become the most important mechant in the colony, having acquired the premises of his predecessors in this position, Macaulay and Babington. By 1846 he was also including palm kernels in his exports.

Because of his wealth and his far-reaching trade connections, Heddle was well known in Sierra Leone and its surroundings, his reputation as the "groundnut king" stretching as far as 300 miles beyond the Colony to distant chiefdoms. He also held a prominent position in the Colony itself. In 1845 he persuaded Governor William Fergusson (term of office 1844-46) to let him lead a mission to negotiate a commercial and anti-slavery treaty with the king of the Morea in Soso country (northwestern Sierra Leone) in order to safeguard British trading interests (in which he largely participated) against French initiatives. Impressed by his enterprise and success, Fergusson gave him a seat on his advisory council.

In 1851, he became the first chairman of the Mercantile Association, formed in Freetown to articulate the interests of the business community. He also played an important role in the establishment in 1852 of a mail packet service between Britain and Freetown called the African Steamship Company, controlled by Macgregor Laird. By the 1860s, he owned an impressive amount of property, both in Freetown, and in Bendu, in Bonthe, and on the Rokel River. He put part of his enormous profits into the acquisition of property, whether by purchase of mortgage, from less successful traders.

In 1863 Heddle was appointed to the newly-constituted Legislative Council by Governor Norman

William Macdonald (term of office 1846-52), where he was an outspoken critic of the colonial administration. Among other things, he urged the policy of keeping the French out of the northern rivers.

By 1870, however, he was a sick and crippled man. He left Freetown in that year to settle in Paris, leaving first his nephew and then one of his sons as his agent in Freetown. It is probable that he died in Paris.

C. MAGBAILY FYLE

BIBLIOGRAPHY: Christopher Fyfe, *A History of Sierra Leone*, London, 1962; A.B.C. Sibthorpe, *The History of Sierra Leone,* 1st ed., London, 1868, 3rd edition, London, 1905, reprinted, London, 1970.

HORTON, J.A.B.

James Africanus Beale Horton (June 1, 1835-October 15, 1883), a gifted Krio (Creole), was a surgeon, British army officer, author, educator, entrepreneur, and politician. He was a precursor of 20th century African nationalism.

He was born in the village of Gloucester, near Freetown. His father, James Horton, a carpenter, was an Ibo recaptive, as also was his mother, Nancy. The name "Horton" had derived from that of an English missionary, who had served in Sierra Leone from 1816-21. "Beale" was a name he adopted from a missionary benefactor. Later, when he went to Edinburgh University in Scotland, he was also to take the name "Africanus."

The Church Missionary Society (C.M.S.), which had been active in the area both in evangelization and in educational work, exerted a strong influence on his early years. After attending the village school in Gloucester, James entered the C.M.S. Grammar School in 1847, where he spent four years studying classics, mathematics, astronomy, history, geography, music, and the Bible. In 1851 he was transferred to the Fourah Bay Institution (another C.M.S. venture, later to become the Fourah Bay College and then the University of Sierra Leone) to study for the ministry. Mainly through the efforts of the Rev. Henry Venn, then secretary of the C.M.S. in London, Horton and two others obtained scholarships from the British War Office to study medicine in England. This decision was partly prompted by the high mortality rate among European doctors on the West African coast. Horton spent five years at King's College, London, where he qualified as an M.R.C.S. (member of the Royal College of Surgeons) in 1858. He then proceeded to Edinburgh University for a year, where he qualified as a medical doctor in 1859 with a thesis entitled "The Medical Topography of the West Coast of Africa," which was later published.

In the same year he returned to West Africa to join the British Army Medical Service as staff assistant surgeon, commissioned for service in West Africa only. Passing briefly through Freetown in October 1859, he was posted to service in the British forts on the Gold Coast (now Ghana), serving initially at Anomabu, then at Keta, and then in Accra. Before going to Accra in 1860, he made a detour to visit Lagos, then still an independent kingdom. He was then posted to Anomabu, where he fell ill. After recuperating at Cape Coast, he was then sent to Dixcove.

In 1861 he returned to Freetown, where he married Fannie Marietta Pratt, the daughter of William Pratt, a well-known Ibo recaptive who had prospered in the export trade. The marriage, however, would be a short one, as his wife was to die in 1865.

By 1862 he was back in the Gold Coast, where he served in a number of places, witnessing a serious earthquake in Accra in August of that year, and serving as a medical officer in the campaign against Krobo, a state 80 km (50 mi) northeast of Accra. He also served during the Asante (Ashanti) campaign of 1863-64, caring personally for Gold Coast Governor Richard Pine (term of office 1862-65) when he fell seriously ill and had to return to Cape Coast.

After the campaign he was posted to the Gambia, but in 1866 was able to visit Monrovia, at which time it is thought that he first met Edward Wilmot Blyden (1832-1912), the gifted West Indian who had an outstanding career as teacher, scholar, and diplomat in Liberia and Sierra Leone.

In 1867 he was posted to Accra before, in September of that year, returning to England, where he stayed for almost a year. From August 1868 to 1869 he was back in the Gold Coast, visiting Lagos twice during that time. In May 1869 he was sent to the Gambia to help fight an outbreak of cholera before returning to Cape Coast in August.

In December 1871 he fought a smallpox epidemic at Mumford, east of Cape Coast, in what is now Ghana. He was then appointed civil commandant at Sekondi. When the Asante war of 1873-74 broke out, he was called to service, but fell ill. He was invalided for six months, but continued his service in the later stages of the campaign. He was then stationed in Cape Coast.

In 1875 he was promoted to the rank of surgeon-major. He was also re-married—to Selina Beatrice Elliott. He traveled to Sierra Leone for the wedding, and then returned to Cape Coast. In 1879 he was briefly posted to Freetown. In December 1880 he retired on half-pay, with the rank of lieutenant-colonel.

Horton was one of the first African doctors, and one of the first Africans to serve as a regular officer in the British Army. Because of prevailing racist attitudes, however, he was discriminated against in the service, and this partly explains why he was frequently transferred from station to station. He served in most parts of British West Africa, from the frontiers of Senegal to the Bight of Benin. Under such circumstances, it is not surprising that his application for the vacant post of governor of the Gold Coast in 1872 was rejected.

Horton took his military and medical duties seriously. He contributed to the administration and defense of Britain's growing empire in West Africa. His researches added immensely to the extant body of knowledge about African diseases. Yet he is most remembered for his contribution to education and politics in the West Africa of his day.

He was noted for his scheme for establishing a university in West Africa. His first proposal in 1861 was for the establishment of a small government medical school in Sierra Leone to prepare young Africans, under the tutorship of Africans, in the preliminaries of medicine before they embarked upon medical courses in Britain. He proposed that students aged 20 and less should, in addition to studying Greek, Latin, and mathematics, be taught "anatomy, physiology, chemistry, botany (of Africa); natural history, hospital practice and pharmacy for two years." Since he felt an African tutor was more suitable than a European, he offered to teach in the proposed institution. The War Office, however, rejected the proposal after reference to the British administration on the Gold Coast, which felt that European doctors were to be preferred to African ones. Horton, however, renewed his proposal in 1863, when it had the support of Governor Pine, who felt that racial prejudice in the medical profession should be broken. But the War Office again refused to support the scheme.

Horton had by 1862 begun to advocate a full university for British West Africa. In 1865, after a Select Committee of the British House of Commons recommended limiting British responsibilities in West Africa, and transferring administration to Africans by stages, he restated his plea in a pamphlet, later expanded to a book, entitled *Political Economy of British Western Africa* (1865). He urged the British government to provide this "focus of learning" by improving upon the missionary efforts in Fourah Bay College. He demanded highly qualified teachers and made proposals for a curriculum which should comprise the theory and practice of education,

classics, mathematics, natural philosophy, mensuration and book-keeping, English language and literature, French, German, Hebrew, history in general, mineralogy, physiology, botany, chemistry, moral and political philosophy, civil and commercial law, drawing and music, besides the other subjects "which might be included under the term theology." He emphasized the study of the physical sciences as "closely connected with our daily wants," but did not include the study of Arabic, or of African languages and cultures.

In 1873 Horton joined the supporters of Blyden in campaigning for a university in West Africa. He wrote his views in *The Negro*—a newspaper founded by Blyden that was published in Freetown in 1872-73—and gave unqualified support to Blyden's proposals. He no longer advocated a government-sponsored university at Fourah Bay, but felt that the institution should be established elsewhere to enable day students to attend it. He proposed that the government should, instead, support the university by endowing professorial chairs in the manner of German universities. He now advocated the study of Arabic, as well as other subjects, but again did not include African languages and cultures.

In his will, Horton was to bequeath his house, Horton Hall, in Freetown, for the establishment of Horton's Collegiate High School. He urged that the school's standards should be progressively raised, and that it should be affiliated with an English university. But after his death, it was found that his estate could not support all his bequests, and the high school did not materialize. His idea for a West African university, unlike Blyden's, was, however, a pale copy of British universities.

No less significant for West Africa's future was Horton's contribution to politics. His political writings were produced in conjunction with the attempts of the Fante of the Gold Coast to establish a confederation, at a time when it was expected that the British would withdraw from their West African colonies. As mentioned, this withdrawal had been recommended by the 1865 Select Committee of the British House of Commons, which examined the status of Britain's West African settlements following incidents on the Gold Coast. Horton, who, as mentioned, had traveled widely in West Africa, serving particularly in the Gold Coast, took up the issue of independence that was implicit in the Committee's report. Though his political treatises were in direct response to the Fante efforts, they were generally oriented towards the establishment of modern independent West African nations. His political thinking was formalized in his popular 1868 book, *West African Countries and Peoples*.

He advocated industry, and particularly education through Europeanization as prerequisites for political independence. Even the Gambia, which Horton felt was least prepared for independence, could be taught eventually to achieve it by employing a monarchical system of government with a king chosen by universal suffrage. On somewhat similar lines, and with varying speed, Sierra Leone could follow the example of Liberia. An independent state could also be developed for the Yoruba, centered on Abeokuta, and another for the Ibo, centered on Bonny—both in what is now Nigeria. Some of Horton's suggestions, for example about the Ibo, showed a marked unfamiliarity with some areas. Nevertheless, many of his proposals were ahead of his time.

Horton's comments found near realization in the Fante Confederation of 1867-74. At the time of the disruptions caused by the exchange of British and Dutch forts on the Gold Coast in 1867, and following the 1865 recommendations of the Select Committee, the various Fante communities had set up a confed-

eration to protect themselves, especially against attack by the Asante (Ashanti) further inland in what is now Ghana. Horton saw the possibility of a Fante monarchy (with an educated monarch) supervised by the British. The monarch should be assisted by an advisory council of responsible chiefs and educated men. Chiefs should gradually be excluded from this government, and British supervision should gradually end. It was because British policy on the Gold Coast was vacillating and ineffective that the Fante had come together to form a union. Horton therefore urged Britain to rethink her policies and work towards setting up strong independent African states on the coast. He recommended the Fante Confederacy as a progressive movement which the British should encourage.

But British policy did not view the Select Committee's report with favor. Growing British influence, and the victory over the Asante in the campaign of 1873-74, made the Fante Confederation and Horton's proposals unpalatable to the British, and Horton was branded as an opponent of British policy.

Horton's writings were mainly on politics, medicine, science, and education. His most famous work is *West African Countries and Peoples,* first published in 1868. It demonstrated not only his versatility, but also the fact that he was a product of his times. Unlike his friend Dr. Blyden, he shared some of the Victorian prejudices of his white middle-class counterparts. He believed, for instance, that Africa's salvation should come only from Christianity and imperial commerce, whereas Blyden believed that the only civilizing force would be Islam.

When Horton returned to Freetown on his retirement, a fairly wealthy man, he demonstrated his faith in commerce and education with militant energy. He established a commercial bank to assist local entrepreneurs, since he believed that an African bourgeoisie would emerge, and offered scholarships to promising Africans to study abroad.

On October 15, 1883, he died of blood-poisoning, contracted after a skin infection, erysipelas, had spread to the bloodstream. He left a substantial part of his estate to further scientific education; it was used to endow three scholarships at the Sierra Leone Technical School.

C. MAGBAILY FYLE and ARTHUR ABRAHAM

BIBLIOGRAPHY: Eric Ashby, *African Universities and Western Tradition*, London, 1964, *Universities, British, Indian, African*, London, 1966; Christopher Fyfe, *A History of Sierra Leone*, London, 1962, *Sierra Leone Inheritance*, London, 1964, *Africanus Horton: 1835-1883: West African Scientist and Patriot*, London and New York, 1972; J.A.B. Horton,

The Medical Topography of the West Coast of Africa, London, 1859, Geological Constitution of Ahanta, Gold Coast, Freetown, 1862, Political Economy of British Western Africa, London, 1865, Physical and Medical Climate and Meteorology of the West Coast of Africa, London, 1867, West African Countries and Peoples, London, 1868, reprinted, with an introduction by George Shepperson, Edinburgh, 1969, Guinea Worm, or Dracunculus, London, 1868, Letters on the Political Condition of the Gold Coast, London, 1870, reprinted (edited by E.A. Ayandele), London, 1970, The Diseases of Tropical Climates and their Treatment, London, 1874, 2nd revised ed., London, 1879; Robert July, The Origins of Modern African Thought, London, 1968; David Kimble, A Political History of Ghana, Oxford, 1963; Hollis R. Lynch, Edward Wilmot Blyden: Pan-Negro Patriot, 1832-1912, London, 1967; Davidson S. Nicol (ed.), with an introduction by Davidson S. Nicol, Africanus Horton; the Dawn of Nationalism in Modern Africa, London, 1969; Henry S. Wilson, Origins of West African Nationalism, London, 1969.

HUGHES, W.

William Hughes (18?-1898) was the first African to be appointed as assistant district commissioner when the interior of Sierra Leone was declared a British Protectorate under the leadership of Governor Sir Frederic Cardew (q.v.).

A Krio (Creole) police clerk, Hughes' appointment was an unusual one. Governor Cardew, an ex-Indian Army colonel, generally appointed officers from the Frontier Police (inaugurated in 1890) to act as district commissioners and assistant distict commissioners over the five administrative areas of the Protectorate. In the Sherbro, however, which was within the Colony, he appointed Thomas Alldridge, a European trader of long standing in the area, as district commissioner. Alldridge had his headquarters at Bonthe, on the Sherbro Island, while Hughes was appointed to Imperi, on the mainland.

Imperi had been deliberately kept within the Colony in order to continue vigilant detective work on the series of gruesome murders carried out by members of the secret Leopard Societies that had become active in the area. Hughes, thoroughly acquainted with the laws of the Colony through his police career, was well qualified for the task of assistant district commissioner in a remote outpost.

In 1897, the Sherbro rulers imposed an embargo on all trade passing from their country to Freetown. They did this as an expression of resentment at the proclamation of the Protectorate, as well as against

Cardew's forthcoming house tax, even although they themselves were unaffected by the tax. Hughes, alone in Imperi, and observing the situation closely, reported that there were signs of a concerted outbreak of hostility, as the Sokong (chief) of Imperi was making arrangements with other chiefs to resist the provisions of the Protectorate Ordinance. His report, unfortunately, was treated lightly in official circles.

At the end of April 1898, a few months after opposition to the house tax had led to an uprising in the north, led by Bai Bureh (q.v.), there was a spontaneous and widespread rising in the south. The attacks were specifically directed against all western establishments and persons. Alldridge, alerted to the crisis by the influx of refugees into Bonthe, sent five policemen to Imperi as reinforcement for Hughes. But already murder, looting and destruction on a large scale had taken place, and the kindly assistant district commissioner could not be found. Sokong had in fact taken Hughes inland where, after being tortured, he, together with his wife and his clerk were murdered at Gbanbaia.

After order had been restored, Cardew objected to the rebuilding of the town, destroyed in the colonial counter-offensive later the same year, because of the murder of Hughes which had taken place there.

ARTHUR ABRAHAM

BIBLIOGRAPHY: A. Abraham, Mende Government and Politics Under Colonial Rule, Freetown, 1978; Christopher Fyfe, A History of Sierra Leone, London, 1962.

HUMONYA, MADAM

Madam Humonya (ruled 1908-1918) was a despotic and unscrupulous paramount chief of the Nongowa chiefdom in the Kenema district, who held her position through the support of the colonial administration. She has been remembered as the worst chief in the history of the Nongowa chiefdom.

She succeeded her mother, Madam Matolo, wife of Faba of Dodo, the father of Nyagua (q.v.) of Panguma, one of the most powerful chiefs in the Sierra Leone hinterland. Madam Matolo was appointed paramount chief of Nongowa in 1898 after the upheavals of the Hut Tax War, when the administration was looking for people who had been their allies to replace rulers who had either been hanged for their part in the war, or who had escaped punishment and would not risk reclaiming their chiefships. This led to many women being put forward and accepted as paramount chiefs by the colonial authorities, of whom Madam Matolo was one.

As the threat of punishment receded, the men tried to oust the women rulers or, if unsuccessful, disregarded their authority. In 1903, Governor Sir Charles Anthony King-Harman (term of office 1900-04) was obliged to present a brass staff to Madam Matolo expressing the hope that, with such a token of support from the government, she would find no further difficulty in enforcing her authority over her subchiefs and other subjects.

Senile and incapable, Madam Matolo maintained a precarious hold on the chiefship until her death in 1908, when her daughter Humonya was 'appointed' paramount chief in her place. She in her turn received special support from the administration which she misused to her own advantage, terriorizing her subjects and soon becoming notorious for petty tyranny.

Because of her privileged position with the colonial administration, who treated her as "a sort of paramount chief over the other paramount chiefs of the district," discontent remained bottled up for fear of the consequences of complaining against her. Astutely taking advantage of her relations with the governor in Freetown, Humonya was able to indulge her despotic behavior and make extortionate demands on her

people (vividly remembered by surviving elders) without fear of reprisals.

Matters changed when W.D. Bowden, an administrator of integrity within the colonial context, took over Kenema as district commissioner in 1917. He promptly recorded in the annual district report that "discontent which had been growing for a number of years...(had) found a voice." With his intimate knowledge of local politics in the area, the longer he stayed, the more Madam Humonya's position was threatened.

Well aware that Bowden would demand an inquiry into her conduct, Humonya forestalled him by complaining that the commissioner was hostile to her and was making it difficult to enforce her authority by encouraging intrigues against her. She managed to obtain an audience with Governor R.J. Wilkinson (term of office 1916-22), after which her attitude to Bowden changed, and he complained that she had become "defiant and openly rude." Ironically, it was she who intrigued against Bowden, involving him in a confrontation with the governor.

The situation became progressively more complex. In 1917 two complaints against Bowden were forwarded to the governor who himself visited Kenema in November of that year, requesting Bowden to enquire into charges made by Humonya against six of the principal men in the chiefdom. Bowden recommended that two of the men he banished, a somewhat shocking outcome, since one of them was Humonya's "paramour."

The governor, influenced by Humonya, rejected the findings and held another investigation himself. The results were the same, but rather than confront Humonya, he summarily transferred Bowden to Ronietta district on the highly unreasonable grounds that the commissioner had denied responsibility for peace in the chiefdom, since the two men had not been banished according to his recommendation.

Even the governor's findings, however, revealed that "for years past very serious abuses had been going on." Humonya was found guilty firstly, of failing to appoint a speaker (deputy) and arbitrarily choosing two men as her principal counselors; secondly, of appointing sub-chiefs for five sections of the chiefdom without the consent of the people; thirdly, of oppressing her subjects by excessive fines, forced labor, and misuse of the pillory. It was decided, in respect of the three charges, that the people should choose a speaker, resulting in the election of Amara Jumu of Hanga and the banishment of the two unofficial counselors; that they should choose their own sub-chiefs, and that excessive fines were to be abolished while all remaining fees and fines were to be recorded and receipts issued. Furthermore, no one was to be put in the stocks for more than seven days.

After the governor's departure, there were fresh complaints to the new district commissioner, Lt. Col. H.G. Warren, expressing disapproval of Humonya's 25 messengers and personal clerk. Warren let the people decide what action to take, and the messengers were dismissed. Humonya was allowed to retain the clerk but was obliged to pay his emoluments herself. In spite of a clear case for deposition proceedings to be taken against her, none were made, for while support from the administration was still forthcoming she could cling to her precarious throne.

In December 1918, the new speaker, Jumu, had a violent quarrel with Humonya. It was widely believed that if an election were allowed, Jumu would become paramount chief, but the governor was not in favor of his standing as candidate. A charge of assault was brought against him and he was banished under suspicion of spearheading opposition to Humonya's rule.

A meeting of the tribal authority, however, voted for the resignation of Humonya from the chiefship. Normally under these circumstances, a paramount chief would have been deposed, banished and disqualified from recontesting. But when elections were held in August 1919 Humonya was allowed to recontest while Amara Jumu was not. In the event she polled only 12 votes, being overwhelmingly defeated in favor of Boakei Kekura.

Nevertheless, the district commissioner, J. Carven, who conducted the election was of the opinion that Humonya, that over-ambitious lady, would attempt to stage a comeback "in spite of the fact that the whole chiefdom is against her." But that was in fact the end of her effective political career, and the final conclusion is that, as D. Simpson has put it, "because of her despotism and cruelty, Madam Humonya is still considered to be the worst chief in chiefdom history and many people vow that they will never support another woman for chief."

ARTHUR ABRAHAM

BIBLIOGRAPHY: A. Abraham, *Mende Government and Politics Under Colonial Rule*, Freetown, 1978; D. Simpson, "A Preliminary Political History of the Kenema Area," *Sierra Leone Studies*, July, 1967.

ISA

Isa (18?-1891) was a chief of Kaliere, a province of the Solimana state in the extreme northeast of Sierra Leone. He occupied an uncomfortable position between warring states, and eventually joined forces with Samori Touré, the Mandinka emperor, and his Sofa warriors.

He was probably born early in the 19th century. He belonged to the Samura clan of Kabelia, a political unit founded by his grandfather towards the end of the 18th century. About the middle of the 19th century, Isa became ruler of Kaliere, then part of the Solimana state, the homeland of the Mande-speaking Solima Yalunka.

During the 1860s, trouble occurred between Isa and the rulers of the Solimana state. They believed that he was in league with the Fula of adjacent Futa Jallon, a state intent on destroying Solimana. When a Fula prince was killed in Falaba, capital of Solimana, his golden saddle and sword were given to Isa, who had no idea where they came from. Some years later the Fula, searching for the saddle and sword, found the incriminating objects with Isa, and attacked his town, causing much destruction. Isa then broke off relations with Solimana, marking the break by changing his last name from Samura (also the name of the Solimana rulers) to his maternal name of Turay.

His son, Sayo, determined to be avenged on the rulers of Solimana. In 1882, Isa sent him to join the forces of Samori moving southwards to gain control of the trade route to Freetown, on which Falaba was situated. Through Sayo's trickery, the Sofa attacked and destroyed Falaba after a nine months' siege. Sayo continued to fight the Sofa thereafter, while Isa remained ruler of Kaliere, now part of Samori's empire.

By 1889, however, Isa had begun to regret his cooperation with Samori's forces. Baba, the Sofa general near Kaliere, had captured some of Isa's people without just cause, and, disillusioned, Isa started to shift his allegiance back towards the rulers of the former Solima state, who were hostile to the Sofa. But by this time he was a very old man, afraid of angering the Sofa and bringing about reprisals on his town.

Meanwhile Sayo was away from Kaliere fighting on the side of the Sofa. When he heard of their hostile action towards his father he broke with them and returned to Kaliere, planning vengeance against his former allies. While Isa lived, he remained a restraining influence on his son, but in 1891 he died, leaving Sayo as his successor, still determined to be avenged against the Sofa.

C. MAGBAILY FYLE

BIBLIOGRAPHY: C. Magbaily Fyle, "Solimana and its Neighbors," unpublished Ph.D. dissertation, Northwestern University, 1976.

JOHNSON, O.A.

Dr. Obadiah Alexander Johnson (1849-1920) was a Sierra Leonean who spent the latter part of his medical career in Lagos where he eventually became one of the foremost medical practitioners in the city. It was mainly due to his initiative that a science faculty was inaugurated at Fourah Bay College.

He was born in 1849 at Hastings, in the rural area of Sierra Leone, was was educated at the C.M.S. (Church Missionary Society) Grammar School, at Fourah Bay College, and in medical schools at King's College, London, and at Edinburgh University.

From 1887-89 he held the post of assistant colonial surgeon in Sierra Leone. In 1888 he also served as justice of the peace in Sherbro. Moving to Lagos, he worked as assistant colonial surgeon there from 1889-97. In August 1901 he was appointed a member of the Legislative Council in the colony of Lagos. He retired from the council in December 1913, by which time he had set up in private practice, and had become one of the most fashionable and successful medical practitioners in the city.

Like many of his fellow countrymen who found their own homeland restricted and bereft of opportunities, Dr. Johnson had left Sierra Leone to seek better prospects in Lagos. But he did not forget his native land. From his own experiences at Fourah Bay College, and probably because of the difficulties he encountered in the initial stages of his medical studies, he was acutely aware of the urgent need for a science

school at Fourah Bay, which would permit aspiring medical students to acquire pre-medical scientific knowledge.

When Dr. Johnson died in England in 1920, he left £5,000 to Fourah Bay College for the founding of a science chair. He also left some of his books to the college. Another Sierra Leonean, Dr. John Randle of Lagos, offered to underwrite the cost of retaining a science master at the college for three years.

The foundation stone of the new science school was laid by H.R.H. the Prince of Wales, when he visited Sierra Leone in April 1925. The great debt which the college owed to Dr. Johnson was acknowledged and widely publicized by the principal and some of his staff.

AKINTOLA J.G. WYSE

BIBLIOGRAPHY: A. Macmillan, *The Red Book of West Africa,* London, 1920; *The Sierra Leone Weekly News.*

JOHNSON, P.

Philip Johnson (March 25, 1853-August 21, 1903) was a Krio (Creole) convert to Wesleyan Methodism who spent his life as a pioneer missionary in Tonko Limba country. A man of little education, he was loved and respected both by his spiritual charges and by his fellow clergymen. He spent much time translating religious texts into Limba.

Born at Hastings, in the rural area of Sierra Leone, he was converted to Wesleyan Methodism in 1870. He subsequently served as prayer-leader, Sunday school teacher, exhorter, and local preacher at the Hastings church. At this time he zealously tried to fill the gaps in his education. Later, in 1879, he followed a course in theology under the guidance of a European missionary in Freetown. Already, at this early stage, his character showed signs of the qualities which were later to earn him such high esteem— humility, piety, and devotion to duty.

In 1880, when the Wesleyan Methodist Church established a mission in Forecaria in Tonko Limba country (in northwest Sierra Leone), Johnson was sent there as catechist under James Booth, the pioneer English missionary who later repudiated his calling and turned trader. Johnson's main concern was with the sub-section at Kathiri village, but when Booth was on leave in Britain, he took charge of the entire ministry. Except for a brief interval when the mission's work was suspended because of hostilities between its Limba hosts and their Soso and Temne neighbors,

Johnson spent all the years of his active missionary life in Tonko Limba.

A source of acute mental anguish to this devout man was the yearly examination which a candidate had to take in order to become a fully ordained minister. But because of his scanty education he was exempted from being tested on many of the more involved texts on theology. Moreover, his religious colleagues felt that he was destined for work among a largely non-literate population.

In 1891 the mission was forced to suspend activities as a result of renewed Limba-Soso conflict. Johnson then went to Freetown, where he ministered to the migrant Limba community in the city and its suburbs where, among his congregation, he found refugees from the strife-torn Tonko Limba. By 1893 hostilities had ceased and he was able to return to the field, serving as second in command to another Krio missionary attached to Tonko Limba, the Rev. Philip Hazeley (q.v.).

Johnson's profound knowledge of the Limba language proved to be his greatest asset. He spent much time on translation work and by 1894 had produced a translation of the catechisms as well as a Limba version of the sacramental services. Eventually, he was ordained in Freetown as Native Assistant Minister in February, 1895.

Struck by an attack of paralysis in 1902, Johnson was declared a supernumerary minister the following year. His condition deteriorated until his death in Freetown on August 21, 1903.

E.D. AMADU TURAY

BIBLIOGRAPHY: C. Marke, *The Origin of Wesleyan Methodism in Sierra Leone,* London, 1913.

JONES, E.N.

The Rev. Ethelred Nathaniel Jones (June 28, 1884-March 29, 1954) who from the 1920s, onwards also used the name Laminah Sankoh, was one of the most outstanding and fearless leaders in pre-independence Sierra Leone. Passionately dedicated to the unification of Colony and Protectorate, he founded the People's Party in 1948 towards the end of a long career as a radical churchman, political writer and educator.

He was born at Gloucester in the mountain district of Freetown, the eldest son of Edward Jones, a merchant who exported peanuts (groundnuts) from the Gambia to England, and of his wife Ransolina. Educated at the village school, the Cathedral School, Albert Academy, and the Church Missionary Society (C.M.S.) Grammar School, (now Sierra Leone Grammar School), he graduated from Fourah Bay College with a B.A.

His father wished him to study medicine in England, but contrary to this wish, Jones decided instead to take holy orders, in order to preach and teach among the people. With this in view, he entered Wycliffe College, Oxford, where he studied theology and philosophy, disciplines which colored his thoughts and actions throughout his life.

At Oxford he had a sharp taste of racial prejudice, when, after hearing a sermon in which an Anglican bishop had appealed for candidates for ordination, he wrote offering himself for the ministry. The bishop replied saying that on no account would he lay his hands on a black man's head. Being a regular columnist in the *Spectator*, Jones took up the issue, and wrote to the editor in scathing terms of this open manifestation of racial discrimination within the church. He got little satisfaction, however, for the editor, summoning him to his office and confirming that he was indeed black, lost interest and failed to honor a second appointment to meet.

Jones was eventually ordained a deacon in 1923 by the Bishop of Peterborough who wore white gloves in protection against his "blackness," which he removed after the service. But the earlier episode had so embittered him that as well as his European names he also began using the Temne name Laminah Sankoh. In so doing he was also expressing solidarity with the peoples of the Protectorate, to whom the majority of the Krios (Creoles) were opposed.

He returned home in 1924, but his relations with the church were from the beginning strained. Unorthodox in small matters, such as the arrangement of his vestments, as well as in the content of his sermons, which were searching and provocative, he annoyed his colleagues and irritated his seniors. Later in 1924, he was ordained as a priest, and was appointed curate of Holy Trinity Church. He held the post until 1927, during which time, given the meager resources of the church, his father paid him a stipend. During his curacy, he relieved Bishop T.S. Johnson as lecturer in logic at Fourah Bay College.

In 1927, greatly disappointed at the lack of progressive thinking in the church in Sierra Leone, Jones resigned his curacy and returned to Britain, where he read Education at Oxford. A year later he travelled to the United States, where he taught at Tuskegee Institute in Alabama, Lincoln University in Pennsylvania, and the state college at Orangeburg, South Carolina. In 1930 he returned to Britain once more, where he was active in the West African Students' Union (W.A.S.U.), a political pressure group for self-government, founded through the efforts of H.C. Bankole-Bright (*q.v.*). He became a regular contributor to the W.A.S.U. journal, of which he later became editor. He also made a study of cooperatives in Manchester, from which he gained certain key ideas which had a definitive effect on his social and political thinking.

In the early 1940s he returned again to Sierra Leone where he immediately embarked on political and civic work of all kinds. At the grass-roots level he was concerned to educate his fellow countrymen in their political rights and duties while at the same time he was deeply involved in the political conflict between Colony and Protectorate. He took an active part in the reconstruction of the Freetown City Council and was elected a councillor for the Central ward in 1948. He also gave an extra-mural course in co-operatives in association with the Extra-Mural Department of Fourah Bay College, and was at one time president of the Freetown Adult Education Committee. One of his last official assignments was to be appointed to a commission set up to investigate the financial affairs and future of Fourah Bay College, which the C.M.S. had declared it could no longer support as a private institution.

Laminah Sankoh put into practice ideas gained from his study of Manchester co-operatives, and founded the Sierra Leone Aro (Co-operative) Society. This met with the bitterest opposition from the government, as it appeared to defy the special ordinance decreeing that official permission was essential for the use of the word "co-operative" in forming associations. By using the Yoruba word 'aro', almost the same in meaning, Sankoh had technically avoided the issue. It was believed, wrongly, that his Aro Society was affiliated to the Co-operative Society in Britain, but that could only have been possible had each member paid the necessary £50 to join. But Sankoh's membership was concerned with pennies, not pounds.

Another of his ideas was to establish a "Penny Bank," with a passbook being issued to each of his supporters to enter the penny savings. Unfortunately, it did not become popular, as a result of propaganda by his enemies that he would misappropriate the savings.

In addition to his political field-work, in 1948 Laminah Sankoh, with the assistance of a prominent lawyer, C.D. Hotabah-During, founded a daily newspaper in Freetown called the *African Vanguard*, which continued publication until 1962. He edited this paper until a few months before his death. He also continued to pursue a cherished aim to found an African church whose theology and philosophy would be free of Western accretions and influences. The "People's Church," to which his supporters adhered, was Christian in outlook, but the main accent was on the African approach to God. It was open to anyone, irrespective of creed or nationality.

Meanwhile Sankoh wrote and published work which reflected his characteristic qualities of elegance of style and simplicity. Among his many pamphlets are the *2 Ps or Politics for the People* (dealing with Colony-Protectorate politics), *Recreation, A Root Cause of the Dissension Between the Peoples of the Colony and the Protectorate,* and *Fourah Bay Fund: The Alternative.*

It was, however, in national politics that this committed political philosopher made his most lasting impact. After his second return to Sierra Leone in the early 1940s he initiated the (People's) Forum, a mainly cultural organization intended to examine the views and values held by Sierra Leoneans. It met initially in his house at Wilberforce Street on Sunday evenings, but when the crowds became too large it transferred to the Memorial Hall. The Forum became so popular that the Freetown intelligentsia spread word that Sankoh was a revolutionary.

While almost the entire Colony was misguided enough to uphold a "united country based on segregation and prescriptive rights," this Colony-born man had the courage to stand by his conviction that Sierra Leone was one country, and that its inhabitants should live and work for the common weal.

When it became inevitable that the Stevenson Constitution of 1947, which gave much greater representation to the Protectorate in the Legislative Council, would be implemented (*see* Historical Introduction), the articulate political groups in the Colony formed a federation in August 1950. This was the National Council (N.C.) of the Colony of Sierra Leone. Among its leaders were Dr. H.C. Bankole-Bright, C.D. Hotabah-During, and C.M.A. Thompson. The sole group not represented in the federation was Sankoh's People's Party, founded in 1948, and consisting of liberal Krios (Creoles).

Eight months after the formation of the N.C., the People's Party merged with the Sierra Leone Organization Society (S.O.S.), primarily representing the people of the Protectorate. The new party was called the Sierra Leone People's Party (S.L.P.P.). Formed in 1951, its leadership included Dr. M.A.S. Margai (*q.v.*), Chief Bai Farima Tass, A.J. Momoh, and Kande Bureh. Laminah Sankoh also transferred ownership of the *African Vanguard* to the new party.

Sankoh contested the 1951 elections to the Legislative Council as an S.L.P.P. candidate for Freetown, acting as a spokesman for the Protectorate Africans and the Krios. He was, however, defeated.

The explicit program of the National Council was to oppose the unification of the Colony with the Protectorate because it would spell the end of Krio domination in politics. "We object to foreigners (i.e. Protectorate Africans) preponderating in our Legislative Council," declared their election manifesto, issued in the 1951 election to the Legislative Council. After the council meeting of November 29, 1951, Bankole-Bright, the leader of the N.C., uttered the unfortunate statement that the peoples of the Colony and the Protectorate were like two hills standing opposed to each other which would never meet. Seven months later he went so far as to move for a grant of immediate independence for the Colony.

It was the arrogance and obstinacy of the leaders of the N.C. that spurred Laminah Sankoh to publish in 1952 his most discussed work, *2 Ps or Politics for the People*, in which he proposed his solutions for bridging the widening breach between Colony and Protectorate. His arguments fired the imagination of almost the whole population, causing a stir of unprecedented political fervor among Sierra Leonean Africans.

To the people of the Protectorate he said: "When you think of the Colony, do not think so much of those who have insulted you, those who have said they would not be ruled by gowned men. Think more of those who, like yourselves, are members of the S.L.P.P. and who are working for the unification of country. When you meet to legislate, do not think exclusively of the Protectorate, but of the country as a whole. This [the Stevenson] constitution has put us all in the same boat. We shall either reach our destination together—Freedom—or sink together. I am confident that under your direction the barque will arrive safely in port."

On the other hand his advice to the Colony was: "Change or Perish! By your refusal to adapt yourselves to a changed environment you have forfeited the leadership of the country. In the process of time, after you have rehabilitated yourselves, after you have realized that a man is a man by virtue of his humanity and not by his antecedents or profession, you may succeed in producing a man who is capable of ascending the heights and commanding the allegiance of the whole country."

Like many outstanding men who were in advance of their time, Laminah Sankoh did not live to see the results of his untiring work. His aim was not self-glorification but the unity of his country. After his defeat in the 1951 elections, however, his personal fortunes declined. Convinced of the rightness of his cause, he lost his property in an attempt to save the *African Vanguard*, and as a result was financially ruined.

He died in 1954, poor and broken-hearted, but received a decent and honorable funeral.

D.H. THOMAS

BIBLIOGRAPHY: E.N. Jones (Laminah Sankoh), *The Significance of Our Acceptance of the Municipality Ordinance*, Freetown, 1947, *The Fourah Bay College Fund: The Alternative*, Freetown, 1948, *The Root Cause of Dissension Between the Peoples of the Colony and Protectorate*, Freetown, 1951, *The Two Ps or Politics for the People*, Freetown, 1952; K. Little, *Negroes in Britain*, London, 1947; M. M. Kilson, *Political Change in a West African State*, Cambridge, Massachusetts, 1966; K. Little, *Negroes in Britain*, London, 1947; A.T. Porter, *Creoledom*, London, 1963; D.H. Thomas, "The Black Moses of Sierra Leone's Independence," *Aureol Review*, August, 1969.

KABBA SEI

Kabba Sei (circa 1840-1908) was a Mende war chief of Mando, in Upper Moa, in eastern Sierra Leone, during the late 19th century, who became prominent during the 'Kpo-veh' wars, which occurred in Upper Mende country in the 1880s. He was one of the few chiefs of his time who favored diplomatic methods rather than continuous aggression, and on several occasions he managed to avert or resolve conflicts between warring chiefs.

Born at Potolu, in the main town of Mando which he later rebuilt, he was the third in line of the chiefs of Mando, the grandson of Mendor and the son of Kpana Farley. His contemporaries were the great warrior chiefs Kai Londo (*q.v.*), Nyagua (*q.v.*), Ndawa (*q.v.*), Makavoray (*q.v.*), Mendegla (*q.v.*), and others. Holding the belief that "unity is strength" in 1880, at the time of the Kpo-veh wars, he formed a society called "Tupke," meaning "push," to secure his own authority and as an alliance of neighboring countries against external attack.

When Ndawa, the famous Mende warrior, was expelled from Luawa, today the largest chiefdom in the Kailahun district, after being defeated in battle by Kai Londo, he threatened Mando, Malema and the surrounding countries. Kabba Sei quickly conferred with the chief of Malema to recall the only warrior of note in the area, Ngevau, who was pressing an attack on the Gola in the Liberian highlands. Ngevau returned, stormed the town in which Ndawa had his stronghold, and routed him from the area.

One of Ndawa's lieutenants, however, Mbawulomeh, a powerful Gbandi chief, whose base was in the Liberian hinterland, continued to make predatory raids in the area. He attacked one of Kai Londo's towns, moved on the chiefdom of Guma, where he attacked and killed the town chief Foreka of Bomalu, and encamped at Giuhun Tonagu in Guma. Kabba Sei and Kai Londo thereupon made plans for a concerted attack. Mbawulomeh learned of it and fled for refuge of chief Fobaywulo of Gbandi who refused to surrender the fugitive. He paid for this refusal with his life, for he was killed by Kai Londo. When Mbawulomeh fled to Gbele country (today the Belle chiefdom in Loji country, Liberia), however, Kai Londo gave up the pursuit and returned to his own country.

Shortly afterwards, Kai Londo quarreled with Mendegla of Joru. The actual cause of the quarrel is obscure, but war between these two powerful chiefs would have been a major disaster. Kabba Sei intervened without delay, and invited both of them to meet in his capital town, Potolu, where he brought the misunderstanding to a successful resolution.

On March 30, 1890, Kabba Sei signed a treaty of friendship on behalf of Mando, Dia and Guma with T.J. Alldridge, a trader who had entered government service as a Traveling Commissioner, representing the colonial authorities. When Mbawulomeh reappeared, some five years later, and started causing trouble Kabba Sei was implicated (possibly by misinformation) and as a treaty chief was severely sanctioned.

In 1896, while the Pax Britannica was being extended in the form of a unilateral declaration of Protectorate over the hinterland, Mbawulomeh returned to the eastern frontiers and raided several towns in Luawa, by then under Kai Londo's successor, Fa Bundeh. Fa Bundeh, also a treaty chief, sent word to Major Fairtlough of the Frontier Police stationed at Panguma, that he had been forced to take up arms, contrary to the terms of the treaty signed by his predecessor Kai Londo. The report was presented in such a way as to suggest that Kabba Sei was behind Mbawulomeh's activities, and though Kabba Sei denied any complicity, action was taken against him.

He was forced to flee from his capital when Major Fairtlough with 50 Frontier Police joined up with Fa Bundeh's and Nyagua's warriors and advanced against him. Thereafter, Governor Cardew (*q.v.*) agreed to his arrest and, as a temporary measure, his territory was partitioned between Nyagua and Fa Bundeh.

In March 1898, after Capt. J.E.C. Blakeney, the Frontier Inspector in charge at Panguma, had inflicted a severe defeat on the Sofa and Gbandi allies of Mbawulomeh, Kabba Sei was released, having been made to promise that he would be involved in no more intrigues. A few weeks later, the Mende rebellion against the payment of house tax broke out, but Kabba Sei, in the light of his recent experiences, refused to fight.

He was confirmed paramount chief of Mando after the 1898 resistance had been quelled because "he remained loyal to the government and was of great service....in persuading several of the disaffected chiefs to submit to the dictate of the Governor." Thereafter, he maintained an uneventful chieftainship until his death in 1908.

ARTHUR ABRAHAM

BIBLIOGRAPHY: A. Abraham, *Mende Government and Politics Under Colonial Rule,* Freetown, 1978; K. Little, *The Mende of Sierra Leone,* London, 1951.

KAI LONDO

Kai Londo (circa 1845-circa 1896) was a famous warrior who through the defeat of a great rival in war became the supreme chief of Luawa, in Kailahun district in eastern Sierra Leone. Energetic in peaceful pursuits as well as in aggressive ones, he undertook vigorous internal reconstruction in his territory, building a new town and rebuilding others. Through wars of expansion he extended the boundaries of Luawa creating a powerful state with many chiefs recognizing his overlordship.

He was born at Komalu, the home of his grandmother, near Mano Sewalu, a sub-district of Luawa. His father, Dowii Komei was born and lived at Dukono on the Moa River in Wunde country, today part of the Republic of Guinea.

It was while Dowii Komei, a warrior of repute, was absent on a campaign against the Kissi Tongi and the Vassama Gbandi, both of Loja county of Liberia, that his wife, Kefue Mombeh, gave birth to a baby boy. Dowii had forced the powerful Gbandi chief Kai Londo to capitulate, and sued for peace at Kunjo in the upper Kpombai section of Luawa. It was during the festivities that followed the reconciliation that news of his son's birth reached him, and as a gesture of faith in the new agreement, Dowii at once decided to call the baby Kai Londo. Thus, though the boy was a Kissi he had a Gbandi name.

Kai was brought up in Komalu, his birth place, in the usual manner for a Kissi boy. He was taught the art of war by Kpawi Bundu of Ngiema, in Kailahun district, and later apprenticed as a horn-blower to chief Nyangbe of Medekelema, a large town in the small chiefdom of Bo in Kenema district, southeastern Sierra Leone. Kai made his debut in the war which broke out between Mendekelema and Nongowa, and returned home with the reputation of an outstanding warrior. Once back in Luawa he built a small town and named it Mofindoh, after a town in Njaluahun country, in Kailahun district, where he had been hospitably received on his homeward journey.

During the 1880s, Kai Londo took part in the Kpoveh wars which began with the onslaught of the famous Mende warrior Ndawa against chief Benya of Blama, capital of Small Bo, for raiding the territory of his mentor, chief Makavoray (*q.v.*). It was this war which brought Kai Londo from relative obscurity to the legendary fame which he still enjoys today.

Initially on good terms with each other, Ndawa asked Kai Londo to join him in hostilities against Benya. Benya, however, hearing of the planned attack, fled from Blama and proceeded towards Kono, where he was pursued by Kai Londo and Ndawa. But the expected engagement at Lowama near Kono did not take place for Benya evaded them by taking a different route and returning to Blama.

After this relations between Kai Londo and Ndawa became strained. Kai complained to Ndawa that his slaves were being maltreated by Ndawa's followers, but the latter took little notice of this. Over the distribution of the spoils of war the latent conflict became open. Kai took offense and, refusing to cooperate in any joint venture, again assembled his warriors and set out for Mofindoh ahead of Ndawa, destroying all the bridges in the vicinity. Ndawa, interpreting this as an affront, resolved to teach Kai a lesson. Taking a roundabout route, he went to Ngiehun in Luawa were he invited collaboration from some local chiefs including Faagbandi of Sacambu, Kpaweh of Mende, and Manjakewai and Jobo of Ngeihun.

The Luawa rulers were immediately thrown into terror. When Kai Londo crossed the Moa River and came to the Sewalu district of Luawa he discovered that an emergency meeting of chiefs had been convened at Gbondu to discuss the threat posed by Ndawa. (Among those present were Kpawi Bundu of Ngiema, Mbapa of Sandyalu, Bondo Foyor of Dia, Towai from Liberia, Massa, Mbowa, Jimmi, Sagba and Bendeh.)

Traditions vary as to who took the initiative in asking Kai Londo to become their leader. By some accounts, it was Kai himself who asked the Gbondu

conference members what they would give him if he expelled Ndawa. By others, it would seem that Kpawi Bundu, Kai's instructor in warfare, acted as spokesman, asking Kai to "defend your land." However it came about, they swore to make Kai Londo king of all Luawa should he defeat Ndawa.

Meanwhile, Ndawa had distributed his best warriors at various strategic points. Kai pitched his camp at Golahun in Luawa, where for three weeks he collected as much food as possible, engaging only in preliminary skirmishes with Ndawa's followers. When he was fully prepared, he and his warriors set out for Ngiehun, arriving there shortly before dawn. After going through the stockades surrounding the town, Kai boldly announced himself. Ndawa, lying awake in a hammock, replied "You have met me." In the ensuing combat, Kai defeated Ndawa, who then promised to trouble Luawa no more, and departed leaving behind as hostages a wife and a son.

At Ngiehun, the members of the Gbondu Conference convened a great assembly of chiefs. Kpawi Bundu was once again the spokesman, and after proclaiming that they had all agreed "to give the

country to Kai Londo" as supreme ruler, he went through the ceremony of symbolic handover. First he took a handful of earth and placed it in a piece of white cloth; he then took a gun, loaded it and unloaded it, and passed all these symbolic objects to Kai saying: "Here is your country. Since you defended us, we give all to you. We shall never resist you." Kai replied that he would never condone an invasion or a threat to Luawa, after which there was a great rejoicing.

Kai immediately set about internal reconstruction of his state. On the site of the destroyed Sacambu, he built a new town which was named Kailahun, meaning the town of Kai. He rebuilt other towns destroyed by war and counseled his people to build larger towns for greater safety, while he also had roads made along strategic routes and closely watched. In the interests of internal order he tried to keep the peace by settling disputes amicably, and also arbitrated in disputes among chiefs outside his jurisdiction.

Kai Londo then set out on a war of expansion. He took Vahun in Guma country south of the Moa River, and made war on the Kissi Tengea, compelling them to recognize his overlordship. Further east, he went to Gbele country (the country of the Belle people in Liberia), killing chief Fobaywulo on the way, for refusing to accept his supremacy. He then crossed the Mafessa River beyond the Moa River in the north, and after a successful battle at Wulade forced all the people east of the Mafessa under his rule. He conquered the Gbandi at Papalahun, while Kai Kai, the chief of Kissi Tongi, came of his own free will to Kailahun and pledged himself as vassal to Kai Londo.

The process of enlarging and consolidating Luawa was not without its difficulties. Ndawa, Kai Londo's old enemy, plotted with the three sub-chiefs of Ngiehun who had originally collaborated with him to recall one of Ndawa's lieutenants, Mbawalomeh, from Liberia to help them destroy the new Luawa. Together they captured some of the inhabitants of Tabia, in Luawa, set the town ablaze, and killed chief Kpawi Bundu in cold blood. Kai Londo set out immediately to meet the challenge. Mbawulomeh escaped, but Kai Londo captured the sub-chiefs Faagbandi, Manjakewai and Jobo and administered swift justice, drowning them in the Keeya River with heavy stones tied around their necks.

He then pursued Mbawulomeh through Gbandi country into Liberia, and when he refused to surrender burned many of his towns. On his way home Kai made Fabana Falla chief of Vassama, Keifa ruler over Papalahun, and Molifo over Botema, thus establishing three Luawa sub-chiefdoms. He reached Kailahun with a considerable quantity of slaves and war booty.

Immediately after this, one of his sub-chiefs, Kafula

of Wunde, rebelled against Kai's rule and called in Samori Touré's Sofa warriors to assist him. Once more Kai was victorious, routing the Sofa from their camp at Benduma, from whence they retired to Tecuyama in Kono district, in what is now the Eastern province.

Besides his wars of territorial expansion, Kai undertook a number of campaigns to help oppressed people. He was also concerned to settle disputes inside and beyond his frontiers, and encouraged his people in the peaceful art of food-growing.

In 1890, the British traveling commissioner, T.J. Alldridge, signed a treaty of friendship with Kai Londo. He was highly impressed by his qualities of leadership and has put his opinions of him on record:"... a man of small stature but large intelligence, beloved by the people for miles around, who used to speak of him... as a father... Certainly he was one of the most intelligent chiefs I ever met; powerful and a mighty man of war, but capable of understanding what was for the lasting interest of his people... a chief who was never spoken of except in the highest terms."

In June 1895, Mbawulomeh and Kai were again engaged in war, then the former attacked the Gbandi for submitting to Kai, and then raided parts of Luawa. Kai defeated Mbawulomeh and his allies, Mbawulomeh barely escaping with his life. but during this campaign Kai became ill with dysentery. His speaker (deputy), who was also away on the Liberian front fighting the Gola, hurried home immediately to start making funeral arrangements. Early in 1896 the architect of the great Luawa state died.

Kai Londo's burial was a closely guarded secret. It is said that he died at Dukono and was originally buried there, the body being later removed to Sakona and then to Komalu in Luawa. According to some traditions, however, it was removed to Magbalu, Kai's mother's home, before being carried to Komalu. Following the custom, £12 sterling, many country-cloths, brass bowls and boxes, and perhaps some slaves were buried along with this great ruler.

ARTHUR ABRAHAM

BIBLIOGRAPHY: A. Abraham. *Mende Government and Politics Under Colonial Rule,* Freetown, 1978.

KAI SAMBA I

Kai Samba I (1902-January 3, 1956), originally called Alpha Lalugba Kalei Samba, was a vigorous and progressive paramount chief of Nongowa in southeastern Sierra Leone, who played an important role in both national and local politics. He ruled from 1942 to 1956. Combining foresight with respect for tradition, he pioneered the development of agricultural industry in his district and changed his capital, Kenema, from an insignificant village to a large prosperous urban center.

He was born in 1902, the son of Boakei Kai Samba who was descended from Boima Kahunla, the nephew of the founder of Kenema town. His mother was Musuwa, who was descended from Madam Matolo, wife of King Faba of Dodo. Educated at Bo government school, Alpha Lalugba joined the civil service as a clerk in 1924 and remained in provincial administration till 1942.

In that year elections for the chiefship of Nongowa, in Kenema district, were held, following the deposition of paramount chief Momoh Vangahun. Three years previously, in 1939, Nongowa chiefdom had been astir with allegations of cannibalism against the paramount chief, an explosive issue which also affected the paramount chiefs Saffa Kebbi of Dama, in Kenema district and Momoh Gbow of Njaluahun, in Kailahun district. The trial lasted till 1942 when Momoh Vangahun and Saffa Kebbi were deposed, Momoh Gbow having died before the enquiry ended.

Six candidates contested the election which was won by Alpha Lalugba Kalei Samba. He became paramount chief of Nongowa on February 17, 1942, taking the title Kai Samba I, *Kai* being a modified form of Kaeei or Kalei, meaning 'bone.'

A cool-headed, self-confident and educated chief, Kai Samba was often at variance with his more traditional colleagues. When district councils were inaugurated in 1946, he became deputy president of the Kenema district council, where he put forward various progressive measures. But his efforts were frustrated by his fellow chiefs who disliked his forward-looking ideas, and either lacked his government school education or simply resented his dominance over the affairs of the council.

Kai Samba was also active in the Protectorate Assembly, to which district councils elected members. It was established in 1946 to advise the colonial administration on matters of significance to the Protectorate. Even before its inauguration, however, Kai Samba had organized chiefs' conferences in Kenema, out of which the district councils developed.

Despite set-backs, his achievements far outnumbered those of his contemporaries. A member of the Legislative Council, forerunner of the present House of Representatives, from 1948 to 1951, he also served on the very important Finance Committee to the Executive Council, the predecessor of the modern cabinet. In 1950 he was awarded the King's medal for chiefs.

Unlike most chiefs, he held strong views against the participation of paramount chiefs in national politics as supporters of a political party. The party system, he felt, would seriously undermine the traditional

paternal authority of chiefs over their people, and in line with these views he refused to contest the elections for the Legislative Council in 1951.

Kai Samba is principally remembered for his initiative in modernizing and developing Kenema district and in particular Kenema town. He encouraged the cultivation of cash crops, and pioneered the development of the forest industries, one of the most important industries in Sierra Leone today, with its headquarters in Kenema. He replanned the town with a system of feeder roads, a good sanitation system, and various new social amenities. Under his direction, a park with recreation facilities was built adjacent to the railway station, proving very popular with passengers in transit. The dispensary was expanded into a fully-fledged hospital with a full-time medical officer. Most important of all Kai Samba authorized the building of the Kenema government secondary school in 1952, providing building materials himself to speed up the construction.

Paramount Chief Kai Samba I died of asthma on January 3, 1956, on the eve of signing a committee report recommending the creation of a Kenema Town Council. He was mourned by many, including the large number of "strangers" he had encouraged to settle as traders in Kenema. Kenema town itself, as it stands today, is a lasting testimony to the achievements of one of the most progressive of Protectorate rulers.

ARTHUR ABRAHAM

BIBLIOGRAPHY: C.P. Foray, *Historical Dictionary of Sierra Leone*, Metuchen, New Jersey, and London, 1977; D. Simpson, "A Preliminary Political History of the Kenema Area," *Sierra Leone Studies*, July 1967; A.M. Lavalie, "History and Development of the Institution of Mende Chieftaincy from the Pre-Colonial Period to Independence; A Case Study from Kenema District," B.A. dissertation, University of Sierra Leone, 1976.

KAI TONGI

Kai Tongi (?-1973) was a paramount chief of Kissi Tongi in Kailahun district in Eastern province, Sierra Leone from 1942 to 1952. During his brief ten-year reign he invigorated his backward chiefdom with new life, rebuilding the capital, reforming agricultural methods, and building up a formidable football team. His despotic methods of ruling, though often effective, finally caused a revolt among his people, after which he was deposed.

His grandfather, Kai Kai, had been chief of the small state of Kissi Tongi during the last quarter of the 19th century. When Kai Londo (*q.v.*) was elected king of Luawa, today the largest chiefdom in the Kailahun district, at the Gbondu conference of chiefs, thereby becoming ruler over an enlarged Luawa state, he used force against those states that would not immediately recognize his supremacy. But Kai Kai came of his own free will to Kailahun, Kai Londo's capital, and voluntarily agreed to "sit under him." In this way Kissi Tongi became a province of Luawa.

Kai Kai's son, a great warrior who exerted powerful influence over neighboring Kissi states, persuaded Kissi Tengea and Kissi Kama to come under the ruling of the greater Luawa state, by which services and tribute were rendered by these states to Kailahun, the capital. In 1916, however, the relationship was altered. The Luawa ruler, Boakei Kpundeh, who had succeeded in antagonizing the Kissi sub-chiefs in particular, was deposed, and the administration was decentralized to give greater autonomy to the Kissi areas, although appeals from Kissi courts as well as tribute still went to Kailahun. This was the political position when Kai Tongi was elected paramount chief in 1942.

In 1951, Kai Tongi, whose father was the warrior and ruler Koli Tongi, entered Bo government school, established in 1906 for the sons and nominees of paramount chiefs. After graduating in 1924, he entered the agricultural college at Njala, Moyamba district, Southern Province, where he showed marked athletic ability. Leaving Njala, he was employed by the Agricultural Department but lost his job in the retrenchments caused by the Great Depression.

Because of his unusual abilities, he was soon re-employed as a quarter-master's clerk. He also made his mark as a sportsman, in cricket as well as football, and became a member of the Royal West African Frontier Force cricket and football teams.

In 1938 when Kai's elder brother Ansuma, chief of Benduma section of Kissi Tongi, died, he returned home to take his place at the request of the people. A few years later the paramount chief, Foloba, died and in December 1942, Kai Tongi was elected paramount chief of Kissi Tongi.

Though Kissi Tongi at this time was poor and backward and suffering from the after-effects of famine, Kai was determined to transform his chiefdom into a model state, by force if necessary. He took up his new functions with energy, one of his first constructive steps being to stop tribute and appeals going to the Luawa court. As a paramount chiefdom, he held that Kissi Tongi should not be subject to any other chiefdom. In his determination to infuse life into the society, he decided on a new site for his capital, Buedu, declaring the old site to be unhealthy. The new town was planned on a grid system. Kai carried out a thorough survey on the main streets basing his survey on a system of compounds, each compound measuring 60 feet by 80 feet and comprising a "modern rectangular" dwelling house (traditional round houses were forbidden), a kitchen and a lavatory. To ensure that the old site was abandoned, Kai Tongi made it an offense either to erect new buildings on it or repair old houses.

He marked out places for public works to be carried out by communal labor from the whole chiefdom, building a market, a mosque, a church, a school and a hospital. And he was insistent on high standards of sanitation, decreeing that all houses were to have a proper sewage system and must be well-ventilated.

Though his practical measures were progressive, Kai's political methods were not enlightened. He came to be regarded as despotic by many people, not least his subjects. Obsessively concerned with hard work, he stopped the use of hammocks for relaxation as "it encouraged laziness." His concern with morality, dress and personal conduct was equally intense, and led to stringent measures, such as corporal punishment administered to anyone appearing in the capital with the body exposed, as was the custom for farm-workers. The communal shop, which he set up to provide the basics of modern living and in which all his subjects had to sell their goods, also included a tailoring section. This was to ensure that scantily clad farmers coming in to sell their produce would return properly dressed, after being flogged and forced to buy clothing!

By sheer force of personality, Kai Tongi in 1946

persuaded the army at Moa Barracks, at Daru in the Kailahun district, to sell him a used generator for £800 which he used to provide electricity for Buedu, thus making it one of the first provincial towns in Sierra Leone to have an electricity supply. Bo, the provincial capital, was only in the process of having electricity installed at the time.

Visiting Buedu a few years after Kai Tongi had built it, a British traveler recorded: "It is laid out on sound principles of town planning, each house in its own compound with a separate latrine, the roads broad and awaiting only the growth of young trees to become shady boulevards. And it is lit by electric light from Buedu's own power station. Schools, cemented wells, and dispensaries meet every requirement of welfare and health planning."

As an agriculturist, Kai was concerned to increase the productivity of his chiefdom and introduced extensive programs using new agricultural methods. Every adult male was forced to work a farm of his own as well as the communal family farm. He insisted on swamp rice farming and actively encouraged the growth of cash crops, leading the way by establishing the largest cocoa and rice farms as well as an extensive poultry farm and orchard. In line with his insistence on hard work from all his followers, his wives, usually clad in uniforms, worked long hours daily on his farms.

Not only in economic affairs but in social life as well, Kai was immensely active. He organized the first known dance troupe in the region, called "Kai's dancers." This troupe, a gift from a Gbandi chief in Liberia, became famous, accompanying Kai wherever he went. It specialized in a particular kind of display known as "Fango Loli", and by bringing both the chiefdom and its ruler admiration and respect, added to his sense of overweening self-importance.

Still maintaining his keen interest in sport, Kai encouraged football to an unprecedented degree. The team he built up was virtually invincible in Kailuhun district. On one occasion, as a gesture of encouragement and the show that he was in earnest, Kai had a football field constructed in seven days.

When the Protectorate Assembly was established in 1946 as a debating forum for Protectorate interests Kai Tongi was elected as a member. As the moving spirit behind the modernization of Kissi Tongi he had antagonized a number of people, including a district commissioner, for he would allow no one to stand in the way of the progress which he forced on his subjects. The demands he made for unpaid labor for his extensive farms were the source of bitter discontent.

Matters came to a head in 1951 while he was attending a Protectorate Assembly meeting in Bo. His subjects revolted and accused him of demanding labor without remuneration; of holding court sessions at night; of imposing extortionate fines and levies, and of insisting on compulsory buying and selling at the communal store. Although Kai Tongi employed a solicitor, in the subsequent enquiry he was found guilty and deposition was recommended, although even in colonial circles there were qualms about taking such a step.

True to his nature, Kai refused any offer of a job after his deposition but moved from Buedu to Freetown where he set himself up as a private building contractor and remained till his death in 1973.

One of the most dynamic rulers in mid-20th century Sierra Leone, his importance should not be underestimated. As the author of the *Combey Manuscript* observed in 1948: "As an agriculturalist, Kai Tongi has freed his people from the threats of malnutrition and poverty. While as a psychist he has infused into them new life and strength... Buedu once loathed by many, detested for its unsanitary state, has loomed out as a center for a holiday resort for all sorts of conditions of people... All go in praise of Kai Tongi, the miraculous reformer of the Protectorate age."

This observation is not exaggerated. Although Kai Tongi died two decades after his overthrow, his rule is remembered with nostalgia by the people of Kissi Tongi, while lasting testimony to the achievements of his ten years' rule is still evident in that state.

ARTHUR ABRAHAM

BIBLIOGRAPHY: Anon., "The Combey Manuscript," (written in Kailahun), 1948; M.J. McCall, "Kailondo's Luawa and British rule, 1880-1930," thesis, York University, 1974; S.E. Tanga, "The Role of Paramount Chiefs in Kailahun District with Particular Reference to Late Paramount Chief Kai Tongi of Kissi Tongi Chiefdom," B.A. dissertation, University of Sierra Leone, 1977.

KANFORI

Domin Konteh Kanfori (14th century), a folk hero, was the leader of the earliest wave of Soso migrants into Sierra Leone. This wave was the first of what ultimately became a group many thousands strong which settled in the northwestern part of the country.

The Soso people, who had once been subjects of the ancient Ghana empire, subsequently came under the rulership of the Fulani (Fula) and Mandinka, both large northerly groups. In the 13th century some of them were incorporated into the Mali empire under Sundiata, but others fled to less hostile territory. Kanfori's group, which numbered about 200, consisted of five families who were all related to the leader.

The following traditional account gives a good illustration of the group's movements: "The Sosos were nomads and hunters. They went towards the west with their women and children, moving slowly but never stopping, like ants. They stayed a month, a year, two years in a place and then set out again. They lived by hunting and by gathering corn, roots and wild berries. They were armed with arrows and accompanied by many dogs as fierce as leopards. When they halted they built shelters in the forest near running water and hunted until there was no more game; then they set out once more with their young men and the dogs in front. They also fished in the rivers, drying the fish and eating it on the spot.

"When they rested the Kanfori set up his family round him in huts, and nearby the other heads of families, and fished; the women cooked, gathered wild fruits, prepared skins of wild animals for clothing and protection, made mats and water pots and fetched wood and water."

Finally Kanfori Domin Konteh and his group settled at Domin-ya, which became the chief town for a considerable time after their arrival.

From time to time the newcomers were almost dislodged from their settlement by fresh waves of migrants, but they held fast to their newly acquired territory. One such invading group, the Baga (who now inhabit the coastal region of the Republic of Guinea), decided after a series of clashes with the Soso that it was best to live amicably with them. They agreed to fix boundaries and soon evolved a working relationship.

By the time of Kanfori's death the Soso settlement had been established on a firm foundation. Kanfori was succeeded by his son, Manga Kombeh Balla during whose reign the first Portuguese traders came into contact with the Soso.

E.D. AMADU TURAY

BIBLIOGRAPHY: A.P. Kup, *A History of Sierra Leone 1400-1787*, Cambridge, 1961.

KARIMU

Karimu (18?-1892) was a powerful Soso warrior chief, who waged continuous war with the Limba to defend and extend his chiefdom, using the uncertain relations between British and French over trade and frontier control to build up his own strength.

His father was Sori Gbay, ruler of the town of Samaya in Soso country on the upper reaches of the Small Scarcies. Karimu appears to have followed the traditional warrior's life in his early days, coming into prominence as a war leader in the 1880s.

In 1885, the Sofa warriors of the Mandinka conqueror, Samori, advanced into the northern Sierra Leone hinterland. They destroyed Samaya and captured and killed Karimu's father, Sori Gbay. After their departure Karimu became ruler in his place.

Determined to consolidate his territory, Karimu fought with the Tonko Limba, and Sela Kimba, a Limba chief who had attacked Digi Digi and other Soso towns in Benna Soso country, in what is now the Republic of Guinea. He also became an ally and helper of Almamy Dauda, ruler of Forecaria in Morea in what is now Guinea, likewise embattled against the Tonko Limba, who had attacked his town in the belief that Almamy had aided his fellow Muslims, the Sofa, against them. At the same time the French, intent on diverting trade from this part of the Sierra Leonean hinterland to Melacourie, also in what is now Guinea, were making overtures of friendship to certain chiefs in the area, and Karimu strengthened his position by receiving aid from the French.

During 1888, Karimu, whose warriors consisted of bands of rebels, many of them runaway slaves, continued his attacks on the Limba. He conquered several areas in Tonko Limba and took control of the Soso town of Kolunkuray, which had belonged to Bilali (*q.v.*). As well as Samaya, Karimu had extended his control of Soso towns to Senanaya, Yania and Langa. He also made several reprisal attacks against the Tonko Limba in 1889, claiming that they had allowed the Loko (from the northwest) to pass through their country in order to attack him.

Because of the suspicion of French involvement in the Soso-Limba hostilities, the British colonial administration decided to intervene, and sent the Superintendent of Native Affairs, J.C.E. Parkes (*q.v.*), to try and settle affairs at the end of 1889. Karimu, however, evaded all Parkes' attempts to meet him. Parkes then burnt Kolonkoray, thought to be one of Karimu's strongholds, before leaving the area, and Karimu moved his forces into Morea country, under the rulership of his ally Almamy Dauda. Since this was in territory claimed by the French, he was safe from British investigation. All attempts to get him to move into the British sphere of influence failed, as he knew he would be taken captive if he returned.

While the British were occupied with Samori's movements in other parts of the hinterland, having managed to prevent Soso and Limba attacks on Karimu, the latter was building a strong force undisturbed in territory under French influence. With this force he succeeded in occupying Laminaya by 1890. This town, which had been Bilali's capital, was on the border between Tonko Limba and Kukuna Soso country, and formed a good vantage point for Karimu to strike into the interior. From there he attacked and destroyed many towns in Sela Limba, then under the suzerainty of the Tonko, but his attempts to take Tembu, a town belonging to Fomgboe (*q.v.*), the Loko leader, were repulsed. Along with other neighboring leaders, Fomgboe formed a grand coalition against Karimu, involving Bai Bureh of Kasseh (*q.v.*), Brima Sanda of Sanda Loko, and Bomboh Lahai of Tonko Limba. The town of Laminaya was attacked twice in 1890 but without success.

Attacks and counter-attacks continued throughout 1891, while the joint British-French boundary commission were at work surveying the land in order to establish their areas of control. At the approach of the British boundary commissioner and his party, Karimu feared he would be attacked, but when he received the assurance of the British that this was not their purpose he disbanded his force and tried to make peace with the Limba. The Limba and Loko, however, rejected the presents he had sent as peace offerings and responded instead with a large force against Karimu, who had moved to Benna Soso country in February, 1892. They destroyed many towns, but Karimu managed to escape and retreated further inland into a part of Soso country controlled by the French.

Fighting continued against some of Karimu's followers who had entrenched themselves in fortified camps at Tambi and Kukuna. It required three British expeditions to destroy the fortress at Tambi. After two humiliating defeats, the help of Bai Bureh was sought, and Tambi was destroyed.

By October of 1892 Karimu was dead, having had a notable career as a military leader.

C. MAGBAILY FYLE

BIBLIOGRAPHY: Christopher Fyfe, *A History of Sierra Leone,* London, 1962.

KAYAMBA

Kayamba (who flourished in the mid-19th century), was a powerful Mende warrior, and the founder of Moyamba, 96 km (60 mi) east-southeast of Freetown, which grew to prosperity and prominence in the late 19th and 20th centuries, becoming an important part of the Kpaa-Mende state.

Born on the eastern extremities of Kpaa-Mende country at a place called Yandu, Kayamba made his reputation in warfare, but in time became tired of fighting and embarked on travels towards the coast to found a settlement. During his period of initiation into the Poro, a male secret society among the Mende, he was called Mangowai, but during his travels he was known as Kagbana. Later, however, he came to be called Kayamba, the name by which he is remembered in oral history.

His retinue, when he left his birthplace, consisted of his wife Tangolawai, his chief warrior Gombla, and numerous relatives, warriors and dependents. Some of his followers remained at Yandu intending to join the first contingent once a suitable settlement had been founded.

During his travels, Kayamba heard of a famous soothsayer, Solonto of Gbangbama, who is said to have possessed owls who sang his praises every day, and whose magical potions were prepared with water from a well believed to be fatally poisonous to the non-initiated.

In order to get to Gbangbama, in Moyamba district in the Southern Province, Kayamba had to find a way of crossing the Taia River (also known as the Jong) which is wide; but while he was still trying to solve this problem, he heard of another powerful magician, Sei Molay, who lived at Hemabu in Banta-Mokelle country. He succeeded in meeting Sei Molay, with whom he became close friends and whose daughter, Konya Nallo, he married. Thereafter, Sei Molay led

Kayamba to meet the famous Solonto at Gbangbama.

After "looking ground," or consulting occult powers, Solonto prophesied that Kayamba and his children after him would become great rulers, and that he should look for a place between two hills having a river with many tributaries to establish a settlement, for there his luck and his future lay.

Leaving Gbangbama, Kayamba collected his party from Hemabu, including his new wife Konya Nallo, her mother Noa Nallo, and her brother Fawosa, and proceeded to Gbangbatok in Banta-Mukele country (also in Moyamba district). Here he met and made friends with two important men, Soloni and Yavi Wuja. The latter gave him another wife, named Majoe.

Soon after, Kayamba was asked to assist in a neighboring war. Leaving his wives behind and taking only his warriors with him he marched north, where Loko warriors had made an encampment. But the Loko retreated and as there was no fighting, Kayamba decided to return. On the way back some of his warriors, who had gone hunting, returned with the news that they had discovered a river with six tributaries between two hills.

Kayamba, delighted with this fulfillment of the prophecy, started building homes on the site while some of his warriors were ordered to hurry back to Gbangbatok and collect his family. Before long he was joined by his wives, a blacksmith, Njalawa Kebiwa, and his son by his first wife Tangolawai, Kengi-Mbomeh.

Kayamba wanted to name this settlement after his birthplace, but being dissuaded by his friends and relatives adopted the Sherbro custom of naming it after the river on which it was situated. This river was originally called Yambaisuk, a Sherbro term meaning "overhanging with creepers." Later this name was adapted to the Mende and became Yambatui, and the settlement was called Moyamba, meaning "at the place of the Yamba."

Among the men who had moved with him to Moyamba, Kayamba had an outstanding hunter, Takoyo, with whom he made frequent expeditions into the surrounding forest and along the banks of the Gbangbai, a tributary of the Yambatui. Coming across a very fertile piece of land on the other side of the river, Takoyo decided to make a farm there, but his wives objected to the daily crossing of the river. In view of a minor dispute between himself and Takoyo, Kayamba decided that Takoyo should stay behind at the new site while he returned to Moyamba. The expression "Lo ngi li" (meaning "you stay while I go") became the name of Takoyo's new town, later shortened to "Longi," and anglicized to Lunge.

Moyamba expanded at a phenomenal rate, incorporating typical Mende institutions like the male secret society, the Poro, and the female secret society, the Sande (or Bondo). It is probable that Kayambe died in the 1860s. He left behind six sons. As the eldest, Kengi-Mbomeh, was not old enough to rule, Takoyo acted as regent for a few years until Kengi-Mbomeh, came of age and took over the rulership of Moyamba.

Kengi-Mbomeh's brothers added new sections to the town, greatly increasing its size. With several other villages annexed to it, Moyamba became an important section of the Kpaa-Mende state at the height of its power in the later 19th century. The state is called Kayamba to this day, with Moyamba town itself eventually becoming its capital.

ARTHUR ABRAHAM

BIBLIOGRAPHY: W.H. Fitzjohn, "A Village in Sierra Leone," *Sierra Leone Studies*, December, 1956; B.H.A. Ranson, "The Founding of Moyamba," *Sierra Leone Studies*, January, 1968, *A Sociological Study of Moyamba Town*, Zaire, 1968.

KEBELAI. See BAI BUREH

KEMOKO BILALI

Kemoko Bilali (who flourished in the later 19th century) was a Mandinka from Torong in what is now the Republic of Guinea. He became one of the chief lieutenants of Samori Touré, the Mandinka empire-builder in upper Guinea. As governor of Samori's territories in northern Sierra Leone, Bilali played an important part in negotiations with the British over control of trade routes to Freetown.

Bilali is said to have been captured by Samori in 1875 while he was still a child, and won his master's confidence even as a boy by his distinguished conduct. It was during Samori's siege of Sikasso in the upper Ivory Coast in the 1880s that Bilali proved himself an outstanding soldier and was made a leading general.

During this campaign rebellion broke out in the southern area of Samori's empire, including northern Sierra Leone. Abandoning the fruitless siege, Samori set about the reconquest of his empire and early in 1890 sent Kemoko Bilali at the head of a contingent to subdue northern Sierra Leone. Within a few months, Bilai had accomplished his mission, and became governor of this region, which included parts of Soso country north of Kambia, the former Solima state of Solimana, and large areas of Koranko country in present-day Koinadugu district.

This was an area of great importance to Samori, as the trade routes to Freetown passed through it, and Freetown was his main source of arms. Bilali's major task as governor was to secure these routes, a matter which put him in direct communication with local rulers in the area as well as the colonial administration in Sierra Leone. The latter, keenly interested in trade with the north, were also at this point in imperial expansion very concerned with the activities of the French, who were progressively annexing parts of Samori's empire and claiming them by right of conquest. This alarmed the British, since it meant that Sierra Leone colony would be hemmed in by French control. Negotiations between the British administration and Bilali were therefore stepped up in a bid to persuade him to give up areas west of the upper Niger which they wished to claim.

The British maintained that in 1885 Samori had relinquished all claim to territories between Port Loko, inland from Freetown, and Falaba, in the far northeast. From 1890 to 1892 Bilali, as governor of the area, refrained from interfering south of Falaba and left the responsibility for this part of the trade route to the British. But while the British were anxious to extend this area of non-interference, they failed to protect the trade route which was Bilali's concern, in spite of numerous complaints by him that local rulers were obstructing the flow of merchandise.

In 1891, hostilities broke out between Sayo, the ruler of Kaliere, in northeast Sierra Leone (once part of the Solima state), and Bilali. Sayo, who had once been a Sofa, but had broken with these followers of Samori over a dispute involving his father, Isa (*q.v.*), attacked his former allies and refused to join Bilali when invited to do so. Bilali declared that he would attack Kaliere to punish Sayo, but the British backed Sayo in his refusal to join Bilali on the strength of their 1885 agreement with Samori. Kaliere being north of Falaba, however, Bilali's action was not a violation of the agreement. When one of Bilali's lieutenants advanced towards Kaliere threatening to attack, Sayo fled, and Bilali ordered soldiers to pursue him. He apparently called off the pursuit for he then ordered the detachment to join his master Samori further in the interior.

Nothing further is known of him after this episode.

C. MAGBAILY FYLE

BIBLIOGRAPHY: Y. Person, *Samori: Une Revolution Dyula*, ("Samori: A Dyula Revolution"), Vol. II, Dakar, 1970, "L'Aventure de Porekere et la drame de Waima" ("The Porekere Adventure and the Drama of Waima"), *Cahiers d'Etudes Africaines*, Vol. 18, 1965; C. Magbaily Fyle, "Solimana and its Neighbors," Evanston, Ph.D. thesis, Northwestern University, 1976.

KISIMI KAMARA

Kisimi Kamara (circa 1890-1962), a man of substance and influence in the Barri chiefdom in present-day Pujehun district, is famous for having invented the Mende script of syllabary, the *KiKaKu*, in about 1921.

He was born at Vaana about 1890. He was an Arabic scholar, and is said by tradition to have received a vision of the script in a dream. The first part, KiKaKu, proceeds in groups of three syllables and is clearly derived from Arabic. In all, there are 195 semantics, each character representing a specific sound, and it is written from right to left, another sign of Arabic influence.

Some traditions, however, cast doubt on the validity of ascribing the invention to Kisimi Kamara. They say that as a local chief and man of influence, he merely popularized the script, which was in reality invented by one of his subjects. In these accounts, he figures as an ambitious and clever man, who, being the first to learn the script after it was invented, then used his position to publicize it. Be that as it may, Kisimi Kamara is generally recognized as the inventor of the script, which flourished during the 1920s and 1930s.

The Mende script quickly became popular. Young men learned it eagerly and, as the few surviving people who still know it can recall, it became a fashionable way of communicating with friends on all kinds of subjects. Schools were opened to teach only the KiKaKu. Nostalgically they remember how, after a short period of flowering, the script began to lose ground in the 1940s, for under the influence of the colonial Education Department, the Mende language began to be written in the Latin alphabet. In consequence, pupils at the missionary and colonial schools learned to write Mende using Latin script, and one of the greatest inventions of Mende history passed into oblivion.

Kisimi Kamara himself lived to about 1962. His achievement, though obliterated by colonialism, remains one of the greatest sources of pride for Sierra Leone.

ARTHUR ABRAHAM

BIBLIOGRAPHY: J.T.P. Dalby, "An Investigation of the Mende Syllabary of Kisimi Kamara," *Sierra Leone Studies*, July, 1966; S. Milburn, "Kisimi Kamara and the Mende Script," *Sierra Leone Language Review*, 3, 1964; A.T. Sumner, "Mende Writing," *Sierra Leone Studies*, XVIII, 1932.

KNIGHT, C.

Charles Knight (circa 1799-1879) was an Ibo recaptive, who became the first African to be appointed general superintendent of the Wesleyan Methodist Mission in Sierra Leone.

He was sent to Gloucester, a recaptive village in the mountains near Freetown, about three months after his release from the holds of the slave ship. There he received schooling after which he found employment in Freetown, first as a shop assistant and later as a schoolmaster. While serving as a teacher he was chosen along with another recaptive Wesleyan, Joseph May, for teacher training in England under the sponsorship of the English Quakers.

He left Freetown in 1842, but illness forced him to return to the colony only six months after he had begun his studies. After serving as an assistant missionary from 1844, Knight was ordained a full minister in 1848, and subsequently served in York and Hastings. Ten years later he became head of the Theological and Educational Institution, which trained candidates for church duties as well as for teaching in the Wesleyan schools. Its curriculum was expanded to include algebra, arithmetic and geography in addition to the normal courses in theological education, Latin and Greek.

Together with John Ezzidio (q.v.), a prominent businessman and an active churchman, Knight made extensive plans for the construction of the Wesleyan Church in Freetown, as well as the renovation of many other churches in the city. In the belief that church members had deserted the Wesleyan Mission on account of the dilapidated state of its buildings, he hoped that his program of rebuilding might win them back.

In 1861, Knight, now superintendent of the Freetown circuit, became acting general superintendent of the Mission in Sierra Leone. But when the Rev. Benjamin Tregaskis, an intransigent and overbearing man, was appointed head of the Mission in 1864, Knight entered into the most difficult period of his ministerial career. Through his intolerance and militancy, Tregaskis created considerable disharmony within the Church, and treated his African colleagues with such contempt that, fearing a general revolt of the African clergy in Sierra Leone, the London headquarters prevailed upon him to return to Britain on leave in 1874. In that year Charles Knight replaced him as substantive general superintendent, the first African to hold such a position.

Attempts to discredit Knight's tenure came not only from contemptuous Europeans but also from the rivalry of some Aku (Yoruba recaptive) clergymen. But he maintained a firm hold on his position despite the return of Tregaskis, who joined the ranks of his detractors.

A stern disciplinarian, Knight insisted on high moral standards among his flock. He was also zealous in educational improvement, and was as concerned to raise the standard of teaching at the Mission's schools as he was to improve the work of pupils who attended them. A system of school inspection was established and followed by other changes, such as improved conditions for teachers.

He also planned to extend the Mission's work into the regions beyond Freetown, and started by sending a catechist to Bonthe in the Sherbro, but this project was cut short when Knight fell ill late in 1877 and died on December 13, 1879, aged 80.

E. AMADU TURAY

BIBLIOGRAPHY: Christopher Fyfe, *A History of Sierra Leone*, London, 1962; E. Matei Markwei, "The Rev. Charles Knight in Methodist History," *The Sierra Leone Bulletin of Religion*, June and December, 1967.

KOGBANDI VANGAHUN

Kogbandi Vangahun (18?-early 1890s) was a brave but profligate warrior whose career as a professional fighter was often marred by the distrust provoked by his wild behavior. He eventually became a follower of Nyagua (q.v.), the great Mende chief, and was made one of his sub-chiefs.

Kogbandi was born at Lablama, in Kenema district, in southeastern Sierra Leone, of Gbandi parents, but was expelled from his country as a boy and took refuge with Kendo, ruler of Kpeima in Nongowa country, who made him his page. His promiscuous habits, however soon disgusted Kendo, who took the opportunity of his sister's marriage to a nearby chief, Panda Yohina of Panderu, also in Kenema district, to hand over Kogbandi as a servant.

At Panderu, Kogbandi was respected for his warlike qualities, but once again his licentious behavior gave offense to his chief, who in consequence sent him on many dangerous missions, which Kogbandi bravely survived. When Panda died, he was succeeded by his more powerful nephew Joya, under whom Kogbandi was made leader of the chief's warriors and became prominent at court. But his improper behavior once again caused friction and he fled to seek refuge with Faba of Dodo, in Kenema district.

Frequently interrogated and regarded with suspicion, Kogbandi had to prove his trustworthiness before being accepted by Faba. To do so, he pledged himself to capture Tupulu, a town that obstinately defied the might of Faba and maintained a sturdy independence. Two days after making his pledge,

Kogbandi stormed the town, took possession of it and brought back the leading defenders as captives to Faba. His bid to win the confidence of his master was successful, and he was immediately made one of his principal warriors.

Soon after, news came that the great Ndawa (q.v.) had sacked the town of Panderu and that the chief, Joya, had also died. With permission from Faba, Kogbandi led a force of warriors to bring relief to the beleagured town, routed the enemy, and settled himself there as a professional warrior. For a time he became a follower of Ndawa.

When Faba died at Dodo, Kogbandi returned to serve his son and successor, Nyagua, whom he held in high regard as a great warrior. Together they entered the "Kpo veh" war in upper Mende country, which began in about the 1880s. Kogbandi achieved much in a short time, building new settlements, rebuilding those that had been destroyed, and fortifying those that were vulnerable. Under his leadership, Filo, in Kenema district, rose up again but under the new name of Hangah. Afterwards, the old chief Kaiwa died, and Kogbandi was proclaimed war-chief and protector of the area.

He continued to make warlike forays, round about 1890, until he had the whole of Nongowa country under his protection. This freed Nyagua from concerning himself with campaigns in that area during the "Kpo veh" war. Kogbandi, however, did not live long thereafter, but died the same year.

ARTHUR ABRAHAM

BIBLIOGRAPHY: Arthur Abraham, *Mende Government and Politics Under Colonial Rule,* Freetown, 1978; Max Grovie, *Our Peoples of the Sierra Leone Protectorate,* London, 1944.

KOKELLY, PA. See TOM II, KING

KOKO. See GOMBU SMART

KONKO GBAKU

Bombo Lahai (Bombolai) Konko Gbaku (who ruled from about 1884 to 1911) was the third paramount chief of Tonko Limba. Much of his reign was spent waging a prolonged war with the Soso, and he is best remembered in Limba country for his efforts to repulse the attacks of Karimu (q.v.), a powerful Soso chief.

Konko Gbaku was probably quite young when he succeeded Keleha Horo of Madina to the chiefship in the early 1880s, and may have served in the regime of the warrior chiefs of that territory. His reign witnessed a remarkable incursion of European influences into Tonko Limba. The Wesleyan Methodists established a mission station at Forecaria, then the principal town of the chiefdom; and in October 1889 Konko Gbaku signed a treaty with the British who were intent on out-manoeuvering French efforts to secure Sierra Leone's northern hinterland for themselves.

Differences with neighboring rulers continued throughout Konko's reign, but the most protracted conflict was with Karimu, chief of Samaya, who accused the Tonko Limba people of harboring slaves who had escaped from their Soso owners. As early as the 1830s when Bilali (q.v.) had settled in Tonko Limba with his fellow fugitives from slavery, it had served as a home for these displaced persons. Continuing this long-standing dispute, Karimu launched frequent attacks against Tonko Limba in order to retrieve the runaways. Konko Gbaku, in his attempts to withstand these invasions, enlisted the support of Temne, Loko, and other Limba rulers, but the Soso chief remained unconquered.

Fearing that the French were supporting Karimu's aggressive campaigns, the colonial authorities in Freetown entered the conflict on Konko Gbaku's side. Two attempts by British-led forces to dislodge Karimu from his stronghold at Tambi failed. When a third and more powerful force, augmented by the warriors of Bai Bureh (q.v.), was victorious in 1892, Konko Gbaku was able to turn his attention to the reconstruction of his war-ravaged territory.

For this task he sought assistance from many quarters, notably from the missionaries whom he regarded as a vital link with the colonial authorities in Freetown. The declaration of a British Protectorate over the hinterland of Sierra Leone in 1896 and the hostile reaction which flared up two years later found him deeply involved in his rehabilitation program. As his chiefdom was not strong enough to take part in the wars of resistance, his response to these events was peaceable. He sent protestations of friendship to the colonial administration, which in later years gave him favorable decisions in many boundary disputes with neighboring rulers.

Though an active supporter of the missionaries, it is doubtful whether Konko Gbaku ever became a convert of Christianity. He had many wives, as befitted his chiefly status, and one of his sons, Brima (q.v.), later became a paramount chief of Tonko Limba. He died in 1911, after a reign of about 25 years.

E. AMADU TURAY

BIBLIOGRAPHY: D.P. Chalmers, *Report....on the Insurrection in the Sierra Leone Protectorate, 1898. Part II: Evidence and Documents,* London, 1899; J.J.

Crooks, *A History of the Colony of Sierra Leone, Western Africa,* 2nd ed., Dublin, 1903, reprinted, London, 1972; V.R. Dorjahn and A.S. Tholley, "A Provisional History of the Limba with Special Reference to Tonko Limba Chiefdom," *Sierra Leone Studies,* December, 1959; R. Finnegan, *A Survey of the Limba People of Northern Sierra Leone,* London, 1965; R. Finnegan and D.J. Murray, "Limba Chiefs" in M. Crowder and O. Ikime (eds.), *West African Chiefs,* Ile-Ife, 1970; Christopher Fyfe, *A History of Sierra Leone,* London, 1962.

KPANA LEWIS

Kpana Lewis (18?-circa 1912) was the last Bai Sherbro or ruler of the Sherbro state. A leading member of the powerful Poro society, he defied the colonial administration over the imposition of a hut tax at the inauguration of the Protectorate by using the Poro to force an embargo on trade. After the wars of resistance in 1898, in which he was thought to be heavily implicated, he was considered too dangerous to remain at liberty and ended his days in exile on the Gold Coast.

He was the grandson of the last holder of the title, Kong Kuba, who had signed a treaty in 1825, with Governor Sir Charles Turner (term of office 1825-26) whereby Sherbro country was ceded to the British. Traditionally, the Bai, who resided at Yoni on Sherbro Island, was the ruler of all Sherbro, which consisted of several provinces on the mainland. But by the 19th century, central authority had weakened and many of the chiefs in the provinces had become virtually autonomous in their day-to-day affairs. Kpana Lewis, who reigned from 1879-98, succeeded in asserting his claims of suzerainty over a number of chiefs, using the enormous political power of the Poro society, of which he was a leading member. He was also recognized by the colonial administration in Freetown which claimed, though it did not exercise, jurisdiction over his territory. In 1881 he received a stipend as the direct successor to Kong Kuba.

In 1896 the British government proclaimed a Protectorate over the area adjoining the Sierra Leone Colony. Ordinances to administer it were passed through the Legislative Council, including provision for a hut tax. In protest, Kpana Lewis and a deputation of chiefs went to Freetown to confront Governor Cardew (*q.v.*) early in 1897. After informing Kpana that his territory was part of the colony and therefore unaffected by the Protectorate proclamation, Cardew told the delegation that they would have to obey the provisions of the Ordinance. Deeply dissatisfied, the chiefs returned to their homes.

On his return to Yoni, Kpana Lewis took action by organizing a boycott on trade with Krios (Creoles) and Europeans, enlisting the help of the Poro society, for whom restraint of trade was a customary form of political or economic control. It was reported that the Bai Sherbro had established a post at Kapala, in Sherbro district, "for the purpose of preventing traders passing to and from, where natives are stopped from transacting business in general with the middlemen."

At this point the administration decided on a show of force. In May 1897 a meeting of chiefs was called by T.J. Alldridge, district commissioner of the Sherbro, at which they were informed that severe punitive action would be taken against them if obstruction to trade continued. The Sokong of Imperi replied that being under the orders of the Bai Sherbro he must first confer with him. But when it was learnt that the Bai had issued further instructions to continue the boycott, the acting governor, Col. J.E. Caulfield; advised his detention. Two ordinances were passed, one making it a criminal offense to use the Poro or any similar institution to restrain trade, the other making it possible for the governor to detain Kpana Lewis any time that he saw fit.

In January, 1898, the Hut Tax War started in the north of Sierra Leone. In April it spread suddenly to the south, organized there, it was believed, by the Poro Society. As Kpana was both a leading Poro chief, with suzerainty in some of the rebelling chiefdoms, as well as a known opponent of the Protectorate regime, District Commissioner Alldridge was convinced that he was the brain behind the resistance. Although he disclaimed any knowledge, Kpana was arrested by the governor on May 7, being "treated as suspect, but against whom there seemed to be no evidence." At the end of hostilities, still without sufficient evidence to procure a conviction, he was deported to detention in Accra on July 30, 1899, along with Nyagua (*q.v.*) and Bai Bureh (*q.v.*), also suspected ringleaders of the insurrection.

In Kpana's case the real reason seems to have been that "trade importance is too great to risk any further trouble on the mainland." It was further believed that his resistance to the Protectorate Ordinance arose from the fact that it made his provinces autonomous of the Sherbro state.

On his banishment, Fama Yani, a former rival, was appointed paramount chief with limited jurisdiction over the Sherbro Island alone, which in effect ensured the automony of the paramount chiefs of the Sherbro mainland. Fama Yani could not even use the title Bai Sherbro, for under Sherbro customary law a ruler is made ruler for life and cannot be legally deposed. To legitimize the authority of a successor, the corpse of the deceased must be presented for much visual ceremony.

Although Bai Bureh was allowed back to Sierra

Leone in 1905, the government remained adamant about Kpana Lewis, despite the fact that the Anti-Slavery Society in London took up his case, and questions were asked about him in the British Parliament. In 1910 his son, Kong Kuba, petitioned for the return of his father. But his petition was rejected outright, for Governor Sir Leslie Probyn (term of office 1904-11) was afraid that "if Kpana Lewis returns, the people will regard him as the head of a pagan tribal authority...due to the peculiarity of the tribal laws respecting succession and choice of chiefs...the return of Kpana Lewis will enable his son Kong Kuba alias Herbert Lewis, to commence scheming for the overthrow of Fama Yani, the present Paramount Chief."

Kpana Lewis died in exile around 1912, and with his banishment the Sherbro state lost its last ruler, its sovereignty, and its territorial integrity. The provinces all became autonomous chiefdoms under their own paramount chiefs.

ARTHUR ABRAHAM and CHRISTOPHER FYFE

BIBLIOGRAPHY: A. Abraham, *Mende Government and Politics Under Colonial Rule,* Freetown, 1978; Christopher Fyfe, *A History of Sierra Leone,* London, 1962.

KPOWAMOH-ei-NEPO

Kpowamoh-ei-Nepo (late 19th century), meaning literally "a mad man cannot be coaxed," was the leader of the Tongo Players, a famous Mende institution which used savage methods of crime detection, particularly of witchcraft, in the pre-colonial period. (N.B: In African usage the correct orthography of Nepo's name is "Kpowamɔ-ei-Nɜpɔ.").

Nepo, who rose to prominence during the 1880s and 1890s, is said to have come from the Taiama region, in what is now the Southern Province, but he is believed to have lived at Monghere further to the east "and only came out himself if the palaver was a big one." Possibly a peripatetic Kpaa-Mende institution, the exact origin of the Tongo Players is not known. But whenever suspicious events, such as sudden deaths, frequent disappearance of persons, and so on, baffled the local priests, they were called in. The office of leader was believed to be hereditary, and Nepo himself was held in such awe that if he had to cross a country in a state of war, hostilities would immediately be suspended to allow him free passage.

By the time he came into prominence, "leopard murders" were very common in the Sherbro, and the local rulers were much troubled. It was thought that the murders were committed by people who had used the power of witchcraft to transform themselves into leopards. Contemporary accounts uncritically called these murders "cannibalism," and this inaccurate use of the term has survived till the present day. In actual fact, the outbreaks of murder in the late 19th century were committed by persons disguised as leopards who removed parts of the human body to make "medicines," and there was strong economic and political under-currents connected with them.

The Tongo Players, apparently, had their own intelligence system, and would only respond to a request to perform when all reports had come in. Then they would proceed to the town which had invited them, where they would hold a ceremonial dance round a great fire at night. They would appear, specially robed, with the leader carrying a large horn filled with "medicines." Towards the end of the dance, he called out a number of people, struck them with the horn, and if it stuck to the chest or forehead, that person was found guilty, that is, he was denounced as a "human leopard." The guilty person was immediately set on, beaten severely, and burned to death, while his property and that of his relatives was seized and distributed among the chiefs.

In 1890 there was a fearsome outbreak of "leopard murders" in Imperi in the Sherbro. The rulers reacted vigorously, and, apparently at the instigation of the Rev. D.F. Wilberforce (q.v.), called in the Tongo Players. A gruesome holocaust followed. By a terrible irony, Gbana Bunje, chief of Gbangbama, one of those who had urged calling in the Tongo Players, was himself found guilty of "leopard murder" and was burned to death with more than 20 others. Evidently, rival chiefs bribed the Tongo Players to get rid of their wealthy competitors.

The colonial administration was horrified, and persuaded the chiefs to agree not to call in the Tongo Players again. But in 1891 there was a fresh wave of murders. The outraged chiefs petitioned Captain C.W. Soden, the frontier officer in Imperi, for permission to recall the Tongo Players. Ignoring his refusal, the two most indignant among them, Ka Tegbeh and Ba Shia went ahead and summoned Kpowamoh-ei-Nepo. An even more ghastly holocaust followed, in which at least 100 people were burnt, including Ba Shia. Alarmed that "the cure was getting worse than the disease," the colonial administration decided that both must be suppressed.

Accordingly, Nepo and his Tongo Players were brought to Bonthe on a witness warrant where George H. Garrett, the manager of the Sherbro, was ordered to send them to Freetown for trial. However, he delayed, apparently unwilling to send Nepo for trial. This was because Garrett was opposed to Macfoy (*q.v.*), and therefore favored Nepo, whom he thought also to be opposed to him.

On May 8, 1892, a second order came banishing the Tongo Players from the country. Garrett used it conveniently to release Nepo and others. They returned into the interior whence they came, and nothing was heard of them again. The colonial administration took over the detecting and policing functions of the Tongo Players, but allegations of "leopard murder" or "cannibalism" have never entirely disappeared until the present day.

ARTHUR ABRAHAM

BIBLIOGRAPHY: T.J. Alldridge, *The Sherbro and its Hinterland,* London, 1901; Christopher Fyfe, *A History of Sierra Leone,* London, 1962; F.W.H. Migeod, *A View of Sierra Leone,* London, 1926; A. Abraham, "The Leopard Phenomenon in Sierra Leone," unpublished manuscript.

LAMBOI

Paramount Chief Lamboi (circa 1860-December 26, 1917) was the last ruler of the Kpaa-Mende state before it followed the fate of other pre-colonial states and was fragmented by the colonial authorities.

Lamboi was the younger brother of Madam Yoko (*q.v.*), who had with the support of the colonial administration become the head of the Kpaa-Mende in 1884. When Yoko and her second husband, Gbenjei, went to live in Senehun on the Bumpe River, Lamboi accompanied them and lived with his sister for a long time.

When Madam Yoko died in August 1906, the administration, in gratitude for her unflinching loyalty and support, had Lomboi elected as paramount chief of Kpaa-Mende. By 1900 all other large pre-colonial territorial federations had been dismantled, but in recognition of Yoko's services the government tried vainly to maintain the integrity of the Kpaa-Mende state, although serious cracks and disintegrative forces were already apparent.

A year after his election, Lamboi and his elders elected Mboyawa to be section chief of Moyamba after the death of Momoh Gulama. A year or two afterwards, Lamboi was struck down with paralysis that lasted till his death nearly a decade later. The story goes that in the dry season following the election of Mboyawa, Lamboi discovered a "witch gown" hanging on a tree at Senehun while on a tour of his "chiefdom" (as all territorial units had come to be termed during the colonial period). Such a gown is said

to enable its possessor to gain power, wealth, and fame. He tried to take possession of the gown and in the process was struck with paralysis.

As he was unable to exercise his duties as paramount chief, a regent, Kpungbu Kangaju of Bauya, up-river from Senehun, was elected to act for Lamboi. The official verdict on Lamboi was that he "did not possess the capacity for ruling that his sister had." But clearly the odds were heavily stacked against him. He had inherited a decaying chiefdom, and his paralysis merely made worse a situation in which strong separatist tendencies were already at work, the component sections of the chiefdom having already attained a quasi-autonomy. Even though Kangaju was a willing and hard-working man, the task of controlling the whole territory was beyond him. The district report on Ronietta for 1914 noted that "the chiefdom is extremely loosely held together. It is quite anticipated that on the demise of Lamboi, many of the subdivisions will clamor for separation which, without doubt, will have to be conceded."

On December 26, 1917, the last Kpaa-Mende ruler died, a not unwelcome event. Kapgaju continued in office as regent. In 1919 an election was held, at which Lamboi's son, Lagao Lamboi, lost to Kangaju. At the end of the year, however, it was thought best to let each of the 13 sections of Kpaa-Mende elect their own paramount chiefs, probably in anticipation of administrative re-organization in 1920, and Kangaju returned to Bauya as paramount chief.

With the passing of Lamboi, there passed away also the last of Sierra Leone's pre-colonial states.

ARTHUR ABRAHAM

BIBLIOGRAPHY: A. Abraham, *Mende Government and Politics under Colonial Rule,* Freetown, 1978; B.H.A. Ranson, *A Sociological Study of Moyamba Town,* Zaire, 1968.

LAMINAH SANKOH. See JONES, E.N.

LANSANA, D.

David Lansana (March 27, 1922-July 19, 1975) was the first Sierra Leonean to be commissioned into the Royal (now Republic of) Sierra Leone Military Forces, later to become its first Sierra Leonean brigadier and force commander. In 1967 he participated in an abortive coup d état, but was quickly overthrown by his own officers. (The coup aimed at preventing Siaka Stevens from coming to power, and at reinstating Sir Albert Margai and the Sierra Leone People's

Party [S.L.P.P.].) He was convicted of treason and executed in 1975.

Born on March 27, 1922, at Baiima in the Mandu chiefdom, Kailahun district, he was educated first at Central School and Union College, Bunumbu, Kailahun district, Eastern Province. He then went to Eaton Hall, Cheshire, England, and finally to the Officers' Training School at Chester, England. He enlisted in the army as an officer cadet in 1947, and five years was commissioned. On January 1, 1965, he was made brigadier and force commander of the Royal Sierra Leone Military Forces.

Following the general elections of 1967, Brigadier Lansana declared martial law. He broadcast to the nation on March 21, explaining his action. The elections, he said, had "reflected not political opinions but tribal differences." After the election of ordinary members, while the elections of the 12 paramount chiefs had yet to take place, the two major political parties, the All Peoples Congress and the Sierra Leone Peoples' Party had broken even, each holding 32 seats, with the Independents holding two. Neither had the required majority of 40. Lansana went on to say that tension was building up and that, as chief of state security, he had twice interviewed the governor-general to inform him that "a dangerous situation would be created if he made any appointment (of a prime minister) when neither party had a majority and the elections had still not been concluded." After a third interview, he reported, the governor-general decided to make an appointment despite the brigadier's warning that he would not be able to handle the situation that might arise from such an unconstitutional act.

In conclusion he stated: "I want to make it clear that the Army—and I say this after consultation with my senior officers—does not, I repeat, not intend to impose a military government on the people of Sierra Leone. This country has a record of constitutional government."

In fact, his account both of the figures involved and the constitutional issues raised was not entirely accurate. Not long after his broadcast, the army seized power; the brigadier was arrested by his own senior officers, the Constitution was suspended and a military regime called the National Reformation Council was formed. Brigadier Lansana was later given a diplomatic appointment in New York.

In 1968, a revolt of non-commissioned officers in the army toppled the N.R.C. government, and reinstated the government of Siaka Stevens, which had already been sworn in by the governor-general the previous year when the armed forces declared martial law. Brigadier Lansana left New York to seek asylum in Liberia, but was extradited at the request of the

Sierra Leone government to face charges of illegal assumption and exercise of certain powers. He was convicted and sentenced to five years' imprisonment in 1968.

In 1973 he was released, only to be arrested again shortly after on a treason charge, along with Mohamed S. Forna and 14 other people. After a lengthy trial, Brigadier Lansana was convicted with Forna and others, and was executed at Pademba Road Prisons on July 19, 1975.

CYRIL P. FORAY

BIBLIOGRAPHY: Cyril P. Foray, *Historical Dictionary of Sierra Leone*, Metuchen, New Jersey, and London, 1977.

LAWSON, T.G.

Thomas George Lawson (circa 1814-June 1891) was a chief's son who became the first official interpreter and messenger operating between the colonial administration and the chiefs of the Sierra Leonean interior. So important was his function in maintaining good relations that his informal department was eventually turned into an "Aborigines Branch" of the Secretariat. He was given special recognition at the end of his long career.

He was born probably in 1814, the son of George Lawson, the chief of Little Popo, in what is now the Republic of Togo. It was common practice in the 19th century for chiefs partial to the British to ensure that their sons had an English education and in 1825 Thomas George was sent to England for this purpose. He broke his journey in Freetown, however, becoming the protégé of John McCormack (q.v.), and stayed there for the rest of his life.

McCormack, Lawson's patron and teacher, was an Irishman whose trading activities, particularly with the Temne, had given him valuable knowledge of the people of the interior. He frequently served as representative of the government, undertaking missions and conducting negotiations with chiefs in the northern interior on behalf of the colony. Lawson accompanied McCormack on his trading visits and official missions. Lawson readily learned several languages which stood him in good stead for his later duties as interpreter, as did his personal relations with neighboring chiefs. These became friendly enough for him to marry the granddaughter of Bai Farma of Koya, a chiefdom to the east of Freetown.

In 1846 he entered the colonial civil service in a temporary capacity as government messenger; but in

1852 he was appointed "Native Interpreter and Government Messenger," a post which he held till his retirement in 1886. Because of his "knowledge of the languages spoken by the neighboring nations," "uniform, steady and correct conduct," and the high personal esteem accorded to him by African rulers who had had dealings with colonial officials, he was considered to be the most suitably qualified person for the appointment.

His duties as government interpreter, which also combined the functions of a police inspector, were many and various. He interpreted between governors or colonial officials and local rulers at meetings, and also in the law courts. As messenger, he ensured that Freetown's policies and demands were properly understood by the chiefs to whom they were directed. He also paid out stipends to chiefs, and entertained in his own home, chiefs and other official visitors from areas surrounding Freetown, supervised the education of various chiefs' sons in Freetown, and reported on such topics as "natives," "escaped slaves," "political prisoners," and the arrival of traders. In time, he took on an advisory role and began to initiate policy changes, but here his effectiveness was contingent on the attitudes of governors towards accepting his advice.

As his official duties increased, Lawson's original salary of £100 per annum was progressively raised until by 1882 he was earning £350 per annum. But from the early 1880s when Lawson's health started to break down, reducing him on some occasions to working from his house, the question of a suitable successor had to be raised.

Various officials had been appointed to lessen his administrative burden as age took its toll, including his eventual successor, James C.E. Parkes (q.v.). But he still kept control of the Aborigines Branch, as it became known in 1878.

Lawson's loyalty and devotion to duty was commended by several governors. He was strongly anti-French and always suspicious of French activity, even in the field of religious proselytising. Only once, during the crisis over the implementation of the Masama Treaty in 1879, was his interpretation ever criticized. The Temne chiefs held that the treaty had been drafted as a peace agreement, following their conflict with the Soso, whereas the British authorities held that it was a treaty of cession affecting the coastal area in the Scarcies region. The chiefs also declared that when the terms of the treaty had been discussed, three years earlier, they had not signed it. The situation brought Lawson's reputation as an interpreter into question. He weathered the storm, however, and his interpreting abilities remained respected. In 1883 Governor A.E. Havelock (term of office 1881-84) recommended Lawson be awarded the honor of Commander of Saint Michael and Saint George (C.M.G.), but the Colonial Office did not act upon it.

In 1886, Lawson declared his intention of retiring at the end of the year, a matter which caused concern as to whether his successor in this important task of liaison with the peoples of the interior would be competent to perform his duties with equal skill. Parkes was being groomed to take over his position, and together they produced an account of relations with the surrounding territories ("Information Regarding the Different Districts and Tribes of Sierra Leone and Its Vicinity," a confidential memorandum to the Colonial Office), almost entirely the product of Lawson's rich memory.

Described by Governor Sir Samuel Rowe (terms of office 1877-80 and 1885-88) as "alone and without equal in the history of Her Majesty's settlements on this Coast," Lawson's retirement required special commemoration. It was decided to award him a personal decoration, and in 1886 at an impressive ceremony he was presented with a silver chain and plaque in appreciation of his services. Even after his retirement in December 1886 on a pension of £210 per annum, he continued to give willing advice and to be responsible for hospitality to official visitors from the surrounding areas.

AKIWANDE J. LASITE

BIBLIOGRAPHY: Christopher Fyfe, "European and Creole Influence in the Hinterland of Sierra Leone Before 1896," *Sierra Leone Studies,* June, 1956, *A History of Sierra Leone,* London, 1962; J.D. Hargreaves, "The Evolution of the Native Affairs Department," *Sierra Leone Studies*, December, 1954, *Prelude to the Partition of West Africa*, London, 1966; A.J. Lasite, "The Department of Native Affairs and the Development of British Policy in the Northern Interior of Sierra Leone, 1850-1900," M.A. thesis, University of Sierra Leone, 1975; T.G. Lawson and J.C.E. Parkes, "Information Regarding the Different Districts and Tribes of Sierra Leone and its Vicinity," confidential memorandum to the British Colonial Office, London.

LEWIS, S.

Sir Samuel Lewis (November 13, 1843-July 9, 1903), barrister and member of the Sierra Leone Legislative Council for more than 29 years, was the leading figure of the Krio (Creole) community at the height of its influence. A convinced upholder of the British Empire and even an advocate of the inland expansion of the

Sierra Leone Colony, he was at the same time a tenacious defender of the legally-established liberties of individual Africans, and of his people as a whole.

His parents were Egba recaptives from Nigeria, who were established at Murray Town, in what are now the western outskirts of Freetown, Sierra Leone, in 1828. Within 30 years, William Lewis, his father, like many of his contemporaries had accumulated a modest fortune by trade on the neighboring coasts.

After attending the Church Missionary Society (C.M.S.) Grammar School, Samuel Lewis assisted in his father's business until 1886. During the next six years he studied law in England, being called to the bar of the Middle Temple in 1871. Soon after returning to Freetown in 1872 he was appointed acting-Queen's Advocate (Attorney-General) for 15 months, and although he later twice acted in a temporary capacity as Chief Justice, he declined offers of permanent government employment in order to pursue his highly successful private practice.

His reputation for mastery of detail and powerfully sustained forensic logic soon won him lucrative briefs from all the British West African colonies. Not all his cases, however, were popular ones. Several times he prosecuted African notables—the Sierra Leonean missionaries involved in a murder in Onitsha Nigeria, Chief W.T.G. Caulker, Postmaster J.H. Spaine—and once defended a British official charged with the brutal murder of his African servant. But Lewis believed the operation of established processes of British colonial justice would more truly protect the interests of his countrymen than appeals to racial solidarity.

In 1872, as acting Queen's Advocate, Lewis had taken his seat *ex officio* in the Legislative Council, but in 1882 he became a permanent unofficial member, and worked to develop the limited means by which such members could try to check abuses of power by the governor. He succeeded in establishing the right of councillors to receive information, debate legislation, propose amendments, and in the last resort to appeal to the Colonial Office. By using to the full these constitutional channels to express his reasoned criticisms of authority, he made the Legislative Council an effective organ for expressing the public opinions of middle-class Freetown.

When the financial and frontier policies of Governor Sir Samuel Rowe (terms of office 1877-80 and 1885-88) became unpopular in 1885, Lewis criticized him in council for "going after the chiefs in their own country to beg them for peace." He added to his verbal criticism by collaborating with other African and European critics of Rowe in the short-lived Sierra Leone Association (a discussion group which sought to exert political pressure). Between 1881 and 1885 he published three pamphlets on Sierra Leonean affairs.

Lewis also played a major role in the establishment of the Freetown Municipal Council, which he regarded as a means of training in self-government, though here he was not fully supported by African opinion, which feared the introduction of rates. In 1895 he became the first mayor of Freetown and was re-elected in 1896. In that year, too, he was awarded a knighthood, the first African to be thus honored by a British monarch.

Although Lewis was proud of his African, and specifically Yoruba, descent, the most important influences in his life seem to have been of European origin, notably the Wesleyan Methodist Church, of which he always remained a devout and fervent member. His support of British imperial expansion was not only because he accepted many of the values he believed the British Empire to stand for, but also because, like his friend Edward W. Blyden, he believed Sierra Leoneans might benefit (not only economically) from association with African peoples further inland, and specifically with the Mandinka empire-builder Samori.

In 1894, he welcomed the advent of a governor, Sir Frederick Cardew (*q.v.*), who seemed likely to pursue the vigorous policies of economic development and territorial expansion which Lewis had been waiting for. It soon became clear, however, that the Protectorate established in 1896 was being arbitrarily administered under the influence of military officers, and that the Krios would be prevented from playing any active role within it.

Though lacking any close knowledge of the Mende or Temne peoples, Lewis was very willing to advise them and to try to secure justice for them in their dealings with the unfamiliar machinery of colonial rule. In 1896 his vigorous pursuit of a land case led to a breach with Cardew, who feared for the consequences if British subjects in the Protectorate were encouraged to claim Sir Sam as their governor.

The hut-tax insurrection of 1898 showed that the Krio community was attracting great hostility and suspicion among Africans in the Protectorate, but still more so in the colonial administration. Cardew, indeed, held Lewis and the Krios generally responsible for stirring up the insurrection.

It thus became clear that many of Lewis' hopes for the place of acculturated Africans within the British African empire were to be disappointed. He remained a respected figure in Freetown until his painful death from cancer in 1903, but he must have been a disillusioned man. Though his ideas would have little appeal to the nationalist leaders of the future, in his generation he was an African patriot of courage and distinction.

JOHN D. HARGREAVES

BIBLIOGRAPHY: Christopher Fyfe, *A History of Sierra Leone*, London, 1962; J.D. Hargreaves, *A Life of Sir Samuel Lewis*, London, 1958; A.T. Porter, *Creoledom*, London, 1963.

LUMPKIN, W.R. See BUNGIE, A.

MacCARTHY, C.

Sir Charles MacCarthy (1769-January 21, 1824) was a governor of Sierra Leone in the early 19th century whose period of rule was looked back on as a golden age of internal prosperity. A man of vision and humanity, he was the first to face the task of rehabilitating the recaptive population round Freetown. He also transformed Freetown by an ambitious program of public building. During his governorship he tried to consolidate all British territories in West Africa under one governor-in-chief. He was killed on the Gold Coast in war against the Asante (Ashanti) of what is now Ghana.

Sir Charles came from a family of Irish Jacobites whom the English exiled to France in the late 18th century. His father, whose name was Guéroult, was French but he adopted his mother's surname. At the age of 18 he became a soldier and served in the Irish Brigade of Louis XVI's army until the French Revolution. A Roman Catholic, detesting republicanism, he left France and joined the British army, serving in Flanders, the West Indies and Canada. He commanded the Royal African Corps in Senegal in 1811, and was transferred in 1814 to Sierra Leone as lieutenant governor, being promoted to full governor in 1815.

Since 1808 Sierra Leone had been the center for the British naval campaign against the slave trade. Slave ships captured on the Atlantic Ocean were brought there for adjudication in the courts, and freed slaves were settled in the Colony. The British government, although responsible for them, did little for the freed men whom they regarded as a burden. MacCarthy, however, with a far-reaching vision of Africa transformed into a Christian continent, re-fashioned the miserable settlements round Freetown into villages modeled on the English pattern and added some ten or more new villages in the Colony. By dint of persuading the British government to supply funds (even at a time of retrenchment in colonial expenditure) and enlisting the co-operation of Church Missionary Society (C.M.S.) clergymen and missionaries, he went far towards establishing those African Christian communities whom he dremt would go out to spread the faith throughout the continent.

MacCarthy also obtained money from the British government to pay for improvements to Freetown, where he built most of the large public buildings which are still standing today (through some of his over-ambitious projects were in disrepair by the time of his successor). As a military and naval headquarters, with money being visibly spent on public works, the town attracted European businessmen, while the settlers, mainly Nova Scotians and Maroons, built houses and shops to sell or let to them.

MacCarthy's governorship saw Freetown transformed from an untidy village into an attractive city, with a lively social life. It was also a time of good relations between Africans and Europeans, for he was determined to break down distinctions on grounds of color, one such measure being to appoint a few Settlers to municipal office.

But he was not content merely to govern Sierra Leone. In 1816 British claims in the Gambia were asserted, and MacCarthy founded the town of Bathurst (named after the Secretary of State, Lord Henry Bathurst), now called Banjul. He persuaded the British government to annex the Isles of Los, lying between the Gambia and Sierra Leone, and in 1824, with the British trading forts on the Gold Coast (Ghana) transferred to the Crown, all British territories in West Africa were united, with MacCarthy (now Sir Charles) as governor-in-chief.

Unfortunately, he knew little of the Gold Coast and its politics, and was easily manipulated by the British officials there, some of whom were determined on war with Asante. Ignorant of the country, always optimistic and ready to overlook difficulties, MacCarthy was persuaded to go to war. At the head of his troops he marched out against the Asante, and met them at Nsamankow (Insamankow) on January 21, 1824. For once his optimism failed him. His troops were almost annihilated; he was killed and his head carried in triumph to Kumase.

MacCarthy's ignominious death should not obscure his achievements. His dream for the Sierra Leone recaptives came true. Thanks to his imaginative plans and his determination to carry them out, they were transformed within a few decades of his death into a Christian community leading the kind of Europeanized life he had wanted for them. As he had forseen, they began in the 1840s to return to their own homes along the coast, bringing with them the skills and new ways they had learned. Within a generation or two Sierra Leoneans were scattered throughout West Africa, forming a European-educated elite, and helping to transform its peoples in the way he had intended.

CHRISTOPHER FYFE

BIBLIOGRAPHY: W.W. Claridge, *A History of the Gold Coast and Ashanti,* London, 1915, 2nd ed., London, 1964; Christopher Fyfe, *A History of Sierra Leone,* London, 1962; W.E.F. Ward, *A History of Ghana,* London, 1958.

MACAULAY, J.

'King' John Macaulay (circa 1800-December 5, 1867) was a wealthy Freetown trader in the mid-19th century, and powerful unofficial leader of the Aku recaptives (Yoruba from what is now Nigeria). He played an important role in reducing inter-ethnic conflict in Sierra Leone by persuading the various racial groups in and around Freetown to form multiracial councils to arbitrate in disputes.

Macaulay was a Hausa Muslim who was recaptured between 1815 and 1822 and brought to Freetown. Being an enterprising young man, he quickly prospered as a trader. He was also a man of great physical strength which earned him the nickname of "Atapa," (from the Yoruba word for "kicker") as he was reputed to use both feet and hands in fighting.

It seems likely that in the 1820s he was headman in one of the provident societies started as a means of self-help for settlers and recaptives by "King" Abraham Potts, an African ex-soldier who had settled in Freetown. From the late 1830s onwards Macaulay served in a number of minor positions, including that of policeman, with the colonial administration, and in 1849 was appointed overseer in the Liberated African Department Yard (where recaptives were first brought) by acting Governor Benjamin Pine (later to serve as governor from 1857-60).

More significantly, Macaulay succeeded to the position of king of the Aku on the death of their former king, Thomas Will. Although unofficial, this position as head of the largest and most powerful ethnic group among the recaptives carried great authority; even the rich and influential obeyed their leader under threat of severe social sanctions, such as the denial of burial rites.

Macaulay's success as a trader also contributed to his rise to leadership. By the late 1840s his business was large enough for him to use his own ship to trade with Badagry, Nigeria, carrying cargoes (sometimes illegal) of tobacco and rum. When he retired from government service in 1853 he invested his profits in property and ran a retail spirit trade from his house.

The position of Aku king was one which at times involved Macaulay closely with the administration, to whom he could be very useful in times of crisis, though at others he was not always viewed with favor. In 1843 a serious conflict flared up at the recaptive village of Waterloo between the Aku, the Calabar and the Ibo, (all groups of Nigerian origin), and troops had to be sent from Freetown to restore order. To try and effect a settlement between the contestants the governor sent King Macaulay to Waterloo. Macaulay persuaded the various groups to form a super-ethnic council to include one member from each of the 17 major ethnic groups at Waterloo. The function of this council, which became known as the Seventeen Nations, was to settle all petty grievances as well as helping maintain law and order. Macaulay's Seventeen Nations turned out to be a very manageable form of government, and the organization continued in Waterloo under successive presidents till the end of the 19th century.

In 1851, disputes similar to those at Waterloo broke out between the Aku and other groups at Hastings. War was averted largely through the intervention of King Macaulay who was able to calm the Aku and keep them from fighting. Here, too, he instituted a modified form of the Seventeen Nations council. Gradually this system of local government spread to other villages around Freetown and throughout the colony, being particularly effective in areas where the colonial administration provided little in the way of supervision. In Hastings, the Seventeen Nations in time grew powerful enough to prevent an influential Freetown Krio (Creole), William Grant, from taking over 1,000 acres of land near Hastings village in the 1880s, despite the fact that Grant had obtained permission from the governor.

Macaulay's influence in Freetown, based on his position as Aku king, extended to other matters than establishing the Seventeen Nations councils. In 1847 he was a leading signatory to the petition sent by the colony's local population to the secretary of state in England requesting the recall of Governor N.W. Macdonald (term of office 1846-52), an overbearing and anti-African governor. He was also approached for help by colonial officials. In 1864, the colonial surgeon, Dr. Bradshaw, faced a lawsuit with claims for £200 damages for striking his groom. It was only with Macaulay's assistance that he was able to settle the matter out of court by paying £30.

In the 1840s Benjamin Pine, acting governor while Macdonald was on leave, asked for Macaulay's help over the question of sending newly arrived Aku recaptives to the West Indies. This was official emigration policy which the administration had unsuccessfully tried to implement, but with Macaulay's assistance it was reviewed. In reward for his help, and because he considered him trustworthy, Pine made Macaulay overseer in the Liberated African Department Yard in 1849.

When Governor Macdonald, for whose recall Macaulay had petitioned, resumed office he tried unsuccessfully to remove him from the post. The Colonial Office found his reasons unacceptable, and Macaulay, whom most governors feared rather than respected, stayed on. It remained for a later governor, Arthur Kennedy (terms of office 1852-54 and 1868-72), of similar views to Macdonald, to solve the problem by abolishing Macaulay's post in 1853. This did not, however, appear to lessen his influence in the colony, especially over the Aku.

In his old age Macaulay became a Christian. He was converted by the Rev. James Johnson of Christ Church in Freetown after he became ill in 1862. He gave up polygamy and started attending church regularly, but his new-found religion did not affect his hold over the Aku, many of whom were still Muslims, and he remained effectively King Macaulay until his death on December 5, 1867 after a paralytic stroke. Markets and shops in Freetown closed down for his funeral, and large crowds from all the different ethnic groups, especially his own Aku, turned out to pay him their final respects.

Macaulay had created a kind of informal authority which the administration had been forced to recognize. In 1891 some leading Aku citizens tried to revive this authority by installing Macaulay's son, George, as his successor. But the era when such an arrangement could exist had passed, and the administration refused to recognize him. King Macaulay's sons, however, continued successfully in trade as Macaulay Brothers, and one of them later entered colonial service as Protector of Strangers.

C. MAGBAILY FYLE

BIBLIOGRAPHY: Christopher Fyfe, *A History of Sierra Leone,* London, 1962, (ed.), *Sierra Leone Inheritance,* London, 1964; J. Peterson, *Province of Freedom: A History of Sierra Leone 1787-1870,* Evanston, 1969; A.B.C. Sibthorpe, *The History of Sierra Leone*, 2nd edition, London, 1881, reprinted London, 1970.

MACFOY, S.B.A.

Solomon Benjamin Augustus Macfoy (circa 1843-January 16, 1893) was a Sierra Leone Krio (Creole) who for several years dominated the Sherbro country of Sierra Leone.

He came originally from Kent village, south of Freetown. The story is that as a boy he was thrown overboard from a canoe off Sherbro Island, swam ashore to Jamaica Point, and determined to stay there and make his fortune. Within 20 years he had established himself as a powerful trader, trading on his own, and as agent for a British export firm in Manchester which was sending him annually some £40,000 worth of goods in return for produce.

Small and unimpressive-looking, with little formal education, he was a man of wide ambitions. Hardworking himself, he demanded hard work from others, carrying out his plans with ruthless determination. He extended his business to the mainland, buying up the European and Krio trading establishments along the Sherbro rivers, and building his own bonded warehouse at Bonthe, the main trading center. He had a cargo steamship of his own built for him in England, naming it with his own nickname, *Sherbro Monarch.*

Perceiving that economic control of the country demanded political activity, he extended his influence over the still-independent Sherbro rulers. Here he was able to take advantage of a legal anomaly which made some of the Sherbro mainland technically part of the Colony of Sierra Leone, even though no British jurisdiction was exercised there. Acting within the letter of the law, he lent money to some of the rulers of Imperi, on the mainland opposite Sherbro Island, in return for mortgages on their territories. In 1885 he foreclosed on the defaulting Ka Tegbe of Gendama and began assuming sovereign rights in his country. When Ka Tegbe complained to the British authorities they would do nothing to help him, as they did not want to raise publicly the complicated issues involved.

Macfoy's business declined during the late 1880s, and he mortgaged ten of his trading establishments for £6,534 to a Liverpool firm. Instead he turned to farming, employing labor on a large scale to grow coffee, cocoa, and other plantation produce, first on Sherbro Island, then in Imperi, which he now virtually controlled. When villages stood in the way of his schemes, he evicted the inhabitants and demolished their homes. When the British authorities tried to stop him, he warned them that he had legal rights to the land, and that if they objected they must take him to court, knowing well that they were not going to risk a law case over the status of Imperi.

Eventually a newly-appointed British official, George H. Garrett, determined to put him down, and suspecting him of being implicated in an outbreak of leopard murders in Imperi, proposed he be detained as a political prisoner. Macfoy retained as his legal adviser the leading Freetown lawyer, Sir Samuel Lewis (q.v.), who was able to convince the government that no case could be brought against him.

Macfoy died on January 16, 1893, at the age of 50, after a paralytic stroke which had suddenly struck him down. He was brought first to Freetown to be treated by Dr. Davies, but, discouraged by the prolonged treatment, his relatives later took him to a country doctor in Grassfields, around Brookfields in western Freetown. It was there that the 'Sherbro Monarch' ended his days, a man who had inspired fear rather than love even in his admirers, an outstanding, if ruthless, example of Krio drive and energy.

CHRISTOPHER FYFE

BIBLIOGRAPHY: Christopher Fyfe, *A History of Sierra Leone,* London, 1962; *Sierra Leone Weekly News,* October 10, 1885 and January 21, 1893.

MAKAVORAY

Makavoray of Tikonko (circa 1830-1897) was a powerful warrior-king who played a vital peace-keeping role among warring chiefs in southern Sierra Leone in the second half of the 19th century. Unlike most of his contemporaries, who were interested only in self-aggrandisement through war, this thoughtful ruler often acted as a check on his unruly juniors.

A descendant of Momoh Kukuwa, Makavoray's proper name was 'Meccavolo' meaning 'the day of Mecca,' because he was apparently born on the day a Muslim pilgrim returned from Mecca. He was trained from youth as a warrior, and by the middle of the 19th century had become the ruler of a substantial state centered on Tikonko on the lower reaches of the Bum River. In his turn, he trained two of the most famous Mende professional warriors of the later 19th century, Ndawa (q.v.) and Makaya.

Tikonko, however, was constantly quarreling with its neighbor, the state of Bumpe. For much of the second half of the 19th century, these rival states were either at war with each other, or fighting as allies of opposing groups in the lower Bum basin. Despite this, Makavoray established himself as a leading ruler in the hinterland.

The colonial administration in Freetown was fully aware of Makavoray's importance. Particularly during the 1880s, he was in constant demand to settle disputes in areas outside his own territorial frontiers. In 1886, he organized a special peace Poro (secret society meeting) to bring an end to the war against the Lugbu. He also received repeated appeals from the administration to restrain Makaya and Ndawa, his onetime warrior pupils, from attacking territories dangerously close to British interests on the Gallinas coast in the far south of Sierra Leone. It was not until Makavoray intervened that Ndawa, who had attacked the town of Bandasuma and captured its ruler, Madam Dalo, could be persuaded to release her.

In 1889, there started a two-year period of rapid treaty-making as a way of preparing for the declaration of the Protectorate over the hinterland. In March 1889 Makavoray signed a 'Treaty of Friendship' with Governor Sir James Shaw Hay (term of office 1888-91) for which he received a stipend of £20 per annum. Two months later, at a meeting held at Bandasuma on the Moa River to reconcile differences among rulers, a similar 'Treaty of Friendship' was signed by King Nyagua (q.v.), Makavoray's northeastern neighbor with whom he had quarreled. Preceding the signing, Hay had settled the disagreement between the two chiefs who publicly shook hands and embraced each other.

The administration, who looked to 'treaty chiefs' for cooperation, continued to turn to Makavoray for assistance. Shortly after the meeting at Bandasuma, he had to intervene in a long-standing conflict among Kpaa-Mende chiefs grouped under two ring-leaders, Moigula and Vonjo. Although these were technically sub-chiefs of Madam Yoko (q.v.), chief of Kpaa-Mende, she was powerless to control them. There were serious disturbances in the Kpaa-Mende state, provoked by incidents which occurred on the Mende-Temne frontier. A Temne warrior, Sembu Kamara of Kumrabai, had carried out raids in Kpaa-Mende country at the invitation of his Mende allies. One of his co-fighters had escaped to upper Mende land where he was captured by chief Vonjo, handed over to Makavoray (who had been asked to help in his capture), and sent to Freetown under police escort.

This caused rival factions to form. Many chiefs in lower Kpaa-Mende grouped together under Moigula of Gondama, determined to fight Vonjo for having captured Sembu Kamara's warrior. The colonial administration was uneasy and sent in Frontier Police under Sub-Inspector Charles Taylor, who persuaded some of the chiefs to withdraw their support from Moigula. But the matter did not end here, for Madam Yoko had little authority over her sub-chiefs. Makovoray, asked by Taylor to intervene, persuaded Vonjo to put a stop to his attacks, but Moigula continued to fight and Madam Yoko had to flee to Freetown for protection as the situation deteriorated.

Several meetings were summoned by the administration in Freetown and in the hinterland, but to no purpose. Moigula avoided a meeting that had been arranged at Yele on the Taia River, raided Vonjo's country, and fled to Chief Foray in Kono in the eastern part of Sierra Leone. The administration could do no more except to station police at key points and prevent arms supplies from reaching Moigula. Finally, Makavoray supported Vonjo in an offensive against Moigula and Foray, and hostilities ended around 1893 with the capture of one of Foray's towns by Vonjo.

Makavoray emerged as a warrior-king of unusual statesmanship, able to see beyond immediate issues of territorial squabbling. He lived to see the Protectorate proclaimed in 1896, but died the following year before discontent erupted in the resistance struggles of 1898. He was succeeded by Sandi, one of his relations, all descended from the first founder settler, Momoh Kukuwa.

ARTHUR ABRAHAM

BIBLIOGRAPHY: A. Abraham, *Mende Government and Politics Under Colonial Rule*, Freetown, 1978.

MANA SIAKA

Mana Siaka (?-1872), warrior and slave-trader, was ruler of Vai, or Gallinas, a powerful state situated on the coast between Sierra Leone and Liberia. Much of his reign was spent contesting his sovereignty against Liberian claims for control of his state.

It was under Mana and his father King Siaka, the founder of the state, that Gallinas reached the height of its power. It is believed that King Siaka was the first Massaquoi, ruling from the late 18th century. Massaquoi, meaning 'learned man,' was a term originally used to describe elders in general. Its Mande root is clearly discernible, *Mansa*, meaning chief or king. By the 19th century, however, Massaquoi had acquired a new meaning, through the evolution of the political system, and signified the holder of the imperial crown.

In 1878, the following description of the state regalia was made in a report by two British colonial officials Messrs. Edwards and Loggie: 'The State Property consisted of a white metal crown which the (King) placed on his head, a crimson robe richly laced with gold, a very fine ivory war-horn, heavily ornamented with silver, and the staff of state.' These regalia became the coveted prize for contestants to the 'Massaquoi crown' during the succession disputes of the 1880s.

Mana, like his father, had numerous bands of professional warriors whom he paid with money acquired from the sale of slaves to the most notorious slaver in the Gallinas, Pedro Blanco. Through his wealth and influence he rose to unquestioned superiority over all other rulers in the Gallinas, reinforcing his position through well-chosen marriage alliances with his sub-chiefs. His capital, Gendama, was sturdily built and well fortified, and Mana and his kin lived in houses of European design with European furnishings such as sofas, mirror, and clocks.

As Gallinas grew rich on the slave trade, rice cultivation became neglected, since it was easily obtained from the Sherbro. In 1849, however, the Sherbro chiefs signed anti-slave treaties, and the Gallinas' food-supply was cut off. In 1850, Mana also signed an anti-slave treaty and expelled slave traders from his country. But his new alliance with the British was disrupted when a consular agent, W.A. Parks, was murdered and naval ships bombarded his most accessible towns in retaliation.

Gallinas' sovereignty was in danger, caught in an uncertain situation between Liberian claims and partial British protection. Between 1849 and 1851, the Liberian government signed treaties along the coast as far as the mouth of the River Jong, and claimed all the Gallinas and south Sherbro territories as their own. King Mana had interpreted the treaties merely as treaties of friendship, but in 1860 the Liberian government seized a ship that had brought visitors to Mana for breaking their customs laws. The Sierra Leonean governor, Sir Stephen John Hill (term of office 1854-62) sent a gunboat to retrieve the captured ship.

In 1869 there was a similar incident. Liberian militiamen were sent to seize goods from ships in the

Mano River, but were stopped by King Mana, whereupon the Liberian president, hoping to gain support in the forthcoming presidential elections, sent a further 300 troops who seized a ship and its cargo. But Mana insisted on his sovereignty supported by Governor Sir Arthur Edward Kennedy (terms of office 1852-54, 1868-72) who wished to see the Gallinas rid of Liberian claims.

Kennedy sent a gunboat which brought back the impounded schooner with part of the compensation promised by the Liberians, who, in spite of the fact that they could not pay the full amount, continued to claim the Gallinas. In 1870 they again sent in troops who attacked several towns and plundered some traders. Finally they proposed that an international boundary commission should settle their claims. It was not, however, until 1917 that the boundary between Liberia and Sierra Leone was finally fixed.

Mana's death in 1872 marked the end of the Vai state's period of power. He was succeeded by his brother Jaya—blind, elderly, inebriated and totally unfit to rule. Wars broke out as various contestants aspired to the authority of the Massaquoi crown, but the colonial administration intervened to prevent the resurgence of a state weakened by persistent wars of succession and the decline of the slave trade. Later, in the colonial period, a paramount chief was appointed over the entire Vai state.

ARTHUR ABRAHAM

BIBLIOGRAPHY: A. Abraham, *Mende Government and Politics Under Colonial Rule*, Freetown, 1978; Christopher Fyfe, *A History of Sierra Leone*, London, 1962.

MANKAH, J.

John Mankah (18?-circa 1900) was a Temne who was associated with the Church Missionary Society (C.M.S.) in Port Loko in western Sierra Leone from 1878 to 1896, probably the only Temne man to have had such a long association with a Christian mission during the 19th century. He contributed extensively to the study of the Temne language and translated much of the scriptures into Temne.

The date of Mankah's birth is not certain, but C.M.S. records first mention him in 1846 when it is presumed that, along with two other Temne youths, he was sent to Freetown from Port Loko to continue his education there. Mankah had no doubt come under the influence of the Rev. C.F. Schlenker, a noted German missionary and linguist who pioneered the scientific study of the Temne language. Impressed by

their work, Schlenker must have recommended that the three boys be sent to Freetown for further education.

In 1850 the Port Loko mission was suspended, but in the same year a new Temne mission was opened at Magbele on the Rokel River which was in operation until 1860. It is probable that Mankah served for a while at Port Loko, but was in all likelihood associated with the Magbele mission.

There is little information on his life between the years of 1860 and 1878, so not much can be said with precision about his activities. But he is mentioned again in 1878 when another Temne mission was opened in Port Loko under the charge of the Rev. John Alfred Alley.

From 1878 to 1896 Mankah worked as an assistant to the Rev. Alley, a partnership that was crucial to the survival of the mission, for Alley apparently found it difficult to maintain cordial relationships with other missionaries, whether African or European. But he and Mankah co-operated in translating many portions of the Bible into Temne. From the evidence of the C.M.S. records it seems likely that Mankah did most of the work, since Alley showed no particular linguistic talent.

Mankah was probably one of the very few dedicated Africans to be converted to Christianity by the C.M.S. in all its years of work in Port Loko. Of his personal life it is only known that he had a son who, according to *The Church Missionary Gleaner* of February, 1882, was baptized in England as John England. Mankah died about the turn of the century.

GUSTAV K. DEVENEAUX

BIBLIOGRAPHY: *The Church Missionary Gleaner*, Vol. IX, February, 1882; G.K. Deveneaux, "The Political and Social Impact of the Colony in Northern Sierra Leone 1821-1896," unpublished Ph.D. dissertation, Boston University, 1973; Christopher Fyfe, *A History of Sierra Leone*, London, 1962; C.P. Groves *The Planting of Christianity in Africa*, 4 vols. London, 1948; C.F. Schlenker, *A Collection of Temne Traditions, Fables and Proverbs,* London, 1861.

MANNAH-KPAKA, J.

John Mannah-Kpaka (circa 1865-1945), a member of the powerful Gallinas family of Rogers or Kpaka, was a wealthy trader who later became paramount chief of the Kpaka chiefdom.

The Rogers family were descended from an English filibuster, Zachary Rogers (*q.v.*), who came out in the service of the Gambia Adventurers Company in 1668 and married an African wife belonging to the ruling

Gallinas family of Massaquoi. According to tradition, one of their descendants was fond of sitting on a chair, an unusual act in those times, and became known as Kpaka, after the Mende work 'kpakai' meaning 'chair.' The Rogers family had retained the name of Kpaka till the present day.

John was one of two boys selected by King Mana Siaka of Gallinas, to whom he was related, to be educated in Freetown at the request of Governor Sir A.E. Kennedy (terms of office 1852-54, 1868-72). Accordingly, in 1872 he went to Freetown and attended the C.M.S. Grammar School, where he was enrolled as John Rogers Mannah.

While he was at the C.M.S. Grammar School, he became a monitor and later taught in the lower school. In 1886, he joined the customs department, but as there was no prospect of promotion he resigned after two and a half years and became assistant customs clerk for the firm of Pickering and Berthoud. He was promoted to customs clerk after two years, and eventually became an agent.

In 1895 John returned home to the Gallinas after 23 years' absence to find himself virtually a stranger, his parents and many relatives having died in his absence. He immediately went into business at Mano Salija at the mouth of the River Mano, trading mostly in ivory obtained from the interior.

With the proclamation of the Protectorate followed by the imposition of a house tax, there was general restlessness throughout the country. In February 1898 John was made aware of it while on a trading visit to collect ivory due to him from Koya and Tunka, a few days' march roughly northeast of Mano Salija. He reported to the colonial authorities that a message had been circulated telling every male capable of handling a machete to be present at Bogboabu, the capital of Koya, because the district commissioner, Captain C.E. Carr, was going to be there to collect the tax. He then quietly returned to Mano Salija.

Business affairs took him to Freetown from which he returned in mid-March to find clear signs of general discontent and unrest throughout the country. At two meetings of all the Gallinas chiefs, John exhorted them not to fight, but he was taken by surprise by a sudden uprising at the end of April during which trading stations, colonial establishments and houses were attacked, and his own store was raided. John joined other refugees including five Frontier Police and escaped to Liberia, where, after much trouble, he succeeded in getting a boat to Freetown. At an audience with Governor Sir Frederick Cardew (q.v.) he volunteered to help the administration quell the resistance. Equipped with one rifle and accompanying 20 Frontier Police, he embarked for Cape Mount in Liberia. While he was there, he persuaded chiefs

Gbessay Kai Luseni and Lamin Abdul Lahai of Juring to join him.

But resistance in this area was bound to fade out before long. Thus when John crossed over with his 'force,' there was very little opposition. Before the end of the year, the administration had overcome the resistance and regained control.

In 1913, John Mannah-Kpaka was elected paramount chief of the Kpaka chiefdom. But in 1916 he was deposed, after being convicted and imprisoned for obtaining money under false pretences in the name of the colonial administration. He was later granted free pardon by Governor R. J. Wilkinson (term of office 1916-22), but by this time Momo Rogers had already been elected as his successor. Momo Rogers ruled over a discontented chiefdom until a crisis was reached in 1932, when he too was deposed. John Mannah-Kpaka contested the chiefship against Momo Tibo Rogers, his uncle, though many years his junior. Rogers won the election but agreed to step down for Mannah-Kpaka on condition that he should be his successor.

Always a loyal supporter of the colonial administration, Mannah-Kpaka was appointed in 1934 to serve on the Legislative Council under the provisions of the Slater constitution of 1924, which empowered the governor to appoint three paramount chiefs to represent Protectorate interests. He served on the council until 1939, and ruled successfully over his chiefdom until his death in 1945, when he was succeeded by Momo Tibo Rogers.

ARTHUR ABRAHAM

BIBLIOGRAPHY: M. Luseni and J. Rogers, "The Origins of the Kpakas or Rogers," *Sierra Leone Studies*, December, 1929; J.M. Mannah-Kpaka, "Memoirs of the 1898 Rising," (1939), *Sierra Leone Studies*, December, 1951; A. Simpson, "Biographical Note on Chief Mannah-Kpaka," in *Eminent Sierra Leoneans in the Nineteenth Century*, Freetown, (1961).

MANSA KAMA

Mansa Kama, who lived from about the mid-16th to the 17th century, was a great warrior and one of the earliest Koranko migrants from the present-day republic of Guinea to the hinterland of Sierra Leone. He founded the settlement of Kamadugu, part of the present Sengbe chiefdom and also ruled over Kholifa country, now part of the Tonkolili district.

He is said to be descended from Sundiata Keita, ruler of medieval Mali in central West Africa, and was a member of the Kagbo (another name for Keita) clan. His real name is believed to have been Yira, but because he was a great hunter and killed many elephants, he was called 'kama' meaning 'elephant.'

Towards the end of the 16th century, Mansa Kama moved into the Sierra Leone hinterland from Sankaran country in Guinea in the company of the alfa (Islamic scholar, charm-maker, and teacher) of the Sesay clan. For the first part of his journey he was with Mansa Morifing, the leader of the first Koranko migrants, and stayed with him at Morifindugu before moving on southwards with Morifing's blessings. His next stop was close to the Rokel River where he founded a settlement, Kamadugu, named after him.

By the end of the 16th century Mansa Kama had fought his way from Kamadugu to the coast. He finally made a new base at Rowala, the center of Kholifa country, and stayed there to become ruler of the territory which remained in Koranko hands until it was taken over by the Temne about the 19th century. He is said to have returned periodically to Kamadugu, his original country, where he had left his son Momori Kalko as ruler. The oldest town in Kamadugu was called Kalkoya after him and still bears this name.

When Mansa Kama died he was buried at Rowala where he left all his charms and his regalia of office. The name Mansa Kama then became the title for the ruler of Kholifa and has been retained by the Temne to the present day.

He is still remembered in both Koranko and Temne traditions as the great founding father of Kholifa and Kamadugu countries.

C. MAGBAILY FYLE

BIBLIOGRAPHY: C. Magbaily Fyle, "The Kabala Complex; Koranko-Limba Relationships in Nineteenth and Twentieth Century Sierra Leone," in A. Abraham, *Topics of Sierra Leone History*, Freetown, 1976.

MARGAI, M.A.S.

Sir Milton Margai (December 7, 1895-April 28, 1964), the first prime minister of Sierra Leone, was an outstanding political leader, a pioneer in medical welfare, particularly in midwifery, and an acclaimed surgeon. A man of high integrity and a moderate approach to politics, his influence made possible an alliance between the educated elite and the traditional rulers of the Protectorate, which led to the formation of the Sierra Leone People's Party (S.L.P.P.). Under his guidance, Sierra Leone achieved independence in 1961 with a minimum of upheaval.

Dr. Margai was born on December 7, 1895 at Gbangbatok in the Banta chiefdom, Bonthe district.

He attended the Evangelical United Brethren School in Bonthe and later moved to the Albert Academy in Freetown for his secondary education. As the grandson and nephew of paramount chiefs he retained a strong sense of his native culture while being exposed to Western culture at an early age. He was the first 'Protectorate Native' to attend Fourah Bay College, where his experiences may well have been useful for his future career, but were not likely to have been pleasant. As a Krio (Creole) dominated institution the attitude towards the 'Kossoh' or 'country man' was markedly condescending.

In 1921, Milton Margai graduated with a B.A. in modern history, after which he went to King's College, Durham, to read medicine. He returned to his own country in 1927, being the first person from the Protectorate to obtain a medical degree, and practiced for a short while in Freetown and Bonthe. He was appointed medical officer in the colonial service in 1928 and posted to Bonthe. During the following 22 years of service he served in every district in the Protectorate except Koinadugu.

Throughout his work, Dr. Margai cultivated warm relationships with chiefs and their subjects, which may well have laid the basis for his active interest in politics. He often acted as confidential adviser to the chiefs and when the Protectorate Assembly was instituted in 1946 he served on it as the non-chief member for Bonthe. By this time his standing in the whole Protectorate was very high. It was at his instigation, together with Chief Julius Gulama (*q.v.*), that chiefs' conferences were held in Moyamba, the starting point from which developed the Protectorate Assembly and district councils.

As medical officer in Pujehun, Dr. Margai pioneered his "welfare work in a secret society," although it extended to other areas. With his special skills in surgery and midwifery, he initiated a scheme of instruction in anatomy, babycare, mothercraft, and general handicraft, using the local women's secret society, the Sande, to try and modernize midwifery practices. For five years this scheme proved very successful and was implemented in other stations where he worked as medical officer. To further this work, he published a simple handbook on midwifery in Mende called "A Primer of Midwifery". In 1947 he was made a Member of the British Empire (M.B.E.) in recognition of his midwifery services.

In 1950, Dr. Margai retired from government service as senior medical officer and began to devote more time to politics, in which he had been actively involved since 1946. He did not, however, abandon medical work entirely for he opened a surgery and clinic in Bo.

In the post-war period, his political influence in the Protectorate was crucial, particularly over the two most important quasi-political associations, the Protectorate Education Progressive Union (P.E.P.U.), of which he was deputy President, and the Sierra Leone Organization Society (S.O.S.). Both were founded in 1946 (though the former had existed as an educational advancement society until it lapsed in the 1930s), and though ostensibly associations for cultural development they acted as pressure groups for the growing political aspirations of the educated Protectorate minority. Dr. Margai also founded and edited the first national Protectorate newspaper, the *Sierra Leone Observer*, in Bo.

The politics of this period were characterized by intense rivalry between the Colony Krios and the people of the Protectorate whom they despised, and whose encroachment on important government positions was much feared. A new constitution, proposed in 1947 by Governor Hubert Stevenson (term of office 1941-48) and aimed primarily at giving a majority to unofficial members in the Legislative Council was delayed until 1951, mainly through opposition from entrenched Krio interests. Through Dr. Margai's influence the two main Protectorate organizations merged to form the Sierra Leone

People's Party, of which he was elected first president, sinking their differences to oppose the claims of the National Council of the Colony of Sierra Leone (N.C.). This latter organization was virtually a Krio party, formed mainly to thwart the introduction of the new constitution.

The most rational course of action, in spite of the insulting protests from the N.C.—for example:"We object to foreigners (i.e. Protectorate Africans) preponnding in our Legislative Council"— was to introduce the constitution in 1951. There was direct limited franchise in the Colony, but indirect franchise through electoral colleges in the Protectorate. The S.L.P.P. won a resounding victory. Dr. Margai welcomed Krios into his fold, and thus the Rev. E.N. Jones (Laminah Sankoh) [*q.v.*] and H.E.B. John became stalwart S.L.P.P. members. The party was run by an executive council of six members, of whom Dr. Margai became chief minister.

Disputes threatened the party mainly from younger members who were impatient with his 'go slow' policy. But his astute leadership prevented the S.L.P.P. from destroying itself, although a splinter group broke off in 1958. He achieved a united front of all parties, however, to work out the independence constitution. In 1959 he was awarded a knighthood, and on July 9, 1960 he became the first prime minister of Sierra Leone as well as minister of internal affairs. Three days later, Durham University awarded him an honorary degree.

Sir Milton, far from being 'tribalist' in his politics, had Krios appointed as governor-general and chief justice at independence in 1961, and also had five Krios in his cabinet. Uninterested in material values, he had very little property and cared little for accumulating personal wealth. Despite occasional shake-ups in the political system, Sierra Leone maintained a strong stability during Sir Milton's leadership. When he died on April 28, 1964, that stability was threatened, and the days of his rule are remembered with nostalgia as an epoch of social well-being.

ARTHUR ABRAHAM

BIBLIOGRAPHY: J. Cartwright, *Politics in Sierra Leone 1947-1967,* University of Toronto Press, 1970; M. Kilson, *Political Change in a West African State: A Study of the Modernization Process in Sierra Leone,* Cambridge, Mass., 1966; M.A.S. Margai, *Mavulo Gbembo Golei* ("A Primer of Midwifery"), Freetown, n.d., "Welfare Work in a Secret Society," *African Affairs,* March, 1948; *Shekpendeh,* April 25, 1961; *Sierra Leone Year Book,* 1961.

MARLAY BOKARI

Marlay Bokari (circa 1800-circa 1900) was ruler over the Mara clan of the Koranko in the second half of the 19th century, and was a direct descendant of one of the earlier great leaders. Though his authority did not cover the entire Koranko territory, his influence extended well beyond his own clan and he was in fact described as ruler of all the Koranko.

He was the great-great-grandson of Mansa Morifing of the Koranko Mara clan, who led the earliest Koranko migrants from Sankaran in the present Republic of Guinea into northeastern Sierra Leone, and who gave his name to Morifindugu (now part of the Mongo chiefdom). Tinalei, Marlay Bokari's father, to whom he was born about the beginning of the 19th century, is described in Koranko traditions as the first ruler of all Ferensola (all territory inhabited by that ethnic group), and his son is described as a ruler even greater than his father.

Based on the town of Yindekuma, located in the present Mongo chiefdom, Koinadugu district, Marlay Bokari ruled the Mara of the northern half of Koranko country in Sierra Leone from about the middle of the 19th century, and his influence reached lower Koranko as well. The Koranko Mara of Barawa (now a section of Nieni chiefdom in Koinadugu), and Sengbe (a chiefdom in Koinadugu) continued to accept his authority until the early 1890s, just before the British occupation of the Sierra Leone hinterland. The ruler of Kamadugu, Mori Musa (also called Fina Bala) is described as his nephew.

When the expansionist campaigns of the Mandinka emperor, Samori, reached the Sierra Leone hinterland in the 1880s, Marlay Bokari's domain at Morifindugu was threatened. In 1890, he was captured by the Sofa general, Kemoko Bilali, and taken to Samori. Later he was kept prisoner at Heremakono in Sankaran country, close to his original homeland, but recognizing his importance Kemoko Bilali gave him good treatment.

Meanwhile, his son, Kumba Wulen Lai, was acknowledged as his deputy over the Koranko, while Mori Musa and Boltamba of the Barawa Koranko round Kabala implored the British to intercede with the Sofa for his release.

In 1893, Bokari was set free. He founded a new capital at Kombili, but the unsettled state of the country led him to seek temporary refuge with his lieutenant, Boltamba, in the Wara Wara hills.

By 1895 Morifindugu was recovering from the effects of the Sofa invasion. Under Marlay Bokari's supervision, some 15 new towns were built, and though by then a very old man, from all reports, his authority was still respected. In 1899 he appears as the first paramount chief of Morifindugu, but apparently died the following year to be succeeded by his son Kumba Wulen Lai, then also an old man.

C. MAGBAILY FYLE.

BIBLIOGRAPHY: Y. Person, *Samori,* Vols. I and II, Dakar, 1968 and 1970; C. Magbaily Fyle, review of Y. Person's *Somori, International Journal of African Historical Studies,* Vol. IX, 2, 1976.

MATTURI

Matturi (18?-1936) was a Kono chief whose fighting skills and able leadership gained him the trust of the great Mende leader, Nyagua (*q.v.*), who made him ruler over the south part of Kono in eastern Sierra Leone. He also took a prominent part in repelling an invasion of Kono country by the Sofa, warriors of the Mandinka emperor, Samori Touré.

Matturi was the fifth chief of Jaiama, a town in Nimikoro country in Kono, whose first ruler was Borwai. But for some years the country was in disarray after attacks against the Kono by Nyagua, which caused many to flee and hide themselves in caves in the Nimi hills and then to move secretly northward into Koranko. After nearly a decade, however, they were

persuaded to return to their original homeland by which time Nyagua was undisputed overlord.

Nyagua demanded help from his Kono vassals when the territories of his father, Faba of Dodo, were raided by Ndawa (*q.v.*), a professional warrior who was harassing Upper Mende countries. The Kono ruler, Fato, chose Matturi as an experienced warrior to lead his countrymen against Ndawa's followers on behalf of Nyagua. Taking complete charge of the operation and of all the fighting forces, Matturi carried out his duty with brutal thoroughness bringing back handsome spoils in the way of booty and slaves for Nyagua. "After this, Nyagua openly handed over the ownership of (southern) Kono to Matturi and vowed that as long as he lived, he would not allow any enemies to enter Kono from the south."

With Nyagua's support, Matturi's influence gradually spread wide. He persuaded his elders to get back their remaining people from exile to repopulate the area and cultivate the land. These reconstruction measures were progressing peacefully when Samori Touré's Sofa invaded Kono in 1893. Mounted, well-armed and mobile, the Sofa quickly occupied Tecu-yama and Levuma in Kono, having been warned off Koranko and Konike Temne countries to the north and west of Kono by the British administration in Freetown.

Matturi's Kono warriors killed one of the Sofa spies, and Matturi made the invasion known to Nyagua, who immediately reported to the governor that his territory had been violated. Orders were immediately given for a force to repel the invaders, but before the British expedition could start, Nyagua's warriors and their Kono allies had expelled the Sofa from Tecuyama. The British and the French, both in pursuit of the Sofa, who had retreated west ready to attack other areas on the Konike border, ended up fighting each other by mistake. Eventually British forces drove the Sofa out of Konike and Kono.

After the Sofa invasion, Matturi's standing was immensely increased. He became the first paramount chief of Jaiama Nimikoro when the Protectorate was declared in 1896, and staffs of office were being granted to local rulers by the British. But much of the area he controlled was broken up and turned into a collection of so-called 'chiefdoms,' just as Nimikoro itself was taken away from Nyagua's control.

One of the very few survivors from the 19th century warrior tradition, Matturi remained active well into the colonial period, highly respected by the British authorities for his readiness to embark on local development projects, such as road-building. By the 1920s he was senile, but continued to rule, though his son was appointed regent, until his death at a ripe old age in 1936.

ARTHUR ABRAHAM

BIBLIOGRAPHY: S. Matturi, "A Brief History of Nimikoro Chiefdom," *Africana Research Bulletin,* January, 1973; E.R. Langley, "A Tale of Nimikoro," *Sierra Leone Studies*, December, 1929.

MAY, J.C.

Joseph Claudius May (August 14, 1845-October 14, 1902), a talented Methodist preacher and educator, was the first principal of the Wesleyan Boys High School, Freetown, which under his direction, developed such high standards as to rival the Church Missionary Society Grammar School. An active participant in public life and keen journalist, he started the influential *Sierra Leone Weekly News* which continued in publication for over 60 years.

He was born at Charles Street in Freetown on August 14, 1845, the son of a Yoruba recaptive schoolmaster and Wesleyan minister named Joseph May. At the age of three he went with his parents to MacCarthy Island on the Gambia River where they spent six years. Returning from the Gambia, his father was appointed to circuit work at Wilberforce, York and Wellington, and also took charge for a period of two years at the Training Institution for Wesleyan ministers and lay agents at King Tom.

May was an industrious scholar. One of his ex-teachers at Wellington village school described him as "intelligent and very shrewd for his age." At 14 he left school to take up employment in the business firm of his father's friend, James Macfoy, where he worked with such application that after a year he was practically running the entire business.

Through the request of Quaker friends of his father, who had received part of his own education abroad, May was sent to England for further studies, but his departure was delayed until 1865 by his mother's reluctance to part with her son.

During the six years he spent in England, May took courses at the Borough Road College in London, at Queen's College, Taunton, and at Westminster Normal Training School. His work, especially in classics, mathematics and natural sciences, was highly praised by his teachers, and he also took a keen interest in the art of teaching itself. Like his father before him, May learned Pitman shorthand while he was in England under its inventor, Isaac Pitman.

May had shown an early vocation for the ministry, and had become a local preacher and Sunday school secretary before leaving for England where he became a fully accredited preacher. Four years after his return to Sierra Leone in 1870 he became a minister on probation and was eventually ordained in February 1880.

For the first three years after his return May devoted himself to the task of improving standards in the Wesleyan elementary schools in the Colony. In 1874 the Wesleyan Mission's plans for a boys' high school, proposed before he left for England but delayed by the intransigence of its autocratic superintendent, the Rev. Benjamin Tregaskis, were finally put into action, and May was appointed its first principal. Starting with only eight pupils on the roll, it soon flourished under his kind and inspiring guidance, and by the time of his death many important Africans had gone through the school. The curriculum was strongly influenced by his ideas, which included the introduction of shorthand, the encouragement of music teaching and the development of games and sports. The school came to rival, and in the eyes of some to excel, the much older Church Missionary Society (C.M.S.) Grammar School established in 1845.

A gifted orator, May organized debates and other public functions at which leading Freetown figures aired their views. The most popular lecture series, organized in 1881, featured papers by, among others, Sir Samuel Lewis (q.v.), the Rev. Charles Marke (a Nupe convert to Wesleyan Methodism from Nigeria) and May himself. The topics covered such matters as agriculture in Sierra Leone, racial superiority and religious issues and some of the papers were later published in pamphlet form.

May also took a keen interest in journalism, being himself an accomplished writer. At great personal expense he established the *Methodist Herald and West African Educational Times* in 1882, serving at its editor, together with his brother Cornelius, until 1888 when it ceased publication. He also founded the *Sierra Leone Weekly News* whose first issue appeared on September 6, 1884. With help once again from Cornelius, and from Dr. Edward Blyden who contributed frequently, the paper became possibly the most influential public mouthpiece along the West Coast. Governor Frederic Cardew (q.v.) even held it responsible for stirring up the dissatisfaction which led to the 1898 Hut Tax War. The paper continued in publication until 1951.

Besides his major commitments, May also held a variety of honorary posts. Governor Arthur Edward Havelock (term of office 1881-84) appointed him a member of the board of education and offered him the post of inspector of schools, but this he turned down. He also served as examiner for the civil service of the colony.

A man of strong views on abstinence, and a teetotaler himself, May did his best to promote temperance literature in the Colony, and served on the church's temperance committee. He was for a long time secretary of the Wesleyan synod. He also published a short biography of his father.

In 1887 he married Christiana Bull, a union which produced seven children of whom three died in infancy. Two years after Christiana's death in 1900, May married again; but his second marriage was short-lived for he died one month later on October 14, 1902.

E. AMADU TURAY

BIBLIOGRAPHY: Christopher Fyfe, "The Sierra Leone Press in the Nineteenth Century," *Sierra Leone Studies*, June, 1957, *A History of Sierra Leone*, London, 1962; C. Marke, *Origin of Wesleyan Methodism in Sierra Leone*, London, 1913; J.C. May, *A Brief Sketch of the Life of the Rev. Joseph May*, Freetown, n.d.; J.R. Roberts, *A Character-sketch of the late Rev. J. Claudius May*, (pamphlet), Liverpool, 1912.

McCORMACK, J.

John McCormack (March 24, 1791-March 20, 1865) was one of the few Europeans in the 19th century who spent almost their entire working lives in West Africa. Starting as a timber trader, he acquired a unique knowledge of the Sierra Leone hinterland, and its peoples, especially the Temne. He was later employed as a government agent, playing a vital part in negotiations and treaty-making, and strongly influencing government policy.

He was born in Lurgan, Country Armagh, in Ireland. By the age of about 18 he was already on the West African coast employed as a trading agent, and around 1814 he settled in Sierra Leone where he was to remain almost continuously for 52 years.

McCormack first rose to prominence through the timber trade. In 1816 he shipped the first consignment of African oak from the estuary of the Rokel River to England, the starting signal for the trade, which boomed in Sierra Leone for a brief span of years. He built himself a house on Tombo Island on the Rokel Estuary, complete with wharf and sawpit, where logs received from up the river and from Port Loko further to the north were processed. His lead was followed by other merchants, chiefly European, who settled on neighboring islands, such as Tasso and Bunce, and started trading in timber.

For as long as it lasted, the timber trade provided an important source of revenue for both the Colony and the Temne, whose country supplied the product. McCormack came into close contact with the Temne, thereby acquiring the first-hand knowledge later to prove so valuable to the Colony. He was also able to prove, against prevailing opinion, that the Temne were willing to work hard if offered incentives.

Initially profitable, the timber trade started to decline after the first few years, and with it McCormack's wealth. Nevertheless, he persisted, and as supplies dwindled in Port Loko, which they did by 1830, he and other timber traders began to shift their ground. McCormack built a new factory at Gbinti at the mouth of the Melacourie River, in what is now the Republic of Guinea, where he hoped to tap the forest area, and even proposed a canal to the Scarcies. But the prospects were not sufficiently good, and by the 1830s he was ruined.

His creditors, however, allowed him to keep the beautiful house he had built in Freetown, and his knowledge of the interior regions ensured that he continue to play an important part in the affairs of the Colony. The governor, Sir John Jeremie (term of office 1840-41) quickly appointed him as stipendiary police magistrate. He then became an unofficial government agent, negotiating on behalf of the official agent at Port Loko particularly in matters involving trade disputes.

His influence was also enhanced by being patron and teacher to Thomas George Lawson (q.v.), son of a chief of Little Popo on the Bight of Benin. Lawson had come to live in McCormack's household and had accompanied him up country on several visits, where he too acquired the kind of knowledge which led to his appointment in the colonial administration in a key position in charge of interior affairs.

In his role as government agent (which had started while he was still a trader), McCormack was constantly involved in settling disputes in the area of Port Loko and further north, and signed various treaties with local rulers on behalf of the government. In 1825 he assisted Governor Sir Charles Turner (term of office 1825-26) in settling a disputed succession to the rulership of Port Loko, the first of several such missions over the next three decades. In 1831, he accompanied the colonial secretary on a mission to mediate in the Temne-Loko wars around Port Loko.

In 1837-38, there was trouble in Koya country east of Freetown, part of which had been ceded to Britain (then called British Koya), while the rest lay outside British jurisdiction. The conflict between Mende in the British section and the Temne owners of Koya country had broken out over farming land. In 1841, McCormack, together with Chief Dalla Modu of Madina in Bullom country, was sent to Koya to settle the disturbance. In 1845, Governor William Fergusson (term of office 1844-45) sent him up the Rokel River to mediate in a protracted war between the Temne and Loko. He succeeded in achieving a temporary peace by 1846.

As he grew older, McCormack's diplomatic negotiations were increasingly colored by the religious convictions which he had embraced in later life. By the 1850s he had founded a free-will Baptist Church, a branch of the Church of God, whose congregation met regularly at his house in Freetown. He became deeply concerned about the spread of Islam in the hinterland, which he feared was at the expense of Christianity. Where he was able to influence outcomes, he tended to act against the interest of known Muslim families or ethnic groups, and to pursue the interest of the Temne, whom he hoped were more receptive to Christianity.

His bias against Islam is made clear from the part he played in the series of disputes over the succession to the Alikaliship or rulership of Port Loko, largely caused by the attempts of the Sankoh clan to regain leadership after being ousted in the early 19th century. The Sankoh were Muslim Soso with Muslim alliances in the neighborhood, and had little sympathy with colonial intervention or with the idea of a Christian mission in Port Loko. In 1841, McCormack accompanied Governor John Jeremie to Port Loko, where his views undoubtedly reinforced the governor's dislike of the Sankoh candidate, and led him to prevent a Muslim succession. In 1853, the situation recurred when the Alikaliship was again to be filled, and Major Dillet and McCormack went to Port Loko on behalf of the government to mediate. Again the decision went against the Sankoh candidate.

In 1860 McCormack went yet again to Port Loko, which had been attacked and burned by Muslim Soso forces, and made a treaty with the chiefs of the Bullom shore to the east of Port Loko, reaffirming their supremacy. The following year, now 70 years old, he was sent to look into the Soso-Temne dispute over the rulership of Kambia, on the estuary of the Great Scarcies River. He persuaded the Soso to accept the rule of the Temne candidate, Lamina Barmoi, once again hoping to further Christianity by backing the Temne.

The negotiations in Kambia were McCormack's last important official service in the hinterland. He had since 1850 been given official recognition for his work through an appointment as "first writer" in the colonial secretary's office. This position, second to that of the local colonial secretary, was later re-titled assistant colonial secretary.

In 1862, Governor Stephen Hill (term of office 1854-62) appointed him police magistrate in Freetown, but he was too old for it to be more than a sinecure. In 1864 he left for England, where he died on March 20, 1865.

His grandchildren, of African descent on the maternal side, survive in the famous Easmon family of Freetown, which has consistently provided a line of doctors serving in Freetown and elsewhere in West Africa.

C. MAGBAILY FYLE.

BIBLIOGRAPHY: Christopher Fyfe, *A History of Sierra Leone,* London, 1962; A.J. Lasite, "The Department of Native Affairs and the Development of British Policy in the Northern Interior of Sierra Leone, 1850-1900," M.A. thesis, University of Sierra Leone, 1975.

MENDEGLA

Mendegla of Joru (?-1890) was one of the most powerful Mende warriors of the later 19th century. Using his immense influence over other rulers, he managed to bring about the pacification of the Gallinas in the extreme south of Sierra Leone, an area which was in turmoil through wars of succession. Along with Kai Londo (*q.v.*), he was held in the highest respect by the colonial government for his remarkable abilities as a chief.

Mendegla's state, with its capital at Joru, (on the Moa River, in what is now the Pujehun district of southern Sierra Leone), spread from the Barri country in a northeasterly direction till it bordered on Kai Londo's state of Luawa. Not much is known about his early career, but throughout the 1880s he was well known in official circles. "The names of Mendingrah and Kai Londo are pass words...in the countries through which I have traveled," reported T.J. Alldridge, traveling commissioner, in 1890, "and from what I have seen myself of the way they govern the extensive territories under their jurisdiction—I gladly endorse the high opinions which I am convinced the masses generally entertain towards these chieftains."

During the 1880s the Gallinas had become a hot-bed of disturbance. Trouble started around 1872 when King Mana Siaka (*q.v.*) was succeeded by his blind, senile, drunken brother, Jaya. This opened the way for many aspiring chiefs to aim at the acquisition of the imperial honor of the Massaquoi, the ruling Gallinas family, to which Mana Siaka and Jaya belonged. Rivalries in attempts to succeed to the authority of the Massaquoi led to frequent wars, which by 1885 had become a struggle between parties backing two clear contestants—Fawundu of the Lower Gallinas, and Boakei Gomma, a member of one of the ruling houses, who was supported by the upper chiefs and Mendegla. Boakei Gomma's rivals hired Ndawa (*q.v.*), a famous professional warrior, who attacked Mendegla. He was repulsed but returned again and was killed at Dama, a

chiefdom in Kenema district, by Mendegla's warriors.

Meanwhile the British had been making vain attempts to keep the peace in the Gallinas. T.J. Alldridge, who had been appointed traveling commissioner in 1889 to make treaties, was sent to meet Mendegla at Bandasuma on the Moa River for the purpose of bringing an end to hostilities through a treaty. But before this meeting, Mendegla, whose influence over rulers as far south as the Gallinas was very powerful, had initiated a special "Peace Poro" to end the Gallinas wars. He had sent this "Peace Poro" over an area of about a hundred miles in radius, bearing in mind that the professionals in this war were always hired from the interior. When Alldridge arrived at Bandasuma "all of the chiefs whom I met there had already accepted the 'porroh', which so far as I could learn, had reference to a permanent peace being maintained in the country." Until the colonial takeover in 1896, when the Protectorate was proclaimed, the Gallinas troubles had abated.

At that same meeting in Bandasuma, Mendegla signed a treaty of friendship with Alldridge, who signed further treaties with some of Mendegla's subordinate chiefs, and then moved on inland to establish still more alliances.

Exactly six months after he had signed the treaty, Mendegla died. Various districts were moved to fight, firstly over the burial place of the deceased ruler, and then over the distribution of his property, but the Frontier Police intervened to prevent disturbances.

Alldridge took part in the "coronation ceremonies" of Mendegla's successor, Gbatekaka, the most powerful man in the state. And from Alldridge comes the highest tribute to Mendegla: "That Chief was a magnificent man, about six feet two in height and of unusual intelligence, a great warrior and beloved by the people." Ironically, by pacifying the Gallinas, Mendegla had unwittingly prepared the way for the imposition of colonialism.

ARTHUR ABRAHAM

BIBLIOGRAPHY: A. Abraham, *Mende Government and Politics Under Colonial Rule,* Freetown, 1978; T.J. Alldridge, *The Sherbro and its Hinterland,* London, 1901.

MILLER, F.A.

Frederic Adolphus Miller (July 2, 1862-October 1, 1943) was a civil servant who took an active part in West African politics in later life. A fervent believer in encouraging the young, he befriended and supported the radical political activist Wallace-Johnson (q.v.) in the teeth of conservative disapproval.

He was born at Freetown. His formal education 'began and ended at the first Model School conducted by the Sierra Leone government.' Yet by persistent application he became a well-known public figure, remembered for his prodigious knowledge of English classics and a wealth of apt quotations.

His career had modest beginnings. He worked first as a grocer's assistant, an office boy in a bookshop, and a junior clerk in a lawyer's chambers. After this he became a minor functionary in the colonial civil service, where through hard work and determination he was eventually appointed clerk of the Executive and Legislative Councils, the last black man to hold this appointment during the colonial period. His work was commended more than once, and he received extra compensation. He retired from the civil service in 1922 and ended his career as a laboratory assistant at the Prince of Wales School from 1925 to 1929.

As custodian of official minutes, memoranda and general correspondence between the Colonial Office in London and the local administration, as well as between local and regional administrations within Sierra Leone, he was well placed to know the inner workings of a colonial government. Not surprisingly, he was credited with an encyclopaedic knowledge of civil service matters, and was in fact one of the founders of the African Civil Service Association and became its first president. His signature was to be found on a number of petitions and memoranda, notably one on the high cost of living in 1918.

In later life, Miller became actively involved in politics. He was a foundation member of the local branch of the National Congress of British West Africa (N.C.B.W.A.) and became one of the vice-presidents. He was also made vice-president of a short-lived association of Colony-born and Protectorate-born Sierra Leoneans—the Sierra Leone Aborigines Society. He did not enter the Legislative Council, but played an important and active role as adviser and elder statesman to young and aspiring politicians. He gave respectability to Wallace-Johnson's West African Youth League (W.A.Y.L.), founded in 1938, when he agreed to become the chairman of its central committee.

This was a significant step to take, for at that period of Sierra Leone's history, the rabid emotionalism and radicalism of Wallace-Johnson's political propaganda was too much for the moderately conservative Krio (Creole) elite. Many of the respectable figures who later adorned the W.A.Y.L.'s platform would have shied away, if the elderly and highly respected Miller had not taken Wallace-Johnson under his wing.

For embracing Wallace-Johnson's cause, Miller inevitably incurred the displeasure of his more conservative peers. But he was a man of principle. He believed in what Wallace-Johnson was fighting for, and being himself a tenacious and unyielding fighter, despite his physical disabilities in later life (he became deaf in one ear and partly blind), he refused to be blackmailed by his detractors.

Kind, helpful, and generous, especially towards the young, Miller did all he could to help young people. As well as his political activities he took part in church affairs, representing the Methodist Church on the council of Fourah Bay College. He was also the secretary of the Sierra Leone Chamber of Commerce for some years.

After a full, varied, and successful life, he died on October 1, 1943, and the people of Freetown agreed that Sierra Leone had lost a true and loyal friend "who was a thriving example to ambitious youth of the possibilities of achievement in the way of persevering." His name rarely figures in history books on Sierra Leone. Yet it was people like Miller, unknown, self-effacing, and unsung, whose efforts laid a firm foundation for later political developments in Sierra Leone.

AKINTOLA J.G. WYSE

BIBLIOGRAPHY: M.H.Y. Kaniki, "The Politics of Protest in Colonial West Africa: The Sierra Leone Experience," *The African Review,* Vol. 4, No. 3. 1974; *Sierra Leone Weekly News*; Leo Spitzer, *The Creoles of Sierra Leone*, Ile-Ife, 1975.

MOMOH SANKOH

Momoh Sankoh (?-circa 1890) was a leading member of the Soso Sankoh clan who made several determined but unsuccessful attempts to regain the rulership of Port Loko for his clan. A man of learning, he was also a shrewd and aggressive leader. But for colonial intervention, he might well have succeeded in becoming ruler.

The Sankoh ruled Port Loko, northeast of Freetown on Port Loko Creek, from 1700 to 1817 when the Soso ruler Alimamy Konkori Sankoh was overthrown and beheaded. They were part of the Mandinka immigrant groups who had gradually moved into Sierra Leone from the 16th century onwards, and who by the 19th century were identified with rulership, prosperous trade, and revered Islamic learning and religion.

After the overthrow of their leader, they still aspired to regain political influence in Port Loko, and struggled towards this throughout the 19th century. Probably no single figure did more to help this cause than Momoh Sankoh, a descendant of the beheaded

Alimamy Konkori. He appears to have left Port Loko just before Konkori's overthrow to obtain an Islamic education in the Melacourie region, of what is now the Republic of Guinea, probably in Maligea.

The Sankoh had been removed from power by an alliance between Temne and Mandinka clan interests which was ratified by a solemn agreement limiting the alikaliship or rulership to both clans on a rotating basis, thus excluding Sankoh claims for good.

Throughout the century, however, succession to the alikaliship continued to be disputed. In 1840, on the death of Alikali Fatimah Brimah, three clans contested it—the Kamara, who, contrary to the agreement of 1817, wanted to continue in power—the Bangura, and the Sankoh.

This rivalry threatened political stability in Port Loko, a matter of concern to the commercial interests of the Freetown colony, whose trade in Sudanic produce (other than slaves), such as cattle, gold and hides, flowed more freely if this important intermediary trading center were free from disturbance. But the situation at the end of 1840 was far from stable.

As had happened in 1825, the Colony, in its own interest, openly intervened in the dispute. From January to February 1841, the aggressive governor, John Jeremie (term of office 1840-41) visited Port Loko. He was accompanied by John McCormack (q.v.), an Irish timber merchant who frequently acted as mediator between local rulers and the government, and Dalla Modu, a Soso chief from Bullom opposite the Freetown Colony who also assisted the government in the settlement of disputes.

Jeremie developed a strong dislike for the candidate put forward by the Sankoh, Namina Lahi Sankoh, who openly expressed his objection to colonial intervention and the possibility of a Christian missionary presence in Port Loko. The Bai Foki, a local ruler, apparently also resented Sankoh claims. Thus, after successful negotiations, Namina Modu Bangura was chosen and crowned Alikali in February, 1841. He then signed a treaty of friendship with the British, agreeing to promote commerce and to allow a Christian missionary station to be started in Port Loko. In return he demanded the payment of stipends, including overdue payments.

The Sankoh, undaunted by their defeat in 1841, again challenged the succession when Alikali Modu died in April 1853. This time their candidate was Momoh Sankoh, a man of refinement and superior learning compared to his rival, Mohamadu Alikali, son of Fatimah Brimah Kamara. This favorable comparison was made even by such unsympathetic judgments as those of the Colony's two agents, Major Dillet and John McCormark, who had come to Port Loko to intervene in the dispute. But already before

their arrival the two rivals had taken steps to urge the government in Freetown to support one candidate against the other.

Momoh wrote to the governor that he had already been chosen Alikali. He made it clear that Soso kinsmen in the Melacourie, the Scarcies and Bullom led by Dalla Modu would come to his support should war break out. Mohamadu Alikali, on the other hand, informed the governor through Mori Bundu of Foredugu in Koya, a powerful and respected Temne chief, that he had also been elected Alikali. His candidacy, he claimed, was supported by equally powerful chiefs and sub-chiefs in the Rokel region, the Bai Foki in Port Loko, Bai Kamara, Bai Banta, Dabo and Ebiru. It was evident that the whole area could easily be embroiled in war, with widespread economic and political disorder.

After three anxious days of parleying and negotiation requiring all McCormack's diplomatic skill, the dispute was resolved in favor of Alikali Mohamadu. Momoh Sankoh handed over the turban, symbol of authority, to McCormack in Saindugu, the Soso section of Port Loko, and Mohamadu was crowned Fatimah Brimah II on May 10, 1853.

Fate, however, intervened to break the peace that had been hoped for. In 1856 Fatimah Brimah II died, and Momoh Sankoh again contended for the throne. This claim threatened to provoke severe hostilities between the Sankoh and the Bangura, whose turn it was to succeed to the Alikaliship. In another deliberate intervention by the Colony to protect its interests, Thomas George Lawson (q.v.), McCormack's assistant, was sent in November as mediator in this succession dispute. After treating with the principal chiefs of Port Loko, Lawson came to the conclusion that the Bangura candidate, Yan Kobah, was to be preferred to Sankoh, hardly a surprising outcome given Lawson's anti-Islamic and anti-Soso bias. Yan Kobah was crowned Alikali, and, to the gratification of the Freetown administration, the leading chiefs wrote thanking the governor for his mediation. The following year in March, 1857, Governor Stephen Hill (term of office 1854-62), accompanied by McCormack and Charles Heddle (q.v.), a Eurafrican timber merchant, visited Port Loko to confirm the succession of the new Alikali.

Sankoh, however, was not yet finished. Determined, shrewd, and aggressive, he launched a fierce attack on Port Loko early in 1859, receiving, as in the past, military help from his Soso kinsfolk within Port Loko, in Kambia, and Bullom. In February, Governor Hill reported that part of Port Loko had been burned down by Sankoh and his warriors. Krio (Creole) resident traders complained of terrible losses of property. The administration had to rush reinforcements to help the Alikali and the Temne, which enabled them to repel Sankoh and his allies. Port Loko very narrowly escaped defeat at the hands of the Soso.

This was apparently the last desperate bid by Sankoh and the Soso to seize power in Port Loko. When Alikali Yan Kobah died in 1868 the succession passed without serious dispute to Alikali Moribah Kindo Kamara who was crowned on April 10, 1868, the Colony being represented by Colonel Yonge and T.G. Lawson.

Not much is known about Momoh Sankoh during this period, but it is probable that he was involved in anti-colonial activities. In 1886 he reappears again, arrested among the leaders of the Yoni Temne who had fought against the Colony in Koya and other regions in the Rokel. Deprived of leadership in Port Loko, through colonial intervention, Sankoh decided to fight against colonial expansion in northern Sierra Leone. In a sense, therefore he stands as an early anti-colonial resistance figure.

After he was brought to Freetown, Sankoh was detained, together with other leaders of the Yoni resistance of 1887. What happened to him afterwards is uncertain, though he probably did not live on for long.

GUSTAV K. DEVENEAUX

BIBLIOGRAPHY: Esu Biyi, ''The Temne People and How They Make Their Kings,'' *Journal of the Royal African Society,* Vol. 12, No. 46, 1913; J.J. Crooks, *A History of the Colony of Sierra Leone, Western Africa*, 2nd ed., Dublin, 1903, reprinted London, 1972; Christopher Fyfe, *A History of Sierra Leone*, London, 1962; E.A. Ijagbemi, ''The Freetown Colony and the Development of Legitimate Commerce in the Adjoining Territories,'' *Journal of the Historical Society of Nigeria,* Vol. 2, June, 1970; E.G. Ingham, *Sierra Leone After a Hundred Years,* London, 1894; C. W. Newbury (ed.), *British Policy Towards West Africa,* London, 1965.

MOMO JA

Momo Ja (late 1840s-early 1900s) was a famous warrior and ruler in the far south of Sierra Leone, who, together with his older brother Momo Kai Kai (*q.v.*), controlled the country round Pujehun on the Wanje River. He initially resisted the British over the collection of hut tax, but later assisted them in suppressing the insurrection of 1898.

Born in about the late 1840s, he was the son of a Fula father and a Mende mother. Both he and his brother were warriors, Momo Ja being the commander of his brother's forces whose permanent encampment came to be known as Pujehun, meaning literally ''in the pepper,'' for it was such a hot spot that even the brave were afraid to attack it. By the last quarter of the

19th century, Momo Ja and Momo Kai Kai had established their domination over the Kittam region south of the Bum River. Momo Ja had established his own center of political power by building the town of Sembehun, in Pujehun district.

In 1889 Governor Sir James Shaw Hay (term of office 1888-91) initiated a ''greatly extended policy'' towards the interior of the country with a triple emphasis on road building, policing, and a rapid increase in treaty-making in preparation for the impending Protectorate. Hay visited the Gallinas and Kittam regions in 1890 to explain his policy to the local rulers who agreed to start work on road-making at once, after false assurances that it was not with any intention of taking over control of their country. He asked Momo Kai Kai to rebuild his town of Bendajuma, to the north of Pujehun, which had been destroyed in recent wars, and to build a block house to quarter police. Kai Kai delegated this project to Momo Ja, whose enthusiasm for Hay's new policy got the work completed in four weeks.

In 1888 a ''standard treaty'' had been prepared by the colonial government, which, apart from a restrictive clause preventing cession of territory to any other foreign power, was still a treaty of friendship. This started a boom of treaty-making with local chiefs, which Hay personally administered in the middle

Mende belt. After persuading many important rulers to sign treaties at a large assemblage at Tikonko on the Bum River, Hay was accompanied by Momo Ja, Makavoray (*q.v.*), and other chiefs of significance, to meet Bumpe rulers, who presented a firm barrier against British penetration. The mission, to convince them to sign similar treaties, was successful.

When the Protectorate Ordinance was proclaimed in 1896, Momo Ja, together with various other rulers, decided to see Governor Frederic Cardew (*q.v.*) in person to clarify certain of the provisions. They were at first refused an audience, but Cardew changed his mind and invited their presence. Momo Ja, however, declined. The other rulers were told by Cardew that they would have to pay house tax, a highly contentious matter, whether they liked it or not.

When the collection of the tax began in Bandajuma district, extorted by brutal methods by the Frontier Police, Momo Ja refused to pay. District Commissioner Carr ordered a sergeant and 20 Frontier Police to arrest him and sentenced him to three month's imprisonment with hard labor for non-payment of the tax. Shortly after, he paid up, and the remaining sentence was rescinded.

Thereafter Momo Ja sided with the British, providing military help to suppress the resistance of 1898. Captain Carr recommended him for a present of £10 for his services, which was approved by the governor. He then seems to have reverted largely to trade, from which he grew prosperous, his chief town of Pujehun being ideally located on the Wanje River.

In 1897 he was recognized as paramount chief of lower Krim country, in the Pujehun district. It was thought in official circles that he might even succeed Momo Kai Kai, who was by now very old, as paramount chief of Malene chiefdom, also in Pujehun. Momo Ja probably died early in this century.

ARTHUR ABRAHAM

BIBLIOGRAPHY: Arthur Abraham, *Mende Government and Politics Under Colonial Rule*, Freetown, 1978; "Records of Paramount Chiefs," 1899, Sierra Leone Government Archives.

MOMO KAI KAI

Momo Kai Kai (circa 1812-circa 1900) was a warrior chief in southwest Sierra Leone, who by the end of the 19th century had become the most influential ruler of the southern coastal region. He was a steadfast supporter of the colonial administration through the resistance struggles of 1898 and after.

Born about 1812, he was the son of a Fula father and a Mende mother, and was the older brother of Momo Ja (*q.v.*). He succeeded Momo Fula as chief of Bandajuma in the Kittam district.

In 1889, Momo Kai Kai signed a treaty of friendship with the British for which he received an annual stipend. He was also requested by Governor Sir James Shaw Hay (term of office 1888-91), who was engaged on an expansionist policy of road-building and policing in the interior, to build a block house to quarter police. This was completed within a month. Kai Kai was also in favor of Hay's road-making policy and enthusiastically put his people to clearing roads.

After the proclamation of the Protectorate in 1896, there were many protests from rulers over some of the clauses. In January 1898, Kai Kai, along with several other rulers, decided to see Governor Frederic Cardew (*q.v.*) in person after receiving an unsatisfactory oral reply to queries transmitted to the governor through a delegation in 1897. Cardew made it clear that if rulers refused to pay house tax, the main source of grievance, the consequences would be very serious. After this ultimatum they promised to collect the tax from their people.

Nevertheless, on Kai Kai's return, cattle belonging to him and his people were seized by Captain Hood, the district commissioner of Bandajuma. When Kai Kai protested to Cardew over this violent seizure, the governor wrote back that the action was justified since he believed that the chief and his people wanted to evade payment of the tax.

After this incident, Kai Kai sided openly with the administration. When the resistance movement began at the end of April, 1898, he took no part in it but gave full co-operation to the British. Police were quartered in his town which became the headquarters of the district of Bandajuma. Kai Kai brought in some of his people to augment the flying columns and to help quiet the resistance. In November, he was awarded a silver medal and chain in recognition of his loyal services during the disturbances.

After the resistance struggles of 1898, Momo Kai Kai emerged as the most important chief in the Bandajuma district, the result of his steadfast support of the colonial administration, which in return helped him to extend his territory. He was officially recognized as paramount chief of Malane chiefdom. Aged 90 at the time of the uprisings, it is difficult to see what alternative course he could have followed, and undoubtedly his decision to side with the British paid him well. He died probably about 1900.

ARTHUR ABRAHAM

BIBLIOGRAPHY: Arthur Abraham, *Mende Government and Politics Under Colonial Rule*, Freetown, 1978; Christopher Fyfe, *A History of Sierra Leone*, London, 1962.

MORIBA KINDO BANGURA

Moriba Kindo Bangura (17?-1825) was the forceful Temne leader who overthrew the Soso hegemony over Port Loko (an important trading center), which had lasted from 1700 to 1817. He then became the first Temne Alikali or ruler of that town in more than a century. He also played a decisive part in creating the system of rotating chiefship of Port Loko which continued throughout the 19th century.

Port Loko, strategically placed for commerce on the Rokel River, attracted traders from the interior of the Sudan, as well as Europeans whose main interest was the slave trade. Its commercial importance also drew Mandinka immigrants from the hinterland who spread the influence of Islam through trade, teaching, and the sword.

The Soso, part of the Mandinka ethnic and cultural complex, established political suzerainty over Port Loko in 1700, but by the early 19th century, they appeared to have become oppressive, provoking strong opposition from some Temne and other immigrant groups. About 1806, Alimamy Brima Konkori Sankoh, a new Soso ruler, came to the throne. A devout Muslim and strongly traditionalist, he quickly antagonized several sections of Port Loko society.

Sankoh's open hostility to the Colony aggravated the situation. The Crown Colony, established in 1807 with its seat of government at Freetown, was concerned with the active pursuit of "legitimate commerce" as opposed to the centuries-old slave trade. It was also concerned with the spread of Christianity. Both these values were strongly at variance with those of Port Loko, and Temne society, as well as with Brima Konkori Sankoh's affirmation of tradition, Soso hegemony, and Islam. His exit from power would have been welcomed by the colonial administration. Nor was his position helped by his unpopularity with local Temne and other inhabitants of Port Loko.

Sometime in 1816, a conspiracy seems to have been formed involving the Bai Foki of Port Loko, Moriba Kindo Bangura, and Fatima Brima Kamara. (Fatima Brima was a Temne leader of part-Mandinka descent who led the movement to end Soso hegemony in Port Loko, and who was the main supporter of Bangura.) The Bai Foki was the traditional Temne ruler of Port Loko whose influence had decreased through Soso power. He belonged to the Kanu clan. Moriba Kindo Bangura, according to tradition, was related to the Sankoh Soso clan, but appears to have claimed Temne ancestry. Because he was an outstanding warrior his claim was not challenged. The conspirators aimed to overthrow Sankoh and Soso hegemony, after which Moriba Kindo Bangura was to succeed as ruler. After his death Fatima Brima Kamara was to follow him, and if he too died, someone from the Kamara clan would succeed him.

Tradition had it that, after the agreement had been sealed, Moriba Kindo Bangura visited the Soso homeland in Maligia on the Melacourie River later in 1816, and collected as much information as possible about the Sankoh. Possibly to conteract Soso pretensions as supreme leaders of Islam, he obtained religious recognition there, being granted the title of Alikali (a-quadi), for which it said he paid a price of seven slaves. In return for these he was given a turban to symbolize his new status.

Returning to Port Loko, Moriba Kindo received tacit but wholehearted support from the Bai Foki, who is said to have blessed him. He was also given a drum as a symbol of authority. This, incidentally, the Sankoh also possessed and used for the same purpose.

On the appointed day in 1817, when the Temne and other malcontents supporting the conspirators had made full military preparations, the drum was sounded. Alerted by the noise, the unsuspecting Brima Konkori Sankoh sent his agents to arrest the person who had dared to challenge his authority. The Soso were ambushed and ultimately trapped and crushed in the part of Port Loko called Sain Bugu in which they had concentrated. Brima Konkori Sankoh and many of his chiefs were beheaded, and, according to tradition, only Temne women married to Soso, and their children, were spared.

Fortunately for the Colony, a disputed succession in 1825 called for intervention. In that year Moriba Kindo Bangura died; but instead of the succession passing to Fatima Brima, as stipulated in the solemn pact of 1816, a schemer, Kunia Banna (alias Jack Coby), who was born in Magbele, south of Port Loko, but lived both at Port Loko and Freetown, persuaded the traditional elective council to confirm him as Alikali. Fatima Brima Kamara quite legitimately felt cheated, and was prepared to use force to gain the succession.

The resulting crisis and impending war disrupted the flow of trade into the Colony, a situation which impelled Governor Charles Turner (term of office 1825-26) to set out with troops to Port Loko to intervene in the dispute. He recognized Fatima Brima Kamara, who was crowned Alikali. Turner also secured a treaty favorable to the Colony's commercial and humanitarian interests, ceding land from Port Loko to the Small Scarcies. The system of the rotating chiefship of Port Loko, which Moriba Kindo Bangura had helped to establish, had been upheld, but at the price of colonial intervention.

GUSTAV K. DEVENEAUX

BIBLIOGRAPHY: Gustav K. Deveneaux, "The Political and Social Impact of the Colony in Northern Sierra Leone 1821-1896," unpublished doctoral dissertation, Boston University, 1973; Christopher Fyfe, *A History of Sierra Leone*, London, 1962; H.C. Hodgson, "Historical Sketch of Port Loko," *Sierra Leone Studies*, February, 1932; H.O. Newland, *Sierra Leone: Its People, Products and Secret Societies*, London, 1916; J.A. Songo-Davies, "Origins of the Masinera Chiefdom," *Sierra Leone Studies*, September, 1928.

MORI LAMINA. See BILALI

MORLAI LIMBA, PA

Pa Morlai Limba (17?-circa 1815) was a leading Limba warrior who fought wars of expansion in the early 19th century. He was such a formidable opponent that it required an alliance between a Limba and a Temne chief, as well as the help of powerful Fula newcomers, the Bunduka, to prevent his threatened invasion of their territories.

The Bunduka were a group of Fula from Senegal who served as agents for French slavers on Gambia Island in the late 18th century. They traveled through many areas of northern Sierra Leone, and by the beginning of the 19th century their influence had spread as far as Foredugu on the Rokel River, Sanda Magbolonto, and Dabia (all in the Port Loko area), and Safroko in Bombali district—areas then inhabited by Temne, Loko, and Limba peoples.

With the disappearance of their French principals in Gambia Island—apparently because they found it unhealthy—these slave-dealers decided to remain in Sierra Leone, where through time their numbers were increased by new arrivals from Senegal.

Local people became apprehensive of the growing influence these strangers had in their territories, especially as the Bunduka began to marry the daughters and close relations of local rulers. But in the event they had to be called upon for assistance. It was at this time that Pa Morlai, who came from the town of Laia, near Port Loko, was engaged on his campaigns of expansion and consolidation. His forces had won notable victories and by 1810 he was close to taking the settlement in and around Sanda Magbolonto. As Pa Morlai had relations in this area, it is probable that his attacks were prompted less by personal ambition than by a desire to dislodge the Fula strangers, reputed to have formidable military skills.

Unable to expel the Bunduka because of the nexus of intermarriage, and faced with the prospect of an imminent invasion, Burema Yarri, the Limba chief of Sanda Magbolonto, and his Temne counterpart, Yenkain Kamara, turned to them for military help. They consented, but exacted a stiff price for their co-operation. In addition to a hundred portions of every trading commodity, they were to receive a whole chiefdom (Mafonda) in perpetuity.

Their task, however, was a daunting one, since Morlai was reputed to be "bullet-proof", and his forces considerably outnumbered those of his opponents. The Bunduka called upon Chernor Abass, their leading Islamic scholar, to divine the best way to cripple Morlai's forces. After a period of spiritual withdrawal, it was revealed to Abass that Morlai would only prove vulnerable to golden bullets.

Even so, no Bunduka dared challenge Morlai openly. Instead, when reports reached the anti-Morlai coalition that the dreaded warrior had gone to arrange an arms deal at Mabanta, in the Bombali district, three Bunduka waylaid him in a cowardly fashion at the smithy, where the first golden bullet felled him. A comrade-in-arms rose in his defence only to be cut down by a blow from a Bunduka's sword.

Suleiman Bundu, one of the attackers, decapitated Morlai and, wrapping the head in a bundle of sheets, quickly made for Gbinti at the mouth of the Melacourie River where there were significant concentrations of Fula. There he presented the head to the chiefs of the coalition.

E.D. AMADU TURAY

BIBLIOGRAPHY: E. Hirst, "An Attempt at Reconstructing the History of the Loko People from 1790 to the Present," *Sierra Leone Studies*, 1957; A. Wurie, "The Bundukas of Sierra Leone," *Sierra Leone Studies*, December, 1953; A. Wurie and E. Hirst, *Rassin*, London, 1968.

NAIMBANA. See NEMGBANA

NAIMBANA, J.F. See NEMGBANA, J.F.

NDAWA

Ndawa the Great (circa 1850-July 1888) was one of the most formidable Mende warriors of the 19th century. He waged many campaigns, some in support of allies, but in later life largely as a mercenary and freebooter.

He was born about 1850 at Manjolu in present-day Kpejewa chiefdom in the Kailahun district. From childhood he made clear his determination to become nothing else but a warrior. Accused of having an affair with one of the wives of a local ruler, he was sold as a slave, eventually ending up in the possession of Makavoray (*q.v.*) who taught him the use of the sword.

He soon became a professional, and his first great military campaign is known to history as the 'Kpo-veh' wars (which took place in about the 1880s in Upper Mende country). These wars resulted in the expulsion of Benya of Blama from Makavoray's territories round Tikonko in present-day Bo district.

Benya, a local chief, had several times attacked Makavoray's country, and Ndawa vowed he would teach him a lesson. He invited Kai Londo (*q.v.*), then a little-known Kissi warrior, to join him in hostilities against Benya, and they successfully routed him from Makavoray's lands.

Meanwhile, in the far south of his master's country, Ndawa had built his own military stronghold at Wende, comprising a chain of 13 towns. From here he invited Kai Londo to continue the fight against Benya, who had by this time escaped north to Kono country. Much booty was acquired during this adventure, but Ndawa cheated Kai Londo over the division of the spoils and they quarreled. Ndawa then threatened to destroy the state of Luawa in the far east of Sierra Leone, where Kai Londo had settled, and this led to the famous confrontation at Ngiehun where Kai Londo defeated Ndawa. After this Ndawa promised to leave Luawa in peace.

But other areas had little chance of peace. Ndawa, was hired by rival parties with quarrels to settle. In 1886 he threatened to sack Bundasuma to the south on the Moa River and was only prevented by the action of Governor Sir Samuel Rowe (terms of office 1877-80, 1885-88) who persuaded Makovoray to stop him. The following year, Ndawa and another warrior, Makaya, were hired to fight in the succession disputes in the Gallinas. During this offensive the ruler of Bandasuma, a woman named Malo or Nalo, was captured, and the British customs post at Sulima raided.

This angered Governor Rowe who sent a special service officer, Capt. Coupland Crawford, to Sulima to take charge. He was instructed only to repel attacks, but, under pressure from local people, particularly traders, he overstepped his instructions and led an unauthorized expedition against Largo, Makaya's stronghold. There he released several thousand slaves, and Makaya fled.

Ndawa was at the time absent campaigning in Dama, where he unexpectedly met his end. Breaking one of the conventions of pre-colonial warfare, a young 'war sparrow' (one of the rank and file of the army) attacked the great warrior and severed the main artery in his left heel. "Only a great warrior puts an end to his counterpart," goes the Mende saying. So Ndawa cried out, having taken refuge in the buttress of a large tree, calling on Jemi Lenjeh, the leader of the 'sparrows' and a better-known warrior, to come and 'finish him.''

In this unlikely fashion, in July 1888, the brief but dramatic career of Ndawa came to an end.

ARTHUR ABRAHAM

BIBLIOGRAPHY: Arthur Abraham, *Mende Government and Politics Under Colonial Rule*, Freetown, 1978; Christopher Fyfe, *A History of Sierra Leone*, London, 1962; M. Gorvie, *Our Peoples of the Sierra Leone Protectorate*, London, 1944; N.C. Hollins, "A Short History of Luawa Chiefdom," *Sierra Leone Studies*, June, 1929.

NEMGBANA

Nemgbana (circa 1775-February 11, 1793) or Naimbana, was regent of the Koya Temne in Sierra Leone. By signing a treaty with British settlers he alienated part of his country, unwittingly preparing the way, like many other African rulers, for the European partition of Africa.

In the late 18th century many of the coastal states of Sierra Leone were ruled by Mandinka, Fula, or Soso immigrants from the north. From 1775 an immigrant (probably a Mandinka) ruled the Temne of Koya, an important state which included the Sierra Leone peninsula and adjoining mainland where the harbor and watering place frequented by Europeans was located. These travelers paid customs and other dues to the ruler.

The French traveler Golberry recorded the regent's name as 'Panabouro,' but he was more usually known by the title of 'Nemgbana', meaning regent. Tall, thin, and dignified, he had great influence in the country, but never held the title of king, though Europeans often referred to him as such. His capital was at Robana, up the Sierra Leone estuary. In 1785, he granted a French officer land on Gambia Island, a small island not far from the modern town of Hastings. But it was so unhealthy that the French abandoned it after a few years.

In 1787, prospective settlers from England, sponsored by Granville Sharp (1735-1813), a fervent campaigner against slavery, arrived in Sierra Leone. Nemgbana's deputy, King Tom, who lived on what it today still called King Tom Point, Freetown, let them land. Though Nemgbana apparently consented, he did not make any formal agreement with them, and when King Tom died in 1788 he told them to leave.

In August, however, he changed his mind and put his mark to a treaty by which he gave up all claim to a stretch of territory 9 or 10 miles long, and 20 miles wide. Normally in West Africa rulers only allowed Europeans to settle in return for annual rents, and retained ultimate sovereignty over the ceded place, whether fort, settlement, or hut. But Nemgbana, by this treaty, renounced sovereignty altogether—probably unwittingly, for he could not read English—in return for an assortment of trade goods.

In 1791 King Tom's successor, King Jimmy, quarreled with the settlers and destroyed their town. It was then refounded under the name Freetown by a British trading company, the Sierra Leone Company. Nemgbana permitted them to settle, and acted as landlord and protector. The company's governors, however, refused to make any further agreement with him for the land, maintaining that he had ceded it in perpetuity under the 1788 treaty and had no more rights to it. He

seems to have accepted this situation, and remained on friendly terms with them until his death on February 11, 1793.

During the time he had been negotiating with the French, Nemgbana had sent one of his sons to be educated in France. Another son was brought up a Muslim. A third went to England under the care of the directors of the Sierra Leone Company, and received a strict Christian education. Eventually this son returned with dreams of becoming a missionary in Africa, but fell ill on the voyage and died as soon as he landed. This was Prince John Frederick Nemgbana (q.v.).

By renouncing sovereignty over the Colony, Nemgbana introduced into West African political practice a new principle with far-reaching consequences. It was ultimately to deprive many rulers of their territories.

CHRISTOPHER FYFE

BILBLIOGRAPHY: Christopher Fyfe, *A History of Sierra Leone,* London, 1962.

NEMGBANA, J.F.

John Frederick Nemgbana, or Naimbana (circa 1768-June 1793), the son of Nemgbana (q.v.), regent of the Koya Temne, had an untimely death. Educated in England, where he was known as Prince Naimbana, he expected to become a missionary in his own country, but died on his return.

His elder brother Pedro, also known as Bartholomew, having already been educated in France, his father agreed to send John Frederick to England to be educated at the expense of the Sierra Leone Company. He sailed for England in the care of Alexander Falconbridge, an agent of the company, in the summer 1791. During the voyage Falconbridge's wife, Anna Maria, later to become the author of *Narrative of Two Voyages to the River Sierra Leone* (1794), taught him to read and write, and found him an intelligent pupil.

In England, Nemgbana became known as the "Black Prince." The philanthropist Granville Sharp (1753-1813), a Member of Parliament, a leading abolitionist, and founder of the Province of Freedom colony for freed slaves, took an interest in him. He placed Nemgbana's education in the hands of a Church of England clergyman, living in the country, who was certified by two bishops as an appropriate tutor. The hope was expressed that Nemgbana would become "as useful to Africa as Alfred and the first Peter were to their respective countries,' and his virtues were enumerated in a tract called *The African*

Prince, the cover of which showed him turning away disdainfully from an unsuitable book.

His father, the regent, died in February of 1793, and John Frederick returned to Sierra Leone in the same year, with the intention of preaching the gospel and making converts. Upon his arrival in Freetown, however, he was taken ashore dying, having fallen fatally ill in the course of his return voyage from England. His brother Pedro circulated the rumor that John Frederick had been poisoned lest he reveal the white men's secrets to his countrymen. A long dispute ensued between the ship's captain and the family which increased ill-feelings without shedding further light on the cause of Nemgbana's death.

Writing about Nemgbana in September 1791, Mrs. Falconbridge gave the following description of his appearance and character:

Writing about Nemgbana in September 1791, Mrs. Falconbridge gave the following description of his appearance and character:

> His person is rather below the ordinary, inclining to grossness, his skin nearly jet-black, eyes keenly intelligent, nose flat, teeth unconnected and filed sharp after the custom of his country, his legs a little bandied, and his deportment easy, manly and confident withal. In his disposition he is surly, but has cunning enough to smother it, where he thinks his interest is concerned; he is pettish and implacable, but I think grateful and attached to those he considers his friends; nature has been bountiful in giving him a sound intellect, very capable of improvement, and he also possesses a great thirst for knowledge.
>
> While with me, although it was seldom in my power, now and then I amused myself with teaching him the alphabet which he quickly learned and before we parted, could read any common print surprisingly well.
>
> He is not wanting in discernment and has already discovered the weak side of his patrons which he strives to turn to good account and I dare say, by his natural subtlety, will in time advantage himself considerably by it.

CYRIL P. FORAY

BIBLIOGRAPHY: *The African Prince*, pamphlet, London, circa 1792; Anna Maria Falconbridge, *Narrative of Two Voyages to the River Sierra Leone, during the Years 1791-2-3*, London, 1794; Christopher Fyfe, *A History of Sierra Leone*, London, 1962; A.H.Rose, "Prince Naimbana in England," *Sierra Leone Studies*, June, 1957.

NJIAKUNDOHUN

Njiakundohun (late 18th century-?1860s) was the leader of the first band of invading Mende warriors who moved westwards across Sierra Leone in the mid-19th century. A great warrior and a formidable orator, he and another leader built the town of Senehun on the upper Bumpe River after many wanderings.

Two or three generations before the British established formal rule over the hinterland of Sierra Leone, clans of warriors originating somewhere in the region of Gorama Mende, in the north of present-day Kenema district, migrated westwards in two waves of invaders. They were in ethnic terms a pure branch of the Mende, but due to other cultural influences they spoke the Mende language with a slight variation. Their point of departure is believed to be the town of Kaweya, now derelict, in Gorama Mende.

The areas invaded by these warriors were inhabited by a group of people called the Banta, about whom there are many legendary stories. They have been identified as a "small group of Temne, cut off from the main Temne population during the tribal wars of the 19th century and now fused with Sherbro." Fyfe (see Bibliography) states that when a Fula, the Fula Mansa, became ruler of Yoni Temne, some Temne, afraid of being sold as slaves, fled and settled near the Jong River in the south, and became known as Mabanta Temne. Temne traditions from Yoni hold that the Banta were a Temne group who moved south and conquered the area between the Jong River and the sea, creating a state centered on Gbangbatok, which included Yoni. The date is uncertain but must have been much earlier than the 19th century. What is not in dispute is their Temne connection, since Banta is an isolated dialect of the Temne language.

According to tradition, the Banta were possessed of a powerful fetish, and were river worshipers. It is also said that they were mysteriously transformed into elephants instead of dying when they grew old. When death was approaching, the dying Banta searched for an old deserted farm-house containing four mortars, one pestle, and two winnowers. He put his hands and feet into the mortars, fixed the winnowers to his ears, and the pestle to the front of his head. He then prayed to his gods and was transformed into an elephant—the mortars forming his limbs, the winnowers his ears, and the pestle his trunk. Thus every elephant that was shot spoke a Banta word before dying.

The new Mende immigrants apparently met with opposition from the Banta resulting in a few bloody battles. But, unable to repel the invaders, the Banta took refuge in the south. The older ones were transformed into elephants, and others prayed to their river gods who opened up the rivers to them, so that they disappeared from the world.

Among the first horde of Mende warriors were many famous names—Kaoleh, Tongovila, Momoh Gete, Vanja Lekpeh, Kambayenge, Vonjo, Gbo, Kamagai, Kowa, Nyawa, Sei, and Nijiakundohun, their leader. The company marched on to the town of Gbondou (perhaps located north of present-day Bo district), situated on a crystal river in which were found some powerful magical gems called 'wali,' in Mende. These became objects of worship. After some time spent at Gbondou, they went on to Walihun, in present-day Nyawa-Lenge chiefdom, where they left Nyawa to establish his own settlement. Sei branched off a little further than Nyawa and established Seilenga. Tongovila and Momoh Gete, assisted by Vonjo, one of the hardiest warriors, established Monghere (Lunya), while between Seilenga and Monghere, Vanja Lekepeh and Kambayenge established Mandu (Vanjelu). The main contingent moved to Kpa, then to Liange, now Fulawahun, in Kakua chiefdom, in present-day Bo district. It was from this center that the main party dispersed and founded the various sections of lower Kpaa-Mende, the name which the newcomers had already acquired.

The origins of the name Kpaa-Mende have been variously attributed. It may have been derived from the little town Kpa, through which the party had passed. Migeod (see Bibliography) maintains that 'Kpa' signifies 'different'—thus, 'different Mende.' This interpretation has no support among the Mende. It rests on a phonetic misunderstanding between 'Gba,' which does indeed mean different, and 'Kpa.' The generally accepted explanation is that the invaders had a discipline so strict and displayed such heroic bravery, that the country where they lived came to be called 'Kpai Loh,' conveying the idea of a country inhabited by a hard-hearted people, almost totally lacking in sympathy. From this is derived 'Kpaaloh,' i.e. Kpaa country, and ultimately Kpaa-Mende. The Wunde society (a secret society peculiar to the Kpaa-Mende, and higher than the Poro society) embodies these stern characteristics.

Of the party that moved from the nuclear area at Liange, Njiakundohun was not only the leader, but also the most renowned. As a warrior and orator he was supreme, and he is also described as a 'native lawyer.' He married the daughter of the chief of Kaweya, Maboi Manga, and they stayed some time at Gbograma, in present-day Bo district, where they had four children—Soma, Ali Kongo, Goba and Lamboi. Soma was later known as Madam Yoko (q.v.).

Eventually the family moved on in company with the remainder of the warrior band. Njiakundohun and Kamagai built Senehun (in the upper Kamagai chiefdom), and Vonjo established Gondama (in the Majei chiefdom).

When Soma reached puberty, she was initiated into the Bondo (or Sande) women's society at Senehun, and graduated with the society name of Yoko. Shortly after this she was engaged to Gongoima, a great warrior who lived at Senehun Ngieya, in Kamagai chiefdom, and subsequently married him. It is recalled that he wore a belt of large pealing bells round his waist in order to frighten his enemies in war.

Gongoima loved Yoko so deeply that he wanted her company wherever he went, and took the unprecedented step of having her initiated into the Poro, the men's secret society. After a short spell of happy marriage, Yoko's love for Gongoima began to fade because of his extreme jealousy. The marriage failed, and eventually Yoko filed a successful divorce suit in accordance with native law and custom. She then married the son of Kaoleh of Taiama, Gbenjei.

Njiakundohun died not long after his daughter's second marriage, followed shortly by his wife. So ended the life of the leader who had led the Kpaa-Mende in their greatest period of expansion.

ARTHUR ABRAHAM

BIBLIOGRAPHY: Arthur Abraham, *Mende Government and Politics Under Colonial Rule*; Christopher Fyfe, *A History of Sierra Leone*, London, 1962; F. Migeod, *A View of Sierra Leone*, London, 1926.

NYAGUA

Nyagua (circa 1842-1906) was a warrior chief of great consequence in eastern Mende country, and ruler of Panguma, one of the largest states in the hinterland of Sierra Leone. Despite various co-operative exploits with the British, his relations with the colonial administration were never entirely cordial and his enormous influence was seen as a threat during the uprising against the British in 1898.

He was the son of Faba Kpovowa, a third generation warrior, who had established his rule around the town of Dodo in present-day Kenema district. Apprenticed to a famous warrior Makaya, Nyagua was himself a fighter with a wide reputation before his father died.

In the 1870s, during the Mende war, Nyagua fought a campaign of reprisals against the Kono to the northeast because of Kono attacks against his father's lands. The Kono were routed and he succeeded in capturing much of the southern half of their country. Later, he enlisted the help of his former enemies, now vassals, to overcome Ndawa (q.v.), a marauding professional warrior, who had threatened Faba and attacked one of his towns. Before the expedition set out, however, Ndawa restored the loot taken in battle, but not before a few skirmishes between their respective followers had taken place.

Nyagua founded the town of Panguma, in the northern part of present-day Kenema district, around which grew the later Bambara chiefdom. Other warriors among Faba's forces founded settlements or fought on behalf of defenseless people until a large area of land came under the jurisdiction of Dodo, including the chiefdoms of Nongowa and Gorama in present-day Kenema district, Kpeje in Kailahun district, and other places.

In 1889, Faba died, leaving extensive territories to be governed. After consultation, it was agreed that since Faba's military comrades were growing old, and since Nyagua was a renowned warrior, he should become ruler and take charge of the political administration of this huge state. He personally ruled the province that grew up round Panguma, and appointed administrators for the other provinces from among his father's famous military leaders. Thus Fakoi controlled Dodo, while Kogbandi Vangahum administered Nongowa.

On May 25, 1889, the British travelling commissioner, T.J. Alldridge, signed a treaty of friendship with Nyagua, who was granted a stipend of £20 so long as he honored the terms of the treaty. But a personality clash developed between the two men. Nyagua, unimpressed by the urgency of Britain's grand colonial design, refused to attend a meeting at Alldridge's convenience, and the latter described him as a most arrogant man, unsufficiently courteous to the British government and demanding much ceremonial deference himself.

Nyagua's 'arrogance' was not particularly marked. He co-operated with the British on several occasions. In 1889, he eventually gave up the warrior Makaya, his old master, to the authorities, after some hesitation on account of the opposition of certain up-country chiefs. Makaya had led many raids to the Kittam and Gallinas districts in the extreme south, and together with Ndawa had actually attacked the British customs post at Sulima. Nyagua, moreover, had been helped by the colonial government forces who had destroyed the 13 towns comprising a large military encampment at Wende, which had been blocking his access to the important trade route to the coast.

In 1890 the colonial administration arranged for Nyagua's son, Gbanyeh, to be admitted to the Church Missionary Society Grammar School in Freetown at government expense. When the Sofa (mounted warriors of the Mandinka empire-builder, Samori Touré) attacked two of Nyagua's towns, they lost no time in sending government troops against them, and Nyagua's warriors formed part of the expeditionary force that destroyed the Sofa and killed their leader.

The administration, however, was still suspicious of Nyagua. His traditional quarrels with other rulers were misinterpreted as a determined wish to prevent trade and its profits. And when the Protectorate was declared in 1896 he was viewed with even stronger suspicion. His town of Panguma was exempt from the house tax, which had been imposed along with the declaration. But district commissioner J.E.C. Blakeney, with whom Nyagua was not on cordial terms, reported that there were rumors that the chief had been holding secret meetings with other rulers in the neighborhood with the intention of driving the British from his territory.

Threatened with arrest, Nyagua ordered his subjects to disarm. But official fears were still unallayed. The following month, in May, 1898, he was arrested and held prisoner at Panguma, where a large force of his followers staged a siege in order to rescue him. There were brief skirmishes, but no sustained campaign, and the resistance soon faded out.

Brought to Freetown as a prisoner, Nyagua petitioned that "he did nothing that in his judgment could be construed as rebellious or inconsistent with justice and truth." The attorney general felt that Nyagua's grievances were legally justified, but advised that for security reasons he should be detained for some time. It was intended to have him released at a later date, but the discovery that Nyagua had been sending secret messages to his people, threatening them for not resisting his capture, caused a change of attitude. He was banished by administrative order to the Gold Coast as a political prisoner, along with Bai Bureh (q.v.), the Temne leader in the 1898 rising, and Gbana Lewis, the overlord of Sherbro. He died there in 1906.

ARTHUR ABRAHAM

BIBLIOGRAPHY: Arthur Abraham, *Mende Government and Politics Under Colonial Rule*, "Nyagua, the British and the Hut Tax War," *International Journal of African Historical Studies*, 1972; M. Gorvie, *Our Peoples of the Sierra Leone Protectorate*, London, 1944.

OMARU

Al Haji Omaru (1851?-April 26, 1931) was a Fula trading agent for a French company who became leader of the migrant Fula population in Freetown. A man of progressive ideas, he did much to promote the educational and religious welfare of his compatriots and was held in high esteem by both Christians and Muslims.

He was born about 1851 in the town of Jamburia in Futa Jallon to the north of Sierra Leone, and migrated to Freetown, as did many of his Fula countrymen, where he was employed as interpreter for the firm of the Compagnie Française de l'Afrique Occidentale (C.F.A.O.) around 1880. As a loyal employee he took an active interest in the business of the firm, and soon became a shop-keeper, buying kola nuts for his employers. On several occasions he was given the responsibility of heading commercial missions to the rulers of the northern rivers as well as to Futa Jallon, his original home. These missions were invariably successful.

Throughout the 19th century immigrants (called 'strangers') had been flowing steadily into Freetown, either as commercial agents, traders, or wage-earning laborers. As their numbers increased it became necessary to elect a chief or 'tribal ruler' to look after the welfare of the different ethnic groups. Al Haji Omaru was elected chief of the Fula in Freetown in 1902, and ceremonially installed at Victoria Park (now Sewa Grounds) in the presence of the governor and chiefs. He was given the title of Alimamy or Al Imam.

One of his chief concerns was to establish proper educational facilities for the Fula. He succeeded in getting the government to open a school for the sons of Fula residents in Freetown, where the pupils were taught Arabic and English. It was called Madrasa Islami, and at one time was housed on his own premises in Jenkins Street. Through his interest in education he was selected as a member of the Mohammedan Board of Education, created in 1906 to watch over the interests of Muslim children when the school for the sons of chiefs was established at Bo. He remained a member until the Board was dissolved in 1910.

He was also interested in furthering the religious life of his people. He built a mosque for them in Jenkins Street, and in 1911 he made the pilgrimage to Mecca, where he was given the title of Al Haji, his expenses being paid by the C.F.A.O. in recognition for his loyal services. By this time he was wealthy enough to buy shares in the firm that had previously employed him.

In his later years Al Haji Omaru was also appointed a Justice of the Peace, and when he died on April 26, 1931, not only the commissioner of police and a contingent of the police force, but many representatives of the Freetown community, Muslim and Christian alike, were present at the graveside to pay him their last respects.

ARTHUR ABRAHAM

BIBLIOGRAPHY: Mohammed Suleiman Jallo, "A Short Sketch of the Life and Work of the Late Alimamy Jamburia, Tribal Ruler of the Freetown Foulahs," *Sierra Leone Studies,* September, 1939.

PARKES, J.C.E.

James Charles Ernest Parkes (1861-August 10, 1899) was head of the Department of Native Affairs during the period of preparation for the British Protectorate, declared in 1896. A highly educated Krio (Creole) with an entensive knowledge of the interior of Sierra Leone, he wished to establish a co-operative partnership between British and Krios in the administration of the Protectorate. His ideas, however, did not find favor with the British, who preferred the tougher authority of district commissioners backed by armed forces.

Parkes was born in Freetown in 1861, the son of a disbanded West Indian soldier and his part-Nova Scotian wife. He was educated at the Church Missionary Society Grammar School, after which he worked in the Queen's Advocate department before going to Britain to study law. Illness cut short his studies there, and on his return home in 1882 he was appointed assistant clerk to the commandant of Sherbro. In 1884, he was transferred to the Aborigines Department of the colonial secretary's office and became involved in 'native affairs.'

His knowledge of this subject was gained almost entirely from Thomas George Lawson (*q.v.*), the long-serving government interpreter. The two men co-operated in preparing a long account of the districts and peoples in the vicinity of the Colony and their relations with the colonial administration. Lawson provided the material from his rich accumulation of knowledge and Parkes worked on the compilation. Both men were highly acclaimed for their work.

When Lawson first indicated in 1886 that he wanted to retire, there were doubts as to whether Parkes had gained sufficient respect and trust from the people of the interior to replace such an outstanding predecessor. At the same time, Parkes, dissatisfied with his low salary of £100 per annum, asked to be transferred to another area in British West Africa where he believed he would be better paid.

But as Lawson's retirement became imminent, everything was done to retain Parkes' services. Before he finally retired in 1888, Lawson recommended him as his successor. He was appointed superintendent of the Aborigines Department at a salary of £150 a year. The department was moved from the colonial secretary's office and placed directly under the governor's control.

Parkes' work extended rapidly. He was involved in formulating and implementing new policies of treaty-making, and with the construction of a frontier road, linking important produce-growing areas in the interior. In 1891 the Aborigines Department became known as the Department of Native Affairs with

Parkes as secretary. Once again he demanded a higher salary commensurate with the work he was doing, and in 1893 it was increased to £250 with annual increments of £20.

In 1890 the Frontier Police Force was created with duties to guard the frontier road and keep the peace in the interior. It quickly became a rival to the Department of Native Affairs, Parkes and Captain E.A.W. Lendy of the Frontier Police vying with each other as to which agency should advise the administration on interior affairs, especially concerning the activities of Samori Touré, the Mandinka empire-builder. Parkes was also openly critical of the Frontier policemen in their dealings with chiefs and their people. They tended to act as 'little despots,' he said, when not under official observation.

In November 1892, Parkes suggested that a protectorate should be declared over the area of British influence, and five Krio 'political agents' appointed to administer the different subdivisions. Their role would be to 'advise and direct' chiefs on such matters as clearing roads, implementing new agricultural schemes, and settling disputes. They would also prevent the imposition of severe punishment and see that treaty provisions were honored. Parkes' suggestion of Krio administrators was intended to reduce the influence of the Frontier Police Force, and its rejection was a personal setback for him. The role of the Force increased, whilst that of Parkes and the Department of Native Affairs was correspondingly reduced.

The clash between Parkes and Lendy continued over the question of Samori. Parkes advised the administration to maintain friendly relations with him, but Lendy claimed that, following reports from Frontier policemen, military action was necessary. Conflict between the two men reached its height when Lendy made various unfounded accusations against Parkes, one of which was that he was in receipt of bribes from Samori, and that his reports were therefore unreliable. He also claimed that Muslim members of the Department of Native Affairs were acting as Samori's arms-buying agents in Freetown.

Lendy continued to press for military action, and having persuaded the War Office in London to sanction it, a military expedition was launched. It resulted in the unfortunate events at Waima near the eastern frontier on December 23, 1893, when British and French forces, each mistaking the other for Samori's Sofa troops, fired on each other with many fatal casualties, including Lendy himself.

In spite of Parkes' total denial of Lendy's allegations, Lord Ripon, Secretary of State, ordered an enquiry to be held. This was conducted by the Executive Council in 1894 and it resulted in Parkes being 'unanimously and fully acquitted,' and his public image completely reinstated.

In 1894, Sir Frederick Cardew took up his appointment as governor, embarking on a series of three extensive tours of the interior, accompanied by Parkes. These were in preparation for the declaration of a protectorate which eventually took place in 1896.

Parkes and the governor held different views on taxation in the Protectorate. Accepting the need for taxation, Parkes held that a poll tax was preferable to a house tax and suggested a payment of 20 cents per head. He was also anxious that Frontier policemen should have nothing to do with tax collection, since they roused fears of intimidation. Cardew, however, opposed the idea of a poll tax believing that it could be too easily evaded.

Realizing that the collection of house tax would probably provoke opposition, Parkes suggested that district commissioners should find out the taxable values of the different chiefdoms and leave it to the chiefs to collect the amount, rather than doing it directly with the assistance of Frontier policemen. In this way friction might be avoided. But this suggestion was also rejected, and Cardew's scheme for collection went ahead as planned, resulting in the widespread war of resistance of 1898.

After the appointment of officers of the Frontier Police Force as district commissioners, Parkes' influence speedily declined. His duties were limited to receiving communications from district commissioners, approving payments of stipends to chiefs, recommending the appointment of minor officials such as messengers and interpreters, and making transport arrangements. He was ignored by some district commissioners who wrote directly to the colonial secretary, although the letters were referred to him for comments.

His declining importance was underlined by Cardew in his evidence before the Chalmers inquiry commission, set up after the 1898 war of resistance. Cardew stated that he regarded district commissioners 'as being better able to become cognisant of what is going on in the Protectorate than our official here' (meaning Parkes). He also felt that with uniforms and armed men at their disposal they commanded more respect—a respect, he might have added, induced by fear.

Parkes became ill in early 1899 and applied for leave, but various duties prevented him from going on leave. He died of nephritis on August 10, at the early age of 38. With his death disappeared the Native Affairs Department, which was absorbed into the colonial secretary's office. But it was on his work—and also Lawson's—that later administrators of the Protectorate were able to set up an effective and efficient system of administration.

AKIWANDE J. LASITE

BIBLIOGRAPHY: R.P.M. Davies, *History of the Sierra Leone Battalion of the Royal West African Frontier Force*, Freetown, 1932; Christopher Fyfe, "European and Creole Influence in the Hinterland of Sierra Leone before 1896," *Sierra Leone Studies*, June, 1956, *A History of Sierra Leone*, London, 1962; J.D. Hargreaves, "The Evolution of the Native Affairs Department," *Sierra Leone Studies,* December, 1954; A.J. Lasite, "The Department of Native Affairs and the Development of British Policy in the Northern Interior of Sierra Leone 1850-1900," unpublished M.A. thesis, University of Sierra Leone, 1975.

PETERS, T.

Thomas Peters (circa 1738-June 25/26, 1792) was a courageous Afro-American slave who escaped from his master and eventually became leader of the black emigrants from Nova Scotia to Sierra Leone.

He was of African descent, and worked as a millwright at Wilmington, North Carolina. In 1776, during the War of American Independence, he ran away and joined the British army, becoming a sergeant in the Black Pioneers. At the end of the war he and many of his fellow Loyalists were taken to Nova Scotia where the British government promised them land. But when it was apportioned the white Loyalists got priority, and the former slaves tended to be overlooked. Some were allocated remote patches of forestland, while many received nothing. Without land they feared they would relapse into their former state of slavery.

Peters waited vainly at Annapolis, Nova Scotia, where he had arrived in 1784, without getting his land. Finally, realizing that the Nova Scotian government would take no action, he determined to go to England to complain to the British government. This required immense courage. Poor, barely literate, and without influence, by venturing on board ship he was risking recapture as a slave, should some unscrupulous captain choose to take him to an American port. He also risked reprisals from the Nova Scotian government. Nevertheless, he made the voyage to London in 1791, where he made contact with the directors of the Sierra Leone Company who were seeking settlers for Sierra Leone. With their promises of a new home in Africa for him and his people, he returned to Nova Scotia to recruit emigrants.

Peters assumed that the directors were going to put

him in charge of the scheme. Instead they sent a British naval officer, John Clarkson (*q.v.*), to superintend the embarkation and voyage. This disappointment embittered Peters, and he decided not to co-operate with Clarkson. He sailed for Sierra Leone in one of the emigrant ships in January 1792, with his wife Sally and their children. On landing he sent an official letter to the secretary of state in London, reporting the arrival of the settlers. But he was again rebuffed, and Clarkson was given charge of the settlement.

In Nova Scotia, Peters had been the people's representative and spokesman. In Sierra Leone, Clarkson, realizing he was a potential enemy, subtly undermined his influence by winning their affection and confidence for himself. When Peters tried to persuade them to choose him as their official leader, Clarkson summoned the settlers, denounced Peters as a mutineer, and by a passionate, emotional speech won over his audience. When eventually Peters called for a showdown, asking them to choose unequivocally between himself and Clarkson, no one supported him. Sick at heart, Peters fell ill with the malaria that was decimating the settlement in its first months, and on the night of June 25-26, 1792, he died.

Peters, tragedy had a curious sequel. Would-be historians in the 20th century prolonged his life and invented an imaginary career for him, so that even quite reputable books still repeat fantasies about his becoming a member of the Sierra Leone Legislative Council which was inaugurated in 1863, 72 years after his death!

Nevertheless, Peters' part in the history of Sierra Leone is an important one. Without his initiative the Nova Scotian settlers would never have left Nova Scotia, and without them the Sierra Leone settlement would have failed.

CHRISTOPHER FYFE

BIBLIOGRAPHY: Christopher Fyfe, *A History of Sierra Leone,* London, 1962.

POREKERE

Foray Benia Porekere (18?-December 28, 1893) was an able general who became leader of the Sofa, troops of the great Mandinka emperor, Samori Touré. His activities in northeastern Sierra Leone caused much trouble to both British and French colonial governments.

By 1892, when he became leader, the French had occupied the town of Heremakono, to the northeast of Koranko country. This prevented the Sofa from using their usual route to Freetown, where they obtained arms, and which ran through Falaba and southwest to Port Loko. So Kemoko Bilali (*q.v.*), the Sofa general formerly in charge of the Sierra Leone hinterland, sent Porekere to open a more easterly route through Koranko and Konike Temne countries.

Porekere built a number of strongholds in Konike country in eastern Sierra Leone. He started his assignment by making an alliance with the southern Koranko, whom he had apparently subdued, against the Konike. A number of towns were attacked and destroyed, but Porekere later fell out with the Koranko over the distribution of captives taken in battle, and attacked his former allies.

At this point the Native Affairs Department, wanting to prevent colonial troops being sent against him, intervened. Its head of department, J.C.E. Parkes (*q.v.*) wrote to Porekere warning him off Konike. Porekere obeyed, retired eastwards, and captured Tecuyama and Levuma, two towns claimed by the powerful Mende ruler Nyagua (*q.v.*). It appears that a chief, Tellu of Kuruwa, who had a land dispute with Nyagua, had asked for his assistance.

Although pacifists in the colonial administration were opposed to violence against the Sofa, they could not suppress the report to the Colonial Office that Porekere had attacked Nyagua, a king in treaty with the British. Orders were given for an expedition against him to set out at once.

The French, who had been fighting Samori since 1871, were also determined to put an end to Sofa hegemony and claim former Sofa-controlled areas as French by right of conquest. A French military officer, Lieutenant Gaston-Maxime Maritz, had moved into this area and joined forces with Kono warriors, subjects of Nyagua's, in driving Porekere out of Tecuyama. Porekere then retreated further northwest to Bagbema, from which point he joined in as a mercenary on one side of a land dispute involving two Mende chiefs, Foray and Vonjo. Porekere helped Foray in attacking Vonjo at Tungea.

Meanwhile the British expedition had set out. It was led by Captain E.A.W. Lendy with Captain A.B. Ellis commanding the troops. Hearing of Maritz's activities in the area, Ellis sent an advance warning of their arrival to the French officer. It would appear that this information failed to reach Maritz, who was acting on information from his Kono allies that a large Sofa force was encamped at Waima in eastern Kono country. This force was, of course, Lendy's. British and French each mistook the other for Sofa, and attacked each other at Waima with the loss of a number of soldiers on both sides, including the two commanders, Lendy and Maritz.

A Krio sub-inspector, Charles Taylor, was also on his way with earlier orders to join Lendy on the expedition. But learning that Poekere and Foray were marching towards Tungea, he hurried to meet them there. The Sofa attacked at Varma, a town subject to Tungea, where Taylor was encamped, and were badly defeated by his troops losing 250 dead and 150 taken prisoner. Among those killed was Porekere.

C. MAGBAILY FYLE AND ARTHUR ABRAHAM

BIBLIOGRAPHY: Christopher Fyfe, *A History of Sierra Leone*, London, 1962; Y. Person, "Porekere et le Drame de Waima" ("Porekere and the Drama of Waima"), *Cahiers d'Etudes Africaines,* VI, 18, 1965.

PORTER, A.T.

Arthur Thomas Porter (1834-1908) was a wealthy business man who plied a dubious but profitable trade in supplying indentured labor from Freetown to the Congo (present-day Zaire). He became consular agent for the Congo Free State, but his appointment was terminated after protests mounted in England concerning his activities.

He was born in 1834, the son of an Afro-West Indian father who became manager of the village of

Kent at Cape Shilling, near Freetown, in the 1830s, and a mother of Maroon descent. His career started modestly as an artisan, employed as a mason in the building of Samaria Church during the 1850s. Two decades later he had become a highly successful businessman.

After the abolition of the transatlantic slave trade, and following the successful maneuvers of King Leopold of Belgium for the recognition of his Congo Free State by the great powers at the Berlin Conference of 1884-85, the way was open for the export of indentured laborers to work there. With a flow of immigrants into Freetown from the interior, private contractors were well placed to expedite 'indentured laborers' after signing a contract with them before a magistrate. Given the conditions in which contract laborers worked in the Congo, these contractors were in reality nothing more than slave traders, operating with the blessing of the colonial administration.

Porter was one of the biggest exporters of labor to the Congo. He had a flourishing business at Gibraltar Wharf, below Kissy Street, supplying contract materials for military installations. He found it more profitable, however, to ship laborers without official sanction.

In 1891 complaints were made that laborers shipped to the Congo were being badly treated, and Porter was sent to investigate. He found much dissatisfaction, but also evidence that some of their complaints were exaggerated. In consequence, no official protest was made by the Colonial Office in London. Instead, Porter was appointed consular agent for the Congo Free State in 1893.

Earlier, in 1892, Porter had built an imposing stone hotel in Wilberforce Street, called Porter's Royal Hotel. It was modeled on his recollections of establishments seen in Europe, which he had first visited in 1887, and had a European manageress.

The recruiting of labor for the Congo aroused protest in England. The United States ambassador in London made accusations that Porter was to all intents and purposes reviving the slave trade, and it was reported that he had been contacted to supply labor for the South African mines. When the Congo government terminated his appointment as consular agent, the Freetown administration took stringent measures to restrict the export of laborers. Thereafter effective control was imposed to end a scandalous situation.

After this reversal of fortune, Porter became a devout churchman. On December 7, 1895, he was reported to be among cathedral members signing an address to E.G. Ingham, bishop of Sierra Leone. By the time he died in 1908, he had become a member of the prestigious Anglican denomination, and was described as 'an ardent churchman and Treasurer of the Native Pastorate church.'

ARTHUR ABRAHAM

BIBLIOGRAPHY: Christopher Fyfe, *A History of Sierra Leone*, London, 1962; A.T. Porter, *Creoledom: A Study of the Development of Freetown Society*, London, 1963.

RAINY, W.

William Rainy (circa 1819-1878) was a courageous and distinguished Afro-West Indian barrister who devoted himself to fighting color prejudice in Sierra Leone and elsewhere in West Africa. A passionate defender of political rights, he was the first Sierra Leonean delegate to the Anti-Slavery Conference held in Paris in 1967.

He was born in Dominica in the West Indies about 1819, and migrated to Sierra Leone where he worked at the customs department from 1844-47. He then went to England where he studied law at the Inner Temple, returning to Freetown to set up a private practice which lasted from 1850-71.

Rainy was successful in his work at the Bar in Freetown, and gained considerable popularity in the general community. In the Sierra Leone courts he fought all cases that smacked of color prejudice. One example is the case of Dr. Robert Bradshaw, colonial surgeon. In November, 1864, Rainy brought an action against him for whipping his groom who had left his horse unattended in a rainstorm. Bradshaw sensibly settled the matter out of court with a payment of £30. A similar action was brought by Rainy against the colonial treasurer, Adolphus Pike, for striking his watchman. Certain businessmen retained Rainy merely to prevent him issuing writs against them.

Although he did once appear for the Crown, it was more usual for him to appear against it, as in the case of Whobay of Imperi, charged with the murder of Patience Peters, a recaptive from Popo in Dahomey (present-day Benin). His role was always that of champion of the helpless and oppressed. A shrewd and skillful debater, he often used ridicule to discredit his opponents in court, and occasionally provoked judges to discipline him to the extent, in one or two instances, of being charged and fined for contempt of court.

At a time when petitions were the most effective, if not the only, legitimate means of expressing a sense of public injustice, Rainy became almost a professional organizer of petitions. He was signatory to nearly all petitions to the Colonial Office protesting against colonial officers or unpopular government measures, and fell out with a series of governors—Sir Stephen

John Hill (term of office 1854-62), Major Samuel Wensley Blackall (term of office 1862-67), and even Sir Arthur Edward Kennedy (terms of office 1852-54 and 1868-72), with whom he was initially on very cordial terms.

Rainy's political protests and legal practice were not confined to Sierra Leone. He appealed successfully on several occasions to the judicial committee of the Privy Council in England, and appeared in person in an action at the Queen's Bench in London, thus becoming the first barrister of African origin to plead in the English courts. Through his initiative a number of questions relating to Sierra Leone were raised in the British Parliament. These included the dangers of trials without jury, as in the Sierra Leone Vice-Admiralty court, and the question of the professional competence of Judge Horatio Huggins, whom Rainy had exposed for imposing higher sentences than were legally warranted.

Rainy exercised a major influence, amounting almost to proprietary rights, over several local newspapers, including *The Sierra Leone Observer, The African Interpreter and Advocate,* and *The West African Liberator.* In these, as well as in overseas papers, such as *The African Times,* he attacked his critics and denounced his adversaries.

In 1867, he attended a meeting of the Anti-Slavery Conference in Paris where, as Sierra Leone's first delegate—to be followed by Samuel Lewis (*q.v.*)—he voiced the discontent of all West Africa. In a fiery impassioned speech he underlined the defects and imprecisions in the political rights of Sierra Leoneans. The French government awarded him a gold medal in recognition of the professional services he had given to French citizens who were his clients in Sierra Leone.

When Rainy returned to Sierra Leone he made sure that a local branch of the Anti-Slavery Society was set up in Freetown. In July, 1871, he left for London, a tired and sick man, destined never to return home again. In the same year he emigrated from London to Australia, where he died.

CYRIL P. FORAY

BIBLIOGRAPHY: Christopher Fyfe, *A History of Sierra Leone,* London, 1962; J.D. Hargreaves, *A Life of Sir Samuel Lewis,* London, 1958.

RASSIN, ALIMAMY

Alimamy Rassin (circa 1825-1890), chief of Mafonda, was that rarity among leaders, a resolute champion of peace. Remarkable in any age, his opposition to violence was all the more outstanding in 19th century Sierra Leone, where warrior chiefs were the norm.

He was born in Mafonda in what is now the Sanda Magbolonto chiefdom, Bombali district, in about 1825. He was the son of a Bunduka Fula from the Futa Toro district of Senegal, named Samba Jombor, and a Temne woman named Memuna Conteh. He was brought up in the home of his cousin, Alimamy Ahmadu, chief of Mafonda, since his restless father had left the country before his birth.

Alimamy Ahmadu instilled in the boy a total aversion to war in an age when violent conflicts were common. Rassin did well in the local Islamic school. He was a gifted pupil whose intelligence impressed both his teachers and fellow pupils. News of the child prodigy spread all over Sierra Leone and beyond, and there were frequent emissaries from Senegal seeking to take him back to the ancestral homeland of the Bunduka. Ahmadu, however, refused to part with the boy, who had come to regard him as his real father.

Over the years Rassin won the respect of the citizens of Mafonda, and when Alimamy Ahmadu died about 1845 he was the obvious choice to succeed him. But Rassin would not accept the honor immediately, and for 12 years following Ahmadu's death he remained the uninstalled chief of Mafonda. Meanwhile, in accordance with the Bunduka practice of expressing solidarity with the largely non-Muslim people of neighboring territories, Rassin married Adama Bomboh of Sanda Tenraran, in the Bombali district of what is now the Northern Province, and Ya Dankay, daughter of his uncle, Pa Bassi Conteh of Safroko Temne.

By 1857 the succession could be delayed no longer and Rassin was made chief without serious opposition. From the outset of his rule he made clear his hatred for war and any other form of violence, and set up a fund for the promotion of peace. Under the direction of the treasurer, Pa Santigie Bokari Kamara, this fund was replenished from fines levied in the chief's court. No price was too high for Rassin to pay in order to secure peace in troubled areas. He mediated successfully in political disputes in Sanda Tenraran, Tonko Limba, Yoni, and Bombali Temne territories, and on occasions would send his sons, especially his favorite, Samba, on such peace missions.

By 1885 the forces of the Mandinka emperor Samori had attacked the peoples of northern Sierra Leone, and various of his leading warriors had taken control of settlements in Koranko, Limba, and Temne country. But on reaching Mafonda the invaders were so impressed with the chiefdom's development under Rassin that they withdrew without causing much trouble. The colonial administration in Freetown, equally impressed by Rassin's moves to secure peace in the hinterland, offered him an annual stipend of 2,000 iron bars (a type of currency, one bar being equal to one shilling in the late 19th century). Rassin rejected the offer on the grounds that it was unethical to receive payment for the promotion of peace.

He was also a vigorous promoter of Islam in his chiefdom, and as a true believer did not hide his contempt for non-Muslims, especially those who held to traditional African religions. Like all leading chiefs of the 19th century, he had a large number of slaves whom he kept at a settlement called Miliki, where they engaged in the cultivation of the oil palm, among other things. Their condition was tolerable, and they seldom changed hands once they had become Rassin's property.

His grandson, Ahmadu Wurie (q.v.), once claimed that had Rassin been alive in 1898 he would have averted the confrontation between Bai Bureh (q.v.) and the British during the Hut Tax War. But Rassin died several years earlier in 1890, aged about 65, after a glorious reign of 33 years.

E. AMADU TURAY

BIBLIOGRAPHY: A. Wurie and E. Hirst, *Rassin*, London, 1968.

RAYMOND, W.

William Raymond (1815-November 26, 1847) was the fearless American missionary who first brought western education and the Christian religion to the Sherbro people of Sierra Leone. In the face of overwhelming odds he established and maintained a mission and school, ready at all times to sacrifice his life for the cause of Christianity in which he so fervently believed.

Born at Ashby, Massachusetts, in 1815, Raymond was originally trained for mechanical work but had always had a strong desire to become a minister. After preliminary studies, he entered Amherst College, Massachusetts, where, after two years, his career as a student came to an abrupt end. Always concerned for the socially oppressed, Raymond had spent much of his time teaching black families, thereby incurring the disapproval of the college authorities. An incident, in which he had given a ride to a black girl, ended with his being rusticated. Although such severe measures were not uncommon in the ante-bellum United States, Raymond felt he had been punished quite disproportionately, and a number of his teachers agreed with him but were powerless to help. He moved to Oberlin Collegiate Institute in Ohio, where he completed his studies in theology and classics. Having received his license to preach, he went to Canada, where he lived for a time among fugitive slaves.

Raymond soon developed a passion to go to West Africa and spend his life there. In the meantime, the 'Amistad Africans' (See SENGBE PIEH) were freed by verdict of the U.S. Supreme Court in 1841. These were slaves who had revolted and taken their freedom in 1839, but had been arrested and charged with mutiny and piracy before the United States courts. While preparations were being made to send them home after their acquittal, the Amistad Committee, set up for their protection and welfare, hired Raymond to teach them at Farmington, Connecticut. When arrangements were completed, the Africans were repatriated. They were accompanied by three white missionaries—Raymond and his wife, and the Rev. James Steele, and two black teachers, Mr. and Mrs. Wilson. They had instructions to enter Mende country in Sierra Leone, where most of the Africans had been originally captured, and open up a mission.

The party reached Freetown in January 1842, whereupon many of the Africans promptly disappeared among friends or countrymen. Since there was much warfare in the interior, the missionaries were advised not to attempt to cross embattled territories to reach Mende country. Instead it was decided to open a mission somewhere in Sherbro country at one of the river-based points of entry into Mende country, and await more propitious times. Steele went ahead and concluded a treaty with chief Harry Tucker to establish a station at Komende, 40 km (25 mi) up the Bum River. Meantime, Raymond moved with the ten remaining Africans to York, a village about 32 km (20 mi) south of Freetown. Steele returned from his negotiations in ill health, and immediately returned to the United States, leaving Raymond in charge.

Troubles started almost immediately. Steele had left the mission coffers empty; there were difficulties with the Wilsons who abandoned the mission; Mrs. Raymond became ill, and as the ultimate disaster, their little daughter Jane, died. Penniless and deserted—he had only six cents left when his daughter died—Raymond wrote urgent letters asking for money while the Wesleyan missionaries in Freetown came to his temporary rescue. In 1843, Raymond and his wife returned to the States to ask for funds and assistants. Miss Ann Harndon offered herself as a missionary, and they all returned together to Sierra Leone later that year.

Raymond lost no time in renewing the contact with chief Tucker for the land at Komende, for which the chief was to receive 100 dollars a year in rent. But Spanish slave traders, fearing the effects of missionary activity on their trade, urged Tucker to expel Raymond. A quarrel developed between Raymond and Tucker, settled only by the intervention of other chiefs. Other troubles gathered fast. Miss Harndon took ill and died. Mrs. Raymond had another baby which died within a few days, and she began to have delusions of persecution. Fearing for her sanity, Raymond sent her home. He reported his distress to the Amistad Committee, which showed little sympathy, and thereafter he decided not to approach them with personal problems. Still fired with a fanatical desire to spread the gospel and die for the cause of Christ, Raymond carried on the work of the mission alone.

Throughout the 1840s the Sherbro was torn apart by civil wars, making Raymond's task almost impossible. Yet he refused to give up hope. Realizing the futility of trying to convert warriors or peasants who lived under the threat of war, he confined himself to preaching to the chiefs and people in the immediate vicinity. In this way the so-called Mende Mission was inaugurated in Sherbro country. Raymond had a mission house and chapel built immediately; he hired a few artisans and started cultivation on the mission farm. But the school he had told the chiefs he would start was delayed by financial problems. The impatient chiefs forced his hand by sending their children to the mission to attend the long-promised school. Finally, in July 1846, Raymond could delay no longer, and the school opened with 24 pupils. It was immediately the subject of slanders of the slave traders in the area who told chiefs that the missionary was a liar who had come to obstruct their slave trade.

The school grew rapidly. Pupils were lodged and boarded in the mission compound and clothed at the expense of the mission. A sabbath school was also started which drew sizeable audiences, and Raymond's standing with local chiefs and people was soon high.

At the mission he emphasized the virtues of piety and industry. He also tried to persuade his misson employees to adopt the Christian practice of monogamy. Many of them, true to African tradition, had more than one wife. Raymond promised to build a house for anyone who would confine himself to one wife and marry her under Christian law.

But in some areas he was powerless. Although alcohol and tobacco were prohibited in any mission transactions by the Committee, Raymond found it impossible to dispense with the use of tobacco as a trading commodity, as it was the commonest and also the smallest unit of currency. In order to acquire staple foods, such as rice, for the mission, payment in tobacco was demanded and he was faced with the choice of disobeying the Committee or starving. Food supplies were also threatened by warfare which disrupted the trade routes from the interior, and Raymond and his mission were reduced at such times to living on boiled rice and palm oil.

War also created other extraordinary pressures on the mission. Warriors demanded that Raymond should 'cook for the war,' which he was forced to do in sheer self-preservation. Nevertheless, he continued to act on the abolitionist beliefs of the mission, rescuing many boys and girls from slavery by paying for their freedom and enlisting them in the school. Some of his artisans were run-away slaves. Rather than let them return to slavery when traced by their masters, Raymond paid for their manumission. This added considerably to the expenses of the mission, already chronically short of money to the point of being unable to buy food.

The Committee was totally unsympathetic to the trials of their lone missionary. He was questioned severely and requested at the end of 1846 to cut down the expenses of the mission and if possible close the school. Raymond, convinced of the moral propriety of his actions, refused. He loved the school and regarded the pupils, many redeemed from slavery and without parents, as his own children. His answer to the Committee was that he preferred to die with the children rather than discharge them.

The Committee also accused him of 'trafficking' in tobacco, and turned a deaf ear to his explanations of its role as currency. They saw the matter simply as a breach of rules. At this point Raymond, almost at the end of his tether, considered leaving their service to 'go into the interior where I can live, labor and die unknown.'

In 1846, however, the American Missionary Association was founded and took over responsibility for the Mende Mission. The Rev. George Whipple became the correspondence secretary, and for once Raymond felt he was in touch with a sympathizer to whom he could unburden. "My dear brother" Whipple wrote to Raymond, "sometimes my soul is in an agony for you, alone, and overburdened, crushed with cares, my soul trembles lest your body should sink under all." In a private letter to his wife, Raymond said he was looking ten years older, bald and toothless. Raymond's successor, George Thompson, stated frankly that "Brother Raymond has opened things on a *large scale* and the amount of work performed by him is almost incredible."

In 1847 Raymond was recalled by the executive committee of the Missionary Association. "I am glad" he rejoiced "that the Committee at last see the necessity of our seeing one another face to face." But as fate would have it, they never met. While in Freetown, enroute for home, Raymond took ill with yellow fever, and died on November 26, 1947.

When the Committee heard of his death they proceeded to make a martyr of him. They resolved, with many a high-flown phrase, to have a memorial written to him, which concluded: "In the death of Mr. Raymond the friends of missions have lost a self-sacrificing, devoted and successful missionary; the Church of Christ, a disinterested, exemplary and faithful minister; Africa, a most useful, laborious and true-hearted friend; the colored man, a sympathizing and unprejudiced friend and brother; this 'American Missionary' Association, a most beloved servant and friend; the missionary band, a most heroic, enterprising and fearless brother; and the world, a man of God full of faith in the Holy Ghost.'' True words indeed—but the Committee itself had contributed in no small measure to the hardships which in the end cost Raymond his life.

At the time of his death, the school which he had opened just a year before had over 100 pupils, and the mission establishment a staff of 15. The Mende Mission had mechanical, educational, and agricultural departments as well as the core religious department. Had Raymond not ''opened things on a large scale'' the mission might not have been sustained; and the Sherbro people would in all probability not have gained their lead in western education over other hinterland peoples of Sierra Leone.

ARTHUR ABRAHAM

BIBLIOGRAPHY: Arthur Abraham, ''Sunrise in the Sherbro: the Mende Mission, 1842-47,'' unpublished manuscript, 1977; M. Cable, *Black Odyssey,* New York, 1971.

ROGERS, Z.

Zachary Rogers (16?-1681), an Englishman in the service of the Gambia Adventurers Company, founded a family line that has been prominent in the Sierra Leone region for more than 300 years.

In 1668, Rogers was appointed chief agent of the company in the Sherbro country of Sierra Leone. He retained the post when the Royal African Company took over the trade in 1672, and held it until his death.

His widow then quarreled with the company's officials who maintained that she was withholding property from them. According to tradition she was Jafua-Lue, a member of the Massaquoi family of the Gallinas country, at the southern end of the Sierra Leone coastline, living at Dumagbe—though tradition confusingly records her husband's name as Charles, not Zachary. It is said that one of their family was seen sitting on a chair (a rarity in those days) and was given the name ''kpaka'' (chair) which the Rogers family have since retained.

Zachary and his wife had at least two sons, Zachary and Samuel, who entered the Royal African Company's service in the 1690s, but subsequently moved to their home in the Gallinas country where they traded on their own in rivalry with the company.

Their family became rich and powerful, second only in the area to the ruling Massaquoi family. Some of them lived in European style. Samuel Siaka Rogers, who at the end of the 18th century traded for about 20 years in the rivers north of Sierra Leone, spoke good English, and used to sleep under a mosquito net. In a later generation, James Western Rogers of Jidaro, Gallinas country, used to eat off silver plates.

The great prosperity of the Rogers family came to an end in 1850, when British naval officers persuaded them to make a treaty renouncing the slave trade which had brought them their wealth. Nevertheless they remained, and still remain, an important family in the country.

CHRISTOPHER FYFE

BIBLIOGRAPHY: C.H. Fyfe, *A History of Sierra Leone*, London, 1962.

ROGERS-WRIGHT, C.B.

Cyril Bunting Rogers-Wright (1905-1971) was a barrister and solicitor of the Supreme Court of Sierra Leone, and from the 1950s played a leading part in national politics, holding several cabinet posts.

In 1956 he began the newspaper *Shekpendeh,* of which he was founder and proprietor. He was also the founder and leader of the United Progressive Party, one of the most important opposition parties in the late 1950s. In the 1957 general elections, he was elected member of the House of Representatives for Port Loko East constituency, and became leader of the opposition from 1957 to 1960.

In the United Front Coalition government which was formed to negotiate independence from Britain, Rogers-Wright was appointed Minister of Housing and Country Planning. In the 1962 general elections, he was elected for Wilberforce constituency, and was appointed Minister of External Affairs from 1964-65. From 1965 to 1967, he was Minister of Health, but resigned and joined the opposition All People's Congress (A.P.C.) party shortly before the 1967 general elections. He won the election as A.P.C. member for Wilberforce, but was detained for a time after the military take-over. In the treason trials which followed the return to civilian rule in 1968, Rogers-Wright was leading prosecution counsel for the proceedings, which lasted till 1970.

In 1971, he took ill, and died in Ireland. His remains were brought to Freetown and buried there.

CYRIL P. FORAY

BIBLIOGRAPHY: C.P. Foray, *Historical Dictionary of Sierra Leone,* Metuchen, New Jersey, and London, 1977.

ROOT, B.

Barnabas Root (1846-1877) was a Sherbro who received western education at the Mende Mission school. He went on to study divinity in the United States and became one of a rare group of Africans who took up missionary posts among freed men in the States.

Born in the Sherbro country, Barnabas was taken at the age of eight into the Mende Mission at the request of his father. (The Mende Mission supported by the American Missionary Association (A.M.A.) had been established in 1842 as a haven for the famous Amistad mutineers: *See* SENGBE PIEH.) The young lad proved to be an exceptional student and in 1850 he was chosen by one of the missionaries, John White, to accompany him on a visit to the United States. White had a dual purpose: Barnabas was an outstanding example of the success of the mission, and his presence also enabled White to continue his study of the Sherbro language which he was turning into a written form. Audiences at missionary meetings throughout the Northern states were impressed by the young African's command of the English language and his knowledge of the Bible.

Returning with White to Africa in 1860, Barnabas went on with his studies in the mission school and acted as interpreter for the mission until 1863, when he came to the United States to prepare for the ministry. He graduated in 1870 from Knox College at Galesburg, Illinois, with honors and received a Bachelor of Divinity degree from Chicago Theological Seminary in 1873. Reporting on the commencement exercises for Root's class at the Seminary, the correspondent for *Advance* wrote that "The oration which showed the most thought and the finest culture was by a native of Africa, Mr. Barnabas Root."

In 1873, Root was appointed pastor for a Congregational mission church for freedmen in Montgomery, Alabama. By accepting the appointment, he became a member of a very small and distinctive group, native Africans who served as Christian missionaries in the United States. He was the second of such missionaries commissioned by the A.M.A., the first being Thomas DeSaliere Tucker (*q.v.*), also from the Sherbro country, who was appointed in 1862 to teach in a school for the freedmen on the eastern shore of Virginia.

During their time in the States, Root and Tucker had galling experiences of color prejudice. In 1859, sitting with John White, Lewis Tappan, the treasurer of the A.M.A., and two white ladies at breakfast in a Chicago hotel, Barnabas was ordered to leave by the landlord, because some of the lady boarders refused to enter the dining room "while that black was there." Tappan was incensed by the incident.

Later, at Knox College, Barnabas displayed Christian forebearance with regard to racial prejudice. Writing to George Whipple, corresponding secretary of the A.M.A., in 1868, he said: "In regard to the influence and effect of the prevailing feeling (of) prejudice of which you desire an expression of my thought, it is a subject of which I have had much thought and feeling, but I fear I have looked too much if not altogether on the darkest side of the matter. I have felt it very keenly since I have been here...and I expressed myself freely about it...but I have asked God to show me my duty in this matter and to keep me a humble Christian from the blighting degrading feeling of self-abasement which I see in almost everyone of my race I meet in this country....One great cause of this feeling I think with many is unacquaintance with us or rather not being accustomed to come in daily and familiar contact with the blacks on the part of the whites...."

Root found his work among the freedmen rewarding, and felt that he had been able to help them. After a leave spent in New Orleans in the winter of 1873-74, where he hoped to recover from a chronic throat ailment, he returned to Montgomery, adding the charge of a church in Selma to his existing duties. During this time, he also attended a meeting of the Congregational Association of Illinois, which led to the entire membership of the association boycotting a hotel operated by the Illinois Central Railroad because of its refusal to serve him a meal.

But his heart was not truly in the work in America. In 1868, he declared that he had given himself to God for the benefit of Africa, and from this resolution he never wavered. Accordingly he returned to his homeland in 1874. Always frail in health, he was unable to readjust to the climate of Sierra Leone. Nonetheless, in the last three years of his life he established a new station of the Mende Mission, built a school house, revised a Mende dictionary, and began a translation of the Bible into Mende. He died in 1877.

CLIFTON H. JOHNSON

BIBLIOGRAPHY: The *American Missionary*, October 1877; Clifton H. Johnson, "African Missionaries to U.S. Freedmen," *The Crisis*, November 1971.

SAMURA

Solimanga Samura (who flourished in about the 17th century) was a warrior traditionally famous for his enormous stature. He was believed by the Yalunka Samura of northern Sierra Leone and the Republic of Guinea to be the founder of their clan.

Originally called Dantili Samura, he is said to have been a Mandinka from Mande (in what is now Mali). But according to tradition, this huge warrior failed to make his mark in his own country and left it to seek fame and fortune elsewhere. He traveled southwards with his weapons of war until he reached Firia, the country of the Yalunka Kamara north of Sierra Leone, where he met a Kamara blacksmith, Sa Yere, at work. Tired from his travels, Dantili sat down on a heap of wooden chips which had flown off the hoe handles (solidagina in Yalunka) that Sa Yere was carving.

Onlookers, ascribing qualities of leadership to this man of impressive build, soon started to call him manga (ruler) as he sat on the heap of chips. Thus he came to be called Solimanga, a fusion of solidagina and manga, and his original name Dantili soon fell into disuse.

While he was in Firia, the ruler, Fori Frigi (after whom the country was named), issued a proclamation that four warriors were attacking and robbing people in Firia. They were native Yalunka Kamara, but had disguised themselves and taken strange names in order to prevent identification. In his proclamation Frigi indicated that he would be indebted to anyone who could rid him of the warriors. Solimanga took up the challenge and killed them all.

Through this incident Fori Frigi discovered Solimanga's presence in his country. In gratitude he gave him his daughter Mmame Yeri as his wife. Together with some other relations in the area, he also gave Solimanga a total of 700 males and as many females to form his retinue. These people were of different clans but none were Samura. Through living with them, Solimanga lost his Mandinka culture and became a Yalunka.

For a time he stayed within Firia, where the people were being harassed by the neighboring Fula of Futa Jallon, in what is now the Republic of Guinea. Solimanga and his warriors drove away the Fula so that Fori Frigi was able to extend his territory over the conquered area. Frigi and Solimanga then agreed that the latter should keep any other territory he might conquer from the Fula. In this way Solimanga founded his first town, Kalota, in territory near Firia which he had rid of Fula.

Most of the Yalunka given to Solimanga as followers readily took the clan name of Samura as a mark of honor and association with their leader. But Solimanga had only four sons—Yirisa Yella, Kumbasa, Yeri Fate, and Yana Tagesa. They became the rulers of Solimankhori, (khori means 'country'), the country surrounding Kalota and founded by Solimanga. Thereafter the Yalunka of Solimankhori regarded themselves as Solima Yalunka.

Solimanga died, probably in the later 17th century, and was succeeded by his son Yirisa Yella as ruler of Solimankhori. In the 18th century a state was founded by Yalunka of different clans, led by the Samura, descendants of Solimanga, and centered on Solimankhori. This state was called Solimana or the Solima state, with the capital at Falaba. Today Falaba is still the principal town of the Solima chiefdom, named after Solimanga, in the Koinadugu district of Sierra Leone.

C. MAGBAILY FYLE

BIBLIOGRAPHY: L.H. Donald, "Yalunkayan Foloxi Di," *Sierra Leone Studies,* January, 1968; C.M. Fyle, "Solimana and its Neighbors," Ph.D. dissertation, Northwestern University, 1976.

SARA BAYO

Sara Bayo (circa later 19th-early 20th century) was chief of Katimbo in northern Sierra Leone at the time of invasions by the Sofa, warriors of the conquering Mandinka emperor, Samori Touré. By a lucky stroke of fortune, his territories were spared the worst of the invaders' attacks.

He was born at Katimbo, in the Kasunko chiefdom, in present-day Koinadugu district—an important town in territory which later belonged to a long line of chiefs who traced their roots to Futa Jallon, in which is now the Republic of Guinea. His father, Bayo Seri, in accordance with the custom of ruling families in northern Sierra Leone, sent his son to Timbo in Guinea, then regarded as an important training ground for future chiefs. He may have acquired some Koranic learning there.

When he reached manhood, Sara Bayo returned to Katimbo and became chief in succession to his father, who died shortly after his return. In the 1880s, Samori Touré's warriors swept down on northern Sierra Leone and Sara Bayo's chiefdom was one of those affected. But like many northern chiefs, he considered it unwise to attempt any military confrontation with the more powerful Sofa. Instead he and his people took refuge at Kamiliki, in Koinadugu district, an earlier settlement long since eclipsed by towns like Katimbo and Fadugu, also in Koinadugu. There, safely hidden in caves, Sara Bayo and his elders sent scouts to spy on the movements of the invaders. When their reports seemed favorable enough, Sara Bayo and his people returned to their chiefdom.

The invaders were now stationed at the town of Fadugu, where Sara Bayo, accompanied by two of his elders, met the Sofa war leader, Lankanfali, and in recognition of his military superiority, presented him with gifts—a bowl full of kola nuts, three slaves and three cows. Lankanfali accepted the gifts, but noticing that Sara Bayo's fingers were twisted, declared that his troops had been forewarned not to make war on anybody with such a deformity.

With due reverence towards Sara Bayo and his subjects, Lankanfali had the gifts offered as a sacrifice. The kola nuts were shared and everyone partook of the cow's meat. The slaves were beheaded. Some of the invading forces stayed in the chiefdom even after Samori's empire had been destroyed by the French in the mid-1890s.

The imposition of British rule followed the withdrawal of the Sofa forces from northern Sierra Leone, and Sara Bayo was recognized as paramount chief. Despite the fact that this put him on an equal footing with his pre-colonial overlord, Suluku (*q.v.*) of Bumban, Sara Bayo continued to refer certain matters to him.

He died in the early years of the 20th century and was succeeded by Lamina.

E. AMADU TURAY

BIBLIOGRAPHY: M.R. Lipschutz, "Northeast Sierra Leone after 1884: Reactions to the Samorian Invasions and British Colonialism," Ph.D. dissertation, University of California at Los Angeles, 1973.

SASSABLA, VA FORAY. See VA FORAY SASSABLE

SATTAN LAHAI

Alimamy Sattan Lahai (who flourished in the 19th century), one of the most astute political leaders in northern Sierra Leone in his day, was ruler over a large area round the Great Scarcies River. Throughout his rule this important trading center was embroiled in almost continuous political warfare.

His father was a Soso, his mother a Temne. Lahai's influence was centered on the Kambia region, but spread to Morea country in the north, and sometimes as far as Port Loko to the south and Kukuna to the north. From the early 1850s, when he came into prominence, until the late 1880s, Lahai's activities were decisive in the political development of Kambia town, a vital trading link on the Great Scarcies River.

In 1851 Sattan Lahai signed a treaty with Freetown, essentially to facilitate trade with the Colony. The treaty failed for various reasons. The growing influence of British and Liberated African (Krio, or Creole) traders, and possibly also French traders, supported by British and French authorities, threatened Lahai's political independence. Kambia's role as distributive 'middleman' in the trading process was also endangered by Krio penetration into the interior. Lahai also faced a serious challenge to his authority from Lamina Barmoi, a Temne with strong support from Temne kinsmen in the Small Scarcies and Port

Loko. Fully aware that the British tended to support the Temne in Port Loko against the Soso, Lahai, himself a Muslim Soso, was naturally distrustful of British activities.

Like several other traditional leaders, Lahai resented the British anti-slavery campaign, on both social and economic grounds. In Lahai's case there were good grounds for resentment, since a "free slave state," established in 1838 by Bilali (*q.v.*), reputedly a Koranko, was a haven for runaway slaves from Kambia and other regions. To compound the complexities of the situation, Bilali was supported by the Limba—support which aggravated relations with Lahai, the Soso, and the Temne on the one hand, and on the other the Krios representing British influence. For all these reasons Alimamy Sattan Lahai took a decision in 1856 to expel Colony traders from Kambia and block trade routes from the interior.

With trade at a standstill and war being waged between Temne and Soso, Kambia became politically explosive. The Soso, in support of Lahai, burned the town with the aim of killing his rival Barmoi, who escaped to Mambolo, south of Kambia, still relentlessly pursued by the Soso, also engaged in fighting against the Temne in Port Loko in support of their kinsman Momoh Sankoh (*q.v.*).

Lahai was becoming too powerful for the colonial administration to tolerate. In February 1858, Governor Stephen Hill (term of office 1854-62), accompanied by Commodore Charles Wise, led a naval expedition against him. Kambia was bombarded, and although this somewhat subdued Soso power, Lahai survived the attack and remained a force to be reckoned with. In all probability he supported the Soso attack on Port Loko when it was burned down by Momoh Sankoh in 1859.

By 1861, however, it would seem that the British had succeeded in curtailing the territory over which he ruled. A treaty signed in that year between Lahai and John McCormack (*q.v.*), representing the Colony, referred to him as 'king Rowula,' Bai Farma was recognized as king of Kambia, providing a counterweight to Soso influence through his backing of the Temne.

During the 1860s, some realignment of forces seems to have given temporary stability to Kambia. By the early 1870s, Barmoi had not only been recognized as one of the chiefs of Kambia, but a rapprochement seems to have taken place between him and Lahai. They united to fight against the Limba and Koranko under Bilali in 1872. This again seriously affected trade, and colonial traders pleaded for forceful intervention by the Freetown administration.

Always cautious about intervening, it was not until the discovery of French influence behind the renewed fighting between the Soso and Temne in 1875—the alliance between Lahai and Barmoi having apparently broken down—that colonial action was taken. Governor Samuel Rowe (terms of office, 1877-80, 1885-88), signed the so-called Massamah treaties with several northern chiefs including Bai Farma and Sattan Lahai. These treaties were intended to establish cooperation between chiefs and colony traders, but failed to eliminate the main causes of friction. The chiefs resented the expanding British colonial presence—customs houses set up by the colony which diminished their own revenues and authority. It is probable that the chiefs were encouraged by the large European trading houses, which resented Krio 'middlemen,' and by the French, permanently hostile to British influence, to disavow the Massamah treaties. With one exception, all the chiefs annulled the treaties, in 1879, despite Governor Rowe's placatory visit in April 1878, and proceeded once again to expel the colony traders.

As before, the traders pleaded for intervention from the colony, but the administration favored diplomatic tactics. By this time, Sattan Lahai seems to have had a change of heart, and was more disposed towards peaceful relations with the colony. He sent a mission to Governor Rowe headed by his half-brother, Tom Wilson, after which in Kambia at least the colony traders were allowed to conduct their business under normal conditions.

Lahai's political troubles, however, were far from finished. A Soso from Morea, Tansa Lamina, was attempting to overthrow him and in 1885 burned Kambia, forcing Lahai to flee to Mambolo and seek refuge with Lahai Young, the most powerful leader in the area since the death of the Bai Sherbro. Lahai retaliated and captured the ruler of Samu as a hostage. Lamina in turn threatened to destroy Mambolo and capture or kill Lahai Young. The region of the Scarcies and Melacourie became dangerously disrupted by such attacks and counterattacks, and trade suffered in consequence.

Lahai's reconciliation with the colony, however, started late in 1879, appears to have held good. Lamina, despite his professed cordiality towards the colony, was regarded with suspicion on account of his close friendship with Bokari (q.v.), ruler of Morea, whom the colonial government distrusted. The colony sided with Lahai and Young against Lamina, a decision strengthened by the fact that previous Bai Sherbro of Mambolo had been in treaty relationship with the British.

In 1896 Governor Rowe visited Mambolo to mediate in disputes among chiefs. Young in particular was warned against further interference in the affairs of the Great Scarcies and beyond, and although that area continued to be plagued with political troubles, he

commended him to the colonial administration, who recognized him as Bai Sherbro in 1889.

Alimamy Sattan Lahai continued to rule as a chief in Kambia, but his influence appears to have waned. The date of his death remains uncertain.

GUSTAV K. DEVENEAUX

BIBLIOGRAPHY: G.K. Deveneaux, "The Political and Social Impact of the Colony in Northern Sierra Leone, 1821-96," unpublished Ph.D dissertation, Boston University, 1973; Christopher Fyfe, *A History of Sierra Leone*, London, 1962; J.D. Hargreaves, *Prelude to the Partition of West Africa*, London, 1966; A.B.C. Sibthorpe, *The History of Sierra Leone*, 2nd ed., London, 1881, reprinted London, 1970.

SENGBE PIEH

Sengbe Pieh (circa 1813-1879), also known as Joseph Cinque, was the courageous leader of a revolt by slaves on board the slave ship *Amistad* in 1839, an event which led ultimately to a historic trial in the Supreme Court of the United States and had far-reaching consequences for both that country and Sierra Leone.

Sengbe was born around 1813 in the town of Mani in Mende country, a distance of ten days' march from the Gallinas coast. He is said to have been the son of a local chief. He was certainly a farmer and was married with three children. In 1839 he was captured by four men as he was going to his farm, taken to a nearby village, and then sent to Lomboko, a notorious slaving island off the Gallinas coast, where he was sold to the wealthiest slaver there. He eventually came to be known as Joseph Cinque, a name given him by Spanish slavers in Cuba, and variously spelled Cinquez, Cingue, Sinko, and Jimgua in textbooks.

From Lomboko he was shipped with several other slaves to Havana, Cuba, on the schooner *Iesora*. Jose Ruiz, a Spanish plantation owner, bought Sengbe and 48 others for $450 each to work on his plantation in Porto Principe, another Cuban port 480 km (300 mi) away. Pedro Montez, another Spaniard also bound for Port Principe, bought four children. Although Spain had made the importation of slaves illegal since 1820, the two men loaded their slaves onto the schooner *Amistad* and set out for Porto Principe.

Three days out to sea, Sengbe managed to free himself and his comrades by using a loose spike which he found on the floor of the ship. Under his leadership, they killed the captain (who was the owner of the ship) and one of the crew, but spared the cabin

Courtesy Chicago Historical Society.

A drawing of Sengbe Pieh (Joseph Cinque) addressing his fellow-Africans on the deck of the *Amistad,* after its arrival in U.S.waters in 1841.

boy, Ruiz, Montez, and the second mate, whose life was allowed him in order to have someone to steer the ship. Two of the slaves died in the attack.

Sengbe ordered the new captain to pilot them eastwards towards Africa, but at night he steered westwards or northwards, and after sailing in this fashion for nearly two months, anchored off Long Island. News soon spread concerning the mysterious ship. The *Amistad,* in a hopeless condition, her sails nearly all in shreds, was seized by a United States survey brig. Ruiz and Montez were released, while Sengbe and the other slaves were arrested and charged with murder and piracy. After a preliminary investigation, the district judge ordered that the case be heard before the circuit court at Hartford, Connecticut.

Ruiz and Montez claimed the Africans as their property, while the Spanish consul in Boston claimed the ship, slaves and cargo in the name of the king of Spain, as Ruiz and Montez were Spanish subjects. A committee of Abolitionists, which came to be known as the Amistad Committee, was then formed to defend the prisoners. Their greatest difficulty was to get the prisoners' version of the story. Several attempts to find an interpreter failed, but eventually Professor J.W. Gibbs of Yale Divinity School discovered James Covey, an ex-slave serving on a British naval ship in New York, who was from Sierra Leone and could speak the Mende language.

With a great stir of excitement the Amistad Committee, comprising S.S. Jocelyn, Joshua Leavitt, and Lewis Tappan, a wealthy merchant and die-hard abolitionist, launched a campaign—"Appeal to the Friends of Liberty"—to raise funds for the welfare of the "Amistad negroes," as the captives were popularly called, as well as to pay counsel to defend them.

The abolitionists' position was a delicate one. The Amistad incident was timely, for it provided an issue which united the differences of opinion which had threatened to destroy the abolitionist movement entirely. Moreover, there were a number of people who sympathized with the Amistad case and gave it their support, but were not abolitionists. On the other hand, many influential supporters of the United States government had entrenched pro-slavery interests.

President Martin Van Buren (in office 1837-41), concerned about winning votes from the southern slave-holders in the forthcoming general election of 1840, was in favor of handing the captives over to the Spanish authorities, but this was stopped since there was no extradition treaty with Spain. The district attorney, a personal appointee of the President, claimed that they should be held at the President's pleasure. Van Buren even sent a warship to New Haven, Connecticut, with instructions to seize the prisoners without delay, should the verdict go against them, so that the abolitionists would have no time to file an appeal.

Counsel for the defense urged the President not to have the case decided "in the recesses of the cabinet," where the slaves could not be defended. When the circuit court finally gave its decision in January 1840, it ruled that the United States government had no right to try the captives as the *Amistad* was owned by a Spanish subject; that as the prisoners had been kidnapped into slavery, they were legally free. They should therefore be transported back to Africa from where they had been taken against their will.

Many people contested this decision, among them the President himself, who ordered the district attorney to appeal to the Supreme Court. Meantime, some of the Amistad negroes had taken ill and died. Meanwhile, the survivors were being taught to read and write in classes organized by the abolitionists.

Recognizing the need for a public figure of the highest standing to plead the case of the negroes before Supreme Court, the abolitionists approached former President John Quincy Adams to lead the defense. At 73, and 30 years out of practice, the ex-President was reluctant to accept the case lest he should jeopardize the lives of the Africans by failing to win. He was, however, persuaded to accept the brief, leading to the famous "trial of one president by another." After preparing an elaborate defense, Old Man Eloquent, as Adams came to be called thereafter, addressed the court for a total of 13 hours. In March 1841, the court gave its verdict: the captives were free men and fully entitled to their freedom.

After their acquittal, the Africans were taken to Farmington, an early abolitionist town, in Connecticut, where they received more formal education for the rest of the year 1841. With the President reluctant to provide a ship to repatriate them, the abolitionists assumed complete responsibility for the Africans. To raise funds to charter a boat, they were taken from one community to another, making appearances before sympathetic church audiences, displaying their knowledge of reading and spoken language, and telling the tale of their ordeal.

Towards the end of the year, enough funds had been raised, and the *Gentleman* was chartered to take the 35 surviving Africans to the colony of Sierra Leone, accompanied by five missionaries—two black and three white—to start the so-called Mende Mission with the Amistad Africans. This would promote the work of evangelization already successfully started in Sierra Leone.

The ship arrived in Freetown in mid-January, 1842. Sengbe learned from Mende recaptives that war had ravaged the country during his absence, and that his hometown and most of his family had been wiped out. The hope of locating the Mende Mission near Sengbe's hometown could never be fulfilled.

Anxious to get to their homes and families, many of the Amistad Africans ran away, leaving only ten adults and the four children behind. It was not easy to find a place to start the mission, but finally in 1844 a station was established at Komende on the Sherbro Island. In the course of time the mission established stations on the mainland, one of which was named Mo Tappan (Mo in Sherbro meaning 'at the place of') in gratitude for the selfless assistance of Lewis Tappan.

It is difficult to reconstruct exactly what happened to Sengbe between 1842 and the time of his death. There were many conflicting stories. Like a number of those who escaped from Freetown, Sengbe continued to return to the mission station from time to time. He told the missionaries that on leaving Freetown, he had hurried back to Mani only to discover the charred ruins of the town. In desperation he came to the mission for some time, then disappeared again. Rumors, many and various, circulated about him—that he had become a great war chief, or that he had given up Christianity and become a wealthy slave-trader himself. One of the strongest, which missionaries inclined to believe, was that he had emigrated to the West Indies.

Be that as it may, Sengbe is reported to have died at the mission station. The Rev. Alonzo Lewis, who as a boy had watched the capture of the *Amistad* and followed the case, later enquired from Rev. Albert Miller of the Mende Mission what eventually happened to Sengbe. According to Miller, shortly after his arrival at the Mende Mission in 1878, an old man, unrecognized by anyone, had stumbled into the station. He had announced himself as Joseph Sengbe, and said that he had come there to die. Sengbe had relapsed into paganism, but lived in the vicinity of the mission. He died in 1879 and was buried in the cemetery near the mission station.

The Amistad affair, prompted by the revolt of Sengbe, had far-reaching consequences. By the time the case ended, it had so embittered feelings between the north and the slave-holding south, that it must be accounted one of the events leading to the outbreak of the American Civil War in 1860. The decision of the court was not in itself an attack on slavery, but it drew the abolitionists together and prevented the movement from breaking up. Moreover, the missionary work in Africa precipitated by the Amistad case led to the foundation of the American Missionary Association in 1846 which took over the Mende Mission. This was the largest and most highly organized abolitionist society in the United States before the outbreak of the Civil War.

The Association established hundreds of antislavery churches and schools in the north and the border states of the south, mainly to educate liberated blacks. Thus were born such important institutions as Hampton Institute, and Atlanta, Howard, Fisk, and Dillard Universities, to which countless black Americans owe their higher education. Under the leadership of Sengbe, as the *New Orleans Weekly* put it, "the determination of 53 Africans not to accept enforced slavery launched a movement that resulted in the creation of a tremendous network of institutions in the south that educated the leadership for the modern-day civil rights movement."

It also led to the beginning of American evangelization in Africa and other parts of the world. In Sierra Leone, the American Missionary Association was responsible for bringing western education to the Mende people before the British colonial government introduced it. It also founded some important schools such as the Harford School for Girls in Moyamba and the Albert Academy in Freetown, both still popular today. All these developments owe their origin to Joseph Sengbe, and to his act of rebellion on board the *Amistad*.

ARTHUR ABRAHAM

BIBLIOGRAPHY: John W. Barber, *A History of the Amistad Captives,* New Haven, 1840; Morris Bishop, "Cinque the Noble Mutineer," *New Yorker,* December 20, 1941; Clifton H. Johnson, "The Amistad Incident," in David Driskell (ed.), *Amistad II: Afro-American Art,* New York, 1975; Bernice Kohn, *The Amistad Mutiny,* New York, 1971; Helen Kromer, *The Amistad Revolt, 1839,* New York, 1973; Alonzo N. Lewis, "Recollections of the Amistad Slave Case," *Connecticut Magazine,* II, 1907; William Owens, *Black Mutiny,* Philadelphia, 1953.

SEWA

Manga Sewa (who flourished in the 19th century) was a powerful ruler in northern Sierra Leone, with many commerical links with northern peoples both in Sierra Leone and beyond. In the later part of his reign his country was attacked by Samori Touré's troops, and he lost his life in the siege of his capital, Falaba.

Sewa was a member of the ruling Samura clan of the Solima state, in the extreme northeast of Sierra Leone. He was born in the early 19th century, the second son of Sori Wuleng (also called Asan Yira), then manga (ruler) of Solimana. Sewa became ruler of Solimana in about 1862.

He is credited with the extension of the areas of influence of Solimana to include numerous small Koranko states in northern Sierra Leone. The Koranko of Barawa, around Kabala, southeast of Falaba, and other Koranko as far as Deldugu (part of present Neya chiefdom) paid tribute to Falaba under Sewa. It was also during his rule that the separation of the government of the town of Falaba from that of the state took place. Sewa maintained commercial relations with Futa Jallon, to the far north, in what is now the Republic of Guinea, with Sankaran country, and with the Biriwa Limba, under Almamy Suluku (*q.v.*).

In 1869 Sewa was visited at Falaba by a British explorer and author, Winwood Reade, seeking the source of the Niger. Sewa received him with friendliness, but would not permit him to continue his search. A decade later two French explorers, J. Sweifel and M. Moustier, arrived in search of new openings for trade. He was described by all three Europeans as one of the greatest kings in the hinterland.

Sewa died in September 1884, as the result of the expansionist campaigns of Samori Touré, the Mandinka conqueror. As Samori's armies moved southwards towards Falaba, the Sofa general Nfa Ali sent Sayo of Kaliere (formerly part of the Solima state) to demand Falaba's submission. Unfortunately for Sewa, Sayo saw this as an opportunity to revenge himself for an act of treachery towards his father Isa (*q.v.*), perpetrated by the people of Falaba.

When Sayo reached Falaba, Sewa called his council together to discuss whether to submit to the Sofa or not. The council agreed on submission, and Sewa sent Sayo with this message to Nfa Ali.

Sayo, however, having left Falaba, took red kolanuts, signifying war, tied them up in a cloth and presented them to Nfa Ali with the message that Sewa had chosen to fight. The fate of Falaba was sealed by Sayo's trick. The Sofa surrounded the town and launched an abortive attack, after which they settled down for a siege. After some six months, the people inside Falaba were reduced to eating rats and the soles of shoes. Sewa sent his son and general, Duga, to seek help. Whereas messengers of war were not usually taken prisoner, Duga was captured by the Sofa, who allowed him to send a message to his beleaguered capital, and then killed him.

After this incident, Sewa decided to give in to the Sofa. But his son Sewa Sayo insulted him, calling him a coward, which so grieved Sewa that he decided to commit suicide. He called on all those who would die rather than have a Muslim Sofa lay a finger on them to join him in his armory. There, with his chief wife, and a few elders, he put a lighted torch to the armory and the whole group was blown to pieces. The Sofa then entered Falaba and took possession of it.

C. MAGBAILY FYLE

BIBLIOGRAPHY: C. Magbaily Fyle, "Solimana and its Neighbors," Ph.D. dissertation, Northwestern University, 1976; W. Winwood Reade, *African Sketch Book*, London, 1873.

SHORUNKEH-SAWYERR, A.J.

Alfred James Shorunkeh-Sawyerr (circa 1861-May 18, 1929), bookseller, printer, journalist, and eventually practicing lawyer, was a forceful and outspoken participant in public affairs in the last days of Krio (Creole) influence over colonial policy.

He was born about 1861, the son of T.J. Sawyerr, an established printer and bookseller who had opened the first bookshop in Freetown, and was also a member of the Legislative Council from 1883-94.

After attending the Church Missionary Society Grammar School in Freetown he was educated for six years in Britain, attending the Monkton Coombe College in Bath. Alfred then went into his father's business together with his brother John (*q.v.*). In 1886 he returned to England and was called to the bar at Gray's Inn in 1889. Following a practice of Africanization which became fashionable in Freetown, he changed his name to Shorunkeh-Sawyerr.

An original, independent thinker, Shorunkeh-Sawyerr on his return from Britain joined the Sierra Leone Association. This was originally founded in 1872 as the Native Association, and was mainly concerned to foster the mercantile interests of its members. It was reconstituted and renamed in 1885, after which it addressed itself to wider problems of economics and politics.

Following the depressions of the 1870s and 1880s, which had adversely affected the Colony's economy, traders naturally took an active part in debating possible solutions to economic difficulties. Sir Samuel Lewis (*q.v.*), the prominent Freetown barrister and a leading member of the Sierra Leone Association, presented a memorandum to a meeting of the association on the subject. His main diagnosis, with which all the other members agreed except Shorunkeh-Sawyerr, was that wars in the interior obstructed the flow of trade to the Colony, thereby diminishing its main source of revenue. He put forward a proposal involving peaceful annexation and the declaration of a protectorate over the hinterland, thus acquiring a "permanent jurisdiction" to control the existing "petty wars for which West Africa has become notorious."

Shorunkeh-Sawyerr raised serious objections: "I am altogether opposed to annexation, no matter by what means," he declared. Annexation would undoubtedly be beneficial to "European capitalists" but would seriously distort the development of those territories so annexed, and demoralize and stunt the growth of their peoples, whose interests Sir Samuel had totally ignored in proposals formulated mainly for the benefit of trade. "Civilized nations" in history were usually imperialists who sought their own ends, and offered little advantage to the peoples they exploited. Interrupted by another member, Zochonis, who shouted "Civilization!" he countered with "your rum and gin civilization, I suppose." With a quick piece of repartee, Lewis pointed out that Shorunkeh-Sawyerr's father would never have been able to send his son to England to learn speech-making had it not been for the civilization he now decried.

The association resolved to press for peaceful annexation; but when a mass meeting was organized to petition the Secretary of State for the Colonies, many members refused to support it, fearing that they would be taxed directly to repay the imperial loan required to affect the "peaceful annexation." Thus, the association fell apart.

At about this time, a "new-found African consciousness" expressed itself in the founding of a Dress Reform Society, aimed at popularizing and making respectable loose African robes, more suited to the climate than western dress. Many people also took African names as middle names or as hyphenated prefixes to their surnames. This striving for African origins was in part the work of Dr. E.W. Blyden, who was dedicated to the reshaping of education to include African culture. These views, however, met with fierce opposition from people like Sir Samuel Lewis. Shorunkeh-Sawyerr for his part seems to have held rather inconsistent views on the subject. For despite his change of name he held that Krios were "Black Englishmen" and should behave accordingly.

Meanwhile, he had been pursuing his career in journalism. During the 1880s he published *Sawyerr's Advertising Medium*, and a newspaper pamphlet called *The Sierra Leone Ram*. He and his brother, John, also educated in England, continued to run their father's press and in the 1890s came out with a new magazine, *Saturday, Ho!*, intended to encourage people to read more widely. This magazine continued even after their father's death in 1894. In 1896, Alfred and John went into legal partnership, a venture which apparently succeeded well.

In 1911, Shorunkeh-Sawyerr became a member of the Legislative Council. Intellectually sharp, eloquent, and commanding sufficient legal respect, he seemed the logical successor to Sir Samuel Lewis who had died in 1903. But he lacked the ability to inspire people as a leader.

In any event, times had changed. The days when the colonial administration respected and took note of enlightened Krio opinion were over. Colonialism was fully established, and the Legislative Council, in the 19th century a forum for discussion and debate, lost its democratic character and was reduced to rubber-stamping policies already decided by the governor and his officials.

Although he stayed on as a member until 1924, Shorunkeh-Sawyerr made little mark there. He died in 1929, five years after leaving the Legislative Council.

ARTHUR ABRAHAM

BIBLIOGRAPHY: Christopher Fyfe, *A History of Sierra Leone*, London, 1962, (ed.), *Sierra Leone Inheritance*, London, 1964; J.D. Hargreaves, *A Life of Sir Samuel Lewis*, London, 1958.

SHORUNKEH-SAWYERR, J.C.

John C. Shorunkey-Sawyerr (January 3, 1863-May 29, 1929) was a successful Krio (Creole) businessman and lawyer, partner to his elder and more flamboyant brother Alfred (*q.v.*).

He was born on January 3, 1863, son of T.J. Sawyerr, who started the first bookshop in Freetown and ran a profitable printing press. John attended the

Government Model School, and like his elder brother Alfred, the Church Missionary Society Grammar School in Freetown and the Monkton Coombe College in Bath, England. He studied accountancy and business in Liverpool from 1880-1882, and lived in France for a year to study the French language. Thus equipped he returned home and managed his father's business until 1889, when he left to study law at Gray's Inn, London.

In 1892 he was called to the bar and in 1896 set up in partnership with his brother in the legal firm of Shorunkeh-Sawyerr and Shorunkeh-Sawyerr, which they ran as well as their father's bookstore. By all accounts the legal partnership was a successful and lucrative venture, and the brothers attracted a creditably large clientele.

In spite of the large slice of their time which professional business must have taken, they both found time to engage in numerous other activities. These ranged from politics to a strong interest in esoteric organizations—both were members of the Poro Society and Cabbalistic associations like the Banner Church founded by Professor Abayomi Cole (*q.v.*). They were also keenly and knowledgeably interested in agriculture.

Although the two brothers were inseparable, their

careers followed different paths, and their approach to politics was widely different. Alfred was nominated and became a valued member of the Legislative Council (1911-1924); he was strongly outspoken in his criticism of government policy, yet on certain current political issues he displayed unexpected conservatism. John, by contrast, was reserved to the point of taciturnity, but in his numerous writings and speeches on topical questions, he expressed a quite distinctive radicalism and a strongly pro-African stance.

Though he did not join the local National Congress of British West Africa (founded in 1920, the first organized and articulate group in British West Africa to express open criticism of the colonial system), he addressed meetings of the movement. His text for one such address in 1924 was on high taxation and unrepresentative government. Political tracts, generally written in local newspapers, were part of his literary output, but he also wrote copiously on agriculture.

Keeping up such a range of activities must have taxed his constitution severely, for in his later years he was afflicted with heart trouble and uncertain health. He died on May 29, 1929, exactly eleven days after his brother, and was survived by six children.

AKINTOLA J.G. WYSE

BIBLIOGRAPHY: Christopher Fyfe, *A History of Sierra Leone, London, 1962*; Allister MacMillan, *The Red Book of West Africa,* London, 1920; *Sierra Leone Weekly News.*

SIBTHORPE, A.B.C.

Aaron Belisarius Cosimo Sibthorpe (circa 1840-June 20, 1916) was the first historian of Sierra Leone.

He was probably brought to Sierra Leone as a boy, on a slave ship, as a recaptive, from what is now Nigeria. He grew up at Gloucester village near Freetown. He was educated at the village school, then at the Church Missionary Society Grammar School in Freetown, and at Kissy Normal School. In 1865 he became a teacher at Christ Church, Pademba Road, Freetown.

He showed artistic promise, and exhibited drawings and models at the Sierra Leone Exhibition of 1865. Then he turned to writing, and composed two school textbooks, a *History of Sierra Leone,* and a *Geography of Sierra Leone.* With the help of a visiting school inspector he had them published in London 1868. Both were subsequently revised. Second editions appeared in 1881. A third edition of the *Geography* was published in 1905, and of the *History* in 1906.

As a historian he was a pioneer in an uncharted field, showing the world that the Sierra Leone Colony was a distinctive country, with an articulate people, proud of their achievements. He seems to have had no access to official records in writing his book, but plainly he read widely in printed sources. Not content with a dull political recital, of the type then usual in school textbooks, he enlivened his narrative with details of economic and social life, including lists of commodity prices at successive periods, songs, and proverbs. His *Geography* also included descriptions of village handicrafts and of the prevalent diseases, information not usually found in school textbooks of the period.

In 1869 he moved to Hastings village, east of Freetown, and spent the rest of his working life as an ill-paid teacher and church catechist there, and in the neighboring village of Grafton. He became interested in natural history, discovering in the countryside near Hastings plants and minerals which he believed to be of great economic value. He described his discoveries in a manuscript book, "The Latent Riches of Sierra Leone," but failed to find a publisher for it. Instead he incorporated his descriptions into the later editions of his *History* and *Geography.* This gave them a personal, indeed eccentric, flavor that detracted from their use in schools. Some pages were almost entirely given over to details of the author's own botanical observations. Eventually the schools stopped using them.

Nevertheless, he went on with his scholarly researches, undismayed by lack of recognition and encouragement. He also practiced as a herbal doctor, using medicines of his own making. From time to time he contributed historical articles to the Freetown newspapers. In 1907, at the centenary of the adoption of the Slave Trade Abolition Act, by the British parliament, he delivered an oration which was subsequently published as a pamphlet. In 1909 he published a short book seeking to prove that the Yoruba people were descended from the lost tribes of Israel. But his achievements were little noticed in his homeland. The only public recognition his labors ever received was from a group of Krios (Creoles) in Lagos, Nigeria, who raised a small subscription for him.

On June 20, 1916 he died, and was buried in Kissy cemetery. He was a talented but unrecognized scholar of originality and determination, who lived out his days in humble obscurity, unappreciated by the colonial authorities or by his own countrymen.

CHRISTOPHER FYFE

BIBLIOGRAPHY: Christopher Fyfe, "A.B.C. Sibthorpe: A Neglected Historian," *Sierra Leone Studies* (new series) Vol. X, 1958, *A History of Sierra Leone,* London, 1962; P.E.H. Hair, "A Reference to A.B.C. Sibthorpe," *Sierra Leone Studies* (new series), Vol. XVIII, 1966; A.B.C. Sibthorpe, *The History of Sierra Leone,* London, 1868, 2nd ed., London 1881,

3rd ed., rev., London, 1906, reprinted, London, 1970; *The Geography of Sierra Leone,* 1st ed., London, 1868, 2nd ed., London, 1881, 3rd ed., London, 1905, *The Geography of the Surrounding Territories of Sierra Leone,* London, 1892.

SMART, C.

Charles Smart (18?-circa early 1900s) was an ambitious member of the Loko Smart family which held a high position in Mahera, near the mouth of the Rokel River. In his determination to be free of Temne Koya overlordship, Smart threw in his lot with the colonial administration, and intrigued ruthlessly and successfully to overthrow his enemies.

The famous Loko Smart family, to which Gombu Smart (*q.v.*) belonged, although dominant in Mahera, was nevertheless under the overall rule of Bai Kompa, king of the Koya Temne. The Temne-Loko wars of the mid-19th century had led to the dispersal of the Loko, some of whom found their way to the Colony, and the result was that the Temne now ruled over much of what was formerly Loko country. There still existed a few Loko enclaves, however, of which Mahera was one.

Charles Smart was probably born at Mahera about the 1850s, and was among the many Loko who, wishing for Colony protection, had become Christian. He was educated by the Church Missionary Society, partly in Freetown, and by the 1880s had returned to Mahera determined to rule.

In 1892 Smart, now apparently leader of the Loko Smart family, asked Bai Kompa to make him chief of Mahera, and establish their independence from Koya rulers. Bai Kompa refused, doubtless on account of Charles's Colony and Christian affiliations. Charles then intrigued with the colonial administration, joined the Frontier Police, and had himself installed and officially recognized by the administration as chief of Mahera.

This affront to his sovereignty angered Bai Kompa and his Temne sub-chiefs, an anger that was aggravated by fears that Christianity would spread in their domain, encouraged by Smart. There was now open enmity between Smart, whose loyalties, willingly enough given, were with the administration, and the Temne.

The conflict between the two groups escalated with the declaration of the Protectorate in 1896 and the imposition of a house tax. The Temne were opposed to the provisions of the Protectorate administration, as were other rulers, and particularly opposed the tax, which they determined not to pay. In 1897, however, when Dr. Hood, acting district commissioner of Ronietta, sent a circular to the chiefs of Koya telling them to start collecting the tax, Charles Smart was one of the few who was ready to comply.

Pa Nemgbana, second in command to Bai Kompa, ruler of Koya, is said to have tried to stop him, saying that he, Nemgbana, would take any responsibility if the British came to arrest Smart for failing to collect. Smart immediately reported this to the British authorities, adding that Nemgbana had threatened to kill him if he continued to collect the tax. A British assistant inspector of police was sent to arrest Nemgbana and Bai Kompa, with Smart accompanying them and helping them all the way with information and men. It was on the strength of Smart's evidence that Nemgbana was jailed for 12 months for his defiance of the administration.

Smart continued to exploit opportunities to settle old scores, afforded by the concerted resistance of chiefs to the house tax. He informed the authorities that Serra Bundu of Foredugu, another Koya chiefdom down-river from Mahera, was disloyal, and suggested to the district commissioner that Fula Mansa of Yoni, another 'loyal' chief, be invited to help subdue Bundu. Smart once more accompanied this expedition through Koya country, provoking many skirmishes in which at least 58 Koya Temne were killed.

Enraged at the activities of Smart and his family, the Temne of Masimera revenged themselves by killing his brother, Pa Gombu, at Rokon on the Rokel in Masimera, where he had been collecting tax and blockading the river. The Colony later retaliated by burning Temne towns.

Smart, having played his part in supporting the administration against his Temne opponents and one-time overlords, continued to be supported by the colonial authorities in his position at Mahera until his death which occurred probably early in the 20th century.

C. MAGBAILY FYLE

BIBLIOGRAPHY: Christopher Fyfe, *A History of Sierra Leone,* London, 1962; Sir David Chalmers, *Report on the Subject of the Insurrection in the Protectorate of Sierra Leone, 1898,* London, 1898.

SORI KESSEBEH

Sori Kessebeh (who flourished in the 19th century) was a powerful Loko warrior who left his own country with a number of refugees after the defeat of the Loko by the Temne in the early 1840s. Through his assistance in war to chief R.C.B. Caulker (*q.v.*) of Bumpe, he became chief of Rotifunk, on the higher reaches of the Bumpe River. Despite his affiliations with Islam he was friendly to the Christian missionary movement and sent his son to be educated in Freetown.

Originally known as Sori Kanu, Sori Kessebeh was the son of Sori Kutu, a great warrior king of the Loko who lived around the middle of the 18th century. The Loko at this time had a famous warrior training center in Malal, and their territory spread over an area occupying much of present day Kambia, Bombali, and Port Loko districts. Most Loko warriors trained in Malal, and Sori Kanu was no exception. He had also come under Muslim influence, and was in the habit of covering his war dress with charms called 'Sebbeh'—hence he came to be known as Sori Kesse-beh.

The Loko were slave traders and their major port is still called Port Loko to this day. Soso immigrants who had been allowed to settle in the area gradually usurped power. The neighbors of the Loko, the Temne, plotted secretly and overthrew the Soso hegemony of Port Loko in 1815, installing their own nominee as Moriba Kindo Bangura (q.v.). He died in 1825 and his successor, Fatima Brimah Kamara, mediating in a quarrel between Loko and Temne, made a fateful decision in favor of the Temne that led to a war between the two peoples which lasted for 15 years.

At its conclusion, the Loko were vanquished, push-ed north, and hemmed in between the Mabole and Little Scarcies rivers. Only the Smart family, including Charles Smart (q.v.), remained in a small Loko en-clave surrounded by Temne at Mahera.

At this time, the Loko king was Gbanga Koba-Wa, brother of Sori Kessebeh, who ruled till about 1860. Sori Kessebeh did not get on well with his brother Koba, and being a renowned warrior he accepted the invitation of R.C.B. Caulker, chief of Bumpe, a coastal area south of Freetown, to help him fight his wars. Thus, he emigrated with his followers and was rewarded for his services to Caulker by being given land at Rotifunk, where he became chief.

Here he encouraged farming, and many Loko refugees flocked to the neighborhood of Rotifunk, which soon became an important center of trade. In 1878, Sori Kessebeh allowed the Women's Missionary Association to open a mission station in Rotifunk, under his protection. This was despite his exposure to Islamic influences.

In the 1880s the Yoni Temne threatened the Bumpe district, and in 1882 raided it, but were repelled by Sori Kessebeh with the assistance of police from the Colony and his own 200 Fula residents. In 1886, Yoni, Ribbi, and Bumpe chiefs met in Freetown to make a truce. But there were many personal jealousies existing among them. Even Richard Caulker Kessebeh's

overlord, was suspected of inciting Yoni attacks on Ribbi.

After the rains, hostilities broke out but were more limited in scale, being confined mostly to Yoni desires for a trading center and petty rivalries among the Ribbi and Bumpe chiefs. Yoni attacks continued, however, and in 1887, after incursions into Bauya and Senehun, towns under British jurisdiction, to the south of Rotifunk, followed by an attack on Rotifunk itself, also "British territory," it was decided that the Yoni, formally declared by the British to be the enemy, must be punished. An expedition was sent under Colonel Sir Francis de Winton, supported by over 700 irregulars— Loko under Kessebeh, Mende, Koya Temne, and Fula. The Yoni were defeated and peace concluded at Momaligi.

After the Yoni defeat, Sori Kessebeh took advantage of his friendship with the British and of the missionary presence to extend his territory. When he died in 1897, he was succeeded by his son Santigi Bundu, who had already received his education at the Church Missionary Society Grammar School in Freetown.

ARTHUR ABRAHAM

BIBLIOGRAPHY: Christopher Fyfe, *A History of Sierra Leone,* London, 1962; E. Hirst, "An Attempt at Reconstructing the History of the Loko People from 1790 to the Present," *Sierra Leone Studies,* December, 1957.

SORI SESAY

Almamy Sori Sesay (late 19th century-1970) was a vigorous and enlightened paramount chief of Konike Barina chiefdom in the Tonkolili district of Sierra Leone. One of his main concerns was to persuade the government to build a road to facilitate the marketing of rice which his chiefdom produced in abundance. After many years of campaigning, the road, later to be extended to the Tonkolili-Kona highway, was eventually completed, due in large measure to his efforts.

He was born at Mayopeh in Konike Barina (one of the two Konike chiefdoms in Tonkolili district), a member of the Muslim Sesay ruling family in which he grew up. He appears to have started market operations in rice, for which the chiefdom was noted, on a large scale. By 1930, he had become a successful trader at Magburaka, the nearest big town to Konike Barina and a terminus for the northern branch of the Sierra Leone railway.

When the paramount chief of Konike Barina, Almamy Kanu, died in 1930, Almamy Sori stood as candidate in the subsequent elections. He was opposed by several others, among whom was Ali Fefegura, son of Mirabong Sesay, the last 19th century warrior chief of all the Konike Temne. Almamy Sori won the election but his opponent could not accept defeat and stirred up trouble in the chiefdom during the first two years of Sori's rule. In 1932, Sori took action and had Fefegura banished to Bo by the colonial authorities. Although he eventually forgave him, Fefegura was never allowed to return to Konike Barina.

Lanky in appearance, Almamy Sori was a determined and progressive leader. He made the pilgrimage to Mecca twice during his lifetime, and was nominated unofficial member of the Legislature from 1942 to 1945. He was awarded the Certificate of Honour in 1946 and later of O.B.E. (Order of the British Empire). Successive district commissioners, colonial secretaries, and governors spoke of him in the highest terms. E.F. Sayers, a clear-sighted provincial commissioner in the north, wrote in 1940, that Almamy Sori was "an energetic and progressive minded chief who favors common sense when it and old tradition are in conflict." Another district commissioner stated that the paramount chief had "...a natural dignity and courtesy... [was] very sound and public spirited, [and] ...was prepared to risk unpopularity..." among his subjects for their own benefit. This same district commissioner, however, said on another occasion that Almamy Sori was "impulsive and hasty, quite ready to forget the Native Law and quite prepared to be overbearing." Different situations appeared to bring out different reactions.

One of Almamy Sori's most significant endeavors was his campaign for a road to link his main town of Makali with Matotoka, a town situated on the Bo-Makeni road. Long before the present Tonkolili-Kono highway (completed in 1971) became a reality, he had seen the need for a main artery of this nature. For over 13 years he pressed his case with the colonial authorities, combating their procrastination.

Sori first sent a letter to the district commissioner of Bombali district north of Tonkolili in 1935, requesting the construction of a road whose main purpose would be to assist the marketing of rice which Konike produced so abundantly. The letter stated in no uncertain terms that the paramount chief wanted his people to "get rest [from] transporting loads by head...." He promised labor and financial assistance if only administrative blessing and support were forthcoming.

The colonial authorities showed little interest. A surveyor was sent to examine the area, but no action came of the survey. While the authorities wrangled over cost and feasibility, Almamy Sori again appealed in 1937, this time directly to the governor of Sierra Leone. A survey was again made in 1938 and again the

matter appeared to end there. In July 1939 Almamy Sori tried again, by talking to Governor J.D. Jardine (term of office 1937-41). This brought no quicker action. In August 1940, he wrote again, this time on behalf of all three Konike chiefdoms promising to give all possible help to the project "in order that the chiefdom may gain light."

By this time the project, much discussed on paper by the administration, had expanded to include an extension beyond Makali to Masingbe. Although officially approved, no work was started until the needs of World War II quickened the pace. The colonial administration imposed a rice quota on the provinces in order to feed extra personnel at the important port of Freetown. By 1943, Almamy Sori's report to the provincial commissioner indicated that transporting rice by headloads made it impossible for his chiefdom to fulfill its quota. Thus spurred, the governor in November 1943, ordered work on the Matotoka-Makali road to be started as soon as possible. Only now was the need for a road, expressed by Sori eight years earlier, felt to be urgent.

Work was started in 1944, but with the end of the war the sense of urgency died down, and the difficulties of finding labor and the fact that the road would pass through secret society bush loomed as grave problems. Thus the work was suspended. In 1947, it was resumed, and was finished by June 1948. Finally, Almamy Sori's 13-year-old dream became a reality, amid celebrations in Konike. It was this road that was extended and later remade in 1971 to become the Tonkolili-Kono highway.

Almamy Sori died in 1970 after ruling as paramount chief of Konike Barina for 40 years. He was buried at his capital Makali.

C. MAGBAILY FYLE

BIBLIOGRAPHY: J. Peterson, "The Kono Road Project: An Overview," in the proceedings of the seminar on "Implications of Development on Population," Institute of African Studies, Fourah Bay College, 1975; E.F. Sayers, "Notes on the Clan and Family Names Common in the Area inhabited by Temne-speaking Poeples," *Sierra Leone Studies*, December, 1927; Sierra Leone Government, *Provinces Handbook, 1962,* Freetown, 1963.

SULUKU

Almamy Suluku (circa 1820-1906), chief of Bumban, was a forceful and able leader who ruled over the Biriwa Limba in a large area of northern Sierra Leone from 1873 to 1906. Strongly aware of the commercial importance of his territory, he maintained an uneasy alliance with the Sofa forces of the Mandinka emperor Samori Touré, as well as establishing good relations with the British in Freetown—a game which became increasingly difficult to play once Samori's forces had attacked his country.

Suluku was of the Limba Konte clan, which originated in Sankaran, and was the second son of Sankailay, the gbaku (ruler) of Biriwa Limba country. He was brought up at Bumban, the capital of Biriwa, situated between the upper Mabole and Rokel rivers, and grew up to be a great warrior. While his brothers were made heads of towns by his father, Suluku remained at the capital as kurugba (warrior). As warrior he was responsible for bringing the Safroko Limba under Biriwa rule. Because of his continued presence at the capital and the degree of influence he came to wield, the question of succession in Biriwa was easily determined. When his father Sankailay died in 1873, Suluku succeeded him as ruler, thus becoming the "biggest man in the country," despite his father's earlier nomination of his elder brother Bubu as successor.

Under Suluku, Biriwa included Mandinka and Fula settlements which accepted his authority. These promoted the development of commerce in his territory. As ruler, he appointed his son, Kpebe as governor of the Safroko provinces, while still retaining a large measure of control himself. Suluku's polity was considered one of the largest in Sierra Leone hinterland, extending for "over two days' march." He developed a considered commercial policy to back his political authority, bringing growth to Biriwa. He fostered trade in gold, ivory, and hides from the northern interior which then passed to the Colony through his country thus earning him additional income. Those who robbed traders in Biriwa were punished by Suluku.

He also made alliances with the neighboring Temne rulers of Port Loko, an important trading center on Port Loko Creek, in order to protect trade. These measures earned him the attention of the colonial administration, which sent him annual presents in the 1870s and 1880s to secure his friendship. Since much of the produce sustaining the Colony came from around Biriwa, Suluku's friendship was well worth cultivating.

In 1884, the Sofa attacked Biriwa. Suluku put together a force and defended his country but by November of that year had been defeated by the Sofa general Nfa Ali. The Sofa then stationed a force of occupation in Biriwa which, in collusion with Suluku's Mandinka subjects, planned to bring about Suluku's economic ruin.

Calculating that British interest in commodities coming from Biriwa would spur them on to intervene and save him, Suluku made urgent representations to the Colony. He also enlisted the support of the Alikali of Port Loko, whose trade had been similarly affected, in approaching the British. Eventually, Major Morton Festing, one of the governor's special service officers, persuaded the Sofa force of occupation to leave Biriwa in 1888.

Suluku then re-established his authority over the Biriwa Mandinka who had collaborated with the Sofa. He became hostile to all Sofa traders passing through Biriwa, and stopped the passage of Sofa arms through his country. The colonial administration, interested in the Sofa as a new means of channeling trade to the Colony, sent a mission to Suluku to persuade him against these moves. Suluku merely treated the messengers from the Colony to lavish hospitality, feeding them sumptuously and pressing gifts on them. They returned full of his praises, but without having carried out the purpose of their mission. Suluku continued to play a double game, even while the British sought to administer the hinterland as a Protectorate, though he still maintained a reputation of unswerving loyalty to their cause, which he used to overawe neighboring local rulers.

When the Protectorate was finally declared in 1896, Suluku's tactics could no longer ensure his independence of action. The British imposed a house tax which aroused opposition from local rulers and resulted in the uprising of 1898. Biriwa, as part of the Koinadugu district which was initially exempted from taxation, did not participate actively in the war. But Suluku was reported to have supplied arms secretly to the Temne rulers to help them in the war, apparently to retain his position as a leading chief in the area.

The war of resistance was crushed and the tax again imposed. In the division of the country into administrative districts, the former Safroko Limba province was detached from Biriwa, to which it had owed allegiance, and added to the Temne chiefdom of Mapaki. As tax from each village and town was to be paid to the paramount chief of its chiefdom, the Safroko were expected to pay to Massa Paki, head of the Mapaki chiefdom. Most of the Safroko Limba towns claimed they would not pay him but only Suluku, whom they considered their rightful overlord, thus indicating the loyalty Suluku had inspired in his former subjects. The matter was resolved after a lengthy inquiry which resulted in re-attaching Safroko towns to Biriwa.

Suluku died in 1906. When very old, he was asked by the district commissioner to name his successor. He replied "Suluku will never die." He did so physically, but not in the minds of the Biriwa.

C. MAGBAILY FYLE

BIBLIOGRAPHY: C. Magbaily Fyle, "Almamy Suluku of Biriwa Limba," (forthcoming).

SUMAN

Almamy Suman (circa 1810-1905) was ruler of the Wara Wara Limba in the 19th century. Like many northern chiefs, his country was severely affected by the aggressive activities of the Sofa, warriors of the Mandinka emperor Samori Touré. Despite a treaty of friendship with the British, his area of jurisdiction was much decreased by the turmoils of the Sofa invasions.

He was born in the early 19th century, a member of the Limba Mansaray clan, descended from Ba Foday Mansaray (q.v.), founder of Bafodea, then capital of the Wara Wara Limba state. He had started to rule by the middle of the century, and in the 1870s led his people in collaboration with the Hubu (Fula rebels south of Futa Jallon, in what is now the Republic of Guinea) against the Yalunka state of Solimana in the far northeastern corner of Sierra Leone.

When, in the course of his wars of expansion, Samori's forces reached the Sierra Leone hinterland, Almamy Suman prudently submitted to the Sofa rather than have his country destroyed. In 1886, he joined another powerful Limba ruler, Almamy Suluku (q.v.), to petition the British for assistance in securing the trade routes which had been affected by Samori's campaigns. By 1889, the British colonial government was making moves to sign treaties with more distant rulers in the hinterland, and a treaty of friendship was signed with Almamy Suman as ruler of all the Wara Wara, in 1890.

By this time, the Sofa had recaptured the northeastern part of Sierra Leone which had rebelled against Samori in 1889, and reclaimed it as part of his empire. Sofa activities in Suman's country made him intensely hostile towards them. When Sayo of Kaliere (formerly in the Solima state) fled from the Sofa to take refuge with Suman at Bafodea, the latter closed the trade route to Freetown through his country as a way of revenging himself on the invaders.

The aftermath of the Sofa invasion created unrest which greatly reduced the area under Almamy Suman's rule. Some of his sub-chiefs sided with the Sofa against him in order to secure their independence. The Limba of Bongobong and Kakrima are examples. After the Sofa had left, the Bongobong Limba, determined to be free of his rule, enlisted the help of mercenaries to fight against him.

When the British took over the hinterland as a Protectorate in 1896, Bongobong and Kakrima were regarded as independent of Suman and made separate chiefdoms. Greatly reduced in authority and weakened by the upheavals of the 1880s and 1890s, Almamy Suman died in 1905.

C. MAGBAILY FYLE.

BIBLIOGRAPHY: C. Magbaily Fyle, "Solimana and its Neighbors," unpublished Ph.D. thesis, Northwestern University, 1976.

TAQI, I.B.

Ibrahim Bash Taqi (September 18, 1931-July 1975) was a journalist and politician. His forceful journalism, particularly as a columnist of *We Yone,* organ of the All People's Congress, (A.P.C.) contributed significantly to the fall in popularity of the Sierra Leone People's Party (S.L.P.P.) in the 1967 general elections.

Taqi was born at Ropolo, Tane chiefdom, in Tonkolili district. He was educated at the Prince of Wales School, Freetown and then at Ibadan University, Nigeria, and at Heidelberg University in the Federal Republic of Germany.

In March 1967 he was elected to Parliament as member for Freetown East I constituency, and was sworn in as minister of information in the government of Siaka Stevens, Leader of the All People's Congress (A.P.C.). The National Reformation Council military regime intervened, however, and civilian rule was halted. When it resumed in 1968, Taqi became a government back bencher until he was appointed minister of information and broadcasting in April 1969.

In September 1970 he was arrested and detained under public emergency regulations after he had resigned from the A.P.C. and joined the newly formed opposition party, the United Democratic Party (U.D.P.). After his release in 1973, he was re-arrested in 1974 and charged with treason in the case of Forna and 14 others. He was convicted and executed at Pademba Road Prisons in July 1975.

CYRIL P. FORAY

BIBLIOGRAPHY: Cyril P. Foray, *Historical Dictionary of Sierra Leone,* Metuchen, New Jersey, and London, 1977.

THOMAS, J.H.

John Henry 'Malamah' Thomas (February, 1845-January 17, 1922) of recaptive descent became a prosperous merchant and a leading figure among the Krios (Creoles) of Freetown. He was several times mayor of Freetown.

John Henry, later nicknamed "Malamah", was born at the village of Hastings, near Freetown, in

February 1845 to John and Betty Thomas. His parents were Liberated Africans of the Egba (Yoruba) ethnic group. His father was a subsistence farmer, and his mother a laundress. At the age of three, John's father died, and his mother had to work hard to bring him up. Though his parents were Christians of the Anglican denomination, his mother could not at first afford to send him to the Anglican Day School, which was more expensive. John had to start school in 1849 at the Wesleyan Day school, where the fees were twopence a month. In 1856, however, John joined the Anglican school.

The poverty of his family made it impossible for him to attend school regularly. He had to spend two days of the week helping his mother by doing odd jobs in the neighborhood, such as fetching firewood or cleaning ginger for money. In these circumstances, John had to leave school in 1859, and was unable to attend secondary school. He was, however, said to be good at arithmetic, though not at English grammar.

John entered business after leaving school through the agency of one of his father's friends, a Mr. Thomas Macaulay. Macaulay had a business on the Rio Nunez River, and he took Thomas there to be trained. Board, lodging, and a few shillings' monthly allowance was John's initial renumeration. By 1867, however, the activities of the French on the Nunez forced many Krio traders out of that area. Mr. Macaulay had to transfer his business to the Scarcies River, and took John with him as his clerk. But business was bad for Mr. Macaulay and he wound his company up that very year.

Because he valued John, however, Macaulay recommended him for a job with the Company of African Merchants, Ltd., which had recently begun trading in Sierra Leone. John joined this company in February 1868, and was immediately sent to the Sherbro branch as a bookkeeper. He was there until September 1872, when the company ended its Sierra Leone activities. Again, his assuidity was to pay off, and an agent of the company took him to the branch at Calabar, in what is now Nigeria, again as a bookkeeper.

By this time, however, John Thomas had married Christianna Rollings, the sister of T.J. Rollings, a shopkeeper in Westmoreland Street, Freetown. John went to Calabar with his wife, and it was while he was there that he decided to return home and set up on his own as a trader on the Rokel River. By now he was a reasonably successful man, and the confidence he had gained inspired great hopes of success in him. He had little capital to begin with, however, and a friend, Dr. Robert Smith, loaned him £100 with which he began.

Thomas started trading on the Rokel in December 1872. The loan was quickly paid off, and the business became established enough to compete effectively with other concerns on the Rokel. John built a factory at Malamah on the Rokel, which became the center of his business. From this time on he was nicknamed "Malamah."

A few years later Ernest Vohsen, an agent for the Compagnie du Sénégal, (later the Compagnie Francaise de l'Afrique Occidentale, popularly known as C.F.A.O.), approached Thomas about working for that company. Vohsen, who was the company's agent on the Scarcies, asked Thomas whether he would be willing to take over his functions. Thomas agreed and closed his business on the Rokel. Before taking up the post on the Scarcies, in October 1882 he opened a small shop in Freetown which he left in his wife's charge.

Thomas held the C.F.A.O. agency on the Scarcies until June 1888, when he resigned and returned to Freetown to prosecute his business more effectively. Under his supervision the business expanded and prospered, and Thomas became one of the foremost merchants in the city. He built a beautiful house in East Street (still retained by his grandson), which became known as "Malamah House". It was the first of its kind in Freetown. The decorative carved heads on this house gave him another nickname 'ed ed' (head-head) Thomas. Thomas traded chiefly in cotton fabrics. He invented, and patented in England, his own brand of cotton known as 'Malamah baft'.

Having gained wealth and security, Thomas participated in Freetown society on a grand scale. He dressed elegantly, smoked cigars, played billiards, and often visited England on business or for pleasure. In 1896, his daughter, Christianna, got married to Councillor C.C. Nicole, a Freetown contractor. John Malamah hired nearly half the houses in East Street for the ceremony. Many came from neighboring villages to witness the event, and business in Freetown was virtually at a standstill for several days before the wedding.

Thomas also served both church and state. He was for 13 years warden of Holy Trinity Church at Kissy Road in Freetown. Later he became a treasurer of that church, as well as of the Sierra Leone Native Pastorate Church. In December 1891, he had been appointed charity commissioner by Acting Governor J.J. Crooks, and had become commissioner of the peace in 1894. In the Freetown municipal elections of 1903, he entered the city council for the East Ward. In 1904 he was elected mayor of Freetown, and held that position in eight other years—1905, 1906, 1908, 1909, and 1911-14. In 1907, he was appointed as an unofficial member of the Legislative Council in Freetown. This was a position of high honor as there was usually only one indigenous member of that council.

Malamah Thomas was also president of the Kissy Road Traders Association. Some of his political activities went beyond Sierra Leone, for he became president of the local branch of the National Congress of British West Africa. This was a body, formed in 1920, advocating united political agitation for self-government among the African peoples of British West Africa. He supported the congress both with his time and his money.

John Malamah Thomas died in Freetown on January 17, 1922. He was deeply mourned, and the tribute in the local *Sierra Leone Weekly News* was testimony to the contribution he had made to Sierra Leone's development.

C. MAGBAILY FYLE

BIBLIOGRAPHY: Christopher Fyfe, *History of Sierra Leone*, London, 1962, (ed.), *Sierra Leone Inheritance*, London, 1964; *Sierra Leone Weekly News*.

THOMAS, S.B.

Samuel Benjamin (Abuke) Thomas (1833-1901) was a hard-working businessman who, by frugal living and shrewd investment, amassed a large fortune from which he left a substantial endowment for an agricultural college on his death.

He was born in Wellington, a village near Freetown, which was the home of many other illustrious Sierra Leoneans. Not much is known of his early life. He was educated for the Anglican ministry at Fourah Bay Institution, but turned to business, using as capital the legacy left by his father, a well-to-do businessman himself.

Contrary to the popular notion contained in some history text-books that the Krio (Creoles) of Sierra Leone scorned agriculture and were only interested in white-collar jobs, men like J.A. Songo Davies, J.C. Shorunkeh-Sawyerr (*q.v.*), Professor J. Abayomi-Cole (*q.v.*) and Samuel Thomas developed a keen interest in practical agriculture.

Where others possessed zeal and ideas on the subject, Thomas had the wealth, foresight and dedication to give practical expression to his views. When he died, he left an endowment of over £54,000 for the establishment of an agricultural college to train his countrymen not only in the liberal arts and sound Christian teaching but also in the theory and practice of agriculture. The S.B. Thomas Agricultural Academy, which was established at Mabang on the Ribi River with his money, was completed in 1912.

A plaque in his local church in Wellington commemorates his death in 1901.

AKINTOLA J.G. WYSE

BIBLIOGRAPHY: Christopher Fyfe, *A History of Sierra Leone*, London, 1962; *Sierra Leone Weekly News*.

TOKBA ASANA SAMURA

Tokba Asana Samura (circa 1730-1788) was the courageous leader who inspired the Solima Yalunka of far northeastern Sierra Leone to rise against the oppressive overlordship of the Fula of Futa Jallon, in what is now the Republic of Guinea. He was also the founder of Falaba, chief town of the Solima state, which resisted all attacks for more than a hundred years.

He was born about 1730, the second son of Yima Yella, the manga (ruler) of Solima country. When Asana's older brother, Yella Dansa, became ruler of the Solima in his turn, Asana became his war leader. By this time the Yalunka of Solima country and other Yalunka in the neighborhood had come under the rule of the Fula, who from 1727 on had been waging a continuous jihad (religious war), and were forced to fight with the Fula against other neighboring countries. They were also being heavily taxed by the Fula, and found their overlordship extremely irksome but could see no way to free themselves.

Tokba Asana, however, rallied the Yalunka to defiance. Some time during the 1770s he called together Yalunka elders of Solima, Sinkunia, Dembelia, and Folosaba countries (all in what is now the Koinadugu district) to discuss the odious subject of vassalage to the Fula. He persuaded them all to "eat country bread" (that is, take a binding oath) and thereby swear to free themselves of Fula overrule and to be led by him in this quest.

Under Tokba Asana's leadership, the combined Yalunka force withdrew its support for the Fula in a war against Konde Brima of Sankaran, in what is now the Republic of Guinea. In retaliation, the Fula killed all Solima Yalunka headmen then in Futa Jallon. The Solima responded by killing all Fula in Solima country. Tokba Asana then led the Yalunka in an alliance with Konde Brima of Sankaran, and there started a period of Futa-Solima wars.

It was during these wars that Falaba was founded by the combined Yalunka force under Tokba Asana. After three centers of resistance had been destroyed by the Fula, the Yalunka forces moved southwards and about 1780 established Falaba in an almost impregnable position. Falaba proved its worth, surviving a number of attacks for over a century until in 1884 the forces of the Mandinka conqueror, Samori, destroyed it after a nine months' siege.

Under Tokba Asana, Falaba became the capital of the Solima Yalunka state which came to include all those who had sworn the oath to be led by him in war against the Fula—the Mansaray Yalunka of Sinkunia, the Jawara Yalunka of Dembelia, and the Kamara Yalunka of Folosaba. Thus he became the first ruler of the greater Solima state.

In 1788, the Yalunka forces, still led by Tokba Asana, decided to strike a final blow against the Fula. The two large armies met on the plains of the Herico River, in the Sulima chiefdom, Koinadugu district, and a bloody battle took place, in which Tokba Asana lost his life.

C. MAGBAILY FYLE

BIBLIOGRAPHY: C. Magbaily Fyle, "The Origins and Integration of the Solima Yalunka State," *Africana Research Bulletin*, VI, I, 1976.

TOM II, "KING"

'King' Tom II (late 18th-early 19th century) was the Temne chief who contested the Sierra Leone Company's right to land ceded by his predecessor, thus provoking warfare between the Temne and the newly established Colony. His resistance was finally overcome and resulted in a treaty with the Colony giving it right by conquest to the disputed land.

'King' Tom was the title assumed by Pa Kokelly, a Temne chief from the Rokel River estuary region, who in 1796 succeeded 'King' Jimmy as ruler of the 'watering place' on Bullom Shore, where since the 17th century ships had paid dues to the ruler for water and firewood. His son Henry studied in England at the expense of the Sierra Leone Company.

After 'King' Jimmy's death, 'King' Tom II became 'landlord' of the Sierra Leone Company, being appointed to this position by Bai Farma, his overlord. Upset because the company did not observe the traditional rules governing landlord/tenant relationships, 'King' Tom II refused to recognize the treaties made by his predecessors. Representatives of the Sierra Leone Company tried in vain to persuade him that, by the terms of the treaty of August 1788, the piece of land had been paid for and alienated to them. 'King' Tom maintained that land could not be alienated. He also refused to accept boundary lines laid down by the company, particularly on the western limit of the Colony.

Towards the end of 1799 there was an insurrection among the Nova Scotian settlers, one of whose principal grievances was the imposition of quit-rents to be paid to the company. In their rebellion they found a ready ally in 'King' Tom. Encouraged by refugee rebels, his Temne forces together with Bai Farma attacked Fort Thornton, Freetown, on November 18, 1801, killing an officer, two soldiers, and a number of defenseless persons. Shortly after, on December 2, 1801, the Colony retaliated by attacking and burning down 'King' Tom's towns between Freetown and Cape Sierra Leone. Subdued by this display of Colony force, 'King' Tom retreated to the Northern Rivers, where the Mandinka chiefs tried to mediate between the Temne and the Colony. Nonetheless, Fatima Fodi, the Mandinka chiefs' envoy, encouraged 'King' Tom to resume fighting. Capt. Charles Bullen of H.M.S. *WASP*, whose sailors had participated in the attack on 'King' Tom's towns in December, tried unsuccessfully to make peace. When he sailed away on April 1, 1802, the Temne chiefs, who had promised peace, found it opportune to strike again. Reinforced by Soso and some refugee rebels, they attacked Fort Thornton again on Sunday, April 11, but were driven back within half an hour and expelled from the Colony.

'King' Tom, supported by a Bullom war-chief, continued the resistance on the Bullom Shore, but his ally was soon overcome and expelled from his territory. Now virtually unsupported, 'King' Tom returned to his domain east of the Colony where he and the Koya Temne remained peacefully. In 1807 a final settlement was negotiated at Robis (between the present Wellington and Hastings) between him and the Colony.

The new treaty, signed on July 10, 1807, confirmed the Colony's conquest of the lands west of Freetown. The Temne chiefs also 'ceded' the right to the peninsula to the company, and cession by means of purchase 'was superseded by conquest.'

CYRIL P. FORAY

BIBLIOGRAPHY: J.J. Crooks, *A History of the Colony of Sierra Seone,* Dublin, 1903, reprinted London, 1972; Christopher Fyfe, *A History of Sierra Leone,* London, 1962; J. Peterson, *The Province of Freedom: A History of Sierra Leone 1787-1870,* London and Evanston, 1969.

TOM KEBBIE SMITH

Tom Kebbie Smith (18?-1878) was a man who rose from obscurity to become chief of Mongray in Imperi country on the Sherbro mainland. Holding his position through wealth and influence rather than popularity, he had to contend with serious opposition to his chiefship.

Nothing is known about Tom Kebbie's early life except that he was of humble, perhaps slave, origin, who by dint of personal effort became exceedingly wealthy. He had many dependents, held much land and traded extensively.

When the chief of Mongray died, Tom Kebbie used his wealth and personal influence to get himself elected. But although some chiefs offered him the horse-tail which symbolized authority, the people of Mongray dissociated themselves from his installation, denied him their allegiance, and claimed that he should surrender the horse-tail. Tom Kebbie, however, refused, and insisted that the people should be his subjects. But war threatened, since the late chief's son, Lahai Sheriff, provided leadership for the opposition.

In 1875, Tom Kebbie granted land to one of his dependents. This grant was disputed by one of the chiefs of Mongray, Lahai Golay, who maintained that he had claims to it. He tried to evict the tenant, who appealed to Tom Kebbie after a riot had ensued. Lahai Sheriff made common cause with Lahai Golay, but even in alliance they could not unseat Tom Kebbie, who had formed alliances with some of his opponents' rivals.

An ambitious man, Kebbie aspired to the sovereignty of the country round the Jong and Small Bum rivers. But, as before, there were objections from other chiefs who refused to elect him king, in spite of his affluence, because of his origins.

In 1878, Tom Kebbie died, having failed in his attempts to be elected ruler of Jong. His death was a source of worry to the Colony, as a struggle for his property and slaves was anticipated. Such was the fear of general chaos generated by this and other events that the Edwards-Loggie mission was set up to make a survey of the area with a view to averting trouble.

ARTHUR ABRAHAM

BIBLIOGRAPHY: Arthur Abraham, *Mende Government and Politics Under Colonial Rule*, Freetown, 1978.

TOBOKU-METZGER, A.E.

Albert Emerick Tuboku-Metzger (October 14, 1856- July 20, 1950), though seldom acknowledged by posterity, was in his day one of the most active of leading African politicians. A fervent pro-African, he played an important role in the early years of the National Congress of British West Africa, of which he eventually became president. He was a consistent defender of his countrymen against colonial attitudes of superiority.

Albert was born at Kissy, a village east of Freetown, in 1856. He was the son of an Egba recaptive from Yorubaland who may well have adopted the surname of the local German missionary. As a young man Albert, supporting nascent African 'nationalism' and reacting against Darwinian racism of the late 19th century, added the African surname of Tuboku to his German legacy.

Young Albert attended the Church Missionary Society Grammar School and, in preparation for a career in the church, studied at Fourah Bay College from 1877 to 1881. He took a bachelor of arts degree and then read for a licentiate in theology which he took with first class honors, the only student to achieve this. He later acquired a master of arts degree after teaching at Fourah Bay College for four years from 1881 to 1885.

Tuboku-Metzger was the first Sierra Leone graduate to enter the colonial service. In 1885 he was taken on as a treasury clerk at the ridiculously low salary of £45 per annum, a position and remuneration far below what a graduate in England would expect. He later worked in the registrar-generals office and the police service. As a police clerk he was requested by the attorney general to draft the Magistrate's Court Ordinance (1905), the Summary Convictions Ordinance (1906), and the Court of Requests Ordinance (1906). Finally in 1908 he was appointed African assistant district commissioner with the privileges and powers of a police magistrate. He retired in 1917 with a favorable report on his career, though he was under a heavy cloud in 1916 for over-assessment while carrying out his jurisdiction in northern Sherbro district.

With his wealth of experience and a knowledge of local government without parallel, Toboku-Metzger was often asked for his views, which were always given with precision and confidence and carried considerable weight with his peers.

As a foundation member of the National Congress of British West Africa, the first articulate organization to express open criticism of colonial government, and which was established in 1920, he played a prominent role in the earlier stages of the development of 20th century African politics. He became one of the congress's vice presidents and eventually president, in

which capacity he did much to steer the movement wisely and keep it active. This was so much so that an official memorandum of 1936 admitted that only in Sierra Leone was the congress ideal being kept alive.

In 1924, Toboku-Metzger was elected as rural representative in the newly reconstituted Legislative Council, where his efforts on behalf of his constituents' interests were considerable. Unfortunately he lost his seat to J.G. Hyde, in 1929, but by that time he was an old man in his seventies.

Like other prominent Krios, he was active in many fields. He took a strong interest in church affairs, serving on all the principal committees of the Sierra Leone Church. He was the Anglican representative in the College Council of Fourah Bay College for a number of years, and did useful work as diocesan lay reader.

He could also lay claim to being a local historian. One of his publications, in pamphlet form, was a *Historical Sketch of the Sierra Leone Grammar School, 1845-1935*. He also wrote prolifically on institutions and events in Sierra Leone, particularly in the Protectorate, his articles being published in the leading contemporary paper, the *Sierra Leone Weekly News*. Following his term of office as an assistant district commissioner—the last black man to be appointed to such a post during the colonial period—Albert was regarded as an authority on Protectorate affairs, impressing even Governor Henry Monck-Mason Moore (term of office 1934-37) by the lucidity of his writings.

On the practical side, Albert was a keen gardener and held strong beliefs in the importance of technical education, for which reason he sent his boys to the Albert Academy, at that time the only secondary school which taught elementary science.

By the time he died on July 20, 1950, Toboku-Metzger had witnessed and participated in many of the important events in the development of Sierra Leone politics. For his public services he was awarded first a Certificate of Honour, then an M.B.E. (Member of the British Empire). He was also a justice of the peace.

AKINTOLA J.G. WYSE

BIBLIOGRAPHY: Christopher Fyfe, *A History of Sierra Leone,* London, 1962; A.E. Toboku-Metzger, *Historical Sketch of the Sierra Leone Grammar School, 1845-1935,* (pamphlet), Freetown, 1935; *Sierra Leone Weekly News.*

TUCKER, N.

Nancy Tucker (18?-1908) was a trader from the Kittam in southern Sierra Leone who settled in Sembehun in Bagru country further to the north. From being entertainer to native and later European officials, she rose by somewhat dubious methods to the position of chief of Baru. Having adopted a line of enthusiastic collaboration with the colonial administration over their plans for a Protectorate, she was kept in power by its backing during and after the wars of resistance of 1898.

Nancy was the mistress of Sergeant Coker, a Temne member of the Frontier Police. When the 1896 Protectorate Ordinance was proclaimed there was widespread resentment at the imposition of a house tax. Nancy, however, promised to collect the tax if she were made chief of Bagru, the former chief, Humpa Rango of Dodo, having died a few years previously. With the help of her lover, she was installed as 'provisional paramount chief of Bagru.'

When the time came for the collection of tax, Nancy, like Madam Yoko (*q.v.*) of Senehun, was vigorous in carrying out this duty, even paying out of her own pocket to make it appear that her people were not opposed to the new administration. Like Yoko, she had to be smuggled away from danger under Frontier Police escort to the barracks at Kwelu, further up the Bagru River, for protection against threats of murder by warriors fighting the war of resistance. Later she was sent secretly to Freetown.

After the war Nancy, back in Sembehun, "proved most useful in bringing many offenders to justice." As a result, her position was confirmed by the governor and she remained paramount chief until her death in 1908.

ARTHUR ABRAHAM

BIBLIOGRAPHY: Arthur Abraham, *Mende Government and Politics Under Colonial Rule*, Freetown, 1978; Christopher Fyfe, *A History of Sierra Leone,* London, 1962; F.W.H. Migeod, *A View of Sierra Leone,* London, 1926.

TUCKER, T. DeSALIERE

Thomas DeSaliere Tucker (1844-1903) was one of the early pupils of the American Missionary Association's Mende Mission in the Sherbro. At the age of 12 he was taken to the United States to study, and remained there to make a distinguished career for himself in higher education for black Americans, becoming first president of the State Normal College at Tallahassee, Florida.

Born in the Sherbro country, Tucker was the son of a French explorer father, while his mother was the daughter of chief Harry Tucker. His mother's family had for many years been prominent merchants and slave traders. He received his early education at the Mende Mission, and in 1856 the missionaries took him to the United States where he enrolled in the preparatory school of Oberlin College in Ohio.

Having graduated from the preparatory school, he entered the college in 1860. In 1862, he took leave from the college and went to Virginia to teach the recently liberated slaves in the American Missionary Association's school at Fortress Monroe. He returned to Oberlin and graduated in 1865. He then taught schools for the freedmen, first in Georgetown, Kentucky, and later in New Orleans, Louisiana. He received a degree in law from Straight College of New Orleans (now Dillard University) in 1883, and was a practising attorney in Pensacola, Florida, for four years.

The Sierra Leone missionaries and the officers of the American Missionary Association were disappointed that Tucker did not return to his homeland, even though he had the 'deepest sympathy' for it. He explained that his family connections there would present 'trials and temptations' that would make it impossible for him to live the life of a Christian.

In 1887 he was co-founder with Thomas Vann Gibbs, of the State Normal College (for blacks) at Tallahassee, Florida. He became the first president of this institution which was to evolve into Florida A. and M. University. Of his appointment to the presidency of the school, the editor of the Pensacola *Southern Leader* wrote on August 20, 1887:

> The State Board of Education certainly deserves much credit for the appointments recently made for this school....We have known Professor Tucker for about 18 years and we have never met a more genial, broadminded and sterling gentleman. He possesses first-class qualities as a friend, gentleman and scholar, and commands the respect of all who know him. He is a strong man, morally and intellectually, and the new Normal has a security of success under his charge.

Tucker left Tallahassee in 1901 and went to Jacksonville, Florida, where he resumed his practice of law. He died in 1903, and was buried in Baltimore, Maryland.

CLIFTON H. JOHNSON

BIBLIOGRAPHY: Clara M. DeBoer, "The Role of Afro-Americans in the Origin and Work of the American Missionary Association, 1839-1877," Ph.D. dissertation, Rutgers University, New Jersey, 1973; Clifton H. Johnson, "African Missionaries to U.S. Freedmen," *The Crisis*, November, 1971.

VA FORAY SASSABLA

Va Foray Sassabla, also known as Foray Kallon, (who flourished in about the 17th century) was the ancestral father of the Kallon, a people widely dispersed over western Sierra Leone today, but who originated in present-day Jawe chiefdom in the Kailahun district.

The first settler in Jawe was the leader of a band of wandering Gola hunters (a people living mostly in western Liberia but spreading into eastern Sierra Leone), called Yarvai. Some traditions say that he fought a war with the Mende and Gola; others say he settled there peacefully. When his followers returned later, however, he was full of anxiety because his wife was pregnant, and she did indeed die in childbirth. Yarvai then swore never to return home but to stay near the grave of his wife. Thus the settlement which grew up there came to be called 'Kambama,' meaning in Mende 'on the grave.'

Not long after, a moriman (charm-maker priest) from Kariko in Koranko country, to the northeast of Sierra Leone, arrived at Kambama, apparently on his way to the coast to obtain white paper and salt. He was called Va Foray Sassabla, and he forecast that the virgin woods so common in the area would soon be teeming with settlements, and that "cocks crowing in one village would be heard in another." He decided, before finally settling down, to make a short trip home. There he was told that the best place for him to settle was a spot where the rain water drained in the direction of 'Kon,' i.e., roughly north or northeastwards.

When Va Foray came back he presented Yarvai with two bottles of wine and two heads (casks) of tobacco. He then erected a temporary shelter beyond the Nikagboiyei River, but still bore in mind his instructions. When he saw the spot he had been looking for, he built a hut there under the 'folei' tree, and the village which grew up around him came to be called Folu, a contracted form of 'folei bu,' meaning 'under the folei tree.'

As Va Foray got himself properly settled in, he asked Yarvai for a wife to consummate their friendship. After talking the matter over with his elders, Yarvai agreed to give Va Foray his daughter, Kefuegunde. Va Foray had many sons by this union, all of whom he sent to Koranko to be educated in Arabic. He managed to keep all of them there, except the last, Borbowa, whom he loved most.

Va Foray wanted Borbowa to succeed him, and being very old at the time, explained the situation to Yarvai, who agreed to his wishes. Va Foray fell ill shortly after and died. Borbowa performed all the funeral rites, and as a mark of respect, buried his father right in the middle of his house in Folu.

When they heard of his succession, however, Borbowa's brothers came from Koranko to protest to Yarvai. To appease them, he allowed them to settle in neighboring areas. Some went far afield and settled in Barrie Potoru, Nongowa, and Koya countries, where the Kallons, their descendants, still live today. In Jawe, Yarvai, on his deathbed, handed over control of his rudimentary state to Borbowa. His descendants, the Kallons, have since held a degree of political power in Jawe.

ARTHUR ABRAHAM

BIBLIOGRAPHY: Arthur Abraham, *Mende Government and Politics Under Colonial Rule*, Freetown, 1978.

WALLACE-JOHNSON, I.T.A.

Isaac Theophilus Akuna Wallace-Johnson (February 6, 1894-May 16, 1965), militant trade unionist, journalist and political activist, was one of the few radical revolutionary spirits in the final decades of colonial government in Sierra Leone. In the forefront of various self-determination movements, he was an ardent campaigner for African workers' rights and a dedicated believer in the ideals of pan-Africanism.

He was born in Wilberforce village, Freetown, in 1895. He was educated at the village school and subsequently at the Centenary Tabernacle School, Freetown. At the age of 18 he entered government service as an outdoor officer of the Customs Department. Soon he had persuaded his fellow-workers to strike for better pay, and was immediately dismissed, along with other leading strikers. After his reinstatement, he again pressed for better wages and conditions of service. He was then transferred to the army as records and confidential clerk, and served in East Africa, the Cameroons, and the Middle East.

Demobilized in 1920, he first worked briefly with the United African Company (U.A.C.) and then at the Freetown City Council where he rose to the position of chief clerk at the Water Works Department. His departure from the City Council followed the same pattern as his earlier dismissal. He was discharged for organizing his colleagues to demand higher pay and better working conditions. He then decided to become a sailor, and for the next five years moved round European, Asian, and African ports, during which time he managed to publish *The Seafarer*, a periodical dedicated to promoting the welfare of seamen.

By 1930, Wallace had returned to Sierra Leone. Using the alias of E. Richards, he went in that year as unofficial representative of the Sierra Leone Railroad Workers' Union to the first International Conference of Negro Workers in Hamburg, Germany, where, after a piece of convincing and impassioned oratory, he was elected to the praesidium. In 1931 he went to Nigeria, where he organized that country's first labor union, the African Workers Union. Later in 1931 he was invited to attend the International Labor Defense Congress in Moscow, where, using yet another pseudonym, W. Daniels, he enrolled for a course of study at the People's University.

Wallace-Johnson returned to Freetown in February, 1933, but did not stay long. Moving on to Nigeria, he became editor of the Nigerian *Daily Telegraph* and wrote for the *Negro Worker*, using a variety of pen-names—W. Daniels, E. Richards, Abdul Mohamed Afric, etc. More or less expelled from Nigeria for his militant journalism and trade unionist activities, he went to the Gold Coast where, in collaboration with Bankole Awoonor Renner and Wuta Ofei, he founded the West Coast Youth League and contributed articles to the *Gold Coast Spectator* and the *African Morning Post*, both published in Accra.

In 1936, as the troops of Benito Mussolini, the Fascist dictator of Italy (in power 1922-43) invaded Ethiopia, Wallace published an outspoken article which had serious repercussions for him. It appeared in the *African Morning Post* in Accra under the title 'Has the African a God?'

"Personally" he wrote, "I believe the European has a God in whom he believes and whom he is representing in his churches all over Africa. He believes in the God whose name is Deceit. He believes in the God whose law is 'Ye strong, you must weaken still further the weak.' Ye 'Civilized' Europeans you must 'civilize' the 'barbarious' Africans with machine guns. Ye 'Christian' Europeans you must 'Christianize' the 'pagan' Africans with bombs, poison gases, etc.''

Wallace was arrested and charged with seditious libel for this piece of writing. He was found guilty by the Gold Coast Supreme Court and sentenced to a fine of £50 or 3 months' imprisonment. Wallace paid the fine, but appealed against the conviction. He lost his appeal and finally took the matter to the Judicial Committee of the Privy Council, who, while disagreeing with the charge of sedition, upheld the conviction on the grounds that under the Gold Coast Criminal Code an attack on religion of this nature reflected adversely on the government of the Colony.

While he was in England, Wallace worked at the recently established International African Service Bureau as general secretary, and with the assistance of George Padmore, the Pan Africanist radical from Trinidad, Jomo Kenyatta of Kenya, and others, established the Pan-African Federation whose aim was to promote the cause of African workers. He also founded the *African Sentinel*, and *Africa and the World*. On his return to Sierra Leone in April 1938, 2,000 copies of the *African Sentinel* were seized by the custom authorities in Freetown.

Ceaselessly active, within a year of his arrival home he had formed the Sierra Leone branch of the West African Youth League, whose official mouthpiece, the *African Standard*, was started in January 1939, and had organized the West African Civil Liberties and National Defense League. In addition, he had started eight labor unions—the All Seamen's Union, the Bonthe Amalgamated Workers' Union, the King Tom Docks Workers' Union, the Mabella Coaling Company Workers' Union, the Motorists' Union, the Pepel and Marampa Miners Workers' Union, the Public Works Workers' Union, and the War Department Amalgamated Workers' Union.

Thoroughly alarmed, the colonial authorities did everything to stop Wallace-Johnson's labor union activities. In September 1939 he was arrested and detained under the emergency Colonial Defense Regulations. During detention he was charged with criminal libel for publishing an article in the *African Standard* the previous month entitled 'Who Killed Fonnie?' The article concerned the death of an African who had died tied to a post after being flogged by order of John Henry de Burgh, the district commissioner of Bonthe, Sherbro, who had met with opposition during a tax collecting mission in the area. Wallace's article suggested that the district commissioner was effectively Fonnie's murderer. A judge and three assessors found Wallace guilty of criminal libel and sentenced him to a year's imprisonment, an experience which only added fuel to his

crusading militancy, for during the time of his sentence he wrote a series of poems, later published under the title 'Prison in the Muse,' describing the appalling conditions in the Central Prison at Pademba Road, Freetown. As a protest they had some effect, for they resulted in an official investigation which led to some changes.

On March 19, 1942, Wallace was exiled to Bonthe, where he made constructive use of his enforced idleness by teaching adults to read and write. He returned to Freetown after his release from detention late in 1944. He was then elected representative of Sierra Leone at the World Trade Union Congress in London in February 1945. In September 1945, at a meeting held in Paris, he was elected to the executive committee of the World Federation of Trade Unions (W.F.T.U.) Congress. Along with Kwame Nkrumah, (later to become the first prime minister of Ghana), George Padmore, and others, he helped organize the Pan-Africanist Congress held in Manchester, England in 1945.

In 1951, Wallace entered a different area of national politics, and won the Wilberforce and York electoral district seat on the Legislative Council as a member of the National Council of Sierra Leone (N.C.S.L.). He left the N.C.S.L. to join the United People's Party (U.P.P.), and retained his seat in the 1957 elections to the Sierra Leone House of Representatives. By 1959, he had broken away again, leaving the U.P.P. to form his own party, the Radical Democratic Party (R.D.P.), largely a platform for his own views. By this time Wallace's influence was waning fast, although he was a delegate to the 1960 constitutional talks in London which made final arrangements for Sierra Leone's independence in 1961.

A man of indefatigable courage, hard-working and self-denying, Wallace turned down all attempts to contain his crusading fervor by offers of official posts, although in his final years he was far from well-to-do. He ended his life in Ghana in an automobile accident in May 1965, while attending a conference. He was buried in Freetown, where his funeral drew the greatest crowd of mourners in the country's history. Thousands mourned him as the founder of trade unionism in West Africa, as a fearless militant journalist, as a national political leader, and as one of the pioneering pan-Africanists.

The virtual suppression of Wallace-Johnson by the colonial authorities had long-term repercussions on the political development of Sierra Leone. He had, through the Sierra Leone branch of the West African Youth League, fostered co-operation between the Krios (Creoles) of the Colony and the peoples of the Protectorate. The harassment of the League by the colonial administration, especially during World War II, checked this co-operation, thus delaying the emergence of a political movement in Sierra Leone enjoying mass support.

CYRIL P. FORAY

BIBLIOGRAPHY: John R. Cartwright, *Politics in Sierra Leone 1947-67,* Toronto, 1970; G.B.O. Collier, *Sierra Leone: Experiment in Democracy in an African Nation*, New York, 1970; M. Crowder, *West Africa Under Colonial Rule*, London, 1968; Martin Kilson, *Political Change in a West African State: A Study of the Modernization Process in Sierra Leone*, Cambridge, Massachusetts, 1966; A.T. Porter, *Creoledom,* London, 1963; J.A. Rogers, *World's Great Men of Color*, revised ed., Vol. I, New York, 1972; D.J.R. Scott, "Sierra Leone General Election, May 1957," in W.J. Mackenzie and Kenneth Robinson (eds), *Five Elections in Africa,* Oxford, 1960; Leo Spitzer, *The Creoles of Sierra Leone: Responses to Colonialism 1870-1945,* Madison, 1974, Ile-Ife, 1976.

WILBERFORCE, D.F.

Daniel Flickinger Wilberforce (1856-1927), paramount chief of Imperi, was the first Christian pastor to become a chief. He was educated mainly in the United States of America, returning to Sierra Leone to take up a post at Clark Theological School in Shenge, north of the Sherbro estuary. He wielded a powerful influence throughout Imperi, but was eventually found to have taken an unsavory part in the political troubles of that area.

He was born at Good Hope in the Jong estuary, Imperreh country, in 1856, and was named after a missionary, the Rev. Daniel K. Flickinger of the Mende Mission in the Sherbro. Wilberforce proved capable and trustworthy. When a lady missionary took seriously ill and had to be repatriated to the United States in 1871, Daniel was chosen to accompany her. On his arrival, he worked in the warehouse of the American Missionary Association. His namesake, the Rev. D.K. Flickinger, then secretary of the Mission Board, met Daniel by chance in New York, and immediately took him to Dayton, Ohio, to have him properly educated.

After graduating with honors, Daniel married Elizabeth Harris in 1878. In the same year he was ordained and appointed to serve on the staff of the Clark Theological School in Shenge, eventually becoming principal in 1887. Wilberforce obtained a 100-acre tract of land from his family near Gbambaia, south of the Bagru River, where he opened a school in 1882, which he supervised from Shenge. He had plans for a 'village of Dan,' which never effectively materialized, but the mission establishment there, including his

house, came to be known as 'Danville.' This project was sponsored by the King Street United Brethren Church in Pennsylvania. As its evangelical and educational work grew and flourished Wilberforce moved from Shenge to take over personal control of the Danville mission in 1892.

In 1890, Wilberforce found one of his servants murdered at Gbambaia. There were other similar 'leopard murders' in the vicinity (ritual murders which nevertheless carried political undertones), misleadingly attributed to 'cannibalism.' Wilberforce suggested to the chief that the Tongo Players or traditional witch-detectors, be brought in. A holocaust followed in which over 30 people were burned to death, including Chief Gbanna Bunjay himself.

When the 1898 resistance broke out in opposition to the house tax, imposed by the Protectorate Ordinance, Imperi became the scene of terrible massacres accompanied by the destruction of mission, official, and trading stations. Many missionaries and officials were murdered in cold blood. Wilberforce himself barely escaped with his life after losing much of his property, and his mother and sister were hacked to death while trying to make for Bonthe.

When the hostilities were over, the chief of Imperi and several others were arrested. Wilberforce was appointed paramount chief, after he had assisted the British in quelling the revolt. Through his missionary and educational activities he wielded enormous influence throughout Imperi, and as an educated man in good favor with the colonial authorities, he was well placed to be the intermediary between his people and the administration at this critical period. "There seems to be no alternative," he wrote.

The administration, however, was rudely shaken in its 'civilizing' complacency when a whole series of 'leopard murders' were revealed in 1905. To everyone's amazement, Wilberforce was one of the accused. There was not sufficient evidence to warrant a conviction but, having failed to live up to expectations as a 'civilizing force,' he lost his chieftaincy by administrative order. The fact that he was a naturalized American was now invoked; as a foreign national he could not be paramount chief in a British Protectorate.

When another outburst of leopard activity occurred in 1912, Wilberforce was again arrested. A special commission court was constituted to try the accused persons. Once again, for lack of sufficient evidence, he could not be convicted, but the special commission court had power to recommend the banishment of anyone whose presence was felt to be prejudicial to peace and good order. Wilberforce was thus banished to Liberia. He was later pardoned and he returned to his home and continued missionary work there. His last memorable activity was the closing address which he gave to the 1924 annual conference of the United Brethren in Christ mission. He died three years later in 1927 and was buried in the Danville church cemetery near Gbambaia.

ARTHUR ABRAHAM

BIBLIOGRAPHY: Arthur Abraham, *Mende Government and Politics Under Colonial Rule*, Freetown, 1978; Christopher Fyfe, *A History of Sierra Leone*, London, 1962; G.D. Fleming, *Trial Blazers in Sierra Leone*, Vol. I, Indiana, 1971.

WRIGHT, E.J.

Dr. Ernest Jenner Wright (1892-December 29, 1955) was one of the most distinguished members of the British Colonial Medical Service, and one of the foremost African physicians in medical research of this century. He was the first to draw attention to certain diseases due to malnutrition in Africans in general, and in expectant mothers and children in particular.

The son of a distinguished Sierra Leonean barrister, C.E. Wright, young Ernest was christened Jenner after the discoverer of the smallpox vaccine. He had a boyhood ambition to be an engineer but his father decided against this and steered him towards medicine.

Jenner was educated at Ealing Grammar School, London and St. Francis Xavier College, Bruges, in Belgium. From Bruges, he entered St. Mary's Hospital Medical School, London University. As a medical student he held the post of demonstrator of physics for a year. In 1914 he qualified as a member of the Royal College of Surgeons (M.R.C.S.), and as a licentiate of the Royal College of Physicians (L.R.C.P.), obtaining his Diploma in Tropical Medicine (D.T.M.) in Liverpool the same year. He was then appointed obstetrical assistant at Liverpool University. He later filled the post of resident medical officer, Ladywood Dispensary, Birmingham.

It was at this time that he decided to make his career in Sierra Leone. In 1916 he joined the Colonial Medical Service, where he quickly established himself as a doctor of ability and industry, and ultimately attained the status of specialist physician.

He was a protagonist against avitaminosis and a reputed dietitian, describing the importance of sulphur in foods long before the essential nature of this element in protein was discovered in America.

He was also the first to report the presence in the tropics of rickets, a metabolic disease usually associated with temperate climates, curable by cod liver oil and sunlight. Dr. Wright explained its presence in the tropical climate by the fact that mothers normally carried their young children on their backs elaborately wrapped up, thus preventing sunlight from acting on the skin. Most medical books wrongly state that the first description of tropical rickets was made in India, where it was recorded some years after Wright's original paper. But in Henry H. Scott's *History of Tropical Medicine* some of his discoveries have been recorded and acknowledged.

Another important aspect of his work was the inception and organization of ante-natal, post-natal and infant welfare clinics in Freetown. Popularly known as 'Pikin Daddy,' he could best be remembered by many mothers for the 'Health and Baby Week' which he inaugurated and ran for several years, and it is fitting that his name should have been perpetuated in the 'Under Five' clinic at Race Course.

The Maternity Hospital and Jenner Wright were inseparable. With his Liverpool experience standing him in good stead, he supervised the work there, later handing over responsibility to his daughter, Dr. Sophie Wright (Mrs. Ramanankoto). On his retirement in 1949 he was appointed consulting physician to the Sierra Leone government. Thirteen years earlier he was honored as a Member of the British Empire (M.B.E.), the first African doctor to be so honored.

Wright's interests were scholarly. He possessed the most complete collection of early West African coins in existence. His collection comprised the Gold Coast 'ackey,' half ackey, and a quarter ackey, dating back to the 1850s; a stamped-out dollar of Sierra Leone origin; a Macgregor Laird penny; the Sierra Leone Company 1896 one cent piece, having a lion with a versatile tail on one side, and a white hand shaking a black hand on the other. Except for the guinea of Charles II, he had the complete set of all coins minted for use in British West Africa.

He was also a bibliophile and had one of the finest and most extensive libraries of early books on Sierra Leone. He researched deeply, and was an authority in the early history of Sierra Leone and the West African settlements. Among his collection he had unique specimens of works of mid-19th century Sierra Leoneans, such as J.A.B. Horton (q.v.), and the Rev. George Nicol, a Cambridge graduate of great literary merit.

Jenner Wright spent large sums of money on valuable books and rare objects of interest, building up not only a priceless library but a miniature museum at No. 31, Howe Street, Freetown.

Added to his main interests of medicine, numismatics, and history, was his practical interest in the uses of electricity. He was the first individual in Freetown to install in his home a metal filament and, later, fluorescent electric lights, and he owned a generating plant long before electricity was publicly introduced in Sierra Leone.

Other aspects of technology also interested him. He was the only medical practitioner who possessed an electro-cardiograph in Sierra Leone, and also obtained an early tape recording machine, and experimented with radio receivers. Photography, too, was another hobby in which he was proficient, developing, printing, and enlarging his own negatives. Last but not least, he was the proud owner of one of the first cars in West Africa.

Wright lived a busy public life. He served as chairman and member of two of the Wages Boards of the Labor Department. He knew practically every African seaman whose home was in Sierra Leone for he had to examine each of them before embarkation. During both world wars he attended to sick sailors of all nationalities, and as first chairman of the Sierra Leone Society he was a great asset.

On the domestic side, he and his brother, the Honourable Claude Wright married two sisters. Charlotte, Jenner's wife, was his constant companion and support throughout their 37 years of married life.

In spite of the fact that he was in many respects a pioneer in each of his posts, Dr. Wright was a man of retiring disposition, sensitive, gentle and full of kindness. His dedication to the welfare of his fellow men is impressive, and his whole life an expression of brotherly love. He died in 1955, at the age of 63.

DOMINIC OFORI

BIBLIOGRAPHY: H.H. Scott, *History of Tropical Medicine*, (2 vols.), London, 1939, reprinted, New York, 1974; E.J. Wright, "Psycotherapy and Witchcraft," *Sierra Leone Studies*, January, 1939, "Glanville Town," *Sierra Leone Studies*, December, 1939, "Remarks on the Early Monetary Position in Sierra Leone with a Description of the Coinage Adopted," *Sierra Leone Studies*, December, 1954; *British Medical Journal*, January 14, 1956; *Sierra Leone Daily Mail*, January, 1956; *The Times*, January 24, 1956.

WURIE, A.

Alhaji Ahmadu Wurie (August 27, 1898-June 13, 1977) was one of Sierra Leone's foremost educators in the 20th century. An active politician, he was appointed minister of education in the first post-independence Sierra Leone Parliament.

He was born in Gbinti on the estuary of the Melacourie River. His mother was Ya Bomporro Folah and

his father, paramount chief Bai Sheka Bundu, was one of the principal supporters of Bai Bureh (*q.v.*) during the 1898 uprising against the British.

Amadu Wurie was a foundation pupil of the Bo School in the Southern Province, established in 1906 to cater for the education of sons and nominees of chiefs. In 1916 he was among the first pupils of that school to succeed in the civil service entrance examination. He was appointed an assistant master at the school in 1916, subsequently rising to the rank of senior assistant master in 1925. In 1927 he suggested the formation of the Old Bo Boys' Association (O.B.B.A.), serving first as general secretary and later as president of this organization which was the inspiration for many other old boys' clubs in the country. On several occasions between 1933 and 1935 Ahmadu Wurie served as acting principal of the school, the first African to fulfill such a role.

From Bo he moved on to Koyeima School, Bo district, where he served as headmaster from 1935 to 1942. In the latter year he became education officer, a post he held until 1952 when he was appointed the first principal of the Kenema secondary school. In 1953 he was appointed a member of Port Loko district council and chairman of the Port Loko education authority. In 1955 he was appointed provincial education secretary, Northern Province. Six years later he became a member of the Mine Workers' Wages Board.

By 1961, when Sierra Leone became independent, Ahmadu Wurie had served in most of the districts in the country. His connection with the country's leading political figures dated from his Bo School days. As early as the late 1940s, he had become an active member of the Protectorate Educational Progress Union (P.E.P.U.), which then comprised most of the Protectorate elite. In 1962 he entered Parliament under the Sierra Leone People's Party (S.L.P.P.) banner and was appointed minister of education in recognition of his life-long devotion to teaching. After the cabinet crisis following Albert Margai's appointment as prime minister in 1964, Ahmadu Wurie was one of the few prominent Northern ministers loyal to the new head of government. He later served as minister of the interior. In 1964 he was awarded the C.B.E. (Companion of the British Empire) for his significant contribution to the educational progress of the country.

After the 1967 general election, in which he lost his seat, Ahmadu Wurie retired into private life at Mahera, near Longi, in the Port Loko district. During this period he made a pilgrimage to Mecca. In January 1973 the University of Sierra Leone conferred on him the honorary degree of Doctor of Civil Law.

Besides politics, Ahmadu Wurie also took a lively interest in the history of the country, especially that of his ancestors, the Bunduka, in whose territory he collected many oral traditions. These were published

in the journal, *Sierra Leone Studies.* While in retirement he co-authored (with Elizabeth Hirst) a biography of his grandfather, Alimamy Rassin, which was published in 1968.

He died on June 13, 1977.

E. AMADU TURAY

BIBLIOGRAPHY: C.R. Foray, *Historical Dictionary of Sierra Leone,* Metuchen, New Jersey, and London, 1977; A. Wurie, "The Bundukas of Sierra Leone," *Sierra Leone Studies*, December, 1953, with E. Hirst, *Rassin*, London, 1968.

YOKO, MADAM

Madam Yoko (circa 1849-August 1906) was a fascinating and impressive woman who eventually became ruler of the Kpaa-Mende state. Famed for her beautiful dancing, she became the foremost trainer of girls of ruling families in the initiation rites for the Sande women's secret society. Succeeding to the chiefdom of Senehun after the death of her husband Gbanya Lango (*q.v.*), she became closely involved with the British administration, a connection she exploited to extend her power. Yet despite support from the colonial government, her vast cheifdom showed signs of disintegration and tales of her importance as a Mende chief have been greatly exaggerated.

She is reputed to be the only woman in the history of Sierra Leone to reign as suzerain to one of the pre-colonial states, the Kpaa-Mende, based on the most powerful of secret societies, the Wunde, and founded by war and conquest in the 19th century. This bald fact has led to pretentious claims for her importance, that she was the greatest of the Mende chiefs and that she used both diplomacy and warfare to unify 14 chiefdoms under her personal rule. Such exaggerations, deliberately perpetuated by colonial officials, have merely misled modern writers into historical falsification. Yoko was not and could never have been the greatest Mende ruler: she did not acquire power by traditional constitutional methods, but was installed by the colonial government. Far from integrating the Kpaa-Mende state, she destroyed the organic basis of its unity.

One of four children of Njiakundohun (*q.v.*), a famous Kpaa-Mende leader, Yoko, whose original name was Soma, was born at Gbograma in present day Gbo chiefdom about 1849. The family migrated westwards, and at puberty Soma was initiated into the women's Sande society at Senehun. She excelled in all aspects of Sande training and after graduating with the new name of Yoko, a customary practice, was given in marriage to a warrior called Gongoima, whose infatuation led to Yoko's unprecedented initiation into the men's secret society, the Poro.

Gongoima's extreme jealousy led to a divorce, and Yoko was remarried to Gbenjei, a chief of Taiama on the Taia River. A true and faithful wife, Yoko made up for her childlessness by winning the confidence of her husband, and soon became Gbenjei's 'big wife.'

Taiama at this time was threatened by Bayon, the mystic who ruled the magic-dominated Bumpe (Banta) state based on Mano-Dasse. After a lengthy struggle for survival, the Kpaa-Mende leaders succeeded in defeating Bumpe, annexing it, and killing Bayon, This was Gbenjei's last great achievement, for he died shortly after.

At the funeral obsequies, many of Gbenjei's relations were present, including his nephew, Gbanya Lango, already a famous warrior. Even the Freetown administration had been calling on him for assistance since 1861. At the conclusion of the funeral ceremonies Gbanya took Yoko as his wife, a practice perfectly consistent with custom. They then moved to Senehun where Gbanya was based, and he soon took over the leadership of Kpaa-Mende, controlling one of the largest bands of professional warriors in Sierra Leone.

Yoko, meanwhile, was rising steadily to social prominence. She travelled to Freetown on several occasions, making the acquaintance of colonial officials there. At the same time, she was running her own Sande bush (a clearing in a forested area where ceremonies of training and initiation into womanhood connected with the Sande society took place). It became famous through her position as the wife of the king of Kpaa-Mende. Yoko also increased her influence with officials by giving them the most beautiful girls from her Sande bush as concubines, an important basis for her subsequent acquisition of power.

It is reported that when Gbanya became fatally ill in 1878, he summoned his closest relations and told them he wished to have Yoko succeed him, requesting also that this wish be communicated to Governor Samuel Rowe (terms of office 1877-80, 1885-88). This simplistic account is not borne out by the evidence. There is reason to believe that after Gbanya's death in 1878, Yoko's popularity declined until she used her persuasive powers on the colonial administration to elevate her to the leadership of the Kpaa-Mende state. This, however, did not occur before the death of Gbanya's successor, Movee, in 1884.

When Melville Laborde, acting commandant of Sherbro, was commissioned to make a trip into Mende country in 1880-81, Yoko was apparently neither significant nor powerful enough to deserve a mention in his report. His accompanying map showed the towns he passed through, together with the names of the town heads, and Yoko's name appeared on the map as head-woman of Mowoto, a small town about two hours' journey from Senehun.

In 1882, however, using her pull with colonial officials, and by special arrangement with Governor A.E. Havelock (term of office 1881-84) Yoko was placed in charge of Senehun, capital of Kpaa-Mende. She was officially described as 'subchief of Senehun,' apparently being subordinate to Movee. Being a wily schemer, she began to undermine Movee's authority by attempting to settle disputes on her own, turning to the colonial administration for help in difficult cases, or to protect Colony traders. When Movee died in 1884, Yoko quickly reported disturbances to the governor, who thanked her for her protection of British traders, and sent two constables as reinforcement.

By May, Yoko was described as the 'Principal Lady of Senehun' and a little later as 'Queen of Senehun,' a title which effectively placed her in the position of representing Kpaa-Mende as far as the administration was concerned. This put a stop to attempts to get a traditionally elected ruler. Yoko's leadership, therefore, was largely the creation of colonialism, and her power lay not in customary constitutional law, but in British support.

In 1885, Yoko received a stipend of £10 which was raised in 1894 to £50 "owing to the increase of her power and owing to the able and loyal manner in which she carried on the affairs of the country."

Evidence of her 'great power' was demonstrated in 1894 when she proceeded to Taiama "to crown the successors of two deceased chiefs." Yet other evidence favors the opposite interpretation. It is clear that her sub-chiefs, technically speaking, ignored Yoko and managed their own affairs, and that her influence never spread beyond Taiama. One such sub-chief, Kamande of Bauya openly defied her authority, and the British had to come to her rescue.

After the Yoni expedition of 1886-87, (undertaken by the British to quell the Yoni Temne who had attacked various towns, including two of Madam Yoko's, under British jurisdiction), Kamande was captured and imprisoned. But other chiefs remained defiant. Two of them, Moigula and Vonjo, quarreled, and all attempts at mediation failed. Yoko was helpless, beseeching for colonial intervention to solve her internal problems. This particular conflict was only resolved through the intervention of Makavoray (q.v.) of Tikonko, outside Kpaa-Mende territory. Yoko herself admitted that it was because of the colonial government that she was looked upon as leader.

In 1898, when the Mende decided to fight in protest against the provisions of the Protectorate Ordinance and the imposition of a house tax, Yoko was not informed. She had already gravely displeased her people by asking them to pay the tax, and when war broke out she barely escaped with her life. Acting on information from a relative who had taken part in the council of war that she was the warriors' first target, she took cover in the Frontier Police barracks.

Dr. Hood, acting district commissioner of Ronietta, would not disguise the fact that "the majority of her sub-chiefs are not loyal to her and pay little attention to her orders until my assistance has been rendered." After the war of 1898, however, Yoko "did great work …. in aiding in the arrests of several important chiefs who were responsible for the rising."

It is thus difficult to accept the view that Yoko's power united the Kpaa-Mende under her personal rule. Lacking traditional legitimacy to support her position, the various sections of the state tended to go their separate ways, while the provinces in the east farthest away from British influence became virtually autonomous. For this reason Vonjo, ruler of Mandu, the eastern-most province of Kpaa-Mende and contiguous to Makavoray's state, could not be controlled by Yoko, and turned to an outside ruler for arbitration. This policy of independent action had been in existence for some time before the 1900s, and even the colonial administration was ignorant of the fact that at least three of these distant provinces belonged traditionally to the Kpaa-Mende state. Yoko's overlordship, had in fact started the disintegration of this vast territory.

After the resistance of 1898, Yoko was recognized as 'paramount chief,' a colonial title for the highest traditional authority. Nothing of great significance happened until 1906 when a boundary dispute arose between Yoko and paramount chief Beimba I of Kakua chiefdom. In consequence Yoko lost her birth place, Gbograma to Beimba. Taking this as the greatest disgrace she had ever suffered, she committed suicide in August 1906.

ARTHUR ABRAHAM

BIBLIOGRAPHY: Arthur Abraham, *Mende Government and Politics Under Colonial Rule*, Freetown, 1978, "Woman Chiefs in Sierra Leone: A Historical Reappraisal," *Odu: A Journal of West African Studies*, July, 1974; M.C.F. Easmon, "Madam Yoko: Ruler of the Mendi Confederacy," *Sierra Leone Studies*, December, 1958; C. Hoffer, "Mende and Sherbro Women in High Office," *Canadian Journal of African Studies*, VI, 2, 1972.

YUSUFU, BOMBO LAHAI

Bombo Lahai Yusufu (18?-circa 1940) was the paramount chief of Tonko Limba, in Kambia district, Northern Province. He was deposed by the colonial government for suspected complicity in an anti-British uprising led by Haidara Kontorfili (q.v.). It is still unclear to what extent he was involved.

He was the son of a Limba man, Dauda, and a Fula woman from Timbo, and was descended from the KaBubuya ruling house. He became paramount chief of Tonko Limba in 1922.

In the years immediately following World War I his chiefdom faced serious economic problems, one of which was low agricultural output. People were hard put to pay regular taxes. A plague of locusts continued unabated despite measures taken by the administration to check it. As these proved ineffective, by 1930 the problem had become very acute. At this time news was received that a powerful Muslim with medicine to check the plague was living in a neighboring chiefdom. This is one of the reasons usually advanced by Tonko Limba people to explain the arrival of Haidara Kontofili, a radical religious leader, in Bombo Lahai Yusufu's chiefdom.

As all traditional rulers would do, Bombo Lahai

Yusufu extended a friendly welcome to this important stranger, believing that Haidara's knowledge would be put to the service of his people and save them from further economic hardship. Haidara called upon the people of KaBubuya, and later the entire chiefdom, to offer prayers regularly, and preached a general message urging the return to a life of virtue.

As his following grew Haidara ordered all the local medicine men to destroy their 'swears,' charms and amulets. Many of these traditional healers and diviners, however, refused to carry out what amounted to a death sentence against their profession. The elusive Nkodi, a famous medicine man, who dishonored many promises to destroy his swears, was a typical example of the resistance of this group of specialists.

Apparently Yusufu himself did not give whole-hearted support to this aspect of Haidara's activities, since as paramount chief he had to take part in many religious functions in which these medicine men featured prominently.

As news of Haidara's activities spread, the colonial administration called on Yusufu to expel him from his chiefdom. Lacking any organized military force, the chief was powerless in the face of Haidara's growing popularity. It was only when Haidara had denounced the colonial government and called upon the people to refuse to pay any more taxes that the colonial officials realized the gravity of the situation in Yusufu's chiefdom. Haidara was killed in confrontation with troops sent by the administrtion to arrest him in March 1931.

In the wake of the Haidara affair, Yusufu was accused of complicity in an anti-British uprising. To prove his innocence the chief swore that he would 'eat bread,' a piece of rice flour mixed with 'medicines' eaten when a serious oath is administered, a ceremony no Limba treats lightly. Convinced of the chief's guilt, the administration deposed him in 1931, making him the only important Tonko Limba chief to have been so humiliated under British rule.

Some authors, on scanty evidence, have labeled Yusufu a bad chief, but many reject this view, and members of the KaBubuya house have defended their chief. They hold that Yusufu's deposition was an unwarranted interruption of KaBubuya rule, pointing out that in the traditional political context, Tonko paramount chiefs held office for life, except when found guilty of atrocious crimes against their subjects. The Kamara clan, for example, lost its rights to nominate successors to a vacant chiefship because its members were slave-dealers who sold their people without compunction.

Yusufu retired into private life after he was destooled, and died about nine years later.

E. AMADU TURAY

BIBLIOGRAPHY: V.R. Dorjahn and A.S. Tholley, "A Provincial History of the Limba with Special Reference to Tonko Limba Chiefdom," *Sierra Leone Studies*, December, 1959; R. Finnegan and D. Murray, "Limba Chiefs" in M. Crowder and O. Ikime, (eds.) *West African Chiefs*, Ile-Ife, 1970; B.M. Jusu, "The Haidara Rebellion of 1931" *Sierra Leone Studies*, December, 1954; M. Kilson, *Political Change in a West African State*, Cambridge, Massachusetts, 1966.

CONCISE GUIDE TO SIERRA LEONE NAMES AND TERMS

AKU — The local expression for the Yoruba from Nigeria. From the 1820s onwards, Yoruba recaptives were known as "Aku," a Yoruba word of greeting.

ALABITAYA — A name, meaning "God protect us," given by the Koranko (q.v.) of Barawa (q.v.) to their hiding place in the hills around Wara Wara (q.v.), when they were driven out of their lands by the Kono (q.v.) in the mid-19th century.

ALFA — An Islamic scholar, charm-maker, and teacher. The meaning is the same as for *Mori* (q.v.), but designates a person who is less a scholar than a charm-maker.

ALHAJI — A title given to a man who has made the pilgrimage to Mecca. The equivalent feminine title is *Alhaja*.

ALIKALI — Also spelled "Alkali." The title of the Temne ruler of Port Loko in eastern Sierra Leone. It derives from the Arabic *al qadi,* meaning "judge."

ALMAMY — Also spelled "Alimamy." Usually the title of a paramount chief among the Islamized Temne and neighboring Islamized groups; it is nowadays more commonly used as a first name. It derives from the Arabic *al Imam,* meaning leader of the mosque.

AWUJOH — A feast given as charity by the Krio (q.v.) on specific occasions.

BAGA — A people inhabiting the coastal region of the Republic of Guinea, and numbering about 45,000 in the 1970s. Some Baga live in northern Sierra Leone, to the north of the Great Scarcies River. They are closely related to the Temne.

BAGRU — A Sherbro chiefdom in southern Sierra Leone. When amalgamated with another chiefdom, it came to be called Bagruwa.

BAI — The Temne title for ruler.

BAI FARMA — The title of the rulers of Koya (q.v.), in use from the time of the 16th-century ruler Farma Tami (q.v.) onwards. It is also given as Bai Farima.

BAI KOMPA — The title of the ruler of Koya Temne.

BAI SHERBRO — Ruler of the Sherbro (q.v.), who in former times ruled his people from Sherbro Island. The Bai flourished in the 18th century, but his power declined in the 19th century.

BANTA — The Banta were originally a related group of the Temne who succeeded in creating an empire extending from Yoni in the north to Bonthe in the south. As Banta power declined, Kpaa-Mende invasions in the early 19th century drove a wedge between them. The northern group fused with the Temne (today known as Mabanta Temne), while the southern crystallized into the Mendenized state of Bumpe in the 19th century. Today there are three

(BANTA)	—	chiefdoms of Banta extraction in the southern province—Bumpe, Banta Mokele, and Banta Gbangbatoke.
BARAWA	—	A Koranko chiefdom.
BIRIWA	—	A sub-group of the Limba (*q.v.*), and the name of a Limba chiefdom in northern Sierra Leone.
BOMBO LAHAI	—	The title of the ruler of Tonko Limba (*q.v.*).
BONDO	—	Also spelled Bundu. A female secret society for initiation into womanhood. It is found among most ethnic groups in Sierra Leone. The Mende also call it Sande.
BONTHE	—	The second port of Sierra Leone, located on Sherbro Island. The Bonthe district includes all of Sherbro Island and a part of the adjacent mainland.
BULLOM	—	A group that originally inhabited the entire coastline of Sierra Leone. The Bullom are among the oldest inhabitants of this region. Temne incursions drove a wedge into their territory which divided them into northern and southern groups. The northern Bullom were absorbed by the Temne, with whom they shared many cultural characteristics. The southern Bullom, often called the Sherbro (*q.v.*), are heavily Mendenized.
BUMPE	—	See *BANTA*.
COLONY, THE	—	The Colony of Sierra Leone was formally established by the British in 1808, when the Crown took over authority from an earlier Abolitionist settlement, governed by the settlers themselves, called the Province of Freedom, which had been established in 1787. From 1896 to the gaining of independence in 1961, Sierra Leone was administratively divided by the British into the Colony and the Protectorate (*q.v.*). The Colony consisted of the Sierra Leone peninsula, on which Freetown is located, the Banana Islands (in the Atlantic, south of the Freetown peninsula), the Tasso Islands (in the estuary of the Sierra Leone, or Rokel, River), the township of Bonthe (on Sherbro Island), and nearby York Island. The Protectorate consisted of the remainder of the country.
CONTEH	—	See *KONTE*.
CREOLE	—	See *KRIO*.
EAT BREAD, TO	—	To swear a binding oath in a ceremony at which "country" bread, made from rice flour, was eaten.
FAKAI	—	A Mende farm settlement.
FALABA	—	The capital of the state of Solimana (*q.v.*). "Falaba" is a Yalunka term meaning "talking on," and signifies a place where much discussion took place.
FERENSOLA	—	A Koranko term signifying all territory inhabited by that ethnic group.
FOURAH BAY	—	A bay on the southern shore of the Sierra Leone (Rokel) River, which gave its name to Fourah Bay College, Freetown. The college, the oldest African institution for higher education in the colonial period to be found on the

(FOURAH BAY) — continent, was founded in 1827 by the Church Missionary Society (C.M.S.). In 1950 the C.M.S. surrendered its interest in the college to the Sierra Leone government. In 1966 Fourah Bay became a constituent college of the University of Sierra Leone. The college is now located on Mount Aureol, overlooking Freetown.

FREETOWN — The capital of Sierra Leone. A port city overlooking the finest natural harbor in West Africa, it is located on the Sierra Leone peninsula, on the southern shore of the Sierra Leone (Rokel) River estuary. Named "Freetown" by the Abolitionist directors of the Sierra Leone Company, because it was to be a home for liberated slaves, it was established in 1792 on the site of an earlier settlement named Granville Town, which existed from 1787-89. In 1794 it was sacked by French revolutionaries. In 1808 it became the capital of the British Crown Colony of Sierra Leone, and as such was the base for operations by the British Royal Navy to suppress the transatlantic slave trade between 1808 and 1871. In 1893 it became a municipality.

FULA — Also spelled Foulah. The Fula, also known as the Fulani or Peuhl, are a widely distributed West African people. Numbering more than 6,500,000 in the 1970s, they are found in Senegal, northern Nigeria, Guinea, and other countries. Fula immigrants from Guinea are found all over Sierra Leone.

FULA MANSA — The title of the ruler of Yoni Temne. It derives from the Mandinka term *mansa* (king). The original bearer of the title was a Fula.

FUTA JALLON — Spelled "Foutah Djallon" in countries of French expression. An extensive mountainous area located in the Republic of Guinea, with outliers reaching into Sierra Leone and Liberia. With an average height of 3,000 ft (914 m), it forms the highest land in West Africa, with the exception of Mt. Cameroon.

GALLINAS — Formerly a state, now a chiefdom, in the extreme south of Sierra Leone, taking its name from the Portuguese word "Gallina" (hen), from the number of chickens found in the area. By extension the name "Gallinas" has sometimes been applied to the Vai *(q.v.)* inhabitants of the area.

GBAKU — The Limba word for "ruler."

GOLA — A people with many cultural ties to the Mende (*q.v.*), living mostly in western Liberia, but also extending into eastern Sierra Leone near the coast.

JIHAD — A holy war waged in the name of Islam.

KAGBO — Also spelled Kargbo. A clan of the Koranko (*q.v.*), also found among the Temne and Limba.

KANFORI — The name, apparently a title, of a legendary leader who brought the coastal Soso to their present home.

KASUNKO — A Limba chiefdom, formerly a part of Biriwa Limba.

KELE MANSA — A Yalunka title for a military leader; the literal meaning is "war leader."

KHORI — Yalunka word for "country" or territory especially those countries which constituted the Yalunka state.

KISSI	—	A group in eastern Sierra Leone, on the Liberia/Guinea border, numbering about 50,000 in the 1960s. The Kissi language belongs to the Mel group.
KOLUNKORAY	—	Soso term, later used to name a settlement, meaning "bitter brook."
KONO	—	A Mande group of eastern Sierra Leone, numbering about 105,000 in the 1960s. Like the Vai (*q.v.*), the Kono entered Sierra Leone from the north before the 15th century.
KONTE	—	Also spelled Conteh. A clan of apparent Koranko origin, located in the Limba areas of Biriwa and Wara Wara in northern Sierra Leone. It is also found among the Temne, Kono and Mende.
KORANKO	—	Also spelled Kuranko. A branch of the Mandinka, located in northeastern Sierra Leone, and numbering about 80,000 in the 1960s. The Koranko first entered what is now Sierra Leone from what is now the Republic of Guinea in the 16th century. The Koranko language is of the Mande group.
KOROMA	—	A clan of the Koranko (*q.v.*), and also a clan of the Temne (*q.v.).*
KOSSOH	—	The name given to Mende recaptives and to the area that they initially settled on the outskirts of Freetown.
KOYA	—	A Temne chiefdom located in the vicinity of Freetown, to the east.
KPAA—MENDE	—	The western branch of the Mende (*q.v.*).
KPO-VEH	—	A term referring to the wars which broke out in about the 1880s in upper Mende countries. These wars were so called on account of the custom of stowing the decapitated heads of cowardly warriors in a pot of excrement. Another tradition holds that cowardly warriors were made to carry dung pots on their heads.
KRIM	—	A Bullom group, located on the coast to the east of the Sherbro, next to the Vai. They have been largely absorbed by the Mende and the Vai.
KRIO	—	Also Creole. The Krios are the descendants of recaptives (*q.v.*) and other settlers. Numbering about 40,000, they live mostly in Freetown and in the Western Area (i.e. Cape Sierra Leone and its vicinity, to the south of Freetown). The Krio language, derived from English and from numerous African languages, is the lingua franca of Sierra Leone.
KURUGBA	—	Also spelled Krugba, and called Kugba by the Mende. It is the Temne, Loko, and Limba title for a military leader.
LIMBA	—	A group numbering about 183,000 in the 1960s, living in the north of Sierra Leone. The Limba language belongs to the Mel group. The Limba, who may have originated in the Futa Jallon mountains, are said to have occupied the Wara Wara hills in the 8th century, from where they spread southwards and westwards to occupy areas of Temne and Loko country.
LOKO	—	A Mande group of northwest Sierra Leone, numbering about 65,000 in the 1960s. The Loko are said to have originated in the 16th century as a result of a Mandinka invasion of lands occupied by West Atlantic groups neighboring the Temne.
MALINKE	—	See *MANDINKA.*

MANDE — Linguistic grouping including peoples of the West African savannah and tropical rainforest, speaking Mande languages. Mande peoples are located in Sierra Leone, Guinea, the Ivory Coast, and Mali. In Sierra Leone, Mande groups include the Mandinka, Mende, Vai, Kono, Koranko, Yalunka, Loko, and Soso.

MANDINGO — European name for the Mandinka (Malinke), (*q.v.*).

MANDINKA — Also known as Malinke or Mandingo. A West African group of people, numbering about 1,500,000 in the 1970s, living in Guinea, the Ivory Coast, Mali, Senegal, the Gambia, and Guinea-Bissau. Some Mandinka immigrants from Guinea are located in Sierra Leone. The Mandinka are a Mande-speaking people.

MANGA — A Yalunka title for "ruler."

MANI — A Mandinka group, apparently from the ancient Mali empire (which flourished from the 13th to the 16th centuries), which invaded what is now Sierra Leone in the 16th century, possibly giving rise to the present-day Mende (*q.v.*) and Loko (*q.v.*).

MANSA — The Mandinka and Koranko title for "ruler."

MANSARAY — A clan of apparent Koranko origin located in the Limba areas of Biriwa. It is also found among the Temne.

MARA — A clan of the Koranko (*q.v.*).

MAROON — The original Maroons were slaves, mostly from Asante (Ashanti), who had been taken to Jamaica, where they successfully rebelled and settled in the mountains. They were later captured by the British and sent to Nova Scotia in Canada. From there they were transported in 1800 to Freetown, where they constituted a strong bloc among the settlers.

MASSAQUOI — A predominant Vai lineage. The name is derived from mansa (king), and from Koi, (the sea), an expression made by one of the followers of Duramani Kamara, the first Vai leader, after they reached the sea coast.

MENDE — The largest single ethnic group in Sierra Leone. Living in the south and east, they numbered about 675,000 in the mid-1960s. A small group of Mende also live in Liberia. The Mende, who speak a Mande language, are believed to derive from the Mani (*q.v.*), a Mandinka group which entered what is now Sierra Leone in the 16th century.

MENDE MISSION — This mission was sponsored by what later became the American Missionary Association (A.M.A.) in the 1840s with the purpose of resettling slaves who had arrived in the United States aboard the Spanish ship *Amistad* in 1839. These slaves who had successfully revolted and seized control of the ship, were tried for mutiny and piracy, but were freed by the United States Supreme Court. They were resettled in Sherbro country (usually regarded as Mende). Missionaries from the A.M.A. were sent out with them to found an outpost there. Many other stations were established in subsequent years.

MORI — An Islamic scholar, charm-maker, and teacher.

MORIMAN — Charm-maker priest.

NEMGBANA — The title of the second in command to the Bai Farma (*q.v.*) in the 16th to 18th century coastal confederacy among the Temne and Bullom. It was a Nemgbana, acting as regent, who leased the Freetown peninsula to the British for the founding of the Sierra Leone colony. One source claims the name of the title was "Gbana," but that a holder of the title, trying to display a smattering of English to the British, said, when asked for his name, "name Gbana" (my name is Gbana). This was unwittingly taken to be a single name, Nemgbana.

NIENI — A present-day Koranko chiefdom.

NOVA SCOTIANS — Early Sierra Leone settlers from Nova Scotia, Canada. They had previously fought for the British in the American War of Independence (1775-83) and had then been settled in Nova Scotia for a time after the war, from where they emigrated to Sierra Leone in 1792.

PIKIN — "Child," or "young one." Found along the West African coast, the word apparently derives from the Portuguese *pequenino*, meaning "very little." (*cf.* "picaninny").

PORO — A major secret society among the Mende, Temne, Kono, Kissi, and Vai.

PROTECTORATE, THE — From 1896 until independence in 1961, the Protectorate consisted of the entire territory of Sierra Leone, with the exception of the Colony (*q.v.*). In essence, this comprised the hinterland to the original colony, which in the 19th century had become progressively linked with the British colonial administration of Sierra Leone by a series of treaties.

RECAPTIVES — A term referring to those Africans who were captured and enslaved, then recaptured on the high seas by the British Royal Navy, and subsequently freed in Sierra Leone. After the British abolition of the transatlantic slave trade in 1807, ships of the Royal Navy—first individually, and then, from 1819-70, as an organized force called the African Squadron—patrolled West African waters to suppress the trade. Slave ships intercepted were taken to Freetown, Sierra Leone, where the offenders were tried. The slaves, set free on Freetown soil, were either known as recaptives, or as liberated Africans.

SANDE — The Mende word for Bondo (*q.v.*).

SANDE BUSH — A clearing in a forested area where Sande (Bondo) ceremonies are held.

SCARCIES, THE — The Great and Little Scarcies Rivers in northern Sierra Leone. The Great Scarcies rises in Guinea, flows for about 256 km (160 mi) southwestwards along the Guinea-Sierra Leone frontier, before turning into Sierra Leone to form a common estuary with the Little Scarcies River. The Little Scarcies also rises in Guinea, but, running to the south of the Great Scarcies, flows most of its course through Sierra Leone.

SHERBRO — A people of southwestern Sierra Leone, numbering about 75,000 in the 1960s. A branch of the Bullom, they inhabit Sherbro Island and the adjoining mainland. The Sherbro language belongs to the Mel group. The Sherbro obtained their name from Sherabola, an 18th century Mani king who lived on Sherbro Island.

SIERRA LEONE — The modern version of the name "Serra Lyoa," meaning "Lion Mountains," given to the Sierra Leone peninsula by the Portuguese in the mid-15th century.

SOFA	—	Soldiers of the great Mandinka empire builder, Samori Touré. The term, in Mandinka, initially meant father (*fa*) of a horse (*so*), but was usually applied not only to cavalry but to all soldiers in the army.
SOLIMA	—	A Yalunka people who founded the state of Solimana (*q.v.*).
SOLIMANA	—	A state formed in the 18th century by the Yalunka (*q.v.*). Its capital was Falaba.
SOSO	—	Also spelled Susu. A Mande-speaking group, of whom about 85,000 lived in northwestern Sierra Leone, and 250,000 in the Republic of Guinea in the 1970s. The Soso, a Mande group, traditionally identify themselves with the 13th-century Soso empire of Sumanguru in the western Sudan, from where they are believed to have moved westwards to the Atlantic.
TAMANGANA	—	A Yalunka word for town rulers.
TEMNE	—	The second largest group in Sierra Leone, the Temne numbered about 650,000 in the 1960s. They live in the west and central regions. The Temne language belongs to the Mel group. According to tradition, the Temne were first organized politically on a relatively large scale by Farma Tami (*q.v.*) in the 16th century.
TONGO PLAYERS	—	Mende witch detectors.
TONKO LIMBA	—	One of the main Limba divisions. They are the western branch, and are today found mostly in the present-day Kambia district.
VAI	—	Also spelled Vei. A Mande group, sometimes called the Gallinas (*q.v.*), inhabiting the coastal area of Sierra Leone and Liberia. The Vai numbered about 200,000 in the early 1970s. The Vai language belongs to the Mande group. The Vai are said to have entered Sierra Leone from the north before the 15th century, together with the Kono (*q.v.*). They have close cultural ties to the Mandinka (*q.v.*).
WARA WARA	—	A sub-group of the Limba (*q.v.*).
WONDE	—	Also spelled Wunde. The most important secret society among the Kpaa-Mende. It is more powerful than the Poro (*q.v.*).
YALUNKA	—	A Mande group in the extreme north of Sierra Leone, numbering about 15,000 in the 1960s.

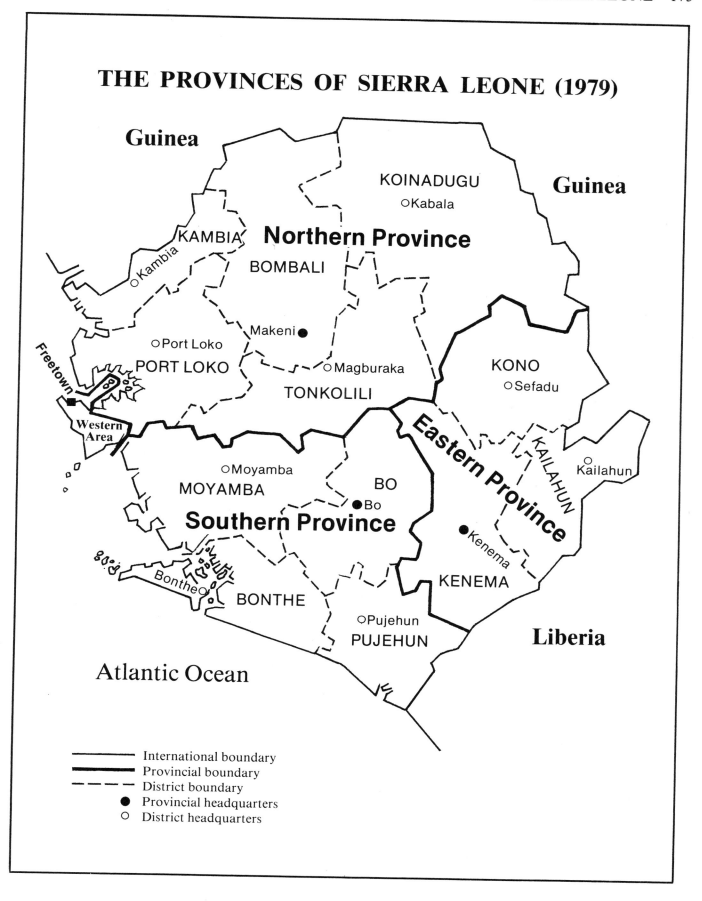

THE PROVINCES OF SIERRA LEONE (1979)

Guinea

Guinea

KOINADUGU

○Kabala

KAMBIA

Northern Province

○Kambia

BOMBALI

Freetown

○Port Loko

Makeni ●

PORT LOKO

KONO

○Sefadu

○Magburaka

TONKOLILI

Western Area

Eastern Province

○Moyamba

BO

KAILAHUN

○Kailahun

MOYAMBA

●Bo

Southern Province

●Kenema

Bonthe○

KENEMA

BONTHE

○Pujehun

Liberia

PUJEHUN

Atlantic Ocean

International boundary
Provincial boundary
District boundary
● Provincial headquarters
○ District headquarters

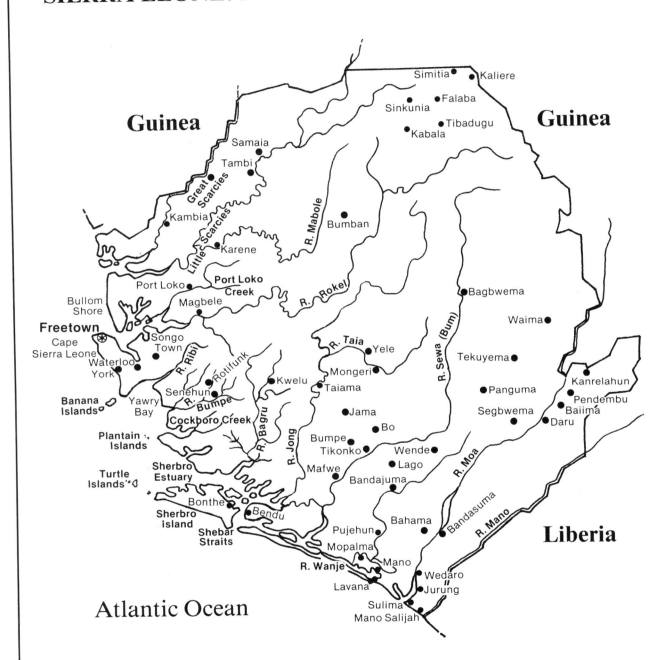

SIERRA LEONE: PRINCIPAL RIVERS AND TOWNS

PEOPLES OF SIERRA LEONE

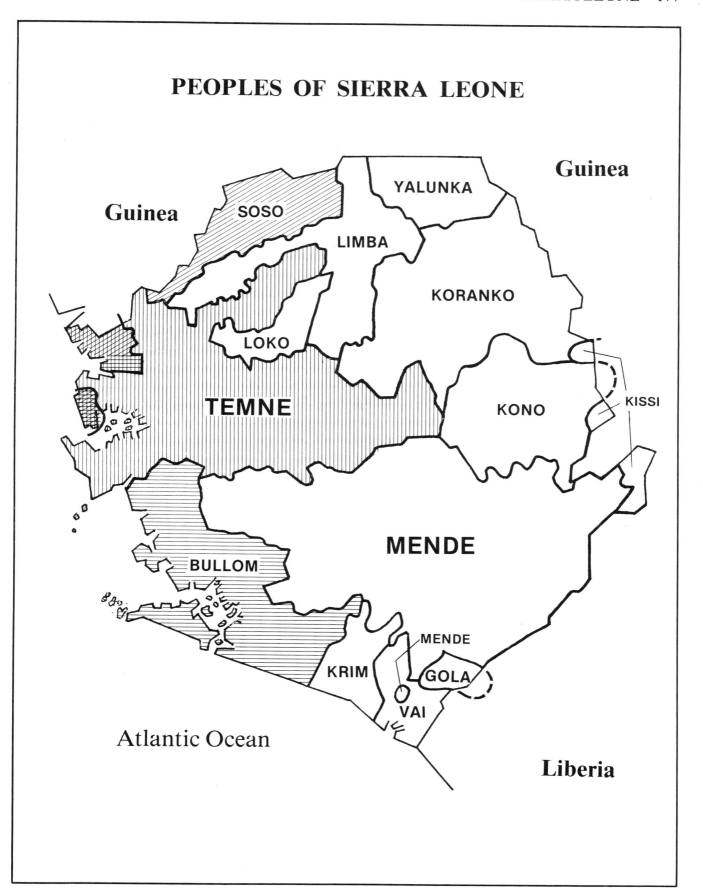

SIERRA LEONE: PHYSICAL MAP

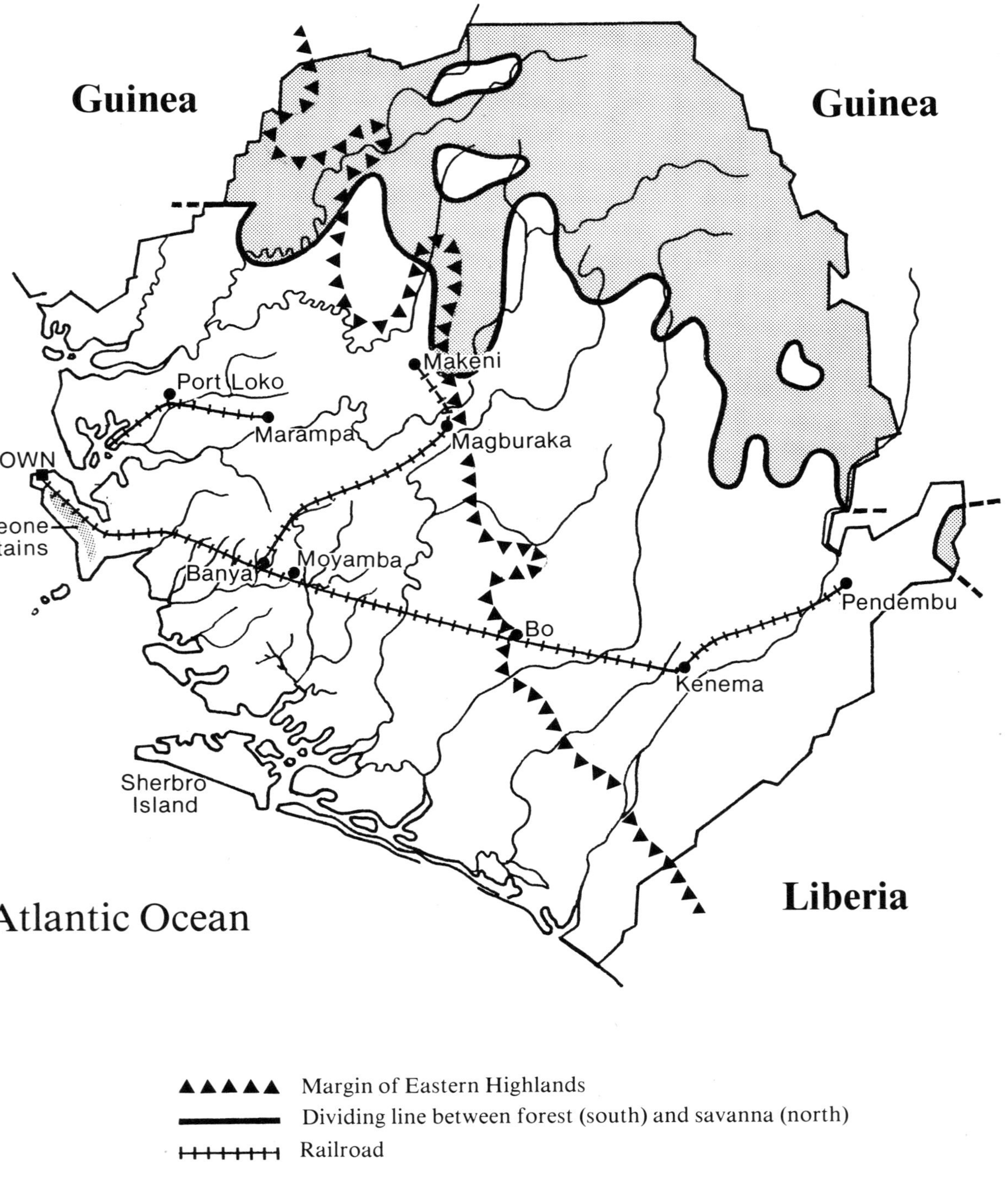

Guinea

Guinea

Makeni

Port Loko

Marampa

Magburaka

FREETOWN

Sierra Leone
Mountains

Moyamba

Banya

Bo

Pendembu

Kenema

Sherbro
Island

Atlantic Ocean

Liberia

▲▲▲▲▲ Margin of Eastern Highlands

――――― Dividing line between forest (south) and savanna (north)

┤┤┤┤┤┤┤ Railroad

ZAIRE—AN HISTORICAL INTRODUCTION

Ndaywel è Nziem

THE Republic of Zaire is located in the heart of central Africa, where it occupies a large proportion of the total area. Its territory of 2,344,885 sq km (905,365 sq mi) is situated in the vast basin which contains the Zaire (Congo) River and its numerous tributaries. The river takes its course almost entirely within Zaire. It rises in Shaba region, in the southwest, after which it forms a huge arc, passing successively through the regions of Kivu, Haut-Zaire, Equateur, Bandundu, and Bas-Zaire, before flowing into the Atlantic Ocean. The central basin, which lies across the Equator in the heart of the country, is almost entirely covered with thick forest. Savanna (tropical grassland) zones extend both north and south from this forest. It is principally in these savanna regions, as well as in the Great Lakes region to the east, that the greater part of the country's population, which in 1974 was estimated at 24,224,000, is settled.

THE PEOPLING OF ZAIRE

This vast territory, drained by many rivers, has without doubt been inhabited by human populations for centuries. Several prehistoric industrial sites have been identified within the territory of Zaire or in its surroundings. Archaeologists have unearthed several vestiges of human activity which reveal and confirm the existence of all the stages of prehistoric evolution in the region. The first of these, the Earlier Stone Age, which may have lasted until about 55,000 BC, is represented by the Oldowan and the Acheulian (Chellean) cultures, of which traces have been discovered not far from Zaire. Then the Middle Stone Age, which emerged in about 40,000 BC and lasted to about 8,000 BC, was represented by the Lupembian (Lupemban) tradition. This, in turn, was followed by the Recent Stone Age, represented by the Tshitolian tradition. Part of the present population, notably the pygmies, may trace its origins to that archaic era of stone-age industries. Archaeologists attribute to them the industries which flourished in the Stone Age. The principal activity at that time consisted in hunting and gathering, a social and economic phase which preceded the emergence of agriculture and stock-raising. Effective food gathering demanded considerable botanical knowledge so that the inhabitants could use effectively the plants found in the country. The transition from food-gathering to agriculture probably took pace by progressive steps, beginning with the

necessity of protecting and sometimes transplanting those forest species which had been identified as being of interest to man. Similarly, hunting could not be practiced without some knowledge of zoology and technology.

The original inhabitants of the region were therefore not uncultured nor unresourceful when the Bantu entered central Africa from the north and west, spreading out over its savannas and into its forests. Migrating probably in the first centuries of our own era, the speakers of the Bantu tongues began to occupy the territory that corresponds to present-day Zaire, decimating and absorbing the original inhabitants. Some of the survivors of these original pygmy groups sought refuge in the ecologically inhospitable forests of the central basin where, independently of one another, they still subsist in separate "islands."

The Bantu were the carriers of several revolutionary innovations, notably new crops and ironworking. Although rudiments of iron technology probably were not unknown previously, they offered major technological advances affecting food production and military effectiveness. Agriculture, scarcely known before the Bantu arrived, henceforth began to spread and diversify as the Bantu speakers introduced cereals indigenous to West Africa, and bananas and yams from Southeast Asia.

The different waves of migrating peoples pushed into practically every region of present-day Zaire. The first migratory movements, which formed the basis of settlement, were followed by numerous internal relocations. It appears certain that these populations initially settled in the savanna, or on the edge of the forests. This last zone was particularly attractive, for it permitted people to obtain forest products without experiencing the problems of living within its confines.

Traces of culturally and technically advanced societies, dating from as early as the year 800 AD, have been identified in the southern savannas and probably existed throughout Zaire. This, at least, is what has been deduced from the findings of excavations at Katoto and at Sanga in the vicinity of Lake Kisale, in southeastern Zaire. The discovery of copper crosses dating from this period not only in Zaire, but even as far away as the shores of the Indian Ocean shows the existence of long-distance commercial links. Cowrie shells and glass beads found in Sanga graves are further evidence of some coastal ties.

Since there was adequate space for expansion and

The Zaire (Congo) River, 4,700 km (2,900 mi) in length, runs in a huge arc through Zaire. Here Wagenia fishermen are seen hauling in a catch from its waters.

U.N. Photo

development, the various Bantu peoples were able to secure territories for themselves and develop as identifiable ethnic groups. Distance and prior linguistic differences were factors in this process of differentiation. Exogamous villages and families, speaking the same language, exchanged wives within a limited geographical area, thus reinforcing the linguistic, agricultural, religious, and social unity of a given region. In time, some groups, especially in the southern savanna, developed political structures unifying them under a common chief or king. In the forest, however, many peoples preserved their similarities through trade and fishing relationships. A few ethnic units maintained their cohesiveness through age-sets or esoteric secret societies which linked the leaders of politically unrelated villages.

In spite of diversification, the lines between ethnic groups were not rigid. Trade, intermarriage, resettlement, conquest, and cooperation all promoted cultural exchanges and borrowings. As groups merged, reformed, grew, or decreased, Zaire's ethnic mosaic resembled a gradually turning kaleidoscope rather than a fixed map.

THE CIVILIZATIONS OF ANCIENT ZAIRE

The period beginning around the year 1000 AD was a time of consolidation after the various peoples had settled in their specific territories. It was to lead to the development of several political micro-societies which may best be described as "chiefdoms." These constituted, in effect, the fundamental units upon which political systems of wider scope were erected. Ancient Zaire, thereafter, developed as an area in which some small existing groups became the subjects of powerful political kingdoms.

It was essentially in the savannas where communication was easiest, trade most advantageous, and the new agriculture most adaptable that the first states appeared. Most frequently these new state structures linked together previously autonomous and decentralized peoples.

At least from the 10th century until the 18th century, what is now Zaire appeared as a confederation of several regions which gave birth to a number of states. One such region was located near Malebo Pool (former Stanley Pool). With its influence spreading as far east as the limits of Kasai, this nucleus gave rise to the coastal kingdoms of the west: Kongo, Kakongo, Ngoyo, Ngola, and Makako. A second nucleus, less well known was located near Lake Mai Ndombe (formerly Lake Leopold II) to the northeast, where the centralized states of Bolia and Ntomba originated. The Kuba kingdom, which emerged to the south of this region, owed its existence to influences both from the west and the north. A third area, centered around the lakes of Shaba (formerly Katanga) was to be the base of the prestigious Luba and Lunda empires. Although mostly situated outside Zaire, another nucleus developed near the Great Lakes of East Africa, giving birth to the Ruanda, Burundi, and Buganda realms. The centralized state of the Shi of Kivu, in Zaire, also owed its origin to this source.

The kingdoms of ancient Zaire all stemmed from clearly defined sources, but each had its own particular evolution. The various kingdoms did not all originate in the same period. Chronologically, the realms of the west coast were the most ancient. In the 15th century, the kingdom of Kongo, was at its zenith, enjoying remarkable prestige. The Lunda and Luba empires, on the other hand, did not reach a similar period of development until, at the earliest, the 16th and, more likely, the 17th century.

But the kingdom of Kongo and the states situated around it (Ngola, Matamba, Kakongo, Loango), were also the first to be confronted with the problems of the intrusion of the Europeans. In 1482, the caravels of King Joao II reached the shores of Kongo for the first time, and the Kongolese had the opportunity to meet with white men. When a second fleet of boats appeared, several Kongolese, thanks to a misunderstanding, were taken to Portugal as hostages. This was the first time that the Kongolese were able to witness, at the source, the marvels of the technology that was beginning to flourish at the time of the European Renaissance. The account given by the hostages after their return to Africa in 1487 greatly impressed the Mani Kongo (king of Kongo) and his court. The king, supported by the majority of the aristocracy, tried to benefit from these technological developments and asked for carpenters and masons from Portugal to build impressive state buildings. He also asked to be baptized so he could share that supernatural force which had created such wonders.

Subsequently, however, king Nzinga Nkuwu (q.v.), who had himself witnessed the first Portuguese landing, felt he had lost something by converting to Christianity. He, therefore, renounced his baptism, while at the same time accepting acculturation, which, in any case, was advancing rapidly within his kingdom.

His successor, Mvemba Nzinga (q.v.), who, in

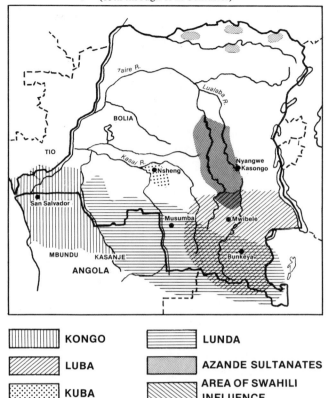

States of the Congo Region
(15th through 19th Centuries)

KONGO
LUBA
KUBA
LUNDA
AZANDE SULTANATES
AREA OF SWAHILI INFLUENCE

imitation of the reigning Portuguese monarch, had been baptized with the name of Afonso, was even more attracted by the prospects of modernization. Hoping to modernize his realm at all levels Afonso reorganized the political establishment and the court, promoted Christianity on a wide scale, and launched a campaign for giving religious instruction to the ruling elite. Several Kongolese young people were sent to study in Portugal while Portuguese professional men and artisans—including architects, doctors, pharmacists, cobblers, and tile-makers—were encouraged to settle in Africa. Acculturation, however, never proceeded in a spirit of equality and cooperation, for the Portuguese used their relationship with the Kongolese to advance their own commercial interests. The whole of the Kongo was regarded by the Portuguese as a source of commercial gain, a land destined to supply the Portuguese with raw materials. In addition, the Americas had just been discovered by the Europeans, and newly-established settlements there held greater interest than did African territories. Labor, however, was needed to consolidate and develop the European holdings in the New World. As the American Indians were unsuited to heavy labor, at an early stage black men from Africa were transported to the Americas. Afonso himself complained about this situation. "Not a day goes by without people being kidnapped to be enslaved," he wrote to his Portuguese royal namesake, "and neither the nobles nor members of the royal family were spared."

But the transatlantic slave trade continued to expand. Thus European influence, to which Afonso himself had opened the door wide, eventually brought about the downfall of the Kongo.

While this first attempt at acculturation was a political setback, nevertheless it brought certain benefits. For example Zaire's first written records date from this period. In agriculture several new crops, notably corn (maize) and manioc (cassava), were introduced, subsequently to spread throughout the country. Commercial activity, furthermore, received considerable impetus, with expansion of overseas trading enterprises as interior merchants took advantage of new coastal economic opportunities.

While the kingdom of Kongo was being ruined by a variety of factors, particularly the burgeoning slave trade, neighboring states attempted to turn the situation to their advantage by expanding their territory and influence. In the 17th century, such states included the Ovimbundu groupings to the south, and the Lunda and Luba empires to the east.

Also located on the southern savanna, the Luba-Lunda cultural complex emerged before 1500. Archeological evidence suggests the Luba people living between the Lualaba and Sankuru rivers are direct descendents of the Bantu people who once lived at Katoto and Sanga. Luba art, music, poetry, pottery, metalwork, and political structures developed early and, throughout the past millennium, were copied or borrowed by neighboring peoples.

According to Luba legends, their state developed when an eastern hunter, a tall handsome man named Ilunga Kalala (q.v.), entered their area and defeated the previous weak and uncouth ruler Nkongolo (q.v.). Supposedly, Ilunga enlarged the state, established an elaborate court structure, instituted royal etiquette, and founded the ruling dynasty whose power and legitimacy were embodied in bulopwe, a spiritual force transmitted by blood through the paternal line. While the story of Ilunga Kalala cannot be accepted as literally true, it does reflect a profound social and political transformation as a ruling elite distinguished itself from the ordinary classes of society. Just when this change took place is not altogether clear although archeological findings at Sanga indicate some class differentiation already by 1000 AD. Presumably, the stories of Nkongolo and Ilunga Kalala developed sometime before 1500.

From the Luba heartland, centralized political structures were transmitted over an extremely wide area of the southern savanna. Sometimes neighboring peoples such as the Kanyok accepted Luba institutions and ideas directly. Even before 1700, minor but ambitious Kanyok chiefs traveled with gifts of tribute to the Luba court, received ritual investiture from the Luba mulopwe (ruler or lord), and returned home claiming superiority over other local chiefs and neighboring peoples who in turn adopted Luba political forms.

The most important carriers of centralized political institutions, however, were the Lunda, living southwest of the Luba. Sometime before 1500—a date confirmed by written evidence from the Atlantic coast—the Lunda acquired certain Luba political customs, thus strengthening the ruling family at Musumba, the Lunda capital. The Lunda ruling family reorganized the court and gained increased magical powers when a Luba hunter Chibind Yirung (q.v.) married the Lunda princess Ruwej (q.v.). Chibind Yirung introduced Luba political customs at Musumba and his descendants have since ruled under the title of Mwant Yav.

From Musumba, the Luba-Lunda political forms spread eastwards to the Lake Mweru area where a Lunda general carved out an extensive kingdom, westwards to Angola, where Lunda lords, known by the title Kinguri, conquered local people to establish the Imbangala kingdom of Kasanje, and northwestwards to the Kwilu river area, where Pende people accepted many Lunda political symbols and titles. While the Lunda disseminated Luba-style political traits, they did not spread other features of the rich Luba cultural heritage. Thus, the many ethnic groups which borrowed, imitated, or were forced to accept Luba-like political centralization, nevertheless retained their own cultural and linguistic diversity.

North of the savanna, in the equatorial forest, lived a culturally homogenous, but politically decentralized people known as the Mongo. The Mongo have lived in the central forest region since before 1000 AD. From Lake Mai Ndombe in the west to the Lomami River in the east, the Mongo shared similar social structures, religious practices, and legends of origin. Although these people spoke closely similar languages, and traced their heritage to a common mythical ancestor named Mongo, until after 1900 local groups were politically autonomous and unaware of belonging to such an extensive ethnic agglomeration. Thus, Mongo unity was maintained, not by conscious and extensive political structures, but by frequent contact as the forest people traveled along the many equatorial rivers and streams, and as they exchanged wives.

East of the Mongo, the Lega people settled the area between the Lualaba River and Lake Kivu. Like the Mongo, the Lega were never united under a single ruler. The Lega, however, were linked together through the semi-secret bwami association. Composed

During the second half of the 19th century, Europeans increasingly penetrated what is now the Republic of Zaire. This drawing, made by a British officer, shows the destruction of "Manuel Vacca's town" by marines of a British expedition led by Commodore Sir William Hewitt, sent against pirates on the Congo (Zaire) River. This illustration was published in the *Illustrated London News* on November 13, 1875.

of the most respected members of Lega society, the bwami association honored and taught humanistic values such as wisdom, generosity, moderation, dignity, loyalty, and cooperation. Elaborate initiation systems were designed to carefully inculcate bwami ideas into the men and women privileged to join the association and to advance into its higher ranks. To aid in teaching the initiates and to provide emblems for bwami members, the Lega manufactured a wide variety of carefully crafted art objects including masks, human statues, animal figurines, stools, and knives.

Northeast, in the Uele river region, ethnic groups have a long and rich history of agricultural development. In the forest, the Mangbetu people cultivate palm trees, bananas, and manioc; many cereals such as millet, sorgho (sweet sorghum), corn, eleusine, and sesame; and also numerous vegetables. North, on the savanna, the Zande too are excellent farmers, although they do not grow bananas and palm trees which thrive only in the more humid forest environ-

ment. Actually, both the Mangbetu and the Zande were relative late-comers into the Uele area which earlier had been settled by Bantu speaking agriculturalists. When the Mangbetu and Zande, (the latter being non-Bantu), pushed into the area, they adopted local agricultural techniques and established conquest states governed by a military elite.

ZAIREAN SOCIETY UNDER FOREIGN DOMINATION: THE 18TH TO 20TH CENTURIES

After 1500, Central Africa increasingly came under the influence and domination of outside powers. Introduced progressively by means of commerce, foreign control climaxed in the 19th and 20th centuries as Europeans, Swahili Arabs, and Nubians used armed force to exploit the area. Frequently, they relied on help from African allies who joined with the interlopers to gain power over their neighbors.

The commercial activity of the 18th century extended virtually throughout the whole of what is now Zaire, as the growing demand for raw materials spread inland from the coast. Slaves, bee's wax, rubber, and ivory, were exported in exchange for products from the industrial world. These exotic imports reached the heart of the country, not only from the Atlantic coast, as in the 16th century, but also from the Indian Ocean and the Upper Nile.

Commerce grew increasingly important, so that Zaire, which at a certain period of her history had appeared to be a grouping of budding states, was changed into a wide territory with well-defined and flourishing commercial zones. As a result, merchants, rather than warriors and kings, became powerful and prosperous.

The central basin, together with what is now the Equateur region, as well as the sub-region of Mai Ndombe, formed an area which was dominated by the Bobangi people, originally a small fishing group from near Mbandaka. This complex was linked to the Atlantic coast by Tio middlemen at Malebo Pool who also supplied trade goods for a second network which was, however, territorial rather than riverine. This was the system of caravan routes that linked the interior regions of Bas-Zaire and Kwango with the coast. Yet another network ran from the coast at Luanda towards Kasai, even extending to the Sankuru River. This network was operated by Imbangala, Ovimbundu, and Cokwe (Chokwe) merchants. In addition, the trade network of the Arabized, or Swahili, merchants extended from the eastern part of the country as far as the Indian Ocean.

It was by these already established routes that European explorers in the 19th century penetrated the interior of the country. Thus, the pre-existing commercial activity facilitated the enterprise by furnishing not only porters, guides, and advisors, but also trade routes.

It was during this period that Leopold II, king of the Belgians, (reigned 1865-1909), took an interest in the country. In 1876 he arranged an international geographic conference, which gathered together the most eminent personalities among those who were interested in the exploration of Africa. At the conclusion of the conference, an "international association for the exploration and civilization of Africa"—known for short as the International African Association (A.I.A.)—was established. The sphere of activity of the new organization was limited to central Africa.

At the same time Henry Morton Stanley (1841-1904), an American journalist of Welsh origin, was completing his extraordinary transcontinental journey, which lifted the veil which had hidden the course of the Zaire River. Upon returning to Europe, Stanley attempted, without success, to interest Britain in his discoveries. Only after being rebuffed by the British did he accept the offers of Leopold II and enter the employment of the A.I.A.

King Leopold II. A picture originally published in the *Review of Reviews* in June, 1892.

The general assembly of the association then established the Comité d'Etudes du Haut Congo, or Study Committee for the Upper Congo. This body sent out an expedition, headed by Stanley, into the area.

When Stanley landed in Africa at the mouth of the Zaire River in August 1879, he ascended the river with the intention of establishing trading posts. But Leopold II's aim of establishing a colony had not yet been achieved. Thus, while the posts were being established in Africa, and treaties were being concluded with the local chiefs, the committee was dissolved to be replaced by an "International Association of the Congo," whose objectives were closer to Leopold's plan. Another step, however, remained to be taken—that of gaining recognition of his enterprise by the great powers of the day. At the Berlin Conference of 1884-85, summoned at the initiative of Otto von Bismarck (1815-98), chancellor of Germany, this goal was achieved. In the course of the sessions of this important conference, the interests of Leopold II, jealously defended, were safeguarded, and the different states represented at the conference recognized the sovereignty of the International Association of the Congo, as it had become known. Thus the Congo Free State (Etat Indépendant du Congo, or E.I.C.), came into being, as the personal trust of Leopold II of Belgium.

The Congo Free State

The newly-created state lasted a total of 23 years, from 1885 to 1908. Leopold, as ruler of the new state, occupied himself with defining its frontiers establishing its administrative organization. Leopold II, who remained in Belgium, was represented in Africa by an administrator general, resident in Vivi, on the Zaire River opposite Matadi. Then in 1886, the local capital was moved 40 km (25 mi) west to Boma, also situated on the north bank of the river. By the decree of August 1, 1888, the country was separated into administrative divisions, which were then further subdivided into districts, each headed by a commissioner. The new state was also equipped with an army, the "Force Publique," whose first task was to combat the Arabized elements in the north east where they exercised control over a considerable part of the territory. In an effort to promote the exploitation of his territory, Leopold began work on a railroad linking Léopoldville (present-day Kinshasa) with Matadi, near the river's mouth, to facilitate the transport of goods and raw materials.

At first economic expansion in the new state was satisfactory for the Europeans, although it was often detrimental to the African population. More than 1,800 persons, for example, died in the course of the construction of the railroad. Before long, however, the Belgian king got into financial difficulties and his activities in the Congo decreased his personal fortune which he had invested in the development of the new state. Besides, from 1902 onwards, an international campaign led by E.D. Morel, an Englishman, was launched against the atrocities being committed in the collection of rubber in the Congo. As the scandal spread throughout the world, it diminished Leopold's prestige and forced him to accept an international commission of inquiry which visited the Congo Free State to investigate the allegations of excesses. Finally, on April 20, 1908, authority over the Congo passed from a reluctant Leopold to the Belgian parliament.

The Belgian Congo

The Congo Free State thus became a colony of Belgium, a status it retained until June 30, 1960. The

Establishing a communications network was one of the preoccupations of the Congo Free State under Leopold's rule. This picture, published in a German publication in the 19th century, shows road-building in progress.

Historical Pictures Service, Inc. Chicago

Historical Pictures Service, Inc., Chicago.

From 1902 onwards, an international outcry arose against the atrocities committed against the African populations of the Congo Free State under Leopold II's rule. The scandal was particularly associated with the practices used in the collection of quotas of rubber. This cartoon, entitled "In the Rubber Coils. Scene—The Congo 'Free' State," was published in the British weekly, *Punch*, on November 28, 1906.

first years of colonization were characterized by a decline in the collection of trade goods and raw materials, the introduction of plantations, and the development of mining industries. The exigencies of World War I (1914-18) required the intensification of this pattern. After the war, from 1920 onwards, the administration of the colony was restructured. Several decrees were promulgated which reorganized chiefdoms, sectors, and "native districts." As a result, large states and ethnic groups were broken down into manageable units, while small and decentralized peoples were joined under chiefs created by the colonizers.

The African populations progressively lost the right to take initiatives on their own, being crushed by the weight of the three facets of colonial power: the administration, the commercial companies, and the missions. Journeys outside one's region of birth, for example, were rigorously regulated and each individual wishing to travel was required to obtain a travel permit. At times Africans rebelled against the strictures of colonial oppression. For example, in 1931 the

Pende people in Kwilu revolted against high taxes, low wages in the palm oil industry, and administrative interference in traditional political affairs.

With the advent of World War II (1939-45), which Belgium entered in 1940, the burden of colonialism became even heavier as Africans were expected to support Allied efforts with increased productivity, especially in the mining sector.

This situation led to the imposition of severe restrictions by the colonial authorities, provoking revolts in several places. In 1941, a miners' strike in Elisabethville (now Lubumbashi) was ended by shooting the strikers. In the same way, a revolt of the soldiers of the Force Publique, at Luluabourg (now Kananga) in 1944, brought on violent repression. The colony as a whole, however, prospered, and an apparent calm reigned throughout its vast territories. Thus, the Belgian Congo was judged to be a model African colony.

After World War II, however, a new political consciousness gripped the Congolese "évolués" (i.e. the first generation of African intellectuals). Subsequently they formed themselves into cultural associations which were either regional in character or consisted of interest groups. These associations included Unelma (Union des anciens élèves des Frères maristes, or Union of Former Students of the Marist Brothers), Assanef (Association d'anciens élèves des Frères des écoles chrétiennes, or Association of Former Students of the Brothers of the Christian Schools), and Abako (Alliance des Bakongo, or the Bakongo Alliance), etc. These associations constituted privileged movements which had the effect of sharpening the nation's political consciousness.

Other circumstances favored the flowering of new ideas. Internally, the pressures applied by the colonial regime created a spirit of unrest that made itself increasingly felt among the population. Then, in 1954, Auguste Buisseret, a politician of liberal tendencies, was appointed minister for the colonies. He inaugurated new administrative policies and dissociated himself from the Catholic Church which ran many educational and social programs in the Congo. The opposition of Catholic missionaries against his policy revealed to the "évolués" for the first time the existence of dissensions between Belgians: Catholics versus liberals, and Flemish versus Walloons.

In 1955, the same year in which Baudouin I, king of the Belgians from 1951, visited the colony for the first time, a Belgian academic named A.J. van Bilsen published the so-called "Thirty Year Plan." In this plan he proposed that the Congolese populations should be progressively prepared for self-government over the next three decades.

In 1958, the Congolese made great progress in

increasing national self-consciousness. On the occasion of the Brussels International Exposition, a great number of Congolese visited Belgium. Coming from different regions of the colony, regions between which movement was most strictly regulated, they were able to meet one another for the first time in the Belgian capital. Some among them took advantage of their visit to become acquainted with the Belgian "Left," which advocated independence for the Congo.

Also, in the course of 1958, General Charles de Gaulle (1890-1970), who had just gained power in France, came to Africa offering independence to French colonies which wished for it. On August 24, he visited Brazzaville, capital of what was then the French Congo, (now the People's Republic of the Congo), on the opposite bank of the Congo River from Léopoldville. Two days after his passage, the governor general of the Belgian Congo, Henri Cornelis, received a petition signed by several Léopoldville intellectuals asking the Belgian authorities to show the same understanding attitude as de Gaulle.

In December of 1958, Patrice Lumumba (q.v.), later to become the first prime minister of an independent Congo, participated in the All-African Peoples Conference, held in Accra, capital of the newly-independent state of Ghana. During his visit he made various contacts with several leaders of Third World countries. After his return from Accra, Lumumba's claims became very precise. "Independence," he declared on December 28, "is not a present from Belgium, but a fundamental right of the Congolese people," One week later, on January 4, 1959, serious rioting occurred in Léopoldville, when an Abako meeting was banned. By that time, the move to independence appeared to have become irreversible.

King Baudouin, therefore, in a message broadcast on January 13, 1959, announced that the colony was going to be led towards independence. From this date progress was rapid, perhaps even precipitous. During 1959, Congolese politicians mobilized support for newly formed parties. In January and February 1960, a Round Table Conference assembled Belgian and Congolese leaders, who agreed to establish June 30, 1960 as the date for independence.

TOWARDS A CONTEMPORARY ZAIREAN SOCIETY

The independence that had been so long awaited came at last, and was joyfully celebrated. But, as might have been expected, because of insufficient preparation of the Congolese, a difficult and laborious phase ensued.

After a mutiny broke out on July 5 in the Force Publique, which had been subjected to great strains

Reproduced by permission of the Twentieth Century Fund, Inc., New York

A street scene in Léopoldville—now Kinshasa, the capital of Zaire.

for several months, rumors spread throughout the country, causing disorder. To expedite the withdrawal of the Belgian troops still in the country, the government of Prime Minister Lumumba requested United Nations intervention. United Nations members, wishing to prevent a direct confrontation between the United States and the Soviet Union in the Congo, agreed to establish a U.N. force, and in mid-July the first U.N. contingents began to arrive. They were to remain in the country until mid-1964.

From 1960-65, the political parties, the government, and National Assembly were all put to the test severely, enduring events without being able to control them. Secessions were declared, public figures were removed from the scene, and numerous civil wars broke out in various parts of the country. Major events during these troubled years included the attempted secession of the province of Katanga (now Shaba), the murder of former Prime Minister Lumumba in January 1961, the 1964 rebellion in Kwilu and in the north and northeastern parts of the country, and the November 1964 attack by Belgian paratroops and European mercenary soldiers on the rebel stronghold of Stanleyville (now Kisangani). Altogether, during the turbulent period from 1960 to 1965, no less than five different governments were to head the country.

Following a final crisis involving Joseph Kasa-Vubu (*q.v.*), president of the Republic, the army high command neutralized the politicians and gave the reins of power to General Mobutu Sese Seko, who thus became president of the Congo in November 1965. With the wisdom of hard-won experience, he put an end to political agitation. This permitted him to initiate a program of social and economic reform and establish a new and solid foundation for Zairean society. On the economic level, efforts were directed towards increasing production and formulating a program for national development. This purpose was aided by two external factors: the rise in the price of copper from 1965 onwards, and the financial and technical aid that was granted for the purpose of stimulating the Zairean economy.

This effort was accompanied by a rigorous administrative reform aimed at strengthening the country internally and internationally. One of the first measures was depoliticizing and reorganizing the provincial administrations. The number of provinces was reduced from 22 to 12 in April 1966, and from 12 to 8 in December of the same year. A new constitution was promulgated on June 24, 1967, replacing the so-called Luluabourg Constitution, which had been in force since 1964. At the same time, through diplomacy, the nation's leaders tried to create a new image for the country and to demonstrate for the world not only that the Congo was prosperous, but also that the disorders and near-anarchy which had characterized the first years of independence were over.

In order clearly to mark the difference between the two epochs, the government decided to dispense with the country's old name of "Congo," and to adopt the name of "Zaire." This was done on October 27, 1971, a date when the national rebirth was also celebrated by changing the name of the river from Congo to Zaire*, by the adoption of a new flag, and by the re-naming of localities and public places. The movement laid claim to a key idea, publicized by the government with the slogan of the "Return to Authenticity." People were encouraged to denounce colonialism and repudiate its worst features and so help to establish a "new Zairean society" which would be modern and authentic.

On November 24, 1975, the new regime marked its tenth anniversary, enabling Zaire to evaluate its experience during the previous decade. Thus, after the passage of centuries, Zaire, born as a republic in 1960, in the course of time progressively reaffirmed its national character.

The personalities who find their place in the pages which follow have lived, each in a different manner and under varied circumstances, through a part of the long national evolution that had been outlined above. Together they bear witness to that long development which has led the descendants of the people of ancient Zaire to constitute themselves into a country whose unity is stronger than any type of unity which past regimes had established, and in which its citizens are able to play an important role.

THE ZAIRE RIVER

The river, which flows for much of its length along the frontier between Zaire and the Congo Republic, is known as the Zaire in the former country, and as the Congo River in the latter. Juridically the river is known as the Congo River, as it retains the status of an international waterway.

AFONSO I. See MVEMBA NZINGA

ALAVER, R.

Raphael Alaver (1898-May 18, 1964), head of the Church of the Holy Spirit (Mpeve) of Esieme, led an important post-independence uprising in the Kwilu district of Léopoldville province (now Bandundu region). Alaver's movement, which attracted many members from among the Nguii people around Mangai (a town on the south bank of the Kasai River 140 km, or 80 mi, northeast of Kikwit), reached a bloody climax in April 1962, when more than 100 people were killed.

Alaver, whose name is a corruption of "Alavear" (which signifies "he who has company") was born in 1898 in Lulaba, northeast of Kikwit, near the village of Eyeme at the place where the Esieme mission, christened Nazareth, was later to be built. His parents were fervent Protestant Christians, and, Alaver grew up with them at Port Francqui (now Ilebo) in an atmosphere of great piety. In 1910, when he was 12 years old, Alaver returned to the Mangai region. According to the "official" accounts which circulated among his followers, he had already wrought several miracles by this time, which allowed him to forecast his own prophetic future. In reality, however, there is little available information about his early career as a prophet, which probably did not come to public attention at this time, as his followers have claimed.

It is alleged that it was at the end of a stay at Oshwe, north of the Kasai River, in the course of which he apparently had contact with exiled Kimbanguists—followers of the prophet Simon Kimbangu (q.v.) who founded the religious movement known as Kimbanguism—that Alaver decided to devote himself to the life of an itinerent evangelist.

This link with Kimbanguism is, furthermore, confirmed by the fact that the "official" account of his life, preserved by his followers, asserts that he met Simon Kimbangu, who strongly urged him to pursue this career. As with Kimbangu, Alaver's unconventional conduct was displeasing to the colonial authorities, who claimed that his actions disturbed public order. In reality, however, they feared confrontation with an independent religious manifestation they would be unable to control. For by invoking Christ as his sole authority, the prophet Alaver stressed separation from Catholic as well as from Protestant religious officials.

One evening in 1952, while praying at a candle-lit cemetery, Alaver was arrested by order of M. Rapp, the territorial agent. He was then banished to Kasongo-Lunda, 420 km (250 mi) to the southwest in the Kwango district of Léopoldville province, where he remained until 1959. These seven years, spent in a region that was near the Kimbanguist stronghold in what is now Bas-Zaire, doubtlessly enabled Alaver to reaffirm his faith. At all events, when he returned to Nguii territory, it was to found a mission, which he named Nazareth, about one kilometer away from the village of Esieme.

Very soon he aroused popular enthusiasm with his teachings, basically drawn from the Bible, but to which he gave pronounced local color. It could be said that the people discovered in him a certain religious identity that they had difficulty in finding in the Catholic cults. The "Christians" of Alaver appealed above all to the Holy Spirit (Mpeve) which they invoked by prayer. When the Spirit came, it manifested itself above all by the delirious movements made by some members, generally young girls. The religion also had therapeutic pretensions: supposedly, several sick people returned from Esieme cured, and sterile women regained the gift of maternity. In the general disorder which followed the celebration of independence, the church of Esieme remained a place of calm and security where ordinary people came to find solutions to their daily problems.

The solidarity among the "Christians" of Esieme was very strong, but it also took the form of opposition to outsiders. For example, certain government functions were challenged because they were viewed as being outside the church. It was thus that the payment of taxes was contested, without, however, becoming the subject of a systematic boycott. The growing sense of unity centered on Esieme, in opposition to outsiders, by 1962-63 became a source of increasing anxiety to the administrator of Idiofa territory, M. Mayilamene. This tension between the religious movement and the public administration finally brought on a conflict which, in its concluding phase, would mark the end of the prophet's life.

The sequence of events began on April 3, 1962. All the "Christians" had been invited to the inauguration of the Alungu church near Mangai. Although Alungu is only a small village, it contained an important community of Alaver's followers, justifying the building of a church second only to that at Esieme. For the occasion, Alaver arrived to preside over the ceremonies. But at the moment when the proceedings were about to begin, an official emissary came to inform Alaver and his followers that the territorial agent of Mangai, the representative of the government in the region, formally forbade the holding of the celebration. The inaugural ceremonies and the blessing of the church were therefore suspended, and Alaver decided to return forthwith to Esieme. Accompanied by his followers, he set out immediately for Esieme.

On the return route, however, the group was again challenged, this time by the territorial agent in person, accompanied by several policemen. The conflict between the two groups degenerated into a pitched battle. The police were repulsed and the territorial agent carried off to Esieme as a hostage.

On the evening of April 3 when, in the course of public prayers, Alaver alluded to the day's events, he announced that he would be arrested and sent to prison, where he would die. At Idiofa, the same evening, the territorial administrator learned that his agent had been attacked, beaten, and imprisoned at Esieme. He immediately decided to intervene militarily, so as to break the force that was jeopardizing the authority of the state. In consequence, the following morning three trucks filled with soldiers left Idiofa.

On April 5, at the time of morning prayer, Alaver's mission at Nazareth was completely surrounded by soldiers, who opened fire and began burning the houses. When the shooting stopped, about 180 corpses were counted, without reckoning the wounded. But during the confusion, the prophet himself succeeded in escaping. He was, however, captured on April 12 at the village of Akwonkwo. Beaten, and with his clothes torn, he was transferred to Idiofa, from where he was sent first to Kikwit, and then to the capital, Léopoldville (now Kinshasa). In Léopoldville he was condemned, with two of his "Apostles," to five years in prison. He later died in Makala prison on May 18, 1964.

After his death, the Church of the Holy Spirit at Esieme continued its activities, and even flourished more strongly than before, attracting a growing membership. In the 1970s, the most important community remained that centered on Esieme, the spiritual capital of the church. Other communities existed at Mangai and Kinshasa.

NDAYWEL è NZIEM

BIBLIOGRAPHY: B. Verhaegen, *Rébellions au Congo* ("Rebellions in the Congo"), Vol. 1, Brussels, 1966, pp. 48-50; H. F. Weiss, *Political Protest in the Congo: the Parti Solidaire Africain During the Independence Struggle,* Princeton, 1967. See also the administrative archives of Mangai, and written accounts by members of the Church of Esieme.

ANTONIO I. See VITA NKANGA

BADJOKO, J.

Joseph Badjoko (circa 1878-1949) served as a colonial agent and territorial administrator for about 40 years, and was chief of Yanonge, on the left bank of the Zaire, 54 km (34 mi) downstream from Kisangani.

As such, he was a member of the African political and economic elite that came into being in Zaire during the colonial era. He belonged to that group of chiefs who used the modern means at their disposal to carve out a unique place for themselves in local society, while serving the cause of the colonizer.

Badjoko (more properly Bodjoko), was the son of Ngemba (*q.v.*), or Mata-Boike, a famous warrior chief of the Bangala people living around the villages at Iboko and Mabale near modern Makanza 200 km (120 mi) north of Mbandaka. He was born at Mpondo (Iboko) a little before 1880.

Because of his family members' relations with the Europeans at the nearby Bangala Station (later Nouvelle-Anvers and presently Makanza), Badjoko, still in his youth, was entrusted by his brother Boike to the explorer-administrator Hodister. Hodister was an agent for Société Anonyme Belge pour le Commerce du Haut-Congo (S.A.B.).—i.e. The Belgian Trading Company of the Upper Congo—a firm collecting ivory and wild rubber. Thus, from Hodister, who employed him as an interpreter, Badjoko received his first training in colonial politics and economics. He later went into the service of Commander Nicolas Tobback, who was in charge of the Stanley Falls station near present-day Kisangani. Soon after his arrival at Stanley Falls, Badjoko, commissioned on a scout mission, penetrated the villages of the Swahili merchants from the East African coast. Taking the name Badjoko ben Salbote, he learned much about the political and economic organization of the "Arabs."

The armed conflicts between the Congo Free State (E.I.C.) agents and the Swahili merchants proved to be the beginning of Badjoko's long and fruitful career with the colonial government. In May 1892 when the Falls station was threatened by the men of Rachid and Kibonge, Badjoko gave a timely warning to Commander Tobback, who immediately took measures to protect the station. He called on Louis Chaltin from Basoko, 200 km (120 mi) to the northwest, for the necessary reinforcements. Following this, and many other, important services to the E.I.C., Badjoko became a trusted ally of the whites: Van Gèle and Malfeyt especially held him in high esteem.

Later appointed chief of Yanonge, Badjoko carried out the duties of a territorial administrator. With soldiers and policemen at his disposal, he brought the regions of the Lokele and Topoke (areas just west of the Lomami River) under colonial rule. He then organized this territory, levied taxes, and performed other normal administrative duties. In the economic realm, he established timber posts along the river, opened inland roads, constructed concrete bridges, and extended the rubber, palm, and coffee plantations. Able to speak both French and English, Badjoko was an effective administrator who was known for his authoritarianism and honesty. Thus, later, his nephew Bando Bodjoko could say of him: "Bodjoko was an extraordinary man, I have never seen his equal. His voice frightened adults and made children cry. But, he would never go back on his word."

As a reward for his services, colonial authorities permitted Badjoko to construct the first brick house at Yanonge. In addition, twice, he was sent to Belgium where he was received by King Leopold II (reigned 1865-1909), and King Albert I (reigned 1909-34). Around 1930, when Badjoko retired after more than 40 years service, the colonial administration gave him an entire village at Lileko 125 km (75 mi) downstream from Kisangani near Isangi and Nasoko. Establishing residence there like a colonial settler, he took care of his plantations and his approximately one dozen trading stations. During his "retirement" he led a comfortable life in the company of his 50 wives.

Two of his children, Jean and Victor Badjoko, studied at the Collège Saint Michel in Brussels, and later were employed by the Institut National pour l'Etude Agronomique du Congo Belge (I.N.E.A.C., or National Institute of the Belgian Congo for Agronomic Studies) as agents at Yangambi 80 km (50 mi) downstream from Kisangani. When Joseph Badjoko died in 1949 at Lileko, his son Jean Badjoko left Yangambi to settle at Lileko and continue his father's work.

Badjoko rendered great services to the colonial administration. He was one of the many Bangala river people who, through their flexibility and skill, effectively contributed towards the progress and modernization of Zaire.

MUMBANZA mwa BAWELE na
NYABAKOMBI ENSOBATO

BIBLIOGRAPHY: *Biographie Coloniale Belge* ("Belgian Colonial Biography"), Vol. 1, "Chaltin," "Hodister," Vol. 2, "Tobback," Brussels, 1948-; F. Flament and others, *La Force Publique de sa naissance à 1914* ("The Force Publique from its Birth to 1914"), Brussels, 1952; "Joseph Badjoko," in *Kongo ya Sika*, April 2, 1950; B. Lokomba, "Contribution à l'étude des institutions politiques traditionelles chez les Lokele" ("Contribution to the study of traditional political institutions among the Lokele"), in *Les Cahiers du C.E.D.A.F.*, series 2, 1972; B. Semopa, "Joseph Badjoko," *Kongo ya Sika*, XI, 12, 1958; Ruth Slade, *King Leopold's Congo*, London and New York, 1962; C. Van de Lanoitte, *Sur les rivières glauques de l'Equateur* ("On the Sea-Green Rivers of Equateur"), Brussels, 1952; J.E. Mumbanza, "Les Bangala et la première decennie du poste de Nouvelle-Anvers: 1884-94," ("The Bangala and the first decade of the station at Nouvelle-Anvers: 1884-94"), unpublished thesis, University of Lovanium, 1971.

BEATRIZ, DONA. See KIMPA VITA

BOLANGWA

Bolangwa (circa 1860-1910), or Bolangbwa, was the first chief invested by the colonial authorities to rule the Bobangi chiefdom located east of the Zaire River, in what is now Equateur region. Formerly a slave, Bolangwa came to rule over territory extending from Irebu at the confluence of the Ubangi and Zaire rivers to Bolobo further downstream.

In the beginning of the 18th century, the Bobangi were only one of many small ethnic groups living in the swamps at the fork of the Congo and Ubangi rivers. During the 19th century, however, as they became involved with the growing slave and ivory trade, the Bobangi expanded along the Zaire River from their original homeland to as far south as the confluence of the Zaire and Kasai rivers. In the 1800s the Bobangi experienced great demographic changes as their population was increased by the acquisition of slaves they purchased from other peoples.

Some of these slaves came to play a decisive role in economic and social life. As among the Bobangi of Bolobo, who were ruled by Ibaka (*q.v.*), a former slave, the Bobangi of lower Ubangi had had a series of chiefs of foreign origin who had also formerly been slaves. Prominent among these were Bolangwa, and his successor, Ensala (*q.v.*).

Bolangwa, of Nkundo origin (a Mongo ethnic group southeast of Mbandaka), was born in a village whose people claimed Eleke as their common ancestor. Since, however, Bolangwa's father had received his wife Bodjimba as a part of the dowry paid for his sister, Nkundo custom decreed that Bolangwa and Bodjimba were the possessions of the sister and her children. Thus, Bolangwa belonged to Balakata, a man from nearby Baminia village. Eventually Balakata sold both Bolangwa and his mother to a Bobangi man named Bobitu.

Bolangwa therefore grew up in the lower Ubangi region. This was at a time when slaves were used on a massive scale for labor on long-distance trading expeditions. This provided them with opportunities to acquire a degree of freedom, as well as to obtain some property of their own. Intelligent and energetic, Bolangwa made the most of these opportunities, and

192—ZAIRE

was able to buy his freedom. He subsequently became a chief, thus joining the political elite.

The agents of the International Association of the Congo (the A.I.C., an organization that was to be renamed the Congo Free State in 1885) penetrated Bobangi country in 1884. Relations between the Association, and later the Congo Free State, and the Bobangi remained good until 1891, despite some tensions arising from the suppression of the slave trade on the Lulonga River. As, however, the Bobangi were located 200 km (120 mi) south of the colonial post at Bangala (presently, Makanza), they remained undisturbed in their commercial activities and their political life.

But, in 1891, when it became the policy of the A.I.C. in Equateur province to impose rubber production quotas, the Bobangi traders withdrew across the Ubangi River to what was then French Equatorial Africa, where they remained for almost seven years. It was not until soon after 1900 that they once more returned home.

It was at this time that Bolangwa made an alliance with the whites to play an intermediary role in attempting to obtain the submission of neighboring groups to the Congo Free State. This submission, however, did not take place without fighting. Clashes took place between the Free State troops, led by Bobangi, and other groups, principally the Bokongo. In this fighting the Bokongo, who fought bravely, lost many men.

Shortly after 1906, the great Bobangi chiefdom, instituted by the Belgians, was founded. Situated on the left bank of the Ubangi, it extended from the river mouth to well beyond the confluence of the Ubangi and Giri rivers, near Bolobo. The chiefdom included not only the Bobangi, but also the Baloi and the Bangele (on the banks of the Ubangi), the Bokongo (between the Ubangi and Zaire rivers), the Mampoko (between the Giri and the Zaire), the Ndjondo (Djundu) from the lower Giri and Ubangi region, and the Makutu and the Mangba (between the Ubangi and the Giri). From local testimony, collected in 1926 by a Belgian administrator named J.B. Delobbe, Bolangwa, who was appointed to rule the new Bobangi chiefdom, enjoyed unchallenged prestige in this period. His authority was, however more fictitious than real in a great part of the vast, but somewhat artificial, chiefdom. After his death in 1910, therefore, government agents divided it into numerous subchiefdoms.

MUMBANZA mwa BAWELE na
NYABAKOMI ENSOBATO

BIBLIOGRAPHY: A. Angles, "Hanssens," in *Biographie Coloniale Belge* ("Belgian Colonial Biography"), I: 479-93 Brussels, 1948-; J.B. Delobbe, "Rapport d'enquête sur la chefferie Bobangi" ("Report of Inquiry on the Bobangi Chiefdom"), Coquilhatville Territory, 1926, Archives of Tervuren, "Renseignements ethniques intéressant la District des Bangala" ("Ethnic Information Concerning the Bangala District"), Coquilhatville Territory, 1926, Archives of the Bomongo Zone; G. Halsteart, "La société politique Nkundo," ("The Political Society of the Nkundo"), in *Etudes Zairoises,* No. 2, June-July, 1974, pp. 85-107.

BUKASA, L.

Léon Bukasa (1925-January 16, 1974), one of the notable figures of modern Zairian song, performed and composed during the eventful decades of the 1950s and 1960s. Some consider him a poet of the colonial period, exalting nature and love of country. He should, however also be recalled as a musician who expressed the hopes and strengths of independent Zaire. Born in Jadotville (the present Likasi) in the

province of Katanga (now Shaba), Bukasa became, in his day, one of the greatest musical celebrities of Kinshasa.

The son of working class parents in a region where the Union Minière du Haut-Katanga ("Upper Katanga Mining Union") exercised considerable power, the young Bukasa entered the working world shortly after he completed primary school. By turn, he was instructed in the trades as a lathe operator, draftsman, and ceramist. He then tried his hand in a totally different area, becoming first a mechanic and then a chauffeur. Later, he learned masonry and even carpentry. None of these professions really inspired him; perhaps this is the reason his success at them was limited. In his leisure time, however, Bakasa devoted himself to fishing and music, two activities he loved dearly. Keeping himself informed about the musical atmosphere of Léopoldville (now Kinshasa), young Bukasa soon realized he would never achieve his full potential as a musician if he remained in Katanga. Therefore, in 1948 he decided to change his environment and he moved to the capital.

At that time, the music world in Léopoldville was experiencing great changes. Moving away from merely constructing melodies out of the traditional repertory, Congolese singers composed more original works, reflecting the problems of their own lives in song. This evolution is partially explained by the integration of modern instrumentation from sources outside Africa. The adoption or adaption of modern dances, the tango, the bolero, the classic rumba, created an increasingly rich atmosphere for the song. In addition to radio transmissions, recording companies brought distant musical themes to the studios, bars, and individual homes in Léopoldville. Bukasa profited from this atmosphere. Soon after his arrival at the capital, he met Bowami who introduced him to the 'Editions Ngoma,' where most of the important singers of the era were being developed. His first recording revealed genuine talent. Since this was the fulfillment, the culmination of his life goals, Bukasa abandoned the trowel and the hammer to devote himself completely to music, taking up with equal pleasure both wind and stringed instruments. He showed himself to be as gifted a composer as he was a singer. From about 1959 onwards, he dedicated his songs completely to themes of national independence, an event which he had the good fortune to celebrate.

Although the country suffered a period of crisis after June 30, 1960, once the Mobutu government restored stability, Bukasa felt the glimmer of new hope. In response, he rewrote his famous song *Ngoo, Congo na biso* ("Ngoo, our Congo") to which he gave the new title *Ngoo, Zaire na biso.*

On the eve of his 50th birthday, after a long illness, one of the most creative figures in Zairian music, Léon Bukasa, died on January 16, 1974.

NDAYWEL è NZIEM

BIBLIOGRAPHY: Lonoh Malangi, *Essai de commentaire sur la musique congolaise moderne* ("A Commentary on Modern Congolese Music") Kinshasa, 1969, *La musique zairoise moderne—hier, aujourd'hui, demain* ("Modern Zairian Music—Today, Yesterday, Tomorrow"), speech to the Festival National de la Culture et des Arts, October, 1976.

BUSHIRI

Bushiri Lungundu (circa 1911-June 23, 1945) was a prophet in the Kitawala movement and the leader of the 1944 Masisi revolt in Kivu province.

Bushiri was born in Orientale province (now Haut Zaire region) in Tshopo village near the town of Bafwa-sende located 200 km (120 mi) northeast of Kisangani on the Lindi River. His father was Salambongo and his mother Eylo. As there was no school in the region, Bushiri did not learn to read or write, but instead accompanied his father to the fields, hunting and fishing.

Not until Bushiri grew old enough to pay a poll tax did he decide to leave his village and seek salaried employment. His first job was as a sawyer with a Mr. A. Lorge for whom he worked from February 1935 until December 1936. Eventually, discontent with his wages of 30 francs per month, Bushiri broke his contract and sought government permission to leave his home area. He had to wait four years before he was granted transfer papers allowing him to move almost 200 km (120 mi) south to the neighboring territory of Lubutu in Kivu. There he was hired again as a sawyer, by the Comité National de Kivu (C.N.Ki.) which sent him to its site in Muhulu, near the Lubutu-Masisi territorial border. At Muhulu, he soon met Kilolo, a follower and teacher of Kitawala. It was Kilolo who introduced Bushiri to Kitawala. Quickly becoming an avid follower of the movement, Bushiri devoted himself entirely to Kitawala, renounced all his possessions, deserted his job in January 1944, and abandoned his second wife, Hatiba.

The Kitawala movement, which Bushiri embraced, was only one of several religious sects spreading throughout the Belgian Congo during the difficult years of World War II. Announcing liberation for people bent under the war effort, these sects promised an end to forced labor and taxes, to prison and the whip, and to misery and misfortunes. Assuring Africans that whites would be expelled from the land and that blacks would become the masters, these movements enjoyed widespread popularity as converts flocked to them.

The Kitawala, more than any other group, became politically aroused and openly hostile to the whites. Derived from the doctrines of the parent sect, the Watch Tower Bible and Tract Society, Kitawala's teachings rejected all forms of organized religion, condemned all civil and religious authority, considered all power as a reflection of Satan's presence, predicted the coming of a second Messiah, and announced the inauguration of a paradise on earth. The perspective offered by such teachings appealed to the oppressed colonial population.

After 1923, the Kitawala's messianic and apocalyptic ideas had been carried into the Belgian Congo by mine workers from Northern Rhodesia and Nyasaland who were employed in southern Katanga. From there, returning Luba and Bemba workers spread Kitawala teachings throughout the eastern part of the colony. In Kivu province, the movement quickly established itself in the areas of Lubutu, a town 200 km (120 mi) southeast of Kisangani, and Masisi, a town 60 km (35 mi) northwest of Goma.

Africans around Lubutu and Masisi, especially the Komo people, were receptive to Kitawala because of the pressures of colonialism during World War II. In 1944, the territorial administrator of Masisi noted many cases of suffering and unrest among the Congolese and conceded that he could offer no solutions to these problems. It is important to note, he wrote, that a large part of the labor force of the territory was out of work. These unemployed, whose numbers swelled with the advent of the war, had once been the clerks, "boys," police auxiliaries, miners, and chiefs working with the colonizers. These people became the first recruits of Kitawala and remained its most ardent supporters.

After embracing Kitawala, Bushiri wandered in the forests for several weeks until he arrived at Utanda, in the Masisi territory, where in February 1944, he began his preaching. He proclaimed himself the Second Jesus, the 'Mukombozi' (Redeemer), and the 'Mufalme' (King) of the world. Calling his teachings 'Mapendo' (love), Bushiri admonished his followers to love one another and to refrain from theft, adultery, and murder. Also, by attacking and destroying fetish cults, Bushiri strongly opposed the traditional sorcerers who sometimes held the peasants in terror. With his principal aide, Alleluya, Bushiri organized his church into 11 degrees, the highest of which he held himself.

Although the prophet's reputation already was very great, he became even more popular when he started to preach revolt against colonial rule. Bushiri ordered a halt to the rubber harvest, pressed his followers not to pay taxes, urged all Africans to leave the mines and workcamps, and encouraged all Congolese to burn all their identity papers. Finally, he announced the time of the white man was over and that the reign of the black man had begun. Chiefs and officials of Utanda not only supported Bushiri, they also encouraged their subordinates to follow him. Bushiri assured those few who still hesitated, because they feared the whites, that he could exterminate the foreigners by magic words alone.

Bushiri Lungundu was not the first to spread the 'good word' of Kitawala in the region. As if to prepare the way, several Kitawala preachers had preceded him. But, it was Bushiri who, through his vivid and radical preaching, was able to translate the people's dreams into direct action. Bushiri Lungundu's following and power increased as his reputation for performing extraordinary acts grew. People believed he could talk to the dead and bring them back to life. Rumor had it that, during a gathering, he multiplied food for his followers.

As Bushiri's support expanded, he became bolder in his proclamations. On February 17, 1944, he ordered his faithful to attack an itinerant colonial agent who was responsible for collecting the rubber harvest. Thus, Mr. De Schryver, an agent in charge of rubber collection, became the first prisoner of the revolts led by Katshaka, 'minister of Bushiri's armed forces.' After De Schryver had been captured and shackled, he was stripped to his underwear and a collar of rubber leaves was hung around his neck. He was told that no one would harvest any more rubber, that no one would pay taxes, and that all whites would be killed and replaced by the blacks. A letter from Bushiri addressed to all whites stated, 'Your time has come. Your well has dried up. God has taken pity upon the Black man and has sent me to save them. If you kill a single Black, you will all perish. The Blacks are superior to you. God wishes it so...' The letter was signed, 'I, Saviour of the world.'

De Schryver's party, which included his "boy," an unarmed soldier, a policeman, and a rubber collector were also arrested. Attempts to free the prisoners, organized by those still loyal to the administration, failed. The loyalists could only alert the territorial authorities of Masisi and Lubutu. Meanwhile, the victorious column of revolutionaries went from village to village rallying the inhabitants to their cause. All who still collaborated with "Bula Matari (the State) were arrested and tortured. Rubber harvest overseers, magistrates, tax-collectors, and policemen were singled out for punishment. Not uncommonly, Bushiri himself, or one of his aides, ordered executions. Fatalities following torture were equally frequent. No white was killed, however, and in addition to De Schryver, only two other European agents of

C.N.Ki. were arrested. Even these men were held by followers of Bushiri for only two days.

Government action taken to repress the revolt was fierce, brutal, and immediate. The district commissioner and the territorial administrator mobilized more than 100 officers and soldiers of the Force Publique (F.P.) to subdue the revolt. In vain Bushiri tried to avoid a showdown between his followers and the elements of the F.P. by proposing a truce with the district commissioner who was pursuing him. Bushiri's message to the commissioner said, 'I want you to know that if you wish for an agreement on these matters, come to me peacefully. Above all do not advance in a hostile manner. Take heed... Come here so that we may confer and agree upon terms. I would be willing to concede one half of the region, I will keep the other.'

Bushiri attempted to rally the black Force Publique soldiers to his cause by encouraging their desertion. 'I do not want you to take part in my war against the whites,' he wrote in one of his letters, 'since it is for you that I have come. If you take part in this war, you will all die. I have come to save you....'

The appeal was in vain. The military operation, launched against Bushiri at the end of February 1944, was completed quickly. On March 16, a few days after his headquarters in the village of Kubasa was destroyed, Bushiri himself was arrested. His aide, Alleluya, was taken prisoner on March 30. In all, more than 180 members of the Kitawala movement were taken prisoner and incarcerated at Iterbo, 80 km (50 mi) west of Masisi. The trial, which began on July 3, 1944, concluded with 72 death sentences, 48 life terms, and 46 terms ranging from 50 years down to five years in prison. Only 15 defendants were acquitted. At the suggestion of the king's prosecutor of Kivu, the death sentences were commuted to life imprisonment. Reasoning that mass executions could only do further damage to the spirit of the indigenous population, the prosecutor stated 'We would appear, without a doubt, to be the cruel and unjust masters. The indigenous population will make martyrs of the executed criminals. Let us guard against widening the gap between our wards and ourselves. Let us be lenient.' The death sentences of Bushiri and his aide, Alleluya, were upheld, however. They were hanged publicly at Iterbo on June 23, 1945.

The repression of the revolt caused an unknown number of deaths among the people. Members of the Force Publique committed many atrocities, especially in Kasese. On the order of a F.P. sergeant, hundreds of Kitawala militants were killed where the present Kasese traffic circle is located. After this massacre, the administrator, disgraced and relieved of his duties, committed suicide by shooting himself in the head. He was the only European 'victim' of the revolt of Masisi.

By publicly hanging the black messiah, the redeemer, the second Jesus, and by bringing severe reprisals against his followers, the colonial authorities hoped to end the movement's religious, social, and political strength, which Bushiri had so successfully channelled and guided. Moreover to quash any future Kitawala resistance, the region was placed under martial law until July 1947.

Despite the various steps taken by the authorities, however, the Kitawala sect not only survived, but spread geographically, socially and ideologically. Although Bushiri was dead, his influence in the region remained.

YOGOLELO TAMBWE ya KASIMBA
and HANGI SHAMAMBA

BIBLIOGRAPHY: D. Biebuyck, "Kimu Society and Kitawala," *Zaire*, Vol. XI, No. 1, January, 1957, pp 7-40; M. Lovens, "The Revolt of the Masisi-Lubutu," *Cahiers du C.E.D.A.F.*, Nos. 3 and 4, 1974; F. Van Langenhove, *Consciences tribales et nationales en Afrique noire*, ("Tribal and National Consciousness in Black Africa"), Brussels, 1960. Ally S. Gambo, "L'extension du Kitawala au Kivu et dans la Haut Zaire, 1940-60, Cas de la Revolte de Masisi" ("The extension of Kitawala to Kivu and Upper Zaire, 1940-60, The Case of the Masisi Revolt"), history thesis, Université National de Zaire (Lubumbashi), 1974. See also court documents of the trial of Bushiri at Iterbo, and other official reports and documents.

BUSIMBA

Monsignor Busimba Mikararabge (1912-September 7, 1974), the first bishop of the diocese of North Kivu was influential in helping to develop that region during the first decade of independence.

Busimba was born in the town of Rutshuru, 60 km (35 mi) north of Goma, where he went to primary school. In 1922, Busimba left Rutshuru for Rugari, 30 km (20 mi) south, to begin Latin studies which he completed at Kabagayi, Rwanda, in 1932.

Remaining in Rwanda, he studied philosophy and theology at the seminaries of Kabagayi and Nyakibanda. After graduation, he was ordained a priest on August 15, 1940 in Rugari, where he had first entered secondary school 15 years earlier. The young priest was assigned to various pastoral duties in Katana, Nyangezi, Rugari, and Goma. In 1960, when an autonomous diocese was established in North Kivu, Busimba was chosen as its bishop and, on May 8, he was consecrated in Rome by Pope John XXIII.

Throughout his pastoral life, Busimba was known for his sincerity and for his concern for community welfare. Under his direction, the North Kivu diocese developed sound scholastic, medical, agricultural, and social services vital to the region's development. During the early years of independence, also the beginning of his career as bishop, when mercenaries operated in Kivu, Busimba displayed his courage and vision by continuing to expand the religious and social programs of his diocese.

Monsignor Busimba died during the night of September 7, 1974 after a long and painful struggle with cancer. Monsignor Ngabu replaced him as head of the diocese of Goma.

NDAYWEL è NZIEM

BIBLIOGRAPHY: *Jua* (Kivu weekly) No. 44, September 14-20, 1974.

CHIBIND YIRUNG

Chibind Yirung (folk hero, who may have flourished circa the 17th century), the reputed founder of the Lunda (Aruund) state, is described by tradition as a hunter from the land of the Luba. Thus, he closely resembles Mbidi Kiluwe (*q.v.*) and Mwamba Ciluu, also hunters from the east who supposedly founded the Luba and Kanyok states. Stories of these hunter chiefs seem very old and may date back to before 1600.

According to legend, Chibind Yirung left the Upemba area in the Luba territory, traveling west to the Nkalanyi (upper Mbuji) Mayi region, where he set up camp on the banks of the nearby Kasidishi stream.

There he traded game to the Lunda in exchange for bamboo wine. Soon, however, Chibind Yirung was discovered by a Lunda nobleman, Nchakal Makal, who introduced the stranger at the court of Queen Ruwej.

Queen Ruwej fell in love with the hunter and married him over the objections of her brothers, Chigud and Chiyam.

The brothers' wrath grew even more when

A Cokwe (Chowke) statue representing Chibind Yirung.

once—during her menstrual period, when she was ritually unable to function as queen—Ruwej gave Chibind Yirung her "Rakam," a sacred bracelet symbolizing royal power. In spite of the new political authority he had acquired at the Lunda capital, Chibind Yirung still had to use force to subdue the surrounding chiefs of the land, who were held in high esteem by the common people.

Although Chibind Yirung's victories allowed him and his descendants to introduce strict rules of protocol and etiquette at the court and to reorganize Lunda socio-political structures, his actions also led to the widespread dispersal of Lunda-related people in Central Africa. Angered by Queen Ruwej's acquiescence to the newcomer, her two brothers left the Lunda heartland: Chigud to found the great commercial state of Kasanje in Angola; Chiyam to rule the Lwena in what are now Zaire and Zambia.

Legend says that Chibind Yirung and Ruwej had no children.

At Ruwaz, Chibind Yirung married a Mukachilund girl, Kamong Lwaz, who bore him three children. The oldest, Yav a Yirung, became the founder who gave his name to the Ant Yav (plural of Mwant Yav) dynasty. Traditional sources do not agree on how Chibind Yirung met his end. Some people contend that he was chased from the Nkalanyi region; others believe that he died and was buried on the right bank of the Kasidishi River.

The folk hero, Chibind Yirung is credited with bringing a new order to the Nkalanyi region. The Lunda believe it was this reorganization and revitalization which enabled them to rise from anonymity and play an important role in the history of Central Africa.

NDUA SOLOL KANAMPUMB

BIBLIOGRAPHY: M.L. Bastin, *Tshibinda, Ilunga, héroes civilisateur* ("Tshibinda, Ilunga, Civilizing Hero"), Tervuren, 1966; Edouard Bustin, *Lunda Under Belgian Rule, the Politics of Ethnicity,* Cambridge (Massachusetts), 1975; H. Dias de Carvalho, *Expediçao ao Muatiamvu, Ethnografia e Historia traditional dos provos de Lunda* ("Expedition to Muatiamvu: Ethnography and a Traditional History of the Lunda Peoples"), Lisbon, 1890; L. Duysters, "Histoire des Aluunda" ("History of the Aluunda"), *Problèmes d'Afrique Centrale*, XII, 40, 1958, pp. 76-98; Methodist Mission, *Ngand Yetu* ("Zaire"), Cleveland and the Transvaal, 1963; P. Pogge, *In reiche des Muata Yamvo* ("In the Kingdom of the Mwant Yav"), Berlin, 1880; Victor W. Turner, "A Lunda Love Story and its Consequences," *Rhodes-Livingston Journal*, XIX, 1955, pp. 1-26; J. Vansina, *Kingdoms of the*

Savanna, Madison, 1966; E. Verhulpen, *Baluba et balubaisés* ("The Baluba and the Balubaized"), Anvers, 1936.

DIOGO I. See NZINGA MPUDI

DISENGOMOKA, E.A.

Emile Adolphe Disengomoka (March 31, 1915-March 15, 1965), educator, civic leader, and novelist, was the first Congolese to receive his Régent Litéraire which is equivalent to an M.A.

Born at Kingemba in the present Ntimansi collectivity of Lower Zaire, Disengomoka spent his early years at Kimpese, 65 km (40 mi) southwest of Thysville (now Mbanza-Ngungu), where his father earned a pastor's diploma at the Evangelical Training Institute in 1922, and at Ngombe Lutete, 40 km (25 mi) north of Mbanza-Ngungu, where his father was pastor of a Protestant church.

After completing primary school at Ngombe Lutete in 1928, Disengomoka was sent to the Ecole de Moniteurs of Madzia (a school preparing elementary teachers) in the French Congo to learn the French language. In 1931, he returned from Madzia to serve as director of the Protestant primary schools in the Ngombe Lutete region. With the exception of the three years from 1934 to 1937, when he enrolled at the Evangelical Pedagogical Institute (E.P.I.) at Kimpese, Disengomoka continued in his administrative capacities until 1942. After another interlude of studies, from 1942 to 1944 at the Kimpese pastor's school, he worked as headmaster at the Thysville primary school.

In 1949, desiring further education, he went to Belgium where he studied at the Ecole Normale Moyenne of Nivelles (Nivelles Teacher Training College) until 1951. Then he enrolled at the Nivelles Ecole de Regence where he was supported through a scholarship awarded by the Baptist Missionary Society. On July 9, 1954, he received his Régent Litéraire diploma, a degree no Congolese had obtained till then.

On his return to the Congo in 1955, Disengomoka took a position as headteacher of the Ngombe Lutete Central School, the most important Baptist primary school in the Lower Zaire area.

In 1958, he left the rural countryside to settle in Léopoldville (now Kinshasa), where he taught French at the Athèné of Nqiri Nqiri until 1961. In addition to his teaching, he also served for a year as director of discipline at Nqiri Nqiri and at the prestigeous Athèné de Kalina. From 1961 till his death on March 15, 1965, he was principal of the Institut Polytechnique Congolais.

Besides his teaching career, Disengomoka took an active interest in civic duties as a member of the territorial council of Thysville, the provincial council of Léopoldville (1955-58) and the Counseil du Gouvernment Général (Council of the Government General). Also, from 1963-64, he sat on the board of governors of l'Université Libre du Congo (Free University of the Congo). In 1964, he was a member of the constitutional Commission of Luluabourg (now Kananga).

Disengomoka should also be remembered as a writer. He was also perhaps the first novelist in Zaire. In 1942 he published *Ku ntwala* ("The Future"), the translation into Kikongo of an American ethical work, *Right Thinking and Right Living,* by O.R. Winstedt. In 1943 he published *Kwenkwenda* ("Where Shall I Go?"), a novel which was to win a literary award, the Margaret Wrong prize, in 1948. In about 1948 he published a sociological work about family living conditions, entitled *Luvuvamu mu nzo* ("Peace in the House"). Besides these, he wrote several articles in *La Voix du Congolais,* published in Léopoldville. He also wrote some hymns, of which about 15 were published.

In all of his writings, Disengomoka expressed concern for the moral and cultural development of Congolese society. As an "evolué," his ideas reflected the deep attachment of the Congolese élite to education and improvement.

SABAKINA KIVILU

BIBLIOGRAPHY: E.A. Disengomoka, *Ku ntwala* ("The Future"), a Kikongo translation of O.R. Winstedt's *Right Thinking and Right Living,* 1st ed., Kimpesi, 1942, 4th ed., Léopoldville, 1965, *Kwenkwenda* ("Where Shall I Go"), novel, 1st ed., Léopoldville, 1943, 4th ed., Kinshasa, 1965, "Les adeptes de Missions Etrangères au Congo Belge" ("Followers of Foreign Missions in the Belgian Congo"), *La Voix du Congolais,* 1945, "Message de nouvel an," ("New Year's Message"), *La Voix du Congolais,* 1946, "La civilisation au Congo" ("Civilization in the Congo"), *La Voix du Congolais,* 1946 *Luvuvamu mu nzo* ("Peace in the House"), 1st ed., Thysville (?), circa 1948, 4th ed., Léopoldville, 1957, hymns, published in *Kinkunga mia Kintwadi,* Léopoldville, 1956; Donald E. Herdeck, *African Authors,* Vol. 1, Washington D.C., 1973; André Massaki, *E.A. Disengomoka. Zingu kiandi: 1915-1965*, Kinshasa, 1968; Mbololo ya Mpiku, "Introduction à la litérature Kikongo," ("Introduction to Kikongo Literature"), *Research in African Literatures,* Austin, Texas, Fall, 1972; A.E. Sewel, "Disengomoka, the first 'Régent Congolais'," in *Congo Mission News,* October, 1954, J.L. Vellut, "Sources écrites africaines pour l'histoire de l'Afrique Central (dès débutes à 1950)," ("African Written Sources for the History of Central Africa (from the Beginnings to 1950)"), *Likundoli, archives et documents,* 1-2, 1974.

EBEYA

Ebeya Eugène (1919-February 5, 1964), lieutenant colonel and chief of staff of the Armée Nationale Congolaise (A.N.C.), was the most notable casualty of the uprising in Kwilu led by Pierre Mulele (*q.v.*).

Born in Mpokola village in Equateur province, Ebeya was a member of a Zaire River ethnic group often referred to as the Bangala. Since 1886, when the Force Publique (the colonial army) was created, the Bangala people have had a continuous tradition of providing many soldiers to the armed forces. Ebeya was certainly aware of this tradition for he went to school at Nouvelle-Anvers (now Makanza) where the Bangala Station, an important colonial military outpost, had been located from 1892 until 1913. It is not surprising then, that on the eve of World War II and at age 20, Ebeya enlisted in the Force Publique.

During and after the war, Ebeya proved to be an intelligent, dedicated, and disciplined soldier who showed promise as a leader. In the 1950s he was assigned to duties as inspector (chief superintendent) at the Ecole de Cadets (school for cadets) in Luluabourg (now Kananga) where new recruits were sent for specialized training. In 1954, the school commander assessed the future colonel's qualities. He said: "From the time of the school's establishment, First Sergeant Ebeya worked as an administrator on the permanent staff. His high moral values were always an example to our future officers." Prior to independence in 1960, Ebeya's ability earned him the first sergeant's star, which at the time was the highest rank a Congolese soldier could attain.

Following independence, Ebeya climbed rapidly through the ranks, assuming ever greater responsibilities. First he became a "captain commandant" responsible for the 13th Infantry Battalion. A year later, in 1961, he took charge of the Second Division at Léopoldville (now Kinshasa), being given the rank of major. Only a few months later, he was promoted to chief of staff of the A.N.C. In 1962, he was placed in command of the military expedition to Katanga (now Shaba), which began to re-establish the central government's control over the secessionist province. When Lt. Col. Malumba was absent in 1963, Ebeya was made provisional commander of the Third Division, stationed at Stanleyville (now Kisangani). In January 1964 he was administering ongoing business at A.N.C. headquarters in the absence of General Joseph Mobutu, commander in chief.

Since July 1963, the Mulelist partisans had been secretly training in Kwilu, primarily in the Gungu and Idiofa territories south and east of Kikwit.

In early 1964, they broke into open revolt against the established regime. At first, this grass-roots popular uprising was discounted by authorities of the central government. But when the Mulelists attacked military expeditions, civil populations, and industrial centers, where they killed policemen, soldiers, supervisors and civil servants who supported the government, Congolese authorities were forced to commit troops to suppress the rebels.

As the revolt continued, whites fled and general panic among Africans ensued. At Idiofa, 70 km (40 mi) northeast of Kikwit, and Gungu, 70 km (40 mi) southeast of Kikwit the Mulelists fought desperately against the A.N.C. To maintain army morale and help restore order in the Kwilu, Ebeya joined his troops on the battlefield.

Making Kikwit his headquarters, Ebeya prepared his strategy. For the offensive against the Mulelist partisans at Idiofa, he mobilized 100 well-armed soldiers and a dozen helicopters. He also requested additional commando reinforcements from Elisabethville (now Lubumbashi). Although two A.N.C. platoons controlled the road to Kasai, the Mulelist partisans increased their attacks so that by

February 1, 1964, the garrison at Gungu was in urgent need of assistance.

Knowing the road from Kikwit to Gungu was not secure, Colonel Ebeya himself decided to lead a relief expedition to Gungu. On February 5, however, his party was ambushed between Kikwit and Gungu and Ebeya was killed by a poisoned arrow. His mutilated body was brought back to Léopoldville where he was buried in the Kalina (now Gombe) cemetery.

In his eulogy, General Mobutu described the death of Ebeya not only as a deep personal tragedy, but also as a great loss for the A.N.C. Mourning Ebeya as a friend and a faithful supporter, General Mobutu said "At the age of 45, Colonel Ebeya died a soldier. To those of us who are soldiers, his example will continue to serve as a model. He died so that the Congo could live. Let us not forget this. Very soon, I will recommend Colonel Ebeya for our country's highest honors. But for now, the best homage we can pay is to show ourselves worthy of him. Colonel Ebeya, your comrades in arms salute you for the last time."

After Ebeya's death, the Zairian government honored him by renaming an important military camp and a large river boat in his memory. Camp Hardy at Mbanza Ngungu (formerly Thysville) became Camp Lt. Colonel Ebeya while the M.S. *Baron Liebrechts* became the M.S. *Ebeya*.

In the death of Ebeya Eugène, Zaire lost a patriot and a valiant soldier.

MUMBANZA mwa BAWELE na
NYABAKOMBI ENSOBATO

BIBLIOGRAPHY: J. Gérard-Libois and J. Van Lierde, *Congo 1964; Political Documents of a Developing Nation,* Princeton, 1966; Sese Soko Mobutu, *Receuil des discours et harangues du Président de la République Democratique du Congo, Le Lieutenant-Général Joseph-Désiré Mobutu* ("Collection of the Speeches of Lieutenant-General Joseph-Désiré Mobutu, President of the Democratic Republic of the Congo"), Kinshasa, 1970.

EDJUMBU

Edjumbu (circa 1880-1937), an extremely wealthy polygamous trader of the Ndolo people, used his riches, geographical location, and local influence to gain an important position in the government of the Belgian Congo. As a government functionary, his career spanned 20 years and he eventually achieved the rank of chief of the sector.

Inhabiting the swampy grounds between the upper Giri and Moeko rivers, the Ndolo (an ethnic group located not far north of the Zaire River, midway between Mbandaka and Lisala) live primarily from fishing, trade, and agriculture. Their villages and fields are built on land reclaimed from the marshes. In addition to their main crops of bananas and yams, they also exploit the natural palm groves of the region for wine and oil. Although for years the Ndolo regularly had sold palm oil to other river peoples, in the 1880s, with the help of their neighbors the Beka and Sengo, they participated in the "great river trade" whose principal commodity was ivory.

In traditional Ndolo social structure, wealth and power were measured in numbers of "wives." Influential men acquired dozens or even hundreds of women who were then given to less prominent individuals in return for regular payments and work. Thus, ordinary men desiring a wife were dependent upon a few very wealthy Ndolo plutocrats who had legal control over much of the female population.

Born around 1880 in the village of Bokala, located 45 km (25 mi) north of the Zaire River, Edjumbu became rich by assembling a large court of women, some whom he got from other Ndolo families. Although often these wives brought dowries from their maternal kin, Edjumbu gained most of his wealth by transferring his women to other men who were then obligated to give him periodic gifts in return. As he grew more prominent, people seeking special favors gave him women who provided Edjumbu with an ever growing source of income.

Edjumbu's fortunes were also aided by the strategic location of his village, Bokala, which served as a stopping place for many Ndolo and Saw (neighbors immediately to the east) people who were going to the Zaire River port of Moeko. Portuguese, trading for palm oil and palmettos, established their first commercial house at Bokala, which later became the site of the first oil works in the region. Bokala was also an important village for white administrators coming from either Nouvelle-Anvers, the present Makanza located 200 km (120 mi) north of Mbandaka on the Zaire River, or Budjula, 80 km (50 mi) north of the Zaire River where it is joined by the Mongala, to visit the Ndolo or their northeastern neighbors, the Mwe.

Edjumbu quickly took advantage of his location and prominence to offer his services as a guide and supporter to the whites, who were consolidating their authority in the area. A significant figure in breaking Ndolo opposition to European seizure, Edjumbu used his alliance with the whites to advance himself in the colonial government.

Around 1910, the Ndolo region, largely dependent on the sector of Nouvelle-Anvers, was visited by state agents who established the sub-chiefdom of Dolo Botila, which was administered by the chief Basoko. Basoko, in turn, was under the jurisdiction of the larger chiefdom of Engumba (the future chiefdom of Malundja). On September 25, 1915, Edjumbu was invested as a "deputy-chief" of Dolo Botila. Six years later, on September 25, 1921, Edjumbu became actual chief of Ndolo-Bokala, at that time dependent on the Budjala territory.

In 1925, when the first steps were taken to organize the Ndolo into a sector of 'Water Dwellers of the Ndolo,' Edjumbu because of his excellent record of service, was encouraged to become chief of the sector. He had to wait ten years, however, before the projected sector of the 'Water Dwellers of the Ndolo' became a reality.

In 1935, when Edjumbu was recommended for the post of chief of the sector, the Belgian territorial administrator described his candidate in these terms:

> "Edjumbu, is a chief of efficiency rare in his region. Through his 350 wives (he) wields power comparable to one of our high financiers. And he knows how to use it. I believe, however, that it would be preferable not to confer upon him the permanent presidency of the Sector's tribunal. He is too interested in palaver, and his cupidity and cunning mind could chase plaintifs from the court."

Thus, Edjumbu became the chief of a vast sector which included the chiefdoms of Moniongo, Lisombo, Tandu, Dolo-Bokala, Mosangi, and the chiefdom of the Saw. In 1936, Edjumbu had his village, Bokala, named as the sector's seat. Edjumbu, however, served as chief of the sector for only two years before he died in 1937.

His successor, an adopted son Bilolo, had been born to one of Edjumbu's wives by her first marriage. Bilolo, who grew up at Bokala, ruled only temporarily, as he proved unsatisfactory in the office of head of the Sector. He was accused of lacking tact and having no notion of justice. No doubt, Bilolo merely wanted to use the means earlier employed by his father to increase the number of his wives. Bilolo, however, succeeded only in gaining the hatred of the chiefs and dignitaries of other groups. When Bilolo was relieved of his duties in 1940, the administration of the sector was turned over to Djala, a judge of the sector and a native of Bokala.

Edjumbu is remembered as a rich, ambitious, but very able, African chief and colonial administrator.

MUMBANZA mwa BAWELE na
NYABAKOMBI ENSOBATO

BIBLIOGRAPHY: M. Guilmin, "Quelques coutumes matrimoniales des peuples de l'entre Congo-Ubangi" ("Some Matrimonial Customs of the Peoples Living Between the Congo and the Ubangi"), *Congo*, 1922, I, pp. 44-48, "La polygamie sous l'Equateur" ("Polygamy in Equateur"), *Zaire*, 1947, I, 9. pp. 1001-23; Mumbanza mwa Bawele, "La dynamique des systèmes de filiation. Cas des peuples de la Haute Ngiri et de la Moeko," ("The Dynamic of Filiation Systems. The case of the Peoples of Haut Ngiri and Moeko"), speech to the Premières Journées d'Histoire Zairoise, Lubumbashi, April 1-5, 1975, 25 pp.

ENSALA

Ensala (18?-circa 1926), a former slave, rose to prominence in colonial times as ruler over the large Bobangi chiefdom extending from the mouth of the Ubangi River in the south to Buburu, about 120 km (75 mi) beyond the confluence of the Ubangi and Giri rivers, in the north. Ensala, who governed for several decades, succeeded Bolangwa (*q.v.*) when he died in 1910.

Ensala's origins are somewhat obscure. Of either Ngombe or Mongo ethnic background, he was born near the Ikelemba River which empties into the Zaire River near modern Mbandaka. Eventually, he was sold as a slave to a man named Dangi living in Bobangi territory. Dangi in turn was the slave of Moli from Ekango.

In Bobangi society, slaves frequently assumed key roles in commerce, thereby gaining great wealth and power. It was not unusual for a slave to purchase his freedom and rise to a position of political authority. This was true of Ensala, for when Bolangwa died in 1910, Belgian colonial agents selected Ensala to fill the vacant office.

For seven years Ensala ruled the great Bobangi chiefdom as it had been organized in Bolangwa's time. Like Bolangwa, Ensala exercised power only over the Bobangi and their immediate neighbors; the groups north of the mouth of the Giri mainly were left to their own devices. Eventually, in 1918, the colonial government reorganized the Bobangi chiefdom by removing the loosely administered northern areas from Ensala's jurisdiction. Enforcing the provisions of a March 28, 1912 royal decree concerning local government structures, the Belgians transferred the Bokongo, Mampako, Njondo, Bangele, Makutu, and Mangba, sub-chiefdoms to the reorganized Bangala district with headquarters at Nouvelle-Anvers (now Makanza) on the Zaire River. From that time onwards, the Bobangi chiefdom only comprised a series of villages situated on the left bank of the Ubangi from its confluence with the Giri as far as its mouth; these included Loka, Lilanga, Bokwango, Bobangi, Bangala, and Bongwande Lokekia. In 1926, the administrator of the territory of Coquilhatville (now Mbandaka), M. Delobbe, proposed to extend Ensala's authority south to include part of the Ngele ya ntando people of Irebu, located about 80 km (50 mi) downstream from present-day Mbandaka. This annexation, however, never took place.

Not only were the boundaries of Ensala's domain determined by colonial agents, his authority within the chiefdom was also limited by the Europeans. Although Ensala's territory contained a large amount of copal, his people, who were primarily fisherman, never worked to collect the resin. When other Africans came to exploit the copal within the bounds of Ensala's chiefdom, local Bobangi people and chiefs lodged numerous complaints. They even went so far as to demand that tribute be paid to them in return for the copal taken by the "foreigners." The colonial administration opposed any such tax and Ensala was unable to regulate copal production in his land.

In general, both the state agents and the Bobangi people regarded Ensala as a great chief. According to a 1926 administrative report, Ensala enjoyed "great influence among his tribe as well as beyond. Furthermore, he [had] incontestable chiefly qualities; calmness, a certain uprightness of spirit in relation to his subjects, and a great deal of common sense."

The example of Ensala and of other former slaves who became great chiefs in the lower Ubangi region challenges the opinion that all the slaves coming from the Lulonga and Ikelemba river areas and sold among the Bobangi should be considered as human chattel or as social dregs. Their condition was less deplorable than it was thought to be.

MUMBANZA mwa BAWELE na
NYABAKOMBI ENSOBATO

BIBLIOGRAPHY: J.R. Delobbe, "Rapport d'enquête sur la chefferie Bobangi" ("Report of Inquiry into the Bobangi Chiefdom"), and "Rapport d'enquête sur la chefferie Bokongo" ("Report of Inquiry into the Bokongo Chiefdom"), both in Coquilhatville Territory, Archives of the Musée royale d'Afrique centrale, Tervuren, 1926, "Renseignements ethniques intéressant le District des Bangala" ("Ethnic Information Concerning the Bangala District"), Coquilhatville Territory, Archives of the Bomongo Zone, 1926; J.J.C. Lemaire, "Rapport d'enquête sur la chefferie de Djundu" ("Report of Inquiry into the Djundu Chiefdom"), Bomana Territory, Archives of the Bomongo Zone, 1926, "Rapport d'enquête sur la chefferie Mobere" ("Report of Inquiry into the Mobere Chiefdom"), Bomana Territory, Archives of the Bomongo Zone, 1921, "Rapport d'enquête sur la chefferie Mampoko" ("Report of Inquiry into the Mampoko Chiefdom"), Bomana Territory, Archives of the Bomongo Zone, 1921; H. VanDevenne, "Notes Complémentaires, chefferie Bokongo" ("Complementary Notes, Bokongo Chiefdom"), Bomana Territory, Archives of the Bomongo Zone, 1927.

ESEKO

Eseko (18?-1901) distinguished himself in a war of resistance he and other Budja chiefs waged against the militia of the Société Anversoise de Commerce au Congo (Antwerp Trading Company of the Congo) and the troops of the Congo Free State. In this struggle, Eseko led the Eloa people—a branch of the larger Budja ethnic group living in the Mongala and Lulonga river basins north of the Zaire River, about 170 km (105 mi) northeast of Makanza.

One of the most widely publicized aspects of Leopold II's rule in the Congo was the abusive exploitation of Africans by the large concessionary companies. Established in 1892, the Antwerp Trading Company was one such company, which obtained a legal contract to monopolize the rubber trade in the Budja territory. The Antwerp Company, like other concessionary firms, was actually a state within the state, and exercised powers of police and taxation. Taxes were collected in the form of wild rubber that people were forced to harvest in the forest. Because the company's only goal was to maximize profits, it obligated Africans to gather as much rubber as possible. In order to ensure a continuing supply, even when overharvesting threatened to deplete the stock of natural rubber, the Antwerp Company simply applied harsher punishments for non-payment of taxes. During such times of intense pressure, near the end of the 1890s, Africans began to revolt against the rubber companies in the Congo Free State.

In 1898, faced with increasingly heavy rubber demands, and cruel reprisals when unrealistic quotas could not be met, the principal Budja chiefs organized an armed uprising which lasted until 1905. Eseko's Eloa people, who were the first Budja people to have been affected by the rubber trade, were also the first to take up arms against the Antwerp Company. Their attacks were aimed at the white agents of the company and against the company's African workers, who, not being Budja themselves, were especially zealous in collecting rubber and oppressing local villagers.

From the beginning, Eseko displayed brilliant tactics, and encouraged the Budja to modernize their military equipment and to increase their strength. Armed only with spears and shields, the Budja made large-scale surprise attacks, and captured Dundusana, Mankika, and Yakombo—all small isolated Antwerp Company stations. Next, Eseko and other Budja chiefs ambushed armed company units traveling through the region. In the course of these operations, several European agents were killed and large stocks of rifles, revolvers, and amunition fell into African hands. From 1898 to 1900, Free State military officers Lothaire and Verdussen launched retaliatory expeditions, but succeeded only in the rare pitched battles where the numerical superiority of their troops was important. Although several Budja chiefs were arrested, judged, and condemned to death by a military council of war, Eseko, Zengo, Ekwalanga, and other leaders escaped to continue their fight.

Besides showing his skill as a tactician, Eseko demonstrated an ability to attract other Budja people to the cause. Therefore, by early 1900, the resistance had spread into the Mondjamboli area of Budja territory. Mondjamboli had remained aloof from the struggle until September 1899, when police stations were set up at their villages of Yambata and Mandika so that state agents could apprehend any Mondjambili individual who might instigate a revolt. In reaction, and following Eseko's example, the Yambata chief Mandjumba ordered his subjects to destroy gardens around the new stations, causing a food shortage among the state personnel. Mandjumba, who then attacked armed units sent out in search of provisions, was able to kill two European and many African state soldiers.

As the struggle continued, it became more difficult for the Budjas to maintain their resistance. Arms and ammunition became scarce. Both the Congo Free State and the Antwerp Company increased the number of soldiers at their stations. European scouts and their African collaborators discovered several carefully prepared Budja ambushes. Eseko then modified his strategy, abandoning direct confrontations in favor of hit and run guerrilla methods. In order to slow the movements of the pursuing state troops and to give the bulk of Budja forces time to escape, he constructed large fortifications in the main villages. These structures, made of earthen-covered poles measuring 3 to 4 meters high, sometimes enclosed an area 75 meters long and 25 meters wide. In this way, Eseko and his men were able to evade and outlast colonial commanders who could leave the security of their stations for only short periods of time.

In July 1901, Mardulier, who commanded the Bangala district with headquarters at the present Makanza, launched a major drive to gain control over the Eloa Budjas under Eseko. Mardulier's 400-man army gave him a large numerical advantage over Eseko's smaller band of warriors, while the state commander's comparatively unlimited supply of ammunition gave him superior firepower. Even these advantages, however, might not have been enough to enable Mardulier to defeat Eseko had it not been for the complicity of some Africans who led the state

troops to key Budja defensive positions. In the course of his five-month campaign, Mardulier captured Eseko and his two principal companions, Zengo and Ekwalanga. Although all three were executed, the Budja Eloas continued their resistance until 1905, four years after the death of their leaders.

Within the next decade, when the Congo Free State became a Belgian colony, the state took measures to reduce the abuses linked with the rubber harvest. While, in part, the changes in policy were due to international pressure, especially from Britain, and to a realization that rubber supplies were nearly exhausted, the changes also came in response to the actions of Eseko and other African leaders who resisted the domination and exploitation of their people.

MUMBANZA mwa BAWELE
na NYABAKOMBI ENSOBATO

BIBLIOGRAPHY: M. Coosemans, "Lothaire," *Biographie Coloniale Belge* ("Belgian Colonial Biography"), Vol. 1, Brussels, 1948-, "Mardulier," "Verdussen," *Biographie Coloniale Belge,* Vol. II, Brussels, 1948-; F. Flament, et al., *La Force Publique de sa naissance à 1914* ("The Force Publique from its Birth to 1914"), Brussels, 1952; R. Harms, "The End of Red Rubber: A Reassessment," *Journal of African History,* XVI, 1975, "La révolte des Budja (détails)" ("The Budja Revolt [details]"), *Belgique Coloniale,* V, 17, 1900, pp. 197-98; A. Lejeune-Choquet, *Histoire militaire du Congo* ("Military History of the Congo"), Brussels, 1906, "Les affaires du Congo à la Chambre" ("Congolese Affairs in the Chamber"), *Belgique Coloniale,* V, 17, 1900, pp. 193-97, "Les troubles de la Mangala" ("The Mangala Troubles"), *Belgique Coloniale,* IV, 6, 1899, pp. 68-69, E.D. Morel, *Red Rubber,* London, 1906; E. Vandervelde, *Les derniers jours de l'Etat du Congo* ("The Last Days of the Congo State"), Paris, 1909.

GANDANDA GIBANDA

Gandanda Gibanda (circa 1865-October 1931), a prominent Pende chief, was unjustly tortured and executed by colonial authorities following the famous Pende revolt of May and June 1931.

Gandanda Gibanda ruled the chiefdom of Musanga, located southeast of Kikwit. Musanga is one of the several chiefdoms in the Kwilu River area of Zaire with a mixed Lunda-Pende population. Probably founded in the early 1700s by Lunda-related people fleeing slave traders in the upper Kwango River region in Angola, Musanga received its Pende people in the early 20th century. Although the Pende had entered the Kwilu in the 1600s, after being displaced from their former Angolan homeland by the Imbangala people, they settled in the particular Lunda polity at Musanga only around 1903. At that time, the Musanga chief granted asylum to some Pende groups who hoped to avoid the demands of the commercial agents from the Compagnie du Kasai ("Kasai Company"), who were obliging the people to harvest rubber. These Pende were given farming land by the Musanga chief who accepted them as his clients. Since the Pende group was large and very prolific, however, it soon imposed its culture on the ruling Lunda families. As the two groups began to intermarry, Lunda and Pende cultures were merged in the Musanga area.

Gandanda Gibanda, a member of the Kimbai clan, ascended the throne of the Musanga chiefdom during the first decade of the 20th century. Sometime after he took office, Chief Gandanda Gibanda entered into contact with the Belgian colonial authorities, who officially recognized the Musanga chiefdom in December 1920. Gandanda Gibanda, who was invested and decorated with a medallion by the colonial government, always acted with great sincerity towards state officials.

Although Gandanda Gibanda was a decorated chief, he is best known because of the violent death he suffered following the 1931 Pende revolt. This popular revolt was provoked by economic difficulties and social dislocations which the Pende people experienced. As a result of the worldwide depression, palm oil prices fell and the demand for palm nuts declined sharply. Because many Pende men earned their wages gathering palm nuts, they were especially hard hit by fluctuations in the world market. At the same time that wages were going down, taxes remained constant or even rose slightly. Also, during the 1920s, entire Pende villages had been relocated as colonial authorities built new roads or sought to eradicate sleeping sickness. Thus, by 1931, the generally co-operative Pende people, were pushed into a revolt against the government.

This revolt began on June 8, 1931 when some Pende dissidents gathered at Kilamba, 55 km (35 mi) southeast of Kikwit, to protest the taxes being levied. There, they killed the Kandale territorial agent, Maximilien Ballot, who was responsible for collecting taxes. Ballot's body was dismembered and then divided among some high-ranking Pende chiefs and dignitaries. Contrary to reports in the colonial press, this was not done for reasons of anthropophagy (cannibalism). Rather this act was carried out in accordance with an ancient Pende custom requiring that the body of a powerful enemy must be decapitated and the head brought to the chief as a trophy. According to custom, certain parts of the body were kept to increase the power of traditional magic charms. Therefore, the Kilamba rebels dismembered and divided Ballot's corpse. There may also have been, in this deed, a historical concern: the various Pende chiefs and dignitaries wanted to keep the pieces of the 'conquered' white so they might show future generations proof of the Pende people's victory over the European rulers.

Government authorities, quickly and brutally, put down the revolt. The district commissioner in charge of suppressing the uprising had orders not to grant mercy or accept any act of submission before Ballot's head and body were returned. In compliance with these directives, several Pende chiefs and dignitaries were arrested and taken to the Kakobola prison. Subjected to severe atrocities, many died from mistreatment. During October 1931, a court-martial was held at Kandale, 130 km (80 mi) southeast of Kikwit, where the arrested rebel leaders and traditional chiefs were arraigned. These individuals were judged and condemned as "authors or co-authors in the murder of Ballot." All the rebel leaders were executed. Some were first subjected to horrible tortures. Musos Shagindungu, the Pende man who decapitated Ballot, was shot with arrows and buried alive. Mwatha Muhega, who had killed Ballot with an arrow to the chest, was broiled alive over a low fire.

Of all these deaths, perhaps that of the Musanga chief Gandanda Gibanda was the most outrageous. Accused of having hidden Guhulula, one of his subjects who kept a piece of Ballot's body, Gandanda Gibanda was condemned to death. He was turned over to the soldiers of the Force Publique (the colonial army) who subjected him to the lash, cut off his genitals, and placed him naked in the sun. There he died an agonizing death from loss of blood, shock, and exposure. Gandanda's death was especially tragic since he was completely innocent. A year later, in November 1932, the colonial authorities admitted that in reality Gahulula had fled south to Cokwe (Chokwe) country at the beginning of the revolt and that Gandanda had been executed unjustly.

The deaths of Gandanda Gibanda and other Pende chiefs and dignitaries, many of whom were innocent of any misdeeds, are examples of the rash and arbitrary acts perpetrated against numerous people throughout the colonial period.

SIKITELE GIZE a SUMBULA

BIBLIOGRAPHY: F. Mulambu-Mvuluya, *Contribution à l'étude de la révolte des Bapende: mai-septembre 1931* ("Contribution to the Study of the Bapende Revolt: May-September, 1931"), Brussels, 1971, "La révolte des Bapende: mai-septembre 1931. Etude d'un mouvement de résistance des populations rurales congolaise á la colonisation" ("The Bapende Revolt: May-September, 1931. Study of a Resistance

Movement Against Colonization by the Congolese Rural Populations"), *Congo-Afrique,* No. 53, 1971, pp. 115-36; H. Nicolai, *Le Kwilu* ("Kwilu"), Brussels, 1963; B. Verhaegen, *Rébellions au Congo* ("Congo Rébellions"), Vol. 1, Brussels, 1966, pp. 45-46.

GARCIA II. See NKANGA LUKENI

HENRIQUE

Dom Henrique (circa 1495-circa 1526), the son of Mvemba Nzinga (*q.v.*), the Mani Kongo, was the first bishop of the Kongo kingdom and probably the first African bishop of the Catholic Church. His 15 years of study in Portugal made him the most highly educated Kongo person of his age.

Dom Henrique was born in about 1495 at Mbanza Nsundi, 75 km (45 mi) south of Malebo Pool. His father Mvemba Nzinga, or Afonso, was already a Christian whose zeal for the faith was well known.

Although Mvemba Nzinga was not yet in power, as a son of the Mani Kongo (ruler of Kongo) he was recognized as a strong candidate for the throne. Thus, he was sent out of the capital as Mani Nsundi (ruler of Nsundi), a post often given to the heir apparent. In 1506, on the death of the Mani Kongo Nzinga Nkuwu, Mvemba Nzinga replaced his father after a bitter succession war against his brother.

The young Henrique, however, lived only briefly with his family at the capital Mbanza Kongo (later San Salvador), for Afonso included his son in the first contingent of young men sent to study in Portugal. Henrique, therefore, left his family at the age of 11 or 12 to study abroad. In general, most of the Kongo students in Europe did poorly in their studies because they could not easily adjust to the new land. This was not the case for Henrique, who zealously applied himself to the study of theology and Latin.

In 1513, Henrique was part of an important diplomatic mission to Rome. On the advice of King Manuel I of Portugal (reigned 1495-1521), the Mani Kongo Mvemba Nzinga, a Christian king, sent envoys to vow fealty to Pope Julius II (in office 1503-13). Young Henrique was made member of the mission since it was also instructed to request a dispensation with regard to his age in the case of his possible elevation to the post of bishop. Such a dispensation was necessary for, at 19, Henrique was far from the required age for such an office. The Kongo delegation, constituted in Mbanza Kongo, then attached itself to the Portuguese delegation in Lisbon. Together the two groups proceeded to Rome where they presented themselves before the pope.

When the Portuguese and Kongolese representatives arrived in Rome on March 12, 1514, they learned that Pope Julius II, to whom the letters of obedience were addressed from Mvemba Nzinga, had died several months before. Since Leo X (in office 1513-21) had now been elected pope, the envoys had to modify their plans. Although the delegates could not officially present the letters professing obedience to Julius II, they could offer Leo X the gifts they had brought along. The pope accepted the gifts and agreed to grant a dispensation for the consecration of Henrique as a bishop.

After this audience with the pope, Henrique returned to Portugal, where he continued his studies. In 1520, he was ordained a priest and shortly thereafter consecrated as bishop. One year later, in 1521, he returned to the Kongo with the title bishop of Utica (in Tunisia), since the Portuguese opposed the creation of a diocese in Kongo. Although the Mani Kongo hoped that Dom Henrique's presence at Mbanza Kongo would add to the king's power and prestige, the new bishop did not live long after his return. Dom Henrique died in 1526, if not sooner.

The life of the Bishop Dom Henrique serves to remind us that Christianity in the western region of Zaire has very ancient roots. His life also stands as testimony to the existence of a small group of literate Africans who flourished during the golden years of the kingdom of the Kongo.

NDAYWEL è NZIEM

BIBLIOGRAPHY: G. Balandier, *La vie quotidienne au royaume du Kongo, du XVIème au XVIIIème siècles,* Paris, 1965, English translation by Helen Weaver published as *Daily Life in the Kingdom of the Kongo from the Sixteenth to the Eighteenth Century,* New York, 1968; F. Bontinck, "La première 'Ambassade' Congolaise à Rome, 1514," ("The First Congolese 'Embassy' to Rome, 1514,"), *Etudes d'Histoire Africaine,* I, 1970, pp. 37-73; J. Cuvelier, *L'ancien royaume du Congo* ("The Old Kingdom of Kongo"), Brussels, 1946; W. Rabozuk, "Notes sur l'enseignement dans l'ancien royaume du Congo" ("Notes on Teaching in the Old Kingdom of Kongo"), *Likundoli,* Series A-2, 1974, pp. 25-44.

IBAKA

Ibaka (circa 1820-April 1889), rose from slavery to become one of the wealthiest men engaged in the 19th century Zaire River trade. As chief of the Bobangi collection of villages at Bolobo, 260 km (160 mi) north of Kinshasa, he was a leading ally of early white explorers and missionaries who established outposts in his territory.

This man, who took the name Ibaka late in life,

came to Bolobo from the Mboshi people in the nearby lower Alima river region. Perhaps of Teke origin (the Teke are located northeast of Malebo Pool, in the present People's Republic of Congo), Ibaka was sold as a slave to the Bobangi who had penetrated south along the Zaire River to Bolobo from their 18th century homeland between the Zaire and Ubangi rivers.

Ibaka took his name from his Bobangi master, a powerful chief associated with the founding of Bolobo. Until about 1850, the original chief Ibaka had lived in the village of Kutumpuku on the south bank of the Nkene River, northwest of present-day Bolobo. Following an internal dispute, several of Ibaka's notables left the area, crossed over the Zaire River, and took refuge at Bolobo where they established the villages of Manga, Muekuana, Ululu, and Mongo, named after themselves. Several years later, after an overwhelming attack on his village by people from the interior, Ibaka joined his refugee subjects, east of the Zaire River. Despite their former conflicts, Ibaka was able to regain his old authority over all the other Bobangi chiefs at Bolobo. By the 1870s, the agglomeration of 15 Bolobo villages spread over a distance of two miles and contained a population numbering 10,000 people.

The Bobangi population at Bolobo made part of their living from fishing and growing cassava. Their chief livelihood, however, was commerce, and in the middle of the 19th century, the Bobangi of Bolobo were the most successful merchants of the upper Zaire River. Travelling throughout the territory by way of the smallest creeks and affluents of the river, they linked the Tio merchants selling European wares at Malebo Pool with people beyond the Iboko-Mabale agglomeration (at the present Makanza). The Bobangi trading network also included portions of the Ubangi and Giri rivers in Zaire, and the Likouala-Mossaka and Likouala-Aux-Herbes rivers in what is now the Republic of Congo-Brazzaville.

Bobangi commercial expeditions included both men and women travelling in convoys of about ten canoes. The canoes carried small bundles wrapped in mats and containing cloth, copper, brass wire, pearls, guns, and powder, which could be exchanged for ivory and daily provisions. For their food, however, the parties fished and hunted along the way.

The large expeditions never had less than 100 armed slaves and the principal entrepreneurs, who remained at home, often conferred great responsibilities on trusted slaves. Slaves who exhibited qualities of courage and honesty, rose to the positions of managing their master's affairs. For example, the slaves of chief Mangulu worked as his commercial agents at the Malebo Pool. Some slaves gained their freedom and amassed fortunes which equaled or surpassed those of

lineage chiefs. Stanley reported that Lungumbila, a former Bobangi slave, owned merchandise easily worth 75,000 francs.

Eventually the Mboshi slave purchased by the Bobangi chief Ibaka achieved the status of head slave over his master's commercial enterprises. As head slave, he directed chief Ibaka's expeditions to the Ubangi River region.

At the death of chief Ibaka, his head slave continued to manage his affairs and actually took over his master's position. This take-over was made easier because Ibaka's actual heir, Lingenji, was still quite young. In fact, the former slave even took the name of his owner in order to reinforce his prestige. Facing strong opposition from his former master's enemies, the new Ibaka proved his superiority through a series of bloody battles. Muekuanga, one of these rivals, left Bolobo and moved toward the interior on the edge of the forest. From the time of this victory until the whites arrived in 1882, Ibaka exercised uncontested sovereignty over the entire Bolobo agglomeration. Ibaka's adjunct was the wealthy slave Lungumbila mentioned by Stanley.

On November 10, 1882, Captain Hanssens, who, in Henry M. Stanley's absence, headed Leopold II's forces in the Congo Free State, arrived at Bolobo to arrange for the construction of a station. Hanssens wanted a place to re-provision the steamers which would soon be traveling the river. Although the other Bobangi at Bolobo expressed hostility to the whites, Ibaka chose to welcome them. Because he hoped to monopolize the trade of these new 'merchants,' from whom he received many gifts, he gave them some land in an old cemetery and offered them protection.

A few months later, C. Coquilhat, who had met Ibaka for the first time in December 1882, described the Bobangi chief.

"Standing under a temporary veranda, we quietly examine the thick circle of...(Africans) which surrounds us. A person of apparent importance cuts through the crowd which stands aside for him respectfully. He quietly shakes the hand of the Captain and points to me. This is Ibaka, the king of the Bolobo. He appears to be 50 years of age; tall, thin, his muscles worn, his head bent forward, his lips closed and sagging, his eye almost covered by a drooping eye-lid, sunken cheeks;...A huge basket in the shape of an Armenian bonnet, decorated with various copper figures, serves as his head-dress, symbol of royalty and pocket. A goatee ending in tresses elongates his already long face. A string of fetishes hangs crosswise on his chest. This remarkable lord, having asked the names of the newly-arrived whites, offers us his soiled hand with a smile. He sits down and asks for something to drink. He eyes us carefully, asks interested questions about our voyage and especially about the merchandise the boat carries."

In the eyes of his Bobangi adversaries, Ibaka's friendship with the whites made him potentially more powerful. Therefore, these rival chiefs sought ways to antagonize the whites and their African employees. The first signs of overt hostility appeared after the departure of Lt. Orban, the first head of the station who had maintained excellent relations with the Bobangi.

At the beginning of 1883, Gulula, chief of the village next to the newly founded International Association of the Congo (A.I.C.) station, killed two Africans from the garrison. He accused these 'bachelors' of having relations with his wife who sold them provisions. Men from the A.I.C. station did not retaliate at that time because they were too few to be sure of victory.

Again expressing their discontent, the lesser Bobangai chiefs attacked the A.I.C. steamers coming to Bolobo in August 1883. The garrison at Bolobo had just experienced a fire destroying 150 loads of merchandise which had been deposited at Bolobo awaiting shipment to the future stations of Bangala and Stanley Falls (now Kisangani). After the fire, the men stationed at Bolobo were without shelter or provisions. Stanley then came to their rescue. Fighting then broke out on August 22, and peace was not signed until September. Ibaka played a crucial role in the signing of the peace. Arguing that Stanley might relocate the Bolobo

station and, thus, deprive the Bobangi of the A.I.C. trade, Ibaka convinced the other chiefs to accept the treaty which gave Stanley an indemnity.

In 1884, Ibaka extended the scope of his relationships by opening negotiations with Protestant missionaries. After talking with Ibaka, R. George Grenfell of the Baptist Missionary Society (B.M.S.), established a mission at Bolobo in 1889. Grenfell himself was based at Bolobo until 1906. In the years following 1889, B.M.S. workers at Bolobo helped put the Bobangi language into writing and provided excellent schools for the area.

Although the state station at Bolobo was temporarily abandoned, it was reoccupied in 1896. At that time Bobangi relations with the whites entered a new era. These relations, however, only temporarily added to the prestige of the old chief Ibaka, whose importance was diminished by each new contact the whites made with neighboring chiefs. By the end of his life he exercised no real control over his own people, and the Europeans had edged him out of the commerce which had been the mainstay of his power. Nevertheless, the whites remained grateful to him, continued to recognize him with gifts, and accorded him the place of honor at public gatherings. The Bobangi too respected this old man who had cultivated alliances with the whites. When Ibaka died in April 1889, the Bobangi sacrificed seven or eight slaves to accompany him to the other world.

Ibaka was one of the African chiefs who accepted the arrival of the Europeans and tried to use them to augment their own political prestige and wealth. Ibaka also belonged to that group of adroit and determined men from the lowest class who used the influence gained in commerce to rise to the heights of their society.

MUMBANZA mwa BAWELE
na NYABAKOMBI ENSOBATO

BIBLIOGRAPHY: H. Bentley, *Pioneering on the Congo,* Vol. 2, London, 1900; C. Coquilhat, *Sur le Haut-Congo* ("On the Upper Congo"), Brussels, 1888; J. de Witte, *Monseigneur Augouard,* Paris, 1924; H.H. Johnson, *George Grenfell and the Congo,* London, 1908; C. Liebrechts, *Souvenirs d'Afrique-Congo, Léopoldville, Bolobo, Equateur: 1883-89,* ("Memoires of Africa—the Congo, Léopoldville, Bolobo, Equateur: 1883-89"), Brussels, 1909; H.M. Stanley, *The Congo and the Founding of the Free State,* 2 vols., London, 1884.

IKENGE

Ikenge (circa 1850-December 20, 1883) was prominent in the early history of Mbandaka, present capital of Equateur region in Zaire. Like many other chiefs of the region, Ikenge welcomed the first whites to his village, Wangata, hoping to gain political and economic benefits from their presence. But when he realized the Europeans would not bend to his direction, he tried, without success, to force them out of his territory.

Ikenge was chief of Wangata, a village inhabited by the Kundu people, who live in the area southeast of what is now Mbandaka, on the Equator. Wangata was one of about 20 densely populated Kundu towns located on the Zaire River southward from where it is joined by the Ruki River. While these villages vied among themselves for political and commercial advantages, the largest Kundu trade centers were at Mkoli and Bolukwansamba, where Bobangi merchants from Irebu and Lolanga had settled. In addition to the competition between Kundu villages near the river, there was rivalry between the villages of the hinterland and the ones on the river bank. As a result of this, Kundu people from Wangata, whose village originally had been located away from the river, moved closer to the water in order to circumvent other Kundu middlemen.

Ikenge, the chief of the Wangata-Libongas, or riverbank-Wangatas, was described as a small, heavily built man with a short neck and extremely broad shoulders. Having succeeded the former chief Soka Toungi, he cultivated ambitions of gaining great influence throughout the entire Kundu community. To achieve his goals, he relied on magical powers he had learned from his aunt Kungulu, a soothsayer and a healer. Ikenge's best opportunity for advancement came in June 1883 when Henry M. Stanley and other agents of Leopold II's International Association of the Congo (A.I.C.) arrived in the area. Although Stanley began constructing a station near the Ikelemba River on the Equator, Ikenge succeeded in persuading the explorer and his men to relocate to Ikenge's own village. There, he signed a friendship pact, first with Stanley and then with Van Gèle, giving them 200 meters of land along the Zaire River in the southernmost part of his village.

Once the whites had settled, Ikenge tried to reap economic profits from their presence. Besides the rent in the form of gifts he received from the station, he levied taxes on traders from other groups who came to deal with the whites. He was, however, unsuccessful in obtaining help from the station to subject his neighbors and enemies. Since they had not come to serve the interests of one local chief, the whites became alarmed. In a letter Coquilhat wrote:

It did not take the Commander of the Equator Station long to realize that he could not depend in any way on Ikenge. An unimportant person, this chief aspires to great power and wealth; and he thinks the White men have come into the country to help him achieve his aim. We would have readily supported him, if he had peaceful views...and desired an alliance. But while pretending in his speeches that he is a great friend, he causes us a lot of trouble. Not only does he claim the right to tax his neighbors who sell us provisions, he constantly challenges the clauses of our agreement with him...Not satisfied with that, he tried to involve us in a series of unjust quarrels with the most peaceful villages. Fortunately, until now, the other chiefs have been unwilling to join in his activities.

In reaction to Ikenge's provocations, the whites tried to neutralize him by signing treaties with his neighbors: Minkoto, chief of Mbandaka; Mokabo, chief of inland Wangata, and Molila, chief of Mokoli. Molila, in fact, promised them land for settlement should they choose to leave Wangata. At Wangata itself, the whites tried to weaken Ikenge by encouraging competition from two other young men: Isambi and Losala-Djouma. Ikenge, however, refused to give in and defended his commercial rights by levying taxes on all transactions at the station.

Finally, after the Europeans refused to pay any more rent for the station, a struggle erupted which involved Ikenge, the other local Africans, and the A.I.C. station. On December 11, 1883, Ikenge ordered an economic blockade of the station. Forced into action, on December 20 Van Gèle and Coquilhat attacked Wangata village. In the ensuing battle Ikenge, along with five of his men, was killed. He did not die, however, before killing a Zanzibar soldier with his spear. Even though Ikenge had fallen, Wangata's allies kept up the attack and destroyed part of the station before finally retreating.

After Ikenge's death, Chief Molila of Mokoli village became the primary link between the Africans and the Europeans. To encourage Africans to deal with the Europeans, he emphasized the economic advantages they now enjoyed since Ikenge's death had eliminated the annoying taxes. After some time, the other villages followed Molila's example and trade at the station returned to normal. To achieve a lasting peace, however, the whites had to compensate Chief Mokabo, a close relative of Ikenge.

From this time on, the Equator Station became a pole of economic and political activity. In 1886, the newly created Congo Free State transferred the Equator Station at Wangata to the Société Anonyme Belge pour la Commerce du Haut-Congo (S.A.B.; the Belgian trading Company of the Upper Congo). In 1891 the center was moved to Mbandaka village, at the confluence of the Ruki and Zaire rivers, where it was given the name Coquilhatville. More recently, in 1966, Coquilhatville, by then a large city, was renamed Mbandaka. In spite of the many changes, Wangata has been part of this town for a long time and is now the name of one of the city's main areas.

Although personally unsuccessful in his dealings

with the agents of European imperialism, Ikenge was influential in laying the groundwork for the future city of Mbandaka.

MUMBANZA mwa BAWELE
na NYABAKOMBI ENSOBATO

BIBLIOGRAPHY: E. Boelart, "Charles Lemaire, premier Commissaire du District de l'Equateur" ("Charles Lemaire, first Commissioner for the Equateur District"), *Bulletin I.R.C.B.,* XXIV, 1953, pp. 506-35; C. Coquilhat, *Sur le Haut Congo* ("On the Upper Congo"), Brussels, 1888; H.M. Stanley, *The Congo and the Founding of the Free State,* Vol. 2, London, 1885. See also Mobembo Ongutu, "Inventaire des papiers Boelart" ("Inventory of the Boelart Papers"), unpublished thesis, Université Nationale du Zaire, Lubumbashi campus, 1974.

ILUNGA MBILI. See MBIDI

KILUWE

IYONKUM MARCEL

Iyonkum Marcel, or Nesfar, (circa 1924-February, 1964), the deputy mayor of Mangai on the Kasai River, singlehandedly fought the rebel forces of Pierre Mulele (*q.v.*), who attacked his town. By his courage, Iyonkum gave strength to others who then were able to organize a resistance against the rebels.

Iyonkum was born in the small village of Olomo-Pese, located in the strip of forest bordering the Kasai River, about 140 km (85 mi) northeast of Kikwit. Because he was a triplet, his family, which belonged to the Nguii ethnic group, held a feast in celebration when he was born. At that time the baby boy received the name Iyonkum meaning "second in command." Later, at the nearby Catholic mission Mateko, 50 km (30 mi) west of Mangai, where he studied and was baptized, he took the name Marcel. During his stay at Mateko, he also acquired the nickname Nesfar which he kept all his life.

After his schooling, Iyonkum went north to Mokala, a Catholic mission on the Kasai River, where he taught in the primary school. Ambitious to advance beyond the ranks of poorly paid elementary school teachers, he left his job to work as a clerk, responsible for the purchase of palm fruit for the Compagnie Africaine Cooreman ("Cooreman African Company"). He was later employed as foreman of a road-crew in charge of maintaining the road between Mangai and Oveke. He then returned to commerce, this time as a clerk at Port Francqui (now Ilebo).

Iyonkum began his political career in the late 1950s, when the Belgian Congo was moving rapidly towards independence. In the ethnically fragmented Kwilu district of Léopoldville province where Iyonkum lived, the Parti Solidaire Africain (P.S.A., the Party of African Solidarity), organized by Cleophas Kamitatu, Antoine Gizenga, and Pierre Mulele, won the overwhelming support of the people. This support was demonstrated in the December 1959 local elections, which the P.S.A. boycotted, and in the May 1960 national elections, which the P.S.A. carried in the Kwilu. By working diligently for the P.S.A. in his local Mangai area Iyonkum won the attention of the party officials and eventually was given a position of responsibility in the Mangai bureaucracy as deputy mayor.

In the meantime, as troubles spread throughout the newly independent Congo, the P.S.A. split between the more moderate wing loyal to Kamitatu, and the radical branch supporting Gizenga and Mulele. While the moderates concerned themselves with provincial and local politics, the radicals gave more attention to national affairs. Complicated by ethnic divisions, this party split left local Kwilu partisans of Gizenga and Mulele with a deep sense of disenchantment. Then, in 1963, after a visit to China the previous year, Mulele returned to his native Kwilu to organize a popular uprising against the government now controlled by factions unsympathetic to the P.S.A. Conscious that his military initiative could not succeed unless he controlled the Kasai River, which potentially linked the Kwilu area with the Congo (Brazzaville), which was friendly to the government, Mulele sought to capture the river ports of Mangai and Dibaya-Lubwe (a short distance upstream from Mangai).

Successful in taking over several towns near Mangai, the militants' victories were made easier by an almost total lack of resistance. The local people had become convinced the Mulele partisans were invulnerable to bullets and that their leader had the magical ability to be in several places at the same time. Thus, when Mangai was invaded in February 1964, the attack provoked a general rout as the urban population sought refuge in the woods. Some even crossed the Kasai River to find security in the Region of Lake Leopold II (now Lake Mai Ndombe).

Although the mayor of Mangai judged it expedient to leave town, the deputy mayor, Iyonkum Marcel, determined to stay. Wielding a rifle, he dared to fire on the Mulelist partisans. It is not clear if he actually expected to frighten the rebels, or if he hoped, by his example, to instill courage in those who were fleeing the invulnerable attackers. In any case, Iyonkum probably succeeded in wounding, or even killing, a Mulele partisan. As a result the population realized the attackers were not superhuman and the people began to organize resistance on a regional level.

Iyonkum's solitary resistance cost him dearly.

Taken within the hour by the rebels, he was buried alive next to the Mangai post office. In memory of Iyokum's courage, the street beside the place where he died is named after him. Although "second in command," Iyonkum was first in bravery.

NDAYWEL è NZIEM

BIBLIOGRAPHY: B. Verhaegen, *Rébellions au Congo* ("Rebellions in the Congo"), Vol. 1, Brussels, 1966; H.F. Weiss, *Political Protest in the Congo: The Parti Solidaire Africain During the Independence Struggle,* Princeton, 1967.

KABEY a MWANB

Kabey a Mwanb (circa 1850-circa 1895) was chief of the Kaninchin, a small Lunda-related people living about 185 km (115 mi) south of Mbuji Mayi. Oral tradition depicts Kabey a Mwanb as a dynamic chief who organized an effective defense against the Cokwe (Chokwe) slave raiders from what is now northern Angola who were operating in the area during the late 1880s.

Although few in numbers when they still lived in their original northern Angola homeland, the Cokwe experienced a remarkable demographical and geographical expansion after 1850 as peripatetic bands of Cokwe hunters, traders, and warriors advanced northwards in search of beeswax, ivory, and slaves. By the 1860s, Cokwe warriors had become deeply involved in Lunda politics as mercenary allies of various contenders for the office of Mwant Yav (paramount chief). By the 1870s and 1880s, vast numbers of Cokwe people had settled among the Lunda living in southern Zaire. From that time until the early 1900s, Cokwe warriors in search of slaves attacked and terrorized Lunda, Kete, Sala Mpasu, Kanyok, Kalundwe, and Kaninchin villages.

When Kabey a Mwanb came to power in about 1875, he set about to repair and strengthen Kaninchin defenses. As many other people in southern Zaire and northern Angola, had also done, the Kaninchin had for long built elaborate fortifications around their villages. These defenses consisted of a palisade surrounded by a deep dry moat. Forming huge ovals often five or more kilometers in length, such structures afforded an effective protection against intruders. Kabey specially reinforced his capital, a group of eight neighboring villages, by constructing a system of three circular entrenchments enclosing a network of underground passages. Other Kaninchin leaders, including Mwin Muandj (chief of Muandj), strengthened the enormous entrenchments encircling their villages. The Kaninchin also purchased some guns from Lwena and Ovimbundu traders based in Angola. It was at this

time that Cokwe raids increased in number and intensity.

According to local oral recollections, the most serious Cokwe attack on Kabey a Mwanb's Kaninchin came during the reign of the Lunda chief Mwant Yav Mbumb Muteb a Kat who held office from 1874 to 1883. Mbumb, who had used Cokwe mercenaries to gain the Lunda throne, rewarded his Cokwe allies by leading them north against his neighbors. Although the Cokwe destroyed many villages and took numerous slaves, they were unable to defeat the well-prepared Kaninchin. Another time, a party of Cokwe raiders were deceived with a clever ruse devised by the people of Mbangom, a Kaninchin village. Feigning friendship with the Cokwe, the people of Mbangom offered to guide them to Kabey a Mwanb's capital. Instead they led them into an ambush at the fortifications surrounding the royal village. Kaninchin tradition claims several hundred Cokwe were killed and that many others were taken captive for sale to Ovimbundu slave buyers.

Kabey a Mwanb's ability to withstand Cokwe warriors is regarded by the Kaninchin people as the start of a victorious liberation campaign. They assert that his example served as an inspiration for other people to resist the Cokwe. The Lunda, on the other hand, credit Mwant Yav Mushid a Nambing (*q.v.*), who took office in 1887, and his brother Kawel as the individuals most responsible for neutralizing the aggressive Cokwe. In 1898, after a decade of exile in the countryside while the enemy occupied their capital, the two brothers attacked and soundly defeated Mawoka, the most renowned Cokwe war leader.

Although Kabey a Mwanb, who died in about 1895, is not as well-known as the two Lunda resisters, he was able to provide security and hope for his people during an era of widespread turbulence.

TSHIBANGU KABET MUSAS and JOHN C. YODER

BIBLIOGRAPHY: E. Bustin, *Lunda Under Belgian Rule: The Politics of Ethnicity,* Cambridge, Massachusetts, 1975; J.C. Miller, *Cokwe Expansion: 1850-1900,* Madison, 1969; *Ngand Yetu* ("Our Land"), Methodist Church, Elisabethville, 1963; J. Vansina, *Kingdoms of the Savanna,* Madison, 1966. *See also* Musas Samal, "Histoire des Kaninchin. Quelques perspectives sur l'histoire ancienne des Etats Lunda" ("History of Kaninchin. Some Perspectives on the Ancient History of the Lunda States"), unpublished thesis, Université Nationale de Zaire, Lubumbashi campus 1974; Yesela Looyo, untitled report on the history and customs of the Bena Tubeya, archives of Mwena Ditu, 1972; J.C. Yoder, "A People on the Edge of Empires: A History of the Kanyok of Central Zaire," unpublished Ph.D. dissertation, Northwestern University, 1977.

KAJIGA BALIHUTA

Monseigneur Kajiga Balihuta (1922-January 3, 1976), was an outstanding churchman, author, and philosopher.

Born in Rugu he later entered the Catholic secondary school at Mugeri-Katana, 30 km (18 mi) north of Goma, to prepare for a teaching career. Committed to working within the Catholic Church, he attended the seminaries of Nyakibanda and Burasira in Rwanda. After graduation from seminary, Kajiga assumed increasingly broad responsibilities. On November 11, 1953, he was ordained a priest at Mungombe-Kamituga and about the same time he was appointed professor of languages and history at the Mugeri-Katana Catholic school. In 1958, he began work as the primary school director and pastor in the parish of Bobandana. He continued at Bobandana until his nomination and appointment as inspector of Catholic education in the diocese of Goma (North Kivu) on October 1, 1969. In 1974, when the religious educational systems were incorporated into the Zairian government, Kajiga took over administration of the Centre Pédagogique Ntu (Ntu Pedagogical Center), which he had founded in 1967.

Besides serving as a priest and administrator, Monseigneur Kajiga made significant contributions as an author and scholar. The titles of his many publications indicate the wide scope of his interests. (*See* bibliography below). In particular, the *Dictionnaire Swahili-Français, Français-Swahili* (''Swahili-French, French-Swahili Dictionary,'' 1975) is living testimony to Monseigneur Kajiga's intellectual capacities. He was elected a member of the Société des Linguistes du Zaire (''Society of Zaire Linguists''), and counselor to the Société des Historiens Zairois (''Society of Zaire Historians'').

Monseigneur Kajiga Bahihuta's major intellectual contributions were in the realm of African philosophy. Kajiga hoped to study and bring to light the cultural values of the Ntu (African genius), to rehabilitate the Muntu (African man), and give him his rightful role in the broader conception and structure of humanity. The ultimate goal of Kajiga's philosophy was to 'ntu-ize' the African uprooted by many years of colonization and persecution. By Untu, Monseigneur Kajiga meant that which is basic to the Muntu and to Bantu Africa (Black Africa). Thus, Untu philosophy is a defense of the cultural values and linguistic unity of sub-Saharan Africa. Untu is also the life and torch in African man's existence. And Untu is the foundation and basis of a new African humanism. To realize his aims, Kajiga wished to take complete inventory of the different manifestations of the Ntu spirit as expressed in literature, art, philosophy, religion, and social relationships. Convinced of the importance of such a vast and ambitious project, he made a tour of Africa to explain the problem to his African brothers. He held a series of conferences in Cameroun, Nigeria, Gabon, Rwanda, Burundi, Uganda, Kenya, and Tanzania to present his thoughts on the Untu and on Africa's contribution to universal civilization.

Although Kajiga was a competent theoretician, he also was deeply interested in translating his ideas into practical reality. To formulate and disseminate Ntu philosophy, he founded the Centre Pédagogique Ntu, an organization of applied research and a workshop for the production of scholastic materials popularizing Ntu. At this center, he focused his activities on the definition and study of three integrally related subjects: a common national language for Zaire, the reform of a colonial-oriented educational system, and the development of a Zairian cultural philosophy within the broader Bantu (African) experience.

Emphasizing that language is the expression of the most profound beliefs of a people, the basis of thought, and the vehicle of communication, Monseigneur Kajiga supported adopting a national language. He argued that a country without a national language is, in reality, mute. He proposed that Lingala become the future national language of Zaire, because it had a national constituency. It was used in the army, by the police, on the radio, in music, in political dealings, and in tourist exchanges. Taking into account the range of expression and potential for expansion, however, Kajiga stressed that Swahili would play a major role in scientific treatises, and the culture and commerce of the African peoples. Swahili, he believed, would become a future language of the Organization of African Unity (O.A.U.).

As a member of the Commission for Educational Reform in Zaire, Monseigneur Kajiga promoted the use of vernacular languages in the primary and secondary schools. In Kajiga's opinion, such reform was necessary because Zairian students were faced with a double learning task: simultaneously, they had to master the material content of their courses and they had to learn in French, the borrowed language of instruction. This problem resulted in the repetition of grades and a massive attrition rate. Monseigneur Kajiga was conscious of the complexities and difficulties of modifying an educational system built on the language and methods of Zaire's former colonizers, but he was convinced that African children could learn properly only when taught in their own languages.

Kajiga frequently reflected on the basic goals of education. He believed that the aim of all education was to develop capable men, conscious of their duty. He believed that the harmonious development of Zaire would be found in good schools. He knew the competency of teachers was not measured by the number of their diplomas, but by their ability, love for their work, and unselfish dedication for their tasks. It was this ideal which he always promoted, hoping to aid the youth of Zaire to rise, to discover themselves, to know, and to discipline themselves in order to build a nation founded on an authentic Zairian culture.

When Monseigneur Kajiga Balihuta died on the evening of January 3, 1976, after a long and painful illness, Zaire lost not only a philosopher, but also a linguist, an educator, a psychologist and a humanist.

RUDURI KWEZI and
RURIHO MUNANIRA

BIBLIOGRAPHY: Kajiga Balihuta, *Conscience Professionelle* ("Professional Consciousness"), 1963, Léopoldville, *Pour une langue nationale congolaise* ("Toward a National Congolese Language"), Kinshasa, 1967, *Initiation à la Culture Ntu: Grammaire Swahili* ("Initiation to Ntu Culture: Swahili Grammar"), Goma, 1967, *Untu et son apport à l'Universel* ("Untu and its Contribution to the Universal"), Goma, 1968, *Langue d'enseignement et culture nationale* ("The Language of Instruction and National Culture"), Goma, 1971, *Lugha ya Kiswahili* ("The Swahili Language"), Goma, 1972, "Le Centre Pedagogique Ntu" ("The Ntu Pedagogic Center"), *Zaire-Afrique,* No. 72, February, 1973, *Dictionnaire Swahili-Français, Français-Swahili* ("Swahili-French, French-Swahili Dictionary"), Goma, 1975; Kudiri Kwezu, "Untu et son apport à l'Universel" ("Untu and its Contribution to the Universal"), *Le Forum Universitaire,* I, No. 3, March-April, 1973.

KALALA ILUNGA

More a symbol than an actual historical personage, the *mulopwe* (Luba king) Kalala Ilunga (who may have flourished circa 1600) is regarded as the father of the Luba ruling dynasty and as the founder of the Luba empire in northern Shaba region. By reciting his story, the Luba reaffirm the validity of their political system. They consider their form of government as superior to other structures—represented in the Kalala Ilunga tale by his antagonist and foil Nkongolo (*q.v.*). Although it is difficult to date the origins of Kalala Ilunga's story, it seems likely that his life has been described since the 1600s.

According to Luba oral recollections, Nkongolo ruled the Luba from his capital near Lake Boya, 260 km (160 mi) southeast of the modern Mbuji Mayi. One day, Nkongolo entertained Mbidi Kiluwe (*q.v.*), a refined visitor, and a hunter from somewhere in the east. Apparently, Mbidi Kiluwe came from a chiefdom endowed with superior protocol and institutions. In contrast to the ill-mannered and unsophisticated Nkongolo, Mbidi Kiluwe had filed teeth, did not laugh with his mouth wide open, nor eat in public. Handsome and cultivated, he captured the attention of Nkongolo's two half-sisters, Bulanda and Mabela, who both fell in love with this paragon of civilized control, and became his wives.

But an antagonism developed between Nkongolo and Mbidi Kiluwe, the two men serving as symbols for two opposing codes of behavior. Luba legend states that Nkongolo insulted Mbidi Kiluwe who then left. Nevertheless, the innovations he introduced, epitomized by new culinary mores, did not disappear. After Mbidi Kiluwe departed, his wife Bulanda bore a son named Ilunga Mbidi. Because Ilunga Mbidi proved to be very gifted, especially in the military arts, Nkongolo gave him the title of Kalala, general of the royal armies. Luba traditions credit Ilunga Mbidi, known thereafter as Kalala Ilunga with many successful military campaigns which enlarged the boundaries of Nkongolo's empire.

Because of Kalala Ilunga's brilliant military exploits, Nkongolo began to fear his nephew would seek to overthrow him. Although, all Nkongolo's attempts to eliminate the young general were thwarted by Kalala Ilunga's cunning, Kalala Ilunga finally decided to leave his uncle's court. He crossed the Lualaba River, taking refuge in his father's country in the east. After gathering an army, he returned to crush Nkongolo. This triumph may symbolize the victory of a new aristocratic ritual code over the old customs, represented by the vulgar and incestuous Nkongolo, who ate in public and married his own sisters. Thus, Kalala Ilunga's conquest may represent the rise of a new political élite whose members considered themselves superior to other Luba people.

Kalala Ilunga's power (*bulopwe*) and polity are said to have been more impressive than Nkongolo's. The Luba believe Kalala Ilunga enlarged the Luba empire and perfected its internal organization. Whatever the various meanings of Kalala Ilunga's story may be, the tale was, and still is, a kind of political constitution used by the Luba to support their incumbent dynasty, validate their system of government, and justify the extent of their imperial domain.

NDAYWEL è NZIEM

BIBLIOGRAPHY: L. de Heusch, *Le roi ivre ou l'origine de l'Etat* ("The Drunken King or the Origin of the State"), Paris, 1972; S.A. Lucas, "L'Etat traditionnel Luba" ("The Traditional Luba State"), *Problèmes sociaux congolais,* 74, 1966, pp. 88-97; J. Vansina, *Kingdoms of the Savanna,* Madison, 1966; E. Verhulpen, *Baluba et Balubaisé* ("The Baluba and the Balubaized"), Anvers, 1936; A. Van Zandijcke, *Pages d'histoire du Kasai* ("Pages from Kasai History"), Namur, 1953.

KALALA KAFUMBE

Kalala Kafumbe (18?-1895), a leader of the Mulenge people of eastern Kasai, united the decentralized Mulenge clans into a single political organization. Like many other African individuals who rose to prominence in the late 19th century, Kalala Kafumbe owed his power to the guns he was able to purchase, directly or indirectly, from Angolan slave dealers. Thus, Kalala Kafumbe's ascendency set aside traditional Mulenge concepts of political authority.

The Mulenge people are one of the numerous Luba peoples from Shaba who migrated west across the Lubilash River into Kasai. Organized into a multitude of autonomous clans, the Mulenge settled between the Lubi and Mujila rivers, about 60 km (35 mi) southwest of modern Mbuji-Mayi. Except in periods of war, when the Mulenge joined together under the guidance of a military general, the various clans lived relatively independent of each other.

Before the time of Kalala Kafumbe, the Mulenge chiefs were elected by local clan leaders and sanctioned by neighboring rulers. Candidates for office distributed gifts to an incumbent chief and his friends until the chief agreed to turn over his office to the petitioner. Once this agreement was reached, the candidates traveled to the neighboring Kanyok chief who then legitimized the candidate by conferring upon him chiefly power, symbolized by a red parrot feather which the newly invested chief wore on his head. Theoretically, this power derived from the Luba mulopwe (chief) in Shaba who possessed bulopwe (royal power), transmitted through the royal bloodline. While the Mulenge claim they once journeyed to Shaba to receive investiture, since at least the early 1800s, they have gone instead to their close southern neighbors the Kanyok. Supposedly the Kanyok ruling dynasty was founded by Chitend, a woman of Luba royal blood, who thus brought the bulopwe power to Kasai.

Kalala Kafumbe gained control of the Mulenge by circumventing the traditional channels of political advancement. The son of chief Kafumbe Bibau and his second wife, Kalala Kafumbe was sold as a slave to the Kanyinda clan of the Mpuka people. The Mpuka had been introduced to a new religious cult, the lubuku, by the Luba people living immediately to the west in the Lulua River region near modern Kananga. Adherents of lubuku smoked hemp and believed the many small Luba Kasai groups would someday be united under their departed ancestors. The Luba Kasai chiefs Musamba Mputu and Mukenge Kalamba (q.v.) had invented and promoted the lubuku cult in the 1860s. These hemp smokers were also attracted by guns, which until that time had been unknown in the region. As early as 1865, Mukenge Kalamba had established contact with the Cokwe (Chokwe) of what is now Zaire, who supplied him with rifles. The power to unite people into the lubuku groups thus came to be based on force and conquest.

Living with the Mpuka, Kalala Kafumbe became adept in the new military arts. Eventually, these skills earned him his liberty. In about 1875, at the head of a group of soldiers, Kalala returned in triumph to his homeland where his half-brother, Katende Kafumbe, had succeeded their father, Kafumbe, as chief.

Powerful and ambitious in his new position, Kalala Kafumbe demanded that his brother share power with him. Once his brother agreed, Kalala Kafumbe set about to create an army, composed of Mulenge men from every clan. With this army, he conquered the nearby Disho clans and forced the "people of the river" clans among the Mpuka to pay him tribute. Conquered rulers who refused to accept Kalala Kafumbe's demands were brought to his village, Cilundu, and subjected to torture.

To guarantee a constant supply of the guns and ammunition, upon which his power rested, Kalala Kafumbe allied himself with Kasongo Lwaba, also called Fuamba, a Luba Kasai slave trader who lived about 65 km (40 mi) southeast of modern Kananga. Following the example of Mukenge Kalamba, in 1875 Kalala Kafumbe went to the Malange in Angola, hoping to establish direct contact with the Cokwe traders. Thus, the chief of the Mulenge was one of the first to open the Portuguese-African trade to the Luba-Lubilash. From then on, the Cokwe traded directly with the Mulenge, and Kalala Kafumbe's prestige grew.

Kalala Kafumbe also sought to strengthen his position by establishing links with the Europeans who were beginning to arrive in Kasai. In October 1881, when the explorers Paul Pogge and Herman von Wissmann arrived for the first time at Malandje near present day Kananga, Kalala Kafumbe was among the first chiefs to welcome them. He clearly wanted them to recognize him as an important leader. He also greeted the Scheut mission leader, Father Cambier, who arrived on November 14, 1891 to found the parish of Mikalayi, near Malandje. To gain an advantage over his rival Fuamba, in April 1892 Kalala asked the missionaries to found a mission at his village, Cilundu. Accepting the request Father Cambier arrived among the Mulenge on June 2, 1892 to prepare for the establishment of the new mission of Merode (the present parish of Cilundu).

Ultimately, however, Kalala Kafumbe recognized his security depended upon his military organization and not merely his alliances. Because of his many warriors, Kalala was able to repulse an attack from Cokwe raiders and from Panya Mutumbo's Bayembi, who had already ravaged the eastern area of the Luba in the Lubilash River area. After Panya Mutumbo's son was killed by the Mulenge at Cilundu, the discouraged Bayembi returned to their own lands.

By acquiring modern military technology, by recruiting numerous soldiers, and by cultivating powerful allies, Kalala Kafumbe was able to centralize Mulenge political structures and to subject neighboring peoples. The unity he created by force of arms, however, was not enduring. When Kalala Kafumbe died in 1895, he was followed by his son Kalala Kamwanga, who in turn was succeeded by his son Dumba wa Kalala in 1913. After Dumba wa Kalala was deposed by the colonial administration in 1937, Mulenge political organization became increasingly decentralized. Kalala Kafumbe's state, like those polities built by other warrior rulers, was ephemeral. Based on the force of arms and not on the authority of tradition, his work had only a temporary impact.

MALENGU MUBAYA

BIBLIOGRAPHY: L. Mpoyi, *Histoire wa Baluba* ("History of the Baluba"), Mbuji-Mayi, 1966; M. Scheitler, *Histoire de l'église catholique au Kasai* ("History of the Catholic Church in Kasai"), Luluabourg, 1971; J. Vansina, *Kingdoms of the Savanna*, Madison, 1966; A. Van Zandijcke, *Pages d'histoire du Kasai* ("Pages from Kasai History"), Naumur, 1953. See also Malengu Mubaya, "Histoire des Bena Mulenge. Contribution á l'étude des chefferies chez les Baluba" ("History of the Bena Mulenge. Contribution to the Study of Chiefdoms Among the Baluba"), unpublished thesis, Université Nationale de Zaire, Lubumbashi, 1975; J. Oldenhove, "Chefferie des Bena Mulenge" ("The Bena Mulenge Chiefdom"), P.V. 177, "Bakwa Mpata," August 8, 1953, Archives des Affaires Politiques, Mbugi-Mayi.

KALAMBA. See MUKENGE a TUNSELE

KALAU, L.

Louis Kalau (circa 1880-July 31, 1945) served as the officially recognized chief of the Niungu people, a Pende ethnic group of about 5,000 individuals, located east of the Kwilu River opposite the modern town of Gungu, situated about 70 km (40 mi) southeast of Kikwit. Ruling during the uneasy years following the great Pende revolt of 1931, he helped Belgian colonial authorities restore control over the region.

Originally from the upper Kwango River regions of northern Angola, the Niungu people migrated to Zaire under their great chief Kinzungu, after the Imbangala had displaced them from the Kwango area in the 1600s. At first, the Niungu established themselves on the banks of the Lubue River in the Mbanda a Nenga lands, about 70 km (45 mi) east of Kikwit. There however, they fought with the dominant Mbuun people and were again forced to move. During the second part of the 1800s, many Niungu families moved south to live on the right bank of the Kwilu, while other groups moved to Muhanji in the present Idiofa zone. Around 1903-04, many Niungu families asked the great Lunda Pende chief of the Kangu for asylum. He granted them permission to live on his lands west of the Kwilu. Thereafter, these settlers were required to pay the Kangu chief the customary tribute, through the intermediary of a Lunda Pende chief responsible for governing them.

In the early 1900s when the first Belgians, commercial agents of the Compagnie du Kasai ("Kasai Company") arrived, Khenda was the Mwene Mbangu (chief of the Niungu). Giboba Gisenzele succeeded him and was officially invested by colonial authorities on August 20, 1921. It is not known exactly how long Giboba Gisenzele ruled, for at the time of the Pende Revolt in 1931 another man, Galenga Mushigo, was exercising the official duties of chief over the Niungu people. Galenga Mushigo was exiled to the west in 1932, following disclosure of the active part he had taken in the 1931 Pende revolt.

After the Pende revolt, Belgian authorities tried to replace rebel Pende chiefs with loyal rulers. As a literate professing Christian, Louis Kalau was selected to take the office of Mwene Mbangu, or chief of the Niungu. Kalau was elected in 1932. On October 8, 1934, the assistant district commissioner Vandevenne invested him in office and gave him a chief's medallion. Kalau was reinvested in the same position on November 25, 1936.

When the former chief Mushigo returned home after his sentence of exile was revoked on November 23, 1932, he tried to regain his lost power. But the colonial authorities intervened to neutralize Mushigo's claims and to permit Louis Kalau to continue performing his duties as chief.

Louis Kalau was an energetic chief who did not tolerate questions concerning his orders. He also required that his people carefully execute all the work required by the colonial authorities. As a result he was highly esteemed by the colonial government. On July 28, 1935, the territorial administrator Alfred Aerts addressed the following report on Kalau to the district commissioner of Kwango:

> I would like to bring Chief Kalau to your special attention; he is one of the best assets of the Territory: intelligent, literate, very devoted, monogamous; his people are disciplined, his villages very clean, his own in particular is a model.

At the end of July 1935, Kalau suffered a great misfortune when his chiefly coffer, containing the returns of the 1935 tax levies and the chiefdom's own cash reserves, was burned. The colonial authorities, however, were understanding in this affair, for Kalau's unswerving loyalty in the past had won their respect and trust.

Lewis Kalau was an indefatigable traveler who visited every area of his own chiefdom as well as parts of neighboring territories. In his work, he acquired a reputation for being a severe yet impartial judge. Thus, he was greatly feared and respected by his subordinates.

During 1944 and at the beginning of 1945 he actively aided the state in fighting the followers of the Lupambulu sect who were in revolt against the government. A secret society, the Lupambulu group embodied discontent from the earlier Pende revolt (see the Gandanda Gibanda article). The Lupambulu sect was also a predecessor of the later Mpeve uprising, led by Raphael Alaver (q.v.). Both the territorial authorities at Gungu and Catholic missionaries at Totshi, about 25 km (15 mi) to the north, were grateful to Kalau for his help in this matter.

SIKITELE GIZE a SUMBULA

BIBLIOGRAPHY: Archives of the Gungu zone, political dossier for the Gungu sector.

KANYIMBU NEWEJ MPEMB

Kanyimbu Newej, also called Kanyimbu Mpembe a Nkind, (circa 1700-circa 1760) was a great military leader, who extended Lunda influence east to the Lake Mweru region, 750 km (450 mi) from the Lunda capital at Musumba. Holding the title Kazembe (governor), he owed his success to the strength of his army and to the willingness of subjected chiefs to become loyal allies of the prestigious conquering Lunda.

Kanyimbu himself was the son of Cinyat Mfemb, a chief living west of the Lubudi River who had been defeated by Lunda armies just before 1700. After his defeat, Cinyat Mfemb became a faithful official in the Lunda state. Later, his son Ngand a Bilond (q.v.) was given the title Kazembe and instructed to secure the Lunda domain in the Lualaba river area north of modern Kolwezi, where the Kecila salt pans were located. Besides organizing Lunda administration in the Lubudi-Lualaba region, Ngand a Bilond pushed eastwards across the Lualaba into the Sanga, Lomotwa, and Lamba lands, located within a 200 km (120 mi) radius of modern Likasi. Unable to consolidate these lands into an effective polity, Ngand a Bilond died not long after his army had killed the Lomotwa chief Mufunga (the Lomotwa live about 200 km north of Likasi).

When Ngand a Bilond died, in about 1750, his brother Kanyimbu Newej and his general Mushima competed to succeed him as Kazembe. The two rival candidates went to Musumba where Mwant Yav Mukaz Waranankong (who ruled circa 1720-40) appointed Kanyimbu as the Kazembe and gave him white clay and a muyombu (ficus plant) as symbols of his new office. The Kazembe was to rub himself with the clay when appearing before the Mwant Yav, while the ficus was to grow in the capital of the lands which he would conquer east of the region already subjected by Ngand a Bilond. Contrary to what some scholars have claimed, the Mwant Yav did not make Kanyimbu his equal for the very title Kazembe implies subordination. To avoid future disputes involving succession to the title of Kazembe, the Mwant Yav Mukaz decreed that succession within the borders of his empire should follow a direct patrilineal pattern.

The new Kazembe went to the Lualaba River area, where he strengthened his politico-economic relations by marrying Monga, the daughter of Abwid, chief of the land where the Kecila salt pans were located. Then Kanyimbu rapidly organized his army and crossed over the Lualaba into the Sanga, Lamba, and Lemba territories, between modern Lubumbashi and Likasi. Campaigning for an entire year, he gained the submission of the Katanga, Poyo, Kyembe, Mutondo, and Kapondo groups, who incorporated Lunda practices into their political ceremonies and agreed to pay tribute to the Kazembe. During this time he learned that a Luba army, reinforced with Lunda adventurers, threatened his newly-created empire. After defeating the Luba, he received tribute from the Lomotwas of the Pweto region at the northern end of Lake Mweru and from all the minor chiefs on the west bank of the Lualaba. Thus, Kanyimbu controlled the entire region bordered by the Lubudi River in the west and by the Luapula River (currently the eastern boundary of Zaire) in the east. In the north, his land reached the Lomotwa people near Lake Mweru, while in the south it extended as far as the Lamba and Kaonde groups, living almost 160 km (100 mi) south of modern Lubumbashi.

The following year Kanyimbu continued his conquests. He crossed the Luapula above Mwabidima, about 100 km (60 mi) south of Lake Mweru. Once on the other side (in what is now Zambia) Kazembe made an alliance with some chiefs to whom he granted Lunda titles. The Aushi, Kalaba, and Myelemyele (Chawala Makumba) chiefs resisted, however, and were conquered.

Moving south to the Lake Bangweolu area, Kanyimbu subjected the Aushi, who live about 100 km

(60 mi) east of modern Lubumbashi. The Kazembe then installed his subordinate Kashib as their chief. Then Kazembe Kanyimbu marched northeast to defeat the Chishinga, who live just west of Lake Bangweolu, and the Bisa, who are located about 150 km (90 mi) east of the lake. When Mwin Mpand, who had been installed as governor over the Chishinga, was killed by Chungu chief of the nearby Makulu people, Kanyimbu retaliated by killing Chungu and subjecting his people.

He then went down the Luapula to attack the Shila who were commanded by their nkuba (supreme chief). Kazembe Kanyimbu fought Katele, the nkuba's nephew, and seized the territory when Katele took refuge in the nearby swamps.

Having conquered numerous peoples over a vast geographical area in what are now southeastern Zaire and northern Zambia, Kazembe Kanyimbu Newej attempted to consolidate his gains by setting up a permanent capital from which he could oversee his territory. He went down the Luapula River and settled near Lake Mweru at Lunde, the capital of his defeated enemy Katele. There, Kazembe Kanyimbu ruled as a representative of the Mwant Yav and as supreme governor of the region. In his new capital he solemly planted the ficus which Mwant Yav Mukaz had given him at Musumba. During his many years of campaigning, Kazembe had preserved the ficus by planting it at each of his provisional residences. The ficus symbolized not only the spiritual presence of ancestors, but also domination over the land. Thus Kanyimbu hoped to legitimize his regime, and also secure the blessing of the Lunda ancestors.

Kazembe Kanyimbu, however, faced internal opposition to his imperial projects. Many Lunda, not wanting to settle so far from their native land, attempted to desert. The Kazembe prevented their escape, however, by posting guards at the Luapula River crossings. Towards the end of his life, Kazembe Kanyimbu had to deal with ambitious sons who tried to usurp his authority. When one of his sons rebelled, the Kazembe sent another son, Mukej, to punish the offender. Instead of complying, Mukej, who was the general of Kanyimbu's western army, also revolted and set up a separate kingdom north of modern Kolwezi. Mukej, known as the Kazembe of the Lualaba, ruled over the region between the Lualaba and Lubudi rivers.

Kanyimbu Newej Mpemb, the Kazembe of the Luapula River region, died around 1760. Although his body was buried in the Majaan cemetery at his capital Lunde, his hair and nails were returned to his homeland in the Lualaba area.

TSHIBANGU KABET MUSAS

BIBLIOGRAPHY: D.R. Hadelin, "Résumé de l'histoire ancienne du Katanga" ("Summary of the Ancient History of Katanga"), *Bulletin du C.E.P.S.I.* No. 61, pp. 3-42; E. Labrecque, "Histoire des Mwanta Kazembe, Chiefs Lunda du Luapula" ("History of the Mwanta Kazembe, Lunda Chiefs of Luapula"), *Lovania,* XVI (1949), p. 9-33; F. Tanguy, *A History of Baushi,* Ndola, 1943; J. Vansina, *Kingdoms of the Savanna,* Madison, 1966.

KAPEND TSHOMB, J.

Joseph Kapend Tshomb (1889-1950), an entrepreneur, rose from poverty and servanthood to become one of the most prosperous and widely traveled Congolese of his day.

Kapend Tshomb was a member of the Lunda ethnic group living in southwest Shaba, northeast Angola, and northwest Zambia. In spite of the great prestige of the Lunda state, when Kapend was born the Lunda were dominated by Cokwe (Chokwe) traders and warriors who had entered the region after 1850. Mwant Yav (ruler) Mushid a Nambing (q.v.), his brother Kawel, and the Kaninchin chief Kabey a Mwanb (q.v.), began a counteroffensive against the Cokwe in the 1890s, but they did not win an important battle until 1898.

Kapend's father Nambing Kambol Maur, a hunter and blacksmith, was a slave of a Cokwe man. While this did not mean that he was treated cruelly, it did mean that he could not keep all of his income, that he could not marry without his master's consent, that he was not free to move or travel, and that he could be sold to coastal plantation owners should he misbehave. After Kapend's mother died in 1902, Kambol Maur repeatedly tried to escape. When he finally succeeded in getting free, he was executed by the Lunda Mwant Yav because someone accused him of being a troublemaker. His assassins mutilated his body and threw it into the Mwen River, a small stream near the Lunda capital of Musumba, 260 km (170 mi) north of Dilolo.

From about 1904 until 1907 the orphan Kapend and his brother Mawaw were clients of the Lunda dignitary Chot Kabamb. When Kabamb died in 1907, the 18-year-old Kapend entered the Force Publique (the colonial army). The Belgian administrator Buylaert, known as Longo-Longo, discharged him, however, along with many other recruits, for being too young.

Once out of the army, Kapend was the client of Mwant Yav Muteb a Kasang, who ruled from 1907 until 1920. In 1910, when the administrator at Kapanga, the state post near Musumba, was looking for a domestic servant who spoke some Lingala, the Mwant Yav Muteb recommended Kapend. Later, Kapend was sent to the Compagnie du Kasai ("Kasai Company") to learn cooking. He returned to Kapanga as the servant of the local representative of the company. Kapend traveled with his Belgian employer throughout Kasai from Lusambo to Kafukumba, 200 km (120 mi) northeast of Dilolo. In 1913, the Belgian, known as Jebula Mukut, was fired, and Kapend returned to the Lunda capital, Musumba. Because of his association with Jebula Mukut, Kapend became the first African in the region able to talk with the whites in French. This skill won him a job as the Mwant Yav's interpreter, which meant that he, along with Mbaku, the future Mwant Yav Ditend Yavu a Nawej III, (ruled 1951-63), acted as the Mwant Yav's special emissary. In 1915, he took a position as interpreter for the territorial administrator Vandewelde. When Vandewelde was transferred from Kapanga to Kabinda, 200 km (120 mi) east of what is now Mbuji-Mayi, and then to Kabongo, 250 km (150 mi) southeast of Mbuji-Mayi, Kapend accompanied him.

In March 1917, at Kabongo, Joseph Kapend, while still an interpreter, launched his career in commerce. With his savings, he bought small quantities of salt and cloth at Kabinda, or Lusambo, 125 km (75 mi) north of Mbuji-Mayi on the Sankuru River, to be resold by his brothers, Paul Mawaw and Jacques Mulaj, in the area between Kabinda and Kabongo. Against the wishes of Vandewelde, Kapend returned to the Kapanga-Musumba area, again to act as the Mwant Yav's interpreter and counsellor. On November 19, 1919, his wife Kat, the granddaughter of an earlier Mwant Yav, had a son they named Kapend Moise, later known as Moise Tshombe (q.v.). On August 31, 1920, the Mwant Yav died and was succeeded by Kaumb (ruled 1920-51), for whom Kapend continued to work.

But in November 1924, Joseph Kapend quit his job as interpreter, established himself in Sandoa, 130 km (80 mi) northeast of Dilolo, and began to devote himself entirely to business. By that time, he had three children, Moise Kapend, Jacques Mulaj and David Yav. Kapend also built himself a European-style house at Sandoa. Kapend traveled continuously, expanding his business as a merchant and carrier. It was not unusual for him to bicycle or walk as much as 1,000 km (600 mi) from Sandoa north to Lusambo, southeast to Elisabethville (now Lubumbashi), or east to Bukama, 135 km (105 mi) north of Kolwezi. When the State forbade portage in 1928, Joseph Kapend bought pushcarts which he and his workers used to transport merchandise. By 1930, he had saved enough money to buy the car of an American doctor, Arthur L. Piper. The Depression did not affect his business and, in 1937, he bought a Ford truck. Kapend saw his business as a family enterprise. Thus, in 1935, Moise Kapend Tshomb (Tshombe) had entered into commerce after his studies at Kanene, a Methodist school 80 km (50 mi) south of Kamina. Yav also became a merchant when he had completed his studies at Kanene in 1940.

Altogether, Joseph Kapend Tshomb and his wife, Kat, had seven children, four boys and three girls. One son, Jacques Mulaj became a nurse and went on to continue his medical studies at Kisantu, the predecessor of Lovanium University Medical School, 100 km (60 mi) south of Léopoldville (now Kinshasa). Kapend and his family were staunch Methodists and good friends of Mr. and Mrs. John M. Springer, pioneer missionaries in Katanga (now Shaba).

In 1949, Joseph Kapend became the first Congolese to travel outside of Africa at his own expense. Journeying by plane to Belgium, he wanted to see Europe and to find a medical school for his son, Mulaj. When Joseph died in 1950, he was the richest African in the Congo. By his energy and initiative, he had risen from slavery to become an immensely successful Congolese entrepreneur.

TSHIBANGU KABET MUSAS

BIBLIOGRAPHY: Anna E. Lebak, and Daniel Munuung (eds), *Ngand Yetu: Uruund wa Mwant Yavu,* Elisabethville, 1963; J.M. Springer, *I Love the Trail,* New York, 1952.

KASA-VUBU, J.

Joseph Kasa-Vubu (circa 1913-March 24, 1969), was the first president of the Republic of Congo, now known as Zaire. Kasa-Vubu is remembered for his advocacy of Congolese nationalism during the colonial period and for his attempts to preserve Congolese unity during the turbulent first years of independence.

Kasa-Vubu was born at Kinkuma-Dizi, near Tshela, 100 km (60 mi) north of Boma in Mayombe district of the Lower Congo, now Lower Zaire region. For his primary education, Kasa-Vubu attended the Kizu Mission school, a few kilometers northeast of Tshela, run by the Scheut Fathers. He obtained his secondary education at Mbata Kiela Minor Seminary, 75 km (45 mi) north of Boma, where he graduated in 1936. Intending to become a priest, he entered the Scheut seminary at Kabwe just outside Luluabourg, (now Kananga), where he studied philosophy and theology for three years. For reasons which are unclear, Kasa-Vubu was unsuccessful as a candidate for the priesthood. Disappointed, he returned to Mayombe to enroll at the Kangu teacher training school, 60 km (35 mi) east of Boma, where he obtained his elementary teaching diploma in 1940.

After his studies, Kasa-Vubu settled in Léopoldville (now Kinshasa) to teach at the Lemba elementary school. Also in 1941, he married Hortense Ngoma Masunda, who bore him seven children during their many years of marriage. Kasa-Vubu remained a teacher only one year, for, in 1941, he took a job as a clerk in AGRIFOR, a private Belgian company. Then, in 1942, he joined the civil service as a functionary in the Service des Finances (Treasury department).

In Léopoldville, Kasa-Vubu developed an interest in the rights of Africans living under colonial government. Although political parties were unknown in the Belgian Congo, the number of cultural, trade union, religious, and ethnic organizations multiplied greatly after World War II. In these groups, Congolese came together for social activities and discussion. One such association, the Union des Intérêts Sociaux Congolais (UNISCO) was composed of évolués (educated and westernized Africans) who were concerned about racial discrimination, improved social conditions, and rights of évolués. Feeling the need for a spokesman with more than secondary education, one of UNISCO's founders, Jean Bolikango, approached, Joseph Kasa-Vubu. To become a member of UNISCO, Kasa-Vubu needed to be the director of a student association. With the sponsorship of Bolikango, an important leader of Léopoldville's Lingala speaking population, Kasa-Vubu was elected secretary general of the Association des Anciens Elèves des Pères de Scheut (Association of former Students of the Scheut Fathers, ADAPES), an organization of which Bolikango was president. Increasingly, Kasa-Vubu the government clerk became involved in political issues.

Kasa-Vubu's first speech to UNISCO in 1946 was a stirring challenge to the private companies and mission societies which controlled much land in the Congo. His address, entitled "The Right of the First Occupant," argued that since the Congolese, and notably the Bakongo people, had been the first owners of the land, it should be returned to their control. Rather than being understood as a call for political independence, Kasa-Vubu's talk should be interpreted as a plea for the rights of his Bakongo people, an ethnic group proud of their centuries-old contact with western civilization and a group conscious of the inequalities perpetrated by such a relationship. Kasa-Vubu's talk, however, had general significance throughout the Congo, for he was the first Congolese publicly to assert the rights of Africans over their own land.

During the 1950s, Kasa-Vubu devoted his energies to the Alliance des Bakongo (Abako). Formed in the early 1950s as a Bakongo ethnic association to counterbalance the growing influence of Lingala speakers in Léopoldville, Abako aimed at promoting Bakongo culture and the Kikongo language. On March 21, 1954, after Nzeza-Landu, an Abako founder, took charge of *Kongo dia Ngunga*, one of the three Abako-related newspapers, Joseph Kasa-Vubu was elected president of Abako. As leader of Abako, he gained the people's almost reverent respect for being the most forthright and courageous spokesman of Congolese rights.

In December 1955, A.A.J. van Bilsen, a professor at the Antwerp Institut Universitaire des Territoires d'Outre Mer (Antwerp University Institute of Overseas Territories), published a paper calling on the Belgian government to make plans to grant Congolese independence within 30 years. Although Belgian officials dismissed van Bilsen's proposal as idealistic dreaming, the Congolese were deeply moved by a statement concerning their independence within a specific number of years. Responding to van Bilsen, the Léopoldville periodical *Conscience Africaine*, which reflected the thinking of the Bangala elite, printed a *Manifesto* in its July-August, 1956 issue. Generally supportive of van Bilsen's ideas, the *Manifesto* called for sincerity on the part of the Belgians in enacting the economic and political reforms which eventually would lead to an emancipated Congolese society embodying the best of African and Western civilization. Expressing a desire for unity and cooperation, the *Manifesto* rejected the introduction of party politics into Congo. At the same time, the *Manifesto* called for African participation in making plans for the Congo's future.

On August 23, 1956, Joseph Kasa-Vubu responded to van Bilsen and to the *Manifesto*. Rejecting the concept of Congolese society slowly evolving within the strictures of a plan designed in Belgium, Kasa-Vubu argued that the Congolese should be given immediate independence, that they should have full freedom of speech, press, and association, that they should form political parties, and that they alone should decide the future nature of their society and state. Kasa-Vubu's August 23 *Counter Manifesto* was a clear statement of his conviction that real independence would come only when Africans themselves determined their own destiny. Merely assuming places of responsibility within a system bequeathed by the colonial power would only perpetuate the old inequalities and injustices. In this speech, Kasa-Vubu also spoke of a federal structure for the future Congo state. Recognizing the profound ethnic differences within the country, he proposed a federation whereby each region would elect representatives who would "be able to bring about union and trace the program of true democratization of the country."

In response to growing pressures for African participation in the political process, on March 26, 1957, the Belgian government decreed the reorganization of major Congolese urban centers. The governor general was given the authority to designate certain agglomerations as cities which were then subdivided into a number of African and European communes. The adult males of each commune were then to elect a council and a burgomaster. In the first elections, held in December 1957, Abako won 60 percent to 70 percent of the vote, 8 out of 10 burgomaster positions, and more than 120 of the 170 seats on the councils of Léopoldville's African communes. Kasa-Vubu, himself, was elected burgomaster of Dendale commune, now known as Kasa-Vubu zone.

When he was inaugurated on April 20, 1958, Kasa-Vubu made a speech listing important African grievances under Belgian colonialism. Citing the inadequacy of higher education for Africans, restrictions on freedom of the press and of association, and prohibitions against Africans becoming police and military officers, the new burgomaster asserted that Congolese must have control over the affairs of their country. To climax his talk, he demanded general elections and internal autonomy for the Congo. Despite Kasa-Vubu's undramatic oratorical style, the people were greatly excited by his bold proclamations. The colonial government, on the other hand, chastised Kasa-Vubu for making statements that went beyond the scope of a burgomaster's concerns. For the remainder of his term in office, Kasa-Vubu devoted his attention to administrative concerns. He was especially effective in obtaining funding for communal improvements such as low-cost loans for housing.

Although angered by Kasa-Vubu's forthright statements, the Belgian authorities were responsive to African opinion. Thus, in July, 1958, the government appointed a Working Group to assess the situation in the Congo. In its final report, issued in February 1959, the Working Group proposed the gradual incorporation of Africans into the colony's decision-making process. Anticipating the Group's report, King Baudouin, on January 13, 1959, spoke of actual preparations for independence. To achieve these goals, it was decided to hold general elections in December 1959 to select local and regional councils which would act as consultative bodies for the European administrators.

In the meantime, however, other events had overtaken the Belgian government's cautious moves towards giving Africans a voice in their own affairs. In 1958 the International Exposition in Brussels, General de Gaulle's promise of independence to the French colonies, and the All-African People's Conference in Accra gave the Congolese a new sense of unity, purpose, and dignity. Because of improper health certificates, Kasa-Vubu was unable to obtain a visa to attend the All-African People's Conference in December. The Abako burgomaster of Ngiri-Ngiri commune in Léopoldville, however, accompanied Patrice Lumumba (*q.v.*) and Joseph Ngalula to Accra.

Triggered by general unemployment and by police cancellation of an Abako rally on January 4, 1959, widespread rioting broke out in Léopoldville. Perhaps 50 to 100 people, mostly Africans, were killed in the rioting, while several hundred were injured. Blaming Abako for the disorders, the government arrested its leaders including Joseph Kasa-Vubu, Daniel Kanza, and Simon Nzeza-Landu. When the three were released after the Colonial Minister van Hemelrijck personally intervened, they were flown to Belgium in order to prevent further agitation in the Congo. Although allowed to travel freely in Belgium, the Abako leaders were watched by security police and were not allowed to return home until May 13.

While other leaders, including Patrice Lumumba, were forming political parties in preparation for the December 1959 elections, Kasa-Vubu and his reorganized Abako party rejected Belgian efforts to grant gradual independence to the colony. In addition to advocating a boycott of the December balloting, Abako declared independence for the Lower Congo, effective January 1960. This was consistent with Abako's earlier position that new government structures in the Congo must evolve from African political discussions rather than from a blueprint prepared in Brussels. Kasa-Vubu argued that an African provisional government should precede the formulation of fixed institutions and policies which, he believed, would only mirror European patterns and desires. When elections were held in December, the Abako boycott succeeded, and only about 30 percent of the eligible voters cast ballots in Léopoldville, whereas up to 90 percent voted in other areas.

Once the Belgian authorities realized the impossibility of imposing an independence plan on the

Congo, the government arranged a Round Table discussion where Belgians and Congolese together could determine the country's future. When the Round Table convened in Brussels on January 20, 1960, Kasa-Vubu was one of the Congolese leaders demanding that the decisions of the conference be binding on the Belgian government rather than merely consultative. His view prevailed and the participants began laying the groundwork for Congolese independence. Then, demanding that the Round Table be turned into a constituent assembly, Kasa-Vubu withdrew from the proceedings, from January 25 until February 10. This absence caused a split between Kasa-Vubu and Daniel Kanza, who was angered by the Abako leader's actions. During this time, Kasa-Vubu made two trips to Paris, perhaps to consult with French government officials and lawyers, and one trip each to Liège, Belgium, and Aachen, West Germany. In spite of his absences, when the Round Table adjourned on February 20, Kasa-Vubu was one of the six Africans appointed to the governor general's staff. More importantly, the Congo had been promised independence by the end of June 1960. From April 26 to May 16, Kasa-Vubu returned to Brussels for an Economic Round Table preparing for the financial transitions of independence.

In the crucial May elections for the new Congolese Parliament, Lumumba's Mouvement National Congolais (M.N.C.) ran a country-wide campaign, and won more seats than any other party. Since, however, he was unable to control a working majority, Lumumba had to reach a compromise with Kasa-Vubu. Thus, when the Congo received its independence on June 30, 1960, Lumumba was the prime minister while Kasa-Vubu was the president.

Until the eve of Congo independence, Kasa-Vubu had subscribed to the thesis of a federated Congo. As late as December 1959, he had assembled a conference at Kisantu, 100 km (60 mi) south of Léopoldville, where Abako and several other political parties had passed a resolution calling for a loose federal government. As head of state pledged to protect the integrity of the new Congo constitution, however, Kasa-Vubu became a defender of national unity and a symbol of moderation and compromise.

Almost immediately after independence, the Force Publique (national army) mutinied, Katanga province seceded, and the skilled expatriate population fled. Traveling around the country with Lumumba, his political rival, Kasa-Vubu tried to restore order in the turbulent nation. As the situation deteriorated, Kasa-Vubu lost faith in Lumumba's ability to control the fragmented Congo. A member of the Tetela ethnic group from Stanleyville (now Kisangani), Lumumba's desire for a strong central government, his radical attitude towards Belgium and the Western powers, and his more flamboyant style brought him into conflict with Kasa-Vubu. Finally, on September 4, 1960, invoking the president's constitutional power to name and dismiss the prime minister, Kasa-Vubu announced over Léopoldville radio that he was dismissing Lumumba. A deep constitutional crisis developed as Lumumba attempted to revoke Kasa-Vubu's mandate and as parliament annulled the actions of both men. Nevertheless, Kasa-Vubu prevailed by gaining the crucial support of the United Nations, which earlier had sent troops to quiet the Congo. Lumumba was then confined to his residence.

On September 14, General Mobutu announced his appointment of a Collège des Commissaires (College of Commissioners), composed of university students, to act as a caretaker government in Lumumba's absence. Although Kasa-Vubu stood above the day-to-day vicissitudes of Congolese politics, he tried to promote national reconciliation, to restore order, and to encourage the writing of a new constitution. In March 1961, he attended a conference at Tananarive, Madagascar, and in April and May 1961 he went to Coquilhatville (now Mbandaka) in an effort to reach an accord among the competing political parties and secessionist movements.

With Kasa-Vubu as chief of state, and Cyrille Adoula as prime minister after August 2, 1961, order gradually returned to the Congo. In January 1964, Kasa-Vubu appointed a special commission which met at Luluabourg (now Kananga) to draw up a new constitution. When, in that same year, new rebellions against the central government broke out in Kwilu and in the eastern part of the country, Kasa-Vubu turned to Moise Tshombe (q.v.), entrusted him with the office of prime minister, and charged him with quelling the uprisings. The president's relationship with Tshombe, however, was tense. Finally, on October 13, 1965, he dismissed Tshombe and the country was again drawn into a political crisis. Although Kasa-Vubu asked Evariste Kimba (q.v.) to form a new government, the effort failed.

In order to prevent further discord and governmental paralysis, General Mobutu deposed Kasa-Vubu and suspended parliament on November 24, 1965. Withdrawing to his native region, Kasa-Vubu lived quietly on his farm in Lower Congo. On March 24, 1969, he died in the Boma hospital from a brain hemorrhage.

Together with Patrice Lumumba, Joseph Kasa-Vubu played a determining role in the struggle for Congolese independence. A mild-mannered, patient man, he had to face almost insurmountable difficulties once he became president of the Congo. By his tenacity and magnanimity during the secessions, rebellions, internal dissensions, and international tensions, he served as a symbol of unity for the new nation and its fragile central government.

SABAKINU KIVILU

BIBLIOGRAPHY: P. Artigue, *Qui sont les leaders congolais?* ("Who are the Congolese Leaders?"), Brussels, 1961; J. Gérard-Libois and B. Verhaegen, *Congo 1960* ("Congo 1960"), Brussels, 1961; C.A. Gillis, *Kasa-Vubu au coeur du drame congolais* ("Kasa-Vubu at the Heart of the Congolese Drama"), Brussels, 1961; C. Young, *Introduction à la politique congolaise,* Brussels, 1965, published in English as *Politics in the Congo,* Princeton, 1965; C.R.I.S.P. (Center de Recherche et d'Information Socio-Politiques), *Abako, 1950-1960* ("Abako, 1950-1960"), Brussels, 1962; *L'Essor du Congo* (Lubumbashi daily), March 25, 1969.

KASHAMA, N.

Nkoy (Stephane) Kashama (circa 1936-August 1968), chief advisor on cultural affairs to President Mobutu, devoted his efforts to gaining popular support for the Republic of Congo (now Zaire) as a unified nation state.

Nkoy Kashama was the only son of Dominique Kashama, a highly successful Pende merchant from Muli Kalunga. The elder Kashama was esteemed by all, including the colonial authorities who considered him an évolué (a westernized African). When, in 1949, the young Kashama enrolled in the minor seminary of Kinzambi, 10 km (6 mi) north of Kikwit, Dominique Kashama was displeased by his son's choice of vocation. Although he was aware that a seminary was the only place in the Congo his son could receive a solid education, he was unhappy to be deprived of a future business partner and successor. Because Nkoy Kashama was the son of an évolué perhaps the only one to have become a seminarian, the Fathers had to develop a special policy for his living arrangements. As an évolué, he was treated as a white student.

Performing brilliantly, Kashama graduated in 1955. When he decided to become a Jesuit, thus rejecting the career his father had planned, Dominique Kashama felt bitter and deceived.

For two years, Kashama lived as a Jesuit novitiate at Djuma, 100 km (60 mi) northeast of Kikwit, where he devoted his time to study and prayer. Impressed with his diligence and aptitude, his superiors sent him to Belgium, Ireland, and—later—to Oxford University in England. During his years of training, Kashama concentrated on philosophy and economics. While he was abroad his country was experiencing the difficult first years of independence. Although far from home, Kashama Nkoy closely followed events in the Congo. He remained united with all his compatriots. As correspondent for the Jesuit review *Documents pour l'Action* (later *Congo Afrique*), he maintained immediate contacts with local events.

Kashama remained at Oxford until 1967 when he decided to return home and serve his country in a secular capacity. Presented to the president of the republic, he caught the attention of Mobutu who made Kashama his chief advisor on cultural affairs. Meanwhile, Kashama had married a young Thai woman, whom he had met during his studies.

As a government advisor, Kashama directed his attention to encouraging loyalty to the Congo as a "state." Conceived during the colonial era and composed of many ethnic mosaics, the Republic of Congo had not yet become a unified nation. Because of an untimely death, Kashama was not able to implement his ideas, which have been continued by others as policies. When Kashama Nkoy fell ill in 1968, he was sent to the United States for treatment. He returned home uncured, however, and all measures by medical personnel, as well as the best Pende sorcerers, were without avail. He died in August 1968, barely a year after his nomination as the president's cultural advisor. Although some circulated a rumor he had been poisoned, Tabu Ley (Rochereau), the most popular singer in the country, chose to immortalize his name in the well-known song 'Kashama Nkoy.'

NDAYWEL è NZIEM

SOURCES: Interviews.

KASONGO KINIAMA

Kasongo Kiniama (circa 1850-circa 1890) was an African adventurer who participated in the slave trade to enrich himself and to advance his political ambitions. By trading slaves for guns, he was able to increase his power vis-à-vis weaker neighbors whom he terrorized and plundered. But, as other chiefs also began to sell slaves and purchase firearms, Kasongo Kiniama's relative strength declined and eventually crumbled.

Kasongo Kiniama, born in the village of Kamaie, about 170 km (100 mi) southeast of modern Mbuji-Mayi, was the oldest son of Kalulu, chief of the Kamaie people. When Kasongo was about 15 years old, he learned of the presence of Swahili (Arab influenced) traders from the east coast of Africa, who were at the court of Kasongo Kalombo, the Luba Mulopwe (chief) near Lake Boya. The young Kasongo Kiniama went to the Luba capital where the Swahili merchants hired him as a servant. Kasongo Kiniama accompanied his employers to Bunkeya (located about 65 km, or 40 mi, north of modern Likasi), the residence of Msiri (*q.v.*) the former east African trader who had settled in Shaba. On his return in the late 1860s, he followed the Swahili merchants to Kabinda, court of the Bakalebwe, a sub-group of the Songye people. There the chief, Ya Kaumbu, father of Lumpungu (q.v.) had asked the Swahili traders for help to gain the submission of the Bakalebwe-related Tshofa people living about 130 km (80 mi) northeast of Kabinda.

After the Tshofa surrendered to Ya Kaumbu, Kasongo Kiniama left the Swahili traders and returned to Kamaie. With support from the Luba Mulopwe, he replaced his aged father as chief. To consolidate his power, he bought flint-lock rifles from the Cokwe, (Chokwe), Angolan traders who had entered the region a few years earlier.

Once he had collected enough arms, the young chief began attacking his weaker neighbors, the Budi, Gandu, Kileo, and Musoko. After victories against these groups, he crossed west of the Lubilash River and launched an offensive against the Kibetu, Musokatshi, Poyo, Tshitolo, and northern Kanyok. Seeing Kasongo's great strength, the Kalambaie, Shimba, and Cinene surrendered without a fight.

Because the people upon whom Kasongo Kiniama preyed had not yet acquired guns, the Luba adventurer's victories were relatively easy. He was not able, however, to consolidate his triumphs into lasting political gains. For example, in the mid-1870s he came to the Kanyok capital, located 180 km (110 mi) south of modern Mbuji Mayi on the Luilu River. Finding the Kanyok central government weakened by schism, he attacked and killed the Kanyok leaders who had never before seen guns. Once Kasongo Kiniama tried to collect regular tribute, however, he met strong local resistance from Kanyok sub-chiefs. Marching 50 km (30 mi) south from the Kanyok capital to Etond village, his troops were ambushed. Many were killed while the others were forced to flee into the bush.

From Etond, Kasongo Kiniama went north to the area around Gandajika, about 80 km (50 mi) southeast of modern Mbuji-Mayi. Here among the weaker, decentralized Luba people of Kasai, he was able to secure a capital at Musokatshi near Gandajika. Placing his trusted assistant Hiam Kakoba in charge of Musokatshi, Kasongo sent his warriors to ambush and collect taxes from his subjects. To the chiefs who recognized him as suzerain he gave a rifle as a sign of their authority; other chiefs he replaced with his own followers.

From the beginning of his conquests, Kasongo Kiniama had refused to pay tribute to the Luba Mulopwe, Kasongo Kalombo, his nominal suzerain. Thus, in 1885, the Mulopwe assembled his armies and crossed the Lomami River where he conquered Kamaie, Kasongo Kiniama's natal village. Kasongo Kiniama's brother, who fled Kamaie, managed to save himself, but he could not stop the Luba from crossing Kamaie territory and plundering the Bala and the Ba-

koshi on the Lumbebi River, as well as the Kibundji, Kibetu, and Mpata north of the Sankuru River, and also the Nioko. From there he turned his attention to northern Kanyok. On the following day, however, the Kanyok launched a counter-attack and recaptured many of their people who had been taken prisoner. Not wanting to expose himself too much to the Kanyok, who were superior in numbers, the Mulopwe renounced his pursuit of Kasongo Kiniama and returned to his own lands. Kasongo Kiniama, it is said, fled to the Lunda, where he hoped to buy gunpowder. He returned to the Lubilash area only after the Mulopwe's departure.

In the late 1880s, Kasongo Kiniama tried to acquire more rifles, in order to consolidate his authority over the numerous populations between Kamaie and Lubilash. In addition, he wanted additional guns to protect against Swahili troops who were harassing Lumpungu in the north. Thus, in 1889 or 1890, Kasongo Kiniama journeyed west to the Luba Kasai chief, Kasongo Lwaba, known as Fuamba, who lived 65 km (40 mi) southeast of modern Kananga. From Fuamba, he hoped to obtain guns and powder the Kasai Luba had bought from the Cokwe. Kasongo failed in his mission and had to retreat in the face of Fuamba's menacing attitude.

During Kasongo Kiniama's absence, Kabw Muzemb, chief of the Kanyok rallied the people around Musokatshi to revolt against Hiam Kakoba who had remained behind at the capital. When the attack failed, Kabw Muzemb retreated to the safety of his own land. On his return, Kiniama began a reprisal against his own disobedient subjects. He was killed, however, by the Nsona villagers who feigned support for the angry slave merchant. His death, followed by the retreat of his people, marked the break-up of his fief. It was also followed, in late 1891, by the famous bloody invasion by Ngongo Leteta (q.v.) instigated by Ntomena a Mukulu, first wife of Kasongo Kiniama. Sworn to avenge her husband's death, Ntomena first asked Lumpungu for help. When he refused, she went to Ngongo Leteta, who came to fight and plunder the rebel villages around Musokatshi.

MUTEBA KABEMBA

BIBLIOGRAPHY: L. Mpoyi, *Histoire wa Baluba* ("History of the Baluba"), Mbuji-Mayi, 1966; J. Vansina, *Les anciens royaumes de la savanne*, Léopoldville, 1965, published in English as *Kingdoms of the Savanna*, Madison, 1966. See also E. Ngoyi, in "Nianda ya Kale," manuscript collections of Luba writings, Kamponde, 1952; John Yoder, "A People on the Edge of Empires: A History of the Kanyok of Central Zaire," Ph.D thesis, Northwestern University, 1977.

KASONGO NYEMBO I

Kasongo Nyembo I, (circa 1860-1931) was the Mulopwe or chief of the Luba state during a period of great political, social, and economic upheaval. In the late 19th century many of Central Africa's large traditional states were being weakened and fragmented as a new commercial élite, with links to coastal markets and access to modern firearms, gained increasing power. In the Luba empire, this process of disintegration was accelerated by an intensification of fratricidal succession wars. Each individual aspiring to the throne had to fight his brothers, nephews, and uncles in a series of battles which escalated in destructiveness as outsiders entered the struggle in hopes of gaining political or commercial rewards.

Kasongo Nyembo, the son of Mulopwe Ilunga Kabale, who died in about 1870, came to power soon after the death of Mulopwe Kasongo Kalombo in about 1885. Succession was not automatic, however, for Kasongo Nyembo had to fight his brothers Dia Mande and Kumi, and also his nephew Kitumba, the son of former Mulopwe Kasongo Kalombo. Although five pretenders had been killed in battle by 1891, Kasongo Nyembo's brother Kabongo continued the succession dispute by proclaiming himself as Mulopwe over the northern part of the Luba empire. Because the two brothers had about equal forces, a protracted struggle ensued, in which many local villages became unwillingly involved.

Both Kasongo Nyembo and Kabongo sought to gain allies and aid from any source they could find. Mulopwe Kasongo Nyembo maintained contacts with Cokwe (Chokwe) traders from Angola who supplied him with guns and powder, while Kabongo had relations not only with Angolan merchants from Bihé, but also with the agents of Msiri Ngelengwa (q.v.), from East Africa. In 1891 and 1892, Congo Free State expeditions under Delcommune, Bia, and Francqui passed through the area. By recognizing state suzerainty, Kasongo Nyembo gained the favor of these Europeans and achieved a temporary advantage as Delcommune interrupted his journey long enough to make a quick foray against Kasongo's rival, Kabongo. In 1896, however, Kabongo received help from Batetela mutineers from the Force Publique (the colonial army). Fleeing their headquarters at Luluabourg (now Kananga) to the Lualaba and Lomami river regions, they sided with Kabongo, forcing Kasongo Nyembo to seek refuge with the Europeans at Kabinda. After a Belgian force under Malfeyt expelled the Batetela from the region in 1901, Kasongo Nyembo returned and in 1902 settled at Lake Samba, 90 km (50 mi) north of Kamina, where the Free State constructed a station in February 1903.

From the start, Kasongo Nyembo's relations with the Free State were uneasy. Not only did the state agents exact taxes, send soldiers, and insult the Mulopwe's wives, they also pursued an ambiguous policy towards the two hostile brothers. Kasongo Nyembo was especially displeased when they established a station at Kabongo's village near Lake Boya, about 170 km (100 mi) northeast of Kamina. Thus, by 1905, Kasongo Nyembo was engaged in an open revolt against the Congo Free State.

In order to avoid the state agents, Kasongo Nyembo moved first to Lake Samba island and then to a more secure refuge in the bush. When all attempts at peaceful negotiations failed, the state agents organized an unsuccessful police and military expedition to punish the rebellious Mulopwe. Using their usual policy to divide and conquer, they looked for a rival who could win the loyalty of Kasongo's people. When this tactic did not succeed, they tried to draw Kabongo into the conflict but he proved hesitant. Finally, in 1911, the government sought to fragment Kasongo Nyembo's territory by declaring local village chiefs independent from the Mulopwe. The chiefs, however, did not betray the Mulopwe.

The colonial authorities then appealed to troops from Kabinda to subdue Kasongo Nyembo. Making progress towards his refuge, the Kabinda soldiers massacred Luba subjects. Faced with the prospect of even further destruction, Kasongo Nyembo decided to surrender. Thus, in October 1917, the police arrested the Mulopwe in the forest. Afterwards, Mulopwe Kasongo Nyembo was transferred to Kabinda, where he was tried and exiled to Buta, 250 km (150 mi) north of what is now Kisangani in northeastern Zaire.

In 1920, when the Belgians attempted to apply the principles of indirect administration, some officials favored reinstating Kasongo Nyembo. The local administrative authorities, however, opposed his return. Mulopwe Kasongo I therefore remained at Buta until his death from a hernia in 1931.

N'DUA SOLOL KANAMPUMB

BIBLIOGRAPHY: V.L. Cameron, *Across Africa,* New York, 1969; A. Delcommune, *Vingt années de vie africaine* ("Twenty Years of African Life"), Vol. 2, Brussels, 1922; H. Segaert, *Un terme au Congo Belge* ("A Stint in the Belgian Congo"), Brussels, 1919; G. Vanderkerken, *Les societés bantoues du Congo Belge* ("The Bantu Societies of the Belgian Congo"), Brussels, 1920; J. Vansina, *Les anciens royaumes de la savane,* Léopoldville, 1965, published in English as *Kingdoms of the Savanna,* Madison, 1966; E. Verhulpen, *Baluba et Balubaisés* ("The Baluba and the Balubaized"), Anvers, 1936.

KIKOSO GIBANDA MAFU

Kikoso Gibanda Mafu (circa 1875-May 21, 1955) ruled the Pende chiefdom of Shimuna, located on the left bank of the Kwilu River in the present Kasai Occidental region. Installed by the colonial authorities, Kikoso owed his power to the whites rather than to traditional political structures. Not respected by the people he supposedly ruled, Kikoso abused his subjects and, towards the end of his life, even disregarded the commands of the Belgian administrators who had placed him in office.

The Belgians installed Kikoso Gibanda Mafu at the head of the Shimuna chiefdom, which contained about 7,000 people and which extended southwards from Gungu, 100 km (60 mi) southeast of Kikwit. Kikoso was chosen to replace Shimuna Mukimba Mugamba, alias Mukulunzambi, who had been dethroned on December 8, 1922 because of disobedience to the colonial administration. Although Kikoso received his official investiture on March 2, 1923, the Shimuna generally saw him only as an administrative official responsible for collecting state taxes, and for executing governmental orders. In fact, Kikoso was detested by the people who remained loyal to the former chief Mukulunzambi. Although Kikoso belonged to the Manda clan of the Akwa Mbangu family, and technically could have succeeded Mukulunzambi, he was regarded as a usurper who had sold out to the whites. Thus, when Mukulunzambi returned from prison, he continued to exercise his traditional power.

Before dying, Mukulunzambi forbade his subjects to confer the royal insignias on Kikoso. Thus the traditional power of the chief was given, after Mukulunzambi's death, to Sasaposo of the Manda clan of Kahunga. This situation was a source of constant tension because the traditional chief Sasaposo was supported by the people from whom his power came, while the official chief, Kikoso, was protected by the colonial authorities. Kikoso represented the power of the state and, at times, succeeded in overshadowing the traditional chief.

Kikoso was one of the few Pende chiefs who was not dismissed or executed following the revolt of 1931. At the start of the uprising, he sent a letter to the colonial authorities declaring that he would never join forces with the rebels. When the troops ordered to repress the revolt arrived in his village, they found, together with a small flock of goats, pigs, and hens, a note written by Kikoso in which he stated he was not a rebel but that he and his people had fled out of fear. Later, he was the first Pende chief to surrender to the district commissioner, Van der Hallen, at Kakobola. Because of Kikoso, many other Pende chiefs were induced to give themselves up. The government's appeal to surrender was, however, a ruse. Some of these chiefs were placed in a concentration camp and massacred by the soldiers of the Force Publique while others were tried at a drum-head court at Kandale where they were condemned to death or banished to the western part of the province.

Chief Kikoso's loyalty during the Pende rebellion of 1931 won him many favors from the colonial authorities. This led Kikoso, however, to think himself safe from all chastisement. Consequently, he committed violent and reprehensible acts without fearing punishment. In particular, he freely employed the whip against his subordinates, using it to vent his rages. In 1934, when asked by Father Jacques Délaere, then superior of the Catholic Mission of Muhaku, why he behaved in this manner, Kikoso answered without hesitation: "But I have always used the whip. If I am not obeyed, if someone steals, if someone does not work, I use the lash. I have the right to use the lash."

In July 1934, he arrested the Pende chief Mutundu of the upper Kwilu, because the latter had crossed Kikoso's land without permission. Mutundu, who was traveling in response to the summons of the local Belgian authorities, was imprisoned and whipped on Kikoso's orders, thus, provoking a long and bloody conflict between Mutundu's people and the Shimuna. Although he was clearly in the wrong, curiously, Kikoso was not chastised in this affair. From 1932 on, Kikoso had many disputes with the territorial administration. Due to the intervention of the district commissioner, however, he never received more than a simple admonition. Thus, he began to see himself as stronger than the colonial authorities and he constantly mocked the remarks of the territorial agents whom he came to regard as lesser chiefs.

An avaricious man, Kikoso used the chiefdom's treasury for himself. Often large sums were missing and frequently he forced his subjects to pay tribute in cash. Having never been installed in the traditional manner, he could not receive tribute in kind, which was reserved exclusively for the customary chief. Thus, during the tax collection of 1939, he demanded that 50 centimes per taxpayer be paid into his account.

By 1936, Kikoso had completely lost his prestige with the Africans. Members of the Mboka clan were particularly hostile to him, and reacted violently against his illegal exactions. His authority was respected only because people feared the laws imposed by the whites. During the 1940s, however, the agents of the colonial administration began to monitor Kikoso more closely, pressuring him to end his abuses. Resenting this new situation, Kikoso worked to counter these agents' orders and, as a result, he completely neglected the administration of his chiefdom. Although colonial authorities imposed disciplinary sanctions on him, Kikoso never changed his basic attitude. After he died, on May 21, 1955, he was remembered as a chief proudly conscious of his own authority, who abusively used the powers entrusted to him.

SIKITELE GIZE a SUMBULA

BIBLIOGRAPHY: Archives of the Gungu zone, Political File of the Gungu Sector.

KIMBA, E.

Evariste Kimba (July 16, 1926-June 2, 1966) was a political leader during the first years of Congo independence. An early supporter of Katangese rights, he later attempted to form a national government as prime minister under Kasa-Vubu (*q.v.*), and finally was executed for his opposition to the regime of President Mobutu.

Kimba was born at Nsaka village in the Bukama area, about 350 km (200 mi) northwest of Elisabethville (now Lubumbashi). His parents, Monga and Makonga, however, soon moved to Elisabethville where Kimba received his primary and secondary education at the Institut Saint Boniface. For five more years, Kimba continued his education by attending evening classes in sociology, law, politics, and economics. Like his father Monga, Kimba took employment at the Compagnie de Chemin de Fer du Bas-Congo au Katanga (Lower Congo to Katanga Railroad, B.C.K.). At that time, Kimba became an active supporter of the Catholic trade union movement.

In 1954, Kimba joined the Elisabethville newspaper *Essor du Congo* ("Rise of the Congo") as a journalist. An outstanding writer, he was sent to the 1958 International Exposition in Brussels as a correspondent. There, at the Exposition, Congolese intellectuals from all over the country met for the first time, developed mutual ties, and came into contact with the political, social, and cultural realities of the larger world. Like other Congolese, Kimba was greatly affected by his experience at the Exposition.

Kimba's political awareness, however, had developed long before the Brussels Exposition. Living in Elisabethville, he was exposed to the competition and resulting political activities of the various ethnic groups who lived and worked in the Katangan mining center. One of the most numerous and prominent African groups was the concentration of Luba people from Kasai. Relatives of the Luba from Katanga, they had been menaced by African slave raiders in the late 19th century. Seeking protection, these Luba living in Kasai took refuge near Belgian colonial authorities who then recruited them for jobs all over the Congo. Thus, many Kasai Luba came to Katanga where they worked in government and industry and where their presence was resented by Africans native to Katanga.

As early as 1952, Evariste Kimba had tried to encourage ethnic pride among his own Katanga Luba people by forming an ethnic organization. When the Association des Baluba du Katanga ("Association of the Baluba of Katanga," known as Balubakat) was founded in January, 1957, however, another man, Jason Sendwe, was elected president.

In December 1957, the Luba of Kasai scored a great political victory over native Katangan peoples. In an attempt to give Africans a greater voice in their own affairs, Belgian colonial authorities held elections in several major Congolese cities. To the great displeasure of local Katangan ethnic groups, the Luba of Kasai won three of the four burgomaster offices in Elisabethville. Even the fourth position went not to a local man, but to an active trade unionist from Kivu province.

As demands for independence grew more persistent, the Belgian government appointed a Working Group to visit the Congo and draw up plans for the Colony's political future. In October 1958, anticipating the Working Group's visit to Katanga, a large number of "native Katangans" formed a political party called the Confédération des Associations Tribales du Katanga ("Confederation of Tribal Associations of Katanga, known as Conakat") which, they hoped, would promote the interests of local people and counteract the influence of outsiders from Kasai. Unhappy because he had not been chosen president of Balubakat, Evariste Kimba soon joined Conakat and became one of its leading spokesmen. Not long after, on February 5, 1959, Jason Sendwe's Balubakat joined Conakat to form a short-lived alliance of all major Katangan ethnic groups who feared the influence of outsiders. Thus, even members of the Balubakat regarded their Kasai cousins as a threat.

As independence approached, Conakat, led by Moise Tshombe (*q.v.*), allied with white settlers in Katanga to demand a very loose and decentralized government for the new Congo state. This, they felt, was the only way to avoid being dominated by outsiders, especially the Luba from Kasai. After the Round Table talks in January and February 1960, Kimba was appointed to the political cabinet of the Belgian minister resident in the Congo, Ganshof van der Meersch. As deputy chief of the cabinet, Kimba was able to press for the acceptance of the Conakat view. In May 1960, Kimba was elected as a senator from Katanga to sit in the national parliament in Léopoldville (now Kinshasa). Like other elected Conakat officials, however, he refused to participate in this body once independence came in June.

After Congo independence on June 30, 1960, Kimba, together with Moise Tshombe, Godefroid Munongo, and Jean-Baptiste Kibwe engineered a secession movement for the Katanga province. From

July 11, when Tshombe announced that Katanga was separating from the rest of the chaotic Congo, until January 1963, when Joseph Ileo of the central government in Léopoldville arrived in Elisabethville to take over control of Katanga, these men attempted to protect their province and gain international recognition for their government. On September 16, 1960, Evariste Kimba was appointed foreign minister of Katanga. As foreign minister he frequently negotiated with Léopoldville and with foreign powers in an effort to buy time for Katanga. In October 1960, he met with Justin Bomboko, Congo Minister of Foreign Affairs, in a futile attempt to resolve their differences. During a series of Round Table discussions held in Léopoldville, Tananarive, and Coquilhatville (now Mbandaka), Kimba and Tshombe consistently refused to rejoin the national government. Because of their intransigence at Coquilhatville, both men were arrested by the Armée National Congolais (A.N.C.) on April 26, 1961. From there they were taken to Léopoldville and held until June 22.

During 1961, the fragmented Congo government gradually regained strength, and on February 21, the United Nations Security Council passed a resolution authorizing the use of force to remove all foreign military personnel and advisors who were aiding secession movements in the Congo. Then in August 1961, Cyrille Adoula became prime minister of the Congo with broad support from most of the previously divided political parties. Recognizing Katanga's precarious position in the face of U.N. opposition and with a viable government in Léopoldville, Tshombe tried to attract more outside support for his cause. Thus, Kimba was dispatched to Europe where he visited France, Germany, and Italy. About the same time, however, U.N. troops in the Congo began a serious campaign to end Katanga secession. On August 28, 1961, U.N. soldiers stationed in Elisabethville, where they had been placed to prevent disorder, rounded up foreign soldiers engaged by Katanga and tried to expel them from the country. On September 13, the U.N. tried to arrest Katanga's top leaders. Although Tshombe, Munongo, and Kimba all managed to escape, they feared resisting the U.N. soldiers, and thus provoking a military confrontation.

As 1961 progressed, Kimba took an increasingly hard line against reaching any accommodation with Léopoldville or the U.N. In December, he warned the U.N. that Katanga would pursue a "scorched earth policy" if U.N. troops continued their drive into northern Katanga. After Tshombe concluded an agreement with Adoula at Kitona near the mouth of the Congo (now the Zaire) River on December 20, 1961, Kimba challenged the validity of the accord,

claiming it had been made under duress.

During the course of 1962, Katanga weakened, U.N. and A.N.C. troops slowly reintegrated northern Katanga into the Congo, and the earlier tacit Western support for Tshombe dissipated. Nevertheless, Kimba remained firm. When his former rival, Jason Sendwe, now a member of the Léopoldville government, asked him to help reorganize a loyal north Katanga under Balubakat leadership, Kimba refused. In December 1962, a large contingent of the U.N. army took control of Elisabethville. From there they moved northwest through the copperbelt to Jadotville (now Likasi). Still resisting, Tshombe and his ministers retreated to Kolwezi, the nerve center of the mining region. They could not hold out, however, and on January 21, 1963, the U.N. occupied Kolwezi, thus ending Katanga secession. Tshombe himself had fled to Spain, so, on January 23, it was Foreign Minister Evaristé Kimba who formally handed over power to Joseph Ileo, whom the Léopoldville government had sent as resident minister to govern Katanga.

Kimba's career, however, was not over. When rebellions in Kwilu and Kivu threatened the fragile

Congo government in 1964, President Kasa-Vubu dismissed Cyrille Adoula and called upon the exiled Moise Tshombe to form a new government as prime minister. Coming to office on July 10, 1964, Tshombe was charged with the task of reuniting the country and suppressing the rebellions. Pursuing a policy of moderation towards former opposition politicians, Tshombe allowed them to resume political activities.

Thus, in 1964, Kimba formed a political party, the Mouvement Populaire d'Union Africaine ("Popular Movement for African Union," known as the M.P.A.). At the end of 1964, he was nominated president of the Balubakat tribal association, a move which reunited the formerly fragmented Luba of Katanga. This, however, was the beginning of a dispute between Kimba and Tshombe, who feared any real opposition. The Balubakat, strong in northern Katanga, elected Kimba as deputy to the national parliament. As a Balubakat representative in Léopoldville, Kimba found himself among the adversaries of Tshombe's new party, the Convention Nationale Congolais (the "National Congolese Convention," known as Conaco), which was merely a new version of his former party the Conakat.

Because of personal rivalries and because of Tshombe's internationally unpopular use of foreign mercenaries to put down the rebellions, relations between Kasa-Vubu and Tshombe deteriorated during 1965. On October 13, 1965, not long before the scheduled presidential elections in which Tshombe threatened to defeat the incumbent, President Kasa-Vubu revoked the elections, dismissed Tshombe, and called on Evaristé Kimba to form a new government. Parliament, however, dominated by Conaco, refused on two occasions in November to approve Kimba's government. As the political crisis deepened, Lieutenant General Joseph D. Mobutu took power by ousting both Kimba and Kasa-Vubu.

Kimba remained hostile to Mobutu and on May 31, 1966, he was implicated in the Complot de la Pentecôte ("The Pentecost Conspiracy"). Together with Alexander Mahamba, Jerome Anany, and Emmanuel Bamba, he was accused of having attempted to overthrow Mobutu's government. On June 1, 1966, all four were sentenced at an open-air trial in Kinshasa (as Léopoldville, the capital, had been renamed on May 5) and hung publicly on June 2. Kimba left a widow and four children. His thoughts, set down in a manucript entitled "Mes opinions sur les problèmes congolaises" ("My Opinions on Congolese Problems") were circulated posthumously.

TSHIBANGU KABET MUSAS

BIBLIOGRAPHY: *Africa Report,* "News in Brief," passim; *Essor du Congo* (1963-66); *Essor du Katanga;* E. Kimba, "Mes opinions sur les problèmes congolaises" ("My Opinions on Congolese Problems"); *La Voix du Katanga;* "Mission du Kimba à Madrid" ("Kimba's Mission to Madrid"), 1960, from the archives of Shaba; C. Young, *Politics in the Congo,* Princeton, 1965.

KIMBAMBA

Kimbamba (circa 1875-May 23, 1944) was a prominent Pende chief of the Lozo people, living east of Gungu about 100 km (60 mi) southeast of Kikwit. Kimbamba ruled during the colonial era as a close collaborator of the colonial authorities.

Succeeding the former Lozo chief Lubunda, who died in September 1923, Kimbamba received the traditional investiture from the people in 1924. His position as Lozo chief was recognized by the colonial government which confirmed him in office and gave him a chief's medallion on May 18, 1925.

Kimbamba is remembered as a very authoritarian figure whose severity knew few bounds. Referring to Kimbamba, the administrator of Kilembe, just east of Gungu, wrote on September 9, 1926: "This chief is most feared by his people and since he was named chief, a good number of people have fled the village rather than submit to his exactions." Kimbamba was so harsh that, at one point, some colonial authorities considered deposing him. Since, however, many other officials advocated strict treatment of the Africans, Kimbamba retained his title. Nevertheless, territorial authorities occasionally intervened, reminding Kimbamba to exercise moderation so as not to further alienate his subjects. Kimbamba's greatest internal opposition came from Lozo notables of the Manda clan who frequently sought to revoke his traditional power, and who reproached him for allying with foreigners in harassing or mistreating Africans.

In 1931, Kimbamba actively worked with the colonial government to suppress and check the revolt that broke out in the Pende region between the Lutshima and Kwilu rivers, south of Kikwit. His faithfulness won favor in the eyes of the administration. As a result, he was one of the few Pende chiefs retained in office after the 1931 revolt.

As a reward for his continued cooperation, on March 28, 1941 Kimbamba was named chief of the newly created sector of Kinzamba-Lozo, which included about 5,000 people living in the previously separate chiefdoms of Kinzamba and Lozo. He was officially invested in his new duties on June 24, 1941.

As chief of the sector, Kimbamba encountered enormous difficulties in governing his subjects, who became resentful of his role. He also had trouble in relating to the colonial authorities who grew more vigorous in their demands. From 1942 on, his relations with Belgian officials deteriorated because Kimbamba, wanting to act on his own initiative, refused to bend to their wishes. Eventually, on August 9, 1943, he was officially relieved of his duties for having refused to maintain his residence in the capital of the sector. Kimbamba reacted in anger and joined the systematic opposition to colonial power. The territorial authorities, increasingly intolerant of Kimbamba's arrogance, which seemed to grow with age, several times sought to banish him from the region and reduce his influence over the population. Finally, Kimbamba was accused of extortion and of having abused the use of the whip. Arrested and condemned to 12 months in prison, he was incarcerated in the district of Kikwit, where he died on May 23, 1944, following ill treatment.

The life of Kimbamba demonstrates the manner in which colonial authorities used African chiefs to serve their own ends regardless of the resulting conflicts which arose between those chiefs and their subjects. The example of Kimbamba also shows that once the interests of the colonizers had been served, or once the chiefs grew too old, government authorities did not hesitate to dismiss their former auxiliaries.

SIKITELE GIZE a SUMBULA

BIBLIOGRAPHY: Archives of the Gungu zone, Political File for the Lozo sector.

KIMBANGU, S.

Simon Kimbangu (circa 1890-October 12, 1951) was the leader of what is generally considered the most important independent Christian religious movement in central Africa. Although active only a few months before being arrested and inprisoned by the colonial government, Kimbangu developed a following which later developed into a large organized church named "l'Eglise de Jésus-Christ sur la terre par le prophète Simon Kimbangu" ("The Church of Jesus Christ on Earth by the Prophet Simon Kimbangu").

Simon Kimbangu, who belonged to the Kikongo group, was born at Nkamba, a village about 50 km (30 mi) north of the present Mbanza-Ngungu. Both his mother and father died when he was very young so he was raised by his grandmother Kinzembo. Kimbangu attended primary school at the nearby Baptist Missionary Society (B.M.S.) station of Ngombe-Lutete where he was baptized and where he learned about the Bible. For a time he worked as a Baptist evangelist, teaching and preaching in local villages. About this time, he married Marie Mwilu who bore him many children, including Joseph Diangienda, Charles Kisolokole, and Salmon Dialungana Kiangani.

During a flu epidemic in 1918, Kimbangu received

This picture of Kimbangu, taken when he was in prison in 1925, is the only known picture of him in existence.

what he interpreted as the call of God. In an attempt to evade the call, he fled to Léopoldville (now Kinshasa). Because the call continued even in the capital, however, and because life in the large city was difficult, Kimbangu returned to Nkamba where, on March 18, 1921, he received a vision asking him to proclaim the gospel. Other visions followed and Kimbangu finally answered the call to preach and heal. People responded eagerly, bringing many sick to be healed. It was widely reported that Kimbangu performed miracles, cured the infirm, and even was able to raise the dead. Kimbangu became known as a prophet with a special mission from God, and his village of Nkamba was called the New Jerusalem.

In the services he led, Kimbangu emphasized singing, praying, Bible reading, and a sermon. An important element of his ministry was healing and as he laid his hands on the sick, Kimbangu was seized with trembling. Kimbangu's teachings, based on the Bible, centered on three themes: destruction of all fetishes, prohibition of polygamy, and worship of one true God. Identifying God with Nzambi, the African Supreme Being, Kimbangu portrayed God as being closely linked to Africans.

Immediately, Africans from as far away as Léopold-ville, the French Congo, and Angola began flocking to

Nkamba. Because Lower Congo (now Lower Zaire) had been deeply affected by the impact of colonialism, Kimbangu's message was eagerly received. Not only had people from the Lower Congo region been heavily recruited to work on the railroad and plantations, they had also been exposed to intense and often competitive mission activity. As Kimbangu's reputation grew, Africans abandoned their fields, deserted their jobs and journeyed to Nkamba where they listened to an African prophet describing a God who was concerned about the needs they felt as Africans.

Under pressure from the Catholic missions, especially the Redemption Fathers, who feared the excessive zeal of an untrained lay preacher, and from plantation owners, who were disturbed by absenteeism, the colonial administration was compelled to investigate the affair of Simon Kimbangu. On May 11, 1921, the administrator Morel came to Nkamba to assess the situation. Arriving at a time when Kimbangu was preoccupied by a religious experience, Morel was treated rudely and ignored by the prophet. For a time, the colonial government tried to halt the flow of people to Nkamba by prohibiting the transportation of the sick as a hazard to public hygiene. As the pilgrimages continued, however, government agents were ordered to arrest Kimbangu. When the agents arrived at Nkamba, on June 21, 1921, Kimbangu escaped and went to live clandestinely in the village of Nsanda near Léopoldville. During the time Kimbangu stayed at Nsanda, the movement developed xenophobic tendencies and a hostility towards the state. This was in spite of Kimbangu's counsel to submit to the authorities and pay taxes to the government.

On September 14, 1921, Kimbangu was captured at Nkamba where he had returned voluntarily to await arrest. Before a court-martial held in Thysville (now Mbanza-Ngungu), presided over by a single judge, Commander Rossi, Simon Kimbangu was condemned to death for "having disturbed the security of the State and the public peace." Inflamed by a vindictive press campaign launched by *l'Avenir Colonial Belge* ("The Future of Belgian Colonialism"), the political atmosphere in the Congo became extremely tense; machine guns were mounted in Léopoldville to prevent a possible uprising on the part of the African population. In spite of pressure from whites in the colony, King Albert of Belgium (reigned 1909-34) commuted Kimbangu's death sentence to life in prison. Kimbangu was transferred to jail in Elisabethville (now Lubumbashi) where he remained until his death on October 12, 1951.

In prison, Kimbangu was known as a kind, peaceful, and quiet man. While other prisoners expressed anger and resentment at their plight, Kimbangu showed patience and love towards the authorities. While other convicts fought among themselves for larger portions of food, he shared his rations. A fellow inmate, a murderer who later became a Protestant minister, described a dramatic moment when Kimbangu divided his piece of precious meat and distributed it to the other inmates. By this act Kimbangu demonstrated not only his unselfishness, but also his courage because sharing food was strictly forbidden in the prison. After this symbolic act, Kimbangu walked into the warden's office a place which was absolutely off limits to prisoners, saluted the official, and returned to his cell.

Following Kimbangu's arrest, members of the movement found it difficult to continue the teachings of the prophet. Not only were they harassed by government officials who placed Nkamba under martial law and forbade anyone to express allegiance to Kimbangu, they were also troubled by heterodox tendencies as various prophetic personalities arose to claim leadership in the sect. André Matwua began Amicalism in 1926, Simon Mpadi founded the Mission of Blacks in 1939, while Toko Simao Gonzalves started Nzambi Mapapu in 1947. Xenophobic in their preaching, these leaders encouraged Kimbanguists to resist taxes, expect firearms from God, and return to polygamy. In general, Kimbangu's emphasis on the Bible was ignored in favor of direct visions as the primary source of religious authority.

In spite of these difficulties, Kimbangu's son Joseph Diangienda was able to organize the diverse group of people loyal to the exiled prophet into a single Christian ecclesiastical organization. In 1948, Diangienda was allowed to visit his father, who apparently named Diangienda as his successor. From 1951, Diangienda systematically reestablished contact with the followers of the prophet who were organized at Nkamba and Léopoldville under the name Kintwadi. In 1954, Diangienda became leader of Kintwadi. Because the colonial administration officially had ordered tolerance for sects which did not disturb public order or state security, in 1955 the Kintwadists under Diangienda organized public demonstrations in Léopoldville to gain government acceptance of Kimbanguism. From 1955 to 1957, they also tried to build support for their cause in Belgium and other Western countries. Then, in September 1957, Joseph Diangienda published a restatement of Kimbanguism in which he affirmed the politically neutral and exclusively confessional nature of the movement. Finally, on December 24, 1959, Belgian authorities signed a decree lifting the prohibition against the Church of Jesus Christ on Earth by the Prophet Simon Kimbangu.

After the Congo won its independence in 1960, Kimbanguism became increasingly important in the life of the nation. Besides operating a seminary, and primary and secondary schools, the Kimbanguist

Church developed an ambitious program of social services in Lower Zaire and Kinshasa. Together with Protestantism and Catholicism, Kimbanguism was recognized by the Zairian government as a major religious organization. Unlike Protestants and Catholics, however, Kimbanguists relied on their own constituency in Zaire for almost their entire leadership and financial support.

SABAKINU KIVILU

BIBLIOGRAPHY: Efraim Andersson, "Messianic Popular Movements in the Lower Congo," *Studia Ethnographica Upsaliensia,* XIV, Uppsala, 1958; G. Balandier, *La sociologie actuelle de l'Afrique Noire* ("The Present-Day Sociology of Black Africa"), Paris, 1963; J. Banda-Mwaka, "Le Kimbanguisme en tant que mouvement pré-politique chez les Kongo" ("Kimbanguism as a Pre-Political Movement Among the Kongo"), *Bulletin du C.E.P.S.I.,* 1972; E. Bazola, "Le Kimbanguisme," ("Kimbanguism"), *Cahiers des Religions Africaines,* I, 1968; C.A. Chome, *Kimbangu, fondateur d'Eglise* ("Kimbangu, Church Founder"), Brussels, 1960; Levi Keidel, *Black Samson,* Carol Stream, Illinois, 1975; M. Martin, "Le Kimbanguisme" ("Kimbanguism"), *Cahiers des Religions Africaines,* 2, 1968; P. Raymaekers, "L'Eglise de Jésus Christ sur la terre par le Prophète Simon Kimbangu," ("The Church of Jesus Christ on Earth by the Prophet Simon Kimbangu"), *Zaire,* XII, 1959.

KIMPA VITA

Kimpa Vita (circa 1685-July 2, 1706), whose baptized name was Dona Beatriz, founded a religious sect known as the Antonians. The goal of this movement was to restore the fortunes of the once glorious kingdom of Kongo and to Africanize Christianity.

After October 1665, when the Portuguese had defeated the Kongo army, the capital San Salvador was abandoned and the ruling dynasty was split by rivalry between the Ki-Mpanza and the Ki-Nlaza families. Members of these families ruled at three different locations, San Salvador, Bula, 100 km (60 mi) northwest of San Salvador, and Kibangu, south of San Salvador near Ambriz. Within the context of the political confusion and moral dispair which gripped the kingdom in the late 1600s and early 1700s, several religious figures arose wishing to reunify the state and instill hope in the people.

The most important prophet was the young Kimpa Vita, or Dona Beatriz, who believed she had received a visitation from the popular Saint Anthony. According to Kimpa Vita, Saint Anthony became incarnate in her

Kimpa Vita - woodcut

body so that she actually was the saint. Compelled by the Christian God to announce his word and to restore the former Kongo capital San Salvador, Kimpa Vita began preaching in the ruined city.

Rejecting missionary domination over Christianity, Kimpa Vita taught that Jesus Christ actually had been born in San Salvador which she called Bethlehem, that he had been baptized at Nzundi, about 150 km (100 mi) north of the capital, which she named Nazareth, and that Jesus Christ, the Holy Virgin Mary, and Saint Francis were black people of the Kongo. Furthermore, Kimpa Vita prophesied that God would punish the people if they did not immediately return to San Salvador. Initially most of the chiefs did not support her, but the common people, longing for unity and peace, joined the movement in great numbers. They believed that the Christian God was, at long last, responding to the plight of the Kongo kingdom and that he would provide great wealth for the inhabitants.

About the same time, Mpanzu Mvemba, or Pedro IV, who was the Mani Kibangu (ruler of Kibangu), gained recognition as Mani Kongo (ruler of the entire Kongo) and attempted to reunify the once powerful Kongo state. Thus, he sent his general Pedro Constantino with an army towards San Salvador to build villages and plant gardens in preparation for people to resettle the old capital. Hoping himself to gain control of a reunified Kongo, however, Constantino joined with Kimpa Vita against Pedro IV. Pedro IV, who did not want to lose control of his kingdom, came north from Kibangu to defeat the rebels.

Arrested with a baby, whom she claimed had been conceived with her guardian angel, Kimpa Vita was tried for crimes against the crown and the Christian faith. At the instigation of Capuchin missionaries, both she and the child were burned at the stake on July 2, 1706.

Kimpa Vita played a major role in the renewal and reunification of the previously divided Kongo kingdom. Together with Mpanzu Mvemba or Pedro IV, she was responsible for briefly restoring the Kongo in the early 1700s. Although she died shortly after she began preaching, her politico-religious ideas inspired messianic movements struggling against colonial oppression and exploitation two centuries later. The prophet Simon Kimbangu (q.v.) has frequently been regarded as the spiritual and political descendant of the martyred Kimpa Vita.

TSIMBA MABIALA

BIBLIOGRAPHY: G. Balandier, *La vie quotidienne au royaume du Kongo du XVIème au XVIIIéme siècle,* Paris, 1965, English translation by Helen Weaver published as *Daily Life in the Kingdom of Kongo from the Sixteenth to the Eighteenth Century,* New York, 1968; L. de Luques, *Relations sur le Congo: 1700-1717,* ("Narratives on the Congo: 1700-1717"), French translation by J. Cuvelier, Brussels, 1953; L. Julien, "Le Congo et la secte des Antoinens, Restauration du royaume sous Pedro IV et la 'Saint Antoine' congolaise: 1694-1718" ("The Congo and the Antoine Sect, Restoration of the Realm Under Pedro IV and the Congolese 'Saint Anthony'"), *Bulletin de l'Institut Historique Belge de Roma, XXXIII,* 1961, p. 411; W.G.L. Randles, *L'ancien royaume du Kongo des origines à la fin du XIXème siècle* ("The Ancient Kingdom of Kongo from its Origins to the End of the 19th Century"), Paris, The Hague, 1968.

KINGWENGWE KIFOFO

Kingwengwe Kifofo (circa 1875-August 1961) was a forceful Pende chief who tried to protect his subjects against political domination by the Europeans. At the same time, however, he encouraged his people to accept the benefits of Western education and to take advantage of new commercial opportunities made available by the introduction of the colonial system.

Kingwengwe Kifofo succeeded Gandanda (q.v.) to the throne of the Musanga Chiefdom 120 km (75 mi) south of Kikwit, following the Pende revolt in 1931. Gaining traditional election early in 1932, Kingwengwe received a government medallion and was invested into the colonial administration on October 8, 1934 when Assistant District Commissioner Vandevenne was traveling in the Pende lands on a political study mission. He was officially reinvested on December 17, 1936 when the earlier December 5, 1933 decree concerning "native districts" was put into effect in the Pende lands.

Kingwengwe proved to be a great chief whose fame reached beyond the borders of his chiefdom. Loved and respected by his own people, he was feared by the outsiders, both white and black. Kingwengwe was one of the rare African chiefs capable of standing up to the whites. He flatly refused to attend the convocations called by the territorial agents, arguing that, as a great chief living on his own lands, it was not fitting to run to men who were merely visitors in the territory. He further objected to becoming the government's tax collector for the area. On many occasions, he advised territorial agents that, as strangers in the region, they should actually pay him tribute.

Finally, in 1937, he came into open conflict with the territorial agent, Flament, over the issue of tax collection. On January 9, Flament ordered Kingwengwe to collect taxes and to submit regular reports on the 25th of each month. When chief Kingwengwe categorically refused, he was summoned repeatedly to convocations between January 25 and March 11. Although at first the chief made no response, when he received the fifth notice, he sent Flament a letter stating he would not tolerate future appeals and expressing his desire to remain independent. Surprised by the behavior of the chief, Flament asked his superiors to depose and banish Kingwengwe. The colonial authorities, however, rejected Flament's petition for fear of risking a rebellion from Kingwengwe's people. Thus, the government could only withdraw the chief's salary and bonuses and attempt to ignore him.

In October 1940, the Assistant Territorial Administrator Douhet, newly arrived in the region, sought to force Kingwengwe into submission by calling him to appear at Kobo. Chief Kingwengwe sent a messenger advising the assistant administrator to come to the chief's capital at Musanga-Kifwameson, and stating that, as a great chief, he would not come at the beck and call of any little foreigner. His pride wounded, on August 23, 1941 Douhet sought to eliminate Kingwengwe's office by creating a new political unit, the Bwele-Lufuku Sector (present Kobo zone) out of the chiefdoms of Musanga and Ndala. Furthermore, Douhet refused to recognize African officials of the former Musanga Chiefdom. When, on

October 21, 1941, Albert Mabaya was elected unanimously as chief of the sector, Douhet categorically opposed his investiture only because Mabaya was a subject of Chief Kingwengwe. On August 13, 1942, to further humiliate Kingwengwe, the colonial authorities designated Jean Kapita of the Ndongela clan to act as provisional chief of the sector, and on March 31, 1943 they chose Sengula Lumanda of the Nzemba Munene clan to exercise the functions of assistant chief of the sector. Both belonged to the chiefdom of Akwa Ndala.

Chief Kingwengwe accused the colonial authorities of having usurped his power by conferring it upon strangers. He vehemently contested the legitimacy of Kapita's power, because, as a member of the Ndala clan, Kapita belonged to a family considered as clients or tenants on Musanga lands. Chief Kingwengwe organized an active opposition against chief Kapita and against the newly-created sector.

Suddenly, the assistant chief of the sector, Sengula Lumanda, contracted pulmonary tuberculosis, and died in November 1944. Then the chief of the sector himself, Jean Kapita, was stricken with pleurisy and died on December 23, 1944. Popular opinion attributed the deaths to the magical powers of chief Kingwengwe and his former notables, who, it was believed, cursed the two usurpers. The territorial authorities, and in particular Assistant Territorial Administrator Gomez, who was in the region in November-December 1944, listened attentively to these rumors and sought to chastise chief Kingwengwe. Fearful of inciting a general rebellion by arresting and exiling Kingwengwe, the officials merely dismissed him from the execution of his chiefly duties as an invested government functionary. The decree, dated February 7, 1945, stated that by his hostile attitude regarding Jean Kapita, he impeded the smooth operation of the sector.

Despite this decision, Chief Kingwengwe continued to exercise his customary power and to lead his people in resisting European exploitation. Despite the open hostility of the colonial authorities towards him, Kingwengwe was able to take measures, both directly and through intermediaries, to insure that a Musanga native succeeded Jean Kapita. Thus, on October 20, 1945, Fumu Vincent, was provisionally appointed to fill the post of chief of the sector. He was finally confirmed on May 24, 1948, thus ending a long dispute between Kingwengwe and the territorial authorities. Several years later, with the approval of the Administrator Caps, Chief Kingwengwe was restored to his official duties.

Despite his strong opposition to colonial policies, chief Kingwengwe admired certain aspects of Western civilization, especially education. In 1935, the territorial agent of Gungu reported that he was amazed to see literate children in the chiefdom. Not only had Kingwengwe urged all the youth to learn this "marvel of the whites," he, himself, learned to read and write. The primary school built in his capital was one of the most prosperous pre-World War II establishments in the Pende territories. Kingwengwe worked closely with the Catholic missionaries of Kisanji, 150 km (90 mi) south of Kikwit, to develop primary education in the Upper Lufuku river region. In addition to encouraging education, he urged all his subjects to earn money by cutting palm nuts, the principal commercial crop of the region. He also was the first chief of the Gungu territory to own a bicycle. The Nsu brand, which he purchased, became famous in the Kobo sector, as many people imitated their chief by buying an identical bicycle.

Chief Kingwengwe Kifofo spent the last years of his life working to ensure that the rights he had won for the Musanga prevailed in the entire region between the Bwele and Longele rivers. A good part of this region was inhabited by 'tenant' clans, or clients who, occasionally, with the blessing and sometimes with the complicity of the Europeans, attempted to gain power at the expense of the established Musanga élite. When Kingwengwe died in August 1961, he was followed by Musanga Gafugusa, who came to power after a long conflict over succession.

SIKITELE GIZE a SUMBULA

BIBLIOGRAPHY: Archives of the Gungu Zone, Political File of the Kobo Sector.

KINZONZI, A.

Augustin Kinzonzi (May 25, 1901-June 19, 1955) rose to prominence as a Thysville (now Mbanza-Ngungu) merchant and government official during the colonial period.

Kinzonzi was born in the commercially unimportant village of Nsanga-Londe in the present Lower Zaire region, He was, however, introduced to the business world at a very young age when he was hired by a Portuguese merchant. Like the Asians and Greeks in the eastern Congo, the Portuguese in the western Congo established a near monopoly on commerce with the Africans. Familiar with African customs and methods of trade, Portuguese agents were employed by the large commercial houses and the Portuguese language was widely adopted in transactions with the Africans. Through his work, Kinzonzi learned about modern commerce and gained an education. Accompanying his employer to Portugal on two occasions, he attended primary school in Europe.

On his return to the Congo, he established himself as a merchant in Thysville. As did Pierre Disu in the Madimba region and Albert Mpaka at Matadi,

Kinzonzi distinguished himself through his commercial transactions, and his business emerged as one of the prominent firms in the area. Its role as a supplier of foodstuffs, especially manioc, to the urban centers of Matadi and Léopoldville (now Kinshasa) contributed to his growing fortune.

During the Depression, which affected the Lower Congo with great intensity between 1931 and 1934, African merchants in Matadi and Thysville created the Chambre de Commerce Indigène (Native Chamber of Commerce) to protect the interests of African businessmen and to promote foreign trade. In 1934, Kinzonzi became president of this organization.

By the 1950s, Kinzonzi had nine commercial outlets in the Léopoldville Province (now Bas-Zaire region and Kinshasa) towns of Léopoldville, Sundi-Lutete, Mpombo, Thysville, Lufu-Ntoto, Gombe-Matadi, Mfwatu, and Matadi.

The prosperity of his business earned him the confidence of the colonial administrators who awarded him a contract to supply the large prisons of the Thysville area with food. When a "Centre-Extra-Coutumier" (urban area not ruled by a traditional chief) was created at Thysville in 1934, Kinzonzi was named assistant head of the center. He exercised this function to the complete satisfaction of both the administration and the African population. In 1939, Kinzonzi became head of the center, retaining the post until his death. In 1947, he became a member of the Léopoldville Province council, a purely consultant body representing the various European and African interest groups. His loyalty to the colony and his distinguished services were recognized when the government gave him the war medal ("Médaille de Guerre"), the silver medal of merit, and the silver medal of the Order of Léopold II. Finally, on January 19, 1955, Kinzonzi became the first African in the Thysville territory to receive a civic merit card and achieve a status which placed him under the jurisdiction of European rather than traditional law.

During his administrative career, Kinzonzi was able to complete his tasks as a merchant and as head of the "Centre-Extra-Coutumier." As a 1954 report prepared by the territorial administrator indicated, he was highly esteemed by the Europeans as an active and intelligent leader. He was, however, also responsive to the Africans' needs. Many people from his home territory of Manianga were able to secure jobs at Thysville because of his efforts.

Besides his municipal administrative duties and his commercial affairs, Kinzonzi maintained an active interest in regional polities. Thus, he joined the "Alliance des Bakongo" (Abako) which, together with other African political parties, led the Congo to independence.

He died of a heart attack on June 19, 1955.

SABAKINU KIVILU

BIBLIOGRAPHY: Thysville territory, "Rapport sur le fonctionnement du Centre Extra-Coutumier de Thysville, 1937-1956" ("Report on the Operation of the Non-Traditional Urban Area of Thysville, 1937-1956"), Archives of the Sub-Region of the Cataracts at Mbanza-Mgungu.

KIWELE, J.

Joseph Kiwele (1912-November 15, 1961) was a leading musician, educator, and politician in the Katanga Province (now Shaba Region).

Born at Mpala 20 km (12 mi) north of Baudouinville (now Moba), on the shores of Lake Tanganyika, Kiwele went to primary school in his home village. He then went on to Lusaka, 40 km (25 mi) southwest of Boudouinville, for his secondary studies in humanities. He then studied philosophy and theology for five years at the seminary of Baudouinville. Going to Europe for one year, he took courses in harmony, counterpoint, and organ music at the Academy of Liège in Belgium. In 1941-42, after returning home, he taught technical design at the Chemins de Fer du Congo-Supérieur aux Grands Lacs Africains' (Great Lakes Railways, C.F.L.) professional school in Albertville (now Kalemie). He then went to Elisabethville (now Lubumbashi) where he was placed in charge of general education and music at the Institut Saint Boniface.

For several years, he played the Elisabethville Cathedral organ and directed the Petits Chanteurs (Childrens Choir) at the Croix de Cuivre (Copper Cross). Besides being able to play any of the great works of such European classical composers as Beethoven, Handel, and Mozart, Kiwele was a composer who wrote many original pieces. He was considered one of the greatest African composers of his time. Kiwele's most famous work was certainly the "Missa Katanga." He also wrote "La Katangaise," the secessionist state of Katanga's national anthem, which was a hymn to heroes, patriotism, courage, and bravery. Another of Kiwele's pieces, "Te Deum bantou" was an arrangement of Handel's Hallelujah Chorus for choir, organ, and African musical instruments. On the occasion of King Baudouin's visit to the Congo in 1955, he composed the "Hymn to Belgium." In addition, Kiwele collected and wrote down many traditional songs of Shaba ethnic groups, especially those of the Yeke people.

Joseph Kiwele's civic and political activities included membership on the council of the Centre Extra-Coutumier ("Council of the Non-Traditional Urban

Center") of Elisabethville and on the Centre d'Etudes des Probèlems Economiques et Sociaux ("Center for Research on Economic and Social Problems"). He was elected a member of the provincial assembly of Katanga at Baudouinville, and was one of the first Congolese dignitaries to visit Belgium. From July 1960 until his death, he served as Minister of Education and Culture for the state of Katanga, devoting himself to strengthening the Congo Official University. When, in July 1960, this institution became the State University of Elisabethville, he became president of its supreme council.

Joseph Kiwele suffered a cerebral vascular attack in November 1961, and died on November 15 of the same year. He was married and had ten children.

TSHIBANGU KABET MUSAS

BIBLIOGRAPHY: *L'Essor du Katanga,* November 16-20, 1961.

KOLA NGBANDI

Kola Ngbandi, or Great Ngbandi, (who may have flourished in the 17th century), was a renowned folk hero who today is viewed as the incarnation of the Ngbandi people who live along the Ubangi River between Mobayi Mbongo and Yakoma.

According to tradition, Kola Ngbandi is one of seven children of Bangalapumba, the mythical ancestor of all the Ngbandi, who flourished when they still lived in Darfur or Kordofan in the southern part of what is now the Sudan.

Allegedly, during the southwestern migrations of the Sudanese people who came to live in what is now northwestern Zaire in the 1600s, Kola Ngbandi and his brother Gboma settled at Mbongo, in the present zone of Mobayi Mbongo, after crossing the Ubangi River near the place where it joins the Bomou and Bili rivers.

Although Kola Ngbandi and his men distinguished themselves in a series of wars with other groups, they were unable to gain political hegemony, Nevertheless, Kola Ngbandi won the respect of many people from the area. Since that time, people have been proud to associate themselves with Kola Ngbandi by claiming him as their ancestor.

Thus, a group which in the beginning was small, grew considerably through the progressive assimilation of neighboring peoples. By the time the Europeans reached the Upper Mongala River area in 1886, the people who live in the present zone of Businga were called Ngbandi, and the name Mongwandi was given to the ruler of the polity founded at the confluence of the Mongala and the Ebola rivers where Businga is located.

From that time on, for historical, cultural, and linguistic reasons, the name Ngbandi has been extended to the other groups scattered below the northwest loop of the Ubangi River.

Although Kola Ngbandi was not the originator of the whole Ngbandi people as many Ngbandi believe, his name and personality are symbols of the unity linking people who have not lived under a single, centralized political authority.

MUMBANZA mwa BAWELE na
NYABAKOMBI ENSOBATO.

BIBLIOGRAPHY: H. Burssens, *Les peuplades de l'entre-Ubangi,* ("The Small Tribes of the Ubangi Region"), Tervuren, 1958; B. Tanghe, "Histoire générale des migrations des peuples de l'Ubangi," ("A General History of the Migrations of the Ubangi People"), *Congo,* III, 4, 1936, pp. 361-91; G. Van der Kerken, *L'Ethnie Mongo,* ("The Mongo Ethnic Group"), Brussels, 1944.

KOMBO KIBOKO

Kombo Kiboko (circa 1870-May 20, 1942), was one of three Pende rulers selected to participate in an ill-conceived rotating chiefship the colonial government designed to unify 13 small Pende groups living just west of Tshikapa in Kasai.

A member of the extended clan of Gavunji, Kombo Kiboko had governed the Pende chiefdom of Akwa Samba in Kasai. On February 28, 1939, district commissioner of Kasai, E. Vallaeys, appointed Kombo Kiboko together with the Akwa Muvumbi chief Kasangi and the Akwa Kisenzele chief Mbangu, to share the duties of chief of the entire sector of the Pende of Kasai, whose chief town was Kitangwa, located 70 km (35 mi) west of Tshikapa. This sector had been created in 1937 by regrouping all the 13 Pende chiefdoms of Kasai. The rotating triumviate was intended to unify them administratively.

This region by rotation was a source of great political tension among the diverse Pende groups of Kasai. Chiefs of the other families not included in the triumviate were openly very hostile to the three designated rulers, for the overlooked chiefs also wanted an opportunity to exercise the functions of chief of the sector.

When chief Kombo Kiboko died, on May 20, 1942, a vigorous competition for his post ensued. Then the colonial authorities intervened to guarantee order and calm in the sector. Finally the system of reigning by rotation was abolished, and on October 11, 1944, Mafuta Benjamin was named sole chief of the Pende of Kasai.

SIKITELE GIZE a SUMBULA

BIBLIOGRAPHY: Archives of the Tshikapa Zone, Political File of the Bapende Sector.

LANKWAN, A.

Abbé Adolphe Lankwan (1926-June 6, 1965), a highly esteemed Catholic priest in the Kwilu area, became involved with partisans of the Mulele (*q.v.*) rebellion which swept the region from 1963 to 1967. While it is not clear if he willingly supported the uprising, Lankwan's opposition to the excesses of Mulele's followers, cost the priest his life.

Of Mbuun ethnic origins, Lankwan was born at Impanga, 125 km (75 mi) east of Kikwit, to a family of six boys. Like Mulele, he entered the Jesuit Minor Seminary at Kinzambi, near Kikwit, but unlike Mulele, he successfully completed this preliminary cycle of studies. In 1946, he was admitted to the Major Seminary at Mayidi, 90 km (50 mi) south of modern Kinshasa, where he studied philosophy and theology. After the seminary, he returned to his home diocese, where he was ordained a priest on August 8, 1954 at Mwilambongo, 125 km (75 mi) east of Kikwit.

The young priest's many pastoral duties took him to different missions: Mwilambongo, Ipamu, Bethanie. In 1959, he was named superior of the Mission of Ngoso, 50 km (30 mi) northeast of Kikwit, a post he held until 1961.

In addition to his acknowledged pastoral qualifications, his superiors recognized his aptitude for public relations. Thus, as independence approached, Lankwan's bishop ordered him to make rounds in the heart of the diocese and explain to the Christians the implications of the changes the country was experiencing as independence approached. This tour was interpreted by some as political propaganda for the "Parti Solidaire Africain" ("Party of African Solidarity," or P.S.A.) a party based primarily in the Kwilu area.

When Pierre Mulele returned from China in 1963 to begin his revolutionary activities in Kwilu, Lankwan was serving at Ipamu, 130 km (80 mi) northeast of Kikwit, where he was headmaster of the Collège Saint Pierre (now the Institut Nto-bi), a school he had founded a year earlier. When panic started to sweep over Ipamu as Mulele's partisans advanced, the Abbé Lankwan remained calm, reassuring everyone, both African and European. Because his attitude was so reassuring, some have alleged he must have been in contact with Mulele well before the Mulelist attack on Ipamu in February 1964.

The violence of Mulele's bands forced everyone, including Lankwan, to evacuate the area. Although Lankwan sought refuge in Léopoldville (now Kinshasa), his absence from the diocese was short. One of the first to return to the Kwilu, Lankwan went to Idiofa, 90 km (50 mi) east of Kikwit, the headquarters of the diocese.

Around May 15, 1964 the Abbé Lankwan disappeared on the road between Idiofa and Ifwanzondo, a few kilometers to the south. Whether this was an abduction or a deliberate defection no one knows. In any case, Lankwan later resurfaced in Mulele's entourage where he was assigned, under surveillance, to technical tasks such as operating the radio receiver. Later, probably because of the revolutionaries' excesses which he witnessed, he maintained his distance from Mulele and tried to help students, seminarians, and young teachers to leave the zone controlled by the partisans.

When Lankwan's activities became known, he was condemned by the Mulelists and buried alive at Kifuza on June 6, 1965. It is not known, however, if Lankwan's execution had been ordered by Mulele.

In popular opinion, Lankwan is remembered as a priest, who unlike his colleagues, believed in the need for revolution and supported Mulele's action. In 1972, the Catholic Church honored Lankwan's memory by renaming the Collège Notre Dame of Idiofa—a school which prospered remarkably after the Mulele rebellion—the Collège Lankwan.

NDAYWEL è NZIEM

BIBLIOGRAPHY: Archives of the Archdiocese of Idiofa; B. Verhaegen, *Rébellions au Congo* ("Rebellions in the Congo"), Vol. I, Brussels, 1966.

LELEKA

Leleka (circa 1905-September 1975) was one of the greatest chiefs of the Giri river region in northwestern Zaire. For nearly 50 years, he efficiently attended to traditional administration, vigorously promoted road building, and actively worked for the economic development of his territory.

Chief Leleka was born in Bobolo, now Buburu, located 150 km (90 mi) north of Mbandaka on the banks of the Ubangi River. A member of the Liboko family responsible for the local river spirits at Bobolo, Leleka was identified with the power of these spirits.

Although the Congo Free State authorities had founded a state post at Bobolo in 1900, they abandoned the region around 1910. It was only in 1917 that the region of Bobolo was again visited by colonial authorities.

When the region was organized into a chiefdom in 1920, Leleka's oldest brother Mundjokola was appointed provisional chief and then invested as permanent chief in 1921. Very influential in this region of the Ubangi watershed, Mundjokola gained great respect as an impartial judge in resolving disputes. Mundjokola, however, was stricken by sleeping sickness which affected his mind and he opposed the orders of the Territorial Agent Frauquet, who was directing work on the Bobolo-Bomongo road. (Bomongo is located 40 km [25 mi] east of Bobolo.) Thus, the chief was banished to Lisala in 1925.

In 1927, when the authorities realized that Mundjokola's belligerence was a result of his illness, they lifted his sentence. After returning home, Chief Mundjokola died following a fit of madness at the end of 1927.

From the time of Mundjokola's banishment until his death, the chiefdom remained disorganized. When Mundjokola died, his brother, Leleka, was selected as provisional chief. Previously Leleka had worked as an overseer in the French Congo, and had also worked for the Dewagenière firm in Bobolo. As an overseer, he had received great respect from the men he directed. Leleka's new chiefdom included not only Bobolo, but also several downstream peoples: the Mangwa from near Mokolovesi, who were led by Mandongo, and the Lobala to the south, who were under the authority of Mangwaba of Bobeka.

After becoming provisional chief, Leleka showed himself a zealous and aggressive official. In 1929, the Administrator Vandevenne said of him:

> Leleka is young and energetic, He must be watched as he could give way, little by little, to abuses. His actions merit our attention. Leleka visably aspires to progress. For more than a year, he has administered the Chiefdom with authority. His investiture will recognize a de facto situation.

Leleka's official investiture took place in June 1929, and he continued to rule with intelligence and authority. For example, in the 1930s Leleka was able to reduce rising tensions between the Protestants and Catholics in Bobolo by assigning individual catechists to separate geographical territories. Leleka also organized forced labor by entrusting specific tasks to designated groups. Thus, the people on the Ubangi River banks were expected to cut wood for use as fuel on the boats, the Mangwa were required to supply palm oil and nuts to the commercial companies established in the region, and all groups were obligated to help maintain the roads and trails.

In 1940, when all the ethnic groups in the territory around Nouvelle-Anvers, now Mankanza, 200 km (120 mi) north of Mbandaka, were organized into sectors, Leleka became chief of the sector of the Djamba, regrouping the chiefdoms of Buburu, Makutu, Bosira, Bonsambi and Sikoro. He then left Bobolo, his home village, to establish himself at Bonsambi, the sector's capital. Working with the same competence as before, Leleka's tenacity and high standards were especially appreciated.

In 1950, the territory of Nouvelle-Anvers became the territory of Bomongo, with Bomongo on the Ngiri River as its capital. Since Bomongo was chosen as the seat of government, it was necessary to improve the road from Bobolo. This was to enable carts to carry the region's produce to the Ubangi River, especially during the dry season when water traffic on the Giri was impossible. Leleka and his men set to work on the 40 km (25 mi) road, which followed an old track, crossing about 25 kilometers of swampland. The road was open to traffic by December 1950, although it was not finally completed until 1956.

Just as this work was completed, Leleka began work on the 1956 government project to build permanent dispensaries and primary schools at Bonsambi and Bobolo.

When the sectors of Djamba and Lobala-Likoka were merged in 1957 to form the chiefdom of Djamba, Leleka was placed in charge of this new and larger administrative entity. From his headquarters at Bobolo, he was responsible for attending to all the peoples of the Ubangi-Giri region. Among his accomplishments was completing the Mokame-Bokondo road, already started in 1954. In recognition for his work as chief, Leleka was chosen as a member of the Congolese delegation to the 1958 International Exposition held in Brussels, Belgium.

In 1961, however, after independence in the Congo, Leleka lost his position to a young man named Manyaka who had been elected by a newly formed standing council. Leleka left the chiefdom in a strong financial position with assets including cash deposits of one million Congolese francs and many head of cattle. While the retired Leleka devoted himself to fishing and farming, the chiefdom deteriorated markedly and the treasury was drained.

Finally, in order to rectify the situation, Leleka was asked to assume his old post. By this time, the chiefdom was divided by rivalry between the Lobala-Lukoka and the Djamba peoples, and the African population was no longer willing to comply with government directives ordering them to work on public projects. Leleka, too, was older and less forceful, so his efforts to restore the area to its former order and prosperity failed. Nevertheless, Leleka remained in office until 1973. Two years later, in September 1975, he died of a heart attack. Regrettably, this man who had served his nation in so many ways, did not benefit from his work. Leleka died in poverty for, after his retirement, he and his wives and children were left to take care of themselves.

MUMBANZA mwa BAWELE na
NYABAKOMBI ENSOBATO

BIBLIOGRAPHY: Registers of Political Information for the Territories of Bomana (1916-1931), and Nouvelle-Anvers (1939-1958), Archives of the Bomongo zone; Report of Inquiry on the Bubura

Chiefdom, February 27, 1923, Archives of the Bomongo Zone (File for the Buburu Group); verbal information received at Bobolo on October 9, 1973, from Leleka himself; verbal testimony of the citizen Ebebele, former Catholic catechist of Bobolo in 1933, obtained at Botaba in November, 1973.

LONGANGI

Longangi (circa 1860-July 14, 1964) was a forceful and ambitious individual elevated by the colonial government to serve as chief over the politically decentralized Lega people of eastern Kivu. As an agent of the colonial administration, Longangi worked to promote the interests of Europeans in government, companies, and missions. Frequently, this cooperation brought Longangi into conflict with individuals and institutions in Lega traditional society.

Longangi was born in Lega lands about 80 km (50 mi) southwest of Lake Kivu, an area influenced by Swahili traders who had come into nearby regions from East Africa by 1869. Although little is known about his mother Kuntebe, his father Mpaga Munyantangoy was one of the first Nyampara (assistants) of the Swahili merchant sultans seeking to conquer and control the territory. In his search for slaves and ivory, Mpaga Munyantangoy led African soldiers against Kivu villages. When Mpaga was killed by his own men during one of these raids, his employer Musekula, or Musareka, adopted the young Longangi as his own son.

Longangi's adoption into the family of the Swahili adventurer marked the beginning of a long career in trade and politics. Through his contact with the Swahili, Longangi learned to handle a rifle. He also mastered the Swahili language, the future regional 'lingua franca.' At a time when few local Africans could speak Swahili, Longangi became an indispensible intermediary between the East African merchants and the local peoples.

When the Congo Free State established control over the area after 1900, colonial agents were eager to hire men like Longangi as interpreters. From interpreter-police auxiliary, Longangi advanced to a position as the European-appointed chief over the local African population. Since the traditional leaders fled the whites out of fear, by default they allowed Longangi to act as their intermediary with the Europeans.

Despite his humble origins, and despite grumblings from other Lega, Longangi gained increasing political control. In 1924 he was named head of a newly created Basile chiefdom encompassing several Lega clans in the present Mwenga Zone in Kivu. (Mwenga is about 70 km or 40 mi southwest of Bukavu). In 1928, Longangi consolidated his power by ousting Kalenga

Kitoga, a legitimate descendant of Sile, as ruler of Basile (people tracing descent from Sile). Longangi also took over the Wamuzimu chiefdom, although his position as head of the Wamuzimu clans was never accepted as legitimate by the people themselves.

Invested in 1931, as chief of the great Wamuzimu chiefdom established by the colonial administration, Longangi strengthened his authority by installing his own men as village notables or headmen. In villages where the incumbent leaders were hostile, he simply relieved them of their duties and, sometimes, had them banished. Thus, Kalenga Kitoga, the original chief of the Basile, was banished to Rutshuru, 60 km (35 mi) northeast of Goma, in 1922. His son and successor, Kalenga Kyalumba, was then invested as a notable of the Wamuzimu chiefdom, but the antagonism between the two families continued until 1960, when the chiefdom was divided. The southern part, headed by Longangi, kept the name Wamuzimu, while the north, which took the former name Basile, was given to Kalenga Kitonga's grandson, Kalenga Lwango.

For many years Longangi acted as the only representative of the Lega populations of the Wamuzimu chiefdom in dealing with the European administrators, company agents, missionaries, and colonists. All the territorial agents' inspection reports on the Wamuzimu chiefdom contained praise for Longangi. In 1952, the district commissioner of Kivu wrote that Longangi was "the best chief of the Mwenga territory …a man who had done great services during his long career." In 1957, another official described Longangi as "very loyal and devoted to the European cause."

Covering more than 6,225 square kilometers, with a total population of 46,081 in 1953, Longangi's chiefdom was large and wealthy. The southern branch of the Compagnie Minière des Grands Lacs (Great Lakes Mining Company, or M.G.L.), which had mined gold in Wamuzimu since 1932, annually employed about ten thousand men, many from Longangi's territory. Furthermore, the chiefdom was the supply center both for the workers' camps and the city of Bukavu on Lake Kivu, which required large quantities of rice, palm oil, peanuts (ground nuts), bananas, and manioc (cassava).

During the colonial period, Longangi's power increased. Accompanied by an imposing train of guards and porters, he annually crossed his vast chiefdom in a litter. In later years he traveled by automobile. Longangi held palavers, requisitioned supplies and porters, recruited laborers, raised contingents of militiamen, relocated farmers to the areas around the mining camps, and acted vigorously to help the colonists maintain order on the plantations and missions.

A powerful man, Longangi could rely on support from the colonial administration and police. A wealthy man, Longangi was the only African in the territory who owned a vehicle. He was easily able to make up, from his own funds, a deficit of 60,000 francs in the chiefdom's treasury. His wealth was measured in more than money, for in the tradition of a great Swahili ruler, he had an imposing court with a harem which included more than 30 wives, who bore him more than 100 children.

Despite Longangi's great influence, primary power in the Lega lands and in the Wamuzimu chiefdom remained in the hands of the semi-secret Bwami society. Traditionally, social, economic, religious, and moral authority among the politically decentralized Lega was exercised by the Bwami. Lega individuals achieved membership in the Bwami only after a rigorous training period which culminated in an elaborate initiation ceremony. From the Lega perspective, this practice guaranteed that those in authority were persons of exceptional intellectual and moral aptitude. The Bwami, therefore resented Longangi, whom they regarded as a colonial auxiliary who held power by force and coercion rather than by merit and cultural achievement.

Although from the 1920s, the Belgian administration outlawed the Bwami association, neither Longangi, nor any other European appointed chiefs, could ignore or diminish Bwami influence. The Bwami caused difficulties for Longangi. Some Bwami-linked families, notably that of Kalenga, challenged his rule. In seeking to diminish Bwami influence, Longangi cooperated with the missionaries in opposing traditional religion, punishing Bwami dignitaries, forbidding initiation into the Bwami, and returning runaway students to mission schools seeking to re-educate the Lega.

Besides the Bwami, Longangi confronted other religious sects, such as the Mulonge, Punga, and Kinzenze, which appeared just after World War II. Adherents of these sects ignored government authority, escaped from prisons, broke work contracts, resisted taxes, and refused to work as porters. By severely punishing the leaders and followers of these various sects, Longangi and the Belgians made it difficult for them to gain a foothold in Lega lands. Another reason for their obvious lack of success in the region was the stablizing presence of the Bwami society. Thus, novel religious movements had little appeal for the Lega.

Old age finally weakened the powerful chief Longangi. If, in the 1950s Longangi still reigned over the Wamuzimu chiefdom, he no longer governed it. In 1952, the colonial administrators began searching seriously for a successor. Although Longangi's son Diemba, a former driver for the Société de Transport de l'Administration (Administration Transport Company, or S.T.A.), became his assistant, Diemba had neither the stature nor the authority of his father. Thus, on April 10, 1960 the colonial government de-

cided to divide the Wamuzimu chiefdom into two smaller units, a Basile chiefdom and a more restricted Wamuzimu chiefdom. Powerless, Longangi witnessed first the disintegration of his empire and then, after June 30, 1960, the sudden and forced departure of his former supporters, the Belgians. Turning over the real exercise of power to his son, Longangi withdrew to his court where he lived with his old servants.

In 1964 separate anti-government rebellions broke out in Kasai's Kwilu province and in the eastern regions of the Congo. The Kwilu uprising was led by Pierre Mulele (q.v.) while the eastern insurrection was initiated by the Conseil National de Liberation (National Liberation Council), a group composed of former followers of Patrice Lumumba (q.v.). Although the two movements were not linked by a common organization or command, the eastern rebels had tremendous respect for Mulele who, they believed, dispensed magical powers making warriors invincible.

On the morning of June 22, 1964, partisans began an attack on Longangi's court, Kitutu, 120 km (70 mi) southwest of Bukavu. Although Longangi organized the defense of Kitutu, the advancing rebels, who shouted "Mayi Mulele" ("Mulele water," a special water thought to give them magical powers), could not be halted. Thus, Longangi, with all his family, fled to Bukavu. This hasty flight, along with the remorse Longangi must have felt from abandoning his endangered troops, led to the 100-year-old chief's death in a Bukavu hospital on July 14, 1964.

Drawing a lesson for the troubled times after 1960, Longangi advised union and cooperation. "To be strong my sons," he said, "gather yourselves around a single authority. With too many chiefs, you will fight among yourselves and be weak." Longangi's counsel reflected his life's work of attempting to bring previously decentralized peoples under a single, Western-supported government structure.

YOGOLELO TAMBWE ya KASIMBA

BIBLIOGRAPHY: D. Biebuyck, *Lega Culture, Art, Initiation, and Moral Philosophy Among a Central African People,* Berkeley, 1973; C. Delhaise, *Les Warega,* Brussels, 1909; *Rapports Economiques* ("Economic Reports"), 1942-1957, Kivu Province; B. Verhaegen, *Rébellions au Congo* ("Rebellions in the Congo"), Brussels and Kinshasa, Vol. II, 1969.

LUKENI

According to tradition Lukeni (who flourished in the late 13th century) founded the Kongo kingdom. The sources, however, are not unanimous, for some claim it was Lukeni lua Nimi, Ntinu Lukeni, or Ntinu Wene who began the Kongo polity.

Lukeni is said to have been the son of Nimi a Nzinga, who originated the Vungu kingdom, in present Mayombe, north of Boma. Traditions vary in explaining why Lukeni migrated to the south. Following one version, Lukeni fled after stabbing his aunt in the stomach when she refused to pay him tribute. In another story, Lukeni is said to have promised his mother that he would become a Mani (ruler) to avenge an insult from a boatman. And, according to yet a third account, Lukeni, who was the youngest son in a large family, wanted to find a new land where he too could reign.

After crossing the Zaire River with his followers, Lukeni subjugated the Mpemba Kazi region, extended his rule eastward, and named his newly conquered possessions, (located north of modern Mbanza-Ngungu), Nsundi. His maternal uncle went to conquer the Mbatas, who lived where the Inkisi River intersects the present Zaire-Angola border. Once the country south of the Zaire River had been subjugated, Lukeni distributed the conquered territories among his captains as gifts. He settled on a hill called Nkumba a Ngundi, which later became Mbanza Kongo, and then San Salvador. This place is located in Angola about 100 km (60 mi) southeast of Matadi.

Thus Lukeni founded one of the greatest kingdoms of Central Africa, a kingdom which European navigators of the 15th century admired. He was able to impose one culture over a vast territory extending west to east from the Atlantic Ocean to the Kwango River, and north to south from Ngoyo, Kakongo, and Loango, north of the Zaire River, to the Kwanza River in modern Angola.

TSIMBA MABIALA

BIBLIOGRAPHY: G. Balandier, *La vie quotidienne au royaume du Kongo du XVIème au XVIIIème siècle*, Paris, 1965, English translation by Helen Weaver published as *Daily Life in the Kingdom of the Kongo*, New York, 1968; *Biographe Coloniale Belge* ("Belgian Colonial Biography"), Brussels, Vol. II, 1951, col. 975; J. Cuvelier, *L'ancien royaume du Congo* ("The Ancient Kingdom of the Congo"), Brussels, 1946; B. Da Galio, (1700), in L. Jadin, "Le Congo et la secte des Antoniens, Restauration du royaume sous Pedro IV et la 'Saint Antoine' congolaise: 1694-1718," ("The Congo and the Antonine Sect, Restoration of the Realm Under Pedro IV and the Congolese 'Saint Anthony', 1694-1718"), *Bulletin de l'Institut Historique Belge de Rome*, XXXIII, 1961, p. 468-69; A. Doutrelous, *L'ombre des fetiches, société et culture yombe*, ("The Shadow of Fetishes, Yombe Society and Culture"), Louvain, Paris, 1969; W.B.L. Randles, *L'ancien royaume du Congo des origines a la fin du XIXème siècle* ("The Ancient Kingdom of Kongo from its Origins to the End of the 19th Century"), Paris, The Hague, 1968.

LUKWESA ILUNGA

Lukwesa Ilunga (circa 1740-October 1805) came to office as Kazembe (military governor) of the Luapula after Kanyimbu Newej Mpemb (*q.v.*) died in about 1760. While Kanyimba had introduced Lunda control east of the Luapula River (today the southeastern border of Zaire), Lukwesa further extended Lunda rule by political and military means. He established a commercial link with the eastern coast of Africa, allowing the Lunda empire to trade with maritime states.

In about 1750, to avoid a repetition of succession wars for the title of Kazembe, the Lunda Mwant Yav (ruler) at Musumba designated the ten-year-old Lukwesa Ilunga as the next Kazembe. Lukwesa was the oldest son of Idim Kaumb, Kazembe Kanyimbu's brother. When Kanyimbu died, however, Lukwesa's accession was not automatic for he had to dispose of a rival, his uncle Chitend. Once invested as Kazembe, Lukwesa established his capital at Chungu on Lake Mweru, and forthwith began the wars of conquest expected of a new chief. At the head of a large army, whose leaders and Lunda warriors carried small quantities of firearms, Lukwesa enlarged his territory east of Lake Mweru. Returning to Chungu with considerable plunder in captives, ivory and other products, he subdued the Tabwa and the Barungu. He remained at Chungu only a short time, leaving almost immediately to attack the Mambwe people south of Lake Tanganyika. Before departing for war against the Mambwe, he had named his maternal uncle, Chibamb Kasokot, as governor of Chungu with orders to capture alive the Shila chief, Katele, who was hiding in the swamp. (*See* the article on Kanyimbu Newej Mpemb). After an initial fruitless attempt, Chibamb Kasokot succeeded in capturing and killing Katele. In transgressing the Kazembe's order to keep Katele alive, Chibamb had usurped a prerogative reserved to the Kazembe alone, the right to execute another chief. Thus, on his return from Mambwe and Tabwa, where his wife had given him a son, Chibang Chelek Muswa Musapu, surnamed Mai or Mwana-Wut, (meaning son of the rifle), Lukwesa had Chibamb's ears cut off. To escape the anger of the Shila ancestors, who might punish the Lunda for Chibamb's act, the Kazembe moved his capital about 20 km (12 mi) south of Lake Mweru, to Kantapala on the Mofwe lagoon.

Soon after, the Kazembe received the sister of Kawama wa Luemba, the Nkuba or supreme chief of the Shila. This woman, Na-Kituti, had come to ask the Kazembe to punish the Nkuba who had killed her son after an angry exchange of words between the two men. The Kazembe took advantage of her request to put an end to the guerilla activities of the Shila, who, at the Nkuba's instigation, had burned Lunda villages and kidnapped their women. The Kazembe gathered an army under the command of Kalandala, the Lunda governor-commander nearest to the territory of the Nkuba. Kalandala took the Nkuba's capital, Kisenga, discovered the Nkuba's hideout, killed the Shila chief together with his brother Mulumbwa, and brought the enemies' heads back to the Kazembe as trophies. Satisfied, Na-Kituti gave the Kazembe a small basket containing earth and a small vase of water, symbolizing Shila ritual power over the land. Her gift made the Lunda legitimate possessors of the Shila lands where the capital of the Kazembe was located. Thus, Lukwesa conquered the entire countryside around Lake Mweru. This was his last and most important military conquest.

His military expeditions over, Lukwesa Ilunga set out to organize and consolidate not only his conquests, but also those of his predecessors Mutand Yembiyemb (q.v.), Ngand a Bilond (q.v.), and Kanyimbu Newej, into a coherent political system.

To administer his vast kingdom, the Kazembe Lukwesa placed loyal Lunda chiefs in charge of the new provinces. Local non-Lunda chiefs also received Lunda titles and were incorporated with their subjects into the Lunda system. For example, Kalandala and his brother Sa-Ntambw were sent to Kisenga as governors of the Shila while their deputy, Kashing, went to govern the island of Kilwa in Lake Mweru, where he subdued chief Kaponto, and killed chief Mukamba who resisted. Musand, dispatched to reign over the west bank of Lake Mweru, conquered the territories of the Shila chiefs Kambala, Kyana, and Mulenga. Chipep (Kipepa), sent to Pweto at the northern end of Lake Mweru to subdue and govern the Aanza, the northern Shila, and several minor groups of Luba-Hemba, brought these peoples under his authority and established his headquarters at Lunkinda. Kaswup (Kasump) went to the Kalunguishi River about 100 km (60 mi) east of Lake Mweru, where he governed the Tabwa of the Mununga lands and the groups which had been subject to them. Mwilu, placed in charge of the region northeast of Lake Bangweolu, lived at Lwena-lwa-Ntipa and governed the following Bena-Mbeba groups: the Kabanda-Kalibu, Kapema, Ntenke, Kabila-wa-Katafu, Munkanta, Mwana-Katenda and Kitondo.

Three chiefdoms of the upper Luapula river area in Lubunda lands, became provinces headed by representatives. Muland governed the northern Aushi west of the upper Luapula, while Matand, son of Kashib, ruled the southern Aushi.

Kazembe Lukwesa's dignitary, Mwin Pand (a title meaning "Man of the Crossroads"), received the immense Bemba province north and west of Lake Bangweolu. He controlled the chiefdom of the supreme chief of the Bemba which included the Chishinga and the Bisa of Kinyimbe, Kipiko, and Kilando near the Chambezi River.

The Lungu and the two other Tabura groups, who voluntarily paid regular tribute to the Kazembe were allowed to retain their former chief, who were accepted into the Lunda aristocracy as 'perpetual' relatives of the Lunda.

Except for the territories of Musokantanda, between modern Kolwezi and Likasi, the present mining area of Upper Shaba was divided into two provinces. The eastern province, including a large area to the west of the Luapula River, was assigned to Kashib, who lived at Kalundwa, near the Lofoi Falls, about 160 km (100 mi) north of modern Lubumbashi. Kashib governed the Lomotwa and the Lembwe and had authority over the chiefs Ntondo, Kyaba, Sampwe Mwanshya, Katonda, Kimungu, and Mukebu.

The western province remained under the authority of Chiseng, who had proclaimed himself the Kazembe of the Lualaba and who governed the lands between the Lubudi and the Dikulwe rivers. Chiseng's aggressiveness, a trait also manifest in his successors, drew the suspicion of both the Mwant Yav and of the Kazembe of the Luapula. This distrust explains why the Lunda, both of the east and the west, much later refused to aid Kazembe of the Lualaba when the Yeke of Misiri Ngelengwa (q.v.) began to infiltrate the region after 1850.

All the provincial governors regularly sent tribute to the Kazembe of the Luapula, who in turn sent gifts to the Mwant Yav. The Kanongish, Nshind, Musokantanda, Chinyama, Kiamfu of the Kwango, and Mai-Munene chiefs did the same. The tribute the Kazembe of the Luapula received came to him in the form of ivory, salt, copper from Katanga, shells from Lake Tanganyika, wrought iron, livestock, game, and fish.

In keeping with the warrior tradition of former Kazembes, Lukwesa maintained a considerable number of well-disciplined troops, while a well-organized and omnipresent intelligence service daily brought him news from all the corners of his kingdom. This messenger corps, in turn, transmitted his orders and made certain his decisions were carried to every part of the land. For his own security, Kazembe Lukwesa maintained numerous guard-houses and patrols.

The fame of Lukwesa's Lunda kingdom reached the eastern coast of Africa, where it came to the attention of the Portuguese of Mozambique. Around 1790, Lukwesa learned the Portuguese were present at Tete on the Zambezi River. He was then successful in establishing commercial ties with them. In 1796, a mulatto named Manuel Gaetano Pereira came to Kazembe's capital in search of ivory. On his return to Mozambique, he informed Dr. Francisco José de Lacerda e Almeida, governor of the Sena Province at Tete, of the Kazembe's willingness to establish commercial relations with Tete. Pereira further suggested that Lacerda seize this opportunity to open a commercial route towards Angola.

With these two goals in mind, Lacerda organized an expedition of 50 armed men, including 18 Portuguese, and 40 porters. Directed by Lacerda himself, the group had not reached the Kazembe's capital when, on October 2, 1798, Lacerda died and was buried not far from the royal cemetery.

The expedition's chaplain, Fr. Francisco Joao Pinto, led the men on to the court of the Kazembe. Lukwesa graciously received these "children born in the water." The Portuguese, however, disappointed the Kazembe, who alternated between showing them friendship and reproach. Pinto, was unable to impose discipline on his troops, who violated the laws of hospitality, committed murder, and abused the wives of Lunda notables. These actions influenced Kazembe's decision to forbid the expedition to cross the Lunda lands and journey to Musumba, Cassange, and eventually Luanda on the Atlantic coast. Lukwesa explained his decision by citing extreme dangers, such as war, famine, and death, which faced travelers. He also noted that the Lacerda himself had died on the voyage.

In reality, Kazembe Lukwesa turned Pinto back because he wanted to maintain the trade monopoly with Tete, and because he considered Lacerda's successor as a man without political power or authority. He understood, no doubt, the adventurous and frivolous character of the Pinto expedition, which eight months later returned empty-handed to Sena, leaving two of their members to wait for the Kazembe's eventual authorization to proceed to Tete.

Once the countryside was organized under his administration, Lukwesa became not only the principal political chief of the region between the Lualaba River and Lake Nyasa, but also the head of the principal trading power in east Central Africa. His capital, Montapala, became a regular starting point for the three trade networks: Cassange-Musumba-Mantapala; Mantapala-Lake Nyasa-Kilwa; Mantapala-Tete. Thus Lukwesa became extremely wealthy. Pinto described him as follows:

> Kazembe Ilunga-Lukwesa had become, by the fact of his resounding conquests, of his incredible organization, and of his prodigious trade, an African potentate of an unequalled power and unparalleled renown. His court had the splendor of the court of a monarch. The king was in the habit of sitting on his throne, dressed in his clothes of black silk bordered in red or in green. He had a crown on his head, made of red feathers and covered with shells and brilliant prisms. His legs and arms were covered with pearls of diverse colors interlaced with rare shells. On his throne five leopard skins were laid out in the form of a star. Not far from

his throne were placed on supports different sculptures representing figurines. Around the king stood his ministers, messengers, counselors, the ladies of his court, and his pages; troops of armed soldiers stood in rows.

> The parvis of the court was of extraordinary cleanliness; pages weeded without cease the least shoots of grass. Young girls kept up a brazier of burning coals in front of the throne: throwing on it some dried aromatic grasses from which came a light and perfumed smoke.

The Kazembe Ilunga Lukwesa died in October 1805. He was buried in the royal cemetery. His son Chibang Chelek, 27 years of age, succeeded him under the name Kazembe IV Chibang Kanyimbu.

TSHIBANGU KABET MUSAS

BIBLIOGRAPHY: Edward A. Alpers, *Ivory and Slaves in East Central Africa*, Berkeley, 1975; R.F. Burton, *The Lands of Cazembe*, London, 1873; Ian Cunnison, "Kazembe and the Portuguese, 1798-1832," *Journal of African History* II, 1, 1961, pp. 61-76; Francisco José de Lacerda e Almeida, *Travessia de Africa* ("The Crossing of Africa"), Lisbon, 1936; Antonio Candido Pedroso Gamitto, *King Kazembe and the Marve, Cheva, Bisa, Bemba, Lunda, and other peoples of Southern Africa being the Diary of the Portuguese Expedition to the Potentate in the Years 1831 and 1832*, translated by I. Cunnison, Lisbon, 1962; E. Labrecque, "Histoire des Mwata Kazembe" ("History of the Mwata Kazembe"), *Lovania*, XVII, 1950, pp. 34-48; J. Vansina, *Les anciens royaumes de la savane*, Léopoldville, 1965, published in English as *Kingdoms of the Savanna*, Madison, 1966.

LUMPUNGU

Lumpungu (circa 1860-May 22, 1919), also known as Goi Mafula, and later as Chief Muikalebwe was an important Songye chief in what is now Kabinda in the Kasai Region. Ruling at a time when both the Swahili Arabs and the Congo Free State authorities were penetrating into the area, Lumpungu attempted to cooperate with the powerful outsiders without losing his own authority over the Songye.

Born in Makonde village near Kabinda in Kasai, Lumpungu belonged to the Bena Mabala family of the Bekalebwe segment of the Songye ethnic group. His father Ngoyi Kaumbu, or Yankaumbu, a village elder and a hunter, was able to purchase the Bena Mabala military title of "Kembe." To prove himself worthy of the title, Ngoyi Kaumbu successfully fought the formidable Bala warriors who had been terrorizing the region.

Lumpungu standing between two of his officials.

Around 1865, two Bekalebwe groups, the Bena Tshofwe and the Bena Lukashiyi, began a violent quarrel. After experiencing repeated defeats, the Bena Lukashiyi persuaded "Kembe" Ngoyi to help them. Ngoyi, however, also suffered a series of losses. Learning that Mahomed, an Arabized man serving the great Swahili slave trader Tippu-Tib, was among the Belande, Ngoyi solicited Mahomed's aid and was able to beat the Bena Tshofwe. This victory enhanced Ngoyi's reputation as a great Bekalebwe chief. Thus, he was able to pay the necessary gifts for becoming a Yakitenge (supreme Bekalebwe chief). Since Ngoyi died in 1880, however, shortly before his consecration, his younger brother Yamutombo Kaumbu was installed in his stead. When Yamutombo too died, Lumpungu, Ngoyi's fourth son, quickly took advantage of his uncle's death to gain control of the Bekalebwe people. By 1882, when the German explorer Herman von Wissmann was passing through the region on his way across the continent, the majority of the Bekalebwe had already recognized Lumpungu as their chief.

Soon after 1880, Swahili slave raids west of the Lomami River threatened the Bekalebwe people. Too weak to resist, in 1882 they decided to buy security with a heavy ransom. Lumpungu was the one who collected the ransom and took it to the residence of the Swahili merchant Fwamba. Then Lumpungu led his men to the Bemeki Kasongo, where there were great quantities of ivory.

Lumpungu's contact with the Arabized forces led him to believe his people had no alternative except to collaborate with the Swahili forces. Therefore, he became their ally and vassal. As, however, he accompanied and guided the slave traders in their raids, he directed them away from his own people or away from those who had purchased his protection. Although he was forced to give the greater part of the booty to his allies, Lumpungu was able to multiply his own wealth and power. With help from the Swahili traders, Lumpungu had become the uncontested political chief of the otherwise decentralized Bekalebwe people by 1890. The Bena Milembwe, Bena Kibeshi, and Bena Kizubu were his vassals. Other neighboring chiefs, such as Panya Mutombo of the Basanga, Mwana Kankenza of the Beneki Babenga, Kayeye of the Bena Budia, and Katombe of the Bena Kalambayi, although nominally independent, paid for warriors for his expeditions.

Early in 1892, Ngongo Leteta (q.v.), a powerful Tetela chief (the Tetela lived north of Lumpungu), who represented the Arabs west of the Lomami, arrived at Kabinda to ask Lumpungu for help in a new slaving expedition among the Juba Kasai people living in the Lubilash river area. Previously, in 1890, Congo Free State troops had demonstrated their superiority over Ngongo by beating him in battle and by founding a State station at Lusambo, 200 km (120 mi) northwest of Kabinda on the Sankuru River. Unhappy with Ngongo Leteta's attempts to control him, Lumpungu refused to accompany the Tetela chief to the Lubilash. Besides, he was not anxious to enter into open conflict with the power which had just dealt Ngongo a severe blow. Nevertheless, in order not to offend Ngongo, Lumpungu gave him some warriors whom he had ordered to desert in the course of their march. Lumpungu was fortunate not to have been involved with Ngongo for Lt. (Baron) Dhanis inflicted painful defeats on Ngongo on April 23, and May 5, 1892. After this trial of forces both Ngongo Leteta and Lumpungu submitted to the Free State, which set up a station at Kabinda on October 4, 1892.

From that time on, Lumpungu, also known as Chief Muikalebwe, devotedly served his new masters, fighting with them against his former Arab masters in the battle of Chige on November 22, 1892. Later, in 1895, when Ngongo Leteta's former soldiers mutinied against the Free State in the Batetela revolt, Lumpungu again aided the State. After 1892, he took charge of rubber collection and supplied provisions and porters for the government. During the World War I campaign against the Germans in East Africa, Lumpungu provided thousands of porters for duty in Tanganyika.

Although he complied with all governmental demands, his main goal was preserving his interests and his authority over his subjects. He was careful to prevent Europeans from interfering in his relations with his sub-chiefs. He preferred to have the colonialists transmit orders through his own court rather than dealing directly with his subordinates. As best he could, Lumpungu resisted attempts to dismantle his vast chiefdom.

The tendency to regard himself as an independent ally did not please the Belgians. Although, at first, they allowed Lumpungu a great deal of freedom, thus using him to supplement their own thinly spread forces, as their occupation became effective, they restricted his authority. First, they granted independence to some sub chiefs and, second, made it clear to all that Lumpungu, as Chief Muikalebwe, was regarded merely as an agent of the State.

Yet when Lumpungu died on May 22, 1919 from a heart disease, his great domain remained almost completely unexplored by the European intruders.

MUTEBA KABEMBA NSUYA

BIBLIOGRAPHY: L. Mpoyi, *Historie wa Baluba* ("History of the Baluba"), Mbuji-Mayi, 1966; A. Samain, *Grammaire Kisonge* ("Kisonge Grammar"), Brussels, 1908; H. Seghaert, *Un terme au Congo Belge*, ("A Stint in the Belgian Congo"), Brussels, 1919; N.N. Tshikuakua, *Les conquêtes de Lumpungu* ("The Conquests of Lumpungu"), Kinshasa, 1974; J. Vansina, *Introduction à l'ethnographie du Congo*, ("Introduction to the Ethnography of the Congo"), Brussels, 1965; A. Van Zandijcke, *Pages d'histoire du Kasai* ("Pages from Kasai History"), Paris, Namur, 1953; C. Wauters, *L'ésotérisme des Noirs dévoilée* ("The Esoterism of the Blacks Revealed"), Brussels, 1949.

LUMUMBA, P.E.

Patrice Emery Lumumba (July 2, 1925-January 17, 1961), served as prime minister of the Congo during the tumultuous first months after independence on June 30, 1960. An ardent Congolese nationalist, he sought to preserve the integrity of a nation threatened by ethnic conflict, regional fragmentation, labor unrest, bureaucratic collapse, military mutinies, and international interference. Although these difficulties proved insurmountable, enabling his enemies to arrest and assassinate the prime minister, Lumumba is now revered as a heroic martyr who suffered and died for his country.

Born at Onalua village, 300 km (180 mi) northeast of Luluabourg (now Kananga) in the Katoko-Kombe territory of Kasai, Lumumba was of Tetela ethnic origins. After completing his primary education at a Catholic mission, in the early 1950s he became a postal clerk first in Yangambi, 80 km (50 mi) west-northwest of Stanleyville (now Kisangani) in Orientale province, and then in Stanleyville.

Settling in Stanleyville, Lumumba entered the ranks of the évolués (educated and Westernized) class of Africans. An insatiable reader, he continued his education by teaching himself a wide range of subjects including law, economics, and philosophy. Lumumba sought and received immatriculation, a legal status giving him many rights otherwise reserved for Europeans. At that time, his political views were those of a moderate, as is evident from his book *Congo My Country* which he wrote during 1956-57, and which was published posthumously; he admired the achievements of the whites whom he tried to emulate. Nevertheless, he was deeply aware that Europeans rarely regarded Africans as their equals.

He read avidly during this period, and was the dominant personality among the Africans in Stanleyville. He was a correspondent of several newspapers, including *La Croix du Congo,* and *La Voix du Congolais.*

Lumumba showed great energy and organizational skill in numerous Stanleyville cultural, educational, and professional groups. In 1955, he became president of the provincial Association du Personnel Indigène (Association of Native Personnel, A.P.I.C.), president of a section of the Association des Anciens Elèves des Pères de Scheut (Association of Former Students of the Scheut Fathers, A.D.A.P.E.S.), and president of a Tetela ethnic group the Mutuelle des Tetela (Tetela Mutual). When Belgium's King Baudouin made his first visit to the Congo in December 1955, Lumumba gained an audience with the monarch in Stanleyville. In 1956, as secretary of the Amicale des Postiers Indigènes (Native Postal Workers Brotherhood), or A.P.I.C., for Orientale, Lumumba was elected president of A.P.I.C. for the entire Orientale province. He also became president of the Stanleyville Cercle des Evolués (Evolué Club), and president of the Belgo-Congolese cultural group. Also in 1956, Lumumba was chosen as a member of a Congolese delegation taken on a visit to Belgium.

Lumumba, however, had difficulty in Stanleyville when, on July 1, 1956, he was arrested and charged with misappropriating about $2,500 from the post office where he worked. Although Lumumba was judged guilty and given a prison sentence, he maintained his innocence and the local évolué community raised enough money to repay the entire sum and to provide for Lumumba's family during the time he spent in jail. His two-year sentence was eventually reduced to 11 months.

In 1957, Lumumba moved to Léopoldville (now Kinshasa) where he worked as a salesman for the large Bracongo brewery which bottled Polar beer. Energetic and creative, Lumumba organized local Polar Clubs which sprang up all over the city. By August 1958 he had risen to become sales manager for the entire brewery.

Although Lumumba was immensely successful as an advertising agent, rapid changes in the Congo allowed him to use his organizational and promotional abilities in politics, an area just opening to Congolese. After having restructured urban areas to allow limited African participation in municipal affairs, the Belgian government held elections in December 1957 in Léopoldville's African communes. Next, in July 1958, a Working Group of prominent Belgians was selected to examine political developments in the Congo and to make recommendations for the future.

The Working Group was due to arrive in Léopoldville in late October of 1958. Anticipating that event, on October 10, a group of leading Africans, including Patrice Lumumba, Cyrille Adoula, Joseph Ileo, Arthur Pinzi, Gaston Diomi, Joseph Ngalula, and Alphonse Nguvulu, addressed a petition to the Minister of the Congo, Léon Pétillon. The petition criticized the fact that no Congolese had been appointed to the Working Group, called for immediate political reforms, and proposed a step-by-step plan for independence. Although the petitioners came from numerous political and ethnic groups, they presented themselves as the Mouvement National Congolais (M.N.C.). This marked the first official act of the multi-ethnic M.N.C. political party. Originally, the M.N.C. had been intended as a temporary committee speaking only to the issue of the Working Group, but Lumumba succeeded in transforming the M.N.C. into a true political party with himself as president.

Other major events in 1958 had a profound impact on Congolese affairs. On August 24, in Brazzaville across the river from Léopoldville, General Charles de Gaulle offered complete independence for all territories under French rule. De Gaulle's speech had tremendous appeal among the Congolese who began to think in terms of independence for themselves. Also, in 1958, several hundred Congolese from all over the colony traveled to the International Exposition in Brussels. There, for the first time, they shared their views on the colonial situation. This European experience did much to develop among the Congolese, a more militant sensitivity to the problems they faced.

For Lumumba, however, the highpoint of 1958 came at the Pan-African People's Conference held in Accra, Ghana, from December 5 to 13. Along with Gaston Diomi and Joseph Ngalula, Lumumba attended the meeting where he met Kwame Nkrumah of Ghana Sékou Touré of Guinea, and Houphouet-Boigny of the Ivory Coast. Lumumba's friendship with Nkrumah began at this time, and he became a convinced pan-Africanist. On December 11, Lumumba gave a speech in which he appealed to the Universal Declaration of the Rights of Man and to the United Nations Charter as indictments of colonialism. Noting the injustices of the past, he argued for an end to colonialism and called for a strong, united Congo. The work of colonialism he proclaimed, was almost finished and future relations with Europe would rest on cooperation instead of on domination. Lumumba concluded with the words, ''Down with imperialism. Down with colonialism. Down with racism and tribalism. Long live the Congolese nation. Long live independent Africa.'' This conference marked the beginning of a close personal relationship between Nkrumah and Lumumba, who was elected to serve as a member of the Pan-African permanent council. Back in Léopoldville on December 28, Lumumba addressed a popular meeting attended by 7,000 people. There he boldly announced: ''Independence is not a gift from Belgium, but a fundamental right of the Congolese people.''

On January 4, 1959, riots broke out in the capital. Although caused by unemployment and urban discontent, the disturbances were blamed on the Abako party of Joseph Kasa-Vubu (*q.v.*). Kasa-Vubu, along with Jean Bolikango, was arrested and sent to Belgium in an effort to avoid further tensions. Partially in response to the riots, and partially as a result of the Working Group's work, on January 13, 1959, both the Belgian government and King Baudouin made declarations about the Congo's future. These statements promised independence in the not-too-distant future and envisioned a democratic Congolese interim government to implement independence. Following January 13, the colonial powers began allowing more African participation in local and colony-wide affairs.

Fluent in Lingala, French, and Swahili, Lumumba emerged in 1959 as one of the most dynamic and effective Congolese political organizers and orators. In early March, he traveled to Ibadan, Nigeria, to participate in International Week. On March 31, the M.N.C. set up a permanent office in Léopoldville's Kinshasa commune. At that time, Lumumba declared the M.N.C. was in basic agreement with the Belgian government's January 13 statements, which he accepted as a starting point for further negotiations. In April, 1959, a general Congress of Congolese political parties was held in Luluabourg. Dominated by the M.N.C., the Congress set January 1, 1961 as the deadline for a provisional government. The Congress also passed motions calling for the Congo's geographical unity, for chiefs and ethnic groups to submit themselves to larger political parties, for democratic elections and universal suffrage, and for economic assistance to Congolese artisans, merchants, farmers, and middle classes.

Without waiting for the Congress to adjourn, Lumumba went to Guinea for a meeting of the Pan-African Congress permanent council. By late April, he was in Brussels seeking the support of Jean Bolikango and Joseph Kasa-Vubu for the M.N.C. At the same time, he continued to make strong pronouncements about imperialism and Western exploitation of Africa. Back in Léopoldville, the other M.N.C. leaders reaffirmed the January 1961 date for independence, but in Brussels on May 11, Lumumba demanded that a Congolese government be formed in 1959.

Lumumba's growing radicalism, independence, and prominence caused conflict with other M.N.C. leaders, especially Joseph Ileo. Ethnic differences also troubled the party, which sought to gain a nationwide constituency. At times the M.N.C. and Lumumba were cast as opponents of a prominent ethnic group simply because they gained support from that group's local rival. For example, the Luba people of Kasai mistrusted Lumumba because he tried to organize the majority Lulua population living around Luluabourg. As a result of these problems, on July 16, 1959, the M.N.C. central committee censured Lumumba for what they

labeled "personal politics." Also on July 16, Ileo instituted organizational reforms in the M.N.C. which conferred specific duties on other party leaders at Lumumba's expense. When Lumumba replied with counter-charges, a split developed within the M.N.C. The split grew into a firm schism with one wing of the party being known as the M.N.C./Lumumba, and the other wing being known as the M.N.C./Kalonji, after a Luba Kasai spokesman, Albert Kalonji. Although Lumumba and Kalonji continued to cooperate on certain issues, increasingly Kalonji was identified with the group of politicians who advocated federation along ethnic lines. Lumumba, on the other hand, continued to insist on a unitary government oblivious to ethnic differences. Federation, in his view, was simply a subterfuge for separatism and division. Despite their differences, however, Lumumba campaigned for the release of Kalonji when he was put under house arrest in 1959.

In the meantime, national elections were scheduled for December 1959. The purpose of the plebiscite was to choose Congolese people to sit on local and regional consultative councils which would assist European administrators in a slow transition towards independence. Lumumba's M.N.C., like Abako, mistrusted Belgian motives in holding these elections. On October 23-30, the M.N.C./Lumumba held a conference in Stanleyville, where the M.N.C. asked that the elections be postponed and that new talks be held between the Congolese and Belgians. After Lumumba spoke on the last day of the meeting, rioting broke out in Stanleyville and more than 20 Africans were killed. Lumumba was arrested for having incited the disorders and, on January 21, 1960, was sentenced to six months in jail. To completely remove Lumumba from politics, on January 22 the government secretly transferred him to Jadotville (now Likasi) in Katanga.

By the end of 1959, Belgian attempts to lead the Congo towards self-government seemed to have failed. Therefore, abandoning earlier schemes of implementing independence in gradual, imposed phases, the government arranged for a Round Table discussion in Brussels between Congolese and Belgian leaders to determine the colony's future. When the Congolese delegates refused to participate unless Lumumba were present, the M.N.C. leader was released from jail and flown to Belgium.

At the Round Table, lasting from January 20 to February 20, 1960, Belgium agreed to accelerate decolonization, which would be completed before July of the same year. Among the Congolese leaders, two opposing positions emerged concerning the nature of the future national constitution. The "federalists," among them Moise Tshombe (*q.v.*) and Kasa-Vubu, called for strong regional states tied together under a moderate national government. Lumumba and his allies, led by Gizenga of the Parti Solidaire Africain (P.S.A.) argued for a strongly unitary state. In general, the agreements reached at the Round Table favored the "unitarists." The Round Table further determined that, until independence, executive authority would be exercised by the governor general and a staff of six Congolese. Appointed to this executive college, Lumumba received the defense portfolio.

In April 1960, Lumumba visited Nkrumah in Accra, and returned home to announce that the Congo bore Belgium no ill will, but wanted justice and freedom. He also undertook to call a pan-African conference in Léopoldville in August 1960. Because of political difficulties in the Congo, however, the conference never materialized.

As independence drew near, the Belgian government dispatched additional armed forces to the Congo in order to ensure stability. Suspicious that the Belgians actually intended to use the troops for political purposes, on May 18 Lumumba called for an immediate withdrawal of metropolitan soldiers. When Belgium did not comply, Lumumba resigned from the executive college. Fearful of jeopardizing his own political position, however, he soon returned to the college.

On May 21 and 22 nationwide elections were held to choose representatives for provincial assemblies and for the national legislature in Léopoldville. The M.N.C. was handicapped in these elections because, in April, Victor Nendeka, the M.N.C. vice chairman, had broken away from the party, accusing Lumumba of excessive left-wing leanings. Nevertheless, the M.N.C. gained an overwhelming majority in the Orientale province assembly, acquired a position of strength in Kivu and Kasai provinces, and won 33 of 137 seats in the national House of Representatives. Lumumba, himself, was elected as a national deputy from Stanleyville.

Although the M.N.C. had won more seats than its nearest rivals the P.S.A. (13 seats) and Abako (12 seats), Lumumba had far fewer votes than he needed to win a solid base of parliamentary support for his candidacy as prime minister. When W.J. Ganshoff Van Der Meersch Belgian resident minister in the Congo from May to July 1960, first asked Lumumba to form a government, the M.N.C. leader sought to build a broad coalition. This effort failed after Tshombe's Conakat party withdrew from the negotiations. But when Van Der Meersch approached Joseph Kasa-Vubu, he found the Abako leader even less able to construct a government on the diffuse groups represented in the assembly. After a second attempt, Lumumba was able to form a government which was confirmed by parliament on June 23, shortly before independence. In the first cabinet, Lumumba held the post of minister of defense as well as the office of prime minister. As part of the compromise ensuring Lumumba's victory, Kasa-Vubu was elected as the Congo's first president.

On Independence Day, June 30, Lumumba gave an unexpected, dramatic speech to the Congolese people and foreign officials celebrating the occasion. In the presence of King Baudouin, he described the movement toward independence as a struggle involving bloodshed and violence. He also recounted the oppression, humiliation, and privation the Congolese had suffered during the 80 harsh years of colonialism. Calling on aid from all Congolese regardless of ethnic ties, on all elected officials no matter what their political party, and on foreign nations and peoples of goodwill, he pledged his administration would work to build the Congo into a rich, free, and prosperous nation. This, he asserted, would be a significant step towards liberating Africa as a whole.

Immediately after independence, overwhelming problems swept the country, making it impossible for Lumumba's government to function effectively. On July 5, the Force Publique (national army) mutinied against its Belgian officer corps. On July 9, Belgian metropolitan troops intervened to guarantee the safety of Belgian lives and property. On July 11, Moise Tshombe declared Katanga (now Shaba) an independent state. Also during this time, thousands of Belgian businessmen, bureaucrats, and technicians fled the country.

On July 12, in conjunction with President Kasa-Vubu, Lumumba registered a complaint at the United Nations against Belgium, and on the same day the Congo broke diplomatic relations with the former colonizer. When Lumumba approached the American president asking for military assistance to restore order in the country, Eisenhower, at the suggestion of Kwame Nkrumah of Ghana, directed Lumumba to the U.N., which passed a resolution sending military aid to the Congo. On July 15, one day later, the first detachment of U.N. peace-keeping troops arrived to return order to the Congo.

A fierce defender of his country's unity, Lumumba hoped to use the U.N. troops in place of the unmanageable Force Publique. When, however, the U.N. soldiers merely acted to maintain peace and refused to restore the secessionist Katanga, Lumumba made overtures to the U.S.S.R. and other Eastern bloc countries for help in preserving the Congo under a single government. In consequence, some Belgians regarded Lumumba as a communist.

After visiting the United Nations in New York in the last week in July, Lumumbu re-visited Nkrumah in Accra in August, and they signed an accord for the Union of Ghana with the Congo.

Soon, the fragile relationship between the more

Prime Minister Lumumba meets with Dag Hammarskjold, Secretary-General of the United Nations, in New York on July 24, 1960.

conservative and cautious Kasa-Vubu and Lumumba broke down. On September 5, a serious constitutional crisis occurred as the president and the prime minister both dismissed each other. Although the House of Representatives refused to ratify these actions and attempted to reconcile the two leaders, Kasa-Vubu prevailed by gaining support from the U.N., which acknowledged his constitutional right to revoke the prime minister. When, however, Kasa-Vubu named Joseph Ileo to succeed Lumumba, parliament refused to accept Ileo's cabinet.

As the deadlock continued, on September 14, Colonel Joseph Mobutu (now Mobutu Seke Seko) neutralized Kasa-Vubu, the government, and the two Houses of Parliament until December. On September 15, Lumumba himself was placed under house arrest in his official residence. On September 20, Mobutu named a college of commissioners, composed of university students, to act as a caretaker government in Lumumba's stead.

Seeing power slipping from his grasp, Lumumba determined to leave Léopoldville and return to friendly Stanleyville. Although his house was surrounded by U.N. troops and by soldiers of the Armée Nationale Congolaise (A.N.C.—the name of the army was changed after the July mutiny), on the evening of

November 27, Lumumba managed to slip out of custody by hiding on the floor of an M.N.C. station wagon which came to the house regularly. Together with his wife, small son, and several loyal politicians, Lumumba made his way by car out of Léopoldville in the direction of Kasai. Although he managed to get within a few kilometers of friendly territory, on December 1 at about 11 P.M., Lumumba's party was apprehended as it tried to cross the Sankuru River, 100 km (60 mi) east of Port Francqui (now Ilebo). Detained in accordance with a writ signed by Kasa-Vubu and high judiciary authorities, Lumumba and two companions, Joseph Okito, vice president of the Senate, and Maurice Mpolo, minister of youth, were mistreated and sent to Léopoldville. The following day, December 2, the three men were transferred to Camp Hardy (now Camp Ebeya) in Thysville (now Mbanza-Ngungu).

On January 17, 1961, a badly beaten Lumumba, Okito, and Mpolo were flown to Elisabethville (now Lubumbashi), the capital city of Tshombe's Katanga state. The three captives were escorted from the plane by Katangan soldiers who took the men to a house near the airport. Apparently, Lumumba was killed on the night of January 17. Although it is not certain how Lumumba's body was disposed, most likely, he was buried in an unmarked grave near Elisabethville. The blame for the murder of Lumumba must be put on Kasa-Vubu and his colleagues in Léopoldville at the time, and on Tshombe, even though he denied it.

During the entire period he exercised power, Lumumba remained a fervent nationalist, deeply devoted to his country. Like his mentor Kwame Nkrumah, Lumumba believed that political independence needed to be based on economic and social freedom. Thus, he resisted all forms of outside control, calling instead on the Congolese to rely on their own strength. In death, Lumumba became a powerful anti-imperialist symbol. On June 30, 1966, he was proclaimed an official national hero and a martyr for Africa.

K. KHANG ZUBAL, NK. K.

BIBLIOGRAPHY: P. Artigue, *Qui sont les leaders Congolais?* ("Who are the Congolaise Leaders?"), 2nd ed., Brussels, 1961; Centre de Recherches et d'Information Socio-Politiques (C.R.I.S.P.), *Les leaders congolais de 1959-60; ce qu'il sont devenus à travers dix ans d'histoire* ("The Congolese Leaders of 1959-60; What Has Become Of Them Over Ten Years of History"), Brussels, 1969; Jules Chomé, *M. Lumumba et le communisme* ("Mr. Lumumba and Communism"), Brussels, 1961; Philippe Decraene, *Le*

Panafricanisme ("Panafricanism"), 5th ed., Paris, 1976; J. Gérard-Libois and B. Verhaegen, *Congo 1960*, 3 vols., Brussels, 1961; R. Govender, *The Martyrdom of Patrice Lumumba*, London, 1972; G. Heinz and H. Donnay, *Lumumba: Les cinquants derniers jours de sa vie*, Brussels, 1966, English translation by Jane C. Seitz published as *Lumumba: The Last Fifty Days*, New York, 1969; L. de Heusch, "P. Lumumba," *Biographie Belge d'Outre-Mer*, Vol. VI, Brussels, 1967, "Plaidoyer à la mémoire de Patrice Lumumba," ("Plea for the Memory of Patrice Lumumba"), *Synthese*, No. 189, February, 1962; Catherine Hoskyns, *The Congo Since Independence, January 1960-December 1961*, London, 1965; T. Kanza, *Conflict in the Congo: The Rise and Fall of Lumumba*, Harmondsworth and Baltimore, 1972; J. Kizerbo, *Histoire de l'Afrique Noir. D'hier a demain* ("History of Black Africa. From Yesterday to Tomorrow"), Paris, 1972; P. Lumumba, *Le Congo, terre d'avenir—est'il menace?* ("The Congo, Land of the Future—Is it Threatened?"), English translation by Graham Heath published as *Congo, My Country*, London and New York, 1962, *La pensee politique de Patrice Lumumba* ("The Political Thought of Patrice Lumumba"), speeches and documents edited by Jean Van Lierde, with a preface by Jean-Paul Sartre, Paris, 1963, English translation by Helen Lane published as *Lumumba Speaks: The Speeches and Writings of Patrice Lumumba, 1958-61*, New York, 1972; G. Martelli, *De Leopold a Lumumba. Une histoire du Congo Belge: 1877-1960* ("From Leopold to Lumumba. A History of the Belgian Congo: 1877-1960"), Paris, 1964; A. Merriam, Congo: *Background of Conflict*, Evanston, 1961; K. Nkrumah, *Challenge of the Congo*, London, New York, 1967; Jean Rouch, *En cage avec Lumumba* ("Caged with Lumumba"), Paris, 1961; Pierre Vos, *Vie et mort de Lumumba* ("Life and Death of Lumumba"), Paris, 1961; C. Young, *Introduction a la politique congolaise* ("Introduction to Congolese Politics"), Brussels, 1965, published in English as *Politics in the Congo: Decolonization and Independence*, Princeton, 1965.

LUPUNGU

Lupungu (circa 1875-circa 1940s), the son of Ngongo Leteta (*q.v.*) claimed to be the legitimate successor to his father's large domain, straddling the Lomami River southwest of Maniema. The colonial government feared, however, that Lupungu might repeat Ngongo's insubordination against the State, and this prevented him from exercising power as chief. Thus, for most of his life, Lupungu was exiled from Ngongo Leteta's former capital, Ngandu, on the Lomami River, 100 km (60 mi) northeast of Kabinda.

Lupungu was named after Ngongo Leteta's ally and vassal, the great Songye chief Lumpungu (*q.v.*). In fact, F. Dhanis, Belgian commander of the Arab zone, continued calling him "little Lumpungu." Although, on the eve of his execution by state authorities at Ngandu in 1893, Ngongo designated Lupungu as his successor, Lupungu's actual reign over the Tetela and other heterogeneous populations conquered by his father lasted little more than a year and a half, from 1893 until 1895.

On July 4, 1895, Ngongo's former soldiers, who had been integrated into the Congo Free State army, revolted at Luluabourg (now Kananga) and began a rampage through Kasai. Learning that the mutineers planned to come to Ngandu and restore Lupungu to the power and position of his slave raiding father Ngongo Leteta, the whites at Ngandu fled with the young chief to the headquarters of Dhanis at Nyangwe, 100 km (60 mi) northeast on the Lualaba River. Finally, in 1896, Dhanis sent Lupungu, his mother, and 40 Tetela warriors to Stanleyville (now Kisangani).

In the meantime, state agents at Ngandu installed Luhaka, a former nyampara (subordinate) of Ngongo Leteta, as the legitimate ruler. Although Luhaka proved to be capable and, devoted, and an excellent administrator, some colonial officials admitted that Lupungu was the rightful heir to Ngongo. In a letter dated September 3, 1900, Dhanis the vice-governor general of the Eastern Province declared the children of Ngongo Leteta had the right to succeed their father whose cooperation, so badly repaid, had enabled the whites to acquire Maniema, the large Swahili Arab dominated area southeast of Stanleyville.

In Stanleyville, Lupungu completed his education under the direction of Father Superior Gabriel of the Sacré Coeur mission. The Europeans described Lupungu as a very intelligent, affable, quiet, serious, and polite young man. Aware of his legitimate right, Lupungu attempted with his young brother, the ambitious and bold Adolphe Kitenge, to recover control of the Sambala chiefdom of Katako-Kombe, located about 300 km (180 mi) northeast of Kananga. In the face of the European's refusal, Lupungu, in 1908, petitioned high officials at Boma, the colonial capital on the estuary of the Congo River, for permission to return to Ngandu to found a small village in the Lualaba-Kasai district. He argued that this was the country of his birth and that he had not seen it for 12 years. But both the local and central authorities refused his request.

Later in 1912, Lupungu's brother Kitenge clandestinely visited Ngongo Leteta's youngest son, Mauka, living at Katako-Kombe. Realizing Kitenge had come to reclaim control of the chiefdom for himself or for

Lupungu, Luhaka informed the administrator E. Germain, who immediately expelled Kitenge from his territory. But when Luhaka died on July 15, 1919, Kitenge again returned as Lupungu's emissary to challenge the succession of Raphael Senga, Luhaka's oldest son. Initially, Kitenge was successful for, in 1922, the territorial administrator, J. Collaert, asked for Lupungu's recall from Stanleyville. Nothing came of Collaert's request, however, and Raphael Senga was inaugurated as chief of the great chiefdom of the Sambala. In fact, from this time on, Collaert asked higher authorities to forbid Lupungu and Kitenge access to the territory. The European authorities were convinced that their return threatened to unleash a widespread internal revolt in the Tetela chiefdoms of the Sankuru district, since many other local notables considered themselves legitimate successors to Ngongo Leteta.

On November 25, 1932, acting as an emissary for Lupungu, Kitenge renewed his claims to the succession of Ngongo Leteta and encountered the same opposition from the administrative authorities of Stanleyville. The following year, Raphael Senga was decorated with a medal for his role as ruler of the Sambala chiefdom, enlarged in 1933. To further undermine all influence of Ngongo Leteta's sons in the chiefdom, one of the chiefdom's tribunals under Lutundula, an ardent supporter of Ngongo's heirs, was abolished on July 20, 1934. According to the commissioner of the province, Lutundula's court duplicated Luhaka's tribunal, only eight kilometers away. Nevertheless, until his death on June 18, 1936, Chief Lutundula Kilinda refused allegiance to Raphael Senga.

On September 22, 1936, the interim commissioner of the province, F. Wenner, required Kitenge to move his residence to Lueta, about 200 km (120 mi) south of Kananga in Kasai. On November 2, 1936, the order was modified simply to forbid Kitenge to enter the Sankuru district.

When Raphael Senga died on October 25, 1939, after a reign of 20 years, his 16-year-old son Emery Milambu was too young to rule, and the problem of succession recurred. Both Lupungu, who was in Stanleyville, and Kitenge, who was in Léopoldville (now Kinshasa), where contacted by emissaries of the local chiefs Lutundula, Mubimbi, Omeonga, Omana, Lumbuli, and Mundala. On October 7, 1940, the commissioner of the urban district of Léopoldville transmitted a request from Kitenge to A. de Beaufort, the head of the Lusambo province (later Kasai province), urging that he re-examine Lupungu's candidacy. According to Kitenge, Lupungu had promised to forget all his family had suffered for 50 years and to conduct himself as a loyal and obedient chief. The district commissioner, E. Vallaeys, speaking for Beaufort, reported to Governor General P. Ryckmans (term of office 1934-46) that this request should be filed without action because the chiefdom had been assigned to a cousin of the deceased chief Senga Luhaka. Thus Léon Mutambwe, of the Tete Ngomba village, was invested on November 9, 1939. Despite European approval, Mutambwe's selection was not in keeping with the consensus of the African notables.

Faced with the Belgian authorities' clear and categorical refusal to give even a small amount of authority to any of Ngongo Luteta's children, Lupungu was forced to live quietly in Stanleyville until his death. His brother, Adolphe Kitenge who lived past independence, was able to return home after 1960. Kitenge, however, was shot at Katako-Kombe by the soldiers of Moise Tshombe's central government, despatched to put down a rebellion in 1964.

The influence of Ngongo Leteta's sons, Lupungu and Kitenge, endured among populations formerly conquered by their father. Despite their distance from the Tetela territories and the heterogeneous peoples of Katako-Kombe, Lupungu and Kitenge were highly regarded for more than half a century. Their return to the region before independence would certainly have resulted in internal repercussions, even possibly revolts against the colonial administration. That is why the Europeans never permitted them to reign or even to return to their native Katako-Kombe territory.

DIMANDJA LUHAKA

BIBLIOGRAPHY: S.L. Hinde, *La chute de la domination des arabes du Congo* ("The Downfall of Arab Domination of the Congo"), Brussels, 1897. Archives of the Katako-Kombe Territory, Busambala sector file; Archives of the former district of Sankuru, at Lusambo (file on the Ngongo Leteta succession.)

MABERA BENOIT

Mabera Benoit (circa 1890-1922), the Vui (paramount chief) of the Nguii people living along the Kasai River north of Kikwit, cooperated with colonial authorities in their attempt to transform African cultural, economic, and religious patterns.

Born at Nkuriam, 130 km (75 mi) north of Kikwit, Mabera was a member of the family eligible to hold the Nguii office of Vui. At an early age Mabera converted to Christianity, and was baptized as Benoit by the Scheut missionaries at Mpangu, near Brabanta (now Mapongu), about 20 km (12 mi) downstream from Ilebo on the Kasai River. While still at Mpangu, Mabera was called upon to become the Vui by the Nkuriam notables who, acting at the instigation of the colonial authorities, were removing the regent who had held power since the death of the last Vui, Ekwong e Biar.

Although still quite young, Mabera was enthroned as Vui by the kingdom's dignitaries according to customary rites. Shortly afterwards he was decorated with a chief's medallion by the state authorities. At the request of the government, the young Christian Vui moved his court from Nkuriam to Owong, along the Kasai River not far west from the budding center of Mangai. This move was to facilitate access to the Vui's court by missionaries, European traders, and state agents who could only travel by river, since there were as yet no roads in the area.

Mabera's accession to power opened a new era for the Nguii peoples, since, from the time of his enthronement, the new Christian Vui undertook an ambitious program of social, economic, and political reform. A confirmed Christian, he fought an ardent battle against sorcerers. A good number of his subjects converted to the new religion and came to live in the new captial where they could sell the products of their harvest more easily. On the economic level, Vui Mabera urged his people to cultivate corn (maize), pineapples, sugarcane, peanuts (ground nuts), and sweet potatoes—plants which were already known but which had not yet been brought into local cultivation. He also urged his people to make their products more marketable, for example by breaking open coconuts for the white traders who increasingly navigated the Kasai. By this time, about half a dozen white traders had already settled in nearby Mangai. At the request of the state, Mabera built roads making the outlying areas of his kingdom more accessible and, therefore, more attractive for settlement. Politically, the Vui's court was reinforced by the presence of "messengers," put at his disposition by the state and recruited, for the most part, among the new Christians.

In Nguii tradition, Mabera is either seen as the valiant young Vui who tried to modernize his society or as the traitor who served the invading whites. His efforts to impose the new culture were greeted with enthusiasm by the majority of the population. Certain factions, however, particularly people of Oveke and other peripheral villages to the west of Nguii territory, were unhappy with the new ideas, for example with the corvée (forced labor) required for road construction, and especially with new taxes which had just been levied.

Oveke discontent culminated in Mabera's assassination. When Mabera went to enforce tax collection at Oveke, the inhabitants of the village revolted and killed the Vui.

The colonial administration, took advantage of this incident to dismantle the traditional Nguii political structure. After having organized a punitive expedition to prevent the spread of the Oveke rebellion, the government partitioned Nguii territory into several autonomous chiefdoms. Thus, the Vui of Nkuriam simply became one chief among many.

NDAYWEL è NZIEM and ELAGNA IVARI

BIBLIOGRAPHY: Struyf, "Le meurtre d'un chef" ("The Murder of a Chief"), *Missions Belges de la Compagnie de Jésus,* 25th year, 3., 1923, pp. 81-84. Ndaywel è Nziem, "Organization sociale et histoire: les Ngwi de les Ding du Zaire" ("Social Organization and History: the Nguii and the Ding of Zaire"), doctoral thesis in history, Paris, 1972.

MAI MUNENE

Mai Munene (who flourished in the mid-seventeenth century) founded the Lunda-related chiefdom, or state, of Mai Munene, located at the confluence of the Kasai and Tshikapa rivers. Mai Munene is both the name of the polity and the title of all the chiefs who have ruled there.

The creation of the Mai Munene state was closely related to 17th century Lunda expansion begun by Kinguri, who founded the Imbangala kingdom of Kasanje in Angola. Lunda advances continued as Kapenda Mukwa Ambungo created the Shinje state, 250 km (150 mi) south of modern Kikwit, and as Mwene Putu Kasongo (*q.v.*) began the Yaka state, 250 km (155 mi) southeast of Kikwit.

Once Kapenda had settled east of the Kwango, the Lunda court tried to extend its power to the northwest by sending the warrior Mujinga to fight and conquer the Tufia and other people in that area. After Mujinga had been disgracefully beaten, the Lunda rulers at Musumba then sent Kombana Mutombo and Mai Munene against the Tufia. Once the two lieutenants succeeded, Mai was charged with ruling over the vanquished people, while Kombana Mutombo continued west and settled in the region between the Lutshiko and the Loange rivers.

In addition to the Tufias, Mai also subjugated some Tupokoto, Kete, and Bashilange. Mai's attempts to conquer some Pende groups, however, failed completely. In Mai's long, painful war against the Pende, chief Kombo, who commanded the Pende troops, distinguished himself by his bravery and acquired a legendary reputation. The Pende won a complete victory, maintaining their autonomy.

Although Mai Munene's chiefdom later experienced a strong Luba influence, its Lunda origin was never forgotten.

SIKITELE GIZE a SUMBULA

BIBLIOGRAPHY: G.L. Haveaux, *La Tradition Historique des Bapende Orientaux* ("The Historic Tradition of the Eastern Bapende"), Brussels, 1954; M. Plancquaert, *Les Jaga et le Bayaka du Kwango: Contribution Historico-Ethnographique* ("The Jaga and the Bayaka of Kwango: A Historic-Ethnographic Contribution"), Brussels, 1932, *Les Yaka, Essai d'histoire* ("The Yaka: A Historical Essay"), Brussels, 1971; J. Vansina, *Les anciens royaumes de la savanne*, Léopoldville, 1965, published in English as *Kingdoms of the Savanna*, Madison, 1966; E. Verhulpen, *Baluba et balubaisés du Katanga* ("The Baluba and the Balubaized of Katanga"), Anvers, 1936.

MAKANDA KABOBI

Makanda Kabobi (March 16, 1940-September 25, 1972), was a scholar and teacher who became one of the most respected theoreticians in Zaire's unique political party, the *Mouvement Populair de la Révolution* ("Popular Movement of the Revolution" M.P.R.).

Makanda was born at Kayaya, a Lele village south of Ilebo in Kasai. Located in a forest clearing, Kayaya, had gained a reputation as the bastion of opposition to the chiefly aristocracy which dominated the Lele. Makanda's father, Makutu Mimboyo was not an unknown figure. He had been recruited in 1914 as a member of the Force Publique, the colonial army. After World War I, Makutu was stationed at Basongo, 20 km (12 mi) downstream from Ilebo on the Kasai River, where he served as interpreter and orderly. Makutu sent his son Makanda Kabobi to primary schools of the Oblate Fathers of Mary Immaculate (O.M.I.) in Mwembe and then to that in the commercial center of Brabanta (now Mapongu), 25 km (15 mi) west of Ilebo.

A gifted intelligent student, Makanda was recommended for the Oblate minor seminary at Laba, 80 km (50 mi) southeast of Ilebo. He matriculated in 1953, and by 1959 he had brilliantly completed a program of Greek and Latin studies. Makanda then enrolled in the major seminary at Mayidi, about 100 km (60 mi) south of Kinshasa, where he studied scholastic philosophy. In July 1961, however, Makanda left the major seminary to enroll in the department of economics at Lovanium University in Léopoldville (now Kinshasa).

At Lovanium, Makanda began taking an active interest in politics. From 1963 to 1965, he served as president of the Association Générale des Etudiants de Lovanium ("General Association of Lovanium Students," A.G.E.I.). In a Congo, woefully lacking an intellectual élite, the A.G.E.I. became a political training ground for young élite groups, later to exercise responsibilities on the national level. As student president, Makanda oriented his program around examining the ability of the university structure itself to fashion the intellectual élite which the country needed so desperately. As a result of these investigations, university students organized a general strike in 1964. The students demanded greater correlation between the educational format and the real needs of the country, and asked for more student influence on the university administration. This strike had repercussions for both the university and the nation. Not only did it lead to a series of university reforms, it also demonstrated the effectiveness of student political action.

In July 1965, Makanda graduated from Lovanium with a diploma in economics. The same month, he left the Congo for the United States, where he studied social and economic development at the University of

Pittsburgh in Pennsylvania. Makanda then took an interest in human resource planning, which he studied at Columbia University in New York City.

When Makanda returned to Africa in 1968, he first worked as a researcher in the economic and financial section of the National Office of Research and Development (O.N.R.D.). In addition, in 1969 he joined the faculty of Lovanium University, teaching subjects relating to the social and economic problems of education. In March 1970, he left the O.N.R.D. to become, first, economic advisor, and then chief advisor to the political office of the Mouvement Populaire de la Révolution (M.P.R.), the country's single political party. In December 1970, he was promoted to the party post of national secretary for youth. In February 1972, he reached the summit of his career when he was named a political commissioner, thus becoming a member of the political office, (the M.P.R.'s highest organ), as well as one of the regime's chief political theorists.

As a political commissioner, he conceived of creating a "school of the party" the role of which would be to train the party's staff ideologically, to serve as a place for formulating new ideas, and to raise political consciousness.

While serving as a party theorist Makanda actively worked for the success of the first extra-ordinary congress of the M.P.R. held in Nsele (just outside Kinshasa) during May 1972. In these meetings, he presided over the party commission working to formulate future economic options for the country.

On September 25, 1972, several months after this congress, Makanda died unexpectedly. The party school, which Makanda envisioned but never lived to see, was inaugurated after his death. In honor of this brilliant young theorist, the school was named Institut Makanda Kabobi.

NDAYWEL è NZIEM

BIBLIOGRAPHY: Archives of the Institut Makanda Kabobi. Interviews with family members.

MAKITU

Makitu (circa 1856-April 1899), a prominent merchant and caravan organizer, grew wealthy from the 19th century ivory trade between the Atlantic coast and the interior regions of the Congo (now Zaire).

Makitu's village, Mbanza Ngombe, 110 km (75 mi) southeast of modern Kinshasa, lay north of what is now the Zaire River on the plateau crossed by caravan routes between Stanley (now Malebo) Pool, where Tio middlemen purchased ivory from Bobangi river traders, and the Atlantic coast, where Europeans came to exchange manufactured items for ivory.

Because of the numerous cataracts in the Zaire River downstream from the Pool, all the trade goods had to be transported through the Lower Zaire region by porters who were either slaves or hired workers.

Makitu's relative, chief Leteta, who owned many wives and slaves, organized large caravans, and introduced the young Makitu to long-distance commerce. By the time he was 25 years old, Makitu was known in the whole cataracts region as a great merchant and caravan leader. Because of his ability to assure security and provide organization, many small merchants joined his group each time he went to the coast. Thus, Makitu's caravans frequently included 500 porters. Makitu's method of keeping accounts was remarkable. He divided his caravan into sections of 10 to 15 men under the guard of a capita (trusted subordinate). Makitu remembered what and how much he gave to each capita and the latter did the same for each of his individual porters.

Makitu purchased ivory from the Tio at Stanley Pool. Since his father originally had been a Tio slave, Makitu was able to establish close relations with the Tio ivory dealers. Having become very wealthy, around 1882, Makitu separated from chief Leteta to settle in the nearby village of Kindoki. There, as an independent trader, he had several huts stacked to the ceiling with merchandise.

In February 1882, Makitu and Leteta became associated with the Comité d'Etudes du Haut-Congo (Study Committee for the Upper Congo, C.E.H.C.) sent by Léopold II to explore the Congo River. Having observed the difficulties of chief Ngaliema (q.v.) with the committee, Leteta and Makitu were initially very hostile to European penetration into their district. They accordingly held the C.E.H.C. expedition for ransom. Leteta even demanded the head of a European as tribute. Although Makitu was unfriendly, he appeared more approachable than Leteta and, in fact, he often refused to participate in Leteta's attacks. Thus, Capt. Hanssens, Lt. Nilis, and Callewaert, all agents of the expedition, which was led by Henry Morton Stanley began negotiations with Makitu. In October 1882, they made a friendship treaty sanctioned by the exchange of blood. According to the terms of the treaty, the C.E.H.C. agreed to pay a monthly indemnity in cloth to both Makitu and Leteta. The Africans, for their part, accepted the establishment of the Leteta station (named after Makitu's cousin) at Mbanza Ngombe village. The committee agents hoped the station would abolish the customary fees these chiefs had always levied on all caravans. In spite of the treaty, the people of this district often made trouble for Europeans by attacking caravans and stealing their trade goods. As a result, when Sir Francis de Winton, the administrator-general of the Congo Free State, held talks with

Makitu and Leteta during an inspection tour in 1884, he threatened to hang the recalcitrants.

It was not long, however, before Makitu began to view European settlement as an opportunity to increase his ivory commerce. Although his hope quickly evaporated when the Dutch Company established at Leteta began buying ivory directly, Makitu continued to enrich himself from wages paid to his slaves who served as porters on the route to the coast. Resolved, somehow, to profit from the presence of the white man, Makitu made gestures of cooperation. Thus in 1882, he gave his slave Lutunu to Van Gèle, the European head of Leteta station. Makitu, together with chief Leteta, also encouraged Baptist Missionary Society (B.M.S.) workers to establish a base in their area. As a result, in 1884 the B.M.S. founded Wathen station (now Ngombe Lutete) and started a school. In February 1885, Makitu helped transport the steamer *Stanley* from Leteta to Stanley Pool. In 1886, he

Some of Makitu's wives.

moved his village a short distance, from Kindoki to Ngombe Matadi.

Makitu's loyalty to the Europeans won him the first medal in the Congo to be given to a chief. When he received the medal from Commander Nicholas Tobback at the great Makewekwe market in 1888, Makitu's authority extended over 64 villages. When he died, in April 1889 from sleeping sickness, he left about 40 wives and hundreds of slaves.

Makitu was one of the Congo chiefs who increased his power and riches by allying himself with the white man.

SABAKINU KIVILU

BIBLIOGRAPHY: W.H. Bentley, *Pioneering on the Congo,* 2 vols., London, 1900; C. Coquilhat, *Sur le Haut Congo* ("On the Upper Congo"), Brussels, 1888; E. Dupont, *Letters sur le Congo* ("Letters on the Congo"), Paris, 1889; M. Luwel, *Sir Francis de Winton, Administrateur General du Congo, 1884-6,* ("Sir Francis de Winton, Administrator General of the Congo, 1884-6"), Tervuren, 1964; J. Maquet-Tombu, *Le siècle marche* ("The Century Advances"), Brussels, 1952.

MAKOMBE

Makombe (circa 1800-circa 1860) served as Mwami (ruler) of the Shi people living southwest of Lake Kivu. His capital was situated at Kabare, about 10 km (6 mi) west of modern Bukavu.

The son of the Shi ruler Birhenjira and of Mwa Buniagu, Makombe was born at Bushangabuye. In order to protect the young Makombe from the wrath of his step-mother, Mwa Murhwa, Birhenjira sent the boy to Rwanda, where he spent his youth in the court of King Mutara II. There, he received training as a warrior and fought in Mutara's wars at Gisaka and Ndorwa. When Birhenjira died in about 1820, Makombe succeeded him as ruler of Bushi (as the Shi land is known).

As ruler, Makombe profited from his experience in Rwanda. He had to repel the invasions of Mutara II, his former protector, as well as those of Kingeli IV. The most important incident of Makombe's reign, perhaps even of the dynasty, was his victory over the adjacent Havu people. Pushing the Havu north, he fixed the Bushi frontier at Nyabaronge, and placed his son Bigomokaro Karhana in the region of Katana, about 20 km (12 mi) west of Bukavu, to guard the border.

When Makombe died in about 1860, his son Byaterana (circa 1845-1884) succeeded him as ruler.

PILIPILI KAGABO

BIBLIOGRAPHY: Bashizi Chirhagarhula, "Origine et éstablissement des Bashi au Bushi, Kivu" ("Origin and Establishment of the Bashi in Bushi, Kivu"), *Lukundoli,* 1973; Bishikwabo Chubaka, *Essai sur l'exercice du pouvoir politique au Bushi* ("Essay on the Exercise of Political Power in Bushi"), Lubumbashi, 1973; Burume Lwigulira, *Histoire et culture des Bashi,* ("History and Culture of the Bashi"), Kinshasa, 1972; P. Colle. *Essai de monographie des Bashi* ("Essay on the Monography of the Bashi"), Bukavu, 1937, 1972; A. Kagame, *Un abrégé de l'ethnohistoire du Rwanda* ("A Summary of the Ethnohistory of Rwanda"), Butare, 1972; P. Masson, *Trois siècles chez les Bashi* ("The Bashi During Three Centuries"), Bakavu, 1966; J. Vansina, *L'évolution du royaume rwanda des origines à 1900* ("The Evolution of the Rwanda Kingdom from its Origins to 1900"), Brussels, 1962.

MALANGA

Malanga (circa 1880-1965), served as chief of the Bodjinga division of the Lobo (Balobo) ethnic group, living just north of Makanza (formerly Nouvelle-Anvers) about 180 km (100 mi) upstream from Mbandaka on the Zaire River.

The colonial take-over of the Lobo region was directed from Nouvelle-Anvers, although the actual conquest was left in the hands of officers at Bonkula post, founded around 1904. In 1908, as European occupation intensified, the Lobo people were divided into chiefdoms. The Bodjinga were included in the East Balobo chiefdom governed by the notable Matantoko, an older and somewhat listless man.

Malanga, who was only a simple capita (sub-chief) from Bondoko village, came to the attention of the whites as a man capable of running the entire chiefdom. Soon, Malanga became Matantoko's chief assistant and assumed many responsibilities. In a report dated September 30, 1913, the Belgian head of the Bomana post, 90 km (50 mi), north of Mankanza, recommended that Malanga replace the old chief. Consequently, when, in May 1914, the chiefdoms of East Balobo, West Balobo, Bunkula, and Monoki na Taba were transferred to the territory of Moyenne Giri (Middle Giri), Malanga was invested as chief of the East Balobo.

The first days of Malanga's rule were marked by strong opposition to him, which the Europeans, however, managed to suppress. Nyamongwalanga, head of an important branch of the Bodjinga people, also claimed rights as chief and refused to yield to Malanga. As punishment, Nyamongwalanga lost his position as a sub-chief.

The whites appreciated Malanga more for his power than for his moral qualities. Thus, in the report of the inquiry regarding his chiefdom, Malanga was accused of selling women and children and of interfering in the judicial process for his own gain. In 1922, J. Hainaux, administrator of the Nouvelle-Anvers territory, labeled Malanga "a tyrant who exploits his subjects." Malanga's ability to profit by manipulating the courts was demonstrated by the fact that in 1921, he had 54 wives, a gain of 51 wives from the year 1913, when he was still a capita.

Once the region of the Balobo came under missionary influence, some wives of polygamous notables, including those of Malanga, fled to the mission at Nouvelle-Anvers, where they married monogamous Christians. Chief Malanga, like Motengo of Monia and Edjumbu (q.v.) of Bokala, entered into open conflict with the state agents and the missionaries by demanding to be reimbursed for the dowries he had supposedly paid to obtain the women. Malanga's claims were exaggerated for, at a time when dowries rarely exceeded 300 francs, he asked a Christian husband for compensation of 2,333 francs.

Malanga's main function was overseeing the corvée (forced labor) imposed by the colonial regime. This work included upkeep of the river channels and management of the Nouvelle-Anvers-Bonkula-Monia dike. The people were also required to cultivate vast banana plantations to provision Nouvelle-Anvers, Lusengo, and Mobeka, the river's commercial centers. In this region, rich in palm groves, the men were also asked to furnish palm oil and palm nuts and to search for copal. A Portuguese merchant, Gomes Constantino, settled in Bondoko, the principal town of Malanga's chiefdom, to buy these diverse products. This allowed the inhabitants to obtain the cash they needed to pay taxes.

Belgian authorities both praised and mistrusted Malanga. On the one hand, their administrative reports reveal a high regard for his ability, through the use of force, menaces, promises, lies, or praise, to impose his will, and the will of the colonial regime, on his people. On the other hand, the Belgians knew very well that Malanga's only goal was increasing his own power and that he had no real loyalty to the government.

Although the colonial officials knew Malanga used them to bolster his own authority among the Lobo people, they also realized he was an effective leader. Thus, in 1925, when the territorial administrator responsible for all the Lobo wanted to restructure the disorganized Bonkula chiefdom—the Bonkula like the Bodjinga were a Lobo sub-division—he proposed placing Bonkula under Malanga. Also, in 1926 when the Belgians began thinking of grouping all Lobo people into a single chiefdom, Malanga was a strong candidate for the office of chief. He was opposed by two other hopefuls: chief Ebunda (or Ebondo) of the Libiri (or Libele) and Malanga's old rival Nyamongwalanga.

Because of administrative restructuring, creation of a Lobo chiefdom was delayed until 1939, when the Belgians finally set up a Balobo sector (a sector being a larger unit than a chiefdom). Malanga was judged to be the most capable candidate by far, and thus was invested as chief over the entire sector. His capital was established at Bokene village, among the Bokane division of the Lobo.

Although Malanga continued to administer effectively, his population declined. Sleeping sickness, and constant migration towards the Congo (now the Zaire) River, were the principal causes. Also, during World War II, the requirements for manpower to harvest rubber, copal, and palm nuts reduced the number of Lobo people living under Malanga's control. In fact, in 1949, the colonial authorities considered relocating the entire Balobo population to settle them along the river at Makanza, Lusengo, and Mobeka. While many young people agreed to emigrate, the older people opposed the obligatory abandonment of their lands. Malanga continued to administer his sector until 1953, when Balobo was joined with two sectors on the Giri River: those of the Libinza and the Baloi. The new unit was named the Ngiri sector.

Malanga, now old, retired, leaving his post to the young Ebamba Maurice, chief of the Libinza sector. Then, in 1957, the Balobo people were attached to the sector of Nouvelle-Anvers (now Makanza zone). Malanga, however, continued to enjoy great prestige until his death in 1965.

Malanga served the colonizers for 40 years. Because of his dynamism and his many accomplishments, he must be considered as one of the greatest chiefs of the Ngiri area.

MUMBANZA mwa BAWELE na
NYABAKOMBI ENSOBATO

BIBLIOGRAPHY: Reports of Inquiry, Archives of the Bomongo Zone: P.I.E. Delonge, into the establishment of the Balobo Sector, 1939, Nouvelle-Anvers territory; J. Hainaux, into the Balobo-East territory, 1922, and the Bodjinga chiefdom, 1925, Nouvelle-Anvers territory; J.M.H. Wera, into the establishment of the Balobo-East territory, 1914, Moyenne Giri territory; register of political information for Bomana territory, Bomongo Zone (1911-16), and for the Nouvelle-Anvers territory, Bomongo Zone (1917-31).

MALANGI a PHUMBA

Malangi a Phumba (circa 1915-1964) was a celebrated expert in Pende oral tradition and also a trusted and effective political leader.

Born in Kasanji village, 60 km (35 mi) southeast of Kikwit, Malangi was the son of Phumba and Niongewe. He was a member of the Akwa Mushinga people, belonging to the larger Pende ethnic group.

A physically imposing man, nearly two meters tall, Malangi became known for his animated eloquence, which marked him as a ngambi—in Pende society a person with a lively intelligence and wit who is at once an orator, advocate, judge, and expert on tradition. Because of his great knowledge, the Pende, and also their Mbunda Kwese and Sonde neighbors, frequently called on Malangi to settle disputes. He was also a great singer, a troubadour who knew all the popular Pende songs and many songs of the surrounding peoples.

On April 20, 1948, the government created the Kilamba sector, situated about 60 km (35 mi) southeast of Kikwit, and incorporating the Pende chiefdom of Mbangi and much of the chiefdom of the Mushinga. Because of his reputation as an arbitrator, Malangi was appointed as a judge and council member for this sector, a position which increased the respect in which he was held as well as his influence among the common people. In effect, Malangi had been considered for chief of the sector, but was not chosen because he was illiterate. On May 2, 1949, however, he was designated provisional adjunct sector chief responsible for the Kilamba sector tribunal. Then, because he was so highly respected by the people, the administrator, L. Caps placed Malangi in charge of tax collection. To compensate for his inability to read, Caps assigned two clerks to help him in his work. Recognizing Malangi's exceptional abilities, on June 5, 1950 the colonial authorities confirmed him in office as adjunct sector chief.

Besides his political activities, Malangi contributed greatly in bringing the Pende peoples to the attention of the international scientific world. From 1953, he served as the principal informant to the renowned Belgian ethnologist, the Rev. Father Professor Léon de Sousberghe, who devoted the major portion of his research and writings to the Pende.

On June 15, 1959, Malangi lost his position as adjunct sector chief when rural administrative districts were reorganized according to a governmental decree of May 10, 1957. Malangi then returned to his former job as a judge and tax collector.

When, however, Kasanza Mbawvu, who ruled the Yongo people (a Pende sub-group) in Kilamba sector, died on January 2, 1960, the Yongo notables unanimously elected Malangi a Phumba as their chief. On February 2, 1960 Malangi was invested as head of the 5,500 Yongo. He took the name Malangi Kalamba. As chief, Malangi faced opposition from the leader of the Gatshinga family who claimed his clan had a legal right to rule the Yongo. Finally, in July 1963 the dispute was taken before the Kikwit district court. But the rebellion instigated by Pierre Mulele (q.v.) interrupted the proceedings, which were never completed.

During the 1964 uprising, for reasons which are unclear, certain Mbunda chiefs ordered the Mulelist partisans to arrest Malangi. After being beaten hundreds of times with cudgels and whips, and dragged along the ground for an entire day, Malangi was buried alive.

The memory of chief Malangi a Phumba, remained strong among the Pende and the neighboring peoples. After 1964, young Pende musicians wrote songs celebrating Malangi's virtues as a leader and folklore expert.

SIKITELE GIZE a SUMBULA

BIBLIOGRAPHY: L. de Sousberghe, *Structure de parenté et d'alliances d'après les formules pende* ("Structure of Relationships and Alliances According to Pende Formulae"), Brussels 1955, *Les Pende. Aspects des structures sociales et politiques* ("The Pende. Aspects of Social and Political Structures"), Bujumbura, 1963. *See also* Archives of the Gungu zone, political file for the Kilamba sector.

MANDRANDELE TANZI

Mandrandele Tanzi (March 20, 1933-February 12, 1974) served in many phases of political life as a government administrator, as a leading theorist of the Mouvement Populaire de la Révolution ("Popular Movement of the Revolution," M.P.R.), and as a close personal associate of President Mobutu Sese Seko.

Mandrandele Tanzi was born in the town of Watsa, about 600 km (360 mi) northeast of Kisangani. The only son of a family of Logo-Ogambi ethnic origins, he attended primary school in Watsa before entering

the Collège Notre Dame at Dungu, 125 km (75 mi) to the northwest.

During the seven years Mandrandele spent in the boarding school run by the Dominican Fathers, he was subject to a quasi monastical life and received a solid intellectual foundation. This rigid discipline imbued with humanism molded Mandrandele's character and outlook.

In 1955, Mandrandele entered Lovanium University in Léopoldville (now Kinshasa) where he studied political science and administration. Due to his lively intelligence, his unquenchable thirst for knowledge, and his enthusiasm for all that he undertook he accumulated the knowledge he needed for his later political career.

Shortly after receiving his degree in 1960, he was named a director of the central government responsible for preserving order. During the same year, he was appointed to the office of internal affairs. In July 1961, he was nominated as director general of the national Water and Power Distribution Authority (Régie de Distribution d'Eau et d'Electricité—R.E.G.-I.D.E.S.O.). He interrupted his job to go to Paris where he studied business administration. After receiving a business degree, Mandrandele returned home to resume directorship of R.E.G.I.D.E.S.O. until 1965. Although he was constantly concerned for efficiency, he never forgot human values and he never sacrificed people for more efficient operations.

After 1964, he assumed many other duties. Thus he became an administrator of Lovanium University (1964-70), administrator of the National Bank (1964-65), and administrator of the National Institute for Agronomic Research (1964-67). In addition, he served as president of the Société de l'Uélé (Uélé Company), president of the Congolese Trust Company, a member of the government commission for Air Congo, and as a national senator (1965-66). With great erudition, a quick grasp of facts, and ease in synthesizing events, he was able to carry out his many obligations effectively.

When the Mouvement Populaire de la Révolution was created in May 1967 Mandrandele was chosen a member of its political bureau. As a party theorist, he argued that man is called upon to dominate a world of rapid changes. Thus, courageous action and firm convictions were qualities Mandrandele cherished. He subsequently held various party posts, including those of first national secretary (1968-69), political director (1970-74), and people's commissioner.

Within the Mouvement Populaire de la Révolution, he worked closely and faithfully with the party founder, Mobutu Sese Seko. Although he was often the subject of sarcasm and encountered the difficulties faced by anyone in public life, Mandrandele's composure, even temper, and moral strength allowed him to think and act objectively.

He died on February 12, 1974.

ATIWIYA MASIKITA

BIBLIOGRAPHY: Archives of the Political Bureau of the Mouvement Populaire de la Révolution.

MANTANTU DUNDULU

Mantantu Dundulu (circa 1865-February 1938) better known as Nlemvo, was the first Protestant Christian in the Congo, and a close collaborator with William H. Bentley in writing down the Kikongo language.

Born at Padwa in Angola, Mantantu Dundulu, fatherless from the day of his birth, was raised, according to the customs of his society, by his uncle, Tulante Mbidi. His uncle was both chief of the village of Lemvo and a merchant in ivory and slaves.

In 1879, King Don Pedro V of the Kongo, accompanied by W.H. Bentley, a missionary of the Baptist Missionary Society (B.M.S.), traveled to Lemvo. It was in this village that Bentley, who was learning Kikongo, discovered Mantantu, who spoke the language extremely well. Bentley found in him an excellent interpreter and made him, with the blessing of his uncle, his collaborator.

Quickly learning to read and write, Mantantu accompanied Bentley on most of his voyages. It is thought that the name Nlemvo, which means obedience and also indicates his native village, was given to him by Bentley.

On April 30, 1882, Nlemvo converted to Christianity. His baptism, however, did not take place until six years later, on February 19, 1888. Thus he became the first person to be baptized at the Wathen station (now Ngombe-Lutete), located 50 km (30 mi) north of Mbanza Ngungu.

In the beginning, Nlemvo helped the English missionaries to build a school at the old Kongo kingdom's capital of San Salvador, and in 1883 he helped in the construction of the B.M.S. at Stanley Pool (now Malebo). Then, he worked with Bentley to compile a "Dictionary and Grammar of the Kongo Language." In the course of this work, he accompanied Bentley to England in April 1884. During his European stay, Nlemvo was received, with eight other "Congolese," by King Léopold II of Belgium. As a result of his protracted absence, his family grew concerned, thinking he had been sold as a slave. So, at the end of his translation work, he returned to his own village until Bentley came back. Later he participated in the exploration of the tributaries of the Kasai, in the company of the missionaries George Grenfell and Bentley.

After his baptism in 1888, Nlemvo married Kalombo, a Christian woman originally from the Kasongo region in eastern Congo, where the missionaries had freed her from slavery. Nlemvo and Kalombo lived in Kivianga, a Christian village created on the land grant of the B.M.S. station at Ngombe-Lutete in 1882. This village, like most of the newly founded Christian villages, grouped together an ethnically heterogeneous population. Before his marriage, Nlemvo had lived there with his three sisters. Nlemvo's interethnic and religious marriage, was but one example of a profound transformation instituted by missionaries in Kongo society. Nlemvo himself had become a true "detribalized man" as was evidenced in his refusal to become chief of his village after the death of his uncle in 1887.

Nlemvo collaborated in the translation of the New Testament into Kikongo. To assist Bentley in this difficult undertaking, he went to England, for the second time, between December 1892 and September 1893. Then, when Bentley, weakened by illness and work, returned to England permanently, Nlemvo accompanied him in order to complete the translation of the entire Bible from English to Kikongo. During his third European stay, he underwent eye surgery intended to correct a disease threatening his sight. Unfortunately the operation ended in failure and Nlemvo returned home in 1905 without having been cured.

In spite of eye problems, Nlemvo continued his rich literary career. He assisted in a revision of the Bible in Kikongo, published in 1926; he took an active part in Mrs. Bentley's translation of the Proverbs and Psalms; he worked with M. Jennings in translating Stakler's book on the life of St. Paul and the Acts of the Apostles into Kikongo; and he translated, from English to Kikongo, the book entitled "Peep of Day." Finally, Nlemvo wrote an autobiographical sketch entitled "Mpungwilu".

In November 1937, the colonial administration informed the first Protestant Christian of their intention to honor him with the gold medal of the Royal Order of the Lion in recognition of his services to the state. Unfortunately Nlemvo died in February 1938, so the medal was presented posthumously to his son in July 1938.

A major African literary expert, Mlemvo's primary contribution was in the work of translating, the importance of which remains appreciated even in the present day.

SABAKINU KIVILU

BIBLIOGRAPHY: W.H. Bentley, *Pioneering on the Congo,* 2 vols., London, 1900; Slade, *English-speaking Missions in the Congo Independent State,* Brussels, 1959.

MANUEL, DOM

Dom Manuel (circa 1430-1510), the Mani Soyo (ruler of Soyo), was one of the first officials in the kingdom of Kongo who sought to understand and exploit the novel technological and spiritual powers introduced by the Portuguese after 1482.

Along with Nsundi, Mbata, Mbamba, Mpungu, and Mpembe, Soyo was one of the six provinces in the kingdom of Kongo. Soyo, however, claimed to be the most important province because it was located on the coast and because Mpinda at the mouth of the Zaire River was Kongo's main harbor. After the Portuguese explorer Diogo Cao arrived in 1484, this pre-eminence increased since all European traffic passed through the Mani Soyo's domain.

Very little is known about the personality of the Mani Soyo, who eventually took Dom Manuel as his Christian name. When Diogo Cao landed, he was already an old man. His enormous political presitge was evident from the first, since the Mani Kongo (ruler of the Kongo) Nzinga Nkuwu referred to him as "uncle." Rather than expressing actual blood ties, the title "uncle" indicated a political relationship which obligated the Mani Kongo to give respect and deference to the Mani Soyo.

Since he lived near the harbor on the Zaire River, the Mani Soyo was the first high-ranking Kongo dignitary to receive envoys from King Joao II of Portugal (reigned 1481-95). Like Mani Kongo Nzinga, he was greatly impressed by the wonders of European technology and by Christianity, which he believed was the supernatural force energizing this powerful new culture. The Mani Soyo attempted to compete with his superior, the Mani Kongo, for control of Portuguese knowledge and spiritual strength. So eager was the Mani Soyo that when a group of masons, carpenters, and missionaries requested by Nzinga, landed at Mpinda on March 29, 1491, he detained the delegation and demanded to be baptized immediately. Pleading that his advanced age made it unlikely that he could live much longer, and pretending that the Mani Kongo had granted his approval, the Mani Soyo accomplished his goal and was baptized on April 3, 1491.

Because his baptism preceded that of Mani Kongo Nzinga, the Mani Soyo hoped to gain an advantage with the Portuguese. His choice of Dom Manuel as his

Dom Manuel's baptism.

new Christian name reflected his belief that two people bearing the same name were unified in a particularly intimate relationship. By selecting the name of the prince heir to the throne of Portugal, Dom Manuel, the Mani Soyo obliged the Mani Kongo and his wife to take the names of Joao and Eleanor, the Portuguese royal couple who were old and would soon be replaced by the crown prince.

Both the Mani Soyo, Dom Manuel, and the Mani Kongo regarded baptism as an esoteric rite conferring special magical powers on the recipient. Thus, neither ruler wanted other notables to be baptized. Although Mani Kongo Nzinga abandoned his Christian religion, Dom Manuel remained faithful.

In the 1506 succession wars between Nzinga's sons, the Christian Mvemba Nzinga (*q.v.*), also known as Afonso I, and the traditionally oriented Mpanzu a Nzinga (*q.v.*), Mani Soyo Dom Manuel strongly supported Afonso, who eventually won and became a "Christian Prince."

NDAYWEL è NZIEM

BIBLIOGRAPHY: G. Balandier, *La vie quotidienne au royaume du Congo, du XVIème au XVIIIème siècles,* Paris, 1965, English translation by Helen Weaver published as *Daily Life in the Kingdom of the Kongo From the Sixteenth to the Eighteenth Century,* New York, 1968; J. Cuvelier, *L'ancien royaume du Congo* ("The Old Kingdom of Kongo"), Brussels, 1946; W.G.L. Randles, *L'ancien royaume du Kongo, des origines à la fin du XIXème siècle* ("The Ancient Kingdom from its Origins to the End of the 19th Century"), Paris, 1968. Makamu Ngangula, "Les rois de l'ancien royaume du Kongo des origines à 1718" ("The Kings of the Old Kongo Kingdom from its Origins to 1718"), unpublished thesis, University of Zaire, Lubumbashi.

MATEMU a KELENGE

Matemu a Kalenge (circa 1895-September, 1931), popularly known as Mundele Funji, led the famous 1931 Pende revolt against the colonial government.

Matemu belonged to the Pende chiefdom of Mushinga, centered at Lutshima about 50 km (30 mi) south of Kikwit in Kasai. This area had been greatly affected by colonial exploitation. Early in the 1900s, the Compagnie du Kasai and the Force Publique (the colonial army) acted in harmony to force the Pende people to collect and sell wild rubber. In the 1920s the Lever Brothers' Huileries du Congo Belge (H.C.B., Belgian Congo Oil Works) began operation of its palm-oil concession. Pende men were obliged to hire themselves to the company where they received low wages and were subjected to harsh working conditions. For the Pende, the oppression became intolerable when the Great Depression of the 1930s reduced the already low prices and wages the Pende received for their produce and labor from the Huileries du Congo Belge.

Sustained by the people's sufferings, a religious-political movement, the Tupelepele, arose in Pende communities in 1930 and early 1931. Tupelepele leaders proclaimed that dead ancestors would return to liberate the oppressed, that the Europeans would soon leave, that Africans should no longer work for the Europeans nor pay taxes, and that all objects of European origin should be destroyed.

From May 13-16, 1931, some taxpayers in Matemu a Kelenge's village of Kilamba, located near Lutshima, refused to accept work as palm nut gatherers from H.C.B. recruiters. Furthermore, they stopped supplying palm nuts to the Compagnie du Kasai. In retaliation, Burnotte, the territorial agent from Kandale, 120 km (70 mi) southeast of Kikwit, Van Hombeek, the H.C.B. recruiting officer, and Collignon, the Director of the Compagnie du Kasai depot at Bangi, took severe measures against Kilamba. Local villagers were whipped, arrested, raped, or taken hostage, and several huts were burned.

Outraged by the abuses, Matemu a Kelenge joined the Tupelepele sect and encouraged the growth of Tupelepele in Kilamba village. Taking the name Mundele Funji (white-wind) Matemu made Kilamba the main center of Tupelepele opposition to the colonial regime. Mundele Funji, now leader of the entire sect, preached open revolt against the Europeans.

Late in May 1931, violence erupted. On May 29, on orders from the Kikwit territorial agent, soldiers at Kinsenzele village fired into a crowd assembled to protest tax collection. After this attack, which killed more than 10 people, the Pende resolved to arm themselves against the state. This determination resulted in the death of territorial agent Maximilien Ballot at Kilamba on June 8. Ballot had come to Kilamba to supervise tax collection in the rebellious village. When a provocative crowd assembled, Ballot's men shot at the gathering badly wounding two villagers. Immediately, the Pende reacted by firing arrows.

In the melée, Ballot's entourage fled and the agent faced the people alone. As principal leader of the Tupelepele sect, Mundele Funji rushed at the European, striking him twice on the head with his machete. Someone else shot Ballot with an arrow while a man named Musoso Shagindungu cut off his head.

For the people, Ballot's murder signaled the liberating power of the ancestors and proved the truth of the Tupelepele message. Thus, the entire Pende region between the Lutshima and Kwilu rivers actively revolted. So serious was the uprising that it took the colonial government from June 1931 to February 1932 to put down the disorder. More than 4,000 Pende lost their lives in these months.

During the military operations, Mundele Funji led the Pende warriors in a courageous resistance. According to oral history, he cut off the hands of several policemen by using his long double-edged knife. Supposedly he ran as fast as lightning.

Official reports say that Mundele Funji died at Kilamba in August 1931. The most important battle of the Pende revolt, the Kilamba engagement involved thousands of Pende warriors who fought for an entire day. Pende general opinion, however, maintains that Mundele Funji was not killed at Kilamba, but merely changed his identity and lived until about 1965.

Mundele Funji's exploits against European occupation became legendary and were frequently recalled in song and dance. Among the Pende, the 1931 revolt is known as the Mundele Funji War.

SIKITELE GIZE a SUMBULA

BIBLIOGRAPHY: C.C. (Caprasse), "Les événements du Kwango. La secte des Pupelepele [Tupelepele]. Quelques épisodes tragiques" ("The Kwango Events. The Pupelepele [Tupelepele] Some Tragic Events"), *Bulletin du Cercle Colonial Luxembourgeois*, No 8, 1931, pp. 169-73; B. Gusimana, "La révolte des Bapende en 1931 (Souvenirs d'un Témoin)," ("The Bapende Revolt of 1931 (Memories of a Witness),") *Cahiers Congolais de la Recherche et du Développement*, XVI, 4, 1970, pp. 59-69; F. Mulambu-Mvuluya, "La révolte des Bapende: Mai-Septembre 1931" ("The Revolt of the Bapende: May-September 1931"), *Congo-Afrique*, No. 53, 1971, pp. 115-35; Sikitele Gize, "Les racines de la revolte pende de 1931" ("The Roots of the Pende Revolt of 1931"), *Etudes d'histoire africaine*, V, 1973, pp. 99-153. *See also* "Contribution à l'histoire de la révolte du Kwango" ("Contribution to the History of the Kwango Revolt"), *L'Avenir Colonial Belge*, July 30, 1931; "L'affair du Kwango. Le procès des incidents de mai 1931 à Kilamba" ("The Kwango Affair. The Trial for the Incidents of May 1931 at Kilamba"), *Le Courrier d'Afrique,* January 13, 16, and 18, 1934.

MBIDI KILUWE

Mbidi Kiluwe (who flourished circa 1500), also known as Ilunga Mbili, a hero in Luba oral tradition, is thought to have introduced "bulopwe," the unique power of kingship, to the ruling Luba dynasty. Although many Luba regard Mbidi Kiluwe as an historical figure, he can best be regarded as a symbol of political authority and courtly ritual.

According to tradition, Mbidi Kiluwe came from the Lake Mweru region in the east, although his precise origins are obscure. Supposedly, he was the son of a powerful chief, Ilunga Kiluwe, who had two other children, a son, Ndala, and a daughter, Mwanana. Because Mwanana was very dear to her father, he designated her as his successor, rather than his son Mbidi Kiluwe who had popular support.

Mwanana owned a domesticated lion, which Mbidi Kiluwe accidently allowed to escape. Furious, Mwana threatened to have him killed if he did not return her lion. Therefore, Mbidi Kiluwe, who was also a hunter, set out westwards to find the lion. Having lost the beast's track, he stopped in the forest located between the Lualaba and Lubilash rivers to hunt. There, he met the two half-sisters of the Luba ruler Nkongolo (*q.v.*). The sisters fell in love with the stranger and took him to their brother's court.

With hesitation, Nkongolo welcomed the hunter. Nkongolo was fearful because a seer had told him the visitor would introduce the customs of anointed royalty to the realm. This royal innovation, symbolized by the new culinary ritual of eating in private, was not accepted gracefully by Nkongolo. Vexed, the visitor decided to leave the court of Nkongolo, despite the fact that earlier he had married Nkongolo's two half-sisters. Thus, he returned to the east from whence he had come.

Despite Mbidi Kiluwe's departure, the prediction of Nkongolo's seer soon was realized. A child, Kalala Ilunga (*q.v.*), was born of the union between Mbidi Kiluwe and Bulanda, one of Nkongolo's sisters. When he grew up, Kalala Ilunga fulfilled the earlier prophecy by overthrowing Nkongolo, establishing a new dynastic line, and expanding the Luba political domain.

NDAYWEL è NZIEM

BIBLIOGRAPHY: W.F. Burton, *Luba Religion and Magic in Custom and Belief*, Tervuren, 1961; L. De-Heush, *Le roi ivre ou l'origine de l'état* ("The Drunken King or the Origin of the State"), Paris, 1972; J. Vansina, *Les anciens royaumes de la savane*, Léopoldville, 1965, published in English as "Kingdoms of the Savanna," Madison, 1966; E. Verhulpen, *Baluba et Balubaisés du Katanga* ("The Baluba and the Balubaized of Katanga"), Anvers, 1936.

MBUNDU a GAMONI

Mbundu a Gamoni (circa 1870-August 5, 1941) was a great chief of the Akwa Mushinga, a Pende people living about 80 km (50 mi) southeast of Kikwit. Owing his power to the colonial authorities, Mbundu worked as a government agent and was partially responsible for the tensions leading to the great Pende revolt in 1931.

The son of Gamoni and his wife Galumbu, Mbundu a Gamoni was not selected as chief according to the traditional pattern. When in 1919 the Belgians recognized the chiefdom of Akwa Mushinga as a customary political structure, they refused to acknowledge the Akwa Mushinga chief Njila Gamoni. Because, in 1916-17, Njila had revealed his strong anti-colonial attitudes by opposing tax collection in the Mushinga lands, colonial authorities conferred official investiture on Mbundu a Gamoni, who had never been chosen as a customary chief. From 1919, the Akwa Mushinga had two chiefs: Njila, "the customary" ruler, and Mbundu, "the official" leader. Njila held the real power in the eyes of the population, while Mbundu was considered a mere capita (sub-chief) responsible for collecting taxes. Therefore, Mbundu was hated and rejected everywhere.

When Njila died in 1929, Mbundu became a candidate for customary investiture, which, he hoped would allow him to exercise real power over the Mushinga. Traditionally, Pende chiefs were selected from among several eligible clans. The basic rule in matters of succession was that each clan eventually came to the throne in turn. Since Mbundu and Njila were from the same clan, the Ngiamba, Mbundu's candidacy was contested by the other clans. The chiefdom's council of notables also rejected Mbundu as chief. Then Mbundu appealed to the Kandale territorial authorities (Kandale is about 130 km, or 75 mi, southeast of Kikwit), who obliged the Mushinga to accept him. The Kashinga and the Kasanji clans, however, opposed this ruling.

In 1930, the Kashinga and Kasanji clans refused to pay the taxes, which they regarded as a tribute to a usurper. Therefore, chief Mbundu and the Kandale territorial agent, Burnotte, had several recalcitrant tax payers flogged and led about by a rope tied around their necks. Very discontent with this treatment, the Pende villagers resolved to defend themselves in the future. In May 1931, acting on orders from Kandale territorial authorities, who wanted Africans to prepare for the 1931 tax collection, chief Mbundu toured the villages under his control. Mbundu's passage through the village of Kilamba, 80 km (50 mi) southeast of Kikwit, inhabited by members of the Kashinga and Kasanji clans, provoked a popular uprising. Matemu a Kelenge, (q.v.), known as Mundele Funji, leader of the Tupelepele sect, which was then active in the Pende villages between the Lutshima and the Kwilu rivers, preached the imminent departure of the Europeans, systematic opposition to the tax levy, and categorical refusal to work for the Europeans. Mundele persuaded the inhabitants of Kilamba to chase Mbundu out of their village. The people followed Mundele Funji's in-

structions by beating Mbundu and throwing stones. When chief Mbundu lodged a complaint about the incident, government officials decided to send territorial agent Maximilien Ballot to collect the 1931 tax levy in the Kilamba region.

Accompanied by chief Mbundu, a soldier, and three messengers, Ballot arrived in Kilamba on the morning of June 8, 1931. Realizing the intensity of local hostility, Ballot ordered his troops to fire on a crowd assembled in Kilamba, where they had come to protest. After two villagers had been badly wounded, the crowd turned and fired a large number of arrows. Panic-stricken, the decorated chief Mbundu, the soldier, and the messengers who had accompanied Ballot fled. Then Mundele Funji, the main rebel leader, fell on Ballot, striking him twice on the head with a machete. Chief Musoso Shagindungu subsequently decapitated the European. Ballot's murder at Kilamba touched off the greatest uprising in the history of the Belgian Congo, as the entire Pende region between the Lutshima and the Kwilu broke out into open rebellion. Harshly suppressed by the colonial regime, the Pende revolt cost the lives of more than 4,000 Pende, and several dozen soldiers of the Force Publique (the colonial army).

Ironically, during the repression of the revolt, chief Mbundu a Gamoni, together with several other Pende chiefs and notables, was arrested for having "handed over" territorial agent Ballot to "his blood-thirsty subjects." He was whipped, almost to the point of death, in the camp at Kabobola, and also during the court marshall at Kandale. Later incarcerated in the prison of Kikwit, the Force Publique tortured Mbundu, putting out one of his eyes.

On February 18, 1932, he was banished to the Banningville area (now Bandundu) with 69 other Pende chiefs and notables. When the Belgian parliament and king, Albert I, (ruled 1909-34), learned of the cruel treatment the Pende had received from the colonial troops and authorities, they demanded redress. Thus, chief Mbundu and the other detainees were released on November 23, 1932, after they had formally promised the government to renounce all future political activity and to remain submissive.

As soon as he returned home, chief Mbundu was officially relieved of his power by the colonial authorities, who replaced him with a man named Khay from the Kihanji clan. Khay received official investiture on October 8, 1934. Upset by the manner in which he was repaid for his many past services, Mbundu categorically refused to return the insignias and symbols of his customary power. Thus neither Khay, nor the two other chiefs who succeeded him during Mbundu's lifetime, (Kingufu in 1938 and Sangu in 1939), received customary investiture.

To avoid a new confrontation, the colonial rulers,

realizing chief Mbundu's great influence, recognized him as the customary chief of the Mushinga. They even acknowledged that the chief upon whom they had conferred official investiture and chief Mbundu, who retained customary authority, would work together for the proper functioning of the chiefdom. Although Mbundu ostensibly accepted this arrangement, in secret he incited his followers to disobey the orders from the "official" chief and from the colonial power.

Chief Mbundu a Gamoni died on August 5, 1941 after having given the insignias and symbols of customary power to the notable, Kingulu, of his clan (Ngiamba). Therefore, Kingulu was regarded by the population as Mbundu's successor and true customary chief, while Sangu, who had received official investiture, was considered a mere capita (sub-chief) of the Belgians.

Mbundu a Gamoni was uncontestably a very great chief. He acquired great renown throughout the Pende lands and in the neighboring areas at the time of the Pende revolt of 1931, in which he found himself indirectly implicated. His memory remained still very much alive decades after his death.

SIKITELE GIZE a SUMBULA

BIBLIOGRAPHY: Sikitele Gize, "Les racines de la révolte pende de 1931" ("The Roots of the Pende Revolt of 1931"), Etudes d'Histoire Africaine, V, 1973.

MIGWA KASANZA

Kangu Migwa Kasanza (circa 1870-August 28, 1953) was a chief of the Lunda-Pende chiefdom of Kangu, located 100 km (60 mi) southeast of Kikwit.

Migwa Kasanza was appointed chief after the death of former chief Kangu Kumbi Lumbombo in April 1929. He received customary investiture in 1929 and was decorated with a medal and officially invested by the colony on May 15, 1930.

Although Chief Migwa sympathized with partisans of the Pende revolt, which broke out in the region between the Lutshima and the Kwilu rivers in May 1931, he could not actively support the rebels because soldiers of the Force Publique (colonial army) impressed him into service as a porter. Because Migwa was mistreated and publicly humiliated during the military operations, for the rest of his life he remained very suspicious of European authority. When Migwa was accused of being disloyal to the government, the district commissioner of the Kwango, Van der Hallen, on February 24, 1932, took measures to revoke Migwa's official duties and banish him to the Banningville area (now Bandundu). Since Migwa never received official notification of this measure, he continued to exercise his functions. Finally, other Belgian officials intervened on his behalf, obtaining a cancellation of Van der Hallen's order. Van der Hallen, in fact, had been suspended from his duties because of the numerous abuses he had engaged in to repress the Pende revolt.

On October 24, 1936, Migwa Kasanza was reconfirmed in his official functions.

Chief Kangu Migwa Kasanza tried to collaborate with the Belgian authorities. Nevertheless, he disliked certain humiliating tasks, such as collecting taxes and supervising corvée (forced labor) for the colonial authorities. In the 1940s, when the tensions of the 1931 revolt had calmed, chief Kangu Migwa Kasanza, refused to continue in the role of capita (sub-chief). In 1940, he objected to collecting taxes or to overseeing the rubber harvest. In retaliation, the government withheld his salary after May 8, 1940.

In 1944, chief Migwa Kasanza supported the Lupambulu sect, active at that time in the Pende region. He protected Lupambulu members whom the Belgians wanted to arrest. Hoping to discipline the chief, the territorial administrator, Bomans requested higher authorities to banish Migwa and several other leaders of the Lupambulu sect from the Pende lands. Because of Migwa's numerous past services, however, the affair was quashed. But ever afterwards the Belgian authorities at Gungu characterized Migwa as "cunning" and untrustworthy. From that time these authorities favored his internal rivals who they hoped could sap his power.

When the sector of Gungu was created on April 20, 1948, government officials did their best to prevent Migwa from retaining any power. In selecting African officials for the new sector, they favored members of rival families. Therefore, chief Migwa Kasanza spent the remaining years of his life defending the Kangu Lunda rights on the lands they had inherited from their ancestors, lands that certain "client" clans, whom they had allowed to settle there around 1903, sought to appropriate.

SIKITELE GIZE a SUMBULA

BIBLIOGRAPHY: J. Vansina, Les anciens royaumes de la savane, Léopoldville, 1965, published in English as Kingdoms of the Savanna, Madison, 1965. See also Archives of the Gungu zone, Political File on the Gungu Sector, and Archives of the Feshi zone, register of political information for the Kianza chiefdom.

MISHA miSHYAANG MATUUM

Misha miShyaang Matuum (who flourished in the early 17th century) ruled as king early in the history of the Kuba, an ethnic group living east of the confluence of the Kasai and Sankuru rivers.

Of Lele origins—the Lele live just west of the Kuba across the Kasai River—Misha came to the Kuba throne following a succession crisis. The incumbent dynasty, founded by Mboong a Iyool at the end of the Kuba migrations, ended when Lashyaang Latot Landoon was killed accidentally near the present village of Kosh, several kilometers from the capital, Nsheeng (Mushenge), located 75 km (45 mi) east of modern Ilobo.

Because there were no male heirs in the royal Matoon clan, and the women who might have risen to the throne were ineligible following a scandal precipitated by an ill-disposed queen, the throne was vacant. Thus, after having won two earlier succession quarrels, the Matoon clan risked losing the throne permanently. Therefore, they called on Misha miShyaang Matuum, the son of a Bushoong princess, Shyaang a Mbul, married to a local Lele man according to some, or in exile with her son among the Lele, according to others. It is possible that Misha miShyaang was of the Matuum or Ntuun clan, called Matundu among the Lele of the east, where they reign to this day.

Oral tradition indicates that Misha miShyaang was so uncouth that it was necessary to teach him how to behave as a ruler. Suspicious, he came to council meetings armed with bow and arrow. Although Misha never felt secure among his Bushoong subjects, he was able to reorganize the Kuba kingdom and recapture regions his predecessor had abandoned to the Kete and the Pyaang. Although tradition portrays Misha miShyaang as an individual ruler, in actuality he symbolizes an entire dynasty, a dynasty deposed by Shyaam aMbul aNgoong (q.v.). Shyaam aMbul is recalled as a conqueror who came from the Kwango-Kwilu region. Either the son of a slave or the offspring of a legitimate Bushoong prince, he brought important innovations to the Kuba after making a voyage into the Kwango area. Supposedly Misha miShyaang banished Shyaam from the kingdom. Taking refuge among the Kel, Shyaam was hidden by Mbakam Mashiing, who refused to deliver him to the envoys of the nyim (ruler). (To this day, an enemy of the nyim, fleeing to the Kel, receives sanctuary.)

Returning to the capital, Shayaam hid with Kaan Kabady at Mbaanc. When the king asked about Shayaam, Kaan Kabady implied that Shayaam was dead by declaring that he was underground. Put to the test of poison to prove the truth of his declaration, Kaan Kabady did not die, for Shayaam was indeed underground in a large, covered well. Misha miShyaang was tricked again when he invited to his capital the wearer of the new Nyeeng mask, who had appeared at Mbaanc. The masked man was his enemy Shyaam, who profited from his stay in the capital to bury

charms. The magical power of the charms enabled the interloper to dethrone the reigning nyim, Misha miShyaang. Misha miShyaang fled with his wives and children. Several days later his family hung themselves in the plain of Nga Shiim. After a prolonged stay in the forest, Misha miShyaang himself died after being caught in a trap for animals.

BELEPE BOPE MABINTCH

BIBLIOGRAPHY: Belepe Bope Mabintch, ''Les conflits de succession au trône dans le royaume kuba'' (''Conflicts for Succession to the Throne of the Kuba Kingdom''), *Etudes d'histoire africaine*, IX, 1977; E. Torday and T.A. Joyce, *Notes ethnographiques sur les peuplades communement appelés Bakuba, ainsi que les peuplades apparentés; les Bushongo* (''Ethnographic Notes on the Group Commonly Called Bakuba, as well as Related Groups; the Bushongo''), Tervuren, 1911; J. Vansina, *The Children of Woot,* Madison, 1978.

MOPIPI MULONGEKI

Mopipi Mulongeki Paul (1904-May 8, 1976) ruled as chief of the Bakisi polity, a subdivision of the Lega people, who live 150 km (100 mi) west of Lake Kivu.

Mopipi Mulongeki, called Kyabunda, was born in 1904, the year Shabunda post (located 160 km, or 100 mi, west of Bukavu and known as Kyabunda in the Lega language) was established. Since the 1860s, when Swahili traders penetrated into the area, the Mopipi family had gained political prominence among the previously decentralized Lega people. Together with several other families, the Mopipi continued to exercise authority during the period of Belgian colonialism.

Mopipi Mulongeki Paul was the son of chief Mopipi Mutimana (q.v.), who ruled the chiefdom of Banabanga from his capital at Shabunda. As a young boy, Mopipi Mulongeki attended a special school in Stanleyville (now Kisangani). The school, established for children of officially invested chiefs, was intended to educate future chiefs in an environment isolated from the customary political atmosphere. After spending eight years as one of the first students at the Stanleyville institution, Mopipi Mulongeke was recalled to Shabunda to succeed his father, who died suddenly of dysentery on May 5, 1930. On July 21, 1930, Mopipi Mulongeki officially was invested as chief over the Bakisi.

As chief, the young Mopipi did not live up to the expectations of the Belgian administrators. In 1932, a government report characterized Mopipi as ''more careless than devoted, does not respond to the directives he supposedly acquired through his professional education. Without the intervention of the territorial," the report went on to say, "his chiefdom would show a state of indescribable decay. He visits only under duress the regions under his authority, does not encourage cultivation of the required crops, neglects the smooth operation of his chiefdom, and, despite repeated recommendations, he curbs none of his wasteful spending habits."

In 1935, disciplinary action resulted in the loss of two months without pay. In 1937, Mopipi Mulongeki was condemned to one year of penal servitude for misappropriating 62,000 francs from the revenues collected in his chiefdom. In 1942, government authorities seriously considered removing Mopipi from office. Finally, in September 1945, he was arrested and dismissed.

Nevertheless, while serving as chief Mopipi contributed greatly to progress in the Bakisi region. During his tenure, the first motor road linked the important center of Kindu to Shabunda via Kalima. Plans were also made for Shabunda-Kigulube-Bukavu road.

Mopipi Mulongeki mobilized villagers to survey and construct these roads. He also recruited young men to work in the newly operating mines of the territory, encouraged his people to work for colonial settlers, and transplanted entire villages of farmers near the mining camps to grow provisions.

Mopipi Mulongeki acted as an intermediary between the Europeans and the African population. Besides knowing how to read and write Kilega and Kingwana, he had a good command of French. Thus, many people sought out Mopipi, asking him for favors and advice.

In administrative matters, he retained the four great notables who had been in power under his father. He was, however, quick to dismiss officials who did not support him. Often they were imprisoned or banished to another part of the colony. Thus, he established a powerful network of servants devoted to his cause.

Mopipi Mulongeki's power and popularity disturbed the local territorial administration. Increasingly, the African chief ignored the advice of territorial agents, conducting the affairs of his chiefdom as he pleased. Thus, a government report noted: "The chief Mopipi sends away tax-payers who were bringing him their taxes....Furthermore, he is not interested in the normal operation of the principal tribunal of his chiefdom and does not apprehend the natives called before the police tribunal." It was true that Mopipi sent away tax-payers incapable of paying their taxes, but took it upon himself to pay in their place. In cases of not seeking out criminals, he was merely following the Swahili dictum which says: "A chief does not

arrest the thief; it is not for the chief to pursue." Mopipi's philosophy of government, while practical and just, was contrary, to the interests of the colonizers.

Although Mopipi received a medal of merit for his loyal service during World War II, he was discharged from office in 1945. Then, in 1946, he was condemned to seven years in prison for "extortions and diverse infractions." He was banished first to Masisi, 125 km (75 mi) north of Bukavu, then to Lusambo, 150 km (90 mi) northeast of Kananga, and, from 1952, to Elisabethville (now Lubumbashi). To earn a living in Elisabethville, he became a bailiff at the district court.

In Mopipi's absence, the colonial government restructured the Bakisi chiefdom in an attempt to reduce the power of the African rulers. The number of artificial chiefdoms created by the Belgians was increased from four to nine. Nevertheless, Mopipi's popularity was deep and widespread. Although Kyalala André, who headed the Bikiunga chiefdom, replaced Mopipi as chief over the Bakisi sector and resided at Shabunda, he had to live with constant police protection. When he traveled from his headquarters, which was rare, he had to rely on an armed escort and he was forced to bring provisions with him as no village would feed him. Also, he constantly feared he would be poisoned. To maintain calm and order in the sector, the administration was obliged to banish all Mopipi Mulongeki's principal collaborators and partisans.

Mopipi's popularity survived his long and distant exile. In 1959, he returned home following a general suspension of banishment orders.

Upon Mopipi's arrival in Kivu, the permanent college of the Bakisi district forced Kyalala to resign on May 20, 1960, and asked Mopipi to resume leadership of the district. This came after an April 1960 plebiscite, organized by the administration, to determine which of the two rival chiefs had the most support. Mopipi had won by a large majority.

On June 1, 1960, the district commissioner of South Kivu reinvested Mopipi as chief of the Bakisi. In compensation for abandoning his office, Kyalala obtained a capital allocation of three hundred thousand francs from the treasury of the chiefdom. Mopipi saved, at the last minute, the power of his family. For, after June 30, 1960, the government of independent Zaire recognized only customary chiefs who had held office prior to independence.

Despite opposition from part of the Bakisi population, chief Mopipi managed to maintain himself at the head of a united chiefdom. Not only did he have the endorsement of a large majority of the population, he could also count on support from his younger brother, Mopipi Bitingo François, an elected national deputy, vice president of the House of Representatives, minister of agriculture in Ileo's provisional government, and, after 1965, a people's commissioner. Mopipi Bitingo pleaded the case of the Bakisi and of his brother Mopipi Mulongeki. United around Mopipi Mulongeki, the Bakisi confronted the 1964 Simba rebels, who were opposing the central government, with courage, determination, and success. Mopipi's authority increased even more after the new regime under General Mobutu ended all power disputes in the Bakisi chiefdom, thus reinforcing Mopipi's control.

Chief Mopipi Mulongeki's last act was to assure his brother's succession to his throne. Aged, weakened by illness, and no longer able to assume the responsibilities of chief, in 1971 he named his brother, Mopipi Bitingo, as permanent secretary of the Bakisi chiefdom. Finally, on January 4, 1976, with the assent of the regional authority of Kivu and the sub-regional authority of South Kivu, the old chief abdicated in favor of his brother, who earlier had been discharged from all political activity on the national level.

Several months later, on May 8, 1976, Mopipi Mulongeki died in the Shabunda hospital.

YOGOLELO TAMBWE ya KASIMBA

BIBLIOGRAPHY: Kaswa Bora Yuma, "Biographie du Grand Chef Mopipi Mulongeki" ("Biography of the Great Chief Mopipi Mulongeki"), manuscript, May 9, 1976. Mulolwa Kangadjo Munganga, "Evolution administrative de la Collectivité des Bakisi: Zone de Shabunda," ("Administrative Evolution of the Bakisi Collectivity: Shabunda Zone"), thesis, Lubumbashi, 1975.

MOPIPI MUTIMANA

Mopipi Mutimana (circa 1875-May 5, 1930), a chief of the Lega people living southwest of Lake Kivu, acted vigorously to modernize his land and people.

Before the late 1800s, the Lega had no centralized political institutions. Instead, they were led by members of the semi-secret Bwami society which maintained legal, moral, religious, and artistic standards in Lega society. When Swahili traders arrived in Lega territory in the 1860s, they engaged local men who acted as banyampara (agents) to aid in collecting slaves, ivory, food, and porters. These agents eventually assumed the role of political chiefs.

Mopipi Mutimana's father Kangadio, a leader of the Lega Banabanga clan, acted as a friend of the Swahili. Although when the Swahili first entered the area, they established their main station at Kyoli (later Shabunda), 160 km (100 mi) west of Bukavu among the Lega Bangoma clan, because of Bangoma hostility, the Swahili soon allied with Kangadio and the Banabanga. In appreciation for Kangadio's support, the Swahili interlopers selected his sons Mutimana, Kinganda, and Itanganika as agents.

Kangadio's son Mutimana earlier had adopted Swahili culture. Not only did he speak, read, and write the Swahili language, he also embraced the Islamic faith. As an Arabized individual, Mutimana placed himself in opposition to members of the Bwami society who resisted modernization. As an agent, Mutimana took the name of Mopipi in memory of another brother who had been killed, probably while helping the Swahili in an ivory raid.

Although Mopipi's appointment as an agent practically coincided with the Swahili defeat in 1894, the Banabanga leader quickly attached himself to the victorious Congo Free State. Since the Bwami dignitaries, the traditional Lega élite, resisted any association with the Europeans, the Free State officials relied on Mopipi Mutimana as their intermediary in dealing with the Lega.

Mopipi retained the respect of the colonizers throughout his life. In 1924, a territorial administrator described him as an "excellent chief, a perfect judge, and a shrewd politician." Mopipi's literacy also won him praise. Already in 1917, Mopipi had been decorated with a silver medal, while in 1923 he was officially invested as a chief. In 1928, he received the decoration of the order of the Lion.

As an official civil servant, Mopipi supervised rubber collection, labor recruitment for the mining companies, and the production of rice and palm-oil. He also helped enlist young men in the Force Publique (colonial army). In all his dealings, Mopipi was fair and just. When there was work to be done or rewards to be gained, he made sure that everyone was treated equally. Mopipi's impartiality extended even to members of his own family.

Mopipi gained the admiration and confidence of both Africans and Europeans. When he died in 1930, the people observed two days of silent mourning and the territorial administrator attended his funeral.

YOGOLELO TAMBWE ya KASIMBA

BIBLIOGRAPHY: Mwepa N'Kingi Kasali Wabanga, "Biographie du Citoyen Mopipi Mulongeki, Chef de la Collectivité des Bakisi (Zone de Shabunda). Région du Kivu" ("Biography of Citizen Mopipi Mulongeki, Chief of the Bakisi Collectivity (Shabunda Zone, Kivu Region), mimeographed, Shabunda, 1973.

MOPOIE BANGEZEGINO

Mopoie Bangezegino (circa 1845-April 15, 1916), a Muslim chief of the Zande people, living between the Uele and Bomou rivers in northern Zaire, forcefully resisted the encroachment of Europeans into his domain. Mopoie's second name, Bangezegino means "he who does not want the white man."

After 1850, the Zande people became allies of Muslims from the north, who had entered the Sudan and Zaire in search of slaves and ivory. Since the 1820s the Sudan had come under Egyptian influence, but in 1883 and 1884 a fervent Muslim sect known as the Mahdists launched a religious war against the modernizing Egyptians and their English allies. Repercussions of the Mahdist uprising reached south of the Bomou River where the Zande chief Powpwo or Poyo, Mopoie Bangezegino's brother, was killed in the disturbances.

Succeeding Powpwo, Mopoie settled at the confluence of the Bengaro and Bomou rivers, not far from where the borders of modern Zaire, the Central African Empire, and the Sudan intersect. In 1894, officials of the Congo Free State, intending to push northwards into the Bahr-al-Ghazal region of the Sudan, established a state post in Mopoie's territory. Sultan Mopoie did not oppose this action for he hoped to ally with the Europeans against his northern rivals. Free State authorities, however, soon abandoned the station.

Meanwhile, Mopoie Bangezegino took possession of extensive territories around the Gurba River, about 175 km (109 mi) north of modern Isirio. Because he was trying to increase his domain, Mopoie came into conflict with the Free State. Shrewdly aware of the rivalry between the Belgians, French, and British, Mopoie was able to play the various European forces against each other. Although he never broke relations with the Congo Free State, he did not permit the Belgians to enter his land. In 1902, he refused to attend an audience with District Commissioner Chatlin.

When, in 1902, the Free State decided to build a post in Mopoie's territory, the Zande Sultan asked his cousin Sasa to aid him in resisting. When Sasa refused to help, Mopoie was forced to capitulate and accept the establishment of the Sili station, 40 km (25 mi) northwest of the confluence of the Uele and Gurba rivers. Nevertheless, he would not cooperate with the Europeans by selling them food, ivory, or rubber. Instead, he traded with French merchants living north of the Bomou River. In 1911, the Belgians launched a campaign against Mopoie. The Sultan then fled, with his people, just across the border into French territory, where he settled about 50 km (30 mi) west of the Sudan frontier.

Mopoie, however, was no more submissive to the French than he had been to the Belgians. Early in 1916, having been warned by the Belgians that Mopoie intended to revolt, the French tried to arrest the African leader. They were not successful and, on February 11, 1916, Mopoie attacked and burned the French station in his area. Only after the French called on reinforcements from the neighboring Belgian and British governments were the Europeans able to defeat Mopoie Bangezegino. Mopoie was killed on April 15 while attempting to escape French riflemen.

TSHUND'OLELA EPANYA SHAMOLOLO

BIBLIOGRAPHY: N.O. Coosemans, "Mopoie Bangezegino," *Biographie Coloniale Belge*, Vol. 2, Brussels, 1951; R. Cornevin, *Histoire du Congo, Léopoldville-Kinshasa* ("History of the Congo, Léopoldville-Kinshasa"), Paris, 1970; P. Salmon, *La dernière insurrection de Mopoie Bangezegino*, ("The Last Uprising of Mopoie Bangezegino"), Brussels, 1916, reprinted, 1969.

MOTENGO

Motengo (circa 1890-1941), a chief of the Monia people who live on the upper Giri River, became famous for his many wives and children.

The area north of modern Mbandaka is inhabited by numerous small ethnic groups, renowned for their fishing. The Monia, located about 250 km (150 mi) north of Mbandaka in the Giri marshes, belong, with the Bonyange of the Moanda region, to the Waku ethnic group. Their language and customs unite them with the Nkato or Libinza to the south, although they live adjacent to the Jando and the Mwe who are settled on both sides of the Giri.

Motengo, born around 1890, is considered by many inhabitants of Monia and the surrounding area as the son of the notable Ekwakola, who was a leader of the Monia people when the Europeans reached the region in 1900. In truth, Motengo was of Ngombe origins for he was born in Molei, a village about 50 km (30 mi) north of the Monia. It is reported that he was purchased by a Mwe man from Limpoko who was at Molei to sell bananas. Because young Motengo earlier had committed a petty theft, he had been reduced to servitude and legally could be sold. His new master from Limpoko gave him to Likumbelo, chief of Bomole, among the Mwe people. Limpoko, in turn, gave Motengo to his friend, Ekwakola, a Monia notable who had gone to Bomole to take part in a "kola" fellowship meeting there. Obedient and intelligent, Motengo soon was integrated into Ekwakola's family as a son. Although Motengo eventually gained a high place in Monia society, he never forgot his

Molei origins. Throughout his life, he regarded the inhabitants of Molei as his brothers and his descendants consider themselves members of the Molei family.

In 1900, the Congo Free State official Sommelier, known as Limpanya, together with his Libinza allies: Molonga, Nzamba, Mungembe (q.v.), and Loweya, attacked the Monia, who had refused to accept European occupation. Panic-stricken, the Monia made an accommodation with the Belgians through the intermediary of chief Monoko na Ntaba, who ruled the Mampoko living at the confluence of the Giri and Ubangi rivers. A certain Lilamba, who led the Monia delegation, was selected by the Europeans as capita (sub-chief) over the Monia, but he died soon afterwards. Lilamba's replacement Ebamba was soon killed in a battle against the Djando Maboko. Thus the old chief Ekwakola—Motengo's master—was designated by the colonizers to receive the chief's medal.

From 1904 to 1913, the Monia were attached to the Giri sector, whose chief-town was Musa. Both the Monia and the Mwe came under the authority of chief Molonga, a Libinza man sent by the European administrator at Musa to subdue the Monia people. Thus, Molonga was invested chief of the Monia and the Mwe. With his Libinza henchmen, Molonga ravaged the area by seizing chickens, goats, and crops, capturing young men whom they sent to Libinza villages as slaves, and taking the wives and daughters of those who refused to pay their taxes. The name, Molonga, became, among the Monia and Mwe, a symbol of the hatred they felt for all the Libinza people.

Although chief Ekwakola married Molonga's daughter Mwamolanga so as to live in peace with the Libinza ruler, the Monia never accepted the Libinza. In 1913, the sector of the Giri was divided into three parts, the Monia being attached to the Upper Giri sector. This provided an opportunity for the Monia to rid themselves of Molonga, who was from the Lower Giri. Molonga lost his power following a general revolt in the Mwe region, an uprising instigated by Ekwakola and his son Motengo. With help from the whites at Musa and Nouvelle-Anvers (now Makanza), Ekwakola defeated Molonga and gained much prestige among the peoples of the Upper Giri area.

Ekwakola's adopted son Motengo received the chief's medal in 1915. From that time on, he helped the Europeans organize the Mwe, who were then attached to the Monia, into administratively viable chiefdoms. Soon Motengo became known as the greatest chief of the region. Hoping to cultivate his friendship, or merely to avoid his wrath, people brought him presents and offered him their daughters in marriage. When individuals could not pay the taxes required by the colonial government, Motengo paid in their place. Then, in compensation, he demanded a woman.

Even though Motengo had only two wives when he became chief, eventually he was able to assemble a "harem" of more than 300 women. Some of these he offered as wives to his nephews and sons. Those remaining women were permitted to take "lovers" in the village and to have children. Although these relationships were actually marriages, the children were customarily and officially recognized as Motengo's offspring. Thus, he was able to acquire an immense family of supporters.

In 1940, the colonial government created the Bamwe sector with Bomole as its chief town. Although Motengo was appointed chief of the sector, he served only a short time before his death in 1941.

MUMBANZA mwa BAWELE na
NYABAKOMBI ENSOBATO

BIBLIOGRAPHY: M. Guilmin, "Quelques coutumes matrimoniales des peuples de l'entre Congo-Ubangi" ("Some Matrimonial Customs of the Peoples Between the Congo and the Ubangi"), *Congo*, I, 1922, pp 44-48, Konga ya Bamey mwa Mokoma, "Etude sur les institutions traditionellés des gens d'eau" ("Study on the Traditional Institutions of the Water People"), thesis, Université Nationale du Zaire, 1973.

MPAGNI

Mpagni Bobuanabongwe (circa 1875-June 8, 1947), a member of the Boma ethnic group, living between the Zaire river and Lake Mai Ndombe, rose to prominence as a merchant, chief, and traditional historian.

Mpagni was born at Bomejuri village. Before he was 20 years of age, he took an active part, with his father, in the regional trade linking Stanley (now Malebo) Pool and Lake Léopold II (now Lake Mai Ndombe). Then, from 1901 to 1904, Mpagni studied the Bible at Tshumbiri, a Baptist Missionary Society station, 50 km (30 mi) south of Bolobo, on the Zaire River. It was there he learned to speak Bobangi and Lingala. The training Mpagni received at Tshumbiri was of great value to him in his later commercial and political dealings.

In 1908, he was chosen as a leader of his Shaa Kempinu clan. After gaining customary authority, Mpagni was recognized and invested by the colonial authority as ruler of the Mpelu Baboma chiefdom not far from Bolobo. Mpagni continued in his capacity for 20 years. As a firm friend of the whites, his influence and authority greatly contributed to the spread of colonial domination.

In 1928, the Mpelu-Baboma chiefdom was dissolved when the colonial authority created the great chiefdom of Baboma-North, placed under the authority of the Sengele people living just west of Lake Léopold II. Consequently Mpagni lost his office as chief of Mpelu-Baboma, and his government medallion was taken back. Angered at being rejected by the whites for whom he had worked so hard, Mpagni petitioned the district commissioner at Inongo, on the eastern shore of Lake Léopold II, to reverse the dismissal. Mpagni argued that he was the most influential man in the region, and that the Sengele were late comers who had arrived in the territory long after the Boma people had settled the lands.

After five years of negotiations, having received no satisfaction from the commissioner, Mpagni organized a resistance against the government. Beginning in 1933, he urged all the inhabitants of his former chiefdom to wear raffia loin-cloths and to smear their bodies with white kaolin (clay). By these actions, Mpagni sought to demonstrate that the Boma people wished to return to their ancient customs and that they were too poor to pay taxes. Accused of causing trouble, Mpagni was banished to the territory of Kiri, about 100 km (60 mi) west of Lake Léopold II.

Mpagni's banishment only increased the unrest in Mpela Baboma, and the region's inhabitants systematically opposed the administration's orders. Forced to reconsider their decision, the authorities soon liberated Mpagni, who returned to his village at Bomejuri. In 1937, the former chief resumed his commercial activities. Retaining his people's loyalty, Mpagni soon was invested as a notable of Mpoko. That same year, Mpagni met the territorial administrator R. Tonnoir, who became an expert in Boma history. At Tonnoir's request, Mpagni recounted Boma oral traditions, thus enabling Tonnoir to write his first work, *La pierre du feu* ("The Fire Stone"). Mpagni was extremely knowledgeable, not only in Boma tradition, but in the history of the entire Lake Mai-Ndombe region. Tonnoir described his as "a grey-haired notable, fully conversant with an inexhaustible repertory of traditional stories, one of the guardians of the oral tradition, and narrator of the *Pierre du feu.*"

Mpagni continued to prosper during the last years of his life. Becoming one of the region's wealthiest men, he was the first Boma individual to purchase a bicycle and a sewing machine. One of his four sons also became a trader, rising to become one of the greatest Boma merchants.

Mpagni died on June 8, 1947, after a long and painful illness.

BEKIMI BONZEKE

BIBLIOGRAPHY: R. Tonnoir, *La pierre du feu* ("The Fire Stone"), Léopoldville, 1939. *See also* "Dossiers des renseignements politiques sur la cheffeire des Baboma-Nord" ("Political Information Files on the Boboma-North Chiefdom"), Archives of the Mushie Zone.

MPANZU a NZINGA

Mpanzu a Nzinga (circa 1460-1506), a contender for the throne of the Kongo kingdom in 1506, advocated a return to traditional religious values, thus reversing the initial acceptance of the Catholic religion and Western culture. Mpanzu, however, was defeated by his brother Mvemba Nzinga (*q.v.*) who welcomed the Portuguese as his allies.

Probably born between 1456 and 1460, Mpanzu a Nzinga was the son of Nzinga Nkuwu, the king of the Kongo who welcomed the Portuguese explorer, Diogo Cao, who landed at the mouth of the Zaire River in August 1482. While the king, the queen-mother and the king's other son, Mvemba Nzinga, embraced the Catholic faith and took respectively the first names of João I, Eleanor, and Afonso, Mpanzu a Nzinga remained faithful to his traditional beliefs.

Mpanzu's adherence to custom won him the sympathy of the common people and of a large part of the nobility who supported him as the heir apparent to the throne. These partisans persuaded the king to abandon Christianity and to designate Mpanzu as his successor instead of Mvemba Nzinga, a fervent Christian.

The king returned to his traditional religion for several reasons. First, the Portuguese auto-da-fés (burning of heretics) stirred unrest among the people. Second, the king found it difficult to abandon polygamy, a practice enabling him to forge alliances which reinforced his power. Third, he concluded that the white man's material power was not due to the efficacy of Christianity. Thus, around 1494, only three years after his baptism, Nzinga Nkuwu forced most of the missionaries and Portuguese to leave Mbanza-Kongo (the capital, later named San Salvador). The Europeans then went to live in the province of Nzundi (located north of Mbanza-Kongo on the Zaire River) which was governed by Mvemba Nzinga. Mpanzu Nzinga, meanwhile, established Mpangu province (located between Mbanza-Kongo and Nsundi), which he administered, and surrounded himself with traditionalists.

Mpanzu's partisans brought many accusations against his rival Mvemba Nzinga, who destroyed traditional religious objects that had been venerated for generations and supported the new religion with great zeal. Therefore Mvemba Nzinga was dismissed as governor of Nsundi by the king. Although he managed to exonerate himself and receive pardon, he again fell into disgrace and was summoned to Mbanza-Kongo for discipline. Mvemba Nzinga, however, was able to delay his arrival in the capital, and the old king died before confronting his son.

After Nzinga Nkuwu's death in 1506, an intense succession dispute erupted. Some authors, for example Batsikama, believe that, strengthened by popular support and by the Mani-Vandu (spiritual chief of the earth and traditional priest of coronations), Mpanzu a Nzinga succeeded Nzinga Nkuwu as the invested king before his brother Mvemba Nzinga was able to gain power several months later, probably in 1507. Cuvelier, however, claims the war of succession, which brought the Christian Mvemba Nzinga to the throne, began immediately following the death of the king.

What is certain is that Mpanzu's refusal to convert to the Christian religion won him the hostility of the Portuguese who defended Mvemba Nzinga. Because of Portuguese help, the followers of the new religion, despite their small numbers, crushed Mpanzu's more numerous partisans. Mpanzu was killed and Mvemba Nzinga became king. Although the conquerors attributed their success to divine intervention, their victory is best explained by the fact that they had Portuguese artillery while Mpanzu's forces had only traditional arms. Mpanzu's death marked a turning point for the Kongo kingdom. With the accession of a "Christian prince," Portuguese exploitation, under the guise of Christianization, increased dramatically.

Mpanzu a Nzinga was a farsighted chief and a fierce defender of custom. Unlike his Christian brother, who kept him from the throne, he correctly interpreted Portuguese intentions in the Kongo. The Portuguese hid behind their religion in order to destroy Kongolese society. After Mpanzu a Nzinga's defeat, the Portuguese gained increasing control over the affairs of the kingdom. Perceiving the disastrous consequences of cultural assimilation, and advocating respect for traditional values as a basis for harmonious development, Mpanzu a Nzinga can be considered the precursor of authenticity.

TSIMBA MABIALA

BIBLIOGRAPHY: G. Balandier, *La vie quotidienne au royaume du Kongo du XVIème au XVIIIème siècle* Paris, 1965, English translation by Helen Weaver published as *Daily Life in the Kingdom of the Kongo from the Sixteenth to the Eighteenth Century,* New York, 1968; R. Batsikama, *Voici les Jagas ou l'histoire d'un peuple parricide bien malgré lui* ("Here are the Jagas or the History of a People Parricide Despite Themselves"), Kinshasa, 1971; J. Cuvelier, *L'ancien royaume du Congo* ("The Ancient Kingdom of Kongo"), Brussels, 1946; W.G.L. Randles, *L'ancien royaume du Congo des origines à la fin du XIXème siècle* ("The Ancient Kingdom of Congo from its Origins to the End of the 19th Century"), Paris, The Hague, 1968.

M'SIRI NGELENGWA

M'Siri (or Mushidi) Ngelengwa (circa 1830-December 21, 1891), a Nyamwezi interloper from east of Lake Tanganyika, established a vast commercial and political empire in the Shaba region.

M'Siri was born to Kalasa Mazuri and Manena Lyabanza in about 1830. Kalasa Mazuri, chief of Usumbwa province of Manua Sera, which Mirambo ruled after 1856, had worked for Swahili merchants as a porter. After a time, Kalasa forced another Nyamwezi trader, a man named Kafasia, to give up his commerce to Itabwa and the kingdom of Kazembe, in the Lake Mweru and southwestern Lake Tanganyika area. Once Kafasia relinquished his monopoly, Kalasa Mazuri became the kirongozi (caravan chief) for those territories. In about 1830, accompanied by his cousin Magulu, Kalasa led a caravan south to Shaba, where he hoped to purchase copper ingots. Although the Nyamwezi, known as the Yeke (hunters) in Shaba, could smelt and work iron, they did not yet know how to refine copper, a skill they learned later from the conquered people of Shaba.

The Yeke arrived in Shaba where they were well received by chief Katanga of the Lamba, about 30 km (20 mi) east of modern Likasi, as well as Pande of the Sanga (situated near Likasi), chief Sampwe of the Lomotwa who lived about 160 km (100 mi) north of Likasi, and chief Kinyama of the Aushi (settled east of the Lomba along the Luapula River). Kalasa made alliances with these chiefs by sealing a pact in blood. Leaving many Yeke in the region, Kalasa returned to Usumbwa with much copper, and ivory, and possibly many slaves. On his last journey to Shaba, Kalasa presented his son, M'Siri Ngelengwa, to the chiefs of the region. Thus, Ngelengwa inherited his father's commercial network. Previously, he had worked as a porter in Swahili caravans.

In 1856, M'Siri passed through the capital of Chinyat Munona, Kazembe (Lunda governor) of the Luapula river area. Despite opposition from his notables, Chinyat granted him passage through his land because the Nyamwezi adventurer gave the Kazembe a vaccine against smallpox, which had been ravaging the area. From the Kazembe's domain, M'Siri went on to live at the court of old chief Katanga. Welcoming this son of his friend Kalasa, chief Katanga gave M'Siri Ngelengwa numerous copper ingots, two daughters in marriage, and some land near the Lutipuka stream.

Having established a foothold in the area, M'Siri

Ngelengwa moved quickly to gain political control. No other chief in the region, not even the powerful Kazembe of the Luapula, was able to stop him. Once he had settled in chief Katanga's domain, other Nyamwezi from Usumbwa joined him. With many guns and a large number of fellow countrymen, M'Siri became a potent political force.

At first, M'Siri used his strength to regulate local quarrels. For example he helped chief Katanga by pillaging the village of a disobedient sub-chief Kapema. Following this action against Kapema, chief Pande Mutaba of the Sanga asked for M'Siri's aid in punishing the rebellious chiefs Kyana Kyamu and Sangatile. M'Siri returned from his Sanga expedition with a considerable booty of slaves, which he shared with his suzerain, Katanga. In addition, he dispatched slaves, ivory, and copper to Usumbwa in Tanzania. Recognized as the major police force in Shaba, he was greatly feared by local chiefs.

When old chief Katanga died, soon afterwards, M'Siri laid claim to Katanga's office by purchasing fabric for the burial shroud. In the ensuing battle for succession, M'Siri killed Katanga's sons and gained recognition as chief of the Lamba of the Katanga in about 1860. Shortly thereafter, M'Siri progressively took over Pande's lands. In the name of friendship, Pande offered M'Siri a portion of his lands. Convinced of his ability to conquer Pande completely, M'Siri refused the gift, agreeing instead to receive a mission of the Sanga notables. In the end M'Siri eliminated all the Sanga who opposed him and forced chief Pande to give him the emblems of power. Thus, M'Siri was recognized as the legitimate Sanga ruler, while Pande spent the rest of his life in captivity. Having become the supreme chief of the Lamba and the Sanga, M'Siri received obedience from chiefs Sampwe and Kinyama, fought the Luba, and appropriated the land between Lake Kisale and Lake Mweru.

Although eventually, the Kazembe sent warriors to control the Yeke aggressor, he acted far too late. Kashib, the Kazembe's Lunda governor over the land between the Luapula and the Lualuba rivers, betrayed the army charged with deposing and expelling M'Siri. Led by the nephews of the Kazembe Mongo Sunkutu, the army fell into a snare laid by M'Siri and Kashib. The army was exterminated and, from then on, the Kazembe of Luapula was completely cut off from Musumba, the Lunda capital, from which his conquering ancestors Kanyimbu Newej Mpemb (*q.v.*) and Lukwesa Ilunga (*q.v.*) had come. As a result of this great defeat, almost all the local sub-chiefs, even the Kazembe's supposed Lunda relatives, declared their allegiance to M'Siri.

M'Siri drew his strength from the carbines and powder which he received from the Wangwana (Swahili) in exchange for slaves, copper and ivory.

While he was fighting with the Kazembes of Luapula, he was careful to send gifts to the Swahili merchants who were also his potential enemies. In addition, he dispatched presents to the Lunda Mwant Yav (supreme chief) who provided him with a link to the Atlantic trade. Within Shaba itself, M'Siri demanded a constant flow of tribute from the peoples he had defeated.

The death of M'Siri's father in about 1880 resulted in discontent and schism among the Yeke in Shaba. When Kalasa Mazuri died in his homeland, M'Siri was asked to return and reign over Usumbwa. Although his brother, Kabebe, wished to replace him in Garanganza (the name of M'Siri's state), M'Siri refused to return home and proclaimed himself ruler of Garanganza. Many Yeke, who had come with M'Siri, were greatly disappointed by this deed because they supported yet another man, M'Siri's cousin Mutimbi, for the rulership. When Mutimbi's partisans rebelled, M'Siri and his brother, Kabobo Lukulu, attacked them at Kapolowe. Initially suffering defeat, M'Siri renewed his attack and pushed his rivals across the Luvua River which leads out of Lake Mweru. Once the Mutimbi faction had been expelled, M'Siri attacked the Bena Mitumba, and established his capital Bunkeya, 75 km (45 mi) north of modern Likasi, on their territory.

From 1880 to 1886, M'Siri's state, then at the peak of its power, grew in size following through campaigns against the Luba east of the Lualaba River. M'Siri captured many slaves and the entire southern part of the Luba empire—save the Lake Kisale chiefdom of Kikondja—yielded to the Yeke army commanded by the Swahili, Said bin Ali. Although the superiority of M'Siri's firearms and Swahili auxiliaries was crushing, a campaign against the Luba chief, Kayumba, was aborted as M'Siri had to contend with rebels among the Bena Mitumba and the Lamba. In addition, a small war against the Kazembe of Lualaba (not to be confused with the Kazembe of the Luapula to the east) was halted quickly so as not to jeopardize trade routes through the Lunda empire and Bihé in Angola.

After 1886, M'Siri's empire weakened. With the half-brother of Kazembe Kanyimbu Ntemana, M'Siri launched a series of fruitless campaigns against the Kazembe of the Luapula. Not only did Kanyimbu Ntemana capture and kill his traitor brother, he also defeated the Yeke army. As M'Siri grew older, his regime became more repressive and cruel. Thus, local populations, notably the Sanga, began a series of rebellions which undercut M'Siri's authority. The Sanga, Lamba, and Lunda people in M'Siri's domain were increasingly able to obtain guns and powder from Ovimbundu and Lwena traders who were often promoted political instability in order to obtain more slaves. At the same time, in retaliation for the high-handed manner in which M'Siri treated them, the

Swahili merchants progressively refused to supply the Yeke ruler with powder. By 1890, M'Siri's men found it unsafe to travel far from the capital, Bunkeya. Sensing that he could not hold out much longer, M'Siri envisioned returning to Usumbwa, and even negotiated for protection from his old enemy the Kazembe.

But M'Siri was unable to escape before being destroyed by a new European power. Already on February 14, 1886, the British missionary Frederich Arnot arrived in Bunkeya. Then, in 1891, several expeditions of the Congo Free State reached M'Siri's capital. When, on December 21, 1891, M'Siri refused to submit to Capt. William Stairs, the old chief was shot by a Belgian captain, O.P. Bodson.

TSHIBANGU KABET MUSAS

BIBLIOGRAPHY: H. Capello and R. Ivens, *De Angola a contra-costa* ("From Angola to the Opposite Coast"), 2 vols., Lisbon, 1886; R.J. Cornet, *Katanga,* Brussels, 1943; J. de Hemptinne, "Les mangeurs de cuivre du Katanga" ("The Copper-Eaters of Katanga"), *Congo,* I, No. 3, 1926, pp. 372-403; E. Labrecque, "Histoire des Mwata Kazembe" ("History of the Mwata Kazembe"), *Lovania,* XVIII, 1951, pp. 18-67; D. Livingston, *Last Journals,* London, 1874; J.A. Moloney, *With Captain Stairs to Katanga,* London, 1893; J. Vansina, *Les anciens royaume de la savane,* Léopoldville, 1965, published in English as *Kingdoms of the Savanna,* Madison, 1966; A. Verbreken, *M'Siri, roi du Garangange* ("M'Siri, King of Garanganza"), Brussels, 1956.

MUKENGE a TUNSELE

Mukenge a Tunsele (circa 1830-1898), also known as Kalamba, dominated the Lulua people during the entire second half of the 19th century. His political importance is closely tied to the long distance trade between Angola and Kasai and to the arrival of the whites in his region. During the first years of the European penetration, Mukenge profited by associating with them. Eventually, however, he came into direct conflict with the agents of the Congo Free State who drove him from his lands.

Mukenge, son of Tunsele, belonged to the Bena Kashyye clan of the Luba people living in Kasai. Originally from Shaba, the Luba migrated to Kasai where some of them settled in the Lulua River valley near modern Kananga. In the 19th century, relying on guns and commercial contacts with Angola, the Luba along the Lulua gained hegemony over other groups located elsewhere in Kasai. Thus, by the end of the 1800s, the Lulua population came to be recognized as a distinct ethnic group. Mukenge a Tunsele played a crucial role in this development.

In the mid-19th century, the Lulua lands experienced considerable social upheaval as hemp smokers established a new community "Lubuku"—a veritable cult promoting hospitality, happiness, and peaceful relations among all the Lulua people. About the same time, Cokwe (Chokwe) merchants from Angola introduced guns into the area. This created new commercial possibilities and led to a realignment of traditional political powers.

Quick to take advantage of the new lines of association provided by the Lubuku and of the new military power made possible by firearms, Mukenge had become a leading figure among the Lulua by 1875. Besides attempting to integrate the Lulua into the Luso-African trading network he also tried to subdue formerly independent groups by force of arms. Mukenge's commercial and military reputation, together with his renowned personal characteristics of energy, generosity, wisdom, tall stature, and handsomeness, earned him the nickname "Kalamba" (unmatched, without peers).

While he had many more rifles, Mukenge had not yet succeeded in dominating the other Lulua chiefs when the German explorers Paul Pogge and Hermann von Wissmann, reached his lands in 1881. Kalamba, who claimed the whites were his departed ancestors, welcomed Pogge and von Wissmann into his village. In actuality, he hoped to use them as commercial partners and as allies against neighboring chiefs.

In order to gain favor with the whites, Mukenge accompanied von Wissmann to the Swahili headquarters Nyangwe, about 450 km (270 mi) to the northeast of the Lualaba River.

Although von Wissmann journeyed on to eastern Africa, Pogge remained to live with Kalamba from July 21, 1882 to November 9, 1883. Kalamba's close ties to the whites increased his prestige in the land. It also seems that he hoped to model his village of approximately 2,000 inhabitants into a city like the Swahili Nyangwe.

In 1884, several months after Pogge's departure, von Wissmann returned to the Lulua as a representative of the Association International du Congo (A.I.C.). With Kalamba's help, he founded the post of Luluabourg-Malandji (now Kananga), near Kalamba's village. Hermann von Wissmann, who depended on Kalamba as much for the construction and the provisions for his men as for the security of the new station, was eager to gain the African chief's favor. Thus, he helped make war on Kalamba's neighbor, Mputu. Later von Wissmann called together all the Lulua chiefs and ordered them to swear obedience and pay tribute to Kalamba who soon became the most powerful African ruler in the area.

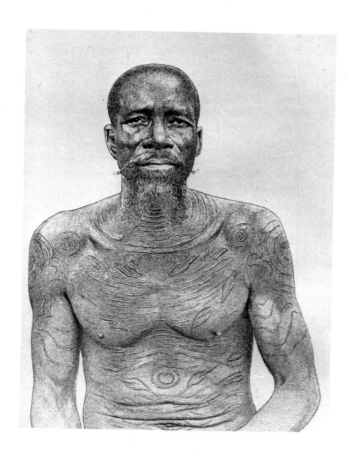

In 1885, Kalamba and 150 of his men traveled to the Stanley (now Malebo) Pool with von Wissmann who was carrying out King Leopold II's request to explore the Kasai River. When the party returned home aboard a state steamer instead of in dug-out canoes, Kalamba's prestige reached its peak.

When Paul Le Marinel and Oscar de Macar replaced von Wissmann at Luluabourg, they continued von Wissmann's policies for some time. Thus, Kalamba used them as his auxiliaries against Mwamba Mputu, chief of the Bakwa Mushilu.

Kalamba appeared as a very powerful man in the eyes of the Bena Lulua, because he commanded both Africans and Europeans. He imposed his rule over all the Lulua people, who paid him an annual tribute, which he used for trade with Angolan merchants and with the Congo Free State station.

In about 1890, however, the Belgians changed their strategy in an attempt to control Kalamba and expel his Angolan allies. Under orders from Lienart, Congo Free State troops began attacking Cokwe merchants in an attempt to halt Angolan commercial competition in their territory. Then, the government station appropriated all the tribute destined for Kalamba. Also, Kalamba's men were forced to seek work at the state post and to pay taxes to the Europeans.

At the beginning of 1891, Kalamba, angered by these actions, resolved to drive the whites and their African allies from his lands. A series of small incidents between the Bena Lulua and the Luluabourg station were preludes to a much more profound break. For their part, the state agents decided to remove chief Kalamba from his lands, as he had become an obstacle to their program of domination and exploitation.

Therefore, the Kasai area was occupied by two opposing camps: first, the State troops established at Luluabourg and Lusambo, 160 km (100 mi) northeast, and, second, the many Lulua clans and their Cokwe allies. Kalamba fought the Europeans from 1891 to 1895. The long Lulua resistance can be explained by the fact that the state troops were not numerous enough or sufficiently disciplined to defeat Kalamba's warriors. Supplied with arms and munitions by the Cokwe, the Lulua often took the initiative in battle. In the end, however, the inferiority of their arms forced them to retreat.

In 1891 Kalamba left his lands and his goods to settle 80 km (50 mi) southwest of Luluabourg, across the Miao River. For three years, while Free State agents watched, he prepared his revenge. In June 1895 Kalamba and his Cokwe allies attacked the post at Mukabua. Although the troops of Commander Michaux pushed Kalamba's forces back, Michaux suffered heavy losses and was obliged to return to Luluabourg.

When the Tetela soldiers of the Luluabourg garrison rebelled on July 4, 1895, Kalamba hoped to profit from the resulting Free State weakness to regain his own lands. He was unsuccessful, however, for in July 1896, as the Lulua chief, his 800 men armed with rifles, and some Cokwe allies were crossing the Miao River in the direction of Luluabourg, Commander Michaux and his 400 men blocked the road. Avoiding a direct confrontation, the Africans inflicted heavy losses on the Free State soldiers by taking pot shots from the bush. Perhaps, had Michaux not used a Nordenfeld cannon, a previously unknown weapon which caused great panic among the Africans, Kalamba might have been victorious.

Following the battle with Michaux, Kalamba retreated across the Kasai River, where he died in 1898.

Kalamba's son and successor, Tshisungu Kalamba, remained a threat to the Free State. In 1906 he attacked and destroyed a trading depot of the Compagnie du Kasai at Mai-Munene, southwest of Luluabourg on the Kasai River. Repulsed by government troops, Tshisungu Kalamba sought refuge among the Cokwe.

In 1907 the whites, asked for peace and invited Tshisungu Kalamba to return to his lands. It was not as a vanquished chief that he came home in 1909. The Lulua and also the whites gave him a triumphant welcome. Mukenge Kalamba's son, Tshisungu Kalamba, died in 1916.

The life of Kalamba exemplifies a generation of

chiefs who dominated central Africa at the middle of the 19th century. Owing their power to the control of commercial activities, they accepted the whites peacefully, thinking they could use them to increase their trade and political domination. At first, the Europeans encouraged these aspirations. But when the newcomers had gained a foothold, they changed their strategy and the Africans understood that, in fact, they had been mistaken. Attempts to drive the Europeans from the lands failed nearly everywhere.

LUKENGU TSHIPANDA wa MUKENYI and
MUMBANZA mwa BAWELE
na NYABAKOMBI ENSOBATO

BIBLIOGRAPHY: Flament et al., *La Force Publique de sa naissance à 1914* ("The Force Publique from its Birth to 1914"), Brussels, 1952; A. Mabika-Kalanda, *Baluba et Lulua, une ethnie à la recherche d'un nouvel équilibre* ("Baluba and Lulua, an Ethnic Group in Search of a New Balance"), Brussels, 1959; O. Michaux, *Carnet de campagne. Episodes et impressions de 1889 à 1897* ("Campaign Notebook. Episodes and Impressions from 1889-1897"), Namur, 1913; Ntambwe Luadia-Luadia, "Les Luluwa et le commerce luso-africain: 1870-1895" ("The Lulua and the Luso-African Trade: 1870-1895"), *Etudes d'Histoire Africaine*, VI, 1974; M. Storme, *La mutinerie au Kasai en 1895* ("The Kasai Mutiny of 1895"), Brussels, 1970; A Van Zandijcke, *Pages d'Histoire du Kasai* ("Pages from Kasai History"), Namur, 1953; H. von Wissmann, *My Second Journey through Equatorial Africa from the Congo to the Zambezi (1886-1887)*, London, 1891.

MULELE, P.

Pierre Mulele (July 25, 1929-October 9, 1968) led a bloody insurrection in the Kwilu area from December 1963 to April 1964. Because of his role in the Kwilu uprising, Mulele gained the status of a semi-mythical revolutionary endowed with magical qualities. Thus, many later insurrection movements, even those in areas outside the Kwilu, were labelled "Mulelist."

Pierre Mulele was born at Kulu-Matandu about 80 km (50 mi) southeast of Kikwit. He received his secondary education at Kinzambi, just north of Kikwit, and at Leverville, about 40 km (25 mi) northwest of Kikwit. Following secondary school, he entered the police force and, still later, he worked as a government clerk.

Mulele, who belonged to the Mbunda ethnic group, became involved in political activities as the Belgian Congo moved towards independence. In 1959, he was appointed deputy secretary-general of the Parti Solidaire Africain (P.S.A.), a Kwilu-based organization led by Antoine Gizenga from the Pende people. During the same year, Mulele traveled to Guinea where he met Gizenga's future advisor, Blouin. In preparation for the transfer of the colony's government into African hands, Mulele took part in the April and May 1960 Round Table conference held in Brussels, Belgium, to discuss future economic affairs. When countrywide elections were held in May 1960, Mulele was elected on the P.S.A. ticket as a deputy to the national Parliament in Léopoldville (now Kinshasa).

The new Congo Prime Minister Patrice Lumumba (*q.v.*), who tried to select a broadly representative cabinet, appointed Mulele to the key post of minister of education and fine arts. After Lumumba's government was dismissed by Kasa-Vubu (*q.v.*), Mulele joined Gizenga in Stanleyville (now Kisangani) where Lumumba loyalists had gone in November 1960 in hopes of regrouping their forces and regaining control of the national government. One of Mulele's first duties was to visit Cairo, where Gizenga expected to receive support from the Egyptian president, Gamal Abdel Nasser (in office 1956-70). Upon his return to Stanleyville, Mulele assumed ministerial duties in Gizenga's government.

In the meantime, efforts were being made to

reconcile the rival politicians from Léopoldville and Stanleyville. Thus, in July and August 1961, Pierre Mulele went to Léopoldville to sit in parliament which had been reconvened at Lovanium University. Attempting to form a new government for the paralyzed nation, the parliament elected the moderate Cyrille Adoula, as a compromise candidate acceptable to both the Léopoldville and Stanleyville factions. Gizenga, however, who had been chosen vice premier, soon broke with Adoula, and returned to Stanleyville in October. Again Gizenga established an opposition government. And, again, Mulele traveled to Cairo to gain international recognition for Stanleyville. Gizenga, however, was arrested on January 20, 1962, and his regime came to an end.

Nevertheless, Mulele continued to oppose the Léopoldville government. In March 1962, Mulele traveled to the People's Republic of China, where he studied revolutionary tactics for peasant societies. He also made a trip to his home area of the Kwilu, where he renewed contacts with the local people. Having spent much of 1962 and early 1963 abroad in Communist countries, Mulele returned to the Congo in July 1963, to begin organizing a popular uprising against Adoula's government.

Traveling clandestinely to his home territory of Kwilu, he began preparing the local people for a guerrilla war. In his efforts, Mulele drew on Mbunda and Pende people, who earlier had supported the P.S.A., and who now felt alienated by the national authorities in Léopoldville. Appealing to rural people disappointed by the results of the 1960 independence, Mulele and his partisans promised a second independence which would benefit ordinary people and not just the powerful politicians. For the activists, who would lead the uprising, Mulele relied on the youthful generation, to whom he gave intensive ideological preparation. Once the rebellion began, terror reigned throughout the Kwilu, especially around the towns of Gungu, 100 km (60 mi) southeast of Kikwit, and Idiofa, 100 km (60 mi) east of Kikwit.

Also in 1964, rebellions led by other individuals trained in China broke out in the eastern part of the Congo. But as Benoit Verhaegen has observed in his book *Rébellions au Congo,* ("Rebellions in the Congo"), the Kwilu insurrection was very different from the other movements. This was because the Mulelist leaders meant to destroy the very basis of existing social, economic, and political organization, and rebuild a new society. According to Verhaegen, only in the case of the Kwilu can the term revolution be used instead of rebellion.

The new society Mulele intended to build was based on a Marxist model. To gain his end, Mulele sought to paralyze the country's political, economic, and judicial machinery. Thus, his partisans seemed bent on destroying everything—bridges, schools, and hospitals—necessary for the normal operation of society.

A charismatic leader, Mulele claimed to have the gift of ubiquity, and to be able to hear and reveal everything, even peoples' hidden intentions. Although Mulele's personality was in part responsible for his movement's appeal, the insurrection made rapid progress because of the great dissatisfaction with national and provincial political leaders that was evident in the countryside.

Mulele soon discovered, however, that it was much easier to instigate an uprising than to complete a revolution. First, he was unable to control the movement he had launched because it had assumed such a large scope. Second, he was unable to satisfy the immediate needs of the people for food, medicine, and consumer goods. Finally, he met resistance when he tried to expand his following beyond the Mbunda and Pende ethnic groups. Soon his partisans directed tortures and executions against people who were not of Mulele's ethnic group, as well as against those who did not endorse his movement. In order to prevent "genocide," some early rebel leaders left Mulele to join the government forces. By April 1964, the national army had regained control over most of the Kwilu, although partisan pockets continued for months afterward. In fact, the threat of a Mulelist uprising remained until Mulele's death in 1968.

After his militia fell before the government troops, Mulele took refuge in the forest, accompanied by some faithful collaborators. Then, on September 13, 1968, he re-emerged in Brazzaville, capital of the Republic of the Congo, across the river from Kinshasa. Learning of Mulele's presence, the government council of Kinshasa, in the absence of the head of state Mobutu, who at the time was on an official visit to Morocco, dispatched Foreign Minister Justin Bomboko to Brazzaville to persuade Mulele to return to the Congo. By promising Mulele that he would receive the amnesty that the president of the Republic had granted to all political prisoners, Bomboko convinced the rebel leader, and also the government of the Congo (Brazzaville), that it was safe for him to come home. Thus, Mulele crossed the river with Bomboko on September 29, 1968.

On October 2, 1968, however, after Mobutu had returned from his Moroccan trip, he announced at a rally that he was categorically refusing amnesty to "war criminals" and, consequently, that Mulele would be tried. On October 3, the political bureau of the Mouvement Populaire de la Révolution (M.P.R.) confirmed this decision. On October 8, a court martial appointed by presidential decree and composed of three anonymous army officers, condemned Mulele to death. Although Mulele asked the head of state for a pardon, the plea was rejected and Mulele was executed at dawn on October 9.

Pierre Mulele stands as a symbol of the frustration and despair ordinary Africans felt after their dreams of a better life after independence were not realized as fully as they had hoped.

SIKITELE GIZE a SUMBULA

BIBLIOGRAPHY: P. Artigue, *Qui sont les leaders congolais* ("Who Are the Congolese Leaders"), Brussels, 1961; R. Beckmans, "Afrique-Actualité, Septembre, 1968" ("African News, September, 1968"), *Congo-Afrique* No. 29, November, 1968, pp. 477-81; R. de Decker, "Afrique-Actualité, Octobre, 1968" ("Africa News, October, 1968"), *Congo-Afrique,* No. 30, December, 1968, pp. 529-33; *Essor du Congo* (a Lubumbashi daily), October 3-5, 9-11, and 17, 1968; B. Verhaegen, *Rébellions au Congo* ("Rebellions in the Congo"), Vol. 1, Brussels, 1966; C. Young, *The Politics of Cultural Pluralism,* Madison, 1976.

MUMBENDU

Mumbendu (circa 1880-April 1915) served the Belgian colonial administration as chief of Bomana, an extensive, arbitrarily-created territory along the Giri River in the northeastern part of Zaire.

Mumbendu was born in the village of Bomana (located on the Giri River 160 km or 100 mi north of modern Mbandaka), an agglomeration of separate hamlets containing the following family groups: Bomoko, Bonsobo, Mokondola, Bolinga, Modjoka, Bonkombi, and Boyombo. From the end of 1898 until early in 1899, the Congo Free State established a station at Bomana. At that time, the young Mumbendu enlisted as a soldier in the Force Publique (colonial army). When his military service was over, he returned home to Bomana where he served as an intermediary between the African population and the Europeans.

Probably between 1908 and 1910, Mumbendu received investiture, from the colonial government, as head of the newly formed Bomana chiefdom. Extending about 120 km (75 mi) along the Giri River, Mumbendu's domain also reached inland to the Ubangi-Giri watershed in the west, and to the Zaire-Giri watershed in the east. This heterogeneous, non-traditional chiefdom included the Loi, Kikila, Mbonzi, and Jamba peoples—ethnic groups too small to be administered efficiently as single units.

Like chief Mungembe (*q.v.*), who governed the remaining area of the lower Giri, Mumbendu had little knowledge or affection for much of his land. To gain acceptance from his subjects, he often found it necessary to use force. Along with similar chiefs imposed by colonial officials, Mumbendu, aided by Ekita of the Bomongo people and other armed adventurers, attacked disobedient villages, capturing many women and children, whom he sold to the Boloki and the Bobangi river people from near Coquilhatville (now Mbandaka). In exchange for the slaves, Mumbendu received rifles which came from the nearby French territory.

The Jamba people, especially the warrior Ekonda of Sikolo, resisted Mumbendu's conquests. Despite his superior weapons, Mumbendu feared to visit the Jamba villages, located west of the Giri River from his capital, Bomana. Mumbundu's campaigns against his fellow Africans were either encouraged or permitted by the Europeans. Since the state posts responsible for overseeing the region were situated 160 km (100 mi) upstream at Bomboma and Musa, Mumbendu was free to rule as he wished.

With the re-establishment of a state post at Bomana in 1911, Mumbendu's freedom of action was greatly curtailed. Forbidden to use force, as he had done in the past, Mumbendu worked hard to satisfy his European masters and supporters. Thus, he made frequent visits to the scattered river villages in his chiefdom. His main concerns were tax collection, village sanitation and up-keep, and the construction of way-stations along the roads.

In the years after 1911, administrative reorganization gradually reduced Mumbendu's authority. First, to facilitate the administration of his large chiefdom and to avoid unnecessary travel, the European head of the Bomana post divided Mumbendu's domain into four groupings, each with its own messenger: Ekita of Bomongo, Sikandja of Koli, Siniaki of Botshongo, and Sako of Mobena. Although this avoided sub-chiefdoms which would have seriously fragmented Mumbendu's power, the new formula was but a step in the process of diminishing Mumbendu's political role. As other ambitious Africans urged the whites to give them more authority, the territory was reorganized in 1914. At that time, Bomana was divided into four independent units: Bomana and Bobena along the Giri River, and Kikoro and Mokondo between the Ubangi and Giri rivers.

By this time, however, Mumbendu was more concerned about his failing health than about his diminished land. Stricken with the sleeping sickness which had swept the Giri region, he went to local hospitals for treatment. In December 1913 he traveled to the Protestant mission at Bolobo 450 km (300 mi) south on the Congo River, while in July 1914, he went to the Ikiko mission on Lake Leopold II (now Lake Mai Ndombe), seeking a cure. During this time, he nevertheless tried to carry on his work as chief. He died in April 1915.

Succession was complicated by the fact that Mumbendu's brother had also died from sleeping sickness a few months earlier, while his son Mohua was only five years old. Although Mumbendu had wanted his principal collaborator Ebenga to follow him in office, Ekwete, a relative of the deceased chief, was invested in office on August 1, 1916.

MUMBANZA mwa BAWELE na
NYABAKOMBI ENSOBATO

BIBLIOGRAPHY: Registres des renseignements politiques ("Registers of Political Events"), 1911-16, and 1916-31, Bomana Territory, Archives of the Bomongo Zone; H. Vandevenne, "Rapport d'enquête sur la chefferie Bomana" ("Report of Enquiry on the Bomana Chiefdom"), Bomana Territory, 1927, Archives of the Bomongo Zone.

MUMPEMA

Mumpema (circa 1880-1945) served as chief of the Mampoko people from 1910-45, during the colonial epoch.

Inhabitants of the lower Giri, the Mampoko formerly lived in the forests between the Zaire and the Giri rivers, about 100 km (60 mi) north of modern Mbandaka. Originally they were known merely as the Tendele and the Bokwango people. Around 1850, some Tendele and Bokwango left the forest, the Tendele to settle on the banks of the Giri, at Ndjondo and Bokwekete and the Bokwango to settle in the area around Ekongobololo, Bwanda, Mokoto, Bobole, Monono and Boyeka. Only after they had arrived on the banks of the Giri did they receive the name Mampoko, meaning "peoples from the vast banana plantations."

When the Europeans arrived in the later 19th century, the patriarch and leader of the Mampoko was Ekonda. From 1891 onwards, the Mampoko were part of the Equateur region. Several years later, through the intermediary of the Bobangi chief Bolangwa (q.v.), they entered into contact with the whites of Coquilhatville (now Mbandaka). Thus, from 1908, the Mampoko, with their southern neighbors, the Bokongo and the Mobele, were included in Bolangwa's vast chiefdom of the Bobangi. Soon, however, the Belgians decided to separate some of the semi-autonomous lower Giri river peoples, including the Mampoko, into sub-chiefdoms. Because of his advanced age, the government passed over Ekonda, the oldest member of the oldest clan, in favor of Mumpema, the oldest individual of the junior family in the

clan. Mumpema was invested in 1910 as leader of the Mampoko sub-chiefdom. In 1918, the sub-chiefdom of Mampoko was detached from the Bobangi polity and made a separate chiefdom dependent on the territory of Bomana, whose headquarters on the Giri were located 160 km (100 mi) north of modern Mbandaka.

As a government official, Mumpema gained an excellent reputation for administering justice. His territories also had little difficulty in paying their taxes, perhaps because of the existing commercial ties with nearby French Equatorial Africa. In comparison to peoples further inland, Mumpema's subjects were considered more advanced.

Because of Mumpema's outstanding abilities, the neighboring chiefdoms of Bokongo and Mobele were gradually incorporated into his domain. Not only were Bokongo and Mobele declining in population, but they also suffered from a lack of effective leadership. After chief Bei of Bokongo died in 1922, no one was invested to replace him until 1927. In Mobele, the people were governed by the ineffectual Mompena. Thus, in 1929, Mumpema's Mampoko chiefdom was enlarged to incorporate Bokongo, Mobele, and also Ndondo.

In 1940, Mampoko, along with Bomana and Mobena to the north, was organized into a new administrative unit, the sector of Baloi. Musoma, also known as Limania, the chief of Mobena, became provisional sector chief with authority over Mumpema. By this time Mumpema was very old, and his power had decreased considerably. Nonetheless, his own subjects, as well as other Africans in the lower Giri area, and also the Europeans, all continued to hold him in high esteem.

One of the greatest chiefs of the Giri region during the colonial era, Mumpema died in 1945 after having governed his land for more than 30 years.

MUMBANZA mwa BAWELE na
NYABAKOMBI ENSOBATO

BIBLIOGRAPHY: J.B. Delobbe, "Rapport d'enquête sur la chefferie Bokongo" ("Report of Enquiry on the Bokongo Chiefdom"), Bomana Territory, 1926, Archives of the Bomongo Zone, "Rapport d'enquête sur la chefferie Bobangi" ("Report of Enquiry into the Bobangi Chiefdom"), Coquilhatville Territory, 1926, Archives of Tervuren; P. Delogne, "Report d'enquête préalable á la création du secteur des Baloi" ("Report of Enquiry Preliminary to the Establishment of the Baloi Sector"), Territory of Nouvelle-Anvers, 1939, Archives of the Bomongo Zone; J.J.C. Lamaire, "Rapports d'enquête sur les chefferies Mampoko, Bokongo, Djundu, et Mobere" ("Reports of Enquiry Into the Chiefdoms of Mampoko, Bokongo, Djundu, and Mobere"), Bomana

Territory, 1921, Archives of the Bomongo Zone; H. Vandevenne, "Notes Supplementaires sur la chefferie Bokongo" ("Supplementary Notes on the Bokongo Chiefdom"), Bomana Territory, 1927, Archives of the Bomongo Zone.

MUNDELE FUNJI. See MATEMU a KELENGE

MUNGEMBE

Mungembe (circa 1870-1949) worked as an agent of the Belgian colonial power to bring government control and administrative order to the politically decentralized peoples living in the Giri river region, east and north of modern Makanza (located 200 km or 120 mi north of Mbandaka on the Zaire River). Although a member of the Libinza people who are settled on the Giri east of Makanza, Mungembe traveled up and down the river aiding European officials in their task of pacification and administration.

Mungembe was born at Molanga, a village on the left bank of the Giri, in about 1870. Because his father died while he was still small, the youth was raised by his father's maternal uncles, who had paid his mother's dowry. Mungembe grew up in his uncle's village of Bosilela, about 200 km (120 mi) north of Mbandaka, where he became a close friend of two other young men, Nzamba and Molonga. The three earned a reputation as good warriors.

On August 21, 1897, Lt. Wilvert became the first European to reach Giri by way of the Mabale stream, which cut across the marshy land from Nouvelle-Anvers (now Makanza). Late in 1897 the Bosilela elder Matabakemba, hoping to protect the Libinza from the aggressive Likoka people west of the Giri who were terrorizing the region, approached Wilvert asking him to establish a station at Bosilela. Thus, in 1898, the Europeans from Nouvelle-Anvers founded a post at Bosilela, which they called Bosesera.

Matabakema was recognized by the whites as chief of Bosilela as well as of all the Libinza people. When he died, not long afterwards, his son refused to succeed him as an agent of the Congo Free State. Thus, Sommelier, or Limpanya as he was called by the Africans, who was head of the post at Bosilela, selected Nzamba, Mungembe's close friend, as the next chief. Thus, Nzamba, Mungembe, and Molonga joined the Force Publique (colonial army) and worked to conquer the countryside for the Europeans and the Libinza.

Sommelier and his African allies were successful because their guns demoralized the warriors of the other peoples of the interior. The once-dangerous Likoka, especially affected by these events observed wryly that: "The Bansongo [the Likoka name for the Libinza] whom we once captured, almost without using weapons, have become strong because of their rifles." Small village communities, formerly independent, came under the authority of Sommelier and "chief" Nzamba. The bloody campaign, which lasted for nearly three years, resulted in the death of many Giri people. The Ndobo, who live just south of the Libinza, were especially hard hit.

As the whites extended the area they controlled along the Giri River, they decided to divide the administrative tasks among Nzamba and his two associates. Nzamba retained his authority over the Libinza, the Mbonzi, and Likoka; Molonga was dispatched north to Monya, where he was placed in charge of the Mwe people; while Mungembe went even further north to the Mwe and Ngbandi of the upper Giri region. Not long afterwards Mungembe was transferred to Bonyange on the Moanda River, where he governed the Biwaku.

In the absence of close supervision from the Free State officials, Nzamba, Molonga, and Mungembe gathered groups of Libinza men armed with rifles and subdued the peoples living along the Giri River. As they worked to create large fiefdoms for themselves they captured hundreds of slaves, especially women, and took booty from the villagers.

In 1906, Nzamba was arrested for his many atrocities and exiled to Boma near the mouth of what is now the Zaire River. Since Molonga wished to remain in the more isolated upper Giri region, Mungembe was selected as chief of Bosesera.

In 1911, colonial officials asked that Mungembe relocate to Bolongo, west of the Giri. Then, in 1914, Molonga was driven out of Monia in the north by the people he had been exploiting. When he returned to his home area among the Libinza, Mungembe's domain was divided into two parts: the northern section given to Molonga, while the southern part still remained in Mungembe's hands. Six years later, in 1920, Molonga again had to flee from the people he ruled. Finally, in 1922 he committed suicide in order to escape arrest and exile.

Mungembe, too, faced unrest and discontent on the part of his African subjects. From 1922 to 1925, supported by Salomon Mohila, a literate former soldier who was chief of the Mosubi people, the Bokwala and Wambala areas of Mungembe's chiefdom tried to oust their ruler. Mungembe was able to retain his post only because he received strong support from the Europeans. But in 1925 Mungembe was made a subordinate chief in a newly formed Libinza sector, headed by Mohila. Although Mohila and Mungembe had been rivals, Mungembe worked as his former enemy's loyal subordinate.

Gradually, Mungembe's village and the populations he governed became relatively unimportant. The sleeping sickness epidemics of the 1920s and 1930s seriously depleted the number of people in Mungembe's territory. An even greater cause of population decline was the substantial out-migration from the Giri area to the growing Congo River towns of Lokolela, Irebu, Coquilhatville, and Lolanga. As early as 1913, Libinza people had left the area to earn a better living elsewhere and to escape harassment from local officials. Individuals who remained around the Giri were forced to pay taxes, cut wood for the small steamers plying the river as far north as the confluence of the Giri and Moanda, maintain the channels linking the Congo and Giri rivers, supply provisions for the government post at Bomana, 160 km (100 mi) north of Mbandaka, and search for copal. Because Mungembe could not halt the flow of people from his land, he was frequently accused of incompetence or of encouraging his subjects to leave.

As a chief serving the colonial power, Mungembe grew wealthy. Through various means, he acquired about 100 wives. Since he sometimes shared these women with European visitors, some of Mungembe's children were mulatto. Mungembe also gained many slaves, taken primarily from the upper Giri area. Some were resold to the Likoka people, others served Mungembe, continuing to work for him even after they were officially freed by the government.

When Mungembe died in 1949, his grandson, Ebamba Moboko Moi-Molanga, succeeded him. Ebamba ruled at Bosesera until 1950, when he became chief of the entire Libinza sector.

MUMBANZA mwa BAWELE na
NYABAKOMBI ENSOBATO

BIBLIOGRAPHY: Files of the Libinza Sector and the Bosesera Chiefdom, Archives of the Bomongo Zone; "Registre des renseignements politiques du territoire de Bomana" ("Register of Political Information on the Bomana Territory"), 1911-16, Archives of the Bomongo Zone; interview with Ebamba Moboko (born 1922), grandson of Mungembe, on September 29, 1973.

MUSHID a NAMBING

Mushid a Nambing (circa 1856-1907), son of Mwant Yav (Lunda ruler) Mbumb Muteb a Kat (ruled 1874-83) and of Nambing, assumed political prominence after the death of Mwant Yav Mudib in 1885. Mushid dominated what might be called "the last days of the Lunda empire," a period characterized by a long succession crisis, Cokwe (Chokwe) incursions from

Angola, and the arrival of Congo Free State forces in Uluund (Lunda country).

During the confused succession struggles of 1885, the designated Mwant Yav, Samabiamb, who was living in southern Uluund, withdrew from the contest. The weak and indecisive Mwant Yav Mutand Mukay (ruled 1886-87) was then able to hold power for only a short time, as other claimants competed for the Lunda throne. Among the hopefuls were Mbal a Kalong, son of Mwant Yav Nawej a Ditend, and Mushid a Nambing. When the Chitentam (Lunda council) chose Mbal a Kalong as the next Mwant Yav, Mushid decided to seize power with the help of armed Cokwe traders and slave raiders from Angola. Mwant Yav Mbal a Kalong was eliminated after reigning for two months, and Mushid assumed power in 1887.

Mwant Yav Mushid a Nambing established his capital at Kawend on the River Mwema, about 250 km (150 mi) north of modern Dilolo. Then, in 1887, Mushid was attacked by his former Cokwe allies who accused him of not having rewarded them for their help. The battle of Kawend ended with a Cokwe victory, after which their ten year occupation of Uluund (1887-97) began. Mwant Yav Mushid, with some members of his court, took refuge in the Upper Lubilash region where, together with his brother Kawel or Mulaj, he organized the reconquest of his homeland.

In 1896, at Kalambakatshak, on the right bank of the Kasidishi stream, Mwant Yav Mushid received Lieut. Oscar Michaux of the Congo Free State. The two men signed a treaty in which Mwant Yav Mushid recognized the sovereignty of the Free State on condition that the latter would provide him with help in his struggle against the Cokwe. This collaboration enabled the Lunda to recover part of their territory, and allowed the Free State to establish stations in the area. In 1902 de Clercq founded Kapanga, near the Lunda capital, while in 1903 Verdick founded Dilolo and Katola (the latter being located midway between Dilolo and Kapanga).

The demands and exactions of European occupation resulted in strained relations between Mwant Yav Mushid and the Congo Free State agents. Thus, with encouragement from his brother Kawel, Mwant Yav Mushid revolted in 1903. Taking advantage of internal dynastic quarrels, Free State officials then supported Muteb a Kasang, a docile member of the royal family, as Mwant Yav in Mushid's place. The insurrection soon became a civil war, with the partisans of Mwant Yav Mushid on one side and Muteb a Kasang (who was to be Mwant Yav from 1907-20) and the Free State on the other.

Although, for a time, Mushid and his brother Kawel succeeded in eluding Muteb and his allies, in 1907, they fell into an ambush and were captured. Mushid was made a prisoner, while Kawel, who tried to escape, was killed. Mwant Yav Mushid was later executed. His body, weighted down with a stone tied to the neck, was cast into the Lulua River at the Ibond ford.

Because of their courage and determination Mwant Yav Mushid and his brother Kawel, remain symbols of Lunda ethnic pride.

N'DUA SOLOL KANAMPUMB

BIBLIOGRAPHY: H. Dias de Carvalho, *Expediçao ao Muatiamvu. Ethnographia e história dos povos da Lunda* ("Expedition to Mwatia Mvu. Ethnography and History of the Lunda People"), Lisbon, 1890, *Memoria, A Lunda ou os Estados de Muatiamvu* ("Note on Lunda, or the State of Muatiamvu") Lisbon, 1890, *Descripçao da viagem a Mussumba do Muatiamvu* ("Description of a Voyage to Mussumba of Muatiamvu") Vol. IV, Lisbon, 1894. See also "Rapport d'enquête, Guerre intestine des Lunda a l'époque de Mwanta Yamfa" ("Report of Inquiry, Civil War Among the Lunda in the Time of the Mwant Yav"), manuscript, 1916, Archives of the Shaba Region, Lubumbashi; L. Duysters, "Histoire des Mwata Yamvo" ("History of the Mwant Yav"), manuscript, 1927, Archives of the Shaba Region; Gome, "Notice sur les populations du district de la Lulua" ("Note on the Populations of the Lulua District"), 1913, Archives of the Kapanga Zone.

MUTAND YEMBIYEMB

Mutand Yembiyemb (16?-circa 1710) was an important agent in the 17th century expansion of the Lunda empire, the capital of which was at Musumba, 240 km (150 mi) north of modern Dilolo.

Late in the 17th century, the Lunda Mwant Yav (ruler) Muteb a Kat organized a military expedition toward the southeast. He entrusted command of the expedition to his paternal uncle, Mutand Yembiyemb. Given the military title of kazembe (governor), Mutand was ordered to end the insubordination of the Kosa, or Ako, people. Although they were Lunda who supposedly had settled west of the Lubudi River in the time of Chibind Yirung (q.v.), the Kosa refused to recognize the authority of the Lunda paramount the Ant Yav (plural of Mwant Yav). In the late 1600s, the Lunda-speaking Kosa were ruled by Muin Cibalak and his nephew, Cinyat Mfemb, who was second in command.

After some years of fighting, the Kosa yielded to Mutand Yembiyemb who also subjected the Lukoshi, and defeated the Ambwela on the Lukoshi River.

Then, Mutand established his headquarters at Cinyat's old capital, located just north of modern Mutshatsha, about 300 km (200 mi) southeast of Musumba. From there he ruled the Lunda groups who had immigrated earlier and who dominated the existing populations. Mutand also imposed his authority over Musokantanda, chief of the Ndembu-Kosa people, living near modern Kolwezi. After this, Mutand sent his son Kafirind, with the now-loyal children of his one-time adversary, Cinyat Nfemb, to subdue the Sanga, a Luba and Lunda-related group living northwest of modern Likasi. After the Sanga had been subdued, the Lunda attacked and defeated Luba chiefs who were raiding Sanga land.

Many non-Lunda people were won over to Matand Yembiyemb by Lunda prestige and by the Lunda ability to provide security against outside raiders. These non-Lunda groups reinforced Kazembe Mutand's army. This army's march, therefore, became a real migration as women and children followed the army, and as families settled with their clan leaders on the conquered lands.

After his campaigns, Mutand returned to his headquarters, Cinyat's old capital, where he ruled as governor-general of all the conquered territory. His generals oversaw the provinces which they themselves had conquered. They owed Mutand tribute, part of which regularly was sent to Musumba.

In the meantime, the former ruler Cinyat Mfemb was dispatched to Musumba, where he received good treatment from the Mwant Yav. While Cinyat was staying at Musumba, a fire, supposedly caused by the head blacksmith Rubund or Lubunda, broke out. In fear, Rubund fled towards the south-east, crossed the country controlled by Mutand, and settled among the Sanga, who authorized him to pursue his profession as a blacksmith. Here, Rubund no longer worked with iron but copper, extracted by the subjects of the Sanga chief Pande and the Lemba chief Katanga. (Pande—Mpand means fork in Lunda—had once been the war name of the Lunda conqueror, Mutombo Kola whose descendants ruled the Sanga in the 1600s). Katanga, who lived east of what is now Likasi, was a Lunda chief ruling over the Lemba, a group supposedly composed of Lunda immigrants from an early period.

Not long after Rubund's flight, Kazembe Mutand sent tribute to the Mwant Yav in the form of cone (conus) shells from the Indian Ocean and copper bracelets from the Shaba area. When Kazembe Mutand's emissaries mentioned chief Pande, chief Katanga, and the blacksmith Rubund as the manufacturers of the copper bracelets, Mwant Yav Muteb dispatched a trusted official, Mushid, to look for Rubund. Mushid was given the title of Kazembe with the same powers as Mutand Yembiyemb. Mushid got lost, however, and went down the Zambezi River, where he probably was killed by the Lozi. Mwant Yav then sent Cinyat Mfemb to Mutand Yembiyemb with orders to occupy the Kecila rock-salt mines (north of Musokantanda), and the copper mines of Pande and Katanga. Cinyat was also asked to bring Rubund back to Musumba.

Mutand Yembiyemb headed the expedition, while Cinyat acted as second in command. After surrendering without resistence Pande led the Lunda to Chief Cibwid who controlled the Kecila rock-salt mines. Once Cibwid capitulated, Cinyat, who commanded the Lunda vanguard, seized some salt to send to Mwant Yav Muteb. Mutand confiscated all the consignments, however, although some salt eventually reached Musumba, carried by a secret emissary who denounced Mutand's maneuvers. While Muteb was angered and summoned his Kazembe to Musumba, Mutand was able to justify himself, and then returned to his post in the Lualaba area. Meanwhile, Cinyat, Pande, Cibwid, and Pande a Muvomb went to Musumba, where they were received as important Lunda dignitaries. For his part, the blacksmith Rubund had fled from Kazembe Mutand's expedition, taking refuge in the Luapula region among the Mbeba, where he founded a small chieftainship.

When Cinyat came home from the Lunda capital, Musumba, Mutand Yembiyemb had him arrested and drowned in the Mukulweji River, near his headquarters. Cinyat's children then lodged a complaint against Kazembe Mutand with the Mwant Yav, who thereupon convened the Citentam, (the Lunda supreme council). The Chitentam condemned Mutand, replacing him with Cinyat's eldest son, Ngand a Bilond (q.v.).

Ngand a Bilond, ("Land of Metal"), whose real name was Idim, received the title of Kazembe and was commissioned to kill Mutand Yembiyemb. Caught between the forces of Ngand a Bilond and of Kanyimbu Newej Mpemb (q.v.), the new Kazembe's half brother, Mutand Yembiyemb fled to the south in about 1710, and was never heard from again.

TSHIBANGU KABET MUSAS

BIBLIOGRAPHY: F. Grévisse, "Notes ethnographiques relatives à quelques populations autochtones, du Haut-Katanga industriel" ("Ethnographic Notes Concerning Some Native Populations of Industrial Upper Katanga"), *Bulletin du C.E.P.S.I.,* No. 32, 1956, pp. 65-207; E. Labrecque, "Histoire des Mwanta Kazembe" ("History of the Mwant Kazembe"), *Lovania,* XVI, 1949, pp. 9-33; M. McCulloch, *The Southern Lunda and Related Peoples,* London, 1952; *Ngand Yetu* ("Our Country"), Elisabethville, 1963; J. Vansina, *Les anciens royaumes de la savane,* Léopoldville, 1965, English translation published as *Kingdoms of the Savanna,* Madison, 1966. See also J. Hoover, "The Seduction of Ruwej; Reconstructing Rund History (The Nuclear Lunda; Zaire, Angola, Zambia)," unpublished Ph.D. dissertation, Yale University, 1978.

MUYANGALA

Muyangala (circa 1875-February 3, 1950) was chief of the Pende Akwa Ndala people, living along the upper Bwelo Milondo River, 100 km (60 mi) south of Kikwit, holding this position from 1932-50.

Originally from Nzemba Munene village and the Akwa Hago clan, Muyangala was elected Mwene Kongo (Akwa Ndala chief) in 1932. His predecessor, Mwene Kongo Kabemba, had been removed following the great Pende revolt of 1931, and eventually died in prison.

Mwene Kongo Muyangala received customary investiture from the local people. In addition, he was officially invested and decorated with a medal by the district commissioner, Vandevenne, on October 8, 1934. (He was re-invested on December 17, 1936.)

Muyangala was an energetic chief who worked hard in the service of the colonial administration and promoted the development of his chiefdom. His situation forced him, at times, to be very severe with his own subjects who did not bend promptly to colonial demands.

In the end, however, he was subjected to humiliation from the territorial administration, and therefore refused to cooperate with the government. In 1937, he refused to attend a series of meetings with the territorial agent Malvoz, who was in charge of his region. When he was summoned, in August 1937, to explain his conduct to the territorial administrator at Gungu (located about 80 km, or 50 mi, southeast of Kikwit), Muyangala did not go. As a result, the government punished him by withholding his salary for three months. In 1939 Muyangala refused to supervise the cultivation of fields, required by the government. Therefore, on September 27, 1939, the territorial administrator, J.B. Bomans, proposed to the Kwango district commissioner that Muyangala be dismissed from office. After taking into account the services he had rendered, however, District Commissioner Peigneux retained Muyangala, after severely rebuking him. But Mwene Kongo Muyangala was deeply angered and, ever after, he took advantage of every opportunity he could find to impede the smooth operation of colonial government.

When Muyangala died on February 3, 1950, he was succeeded by Mukwakeza, a man of the Kigudi clan, from Lusanga village.

SIKITELE GIZE a SUMBULA

BIBLIOGRAPHY:"Dossier Politique du Secteur de Kobo" ("Political File of the Kobo Sector"), Archives of the Gungu Zone.

MVEMBA NZINGA

Mvemba Nzinga (circa 1461-1543), also known as Afonso I, ruled as Mani Kongo (king) of Kongo from 1506-43. He came to power soon after the arrival of the first Europeans in 1482. Having adopted Christianity, Afonso I tried to strengthen his dynasty and his country by modernizing and proselytizing the Kongo. Because Portugal was more interested in exploitation than in cooperation, his efforts failed.

Mvemba Nzinga was the son of Nzinga Nkuwu, the king of the Kongo, who received representatives of the Portuguese navigator Diogo Cão who landed at the mouth of the Zaire River in 1482. Cão was the first European to visit the Zaire area. Hoping to benefit from the power and wealth of the Portuguese, Nzinga Nkuwu converted to Christianity and was baptized with the name of the reigning Portuguese king, João. At the same time, in July 1491, Nzinga Nkuwu's son, Mvemba Nzinga was baptized as Afonso, the name of the Portuguese prince who was heir to the throne.

Mani Kongo Nzinga Nkuwu quickly returned to his traditional beliefs. One of the causes for this was his attachment to the institution of polygamy, which, as king, he needed to gain wealth, increase his prestige, and form alliances with other political leaders. Also, when, earlier, Nzinga had burned traditional religious symbols, he had incurred the anger of his people, who had begun looking to his unconverted son Mpanzu a Nzinga (q.v.) as a replacement.

Because he was governor of the province of Nsundi, lying across what is now the Zaire River, mid-way between modern Kinshasa and Matadi, Mvemba was the heir apparent to the office of Mani Kongo. In his capital, Mbanza-Nsundi, he welcomed those priests and Portuguese agents who had been obliged to leave the Mani Kongo's capital in about 1495 after the monarch had renounced Christianity. He also had traditional objects of art, considered by the Portuguese to be diabolical, burned. Such destruction, however, greatly displeased many people in his realm.

On Nzinga Nkuwu's death in 1506, Mvemba Nzinga fought with his brother, Mpanzu, the leader of the conservatives, who hoped to take power. Victorious in the struggle, the Christian Mvemba Nzinga and his partisans attributed their success to divine intervention. In truth, Mvemba won because of aid from Portuguese weapons. This battle was a landmark in the history of relations between the kingdom of the Kongo and Europe.

As king, Mvemba Nzinga worked zealously to convert his kingdom to Christianity. Portugal, which had supported his candidacy against Mpanzu, answered his requests for missionaries. Mvemba, or Afonso I, also sought to modernize his kingdom. Perhaps his most notable efforts were in education. By 1516 he had founded schools, for both boys and girls, at Mbanza-Kongo, (renamed San Salvador). He also sent young boys of noble birth to Portugal to study. One of his sons Dom Henrique (q.v.) studied in Portugal, and was consecrated a bishop in 1518. Mani Kongo Mvemba Nzinga also called on Portuguese masons, carpenters, and joiners to renovate royal architecture. He further solicited the skills of European chemists, doctors, schoolmasters, jurists, and specialists in court protocol.

But Mvemba Nzinga's efforts quickly ran into a series of unexpected difficulties. The Portuguese technicians, once in the Kongo, worked indifferently, and did not follow the instructions of the country's king. The efforts of Christian missionaries did not benefit the kingdom as much as Mvemba Nzinga had hoped. And, finally, European ships' captains traded along the Zaire River without regard to the Kongo's commercial laws.

Mvemba Nzinga asked the king of Portugal, Manuel I (reigned 1495-1521), to send an emissary with special jurisdiction over the Portuguese nationals in the Kongo. In consequence, in 1512, Manuel codified a program of Christianization and acculturation for the Kongo and sent out an ambassador with a "regimento" (a regulation or systematic statement).

The "regimento," however, failed in its purpose for several reasons. First the plans for cultural change could not be achieved because they were on such a large scale and because there were comparatively few artisans and missionaries to carry them out. Second, most Portuguese were interested mainly in economic gain. Finally there was a fundamental ambiguity in Portuguese policy toward Africa. Portugal wished both to aid the Kongo but at the same time to exploit it economically. Although claiming to treat the Kongo as an equal, Portugal attempted to limit the Kongo's sovereignty on several levels. Commercially, it refused to restrict Portuguese traders who circumvented the Kongo's laws; in the judicial domain, it tolerated illegal activities of the Portuguese living in the Kongo; in the religious sphere, it sought to abolish traditional customs.

The Portuguese were not satisfied with gaining commercial and religious dominance in the Kongo. They also wished to exploit the precious minerals, which they erroneously believed to be abundant, as a result of impressions given by the unlucky envoys of Mvemba Nzinga. Both Manuel, in 1520, and his successor, Joao III (reigned 1521-57), in 1530, had received gifts of several silver manacles from Mvemba Nzinga. The Portuguese consequently believed the

Kongo was filled with mines. (Even as much as a century later, the Portuguese were to wage a disastrous war against a king of the Kongo who refused to surrender his mines to them.)

During the reign of Mvemba Nzinga, the slave trade began—ruining the interior of the country, not so much in demographic terms as on an institutional level. The Portuguese sent to help educate and modernize the Kongo, chose instead to take part in this very profitable activity. The Portuguese of São Tomé island, who received a trade monopoly for Central Africa from Portugal scorned any attempts on the part of the Mani Kongo to halt or even regulate the slave trade within his kingdom. Portuguese adventurers in the Kongo had close links to São Tomé. On Easter Sunday 1539, these adventurers even tried to kill the Mani Kongo as he attended mass. The king barely escaped.

In about 1843, Mvemba Nzinga died, after a long reign of almost 40 years. He is remembered as an inspired builder, and a sincere ruler with a great vision. He was, nevertheless, naive, lacking the decisiveness and political cunning needed to outmaneuver the Portuguese. Some of his actions led to the eventual downfall and ruin of his land. By seizing office through the force of arms, he inaugurated the violent struggles for succession which were to divide the Kongo during the second half of the 17th century. By revealing the existence of mines in his lands, he aroused Portuguese cupidity, with disastrous results. Finally, in his numerous campaigns to abolish traditional religion, he destroyed many examples of Kongolese art.

TSIMBA MABIALA

BIBLIOGRAPHY: G. Balandier, *La vie quotidinne au royaume du Kongo du XVIème au XVIIIème siècle*, Paris, 1965, English translation by Helen Weaver published as *Daily Life in the Kingdom of the Kongo from the Sixteenth to the Eighteenth Century*, New York, 1968; R. Batsikama, *Voici les Jagas ou l'histoire d'un peuple parricide bien malgré lui* ("Meet the Jagas, or the History of a People Parricide Despite Themselves"), Kinshasa, 1971; J. Cuvelier, *L'ancien royaume du Congo* ("The Ancient Kingdom of the Kongo"), Paris-Bruges, 1946; W.C.L. Randles, *L'ancien royaume du Congo des origines a la fin du XIXème siècle* ("The Ancient Kingdom of Kongo from its Origins to the End of the 19th Century"), Paris, The Hague, 1968.

MWANANDUNGU

Mwanandungu (who flourished in the mid-19th century) is recalled in oral tradition as one of the leaders of the Lobala people when they migrated to the present location on the left bank of the Ubangi River, about 175 km (100 mi) north of modern Mbandaka.

The Lobala are one of the many river or fishing peoples of the region between the Zaire and Ubangi rivers, whose history is complex, and only partially known.

Like the Likoka-Ntanda who live immediately to the east of them, the Lobala claim to have come originally from the left bank of the Giri River in the region of Mobele. According to oral tradition, the Lobala emigrated in small family groups led by men such as Bongombe and Iteno, who brought the Nkungu (now Bolebo) group, or Itumba, who led the Mokame. Mwanandungu, together with his father and grandfather, is remembered as a leader of the Ikwangbala family of the Lobala.

Supposedly, in the original Lobala migration from Mobele, the Ikwangbala traveled with the Mantele, Bosoko, Bokeka, Nyonyo, and Ikembe families. Guided by their common leader Munkata, they stopped at Mufondu, Mabenzo, Bonyoyi, Kwese, and Nkombe before separating when they reached Bokombe.

One part of this larger migration then followed Mboloyamato (meaning "prow of a dug-out canoe"). When Mboloyamato died, at Bokembe, on the crest of the Ubangi-Giri watershed, his son Mwanandungu took charge of the group. As the people no longer traveled by river and stream, for a time they forgot how to use dug-out canoes.

Under Mwanandugu, they attacked the Bonzembo, the principal clan of Nseka, or Mokolo, who had preceded them in this migration. Pushed to the banks of the Ubangi, the Bonzembo then fought the Bondongo, who, in turn, went further north, towards the present side of Dongo, located about 275 km (185 mi) north of what is now Mbandaka on the Ubangi River. Mwanandungu's people stopped briefly at Bibete before finally settling at Ikwangbala near the Ubangi.

One day, while the people were living at Ikwangbala, Mwanandungu's slave, who was out hunting with his dogs, discovered the Ubangi River. Carrying a large fish, he returned with news of the river previously unknown to them. The desire to catch more such fish caused Mwanandungu and his men to abandon the old site of Ikwangbala and settle on the river bank. The new site was also called Ikwangbala, and this name became the name of the clan. The Ikwangbala, however, who did not yet know how to fish in this great river, had to come to terms with their earlier rivals the Bonzembo, in order to exchange their bananas for fish.

According to H. Vandevenne's inquiry in 1928, the migrations of Ikwangbala, under the leadership of Mwanandungu, had taken place 50 to 60 years earlier. It seems, however, that they took place earlier still, and well before 1870, for when Bobangi traders began to visit the region around 1880-90, the members of the Ikwangbala clan were solidly entrenched, and had long been accustomed to life on the water.

Besides explaining when and why the Ikwangbala settled on the Ubangi River, oral traditions about Mwanandungu also describe the Ikwangbala family's relation to nearby Lobala people. According to oral records, once Mwanandungu died, his sons and relatives dispersed, spreading out "as embers scatter."

For example, Ikwango, having killed several men in his own village, and being unable to pay restitution to the injured families, was forced to leave Ikwangbala. Ikwango founded another village called Ikwangbala bongondo fa Ikwango ("Ikwangbala, created by Ikwango"). This village, which has since disappeared, was located near Kungba beyond Imese 220 km (140 mi) north of Mbandaka, on the Ubangi.

Itongo, another notable and the grandson of the original leader Munkata, settled among the Lobala Mpoko, where he founded the family called "Ikwangbala created by Itongo."

Ikwangbala people also appeared west of the Ubangi in what is now the People's Republic of the Congo. When Mwanandungu was still alive, he gave one of his daughters to a man named Bondongo, who lived west of the river. This marriage was intended to bring peace between the two groups. Afterwards, one of Mwanandungu's grandsons from this union founded a village called Ikwangbala, and located in what is now the People's Republic of the Congo.

Even after Mwanandungu had separated from other leaders—such as Ingende and Ibito, who founded Bokweye, Nyambaka, who founded Nyonyo, and Mokoma, who founded Ikembe—the Ikwangbala clan retained some influence over these diverse Lobala groupings.

Although oral histories of Mwanandungu and his kin may reflect social arrangements rather than factual events, such stories reinforce the prominent position of Mwanandungu's family in the Lobala area. Thus, when the Lobala chiefdom was created by the colonial government in 1928, the ruler was chosen from among the descendants of Mwanandungu. There was no opposition to this from the other groups.

MUMBANZA mwa BAWELE na
NYABAKOMBI ENSOBATO

BIBLIOGRAPHY: H. Vandevenne, "Rapport d'enquête sur la chefferie des Lobala, No. 1: Les Lobala" ("Report of Enquiry into the Lobala Chiefdom, No. 1: The Lobala"), 1928, Bomana Territory, Archives of the Bomongo Zone.

MWANZA KASONGO. See
NGONGO LETETA

MWATHA KOMBANA

Mwatha Kombana (who flourished circa the 17th century) founded a Lunda-related chiefdom in the region between the Lutshiko and Loange rivers, about 160 km (100 mi) southeast of Kikwit. Begun as part of a general 17th-century pattern of Lunda conquest and expansion, the Kombana polity had a significant influence over the entire region between the Kwilu and Tshikapa rivers.

Some oral traditions claim that Lunda expansion began with Kinguri, who, in protest against the marriage of his sister Ruwej a Nkond (q.v.) with the Luba Chibind Yirung (q.v.), left Lunda territory to settle elsewhere. Moving westward, he was responsible for founding the Kasanje state which his son, Kasanje Ka Imba, consolidated on the Kwango River in the early 17th century. Later the Shinje state was founded by Kapenda Mukwa Ambungo, and the Yaka state by Mwene Putu Kasongo (q.v.).

It was by following the example of Mwene Putu Kasongo that Mukelenge Mutombo (cousin of Chibind, or of Ruwej, according to some tradition—or the favorite son of the Mwana Uta, under Chibind Yirung or Ruwej, according to others) left the Lunda area in search, like Kasongo, of Kinguri. He left Lundaland at the same time as Mai Munene (q.v.), Chibind Yirung's cousin, and moved towards the northwest. The most likely story is that Mukelenge Mutombo did not leave Lundaland of his own initiative, but was sent, together with Mai Munene, by the Lunda court at Musumba to fight the Tufia people. Earlier in this era of Lunda conquest, Ruwej had sent her maternal uncle Mujinga north to fight the Tufia. Mujinga had been beaten shamefully, thus discrediting the court of Musumba. Therefore, Chibind Yirung sent "his son" Mukelenge Mutombo and Mai against the Tufia, whom they defeated. After the victory, Mai settled at the confluence of the Tshikapa and the Kasai. Mukelenge Mutombo, accompanied by several of his clans (Shakatwala, Kakinga Mutombo, Mwadi a Ngoya, and Kabeya), continued westward in hopes of finding Kinguri.

Mukelenge Mutombo, however, never realized his original intentions for, after crossing the Lovua River, in about 1650, he settled at the confluence of the Loange and the Lutshiko rivers. There, he dislodged the Pende people who had just come to the area. Founding a chiefdom, Mukelenge Mutombo took the title Mwatha (ruler) Kombana ("one who gives generously"). Through a common practice known as positional succession, all later rulers of the chiefdom took the same title. Thus, Mwatha Kombana came to represent an office rather than one specific individual. Sometimes the Kombana rulers were also called Mwatha Yamvu, a title identifying them with the prestigious Lunda Mwant Yav.

After this event, some clans who had accompanied Mukelenge Mutombo continued westward. One of them, under the leadership of Shakatwala, founded the Lunda chiefdom of Mwe Nzila, or Shakatwala.

Mukelenge Mutombo was the first Mwatha Kombana. In chronological order the rulers who succeeded him were: Kambakamba from the Shakatwala family, Kotoi from the Mweni Mavu family, Motatshinga from the Mweni Lukanda family, Kapata from the Shakatawala family, Ilunga from the Kawaya family, Kabeya from the Mbaji a Ngoi family, Muteba Tshibindu from the Shakatawala family, Kapata Fungi from the Kapenda Tshibudi family, Lunga from the Shimbundu Makata family, and Muloshi from the Shakatwala family.

Kabeya was chief when the Cokwe (Chokwe) from Angola began invading the land in the last half of the 19th century. This Cokwe intrusion marked the beginning of a period of decadence in the Kombana chiefdom. The last named chief Muloshi ruled in 1936.

Strongly influenced by the Pende, the Kombana Lunda have adopted the Gipende language and many Pende cultural forms. Nevertheless, they have never forgotten their Lunda origins in Shaba. Even in the 20th century, the Mwatha Kombana claims to rule with authority delegated from the Lunda Mwant Yav.

SIKITELE GIZE a SUMBULA

BIBLIOGRAPHY: L. de Sousberghe, *Les Pende, Aspects des structures sociales politiques,* ("The Pende, Aspects of Socio-Political Structures"), Bujumbura, 1963; G.L. Haveaux, *La tradition historique des Bapende Orientaux* ("The Historical Tradition of the Eastern Bapende"), Brussels 1954; M. Planc-quaert, *Les Jaga et les Bayaka du Kwango, Contribution Historico-Ethnographique* ("The Jaga and the Bayaka of Kwango, a Historico-Ethnographic Contribution"), Brussels, 1932, *Les Yaka Essai d'histoire* ("The Yaka. An Historical Essay"), Brussels, 1971; I. Struyf, "Kahemba, Envahisseurs Badjock et Conquérants Balunda" ("Kahemba, Badjock Invaders and Balunda Conquerors"), *Zaire* II, 1948, pp. 351-90; J. Vansina, *Les anciens royaumes de la savane,* Lèopoldville, 1965, published in English as *Kingdoms of the Savanna,* Madison, 1966.

MWENE PUTU KASONGO

Mwene Putu Kasongo (who flourished in about the mid-17th century), a Lunda from western Shaba, subjected the Yaka people living along the Kwango River, southwest of modern Kikwit.

Kasongo's activities among the Yaka were only part of a larger 16th and 17th century Lunda pattern of conquest. Lunda expansion started with Kinguri, who, in protest against the marriage of his sister Ruwej a Nkond (*q.v.*), to the Luba interloper Chibind Yirung (*q.v.*), left Musumba, the Lunda capital (located 240 km, or 150 mi, north of modern Dilolo). Kinguri migrated to the southwest where he hoped to found a state to use as a base to destroy the Lunda kingdom of Musumba.

Kinguri and his men went as far as Luanda, on the Atlantic coast, where they put themselves at the service of the Portuguese. Some of his men later left the coast and moved, under the leadership of one Kulanjinga, back towards the east. They settled on the east bank of the Lui River, a tributary of the Kwango. It was the men of this group of emigrants who later built the famous state of Kasanje on the Kwango River in Angola. This state subsequently played a determining role in the trade relations of the Portuguese African zone by serving as an intermediary or broker state between the coastal regions and the hinterland.

According to certain traditions, it was with the aim of finding their uncle Kinguri that Kasongo and his elder brother Lukundo Sango left Musumba and journeyed toward the west. On their way, the two brothers and their men had to fight hostile people who wanted to block their progress. The fierce opposition came from the Suku and the Holo, located about 350 km (200 mi) southwest of modern Kikwit. After indecisive but bloody battles in the region of Tungula Falls and along the right bank of the Wamba River, the emigrants concluded they could not go any further without additional support from Musumba.

Kasongo therefore left his elder brother Lukundo, the titular leader of the expedition, on the banks of the Wamba, and went back to the Lunda capital for reinforcements. But when he returned, leading a strong army of Lunda warriors, Kasongo did not go back to his elder brother. Instead he traveled towards the northwest, probably hoping to avoid control from Musumba's control, and with the intention of building his own kingdom.

Some Lunda traditions from the Kwango-Kwilu area claim that Kasongo left Musumba at the same time as Mai Munene (*q.v.*) and then he, together with Kisanda Kameshi and Mukelenge Mutombo, participated in Mai Munene's expedition. After conquering the region between the Tshikapa and Kasai rivers, Mai Munene settled at the confluence of the two rivers and organized the Lunda state of Mai Munene.

Kisanda Kameshi went to the region of the upper Lovua, where he founded several chiefdoms, and appointed his brothers and some of his close relatives as chiefs. He himself moved towards Luajimu where he built the Lunda state of Kahungula, situated 100 km (60 mi) south of Mai Munene. His people adopted the name Lunda Amukundo, and he himself took the title Kahungula (meaning one who removes obstacles from his path).

Mukelenge Mutombo crossed the Lovua to conquer the region between the Lutshiko and Loange rivers, where Pende people had just settled. With help from the Pende, he founded a Lunda chiefdom. He himself took the title Mwatha Kombana (q.v.), which also became the name of his polity, which was located about 160 km (100 mi) southeast of what is now Kikwit.

As for Kasongo, he continued westward, crossed the upper Kwilu River, and established several Lunda settlements. After staying there for a long time, he pushed on towards the west, reaching the Kwenge River. According to the traditions of the Lunda of Kwango, Kasongo and his men had difficulty crossing this river on account of its width, its swampy banks, and the many crocodiles. Traveling for many days along the right bank in search of a passage, they arrived at the Kwenge's five falls. Because it was the dry season, the river was low and they were able to build a bridge with stones. Their crossing, however, was marred by one painful incident, Mwaku, Kasongo's young brother, died in the falls. The Lunda of Kwango still have a vivid memory of this crossing. The place or the ford where Kasongo forded the Kwenge is still remembered as the "Kasongo Lunda passage."

Settling several Lunda families in the region between the Kwilu and the Kwenge, Kasongo charged them to occupy the conquered land, to make the inhabitants recognize his authority, and to pay tax to him. One of these Lunda families, that of Mwene Kalunga, was active in contributing towards Lunda expansion in that area.

After crossing the Kwenge, Kasongo and his men settled temporarily west of the river at a place called Nzofu Lukunda, in the region where the Kwenge and its tributaries, the Tendwala and the Wovo, flow. With Nzofu as their base of operations, Kasongo and his men raided the regions of the upper Kwenge for several years.

In his effort to settle as far from original Lunda homeland as possible, Kasongo left the Kwenge and, with some of his followers, went further west. Reaching the Kwango River, where the Tùfu and the Yonso flow, he settled on the right bank of the Kwango at the place now called Kasongo Lunda (located 200 km or 120 mi southwest of Kikwit).

Once settled, he conquered the Yaka people, who had occupied the land for a long time. After the Yaka had been subjugated, Kasongo modeled their administration on the model of the Lunda state of Musumba, with a decidedly hierarchial power system, and succession through the male line.

Having learned, as soon as he arrived in Yaka land, that the area west of the Kwango belonged to Mwene Putu (the King of Portugal) Kasongo decided to take Yamu Mwene Lunda Putu Kasongo as his title—a title which his successors still bear. They are, however, often called Kiamfu, which is a deformation of Yamwu, or else Kasongo Lunda, or simply Mwene Putu. Kasongo's arrival on the Kwango and his subsequent conquest of the Yaka probably took place soon after 1650.

Traditions of the Lunda and of other people of the Kwango-Kwilu, region describe Kasongo as a great conqueror, a man of exceptional courage, and a great political organizer. The Yaka state, which he built by introducing socio-political structures from his homeland, soon became the most powerful and extensive of all the Kwango-Kwilu polities. Essentially a military state, by the 18th century it covered much of the territory from Kwango to Lutshiko.

A western counterpart of the kingdom of Kazembe in the eastern section of the Lunda empire, Kasongo's state played a determining role in the political and economic relations of Kwango-Kwilu regions. On the political level, the Yamu Mwene Putu subjected the people of these areas, making them his vassals and obliging them to pay tribute. This Lunda-Yaka hegemony was imposed by arms. On the commercial level, Yaka country came to serve as an intermediary between the merchants from the coast and traders from the hinterland. The Yaka jealously controlled the trade route which, from the coast (Ambriz), passed through the capital of the Kiamfu, then through the territory of Mwene Kongo, chief of the Suku, before it reached the capital of Mwatha Kombana, the Lunda chief of Lutshiko.

During the 17th and 18th centuries, slaves and ivory were the main commercial products in Central Africa. In Yaka country, the Mwene Putu (the title refers to all the successive office-holders) maintained a monoploy on these products. He also made certain never to allow the Pombeiros (Angolan merchants) to cross the Kwango River. In order to ensure supplies for the slave trade with the Atlantic coast, he started acquiring and selling men in his own kingdom. Later, when the trade increased, the Mwene Putu raided his neighbors, thus causing great damage to Kwango-Kwilu society. Faced with incessant slave raids by Yaka warriors under their Kiamfu, many Suku, Mbala, Pende, Hungaan, and Mbuun people fled from the Upper Kwango to seek refuge in the northern and eastern regions. These migrations explain, to a large entent, the dense concentration of people in the mid-Kwango and Kwilu areas.

SIKITELE GIZE a SUMBULA

BIBLIOGRAPHY: G. L. Haveaux, *La tradition historique des Bapende Orientaux* ("The Historic Tradition of the Eastern Bapende"), Brussels, 1954; H. Nicolai, *Le Kwilu, Etude géographique d'une region congolaise* ("Kwilu. A Geographical Study of a Congolese Region"), Brussels, 1963; M. Plancquaert, *Les Jaga et les Bayaka du Kwango. Contribution historico-ethnigraphique* ("The Jaga and the Bayaka of Kwango. An Historico-Ethnographic Contribution"), Brussels, 1932, *Les Yaka. Essai d'histoire* ("The Yaka. An Historical Essay"), Brussels, 1971; I. Struyf, "Kahemba. Envahisseurs Badjock et Conquérants Balunda" ("Kahemba. Bajock Invaders and Balunda Conquerors"), *Zaire,* II, No. 5, 1948, pp. 351-90; H. Van Roy, "L'origine des Balunda du Kwango" ("The Origin of the Balunda of Kwango"), *Aequatoria,* No. 4, 1961, pp. 136-41; J. Vansina, *Les anciens royaumes de la savane,* Léopoldville, 1965, published in English as *The Ancient Kingdoms of the Savana,* Madison, 1966.

NABIEMBALI

Nabiembali (circa 1815-1860), expanded and ruled the Mangbetu state when its power was at its zenith.

Located on the Bomolandi River, a tributary of the Uele, about 400 km (250 mi) northeast of what is now Kisangani, the Mangbetu people are Sudanic-speaking groups who penetrated into the forest areas of Zaire before 1800.

Nabiembali was the son of Manzika, the chief who led the Mangbetu people out of the forest and northwest toward the regions they presently occupy. From his youth, Nabiembali distinguished himself in hunting, dancing, and war. He was already highly regarded when he took power in about 1830 after his father died.

Upon coming to power, he quickly extended his domain by conquering a large territory which reached northwest as far as the mid-Uele River at what is now Niangara.

Nabiembali, however, is remembered even more for his administrative innovations than for his conquests. A shrewd organizer, he allowed the chiefs of conquered tribes to reign securely under his authority. By allowing a great deal of autonomy to subjected chiefs, he showed much more flexibility than his Zande neighbors to the north. Once they had taken an area, the Zande leaders immediately replaced the chiefs and notables of the conquered populations with their own relatives. Nabiembali was aware, at the beginning of his reign, that he could not possibly apply the Zande system to his conquests, his family being too small. Later, when his sons, and grandsons increased in number, he shifted to the Zande pattern of placing family members in key offices. Nevertheless, he had prepared for this transition long in advance for, from the start of his reign, after each victory he took a wife from among his new subjects. The children born of these unions were raised in the royal residence. When they grew old enough to govern, Nabiembali appointed them to rule over their mother's people. While Nabiembali could reasonably expect these new chiefs to be loyal to him, they were usually received with enthusiasm by the local people, who considered them family members rather than usurpers.

Order and peace reigned in Nabiembali's time, an era marking the height of the Mangbetu power. Later rulers never succeeded in restoring the glory of that age. Nabiembali himself lived long enough to see signs presaging the approaching disintegration. The Mangbetu state had always been a fragile grouping of disparate people. Frequently, ambitious political figures sought support from one or more of the component elements in order to challenge the central government.

During Nabiembali's own lifetime, and after his death when his sons sought to take power, rivalries, dissensions, murders, and internal wars threatened to destroy Nabiembali's work. In about 1800, his oldest son, Tuba, dethroned Nabiembali and took power. Although Nabiembali did not long survive these events, before dying he formally disinherited his sons. Then secretly calling his confidant, a young man named Dakpara, he gave him the royal hammer, a symbol of authority and legitimacy.

After Nabiembali's death the Mangbetu state fragmented—first into two parts, and then into a multiplicity of small chiefdoms, ruled by his many competing sons. Internal forces of division were intensified by the arrival of slave traders from Egypt and the Sudan. These traders profited by supporting one faction against another, thereby gaining the slaves who were generated by the fighting which followed.

TSHUND'OLELA EPANYA SHAMOLOLO

BIBLIOGRAPHY: R. Cornevin, *Histoire du Congo des origines préhistoriques à la République Démocratique du Congo* ("History of the Congo from its Prehistoric Origins to the Democratic Republic of the Congo"), Paris, 1970; P. Curtin, S. Feirman, L. Thompson, and J. Vansina, *African History,* chapter 14, Boston, 1978; A. de Calonne-Beaufaict, *Azande, Introduction à une ethnographie générale des bassins de l'Ubangi-Uele et de l'Aruwimi* ("Azande, Introduction to a General Ethnography of the Ubangi-Uele and Aruwimi Basins"), Brussels, 1921; P. Denis, *Histoire des Mangbetu et des Natshaga jusqu'à l'arrivée des Belges* ("History of the Mangbetu and the Natshaga until the Arrival of the Belgians"), Tervuren, 1961; J. Ki-Zerbo, *Histoire de l'Afrique noire. D'hier à demain* ("History of Black Africa: From Yesterday to Tomorrow"), Paris, 1972.

NAWEJ a DITEND

Nawej a Ditend (circa 1800-1852) ruled as the Lunda Mwant Yav (supreme chief) at a time when commercial and political relations between the Lunda and Angolan peoples were intensifying.

The son of Ditend and grandson of Mwant Yav Chikomb, Nawej assumed power, perhaps in about 1810, after succession struggles in which he fought

Isindji and Mulaj who were also candidates for the throne.

Trade between the Lunda empire and Angola increased during his reign. Luso-African caravans began visiting Musumba, the Lunda capital, situated 240 km (150 mi) north of what is now Dilolo. Leaders of these groups were Manuel Gomes Sampaio (Campacala), Romao, Antonio Bonifacio Rodrigues, Francisco Pacheco, and Joaquim Graça (who remained at Musumba from 1843 to 1846), a trader from Golungo Alto (who stayed from 1846 to 1847), and Lourenço Bezzera Corraia Pinto, (who established an agricultural plantation in 1850).

In the 1840s the price of slaves declined while the price of ivory increased dramatically. To increase his ivory production, Mwant Yav Nawej a Ditend called on help from Cokwe (Chokwe) hunters, whose settlement in southern Lunda lands often caused frictions which degenerated into conflicts with local Lunda chiefs. Mwant Yav Nawej a Ditend's intervention temporarily brought a precarious period of peace.

Mwant Yav Nawej's commercial methods were troubling both to his own subjects and to the visiting traders. Supposedly, all the commercial dealings within Lunda territory were under the monopolistic control of Mwant Yav or the landed aristocracy. In consequence, many a trader suffered when he found his property confiscated as a fine by Nawej a Ditend. Likewise, local Lunda villages were pillaged, since Nawej often "paid" for trade goods by allowing Angolan merchants to raid villages which had not paid enough tax to the Mwant Yav.

When he died in 1852, Mwant Yav Nawej a Ditend had gained a reputation as a cruel, harsh ruler.

N'DUA SOLOL KANAMPUMB

BIBLIOGRAPHY: I. Cunnison, "Central Bantu historical text, II., Historical tradition of the Eastern Lunda," *Rhodes Livingstone Common,* IX, 23, 1962; H. Dias de Carvalho, *Expediçao ao Mwatiamvu. Ethnografia e Historia tradiçional des povos de Lunda,* ("Expedition to Mwatiamvu. The Traditional Ethnography and History of the Lunda Peoples") Lisbon, 1890; H. Drum, *Lueji va Konde,* Brussels, 1932; L. Duysters, "Histoire des Aluunda" ("History of the Aluunda"), in *Problèmes d'Afrique centrale,* XII, 40, 1958, pp. 76-98; *Ngand Yetu* ("Our Country"), Cleveland (Transvaal), 1963; P. Pogge, *Im Reiche des Muata Jamvo* ("In the Realm of the Mwant Yav"), Berlin, 1880; L. Van Denbyvang, "Notice historique sur les Balunda" ("Historical Note on the Balunda"), in *Congo,* Vol. 1, 1937, pp. 426-38, 548-62, Vol. 2, pp. 193-208; J. Vansina, *Les anciens royaumes de la savane,* Léopoldville, 1965, published in English as *Kingdoms of the Savanna,* Madison, 1966.

NGALIEMA

Ngaliema (circa 1850-circa 1900), a former slave, rose to become the richest and most powerful merchant at Malebo Pool (formerly Stanley Pool) in the late 19th century, at the time when Europeans were entering the area. Belonging to the Tio or Teke people, originally living north and west of the Pool, Ngaliema acted as a middleman between the Bobangi traders from upriver and the caravan leaders from the lower Zaire river region.

In order to take advantage of the growing trade, many subjects of the Makoko, the Tio chief, withdrew from his authority to create a new source of authority, based on wealth and weapons, in Hum territory on the southern bank of the Pool. When the Europeans came to settle the country in 1881, Ngaliema was among the most powerful men at the Pool. But the people he controlled finally took advantage of the European presence to challenge his power which was thus undermined by the Europeans, who introduced trade controls and taxation.

Ngaliema was born in Tio country, on the northern bank of the Pool. Like two of his brothers, he became a slave of one Bamaku, a Tio trader who had settled south of the Pool. After the death of his master, Ngaliema was freed and even inherited part of his master's property. Ngaliema's case was not unusual, for among the Tio slavery was an extremely prominent institution, as families purchased slaves in order to increase their numbers. On the other hand, it was also extremely easy for a free Tio to fall into slavery. In order to pay debts or fines, Tio families frequently sold one of their own kin to another family wishing to buy and adopt a new member. Merchants also acquired slaves who worked in their businesses.

At that time, the whole of the southern bank of the Malebo Pool was occupied by a number of Tio villages—notably, Kimpoko, Kimbangu, Kindolo, Kinshasa, and Kintambo. The rich traders in these towns had become practically independent and no longer obeyed the Makoko of Mbe, (the nominal Tio capital north of the Pool). South of the Pool, the Hum people, who had controlled the land, allowed the powerful Tio traders to settle in their villages.

Following his master's death in the early 1870s, Ngaliema quickly enriched himself through the ivory trade. Like other Tio brokers, he bought goods from the Bobangi river traders and resold the products to Bakongo and Bazombo caravan leaders who linked the Pool to the Atlantic coast.

Following a dispute with Nchuvila, the Hum chief of Kinshasa village, located south of the Pool, on the site of modern Brazzaville, Ngaliema went to settle at Mfua, and continued his trade there. The inhabitants of Mfua resented his success, however, and trade at Mfua was not as profitable as it had been at Kinshasa. Thus, Ngaliema decided to relocate at Kintambo on the present Mount Ngaliema. Kintambo village, inhabited by a certain number of Tio, was under the leadership of the Hum chief Ngako, the brother of Nchuvila. Before settling there, Ngaliema had to recognize Hum authority over the land by giving an ivory tusk to each local chief.

Before long, Ngaliema gained enormous wealth through the ivory trade. His riches enabled him to buy slaves and rifles for his caravans. Through alliances

based on marriages, he befriended a number of the Hum rulers of Lemba and Kimbangu villages, located between the Funa and Njili streams. These relationships strengthened his position in the country, to the detriment of Chief Nchuvila of Kinshasa. After Nchuvila had died and been succeeded by the ineffective Ngako, Ngaliema became the most important Tio chief, and the master of Kintambo.

Ngaliema's followers included a considerable number of Tio sub-chiefs, who had attached themselves to his commercial enterprise. Ngaliema's subjects, estimated at 3,000 men in 1881, had about 450 rifles, while Ngaliema himself had 150. Thus, the Tio were easily able to dominate the other peoples, who did not have many guns. Nevertheless the Tio, whose only occupation was trade, depended on the local Hum for their food supplies, especially manioc. Through this relationship, the Hum were able to exert some control over the more powerful Tio.

Although when the Europeans arrived in the region in 1877, Ngaliema had not yet gained complete control over the inhabitants of the area, he was recognized as the richest and most important chief. Like many Tio leaders who had become rich through trade, Ngaliema had created a kind of royal court with ceremonies, strict protocol, and special dress. The insignia of his authority were no longer traditional.

In March 1877, Ngaliema who also used the name Itsi, met the Anglo-American explorer, Henry Morton Stanley (1841-1904), who had been sent to central Africa by the *New York Herald* and the London *Daily Telegraph* in order to complete Livingstone's work.

Introducing himself as the chief of Kintambo, Ngaliema made a blood pact with Stanley, gave the explorer gifts, and provided necessary information about travel towards Boma.

When Stanley returned to Malebo Pool in August 1881, as the leader of King Leopold's Comité d'Etudes du Haut-Congo (Study Committee for the Upper Congo River) he faced opposition from the Tio, who had signed treaties with the Franco-Italian explorer Savorgnan de Brazza (1852-1905). Opposition also came from the Bakongo and Bazombo caravan leaders, who feared the whites were destroying their monopoly over transport between the coast and the Pool.

Chief Ngaliema and his followers, however, welcomed Stanley, doubtlessly in hopes of gaining an advantage over the chiefs of Kinshasa and Mfua, and perhaps also out of respect to obligations of hospitality towards a blood brother. After receiving gifts from Stanley, Ngaliema promised him land for future settlement. Ngaliema was therefore attacked by the Tio, Hum, Bakongo, and Bazombo, who resented direct European intrusion into the commercial domain. In the face of strong African opposition to working with the whites, Ngaliema temporarily reversed himself by sending Stanley's subordinates out of the Pool area. For some time he opposed white settlement in his territory.

After a time, the Hum people, who were the owners of the land, expressed tolerance for the Europeans. Ngaliema took advantage of this shift to encourage white settlement. In November 1881, the whites located at a nearby hill the Africans called Konzo Ikulu. At first the Europeans referred to the hill as "Mount Léopold." Later it became "Mount Stanley."

Relations between Ngaliema and his newly arrived neighbors were at first uneasy, being characterized by mutual distrust. The Europeans, who sought to consolidate their position, avoided armed confrontation, and played on the rivalries between the various African groups. Nevertheless, for a time, the Bakongo and Bazombo buyers continued their trade as in the past. Ngaliema therefore benefited from the ivory trade as well as from the rent which Stanley's station paid. But he was no longer free to impose his will on the other African groups, since the Europeans regulated local political affairs.

After 1885, European competition began to affect traditional patterns of trade around the Pool. Taking advantage of agreements reached at the 1885 Berlin Conference, other commercial houses from the coast and the lower Congo River—the Dutch company N.A.H.V., the French company Daumas and Co., as well as new companies like the Société Anonyme Belge pour le Commerce du Haut-Congo (Belgian Commercial Company for the Upper Congo) became established at Malebo Pool. Increasingly, Bazombo and Bakongo brokers played a lesser role, and the Tio were undercut as middlemen between the upriver Bobangi carriers and the European trading stations.

In the end Ngaliema regretted having allowed the whites to settle at the Pool. But it was too late for military action. He no longer had reliable supplies of arms. Eventually, as commercial companies introduced river steamers, they were able to bypass both the Tio and the Bobangi.

Politically diminished and economically ruined, all the Tio chiefs, including Ngaliema, began a massive exodus from their villages on the southern bank of the Pool in 1891. Refusing to submit to the demands of taxation and forced labor which had been introduced by the Congo Free State, Ngaliema crossed the Pool in September 1891, and returned to his old home. From then until his death, he never regained his commercial power.

In order to perpetuate Ngaliema's memory, the government of modern Zaire erected a monument to him on the hill where, 95 years earlier, Stanley had founded the first Upper-Congo station, near the village of Kintambo, and which had become known as "Mount Stanley." This hill, the headquarters of Zairian state institutions, was re-named Mount Ngaliema, in honor of the great Tio merchant.

MUMBANZA mwa BAWELE na
NYABAKOMBI ENSOBATO

BIBLIOGRAPHY: H. Bentley, *Pioneering on the Congo,* Vol. 1, London, 1900; F. Bontinck, "Tippo-Tip et Ngaliema" ("Tippu Tib and Ngaliema"), *Ngonge Carnets des Sciences Humaines,* No. 27, 1972, pp. 6-10; C. Coquilhat, *Sur le Haut-Congo* ("On the Upper Congo"), Brussels, 1888; J. de Witte, *Vie de Monsieur Augouard* ("The Life of Monsieur Augouard"), Paris, 1924; H.M. Stanley, *Through the Dark Continent,* Vol. 2, London, 1878, *The Congo and the Founding of its Free State,* Vol. 1, London, 1885, *In Darkest Africa,* Vol. 1, London, 1889; J. Vansina, *The Tio Kingdom of the Middle Congo, 1880-1892,* London, 1973.

NGAND a BILOND

Ngand a Bilond (circa 1700-circa 1750) was responsible for consolidating and extending the Lunda empire in both the Lualaba River and the Lake Mweru areas of what is now the Shaba region. As Kazembe (governor) of vast eastern regions, he conquered local people and integrated them into the Lunda system.

Ngand a Bilond was the son of Cinyat Mfemb, who ruled the Kosa (Ako) people, living just north of what is now Mutshatsha, about 100 km (62 mi) west of what is now Kolwezi. Although originally not within the Lunda empire, the Kosa were defeated by the Kazembe Mutand Yembiyemb (q.v.), who established his headquarters at Cinyat's capital. Cinyat and his family then became loyal vassals of the militarily powerful and ritually prestigious Lunda.

Mutand Yembiyemb, however acted treacherously by withholding information about the source of salt in his newly-conquered land, and by killing Cinyat Mfemb, who had informed the Mwant Yav of his insubordination. After removing Mutand Yembiyemb from office, the Mwant Yav replaced him with Ngand a Bilond (meaning "land of metal"), whose given name had been Idim a Kaumb. The new Kazembe, Ngand a Bilond, then launched a campaign against Mutand, who fled south and was heard of no more.

After the disappearance of Mutand, Ngand a Bilond organized the administration of the conquered land, between the Lubudi and the Lufira rivers. Meanwhile, to the north of Kecila (near what is now Kolwezi), his commanders created armed chiefdoms, or military marches (i.e. border regions), to stop the incursion of the Luba Samba. Some years later, Ngand a Bilond crossed the Lualaba River with a large army. He then went through Sanga and Lamba territories, adding to his forces with local contingents and levying tribute from the people subjected to his rule.

As he pushed eastward, Ngand a Bilond learned that it would be difficult to cross the Luapula River. Thus, he decided to go north around Lake Mweru. Arriving at the Kundelungu, he met resistance from chief Mufunga's people, the Lomotwa, who were supported by Luba forces. The Lundas first entrenched themselves, and then attacked the Lomotwa, who surrendered after two days of fighting. The Lomotwa chief Mufunga was decapitated by Mushima Kainda, chief of the Kaonde people, who had rallied to the Lunda invaders.

But, on the following day, Ngand a Bilond fell ill. He died some days later.

TSHIBANGU KABET MUSAS

BIBLIOGRAPHY: F. Grévisse, "Notes ethnographiques relatives a quelques populations autochtones du Haut-Katanga industriel" ("Ethnographic Notes Relating to Some Native Populations of Industrial Upper Katanga") *Bulletin du C.E.P.S.I.,* No. 32, 1956, pp. 33-207; R. Hadelin, "Résumé de l'histoire ancienne du Katanga" ("Summary of the Ancient History of Katanga"), *Bulletin du C.E.P.S.I.,* No. 61, pp. 3-42; E. Labrecque, "Histoire des Mwate Kazembe, chefs du Luapula" ("History of the Mwate Kazembe, Chiefs of Luapula"), *Lovania,* XVI, 1949, pp. 9-33; *Ngand Yetu* ("Our Country"), Elisabethville, 1963; J. Vansina, *Les anciens royaumes de la savane,* Léopoldville, 1965, published in English as *Kingdoms of the Savanna,* Madison, 1966.

NGANKABI

Ngankabi (18?-1892) was the powerful Nkum'okare (queenmother) of the Bantote clan, the ruling élite over the Nunu people, living north of the Mfimi River, which links Lake Mai Ndombe (formerly Lake Léopold II) to the Kasai River. Although little is known about the many other women who influenced Central African history, Ngankabi was a celebrity who, during the 1880s, played a remarkable political and economic role in the lower Kasai river region.

She was the daughter of Nganzulu, and a member of the Bantote clan, from whose ranks the Nunu chiefs were chosen. The earliest written description of Ngankabi comes from the Anglo-American explorer, Henry M. Stanley (1841-1904), who met her at Mushie, on the Mfimi River, in May 1882. Stanley characterized Ngankabi as a brown and frizzy-haired version of Martha Washington (i.e. the wife of George Washington, first U.S. President), a square-shouldered woman about 1.7 meters (5 feet 6 inches) tall. When Stanley met Ngankabi she was wearing a large grass skirt and was barefoot. Ngankabi's Belgian biographer, Father Storme, qualified Stanley's description as an exaggerated and idealized account written by a journalist. The Protestant missionaries G. Grenfell and T. Comber, however, who visited Mushie in July 1884, spoke of Ngankabi as a "strong minded woman."

Stanley gave her the title of "Queen of the Ouaboume" ("Boma people"). This title, however, has been disputed: first because the people of Mushie are not Boma, although the Belgian colonial administration strove to make them a sub-tribe of the Boma-North; second, Ngankabi was not a "queen" in the sense in which Stanley meant the word, since Nunu society, although strongly holding to matrilineal succession, does not allow women to govern the community in the executive sense.

Nevertheless, at the time of the European penetration, Ngankabi was not only the oldest woman of the Bantote, but also the mother of Bokoko, the reigning chief. These two attributes gave her great influence. As eldest woman of the clan she was considered "mother" of all the Bantote, and as such had custody of all the clan's magical fetishes. She also "owned" the clan's soil and water. Furthermore, as mother of Chief Bokoko, she had much influence over the political process. Taking advantage of her strong position, Ngankabi relegated her son, a legitimate chief according to custom, to a secondary position on the political scene, while she herself assumed major commercial and diplomatic responsibilities.

Ngankabi participated in the great Zaire River trade, based on interregional commercial exchanges. The principal artery of trade was the river itself, fed by tributary and secondary channels, such as the Alima, Likouala-Mosaka, Nkene, Ruki-Busira, and Kwa-Mfimi which flowed out of Zaire's central basin. Located at the confluence of the Mfimi and the Kasai, Mushie's geographic position enabled its inhabitants to take an active role in river commerce. The Nunu of Mushi were thus able to act as intermediaries between the Bakutu, (merchants on the Mfimi and Lukenie rivers and on Lake Mai Ndombe), who descended the Mfimi as far as Mushie, and the Bobangi traders, who ascended the Kwa River with trade goods obtained in the markets at Malebo Pool (in what is now the Kinshasa area).

As the eldest of the Bantote, Ngankabi had the right to commissions on transactions taking place in the clan's domain. From these commissions she acquired many European goods, as well as immense quantities of ivory, and large numbers of slaves. These possessions allowed her to develop further commercial relations. Also by sending some of these goods as gifts, as well as dispatching emissaries, to other Central African leaders, such as Ngaliema (q.v.) of Kintambo, Gobila of Msuata, and Keboke of Misongo—Ngankabi developed strong diplomatic ties.

This opening to the outside world enabled Ngankabi to become one of the most important individuals in the Zaire river area. Thus, all the Europeans—H.M. Stanley, Col. Sir Francis de Winton, George Grenfell, T.J. Comber, Massari, and A. Delcommune—who reached Mushie in the 19th century, sought to contact her. Moreover, Ngankabi received the visitors cordially. From June 3 to June 6, 1882, she housed Stanley, who had fallen ill on his return from exploring Lake Mai Ndombe.

Ngankabi also maintained good relations with the missionaries of the Berghe-Sainte-Marie station—founded in May 1886, at the confluence of the Kwa and Mfimi rivers, by Father Augouard, a Frenchman. In 1888, the site was taken over by the Belgian Scheut Fathers. Ngankabi even concluded a treaty with these missionaries in February 1891, on the occasion of the liberation of Nsungu, her great-grandson and "crown prince" of the Nunu. Nsungu had been kidnapped by soldiers of the Congo Free State commanded by Ponthier. Nsungu had been released thanks to the intervention of the missionaries. He was returned to his parents at a ceremony held on February 27, 1891, at Berghe-Sainte-Marie. The missionaries took advantage of this occasion to require Ngankabi to sign a treaty by the terms of which the Nunu renounced hu-man sacrifice, the trial by poison ordeal, the slave trade, and other practices opposed by the missionaries.

Ngankabi died, according to Storme, at about the end of 1892. She was buried at Nkieme in the cemetery of her clan. Her name remains associated with the period of Nunu economic prosperity and glory.

MFIRI MAPESA

BIBLIOGRAPHY: W.H. Bentley, *Pioneering on the Congo*, Vol. II, London, 1900; A. Delcommune, *Vingt années de vie africaine*, ("Twenty Years of African Life"), Vol. I, Brussels, 1922; H.M. Stanley, *The Congo and the Founding of its Free State*, 2 vols, London, 1885; M. Storme, "Ngankabi," *Biographie Coloniale Belge*, Brussels, Vol. IV, 1948-68.

NGEMBA

Ngemba (circa 1820-September, 1886), also known as Mata-Boike, was a famous warrior-leader of the Iboko and Mabale people, living at Makanza on the Zaire River, about 200 km (120 mi) north of what is now Mbandaka. Through his relations with the Anglo-American explorer Henry Morton Stanley (1841-1904) and Camille Coquilhat (governor of the Congo Free State from 1891-92), Ngemba played a significant role in opening Central Africa to European expansion. Because of his contacts with the colonialists, the Iboko and Mabale people, subsequently called Bangala by the whites, became key actors in the modernization of the Congo state (now Zaire).

The Iboko once lived at the confluence of the Ubangi and the Giri rivers. In the early 18th century, they migrated from that region to settle at Wambala on the mid-Giri. Then, under the leadership of Lokole, Ngemba's grandfather, the Iboko traveled east along the Mabale channel until they reached the right bank of the Zaire River, where the group broke into two parts. Lokole, leading the northern section, settled at the present site of Makanza. The southern section, however, were attacked by the Boloki, another group of Giri river people who had arrived in the area some years before. Those southern Iboko, who managed to escape from the Boloki, rejoined Lokole's northern group. The Iboko then allied with the Mabale from Djongo, on the crest of the Zaire and Giri rivers.

Together, the Iboko and Mabale attacked the Boloki, forcing the Bobeka division of the Boloki northeast to the mouth of Mongala River, 80 km (50 mi) northeast of Makanza. After driving away some Ngombe groups who earlier had settled on part of the land, the united Iboko and Mabale gained firm control over the Makanza area. The union between the Ibokos and the Mabales was further strengthened by numerous exchanges of women and by the need for cooperation against the Boloki of Bobeka, who constantly were trying to avenge their earlier defeat.

It was in this atmosphere of conflict that Ngemba was born. His father, Matamumbete, died in a fight against the Bobeka. Matamumbete's brother Boike then took charge of military operations against the Bobeka. He also gained control of the political and economic affairs of the Iboko and Mabale.

When Ngemba (also known as Engwangola) succeeded his uncle Boike, the Ibokos and Mabales were experiencing demographic expansion (in 1885, Coquilhat estimated this growing population at about 30,000). Thus, some units detached themselves and occupied small areas almost as far east as the Mongala River. In addition, the Iboko were enjoying economic prosperity because of the growing tide of commercial activity on the rivers. The Iboko region was the most important ivory market in the region. These facts combined to give another turn to the old political rivalries. Ngemba, who had taken the name Mata-Boike, meaning great prophet, or soothsayer, took advantage of Iboko demographic, military, and commercial growth to increase his own political power. Through trade, his sons acquired many guns. Thus, Ngemba, an able strategist, led his men to many victories over other peoples of the region. Although Mata-Boike ruled the Iboko-Mabale groups, he made no attempt to govern the other inhabitants of the river between Losengo, upstream from Makanza and Bonsembe, downstream. Nevertheless, those peoples sought his protection or at least tried to live on good terms with him. Thus Coquilhat could write: "Mata-Boike was governing one of the largest states on the shores of equatorial Congo." His old enemies, the Bobeka, even though under the effective leadership of Monoko mwa Nkoi, could not stand against Mata-Boike. They had abandoned their river villages, some years before the Europeans arrived in 1883, to settle on the lower Mongala River, about 25 km (25 mi) further east.

In internal politics, Mata-Boike was a skilled arbiter rather than a supreme decision-maker. His power was by no means absolute; important decisions for the whole community came only after long public palavers between the chiefs and the notables of the confederation. In giving the last word, Mata-Boike expressed the consensus of such meetings. In commercial dealings, he exercised a virtual monopoly. Because of his prestige, most of the merchants from upstream came to trade with him at Makanza.

When Stanley arrived in Iboko-Mabale territory in February, 1877, Mata-Boike's men attacked the expedition. From that time on, the Iboko and Mabale people were labelled "the Bangalas" in European writings. Their courage, which earned them the nickname "the Ashantis of the Livingstone River," focused European attention upon them.

Thus, when Stanley—who in the meantime had begun working for King Leopold II of Belgium, (reigned 1865-1909)—returned to the Iboko people in October 1883, one of his main objectives was to gain their friendship and to use their power to dominate other groups in the region. Mata-Boike now welcomed the Europeans traveling from the Equator station (now Mbandaka) to Stanley Falls (of what is now Kisangani). But when the Europeans tried to settle at Iboko in January 1884, they faced a strong opposition from Mata-Boike's subjects. The second attempt to settle there in May that same year also would have failed had Mata-Boike himself not decided to receive the Europeans at Makanza. Mata-Boike's decision was based on economic and especially political considerations. Since he was then old and unable to lead an expedition against the Bobeka, he wanted to use his guests as allies to annihilate his enemies once and for all. He failed, however, to achieve his goals. Not only did the Europeans at Makanza, (then called Bangala Station) refuse to fight the Bobeka, they also broke the economic monopoly that Mata-Boike had previously won for himself. From that time onwards, and especially in 1888, the Bangala Station assumed control of the river trade.

Ngemba, shaking hands with Coquilhat - a picture taken in about 1890.

In spite of his disappointments, Mata-Boike—of whom Stanley said, "he must have been erstwhile the most astonishing specimen of physical virility which could possibly be found in Equatorial Africa"—honored his commitments to the Europeans and did not attempt to repel them. Doubtlessly because of the friendship he developed with the first chief of the station, Camille Coquilhat, Mata-Boike gave material aid to the new station, and tried to regulate the relationship between his subjects and his guests. From the beginning, he offered the Europeans some of his men, including his own children, to guide them in their numerous observation missions around the country. Thus it was owing to Mata-Boike's assistance that the Europeans were able to strengthen their position at Iboko and then throughout the whole of the region. Having grown accustomed to accompanying the white men on their trips, Mata-Boike's children were the first, in the whole Congo Free State, to go into service as wage-earners and as soldier-workers on the European stations along the Congo (now the Zaire) River. This process, which started on July 14, 1885, was strengthened as time went on. Mata-Boike's people were to become trusted recruits in the army and the militia of the concessionary companies, as well as workers on the crews of steamers, and employees in the other services at the various stations.

The Bangala station increasingly gained favor from the colonial authorities, and especially from Vice-Governor General Camille Coquilhat. It became the most beautiful station in the Congo, and the most important center in the region. Workers at Bangala station—called Nouvelle-Anvers after 1890—gathered "abandoned" children or "orphans" to train them in one of the first schools of the country. It was also from Nouvelle-Anvers that Lingala, one of the four vernacular languages of Zaire, developed and spread.

Mata-Boike, however, died in September 1886, two years after the station was established. Thus, he did not live to see the results of his actions. His role, however, was important for the latter history of this station. After staying in Iboko for 15 months, Coquilhat wrote:

> ....I see in Mata-Boike a wise, benevolent, and superior man, who vaguely sensed the progress which white men could bring to his country. As a Bangala, he was a faithful friend and through the reconciliation role he had assumed, he was the co-founder of our establishment.

Mata-Boike was laid to rest in the land of his ancestors, near the state station, between two giant palm trees, which were planted at his burial.

His son Boike succeeded him in October 1886, and continued his father's policy towards the Europeans. A tactful man, Boike rendered good service to the colonial state. Congo Free State agents often accepted his sound advice. He went to Belgium in 1848 with a group of 39 other Bangalas to attend the Antwerp Exhibition.

By allowing the European agents to settle at Makanza, and by supporting them in many instances, Mata-Boike, although he lost his own authority, greatly contributed towards the consolidation of the authority of the new Congo state. The role played by the Bangala station was one of the most important in the upper Congo, and even in the rest of the country. This collaboration with Europeans, far from being treason against his people, was considered by Mata-Boike to be the opening of a new era.

MUMBANZA mwa BAWELE na
NYABAKOMBI ENSOBATO

BIBLIOGRAPHY: "Traité passé entre Mata-Boike et E. Hanssens, le 7-5-1883" ("Treaty Concluded Between Mata-Boike and E. Hanssens, May 7, 1883"), *Archives Africaines*, A.I. (1377) h, Brussels; "A propos d'un voyage de Congolais en Belgique" ("About a Voyage of Congolese to Belgium"), *Belgique Coloniale* I, 5, 1895, pp. 37-38; C. Coquilhat, *Sur le Haut Congo*, ("On the Upper Congo"), Brussels, 1888; E. Hanssens, "Les premières explorations du Haut-Congo" ("The First Explorations of the Upper Congo"), *Congo Illustré* I, 1892; "Le Capitaine Hanssens chez les Bangala" ("Captain Hanssens Among the Bangala"), *Mouvement Géographique* I, 1884, 9, p. 35; "Le lieutenant Coquilhat chez les Bangala" ("Lieutenant Coquilhat Among the Bangala"), *Mouvement Géographique* II, 23, 1885, pp. 90-91; "Mort de Mata-Boike" ("Death of Mata-Boike"), *Mouvement Géographique* III, 26, 1886, pp. 107-108; J.E. Mumbanza, "Ya-t-il des Bangala? Origine et extension du terme", ("Are There Bangala? The Origin and Extension of the Term"), *Zaire-Afrique*, No. 78, pp. 471-483; H.M. Stanley, *Through the Dark Continent*, Vol. 2, London, 1878, *The Congo and the Founding of its Free State*, Vol. 2, London, 1885; R. Stanley and A. Nemue, *Exploration Diaries of H.M. Stanley*, London, 1961; G. Van der Kerken, *L'Ethnie Mongo* ("The Mongo Ethnic Group"), Vol. I, Brussels, 1944; H. Ward, *Five Years with the Congo Cannibals*, London, 1891 reprinted New York, 1969; J. Weeks, *Among Congo Cannibals*, London, 1913; J. R. Werner, *A Visit to Stanley's Rear Guard at Major Bartlett's Camp on the Aruwimi with an Account of River Life on the Congo*, Edinburgh and London, 1889.

NGONGO LETETA

Ngongo Leteta (circa 1850-September 15, 1893) was a powerful slave trader from the Tetela ethnic group, located in the Lomami river region east of Lusambo. An auxiliary of the Swahili merchants, he transferred his loyalty to the Congo Free State in 1892 and helped in the campaign to defeat the Swahili Arabs in the eastern Congo (now Zaire).

Ngongo Leteta, whose real name was Mwanza Kasongo, was probably born between 1850 and 1862 in the village of the chief Pena Mwimba, on the right bank of the Lomami River. He was to take the two names Ngongo and Leteta much later. "Ngongo" was the name of a great rival Tetela chief east of the Lomami, a chief who fiercely opposed Mwanza Kasongo before yielding to him. Leteta was a nickname in Otetela (the Tetela language) that the people gave him to indicate that he never remained in the same place but that he was always traveling or on a military expedition.

While still very young, Mwanza Kasongo accompanied Pena Mwimba's daughter to the Songye village of Kilembwe, on the right bank of the Lomami, where he grew up in the chief's court. Soon, he gained a reputation as an outstanding warrior, being characterized by exceptional bravery, ability, and speed on military expeditions. In spite of his youth, he was named military chief of the region. He was then adopted by chief Kilembwe, who regarded him as one of his own children.

Around 1874, Tippu Tib, the great Swahili Arab trader from East Africa, arrived in the region to purchase ivory tusks, parrots, and slaves. At that time chief Kilembwe delegated Mwanza Kasongo and several other men to go to Tippu Tib with gifts, and to make an act of submission. Afterwards, Mwanza accompanied Tippu Tib to his headquarters at Kasongo, located on the Lualaba River, about 110 km (65 mi) north of Kongolo, where he entered the Swahili merchant's employ.

Shortly thereafter, Tippu Tib placed Mwanza Kasongo under the orders of his representative in Tetela territory, Dadi ben Ndoe, known by his African name, Tshungu. Mwanza gained favor with his new patron, who made him his alternate. To put Mwanza's honesty to the test, Dadi ben Ndoe entrusted him with a great quantity of salt, beads, and cloth, which he was to barter for elephants' tusks, parrots, leopard skins, and slaves in his home region. Mwanza took the trade goods and exchanged them for the desired products. After this, Dadi treated Mwanza henceforth as his own son.

Receiving more and more trade goods, and increasing his territory, Mwanza Kasongo went to settle with the Tetela chief Kitate, on the right bank of the Lomami, where he lived for some time. Bartering his goods for the local products Mwanza surrounded himself, little by little, with ambitious young men, among them his successor Ngongo Luhaka (*q.v.*).

When he had completed his purchases, Mwanza Kasongo returned to Dadi ben Ndoe, telling him of the abundance of wealth and goods which were to be found in Kitate's region. Although, at first, Dadi was skeptical, he eventually gave Mwanza trade goods as well as rifles and munitions, and men who knew how to use weapons.

From this time on, Mwanza Kasongo was no longer a simple merchant, but also a slave dealer. While continuing to trade with the local population, he also stole their property and ambushed the roads. On several occasions, he traveled through all the Tetela regions between Kibombo (located about 200 km or 120 mi north of Kongolo, near the Lualaba River) and the Lomami River, raiding for slaves and ivory. It was at this time that he received the name "Leteta".

When Dadi, who had been Tippu Tib's representative in the Lomami area, died in about 1889, Leteta immediately took his place. Shortly thereafter, however, he faced a general uprising of the population, who wished to profit from Dadi's death to escape from the domination of the Arabs and their lieutenants. The ease with which Leteta put down the revolt caused Tippu Tib to appreciate his new agent's talents as a warrior.

Soon after this, Leteta received a large number of rifles and munitions. After Tippu Tib he thus became the possessor of the largest quantity of weapons in the area. Aware of his superiority and strength, Leteta decided to conquer all the chiefs from Kibombo to the Lomami River. Having subdued the region, he settled in Ngongo l'Okole, where he took the surname, Ngongo.

Mwanza Kasongo, now Ngongo Leteta, then crossed the Lomami, made a first incursion against the Tetela of Sankuru, and went to settle at Kitenge Ngundu, his future capital which was located on the Lomami River directly east of Lusambo. By settling here, Ngongo Leteta hoped to control both banks of the Lomami. This aim, however, was not to be realized as his rule was challenged by the arrival of the Europeans.

Around 1890, emissaries brought Ngongo Leteta news that a strangely shaped boat had transported men called "the white spirits" to Lusambo on the Sankuru River. The newcomers were agents of the Congo Free State, who were setting up a station in order to halt Arab expansion towards Kasai. Curious about the whites, Ngongo decided to travel to Lusambo. He was accompanied, according to custom, by a large entourage, marching to the sound of drums and tom-toms. The whites interpreted this pomp as a declaration of war and attacked Ngongo who, surprised by this unexpected reception, suffered a defeat and returned to his capital.

Since settling at Kitenge Ngundu, Ngongo Leteta

had pursued policies somewhat independent of those of the Arabs. To guarantee his freedom, he then determined to find new sources of supply for rifles and munitions. Thus, he resolved to contact the Cokwe (Chokwe) traders from Angola, who were operating in Kasai.

In the meantime, at the beginning of 1891, he was visited by the wife of Kasongo Kiniama (q.v.), who wished to avenge the death of her husband, the great slave raiding chief from Musakatshi, (near modern Gandajika), who had been killed by an uprising of his sub-chiefs. Invited by Kasongo Kiniama's wife to punish the rebellious vassals, Ngongo Leteta made an incursion against the Luba of Kasai, where he received submission from several chiefs. Having captured thousands of slaves, he believed that the proper moment had arrived to enter into contact with the Cokwe, through the intermediary of Mukenge Kalamba (q.v.), chief of the Bena Lulua. Ngongo hoped to sell his captives for arms and thus free himself from Arab tutelage. But when Kalamba refused to deal, Ngongo was forced to set up a slave-market where he sold thousands of Luba slaves.

Returning to Kitenge Ngundu, Ngongo Leteta then went to Kasongo to deliver the products of his incursions into Kasai. There tradition reports, the Arabs were so surprised by the great quantity of goods that they advised Sefu, Tippu Tib's son living in Kasongo, to put Ngongo to death as his power could overshadow theirs. Although he was not killed, Ngongo Leteta was arrested, severely judged, and punished. This incident ended his alliance with the Arabs, and when he returned to Kitenge Ngundu at the beginning of 1892, he ceased trading with the Arabs.

Until this time, he had paid tribute to the Arabs in exchange for arms. Now, Ngongo revived his old project and sought to enter into relations with the Cokwe. But, this time, avoiding Kalamba, the great chief of the Bena Lulua, he mobilized his forces and took the route to the south. During this journey, the troops of Ngongo Leteta were attacked twice and beaten by the troops of the Congo Free State. Finally, Ngongo Leteta gathered his men in an attempt to end, once and for all, interference from the Europeans. But when he faced the forces of the Congo Free State at Batubenge, near the confluence of the Lubilash and Mbuji-Mayi rivers, his army was defeated on May 9, 1892.

Humiliated by the Arabs, beaten at the head of his army, having failed in his attempt to contact the Cokwe, and abandoned by his two most powerful allies, Penya Mutombo and Lupungu (q.v.), who had surrendered to the whites, Ngongo halted his resistance and allied himself with the Free State. Since the Arabs probably intended to kill him, Ngongo had no other choice.

On September 19, 1892, Ngongo Leteta finally broke with the Arabs, and signed a treaty with the Congo Free State. His alliance with the Europeans had disastrous consequences for the Arabs. The State began a campaign against Sefu, which ended in the capture of the Arab posts at Nyangwe and Kasongo, on the Lualaba River. Ngongo Leteta actively participated with his men in the Belgian troops' efforts, and, according to Hinde, it was "in large part due to his vigilance and to his energy that success was won during the first phase of the campaign against Sefu."

A year after the conclusion of his alliance with the Europeans, however, Ngongo, who had rendered innumerable services to the Congo Free State, was accused of treason, arrested, and incarcerated by the head of the post of Kitenge Ngundu. Judged by a hastily-assembled court martial, he was condemned to death on September 14, 1893, and executed on September 15. The legitimacy of this execution was immediately and sharply criticized. Perhaps the whites, no longer having need of Ngongo Leteta, preferred to eliminate him. Whatever the reasons given to justify his execution, it would remain an unfortunate episode in the history of the European penetration. But it was a gross political error which resulted in violence and bloodshed for a decade. Among the consequences were the military mutinies, commonly called the Batetela revolts. These revolts, of Ngongo's former soldiers, took place in 1895 at Luluabourg (now Kananga) in 1897 on the Uele River in the northeast of the country, and in 1900 at Shinkasa Fort, at Boma on the Congo River (now Zaire).

Ngongo Leteta will be remembered as a conqueror who, because of his extraordinary energy, his rapid marches, and his highly disciplined bands, created for himself a large military and commercial domain.

TSHUND'OLELA EPANYA SHAMOLOLO
and LOHAKA OMANA

BIBLIOGRAPHY: M. Coosemans, "Gongo Letete," *Biographie Coloniale Belge*, II, Brussels, 1951, pp. 427-32; L. Delcourt, and A. Dallons, "Les Mongo du Sankuru" ("The Mongo of Sankuru"), *Bulletin des Juridictions Indigènes et du Droit Coutumier Congolais*, XVII, No. 5. 1949, pp. 137-63, No. 6, 1949, pp. 165-90; T. Turner, "Mouvements de résistance chez les Mongo du Sankuru" ("Movements of Resistance Among the Mongo of Sankuru"), *Revue Congolaise des Sciences Humaines*, No. 2, Kisangani, 1971, pp. 59-85.

NGONGO LUHAKA

Ngongo Luhaka (circa 1860-July 15, 1919) worked as the principal assistant of Ngongo Leteta (q.v.).

After Leteta's death, Luhaka succeeded his master as ruler over the Tetela people, living around Katako-Kombe, located 350 km (210 mi) northeast of what is now Kananga.

Luhaka was the son of Epunga, and the nephew of Mutohembe, chief of Mulamba Lowa, a Tetela village east of the Lomami River. At the time of the invasion of Swahili slavers into the Maniema region, in an attempt to prevent plundering in his territory, chief Mutohembe dispatched Luhaka to Ngongo Leteta, an African auxiliary of the Arabs. At that time, Ngongo was among the Songye people of Imbiadia, southeast of Ngandu in the region between the Lomami and the Lualaba rivers. Finding Ngongo at the village of chief Dibwe, Luhaka made offers of submission which were accepted.

Shortly afterwards, Luhaka who was then about 16, went into Ngongo Leteta's service, accompanying his master on slave-raiding expeditions. Some years later, as a reward for his services, Luhaka was appointed to a rank immediately under that of Ngongo Leteta himself. From that time on, having received men, arms, and ammunition, Luhaka was a leading member of Ngongo's raiders. He led many expeditions for his master among the Ahinas, east of the Lomami and among the Eninga a Ndjovus, west of the river in what was to become later the territory of Katako-Kombe. On his return to Ngongo Leteta's headquarters at Ngandu on the Lomami River, 325 km (200 mi) northeast of what is now Kananga, Luhaka was again sent on an expedition against the Luba in the Lubilash river region.

After Ngongo Leteta's submission to the Congo Free State on September 19, 1892, Luhaka, under the orders of Ngongo Leteta, participated in the campaign against the Arab slave and ivory merchants in the eastern Congo (now Zaire). After Ngongo Leteta was executed for treason on September 15, 1893, Ngongo Luhaka was sent to the Konde people in the present zone of Lodja, 300 km (180 mi) northeast of what is now Kananga. From there he was recalled to Ngandu to succeed Ngongo Leteta in 1896. From that time on, he sent his own subordinates to subdue and occupy the Tetela's land, extending from the 5th to the 1st parallel south. These operations made him a great Tetela chief.

In January 1904, as a result of jealousy, and of numerous complaints from some of his subjects, Ngongo Luhaka was removed from office by the colonial government. At first he was relegated to Libenge in the region of Equateur, and then was sent to Lusambo, where he remained a prisoner until 1907. Pleas from those subordinate chiefs who had remained loyal to him, however, induced the government to release him. Once he had returned home, Ngongo Luhaka tried to rule as in the past, without taking into account the profound changes which had taken place.

European agents had set up a state station at Katako-Kombe (May 1904), had freed the local population from Asambala tutelage (1905 and 1911), and were in the process of establishing chiefdoms according to the terms of government decrees of June 3, 1906, and May 2, 1910.

Eventually, illness and the actions of his enemies resulted in his removal from power. In June 1912 Ngongo was stricken with temporary paralysis. In July 1919, he had two apoplexy fits resulting in a general paralysis of his left side. Thus, the Tetela nicknamed him "Ngongo with the moving leg." Finally, he was killed by Shinga I (alias Luhaka), near the Katako-Kombe station, on the night of July 15, 1919. He was buried north of the Lunga River, 9 km (6 mi) south of the present Katako-Kombe station. His son Senga Raphael, who had attended the Lusambo Colonial School, succeeded him, taking the name of "Pene Luhaka."

DIMANDJA LUHAKA

BIBLIOGRAPHY: P. Ceulemans, *La question arabe et le Congo 1883-1892* ("The Arab Question and the Congo, 1883-1892"), Brussels, 1959; L. Delcourt and A. Dallons, "Les Mongo du Sankuru" ("The Mongo of Sankuru"), *Bulletin des Jurisdictions Indigènes et du Droit Coutumier Congolais,* No. 5, September-October, 1949, pp. 135-63, No. 6, November-December, 1949, pp. 165-90; L. Mpoyi, *Histoire wa Baluba* ("History of the Baluba"), Mbuji-Mayi, 1966.

NGONSO, S.

Sebastien Ngonso (circa 1940-October, 1965) was a young Congolese poet whose work expressed the anguish and suffering he experienced in life.

In the 1950s Ngonso was a highly regarded student at the Kizambi minor seminary a short distance northwest of Kikwit, where he was preparing to become a priest. During Ngonso's final year of seminary, a tragic accident upset his plans. In October, while participating in a swimming match, he dislocated his neck while diving, and became paralyzed. Despite the care he received in the hospitals of Kikwit and Léopoldville (now Kinshasa), he could not use his arms and legs.

Ngonso was then sent to Belgium for treatment, where he regained some mobility, and learned how to use a typewriter. Returning to the Congo, he continued his studies, succeeded in his secondary school examinations, and in 1964, entered Lovanium University.

During these difficult years, Ngonso began to write poetry. His work spoke of his perseverance and his struggle for life. Soon, his talent became recognized, not only by his closest friends, but also by a growing audience. His ability was confirmed when he won a prize in a contest sponsored by the French cultural organization, the Alliance Française. His poetry had an accent of truth, making the anguish of a paralyzed man real to all.

At a time when, through his success at the university, he appeared to have won his internal struggle, Ngonso died. In October 1965, on his return trip from a visit to his home village, which he had not visited since 1958, he was killed in an automobile accident.

In memory of Ngonso, a poetry prize bearing his name was inaugurated in 1967 by Lovanium University. Later, his name was also given to a literary circle in Kinshasa.

NDAYWEL è NZIEM

BIBLIOGRAPHY: C. Faîk-Nzuji, "Prix de poésie Sebastien Ngonso" ("The Sebastien Ngonso Poetry Prize"), *Congo-Afrique*, No. 17, August-September, 1967, pp. 346-56, *Prix de poésie Sebastien Ngonso* ("The Sebastien Ngonso Poetry Prize"), Kinshasa, 1968, p. 69; O. Ugirashebuja, "Sebastien Ngonso poète" ("Sebastien Ngonso, Poet"), *Congo Afrique*, No. 4, April, 1966, pp. 194-205.

NKANGA LUKENI

Nkanga Lukeni (ruled 1641-61) or Garcia II, was Mani Kongo (ruler of the Kongo) during a time of military conflict between the Portuguese and the Dutch. By manipulating the European rivalry, he was able to restore some of the Kongo kingdom's former authority.

He came to power in 1641, following the death of Alvare VI (ruled 1636-41). This was in the same year that the Dutch occupied Luanda on the coast. Hoping to free himself from the Portuguese, who exercised their control through missionaries, Nkanga Lukeni concluded a military alliance with the Dutch. The agreement was political rather than religious in nature, for the Mani Kongo never abandoned his Catholic faith to become a Protestant. Nkanga Lukeni also attempted to use the Dutch in his ongoing struggle against rebellious officials in his land.

Nkanga first employed his Dutch allies to subdue the disloyal chief of Nsala, who ruled the area east of the Inkisi River, about 170 km (100 mi) southeast of the Mani Kongo's capital of San Salvador. Then, in 1645, he waged war on the Mani Soyo—Soyo is the territory just south of the Zaire River estuary—who controlled the port of Mpinda. Known by his European name of Daniel da Silva, the Mani Soyo had refused to ask for the traditional confirmation of his

election from the Mani Kongo. But, the Mani Kongo's troops were defeated on April 29, 1645, and again in July 1646. From that time onwards, the Mani Soyo became practically independent of San Salvador.

The Dutch occupation of Luanda enabled the Vatican to send non-Portuguese missionaries to Kongo. Earlier, the Catholic church in the Kongo was under Portuguese protection, and any priests sent there had to have approval of Lisbon. The Portuguese had consistently refused passports for any non-Portuguese priests appointed by Rome. Thus, in 1645, Nkongo Lukeni eagerly welcomed the Italian Capuchin Friars sent by Rome. Hoping to stabilize the dynasty, he appealed to the Vatican to make the office of Mani Kongo a hereditary right of his particular branch of the larger family that was eligible for election. When these efforts failed, Nkanga Lukeni accused the Capuchins of not supporting his cause. Relations between the missionaries and the Mani Kongo became strained when the Europeans began to criticize the king for reverting back to paganism.

After the reconquest of Loanda by Portugal in August 1648, Nkanga Lukeni was obliged to sign a 1649 peace treaty in which he ceded to the Portuguese the island off the coast at Luanda from which the Kongo obtained its shell currency. The treaty also gave Kongolese mineral rights to the Portuguese.

When Nkanga Lukeni died in 1661, Vita Nkanga, known as Antonio I, took power. During Antonio's reign the Portuguese took advantage of the earlier treaty to invade the southern part of the Kongo kingdom, where they hoped to find silver and gold.

Although ultimately unsuccessful, Nkango Lukeni managed for a time to free himself from Portuguese tutelage.

TSIMBA MABIALA

BIBLIOGRAPHY: *Arquivan de Angola* ("Angola Archives"), Vol. II, 2nd series, No. 8, Luanda, 1944, pp. 170-71; G. Balandier, *La vie quotidienne au royaume du Kongo du XVIème au XVIIIème siècle,* Paris, 1965, English translation by Helen Weaver published as *Daily Life in the Kingdom of Kongo from the Sixteenth to the Eighteenth Century,* New York, 1968; *Biographie Coloniale Belge,* Vol. 2, Brussels, 1951, pp. 398-99; F. Bontnick, *Jean François de Rome OFM. Cap. La fondation de la mission des Capuçins au Royaume du Congo: 1648* ("Jean François of Rome OFM. Cap. The Foundation of the Capuchin Mission in the Kingdom of Kongo, 1648"), Louvain, 1964; J. Cuvelier and L. Jadin, *L'ancien Congo d'après les archives romaines (1518-1640)* ("The Ancient Congo According to the Roman Archives: 1518-1640"), Brussels, 1954; L. Jadin, "Le clergé séculier et les capuçins du Congo et d'Angola au XVIème et XVIIIème siècle, conflits de jurisdiction

1700-1726,'' ("The Lay Clergy and the Capuchins of the Congo and of Angola in the 16th and 17th Centuries, Conflicts of Jurisdiction 1700-1726''), *Bulletin de l'Institut Historique Belge de Rome,* Vol. XXXVI, 1964, pp. 206 ff.; W.G.L. Randles, *L'ancien royaume du Congo des origines a la fin du XIXème siècle* ("The Ancient Kingdom of the Congo from its Origins to the End of the 19th Century''), Paris, The Hague, 1968.

NKONGOLO

Nkongolo, a Luba folk hero, (who may have lived in the earlier 16th century), was the legendary Mulopwe (chief) who supposedly laid the first foundations of the Luba empire. Scholars view Nkongolo as the symbol of a dynasty which ruled before the mid-1500s, rather than a specific historical individual. In Luba legend, Nkongolo stands as a foil for later rulers, who developed highly complex patterns of government and courtly ritual.

According to Luba oral tradition, Nkongolo was the son of Kiubaka-Ubaka and Kibumba-Bumba, the original parents of the Luba peoples. Nkongolo subjugated lands east and west of the Lualaba River before settling his capital at Mwibele, on the banks of Lake Boya. Nkongolo, whose name means "rainbow," is reputed to have had pale ("red") skin and, as a child, may have been dedicated to the serpent, which is associated, in the Bantu universe, with the rainbow.

Nkongolo was a very brutal ruler. On the familial level, his life was licentious, and he had incestuous relations with his two half-sisters, Bulanda and Mabela. Unaware of proper chiefly etiquette, he ate in public, laughed with his mouth open, and crudely neglected to file his teeth to a point.

During the course of his reign, an eastern hunter, Mbidi Kiluwe (*q.v.*), visited Nkongolo's domain. This hunter is represented in tradition as the bearer of a superior civilization. He married Nkongolo's two half-sisters, but was not able to remain in Luba territory for long because of the conflict which arose between himself and Nkongolo. After Mbidi Kiluwe's departure, his wife Bulanda bore a son, Ilunga Mbidi, later known as Kalala Ilunga (*q.v.*).

When he grew to manhood, Ilunga Mbidi proved to be such a great warrior that Nkongolo made him a general. The ruler then used his nephew to lead military expeditions and to enlarge the frontiers of the Luba state.

Ilunga Mbidi's success caused Nkongolo to fear the young man as a serious rival. Thus, he sought to eliminate Ilunga, who fled, but returned later at the head of a powerful army. He then had little trouble defeating his uncle, whom he had executed. Power then passed to Ilunga, regarded by the Luba as the founder of their system of government and as the father of the Luba chiefly family.

NDAYWEL è NZIEM

BIBLIOGRAPHY: L. de Heusch, *Le roi ivre ou l'origine de l'Etat* ("The Drunken King or the Origin of the State") Paris, 1972; S.A. Lucas, "L'Etat traditionnel Luba" ("The Traditional Luba State"), in *Problèmes sociaux congolais,* 74, 1966, pp. 88-97; J. Vansina, *Les anciens royaumes de la savane,* Lèopoldville, 1965, published in English as *Kingdoms of the Savanna,* Madison, 1966; A. Van Zandijcke, *Pages d'histoire du Kasayi* ("Pages of Kasayi History"), Namur, 1953; E. Verhalpen, *Baluba et Balubaisés du Katanga* ("The Baluba and the Balubaized of Katanga"), Anvers, 1936.

NLEMVO. See MANTANTU DUNDULU

NSAKU ne VUNDA

Nsaku ne Vunda (a title in use in about the 14th century) was not only the title of a chief, but also the name of a clan living around Mbanza Kongo (later San Salvador) when Ntinu Wene established the Kongo kingdom sometime before 1400. As Nsaku ne Vunda, whose other title was Mani Vunda (chief of the Vunda), or Mani Kabunda, the individual holding this office had a powerful ritual association with the land.

When Ntinu Wene arrived in the area of Mbanza Kongo, he found it occupied by the Vunda clan, which was part of the larger Ambundu ethnic group. The Nsaku ne Vunda's sphere of supernatural influence was very extensive, reaching south to Ndongo, located east of what is now Luanda, Nsaku, as chief of the soil, ensured the land's fertility, made hunting and fishing fruitful, and gave children to the women.

Although originally the holder of the office of Mani Kabunda had exercised political power, under pressure from Ntinu Wene, who came from Bungu (located north of the Zaire River), he lost this political authority. Tradition describes this transition by reporting that Ntinu Wene, who may have been the same as Lukeni (*q.v.*), married Nsaku's daughter. This incorporated the Mani Kabunda's power into, and linked his descendants to the new political system imported from Bangu.

Remaining linked to the supernatural forces, Nsaku's subsequent duties consisted of giving the Mani Kongo a special benediction in order to ensure a calm, and prosperous reign and to keep the spirits favorably disposed to him. Ritually, the Mani Kabunda's functions were expressed when he presided over the Mani Kongo's ceremony of investiture. The ruler in return, paid tribute to the chief who had once reigned supreme in the land.

Most likely, the Mani Kabunda would only participate in the installation of a royal candidate who was acceptable to him. Thus, in later years, he became one of the principal electors of the ruler of the Kongo. Since his voice was crucial in the choice of a new monarch, the Nsaku clan was considered the "eldest" of the senior clans in the kingdom.

After the Christianization of the Kongo, the Mani Kongo Mvemba Nzinga (Afonso I) designated the Mani Kabunda as the Catholic priest responsible for safeguarding religion. This new role merely continued, in Christian form, the Mani Kabunda's traditional functions as the main ritual guardian of the Mani Kongo.

NDAYWEL è NZIEM

BIBLIOGRAPHY: G. Balandier, *Le vie quotidienne au royaume du Kongo du XVIème au XVIIIème siècle,* Paris, 1965, English translation by Helen Weaver published as *Daily Life in the Kingdom of Kongo from the Sixteenth to the Eighteenth Century,* New York, 1968; Batsikama Mampuya, *Voici les jagas ou l'histoire d'un peuple parricide bien malgré lui* ("Here are the Jagas, or the History of a People Parricide Despite Themselves"), Kinshasa, 1971; J. Cuvelier, *L'ancien royaume du Congo* ("The Ancient Kingdom of Kongo"), Paris-Bruges, 1946; W.G.L. Randles, *L'ancien royaume du Congo. Des origines a la fin du XIXème siècle* ("The Ancient Kingdom of Congo. From its Origins to the End of the 19th Century"), Paris, The Hague, 1968.

NYAIYONGWA

Nyaiyongwa (circa 1885-1961) ruled the artificially-created Lobala-Likoka sector, between the Ubangi and Giri rivers northwest of present-day Makanza throughout its entire existence from 1940 to 1957.

The history of Nyaiyongwa and of the Libala-Likoka sector reflects the difficulties the Belgian authorities experienced in trying to "rationalize" their administration over the numerous, small ethnic groups living in the lower Ubangi and Giri regions.

Nyaiyongwa was born at Ikobo, a Likoka village located in the middle of the forest which grows near the channel which empties into the Giri at the Mobusi-Bomwanga village. Before the arrival of the Europeans, Ikobo—an agglomeration of small settlements—was one of the most populated villages in the Giri river region. Its inhabitants were famous warriors, known as the Ngili by the Iboko-Mabale people, of what is now Makanza. Ikobo warriors frequently attacked their eastern neighbors, the Libinza of Mobusi, the Mbonzi, the Lobo and the Iboko-Mabale. In 1898, because of Ikobo raids, Matambakemba of the Libinza village of Bosilela asked the whites to settle in his area.

In response to Matabakemba's request, the Congo Free State officer Sommelier, whose African name was Limpanya, gathered Libinza allies from Bosilela and attacked the Ikobo. the inhabitants of Ikobo then abandoned their village and withdrew deeper into the interior. Although at first they settled at Bakandi, in 1911 the village had to be evacuated following leopard attacks. It was then that the Ikobo people founded the villages of Indonga, Iwondo, Iyombo and Ngombe.

When the colonial government organized the area into chiefdoms in 1908, the Ikobo, together with the Bodjinga, were placed under the authority of their Libinza enemies. Mungembe (*q.v.*) of Bosesera (located on the Giri River 50 km, 30 mi, west of what is now Makanza) became their chief.

Nyaiyongwa's father Mwasamotoko, who had been the Ikobo chief when the people lived at Bakandi, openly resisted Mungembe. Thus, in July 1911 Mungembe removed him from office and installed Niabongonga in his stead. Ikobo opposition to Mungembe continued, however, until 1912, when a Mobusi sub-chiefdom was created with Mohila as its ruler.

Since Mohila's maternal uncles lived at Ikobo, the Ikobo people accepted colonial rule and began paying taxes. But the situation was complicated once again when, in 1914, the Mobusi sub-chiefdom was dissolved and included in the Bokambo chiefdom, under chief Molonga an associate of Mungembe. Molonga, however, was never able to dominate the Likoka, a people he rarely visited. But when Molonga's rule ended in 1920, the Mobusi chiefdom was reestablished. Then, in 1925 Mohila was placed in charge of the entire Libinza sector. Because Mohila was a good friend of the Likoka people, government agents at Bomana, located on the Giri River 80 km (50 mi) southwest of Makanza, unhesitatingly included the Likoka in the larger Libinza polity.

During 1925, state officials made a study of the entire Likoka region. In their subsequent report, they proposed the creation of a separate Likoka chiefdom. Niaiyongwa, who was then chief of the Ikobo village of Iwondo, was one of the three candidates for the office of chief of the suggested new polity. But he was considered to be too young for the post, and Munsasa of Indonga, an Ikobo market village, was appointed instead.

Nyaiyongwa's opportunity to rule came in 1939 when the Belgian colonial government decided to establish a Lobala-Likoka sector which would group these two peoples. Munsasa meanwhile remained head of the Likoka chiefdom, a sub-district of the sector. In order to appease the Bolanga and Bolebo villagers who were unhappy with Ikobo domination—both Nyaiyongwa and Munsasa being Ikobo—the new headquarters for the sector were located at Bokondo instead of at Indonga, Munsasa's village, or at Iwondo, Nyaiyongwa's town. Nyaiyongwa began administering the sector from Bokondo in 1940.

Nyaiyongwa's main tasks as chief were to improve the roads and waterways in the area. Although he was crippled and unable to walk far, Nyaiyongwa personally oversaw these projects. He opened a road from his headquarters at Bokondo to Mokame on the Ubangi River. He also had a road built linking Mokame and Mikolo. These roads allowed the Likoka and Lobala people to export palm oil and palm nuts, the two principal commercial products of the region.

Among his Ntanda subjects (the Ntanda being those Likoka living in the swampy river area), Nyaiyongwa insured the continuous maintenance of water channels. This allowed state officials and commercial agents from Bomongo located on the Giri River, 90 km (50 mi) southwest of what is now Makanza, access to the region. Concerned for his people's welfare, Nyaiyongwa also had the first rural school and the first "bush" dispensary in his sector constructed at Bokondo.

Nyaiyngwa also had a deep understanding of African customs. He frequently conducted traditional legal proceedings, winning the respect of his people. Taking the attitude of a father, he knew how to punish, pardon, and protect his subjects. He also would resist orders from the Europeans when he felt these demands might place an excessive burden on the local people. Nyaiyongwa's profound attachment to traditional values was exemplified by the fact that he, as a chief, never drank water, but only palm wine. Neither would he use a western-manufactured glass, but instead drank his wine from a handmade wooden goblet.

In 1957, the Lobala-Likoka sector was joined to the Djamba sector to the south. Nyaiyongwa, who was now an old man, lost his position, and returned to his home village, Iwondo, where he died in 1961.

MUMBANZA mwa BAWLELE na
NYABAKOMBI ENSOBATO

BIBLIOGRAPHY: J.J.C. Lemaire, "Etude ethnique de tout le groupement Likoka" ("Ethnic Study of the Entire Likoka Grouping"), 1924, Bomana Territory, Archives of the Bomongo Zone; E. Vereecken, "Rapport d'enquête sur la chefferie des Likoka" ("Report of Enquiry into the Likoka Chiefdom"), 1929, Bomana Territory, Archives of the Bomongo Zone. See Also "Registre des renseignements politiques" ("Register of Political Information"), 1911-1916, and 1916-1931, Bomana Territory, Archives of the Bomongo Zone.

NZINGA MPUDI

Nzinga Mpudi (circa 1510-November 4, 1561) ruled from 1545 to 1561, as Mani Kongo (ruler of the Kongo) during a period of confrontation between the kingdom of the Kongo and the Portuguese.

Succeeding Mvemba Nzinga (q.v.), also known as Afonso I, a Christian ruler who ruled from 1506 to about 1543, Nzinga Mpudi took office in 1545 as Diogo I, following a succession struggle with other pretenders.

Soon after taking power, he dispatched Diogo Gomes, a Creole priest, as an ambassador to the Portuguese king, João III (ruled 1521-57). Through Gomes, Nzinga Mpudi hoped to acquire some new missionaries, but especially to renew a 1517 treaty which recognized a royal monopoly on trade and confined Portuguese boats and merchants to the port of Mpinda on the Congo (Zaire) river estuary. This was because, in the 1540s, Portuguese traders from São Tomé island were trying to by-pass the authority of the Mani Kongo.

Gomes was not entirely successful, but he did return with four Jesuit priests. The Jesuits established a school at Mbanza Kongo (now San Salvador) where they enrolled 600 pupils. Relations between Nzinga Mpudi and the Jesuits deteriorated, however, as the Jesuits increasingly sided with the interests of the Portuguese on São Tomé. By 1555 the Jesuits, and also Gomes, had left the Kongo. In 1557 Franciscan missionaries arrived to replace the Jesuits. Their catechism, in Kikongo, was the first written document in the local language.

The conflict with São Tomé eventually led Nzinga Mpudi into war with his southern neighbor, Ndongo. Portuguese traders at his capital, Mbanza Kongo, urged Nzinga to punish the Ngola (chief) of Ndongo, who permitted and even encouraged São Tomé merchants to operate in Ndongo. Although the Mani Kongo sent troops against the Ngola, Kongolese forces were badly beaten in 1556. Unhappily for Nzinga, in 1557 Ndongo established direct relations with Portugal, thus weakening the status of the Kongo kingdom and further thwarting the Kongo's attempts to establish controls over European commerce in central Africa.

Unlike his predecessor Mvemba Nzinga, Nzinga Mpudi was not deceived by the Portuguese. He worked hard to curb foreign intervention in local political affairs, and he tried to maintain authority over trade in his domain. He died on November 4, 1561.

TSIMBA MABIALA

BIBLIOGRAPHY: G. Balandier, La vie quotidienne au royaume du Kongo du XVIème au XVIIIème siècle,

Paris, 1965, English translation by Helen Weaver published as *Daily Life in the Kingdom of the Kongo From the Sixteenth to the Eighteenth Century,* New York, 1968; *Biographie Coloniale Belge,* Vol. 2, Brussels, 1951, cols. 293-94; J. Cuvelier and L. Jadin, *L'ancien Congo d'après les archives romaines: 1518-1640* ("The Ancient Kongo According to the Roman Archives, 1518-1640"), Brussels, 1954; L. Jadin, "Relations sur le Congo tirées des archives de la compagnie de Jésus, 1621-1631" ("Reports on the Congo Drawn from the Archives of the Company of Jesus, 1621-1631"), *Bulletin de l'Institut Historique Belge de Rome,* Vol. XXXIX, 1968, p. 349; W.G.L. Randles, *L'ancien royaume du Congo des origines a la fin du XIXème siècle* ("The Ancient Kingdom of Congo from its Origins to the End of the 19th Century"), Paris, The Hague, 1968; T.H. Simar, *Le Congo au XVIème siècle d'après la relation de Lopez Pigafetta* ("The Congo in the Sixteenth Century According to the Account of Lopez Pigafetta"), Brussels, 1929; J. Vansina, *Les anciens royaumes de la savane,* Léopoldville, 1965, published in English as *Kingdoms of the Savanna,* Madison, 1966.

ONEMA, MAMA

Onema Henriette (circa 1900-August 27, 1967), better known as Mama Onema, was a powerful sorcerer who aided the Armée Populaire de Libération (A.P.L.), or Simbas, during the 1964 Congo rebellions in which the A.P.L. fought against the central government.

A simple peasant fetishist, who spoke no language except that of her Tetela ethnic group (the Tetela are part of the Mongo people), Onema gained prominence during the troubles of the 1960s. In May 1963, bloody conflict broke out at Lodja, 300 km (180 mi) northeast of Kananga on the Lukenie River, between the Tetela of the forest, known as the Ekonda, and the Tetela of the savanna, called the Eswe. Some Eswe leaders asked Onema to prepare a magic power for their young men fighting the Ekonda. Onema mixed some beans with hemp which she gave to the warriors, making them invulnerable to bullets, arrows, spears, and matchets. The Lodja incident gave Onema great prestige; she became known as the greatest fetishist in northeastern Kasai.

The A.P.L. rebellion took place in 1964. On July 15, the Simbas took Kongolo, about 750 km (450 mi) south of Kisangani on the Lualaba River. On July 21 and 22 they captured Kindu, 400 km (250 mi) south of Kisangani on the Lualaba. From there they spread out, hoping to gain control of the eastern Congo. In all their battles, the Simbas relied on magical forces reputed to make them invincible.

Needing a trustworthy sorcerer, Nicolas Olenga, the Tetela general who had invaded Kindu, went to Enyamba, 135 km (80 mi) southwest of Kindu, where he persuaded Mama Onema to accompany him to his headquarters at Kindu. Besides being Olenga's personal sorcerer—reputedly he agreed to pay her three million francs for magic giving him absolute protection—she became the most important doctor for all the Simba forces. At the Hotel Relais, where she spent most of her time, she prepared magic charms, instructed other practitioners, and administered magical potions to Simba soldiers. In private ceremonies, Mama Onema sprinkled a white liquid over the men. Driven through the town in a car, she also baptized civilians, houses, streets, and the river ferry to render them safe in case of an air attack.

Believing in Onema's magical power, young men eagerly enlisted in the A.P.L., and, once in the army, went fearlessly into battle assured that no bullet could harm them. So important was her role in maintaining army morale that before the crucial battle of Beni, 400 km (250 mi) east of Kisangani, Olenga urgently appealed to Onema to sent at least 10,000 amulets to the front. But the A.P.L. was badly beaten at Beni, and Onema lost much of her prestige.

In January 1963, she was arrested near Kibombo, 110 km (65 mi) south of Kindu. Taken to Kinshasa and interrogated, Mama Onema eventually died of illness and old age in a hospital on August 27, 1967.

TSHUND'OLELA EPANYA SHAMOLOLO

BIBLIOGRAPHY: B. Verhaegen, *Rébellions au Congo* ("Rebellions in the Congo"), Vol. 2, Brussels-Kinshasa, 1969.

RUWEJ a NKOND

Ruwej a Nkond (who flourished in the 16th century) was a queen who ruled in the formative period of the Lunda state. She figures prominently in legends regarding the beginnings of the state, which was located in southern Zaire, eastern Angola, and northern Zambia. Although oral tradition portrays Ruwej as an historical personage, modern scholarship emphasizes the symbolic meaning in her story.

According to the Lunda oral record, Ruwej was the youngest daughter of chief Nkond a Matit and his wife Rukombu. In contrast, the Cokwe (Chokwe), who originally lived in northeastern Angola, claim that Ruwej was the youngest daughter of Mwaket of Tumba.

Following the Lunda version, Ruwej succeeded her father because he disinherited his two sons, Chigud and Chiyam. After Chigud and Chiyam had rudely beaten their father, whom they accused of refusing them palm wine, Nkond a Matit designated Ruwej as the heir of the Rukan, the sacred bracelet symoblizing royal power.

When Nkond a Matit died, Ruwej became queen over the Nkalanyi (upper Mbuji-Mayi) river region. She ruled from her capital Musumba, situated east of the Lulua River, about 250 km (150 mi) north of modern Dilolo.

As she was unmarried, the council of Lunda land chiefs proposed to marry her to one of their own number who lived northeast of Musumba. But the marriage did not take place, as Mwin Kanitshin would not renounce his own office, nor would he leave his residence for that of queen Ruwej a Nkond.

In the end, she married a non-Lunda outsider, a Luba hunter named Chibind Yirung (q.v.). While marriage to a local land chief would have symbolized continuity with past practices of government, Ruwej's union with a Luba interloper represented innovative change. According to oral tradition, Ruwej's choice of a husband angered Chigud and Chiyam who left the Lunda homeland to establish new states. This event, thus, marks the beginning of Lunda expansion into Angola and Kasai.

According to Lunda custom, women are forbidden to keep the sacred royal bracelet during their menstrual period. When Ruwej entered her monthly period, she entrusted the bracelet to her husband Chibind Yirung. This act greatly angered many Lunda who then rebelled against Ruwej. The uprising was put down only with the help of Cokwe warriors from Angola. Because of this conflict, large numbers, of Lunda chose to emigrate, rather than accept the new political situation.

According to the Lunda tradition, Ruwej a Nkond had no children by Chibind Yirung. Thus, he married another woman who gave birth to Yav a Yirung (Luseng) whose son Nawej became the first Mwant Yav (paramount chief). When she died, she was buried at the Kavadilongombe River. The chiefs then chose a new Ruwej from among the female descendants of the family of Nkond a Matit. This woman took the name "Swanamurund," a political title which had perpetuated even to this day the memory of Ruwej a Nkond.

N'DUA SOLOL KANAMPUMB

BIBLIOGRAPHY: H. Dias de Carvalho, *Expediçao ao Muatiamvu. Ethnographia e história dos povos da Lunda* ("Expedition to Mwatia Mvu: The Ethnography and History of the Lunda People"), Lisbon, 1890; L. Dysters, "Histoire des Aluunda" ("History of the Aluunda"), *Problèmes d'Afrique centrale*, XII, 40, 1958, pp. 75-98; *Ngand Yetu* ("Our Country"). Cleveland (Transvaal), 1963; J. Vansina, *Les anciens royaumes de la savane*, Léopoldville, 1965, published in English as *Kingdoms of the Savanna*, Madison, 1966; J.L. Vellut, "Notes sur le Lunda et la frontière luso-africaine: 1700-1900" ("Notes on the Lunda and the Luso-African Frontier: 1700-1900"), *Etudes d'Histoire africaine*, III, 1972, pp. 61-66.

RYCKMANS, P.M.J.

Pierre Marie Joseph Ryckmans (November 26, 1891-February 18, 1959), governor-general of the Belgian Congo (now Zaire), and of Ruanda-Urundi (now the separate countries of Rwanda and Burundi), from 1934-46, was the most outstanding colonial administrator in the history of the territory.

Ryckmans was born in Antwerp, Belgium. He was educated at the seminary of Hoogstraeten, and then at the Collège St. Jean Beerkmans. He entered Louvain University where he graduated in law and Thomist philosophy. Although Ryckmans began a legal career in 1913, World War I prevented him from practicing law. Volunteering for the army, he was assigned to the Ninth Line Regiment and distinguished himself in the battle of the Yser. In 1915 he joined the Force Publique (colonial army) of the Belgian Congo, and left for Africa.

Ryckmans took part in the Cameroun campaign against the Germans as a second lieutenant in the Force Publique. He also fought in the East African campaign in Tanganyika, and was mentioned in despatches after the victory of Mahenge. He was promoted lieutenant in the Belgian Army in 1918.

At the end of the war, Ryckmans decided to enter

the Belgian colonial administrative service. He was posted to Ruanda-Urundi, former German territories which had been made League of Nations mandates under Belgian administration. He learned the local language and grew to appreciate the problems faced by the Africans. He therefore became very popular in these territories.

In 1928, Ryckmans decided to leave Africa. Since his marriage in 1921, he had fathered five children and wanted to have them educated in Europe. Therefore, he returned to Belgium and practiced as a lawyer. But his interest still centered on Africa, and during his stay in Belgium from 1928-34, he wrote a series of articles on Belgian colonial policy and practice, attended conferences on Africa, and gave radio talks and lectures on the way of life of the African populations under Belgian tutelage. He was a professor of colonial administration at Louvain University. And because he had practical experience of the Congo and Ruanda-Urundi, his lectures were better appreciated by his audience. He was secretary-general of the Union Royale Coloniale Belge; a member of the Institut Royal Colonial; of the Institut Colonial International; of the Standing Committee of the Colonial Congress; of the Association of Colonial Writers and Artists; and of the Catholic Writers Association.

In 1930, he was appointed a member of a commission of enquiry into the labor problems of the Congo peoples. He specialized in the problems of the province of Kasai. In 1934 Ryckmans succeeded the Duke of Brabant, who had become King Léopold III of Belgium (ruled 1934-50), as president of the National Institute for the Study of Agriculture in the Congo (I.N.B.A.C.). He also wrote his principal work, *Dominer pour servir* or ("To rule through service"), in 1931. It was an insightful study based on his stay in Burundi. In 1934, he wrote *Allo, Congo* ("Hello, Congo"), and *La Politique Coloniale* ("Colonial Policy").

On September 14, 1934, he was appointed governor-general of the Congo in succession to Lt. General A.C. Tilkens (term of office 1927-34). During the 12 years he served as governor-general, Ryckmans was able to put into practice some of the views he had expressed in *La Politique Coloniale*. He dealt first with the deteriorating economic situation, taking steps which offended certain interest groups in the colony. He also dealt with African social problems, and made plans for education and health needs.

When the Nazis overran Belgium on May 10, 1940, Ryckmans was faced with a war situation in the Congo. A government of Belgium in exile had been formed in London, and the Belgian Congo had to contribute to the war effort in order to help free Belgium from Nazi occupation. He had to encourage people to increase the production of raw materials to help to sustain the armed forces. Ryckmans faced a shortage of personnel, since many Belgians had joined the armed forces. A general despondency also prevailed among the Europeans. Ryckmans did his best to live with these problems and solved those he could deal with effectively. His *Messages de Guerre* ("Wartime Messages") which he compiled into a book in 1945, are an eloquent testimony to his faith in the future and his dogged determination to succeed where there seemed to be no hope of success. He also prepared a volume entitled *Etapes et Jalons* ("Steps and Landmarks"), consisting of his reports to the Belgian government.

Ryckmans retired as governor-general of the Congo in July 1946, and returned to Belgium. Before leaving the Congo, he organized, under the auspices of the Association of Universities, a conference entitled *Vers l'Avenir* ("Towards the Future"), in which he voiced his concern for the future progress of the Congo. He stated clearly and forcefully that Belgium should aid the Congo financially, since its development would benefit the Belgians as well. This conference was the origin of the ten-year development plan for the Belgian Congo.

On his return to Belgium, Ryckmans continued his interest in African affairs. He was appointed as the Belgian delegate on the United Nations Trusteeship Council, a post he held until 1957. He defended forcefully Belgium's colonial policy, attacked the anti-colonial parties and factions in the United Nations, and in Belgium, and tried in vain to prevent the U.N. from interfering in the internal affairs of the Belgian Congo. He was swimming against the tide, since this was the period of decolonization in Asia and Africa. By the end of his term of office, the British West African colony of the Gold Coast had become independent Ghana (1957), and before he died a nationalist movement had started in the Congo, with Patrice Lumumba (*q.v.*) as one of its leaders.

He had also held the post of Belgian representative on the U.N. Atomic Energy Commission from 1951 onwards. Here too he showed intense curiosity, and a desire to get Belgium involved in new scientific and technological advances. He gave several lectures in these fields at home and abroad, having been an honorary member in the Moral and Political Sciences section of the Royal Academy of Sciences Overseas since 1955, and having become its president in 1949.

In 1947, his desire for higher education in the colonies led him, together with Monsignor Van Wayemberg, to sign an appeal for the establishment of a university in the Belgian territories in Africa. In 1948, he was appointed to the administrative council of the Congolese University Center at Louvanium, later named Lovanium University. The university was inaugurated in 1953, and Ryckmans was vice-president of its administrative council. He continued to take an active interest in the university's work until his death, and was disturbed by the way Congolese politics were affecting the university.

Two important books which he wrote during this period were *A l'autre bout de monde* ("At the Other End of the World"), which dealt with his visit to Samoa on behalf of the United Nations Trusteeship Council, and *Barabara* ("The Road"), which dealt, in broad terms, with his African experience as a soldier and administrator.

In June 1958, he was offered a post in the 1958-61 government of Belgian premier Gaston Eyskens, but declined it. Yet, in spite of failing health, he decided to serve the Congo to the end, and accepted the presidency of the Working Group for the study of the political problems of the Congo, a body set up in 1958 to deal with political change in the colony. He could not take part in its work, however, because he was at the point of death. He died on February 18, 1959, and was posthumously made a count by King Baudoin. His son André, who died during the distrubances which followed in the Congo in 1960, received the same honor.

L.H. OFOSU-APPIAH

BIBLIOGRAPHY: A. Gille and M. Van den Abeele, "Ryckmans, Pierre," *Biographie Belge d'Outre-Mer,* Vol. VII, Brussels, 1948-; P.M.J. Ryckmans, *Dominer pour servir* ("To Rule Through Service"), Brussels, 1931, new revised edition, Brussels, 1948, *Allo, Congo* ("Hello, Congo"), Brussels, 1934, *La politique coloniale* ("Colonial Policy"), Louvain, 1934, *Messages de guerre* ("Wartime messages"), Brussels, 1945, *Etapes et Jalons* ("Steps and Landmarks"), Brussels, 1945, *Barabara,* Brussels, 1947, *A l'autre bout de monde* ("At the Other End of the World"), Brussels, 1948.

SEMOPA BAVON

Semopa Bavon (circa 1885-March 1, 1933) is remembered as the black apostle of the Giri river region. For 25 years he served as the chief Catholic catechist west of Nouvelle-Anvers (now Mankanza) where he evangelized, taught, and organized for the church which suffered from a lack of European workers.

Semopa Bavon was born at Nioki, a village on the Fumi River about 50 km (30 mi) west of Lake Mai Ndombe (formerly Lake Léopold II). Because Semopa lost his parents, he was numbered among those individuals the Europeans considered as "abandoned" children or "orphans." Thus shortly before 1900, an agent of a commercial house of Nioki took him to the colonial school at Nouvelle-Anvers. There Semopa was expected to undertake military service and to learn useful trades. Being extremely intelligent and of excellent character, he was removed from the school by Father E. de Boeck after three years of outstanding accomplishments. Although Semopa at first worked with Father de Boeck, he was later sent as a catechist-monitor to Bogbonga, east of the Congo (now Zaire) River. At that time Semopa was not yet 20 years old.

Not long afterwards, Semopa was transferred west of the Congo to the Giri river valley, where the influence of the Protestant missions was strong. These missions were established at Bolenge (a few kilometers southeast of modern Mbandaka, on the banks of the Ikelemba River), Lulonga (at the confluence of the Lulonga and Zaire rivers), and Bonsambo (a few kilometers north of Nouvelle-Anvers).

The Catholic missionaries at Nouvelle-Anvers needed an intelligent and energetic man to counteract Protestant influence and to serve as an overseer for the African catechists. For this task, in about 1913, the father superior of Nouvelle-Anvers sent Semopa to Bomana (located southwest of Nouvelle-Anvers), the chief town on the lower Giri. Semopa was expected, first, to install catechists along the Giri River, from Musa and Bomboma to its mouth, and second on the Lower Ubangi to Irebu. While keeping in contact with the mission at Nouvelle-Anvers, Semopa traveled continuously throughout his extensive region to encourage and guide the catechists, and note the progress accomplished. In a few years, he was able to gain back from the Protestants the allegiance of a good portion of the population of the lower Giri territory. By 1922, Catholics were in control of practically four-fifths of the villages in the area.

Before 1910, in the early years of European penetration, colonial practices had favored and intensified the slave trade, which was carried on by the first chiefs imposed by the Congo Free State. With the help of the Belgian administration, Semopa worked to free a great number of these captives whom he taught and baptized.

Because of his education, Semopa maintained close relations with the Portuguese traders, and with the administrative authorities at Bomana. At Bomana itself, he served as a State "clerk" in charge of the station's African troops and the catechumens. He was also called upon to settle palavers (disputes) between the different ethnic groups at the station.

A sociable man, Semopa was able to blend gentleness and firmness, and gained the respect and affection of Africans and Europeans alike. Eventually, all the village chiefs along the Giri became his blood brothers. So prestigious did he become that when going to Nouvelle-Anvers during important festivals, he was always accompanied, like a great chief, by more than a hundred boats manned by catechists and Christians from throughout the Ngiri region. On his arrival at Nouvelle-Anvers, he was received with pomp by his Eminence E. de Boeck, the missionaries, and the Christian congregation of the mother-mission.

Although he devoted his life to spreading the Christian faith, Semopa Bavon nonetheless derived considerable material advantages from his position. He received many gifts from Africans as well as from European merchants, State agents, and missionaries. In 1925 he owned, among other things, a 12 calibre hunting rifle, a rare possession for an African. By the time he died, in 1933, he had accumulated 30,000 francs.

In 1931, at the request of the Reverend Fathers Charles Varhenyen and Dieudonné Brisebois, Semopa left Bomana with 140 catechumens and ex-slaves to found a non-traditional "Christian village" at Libanda just outside Bomana. From there, he continued organizing the central catechumenate of Giri which had been started in 1928 at Bomana.

Not long after moving to Libanda, Semopa died on March 1, 1933.

Semopa Bavon was survived by his wife Moba Georgine—a woman from Uele who was a former student of the colonial school at Nouvelle-Anvers—as well as by their five children.

MUMBANZA mwa BAWELE na
NYABAKOMBI ENSOBATO

SHYAAM aMBUL aNGOONG

Shyaam aMbul aNgoong (ruled circa 1625-1640) is remembered as the founder of Kuba civilization. Living east of the confluence of the Sankuru and Kasai rivers, the Kuba have developed a strong centralized state, complex patterns of government, and a refined artistic tradition.

Shyaam, the son of the woman Mbul aNgoong, was probably not born a member of the Bushoong (the Kuba ruling élite). There are three versions of his origins. Some authorities believe Shayaam was an outsider from the Kwilu river area, probably from the Mbuun or Ding lands, who simply revived the name of the old Matoon ruling dynasty. Other traditions assert that a boy named Shyaam aMbul aNgoong was indeed born to the royal Matoon clan during the reign of Misha miShyaang (q.v.). Finally, the third version reports that Mbul aNgoong was not Shyaam's true mother. Rather, because Mbul aNgoong had no children of her own, she adopted Shyaam, the son of her female slave, and had the slave mother killed.

Tradition tells us, that as Shyaam grew up, Mbul aNgoong impressed on him the fact that the reigning Nyim (Kuba paramount chief) was a foreigner, and that he, Shyaam, was the true heir. Encouraged by the princess Mbul aNgoong, and repulsed by Misha miShyaang's crudeness, Shyaam nurtured the ambition of dethroning him. Shyaam, however, received little other encouragement for his project, possibly because of his own origins. When Misha miShyaang learned of Shyaam's intentions, he put a price on his head. Disguised and feigning madness, Shyaam escaped, reaching the region of the Kwango and Kwilu rivers, where he searched for magical charms which would enable him to dethrone Misha miShyaang and become loved and accepted as Nyim. From the Kwango-Kwilu area, Shyaam arrived among the Kel people (southwest of the Kuba) where he was hidden by Mbakam Mashiing who refused to deliver the refugee to the Nyim's envoys, sent to take him. To this day, an enemy of the Nyim who finds refuge among the Kel is never betrayed.

From Kel, Shyaam went to Mbaanc where he hid

with a man named Kaan Kabady. When the Nyim interrogated Kaan about the pretender's whereabouts, Kaan said Shyaam was underground, implying he was dead. Since Kaan proved the truth of his statement by passing a poison ordeal, people in the capital believed that Shayaam was indeed dead. In truth, however, Shayaam was underground, in a large hole where Kaan had hidden him.

Shyaam then assumed a disguise, and went to the Kuba capital to bury magical charms. Earlier, Shyaam had worn the Nyeeng mask, until then unknown by the Bushoong—a mask which was said to change height according to spectators' requests. The mask fascinated the people, its reknown spread to the Nyim's capital. When the Nyim called upon the people of Mbaanc to show him the new mask, Shyaam arrived in the capital, masked, and danced before his enemy, the Nyim. He then profited from his stay in the capital to bury the charms there.

Shyaam returned to dance in the capital several times. Eventually Misha miShyaang became frightened of him, and fled. Soon afterwards, Shyaam was invested as Nyim in his place.

When Shyaam took power, probably around 1625, he was no longer young. A game, represented in front of his royal statue (a carved wooden statue was made for each Nyim), illustrates the context of his investiture. The game symbolizes the struggle for succession to the throne, a struggle in which the crafty candidate triumphs. During his reign, Shyaam had to contend with ambitious rivals who wanted to overthrow him. Therefore, on several occasions, he moved the site of his capital. It was in Shyaam's time that the Kuba kingdom assumed its classic form, and that the Kuba civilization, with its great originality, took form. The techniques of weaving, wood-sculpture, and metal-working developed during his reign and in the reigns that followed. He also developed a plan for the capital, and is said to have organized the first concentration of peoples in the Kuba lands. Shyaam reformed and enlarged the kingdom to such an extent that he became a cultural hero, a great founder-king. Remembered as a prodigious innovator and a great magician, Shyaam has been credited with all the arts and inventions which could not be attributed to others.

BELEPE BOPE MABINTCH and
NDAYWEL è NZIEM

BIBLIOGRAPHY: Belepe Bope Mabintch, "Les conflicts de seccession au trône dans le royaume kuba," ("The Conflicts for Succession to the Throne in the Kuba Kingdom"), *Etudes d'Histoire africaine,* IX, 1977; J. Cornet, *Art de l'Afrique noire au pays du fleuve Zaîre* ("The Art of Black Africa in the Country of the Zaire River"), Brussels, 1972; J. Vansina, "L'influence du mode de compréhension historique d'une civilisation sur des traditions d'origine: l'example kuba" ("The Influence of the Method of Historical Understanding of a Civilization According to Its Traditions of Origin: the Kuba Example"), *Bulletin de l'Académie Royale des Sciences d'Outre-Mer,* 2, 1972.

SIMS, A.

Aaron Sims (18?-1922), a Scottish missionary-doctor, was a pioneer worker for the Livingstone Inland Mission (L.I.M.) and the American Baptist Foreign Mission Society (A.B.F.M.S.) in the Belgian Congo (now Zaire). He worked from 1882 until 1922.

Sims' interest in Africa began while he was a medical student at the University of Aberdeen in Scotland. Having read the accounts of the Anglo-American explorer, Henry M. Stanley (1841-1904), he had tried to join Stanley's expeditions. After failing, he contacted Henry and Fanny Guinness, co-founders of the Livingstone Inland Mission which had been sending missionaries to the Congo since 1878. Impressed with Sims' practical piety, his scholarly attitude, and his scientific knowledge, the Guinnesses accepted the young doctor and sent him to Palabala, about 15 km (9 mi) east of Matadi. When Sims came to Palabala, the mission station had been destroyed by fire, and had lost three workers because of illness. Had it not been for the arrival of Sims, Palabala probably would have been abandoned.

The goal of the L.I.M. was to extend its work into the heart of the African continent. At first, however, the cataracts between Matadi and the Stanley Pool (now Malebo Pool), as well as hostility on the part of local peoples, made it difficult to advance into the interior. Once Stanley had established the Léopoldville station at the Pool, however, regular transportation and security seemed assured, and the L.I.M. set up a mission station at Léopoldville in 1883.

Sent to Léopoldville, Sims was soon making plans to move even further up the Congo (now Zaire) River. Late in 1883 he traveled upstream to Bolobo, 250 km (150 mi) north of the Pool, as a first step to founding a station in Equateur. He also made plans to begin work at Stanley Falls (now Kisangani).

A small, independently-run mission society, the L.I.M. was unable adequately to finance and supervise the ambitious program it had begun in Africa. Thus, in 1884, the L.I.M. was happy to transfer many of its sites and personnel to the larger, church-supported American Baptist Foreign Mission Society. Thus, Sims joined the A.B.F.M.S. staff.

It was in Léopoldville that Dr. Sims made his greatest contribution to the progress of the A.B.F.M.S. He built the first Protestant chapel in the area, and won the first set of converts for the mission. He was very active as a medical doctor, and treated patients of all religions. In April 1887, he came into conflict with Henry Stanley, who was leading a military expedition to relieve Emin Pasha (1840-92), a German scholar and administrator, serving the Ottoman Turkish government as governor-general of the Sudan, who was threatened by the Mahdist uprising there. Needing transportation, Stanley asked missionaries at the Pool to loan him mission steam boats. Although the British Baptist Missionary Society (B.M.S.) acceded to Stanley's demand, Sims refused the Congo Free State's request to use mission property for colonial advancement. In the end, Stanley had to requisition the steamer, the *Henry Reed,* forcing Sims to turn it over to the government. In addition to his other work, Sims found time to study one of the local languages, Teke, spoken by the Tio (Teke) people, and published a Teke dictionary and grammar. He left Léopoldville in 1895 and was sent to establish a post at Stanley Falls. There he had a colleague called Dr. Hote, with whom he cooperated until the station was destroyed by the Arabs and then abandoned by the Mission.

In 1900, Sims was sent to Matadi where he worked until 1922. Once the new A.B.F.M.S. station had been officially opened in Matadi in 1902, Dr. Sims worked to make the post a showpiece. He won several converts and expanded the stations at Palabala, Lukunga, 110 km (65 mi) northeast of Matadi, and Mbansa-Manteke, 50 km (30 mi) northeast of Matadi. He tried to root out fetishism, polygamy, and "superstitious" practices, and succeeded in raising the moral and spiritual standards of the inhabitants.

He represented the A.B.F.M.S. at several Protestant Mission conferences. One of these was held in 1907, and led to the founding of a school for African pastors and teachers at Kimpese, 110 km (65 mi) east of Matadi. Before this, in 1902, he had represented the A.B.F.M.S. at the Conference of Evangelical Missions in the Congo. This was the first body of the Protestant Council of the Congo (P.C.C.), now known as the Church of Christ in Zaire. In 1910 he hosted a conference of A.B.F.M.S. members at Matadi.

Dr. Sims worked with zeal and dedication against several obstacles. Although the Catholic Church in the Belgian Congo, with the open support of King Leopold II (reigned 1865-1909) showed hostility to the Protestant missions, Sims faced his rivals with resolution and perseverance. His relationship with the Africans was very good, and he became very popular in the country. He made a good impression on all who came into contact with him, but was a puritan who forbade the use of alcohol and drugs. He also combated certain harmful customs, such as the poison ordeal which was often carried out in the Lower Congo region.

Dr. Sims left the Belgian Congo in 1922 and went to Britain for medical treatment. When he died there, in the same year, individuals and organizations in many countries paid glowing tributes to his memory.

MBASAMI MBAMBI

BIBLIOGRAPHY: E.M. Breakman, *Histoire du Protestanisme au Congo Belge* ("History of Protestantism in the Belgian Congo"), Brussels, 1961; R. Cornevin, *Histoire du Congo* ("History of the Congo"), Paris, 1970; A. Sims, *A Vocabulary of the Ki-Teke, as Spoken by the Bateke, Batio, and Kindred Tribes on the Upper Congo: Ki-Teke—English,* London, 1886, 1888; R.N. Slade, *English-Speaking Missions in the Congo Independent State (1878-1908),* Brussels, 1959;

TARA PLACIDE

The Abbé Tara Placide (circa 1930-January 7, 1971) was caught up in the 1963 uprising of Pierre Mulele (*q.v.*) in the Kwilu area of the Congo (now Zaire). Becoming disillusioned with the Mulelists, he escaped, only to be treated with suspicion by his ecclesiastical colleagues. He then continued his religious career by enlisting in the Armée National as a chaplain.

Born in Gampuru, a small village near Djuma, about 100 km (60 mi) northeast of Kikwit, Tara spent his youth in schools run by Jesuit priests. After primary school in Djuma, he went to minor seminary at Kinzambi (just outside Kikwit), and then to major seminary at Mayidi, about 100 km (60 mi) south of modern Kinshasa. In the dry season of 1961, he was ordained to the priesthood in Djuma.

He was assigned to the Atene mission where he was to supervise rural schools. Later he was transferred to the large mission of Totshi, 75 km (45 mi) southeast of Kikwit, where he again administered rural schools. Tara was at Totshi when the Mulele rebellion surprised him in August 1963. At first, he attempted to remain with his parishioners and to continue his work as a priest. Soon, together with his colleagues, he was forced to seek refuge with the army which evacuated the priests to Léopoldville (now Kinshasa). In Léopoldville, Tara suffered great remorse for having left behind his two nieces who were students at Totshi. He then determined to return to Totshi, where he learned the two young girls had been taken by the rebels. Advancing deep into the bush to find and save the girls, Tara was captured by the Mulelists.

The details of what happened during the two years he was held by the rebels may never be known. What is certain, is that, at the beginning, he was taken prisoner, and mistreated, and even tortured. Nevertheless, he expressed admiration for and belief in the ideals and doctrine of Mulele, who was preaching the liberation of the masses. It is believed that, for a time, Tara became part of Mulele's immediate entourage. Supposedly he believed he should continue his role as a priest among the Mulelist partisans. Several times, but in vain, he wrote to the superiors of the diocese and to his colleagues, asking them to send supplies for celebrating mass and annointing the sick.

Gradually, however, the unfolding of the struggle and the behavior of the Mulelist militants caused Tara to become increasingly disillusioned with the revolutionaries. From then on, Tara stayed in the Mulelist camps only to protect the two girls, for whom he felt responsible, and to find a favorable opportunity to escape with them to the government camp. Freedom came after a battle in 1966, which was won by the Armée National. The Mulelist camp was destroyed, and the army evacuated Tara and his nieces to Kikwit.

Once he returned from the bush, however, Tara was viewed with suspicion, especially by his colleagues in the clergy. In addition, he had to explain to the police. After being questioned in Kikwit, he was transferred to Kinshasa where he underwent several more weeks of interrogation. Following his release, he was not allowed to serve as a priest in his native diocese at Djuma. For a while he served at Kenge, but pressure from the church hierarchy forced him to leave that post.

Tara Placide then decided to enter the military chaplaincy. It was his conviction that to be a good chaplain, it was necessary first to be a successful soldier. Therefore, he underwent the rigors of military training, receiving the brevet of commando at Kota-Koli and of parachutist at the center for squad training in Mikondo. Then, with the rank of sub-lieutenant, he was sent as chaplain to the lower Zaire river area, serving Matadi, Banana, Moanda, and Luozi. When he returned as a lieutenant, he was posted to the prestigious camp, Tshatshi, in Kinshasa. There, as in the bush, he gave his best, exhibiting strength of spirit, goodness, and simplicity.

But just when Tara appeared to have established a new way of life with the military, he was killed in an automobile accident on January 7, 1971. He is buried in the cemetery at Djuma.

NDAYWEL è NZIEM

BIBLIOGRAPHY: B. Verhaegen, *Rébellions au Congo* (''Rebellions in the Congo''), Brussels and Kinshasa, 1966; Interviews with members of his family.

THYS, A.

Albert Thys (November 28, 1849-February 10, 1915), a Belgian military officer, directed the planning, financing, and construction of the first railroad in the Congo Free State (now Zaire). A crucial link between Matadi and the Stanley Pool (now Malebo Pool), the railroad facilitated the opening of the Congo to colonial exploitation and development.

The son of a country doctor, Thys was born at Dalhem in the Belgian province of Liège. He was educated at Vise, a town 15 km (9 mi) from Dalhem, and then entered the army becoming a corporal in the Seventh Line Regiment in 1865. He was promoted to second lieutenant at the Military Academy in 1870. In 1872 he joined the Eighth Line Regiment and attended the War College. In 1876, when the Brussels Geographical Conference was held, Thys was promoted to lieutenant and appointed deputy staff officer. On the advice of Col. Viscount Jolly, commander of the Military Academy, the Belgian King Leopold II (reigned 1865-1909), who wanted a suitable officer for his secretariat of Colonial Affairs, selected Thys for the post. Very knowledgeable about the geography and exploration of Africa, Thys soon gained the respect of King Leopold. Baron Greindl became his immediate superior, and Thys was initiated into the financial and colonial policy of the court, where he had easy access to the monarch. He was entrusted with the detailed preparations for the Brussels Geographical Conference under Banning and Baron Greindl. His passion for hard work made him the obvious choice for the post of acting secretary general of the International African Association, after Baron Greindl resigned and before Col. Strauch was appointed to the post in 1878.

So strong was his dedication to work that in 1877, during his honeymoon in Paris, when he learned that the Anglo-American explorer Henry Morton Stanley (1841-1904) had traced the course of the Congo (Zaire) River, he interrupted the honeymoon to help persuade the explorer to accept an appointment as King Leopold's agent in Africa. Thys was promoted to the rank of captain in 1879, when Stanley signed a five-year contract as the representative of King Leopold's Study Committee of the Upper Congo. This committee's aim was to build a railway and a river communications system between the Lower and Upper Congo.

On October 11, 1883 Thys was appointed staff officer to the king and had the opportunity of working closely with him. This relationship proved advantageous in his subsequent career. Stanley had planned to build a railway from Vivi, north of the Zaire River, and Matadi, to Stanley (now Malebo) Pool, but there were financial difficulties. Léopold had to decide whether to use Belgian or British capital for the railway. The initial decision was to form a syndicate in Manchester, England, called the Congo Railway Company, to which the king would entrust the building of the railway. But public opinion in Belgium was against this plan, and it had to be abandoned. In the meantime, Thys actively canvassed Belgian financiers and businessmen, including members of the Belgian Society of Engineers and Industrialists as well as the Brussels and Antwerp Geographical Societies, for a

loan. Once he succeeded in getting Léopold to break the contract with the Manchester company, Thys was able to collect a million francs for preliminary studies from supporters of the project. By the beginning of October 1886 the railway building enterprise entered its second phase, with the establishment of the Congo Company of Commerce and Industry, which was formally inaugurated on February 9, 1887. Its aims were "to study, build, and operate the railway linking the Lower Congo to Stanley Pool...and to survey the Upper Congo to find out its commercial value for the future". These tasks were undertaken by two teams. One, consisting of engineers and topographers under Captain E. Cambier, surveyed the region of the Cataracts, which the proposed railway was to cross. The other, under the command of A. Delcommune, was to assess the commercial value of the Upper Congo and its tributaries. The report advised that the railway should be constructed, since the traffic in goods in the Upper Congo was enough to supply the Cataract Railway, whatever its cost might be.

In October 1888 Thys therefore began to organize the Compagnie du Chemin de Fer du Congo ("Congo Railroad Company"), or C.C.F.C. Its aim was to create trade for the future railway and to prepare economically the areas it was going to serve. In effect, it was one of four commercial companies dealing with the development of the Congo. All four companies had well defined aims, separate capital, distinct councils of administration in Europe, and their own personnel in Africa. But they had a single board of directors, which depended on a board of directing staff common to them all. They worked with a capital sum of 32 million francs.

In June 1889, a magazine supplement called the "White Brochure" was published, with articles on the Congo railway "from Matadi to Stanley Pool". This brochure contained the results of the research work, described the plan for the railway, evaluated its operating cost, and estimated the profits to be gained. In conclusion, the engineers cited the need for capital investment of 25 million francs. German and British financiers agreed to participate in the project on condition that the Belgian government contribute 10 million francs. In spite of Thys' apprehensions, Prime Minister Beernaert brought the matter before the Belgian Parliament. Legislation approving Belgian participation was adopted, after which the Congo Railway Company was created in Brussels on July 31, 1889, with Thys as its administrator.

The actual building of the railway began in March 1890. From the beginning, problems of climate, topography, recruitment, accident, and illness caused great difficulty. Construction was seriously delayed during the initial stages, and the work proceeded in an atmosphere of disenchantment.

Thys was disappointed by these difficulties. Perhaps it was his promotion to the rank of major on September 25, 1892, which raised his morale. A new and crucial phase was now in sight—the crossing of the Palabala range (east of Matadi)—which was achieved in 1893 with much difficulty. In spite of further problems, for example heavy rains at the end of 1893, the project still continued. Thys traveled between Brussels and Matadi to encourage those at work.

Early in 1894, when the hardest phase had been completed, the 25 million franc capital had been exhausted. Thys negotiated with a syndicate of bankers and Belgian corporations to guarantee a further loan. In the heat of the financial crisis, it was Thys who again arranged for a loan of 2,500,000 francs from the bankers, who were to be reimbursed in 1895.

From that year on, the railway enterprise was out of danger. This was due to the Belgian Parliament's vote in favor of the Matadi to Léopoldville (now Kinshasa) railway, to the introduction of work on the bonus system, and to the reorganization of team work. As a result the C.C.F.C. managed to inaugurate the first half of the line—the 190 km (120 mi) Matadi to Tumba section—in 1896. It was on March 16, 1898, a memorable date in the history of the Congo Free State, that the first train arrived at the end of the line at Ndolo, Léopoldville, amidst indescribable rejoicing. The official inauguration took place on July 6 of the same year at Léopoldville.

The railway created many problems for Belgians and Africans alike, but served a useful purpose. It was, however, not structurally perfect, and Thys was planning to improve upon it when he died in 1915. His memory was honored when a key town on the rail line was named Thysville (now Mbanza-Ngungu).

LUMENGA-NESO KIOBE

BIBLIOGRAPHY: R.J. Cornet, *La bataille du rail* ("The Battle of the Railroad"), 3rd ed., Brussels, 1953, pp. 59-67; A. Delcommune, *Vingt années de vie africaine (1874-1893)* ("Twenty Years of African Life (1874-1893)"), Vol. 1, Brussels, 1922; Lumenga-Neso Kiobe, "La question du Chemin de Fer Matadi-Kinshasa au 19ème siècle" ("The Question of the Matadi-Kinshasa Railroad in the 19th Century"), *Zaïre-Afrique*, No. 126, June, 1978, pp. 343-63; H.M. Stanley, *Cinq années au Congo: 1879-1884*, ("Five Years in the Congo: 1879-1884"), Brussels, undated, circa 1885; A.J. Wauters, "Le Comité d'Etudes du Haut-Congo: Coup d'oeil rétrospectif" ("The Study Committee of the Upper Congo: A Glance in Retrospect"), *Mouvement Géographique*, May 21, 1911, No. 21, col. 261.

TSHOMBE, M.

Moise Tshombe (November 19, 1919-June 29, 1969) served as president of the secessionist state of Katanga, and then as prime minister of the Republic of the Congo.

Oldest son of Joseph Kapend (*q.v.*), Moise Tshombe was born at Musumba, 200 km (120 mi) south of Katanga, capital of the Lunda empire of the great chief Mwant Yav, to whose royal line he was related by both blood and marriage. His father was one of the most successful Congolese businessmen of the colonial epoch. As the oldest son, it was young Moise who was to inherit management of the firm "Joseph Kapend Tshombe et Fils." To this end, his father sent him to primary school at the Methodist mission near Sandoa, 90 km (50 mi) south of Musumba, where the family then lived, and on to the Methodist teacher-training institute of Kanene, about 200 km (120 mi) southeast of Musumba, where he obtained a teaching certificate after four years of study. His formal education was completed through a correspondence course in accounting.

At this point, the young Tshombe arrived in Elisabethville (now Lubumbashi) in order to conduct his father's business. In the city, however, the way of life was markedly different from that which the young man had known during his years in the country. He was dazzled. Moise Tshombe visited the enchanting night clubs, spending most of his time ambling through the city, and quickly became popular in the cafés of Elisabethville. His father, who had acquired his wealth by the sweat of his brow, reacted by sending the young spendthrift to manage a series of stores in the bush, far from the bright lights of Elisabethville. Moise, however, who had in the meantime married the daughter of chief Mbaku Ditend (who became Mwant Yav Ditend Yavu a Nawej III, who ruled from 1951-63), did not have his father's success, and the latter had to intervene three times to save Moise from bankruptcy.

In 1951, following his father's death, Moise Tshombe took over as director of the family's interests in Elisabethville. As such, he enjoyed the status of an évolué (Western-educated African), was elected president of the African Chamber of Commerce of Elisabethville, and replaced his father on the provincial council where he held a seat until 1953.

After his father's death he continued with his business; but got into difficulties because Belgian colonial law did not permit Congolese Africans to obtain credit from banks, even when they had landed and real properties. It was this disability which forced Tshombe to enter politics.

When his commercial enterprises began to waver, Tshombe decided to entrust them to his brothers; he entered politics where he finally found great success. In 1956 he founded a Lunda tribal association, approved by the Belgians as a non-political club although it did not hesitate to become a political one. In 1958 Tshombe became regional president of A.C.M.A.F. (Association of African Middle Classes) and president of G.A.S.S.O.M.E.L. (Grouping of Mutual [ethnic] Associations of the Lunda Empire).

In Katanga, as everywhere in the Congo, communal elections were held in December 1957 about constitutional reform concerning the status of cities. In Elisabethville these elections gave three out of four posts of burgomaster (mayor) to the Luba elements originally from Kasai. This victory of the "foreigners" was not well accepted by the "true Katangans" and provoked a movement for solidarity among the Katanga ethnic groups. With a view to confronting the rising Katangan professional and social elements, Moise Tshombe and his colleagues created CONAKAT (Confederation of Tribal Associations of Katanga) in October 1958. The following year relations between those born in Katanga and those from Kasai deteriorated even more. There was an economic recession, and many Africans found themselves without work. Misery was widespread in the industrial centers; the Katanga-born denounced the competing Kasai immigrants. The principal objective of CONAKAT then became the repatriation of 160,000 Luba "foreigners" to Kasai.

For Tshombe, the idea of a federal Congo, permitting autonomy amounting to secession for Katanga, came chiefly from the recession of 1959 and the rising ethnic tensions with the Luba from Kasai. He hoped to see an autonomous state of Katanga in order to stop "ruinous immigration" and to keep a larger portion of mineral profits for the Katangans from whose soil the copper came. In this regard, the rapid rise of the M.N.C. (Mouvement National Congolais, or National Congolese Movement), led by Patrice Lumumba (q.v.), evoked the menace not only of radical, foreign influence but also the continued dominance of a government outside the province and one under the control of Luba-Kasai. (The directing committee of the M.N.C. was composed principally of Luba from the province.) Tshombe's attitude toward the Luba of Kasai earned him the opposition of the related Luba of Katanga, led by Jason Sendwe's BALUBAKAT (Association of Luba of Katanga), a former member group within CONAKAT. Sendwe then formed the Katanga Cartel with the Kasai immigrants and Cokwe (Chokwe) leaders.

Tshombe, as president of CONAKAT, incorporated into his coalition the Katanga Union, an association of white colonists known for their secessionist, or at least

federalist, views. The whites wanted autonomy for different reasons than Tshombe. For them, the principal threat was the radical view of the northern leaders, such as Lumumba and the M.N.C.—i.e. those urging a unitary state. The whites estimated that their interests would be better preserved under an autonomous regime led by a moderate well-disposed to their interests.

From January 20 through February 20, 1960, there was a political Round Table conference in Brussels at which the unitarist thesis of Lumumba's M.N.C. triumphed.

During Tshombe's visit to Belgium in early 1960, he was given very special treatment by Belgian financiers and politicians, and he assured them of his full cooperation after independence. On his return home he had a rousing welcome from the Katangese. He also rejected the offer of Sir Roy Welensky, the prime minister of what was then Central African Federation, for a union between Katanga and the federation. Tshombe himself was a convinced federalist, and stood for a form of confederation—a position he defended during the Round Table Conference. This led people to conclude that he was in the pay of the mining companies. On March 3, 1960, he was invited to Brussels by the Movement for the United States of Europe. He told the members of this organization of his plans for an independent Congo, and asked for their help in achieving his goal.

He then returned to the "Capital of Copper," Elisabethville. In April his party won the provincial elections. On June 17 the provincial government was formed with Moise Tshombe as its president. On the national level, however, his enemy Patrice Lumumba had won the battle for leadership and formed a central government on June 23. Katanga was given two ministerial portfolios; Tshombe judged this share insufficient. At this point, supported by the European community, he attempted to proclaim independence for the copper province before June 30, the date foreseen for the Congo. Belgian counselors and the copper-producing Union Minière du Haut Katanga (UMHK), however, prevented Tshombe from doing so.

The Congo's independence took place on June 30 in an atmosphere of calm, but shortly afterward the soldiers of the Force Publique mutinied in several garrisons throughout the country. Katanga was not spared. In Elisabethville, for example, a revolt erupted on July 9 at Camp Massart. Tshombe called upon the Belgian paracommandos from Kamina, 400 km (250 mi) northeast of Lubumbashi, to save the situation, and on July 10 calm was restored in Katanga. Supported by the European community of Katanga and the Belgian military, Tshombe profited from the reigning chaos in the rest of the Congo to proclaim Katanga's independence on July 11, 1960.

Convinced of a Belgian hand in Katanga's action, the central government in Léopoldville (now Kinshasa) broke diplomatic relations with Belgium on July 14. The Belgian government—without, however, officially recognizing Katanga—supported Tshombe's ambitions by continuing to give his government technical assistance and by maintaining key Belgian personnel within the secessionist state. Tshombe took advantage of the Belgian military who themselves clearly supported secessionism in Katanga.

The copper revenue of Katanga was the major reason for Tshombe's secessionist movement. Complex negotiations followed the declaration of secession, and included the following events:

In September 1960, a Katangan delegation went to Brazzaville and signed an agreement with Joseph Ileo, then prime minister of the Congo, under which Katanga would give its full support to Joseph Kasa-Vubu (q.v.) and Ileo. The form of polity to be established was to be discussed later at a Round Table Conference.

On November 30, 1960, Tshombe was invited to Brazzaville by the Abbé Fulbert Youlu, prime minister (later president) of the Republic of the Congo (Brazzaville), to attend the independence celebrations. It was then suggested that a round table conference should be called in the near future to settle the Congo problem. Tshombe agreed. Tshombe at this time found money to give a present to King Baudouin and Queen Fabiola of Belgium, and was received in audience at the royal palace in Brussels. Some days later, during a banquet given in his honor by a Katangese delegation in Belgium, the Count d'Aspremont Lynden, the Belgian Minister of African Affairs, informed the gathering that the king had awarded President Tshombe the Grand Cordon of the Order of the Crown, and that the honor was in recognition of Tshombe's courage. This decoration made Tshombe unpopular at home, since he was regarded as a dangerous opportunist. But the Belgian government did not officially support his secessionist movement.

In January 1961, Tshombe attended a conference in Tananarive, capital of Madagascar, where most major Congolese personalities, except Justin Bomboko, were present. The conference accepted Tshombe's idea of a federated Congo. He afterwards returned to Elisabethville, and gave a banquet in honor of Kasa-Vubu. But in April 1961, when Tshombe and Kimba went to Coquilhatville for a conference to implement the Tananarive accords, they were arrested on April 26, and charged with treason against the central government. Later, on June 24, 1961, they were released by Kasa-Vubu and Mobutu on the intervention of Fulbert Youlou.

Very quickly the Katanga conflict became internationalized. Pressures of all sorts were exercised in vain on the Katanga government to renounce secession. All attempts for negotiations between the central government and Katanga were similarly doomed to failure. In the end, intervention by the "Blue Helmets" (the United Nations Emergency Force, or U.N.E.F.) put down the Katanga secession. At Kolwezi on January 14, 1963, Moise Tshombe proclaimed the end of Katanga's bid for independence. Following his return to Elisabethville, he left for Paris by way of Ndola in Northern Rhodesia (Zambia). In March he returned to Katanga to recognize the authority of Joseph Ileo, designated by the central government as general commissioner for Katanga affairs. Having recovered the copper province, however, Léopoldville conducted an investigation, Tshombe did not remain sheltered from the inquiries. In June 1963 he returned to Paris, moving on to Barcelona, Spain, then, in November, Madrid.

From abroad Moise Tshombe maintained and multiplied his contacts. From Barcelona or Madrid he addressed the politicians of Léopoldville and their advisors, expressing his desire to serve the central government loyally "without a backward glance to secession or personal ambition." In the meantime the Congolese situation deteriorated. The 1964 rebellion led by Pierre Mulele (q.v.) had won three-quarters of the country, thanks to the parallel action of Emile Soumialot in the east. Just beyond the Congo's borders, the Katanga mercenaries threatened to invade from Angola, and Christophe Gbenye founded a National Council of Liberation (C.N.L.) in Brazzaville (capital of the Republic of the Congo, formerly the French Congo).

In despair of ever reaching an accord with the central government of Cyrille Adoula (in office 1961-64), Tshombe turned to the C.N.L., meeting with its representatives in Madrid on February 22-24. An accord was concluded for national reconciliation and the cessation of all hostilities. Although this accord was never put into effect, the political leaders in Léopoldville, faced with growing rebellion and external pressure, were convinced that Tshombe's return was the only possible solution. On June 26 Moise Tshombe arrived in Léopoldville, and Prime Minister Adoula offered his resignation to the president of the Republic on June 30. Tshombe then formed a new central government, calling for dedication to "the public welfare" and national reconciliation. The forces of rebellion, however, did not disarm. Tshombe had to call on European mercenaries to supplement the Congolese National Army (A.N.C.), which undertook operations for the systematic reconquest of the territories occupied by the insurgents.

These operations succeeded in part. On the diplomatic level, however, Tshombe confronted opposition from African countries, who reproached him principally for having called for aid from the West. In September 1964, the Organization for African Unity (O.A.U.) asked that the "recruitment of mercenaries in the Congo cease immediately" and demanded the expulsion of the mercenaries already recruited.

On October 5 Tshombe, who had gone to Cairo to attend a conference of non-aligned countries, was assigned to a house under surveillance. On his return to the Congo, he attempted to recover his standing. He visited the president of France, Charles de Gaulle, in Paris, was received at the Vatican, and traveled in West Germany, everywhere seeking to win as many allies as possible. Tshombe participated later in the conference of the Joint African and Malagasy Organization (O.C.A.M.) in Abidjan, capital of the Ivory Coast, then went to Brussels where he believed that he had succeeded in finally regulating the contentious Belgo-Congolese economic issues.

New elections took place in the Congo in the second half of 1965. CONACO (the National Congolese Convention) Tshombe's new political party, assured itself of parliamentary control. President Joseph Kasa-Vubu, convinced that Tshombe was going to oust him in the transition to a new constitutional structure, requested Tshombe's resignation. When Tshombe's resignation was not forthcoming, Kasa-Vubu dismissed him from office despite CONACO's parliamentary majority. The situation was confused. Finally, on November 25, 1965, General Mobutu dis-

charged Kasa-Vubu and proclaimed himself president with executive authority for five years.

Tshombe was traveling, on July 1, 1967, by air from Madrid to the Balearic Islands, where he wanted to purchase a property at Ibiza, when the plane was hijacked by an ex-convict called Bodenan, and forced to land in Algiers. Tshombe was put under house arrest by the Algerian government, and an enquiry was held into his activities in the Congo. The Congolese government sent delegations to seek his extradition for trial for offences which included the murder of Patrice Lumumba, but President Boumedienne refused to release him. He spent his days reading, and going for car rides around Algeria with his guards, until he died of a heart attack on June 30, 1960. His wife was allowed to take his body to Brussels, where he was buried on July 4, 1969.

MUTEBA KABEMBA NSUYA

BIBLIOGRAPHY: J. Bourlion, *Tshombe abandonné* ("Tshombe Abandoned"), Brussels, 1969; A. Bouscaren, *Tshombe,* New York, 1967; Centre de Recherche et d'Information Socio-Politiques C.R.I.S.P.), *Congo 1959,* Brussels, 1960, rev. ed., 1961, *Congo 1960,* Brussels, 1961, *Congo 1961,* Brussels, 1968; J. Gérard-Libois, *Sécession au Katanga* ("Secession in Katanga"), Brussels-Kinshasa, 1963; A. Lederer, "Tshombe," *Biographie Belge d'Outre-Mer,* Vol. VII, Brussels, 1973; Moise Tshombe, *My Fifteen Months in Government,* translation by Lewis Bernays, Plano, Texas, 1967.

VITA NKANGA

Vita Nkanga (16?-October 29, 1665), also known as Antonio I, ruled over the Kongo kingdom for a short time in a period when the state was being destroyed by internal revolt and Portuguese aggression. His death, in a battle against rebellious vassals and Portuguese adventurers, marked the beginning of a long period of unrest and instability in the once powerful kingdom.

Vita Nkanga, the son of the Mani Kongo (king of the Kongo) Nkanga Lukeni (*q.v.*), or Garcia II, served as governor of Mpangu, a territory about 100 km (60 mi) northeast of the capital, San Salvador. Wishing to make royalty hereditary in his family, and to assure Vita Nkanga's succession Nkanga Lukeni killed potential pretenders to the throne. Unfortunately for Vita Nkanga, the hostility of his father toward the Portuguese had troublesome consequences during his reign. Wishing to put an end to Portuguese meddling in the internal affairs of the Kongo, Nkanga Lukeni allied himself with the Dutch who had expelled the Portuguese from Luanda in August, 1641. In 1649, after the reconquest of Luanda by the Portuguese, Nkanga Lukeni was asked to cede the territory south of the Kongo, where he obtained the shells which served as money, and to give up the kingdom's reputed silver mines. To the great dissatisfaction of the Portuguese, Nkanga Lukeni refused to sign such a treaty.

Problems with the Portuguese continued after Vita Nkanga came to the throne in 1661 as Antonio I. He too did not wish to transfer the sovereignty of his country and reclaimed, from the Portuguese, lands which had been lost in war. When the Portuguese demanded possession of the mines, Vita Nkanga refused, further angering them.

Only four years after Antonio's accession to power, Wandu and Ambuila provinces, about 150 km (94 mi) south of San Salvador, revolted. When they called on the Portuguese at Luanda for help, Vita Nkanga mobilized his army of 70,000 men, and prepared to fight at the side of his soldiers. The two armies confronted each other at Ambuila on October 29, 1665. Although the battle lasted several hours, the Kongolese, who had only traditional weapons to oppose the Portuguese artillery, were defeated. Vita Nkango, more than 100 Kongolese nobles, and a large part of the population died in defense of the country. Vita Nkanga's head was taken to Luanda where the Portuguese governor buried it with much pomp. After the king's defeat, an era of division began in the Kongo; rival kings arose in several different places, who fought each other mercilessly. A great part of the Kongolese nobility was decimated by these wars.

The reign of the unfortunate Vita Nkanga was catastrophic for the Kongo, but the damage resulted from errors committed by his predecessors. Not only had his own father lacked political acumen, earlier still, in the 1520s or 1530s, Mvemba Nzinga (Afonso I) inadvertently had given the Portuguese the notion that mines existed in the Kongo by sending silver manacles to the Portuguese king. Nevertheless he set an example of patriotism, since he resisted relinquishing any part of his country's sovereignty.

TSIMBA MABIALA

BIBLIOGRAPHY: S. Axelson, *Culture Confrontation in the Lower Congo,* Falköping, Sweden, 1970; G. Balandier, *La vie quotidienne au royaume du Kongo du XVIIIème siècle* ("Daily Life in the Kingdom of Kongo in the 18th Century"), Paris, 1965, English translation by Helen Weaver published as *Daily Life in the Kingdom of Kongo from the Sixteenth to the Eighteenth Century,* New York, 1968; Batsikama, *Voici les Jagas, ou l'histoire d'un peuple parricide bien malgré lui* ("Here are the Jagas, or the History of a People Who Became Paracide Despite Themselves"), Kinshasa 1971, pp. 147-50; J. Cuvelier, *L'ancien royaume du Congo* ("The Ancient Kingdom of Congo"), Brussels, 1946, pp. 240-242; W.G.L. Randles, *L'ancien royaume du Congo des origines à la fin du XIXème siècle* ("The Ancient Kingdom of Congo from its Origins to the End of the 19th Century"), Paris and the Hague, 1968, pp. 117-120; J. Vansina, *Les anciens royaumes de la savane,* Léopoldville, 1965, published in English as *Kingdoms of the Savanna,* Madison, 1966.

WEMBO NYAMA

Wembo Nyama (circa 1870-July 28, 1940) began his career as an auxiliary of the great slave trader Ngongo Leteta (*q.v.*). Later, he became a faithful ally of the Congo Free State, helping them to occupy his Tetela homeland, located west of the Lomami River, and even aiding the Europeans to put down a revolt of Ngongo's former Tetela soldiers.

During Ngongo Leteta's raids into Tetela territory between Lubefu, 120 km (70 mi) east of Lusambo, and the Lomami River, Wembo Nyama was captured and deported to Ngandu, Ngongo's residence located on the Lomami River directly east of Lusambo. After acting as a servant to Ngongo Leteta for several years, Wembo Nyama was elevated to the rank of a village

Wembo Nyama (center).

chief. After Ngongo Leteta's surrender to the Congo Free State on September 19, 1892, Wembo Nyama also gave himself up to the whites.

At this time, Lieutenant F. Dhanis designated Wembo Nyama to escort caravans and resupply arms and munitions to the expeditions which were traveling from Lusambo to Nyangwe, 175 km (100 mi) downstream from Kongolo, or to Katanga (now Shaba) via Ngundu. During the Congo Free State's campaign to defeat and drive away the Swahili slave traders in eastern Congo, Wembo Nyama served to the complete satisfaction of his European superiors. Once the war against the Arabs was over, Wembo Nyama was authorized by Dhanis to settle near the State post of Ngandu.

When in 1893, Capt. G. Augustin began the effective occupation of the Tetela region of the savanna, Wembo Nyama, who came from that area, became his closest collaborator. Wembo accompanied Augustin on all his operations, constantly showing initiative and energy.

Augustin and Wembo Nyama gained control over all the region contained between Lubefu and Lodja, on the Lukeni River 160 km (90 mi) north of Lusambo. As a reward for these services, Augustin placed the populations between the Lunga and Lomami rivers under the authority of Wembo Nyama, who settled near the Lotembo River, several kilometers from the present village of Wembo Nyama, 140 km (85 mi) northeast of Lusambo.

By about 1894, Wembo Nyama and Augustin had already made their influence felt in Tetela country, from Ngandu in the south to the sources of the Lukenie in the north, and from the Lomami River in the east to Lodja in the west. Their pacification expedition had lasted about seven months.

Even after the Tetela had been brought under government control, Wembo Nyama had occasion to demonstrate his loyalty by participating in Free State military operations. In July 1895, Ngongo Leteta's former soldiers, then serving the Free State, mutinied at Luluabourg (now Kananga). Without waiting for a government order, and as soon as he heard that the Tetela soldiers had rebelled and were returning to their homes, Wembo Nyama hastened to the Ngandu post with reinforcements. Along with the other Free State forces, he and his men took a stand on the route between Kabinda and Ngandu. Despite the bloody defeat then inflicted on the Free State troops by the Tetela from Luluabourg, Wembo Nyama nevertheless remained loyal to the government. After the battle he crossed the Lomami, where he rejoined the refugees, including Capt. J. de Sagers, in the village of Lusuna, near Malela about 20 km (12 mi) southeast of Nyangwe. After the group had struggled back to Nyangwe,

de Sagers reported to Commander H. Lothaire that, without Wembo Nyama, neither he nor the rest of the soldiers would ever have arrived.

Commander Lothaire recognized Wembo Nyama to be a man of great loyalty who was knowledgeable about the Tetela lands. He therefore designated Wembo to serve as a guide for the expedition against the still-undefeated rebels. With Lothaire's soldiers, Wembo Nyama confronted the Tetela mutineers, who suffered their first defeat. The post of Ngandu was immediately re-occupied and was then moved about 30 km (20 mi) further south to Tshofa, also on the Lomami River.

Wembo Nyama was again settled near the post, where he built his village. Lothaire gave him some reconditioned guns so that he could support the Europeans more effectively. In 1902, the post at Tshofa was ceded to the Comité Spécial du Katanga (C.S.K. or "Special Committee for Katanta"). Wishing to remain under the jurisdiction of the government instead of under that of the C.S.K.—a vast government and private organization created to administer Katanga (now Shaba)—Wembo Nyama relocated his village near the newly-created state post of Lubefu.

Tired of so much relocation, Wembo Nyama asked permission to settle definitely at Ewango, the place where he was living before the Luluabourg revolt in July 1895. His request was granted, and in 1902 Wembo Nyama resettled his people at the present site of Wembo Nyama village.

On July 30, 1907, Wembo Nyama received a government medallion and was invested as chief of the Eswe, the Tetela of the savanna. This original domain was greatly reduced, however, when in 1911 and in 1914 many of his subordinate chiefdoms were declared autonomous. His power ultimately reduced to control of his own village, Wembo Nyama, as in the past, remained a firm friend of the Europeans in the administration. He also supported the American Methodist missionaries who settled north of his village in 1914.

Wembo Nyama died on July 28, 1940 in the Methodist hospital which had been built in his village. He was succeeded by his son Malu Malu.

DIMANDJA LUHAKA

BIBLIOGRAPHY: J. Miller, *Jungles Preferred*, Boston and New York, 1931; A.J. Reid, *Congo Drumbeat*, New York, 1964; J. Sheffey, "A Great African Chief Reaches Journey's End," *Congo Mission News*, No. 113, 1941, pp. 17-18; R. Slade, *English-speaking Missions in the Congo Independent State, 1878-1908*, Brussels, 1959.

CONCISE GUIDE TO ZAIRE NAMES AND TERMS

ABAKO — The Bakongo Alliance (Alliance des Bakongo), a cultural group, formed after World War II, that was active in promoting political self-consciousness among the African elite in the Lower Congo area.

A.I.A. — The Association Internationale Africaine, or International African Association. It was founded at the instigation of Leopold II , King of the Belgians, (reigned 1865-1909), at the conclusion of the Brussels Geographic Conference of 1876. Its purpose was the "exploration and civilization of Africa." The subsidiary of the A.I.A., the Comité d'Etudes du Haut Congo (Survey Committee for the Upper Congo), was a precursor of the Congo Free State (q.v.).

A.I.C. — See INTERNATIONAL ASSOCIATION OF THE CONGO.

ALBERTVILLE — See KALEMIE.

ALLIANCE DES BAKONGO — See ABAKO.

ANT YAV — Plural of Mwant Yav (q.v.).

ARAB CAMPAIGN — The campaign conducted between 1891 and 1894 by the forces of the Congo Free State (q.v.) against the strongholds of the Arab or Arabized traders, then controlling the eastern regions of what is now Zaire. The defeat of the traders resulted in the suppression of the slave trade in the Congo Free State.

"ARABS," THE — Arab or Arabized elements, often Swahili, who played a major role in the trade of east and central Africa, including the eastern parts of what is now Zaire, until the coming of the colonial powers.

ASAMBALA — Agents of the "Arabs" (q.v.) and Swahili (q.v.) among the Tetela (q.v.).

ASSANEF — Association of Former Students of the Brothers of Christian Schools (Association d'anciens élèves des Frères des écoles chrétiennes), a group founded after World War II that helped to foster political consciousness among the African élite in the Belgian Congo.

AZANDE — See ZANDE.

BA- — A prefix meaning "people," as, for example, "Batetela," meaning "the people called Tetela."

BAKONGO — See KONGO.

BAKUBA — See KUBA.

BAKWANGA — See MBUJI-MAYI.

BALOBO — See LOBO.

BALUBA — See LUBA.

BAMWE — See MWE.

BANDUNDU — (1) One of the eight regions of Zaire, located in the east. (See map on page 330); (2) A town, on the right bank of the Kwango River, a short distance above its juncture with the Kasai River. The capital of Bandundu Region, it was formerly called Banningville.

BANGALA — See NGALA.

BANGI — See BOBANGI.

BANNINGVILLE — See BANDUNDU (town).

BANTOTE — Ruling clan of the Nunu (q.v.) of the Bandundu Region (q.v.).

BANTU — A linguistic sub-group of the Niger-Congo peoples, including about 200 languages spoken in the early 1970s by more than 60,000,000 peoples. The majority of the peoples of Zaire are included in this grouping.

BANYAMPARA — Plural of Nyampara (q.v.).

BAPENDE — See PENDE.

BAS-ZAIRE — The easternmost of the eight regions of Zaire, located on the southern bank of the Zaire River, at its mouth.

BATEKE — See TIO.

BATETELA — See TETELA.

BATETELA REVOLTS — A series of revolts by the Batetela. The first occurred in 1895-96 when Batetela soldiers rose at Luluabourg (present-day Kananga) against the Congo Free State (q.v.). The second occured in 1897-99, when Batetela soldiers participating in the Nile Expedition revolted against their commander, Dhanis.

(BATETELA REVOLTS)	—	The third occurred in 1944 at Luluabourg, and was directed against Belgian authority.
BAYEKE	—	*See YEKE.*
BELGIAN CONGO	—	The colony created on November 15, 1908 when the Belgian Parliament annexed the former Congo Free State (*q.v.*). It continued to administer it until June 30, 1960, when the Belgian Congo gained independence as the Republic of the Congo (Léopoldville), which in 1971 became the Republic of Zaire.
BEMBA	—	An ethnic group, speaking a Bantu language, living in southeastern Zaire and northeast Zambia, and numbering about 150,000 in the 1970s. The Bemba claim to have originated in the Luba (q.v.) empire.
BIFUKU	—	The plural of Cifuku (*q.v.*), a clan grouping among the Luba (*q.v.*).
BOBANGI	—	(1) Also known as the Bangi. An ethnic group of northern Zaire, numbering about 60,000 in the mid-20th century; (2) a chiefdom, founded in 1906 by the Belgians. It included, in addition to the Bobangi people, the Baloi, and the Bangele (on the banks of the Ubangi), the Bokongo (between the Ubangi and Zaire Rivers), the Mampoko (between the Giri and the Zaire), the Ndjondo (Djundu) from the lower Giri and Ubangi region, and the Makutu and the Mangba, (between the Ubangi and the Giri).
BOLIA	—	A centralized state of ancient Zaire, located in the northeast of what is now Zaire, near Lake Mai-Ndombe.
BOMA	—	(1). A river port on the Zaire River, in Bas-Zaire, about 96 km (60 mi) from the Atlantic Ocean. It was the capital of the Congo Free State (*q.v.*) from 1886 to 1908, and of the Belgian Congo (*q.v.*) from 1908 to 1926, when the capital was removed to Léopoldville; (2) An Arab or Swahili term for a fortified enclosure, usually surrounded by thorn bush or a palisade.
BUDJA	—	An ethnic group of northern Zaire, speaking a Bantu language.
BUKALENGE BUA NSALA	—	Literally, "power of the feather." Among the Luba of Kasai, a red parrot's feather was one of the attributes of power.
BUKAVU	—	Known as Costermansville until 1966. A city standing on a peninsula on the southwest shore of Lake Kivu, in Kivu Region, in eastern Zaire, near the Rwanda border.
BULA MATARI	—	A Kikongo expression meaning "breaker of rocks." Originally the name was given to Henry Morton Stanley (1841-1904) at the time of the construction of the railroad from Matadi to Léopoldville (now Kinshasa), which began in 1890 and was completed in 1898. It later came to be applied to colonial agents or to the state in general.

BULEGA — The territory of the Lega, divided between three administrative zones: Shabunda and Mwenga in the sub-region of South Kivu, and Pangi in the sub-region of Maniema, in Kivu.

BULONGO — A military alliance uniting the Luba clans of Kasai against a common enemy.

BULOPWE — The principle of sacred power embodied in by the Mulopwe (*q.v.*), the paramount chief of the Luba.

BUSHI — Name of the homeland of the Shi people, living to the southwest of Lake Kivu.

BUSHOONG — The ruling elite of the Kuba.

BWAMI — A socio-political association among the Lega (*q.v.*), which ensured the cohesion and constituted the strength of Lega society. Suppressed and banned during the colonial era, the Bwami reappeared after independence in 1960.

CHITENTAM — The Lunda (*q.v.*) Council, which elects the Mwant Yav (*q.v.*).

CIFUKU — A clan grouping among the Luba. The plural is Bifuku.

CILOL — A Lunda province.

COMITE D'ETUDES DU HAUT CONGO — *See STUDY COMMITTEE FOR THE UPPER CONGO.*

CONGO — A name derived from the Kongo state—*See KONGO, KINGDOM OF*—and, by extension, used to refer to both the Congo, or Zaire, River (see note on page 188), and to the region as a whole. Having been known successively as the Congo Free State, the colony of the Belgian Congo, and—after independence on June 30, 1960—as the Republic of the Congo, the name of the state became the Republic of Zaire on October 27, 1971.

CONGO FREE STATE — (Etat Independant du Congo, or E.I.C.), which existed from 1885 to 1908. Established as the personal trust of King Leopold at the Berlin Conference of 1884-85, it was taken over by the Belgian Parliament in 1908, after mismanagement and abuses had created an international scandal. It then became the Belgian Congo (*q.v.*).

COQUILHATVILLE — *See MBANDAKA.*

COSTERMANSVILLE — *See BUKAVU.*

CUSTOMARY CHIEF — A traditional chief, as distinct from an officially appointed chief invested by the colonial administration. (*See INVESTITURE*).

E.I.C. — *See CONGO FREE STATE.*

EKONDA — The Tetela (*q.v.*) of the forest.

ELISABETHVILLE	—	*See LUBUMBASHI.*
EQUATEUR	—	One of the eight Regions of Zaire, located in the northwest. (*See* map on page 330).
ESWE	—	The Tetela (*q.v.*) of the savanna.
ETAT INDEPENDENT DU CONGO	—	*See CONGO FREE STATE*
FORCE PUBLIQUE	—	The security force in the Congo Free State (*q.v.*) and, later, in the Belgian Congo. (*q.v.*). Before independence, in 1960, it numbered about 25,000, and was led by Belgian officers. After independence, it became the Armée Nationale du Congo (A.N.C.), or Congolese National Army. The function of the Force Publique was to maintain law and order, protect property, and secure the borders.
HAUT-ZAIRE	—	One of the eight regions of Zaire, located in the northeast. (*See* map on page 330).
IBOKO	—	*See NGALA.*
ILEBO	—	A river port on the right bank of the Kasai, about 20 km (13 mi) from its confluence with the Sankuru. Formerly known as Port Francqui.
IMMATRICULATION	—	A status, created towards the end of the colonial era, in the 1950s, which recognized certain educated Congolese as having the legal status of Europeans.
INTERNATIONAL AFRICAN ASSOCIATION	—	*See A.I.A.*
INTERNATIONAL ASSOCIATION OF THE CONGO	—	The organization which superseded the Study Committee for the Upper Congo (*q.v.*) in 1883, and in the name of which the Congo was occupied by the agents of King Leopold II of the Belgians (reigned 1865-1909). In April 1884 the United States recognized the Association as a sovereign state. In 1885, after the conclusion of the Berlin West African Conference of 1884-85, the name of the Association was changed by decree to the Congo Free State (*q.v.*).
INVESTITURE	—	Ceremony at which a chief was accorded official recognition by the Belgian colonial authorities. The ceremony, at which the chief was given a medal, was designed to inspire the spectators with awe. After investiture, a chief was regarded as being virtually untouchable.
JADOTVILLE	—	*See LIKASI.*
KAKONGO	—	A people located on the lower reaches of the Zaire River, and related to the Kongo (*q.v.*). The Kakongo kingdom was peripheral to the kingdom of Kongo (*q.v.*).
KALANDALA	—	Title of a governor-commander among the Lunda (*q.v.*).

KALEMIE — Formerly Albertville. Town in the Shaba Region in southeast Zaire, on the west shore of Lake Tanganyika. Founded in 1891, it was also known as Lukuga until 1915, when it was renamed Albertville, a name retained until 1966 when it again became known as Kalémie.

KANANGA — Formerly Luluabourg. The capital of the Western Kasai (Kasai Occidental) Region in south central Zaire. It was named Luluabourg in 1884, and was renamed Kananga in 1971.

KANGU — Title borne by the paramount chief of the Pende (*q.v.*). It also refers to the chieftaincy itself.

KANINCHIN — A small group of Lunda-related people living about 185 km (115 mi) south of Mbuji-Mayi.

KANIOK — *See KANYOK*

KANYOK — A Luba-related chiefdom west of the Lubilash River.

KASAI — One of the eight regions of Zaire, located in the south central region. It is subdivided into Eastern and Western subregions (Kasai Oriental and Kasai Occidental). (*See* map on page 330). Before independence it was the province of Kasai, and earlier (1935-47) was known as Lusambo.

KATANGA — *See SHABA*. Formerly the southeasternmost province of the Belgian Congo. One of the richest mining areas in Africa, it attempted to secede from the newly-independent state of the Congo in 1960, but after 1962 was gradually reintegrated into the republic. It was renamed Shaba in 1972.

KAZEMBE — (1) Title of the leader of a military expedition of the Lunda (*q.v.*) empire; (2) The most prestigious political title in the Lunda empire.

KIAMFU — The most prestigious political title among the Yaka (*q.v.*) of Kwango in what is now Bandundu (*q.v.*) Region in western Zaire.

KIKONGO — One of the four national languages in Zaire. The language of the Kongo (*q.v.*) of Western Zaire, it was spoken by an estimated 1,500,000 people in the 1970s. It belongs to the Bantu linguistic grouping. *See also: LINGALA, SWAHILI, TSHILUBA*.

KILEGA — Language of the Lega (*q.v.*).

KILUBA — *See TSHILUBA*.

KIMBANGUISM — A Christian messianic movement, founded by Simon Kimbangu (*q.v.*), which became widespread in the 1920s, and was banned by the Belgian authorities. It nevertheless continued to flourish, and in the 1970s existed as the Kimbanguist Church of Zaire, the largest independent African church. In 1969 it affiliated with the World Council of Churches.

KINGURI — Title of lords of the eastern Lunda (*q.v.*) empire, centered in Angola.

KINSHASA — Formerly Léopoldville. The capital of Zaire, located on the south bank of the Zaire River, at the downriver end of Malebo Pool (*q.v.*). Founded by Henry Morton Stanley (1841-1904) in 1887, it succeeded Boma (*q.v.*) as the capital of the Belgian Congo in 1926. From the time of independence it was also the capital of the Congo (now Zaire), and was renamed Kinshasa in 1966. In 1970 its population numbered about 1,300,000.

KISANGANI — Formerly Stanleyville (until 1966). The capital of Haut-Zaire Region. The nation's second largest inland port, after Kinshasa, Kisangani is a road junction, and the head of navigation on the Zaire River. In 1970 its population was about 230,000.

KIRONGOZI — A Swahili term, meaning leader, particularly the leader of a caravan.

KIVU — One of the eight Regions of Zaire, located in the east. (*See* map on page 330).

KIZENZI — An initiatory sect which, like the similar Mulonge sect, appeared among the Lega (*q.v.*) during World War II. Those initiated supposedly became in their turn "whites" and "masters," were invulnerable to the whip, and were not subject to imprisonment.

KOLA — An association of the peoples of the upper Giri (Ngiri) River, a tributary of the Ubangi in northwestern Zaire.

KONGO — Also Bakongo. An ethnic grouping located in Zaire and Angola, numbering about 1,500,000. In Zaire, the Kongo are located on both banks of the Zaire River, near the mouth. The Kongo speak Kikongo, a Bantu language.

KONGO, KINGDOM OF — A kingdom, founded in about the 14th century, located on the lower Congo (Zaire) River. It was ruled by the Mani Kongo (*q.v.*) from his capital at Mbanza. The kingdom had six provinces—Mbamba, Mbata, Mpembe, Mpungu, Nsundi, and Soyo. After the coming of the Portuguese in 1484, the kingdom was undermined by the slave trade, dissolving into warring chiefdoms in the later 17th century.

KONGOLESE — The subjects of the kingdom of Kongo (*q.v.*).

KONZO IKULU — Also Mount Ngaliema. A hill in Kinshasa (*q.v.*), formerly the site of the residence of chief Ngaliema. Known as Mont Léopold during the colonial period, it was renamed Mount Ngaliema in 1971. It is the seat of the Zaire government, and the residence of the head of state.

KUBA — Formerly a traditional kingdom. A cluster of about 16 small ethnic groups, located in Western Kasai, east of the confluence of the Kasai and Sankuru rivers, and numbering about 75,000 in the early 1970s.

KUMU — An ethnic group in the north and northeast of Zaire, numbering about 20,000, and speaking a Bantu language.

KUNDU — A people living on the equator, southeast of Mbandaka.

KWANGO — District in Bandundu (*q.v.*) Region in western Zaire. Kikwit is the capital.

KWILU — A region taking its name from the Kwilu River, which rises in Angola, and flows generally northwards across southern Zaire to its confluence with the Kwango. Kikwit, the principal town in the area, is on its left bank, and is the head of navigation for shipping. The Mulelist uprising which occurred in this area in 1964, became known as the Kwilu Rebellion.

LAKE LEOPOLD II — *See LAKE MAI NDOMBE.*

LAKE MAI NDOMBE — Located in western Zaire, east of the Zaire River, and 332 km (270 mi) northeast of Kinshasa. It drains into the Kasai River through the Fimi River. It is 130 km (80 mi) long, and has an area of 2,300 sq km (888 sq mi)

LEGA — Also called Rega. An ethnic group of eastern Zaire, speaking a Bantu language.

LELE — A people living just west of the Kuba (Bakuba), across the Kasai River.

LEOPOLDVILLE — *See KINSHASA.*

LIKASI — Formerly Jadotville, until 1966. An industrial center for the copper industry, and a road and rail center, Likasi is located in Shaba (*q.v.*), 140 km (86 mi) northwest of Lubumbashi.

LINGALA — One of the four national languages in Zaire. A Bantu language, it is spoken along the middle reaches of the Zaire River. A trade language, it is widely used in Kinshasa, and is also the language of the army. *See also: KIKONGO, SWAHILI, TSHILUBA.*

LOANGO, KINGDOM OF— A state, founded in about the 16th century, located on the northern periphery of the kingdom of Kongo. In the 17th and 18th centuries, it grew wealthy from trading in slaves and ivory.

LOBO — Also Balobo. A people living just north of Makanza, about 180 km (100 mi) upstream from Mbandaka on the Zaire River.

LUBA — Also Baluba. An ethnic group in southeast Zaire, living in the Kasai, Shaba, and Kivu Regions, and speaking Tshiluba (*q.v.*) and related Bantu languages. The group numbered more than 1,500,000 in the 1970s.

LUBUKU — A religious cult among the Luba, whose adherents smoked hemp.

LUBUMBASHI — Formerly Elisabethville, until 1966. The capital of Shaba Region, it is the third largest city in Zaire, with a population of more than 300,000 in 1970. It is the main industrial center in southeastern Zaire.

LULUABOURG — *See KANANGA.*

LUNDA — Grouping of peoples speaking Bantu languages, and widely distributed over

(LUNDA) — southeast Zaire. The grouping numbered about 1,500,000 in the 1970s. The Lunda empire, located in the southern Kasai river region, was founded in about 1700. Its capital was Musumba.

LUPAMBULU — A secret sect opposed to the Belgian administration which flourished among the Pende during World War II. Its members believed themselves immune to European action against them.

LUSAMBO — (1) The former name of Sankuru (*q.v.*), capital of Kasai Oriental; (2) The former name (1935-47) of the province of Kasai (*q.v.*).

MABALE — *See NGALA.*

MAKANZA — A town on the right bank of the Zaire River, about 904 km (565 mi) from Kinshasa. It was formerly known as Nouvelle-Anvers. It was also the site of the Bangala State Post, founded before 1900.

MAKOKO — The title of chief among the Tio (*q.v.*), or Teke, people.

MALEBO POOL — Formerly known as Stanley Pool. A lake formed by the Zaire River, about 560 km (350 mi) from its mouth, separating Kinshasa (which stands on its southwest shore) from Brazzaville, capital of the People's Republic of the Congo (formerly the French Congo), to the west.

MANGBETU — A Sudanic-speaking people who arrived in the forest area of what is now Zaire before 1800. They are located on the Bomolandi River, a tributary of the Uele, about 400 km (250 mi) northeast of Kisangani.

MANI — A prestigious title among the Kongo nobility which denoted the king (the Mani Kongo), or other high dignitaries of the state, such as the Mani Soyo (*q.v.*).

MANI KONGO — Title of the king of the Kongo. (*See MANI*).

MANI SOYO — Title of the ruler of Soyo, one of the six provinces of the kingdom of Kongo.

MANI VANDU — The title of the kingdom of Kongo, of the spiritual chief of the earth, who traditionally officiated as priest at royal coronations.

MATADI — A seaport on the left bank of the Zaire, and the capital of the Bas-Zaire Region. It is 150 km (93 mi) upstream from Banana, at the mouth of the Zaire River.

MBANDAKA — Formerly Coquilhatville. It is the capital of Equateur Region, and is situated on the left bank of the Zaire River, at the mouth of the Ruki River, 370 km (592 mi) from Léopoldville. Founded by Henry Morton Stanley (1841-1904) in 1883, and originally named Equateur or Equateurville, it was then named Coquilhatville, until it became Mbandaka in 1966.

MBANZA KONGO — Capital of the kingdom of Kongo (*See KONGO, KINGDOM OF*), which flourished from the 14th to the 17th centuries. Located in what is now Angola, it fell under Portuguese influence, and was renamed San Salvador.

MBANZA-NGUNGU — Formerly Thysville. A railroad town in Bas-Zaire Region, 150 km (96 mi) south-southwest of Kinshasa.

MBOSHI — A people of the lower Alima River region.

MBUJI-MAYI	—	Formerly Bakwanga. The capital of the Kasai Oriental (Eastern Kasai) Region. It is a diamond-mining center.
"MBULA MATARI"	—	*See BULA MATARI*
MONGO	—	A people living in the forest south of the main Zaire River bend, and north of the Kasai and Sankuru rivers. Numbering about 2,000,000 in the 1970s, the Mongo include the Bogandu, Bokole, Bolia, Boyela, Ekonda, Mbole, Ndengese, Nkundo, Nkutu, Sengele, and Tetela-Kusu.
MOUNT NGALIEMA	—	*See KONZO IKULU.*
MULELIST REBELLION	—	The uprising in the Kwilu (*q.v.*) region, begun in 1963, named for its leader, Pierre Mulele (*q.v.*). The uprising, sometimes called the Kwilu Rebellion, was quelled by the central government.
MULENGE	—	A Luba people from Shaba who migrated west across the Lubilash River into Kasai.
MULOPWE	—	The title of the ruler of the Luba (*q.v.*). *See also: BULOPWE.*
MUYOMBU	—	A ficus plant, a symbol of office of the Kazembe (governor) among the Lunda.
MWAMI	—	Title of ruler among the Shi, and other peoples.
MWANT YAV	—	Also Mwata Yamvo. The title of the ruler of the Lunda (*q.v.*), belonging to the Lunda dynasty founded, perhaps in the 17th century, by Chibind Yirung (*q.v.*). The plural is "Ant Yav." In the 1970s, the Mwant Yav was located in the Kpanga district of southern Zaire. The meaning of the title is "Lord of the Vipers."
MWE	—	Also Bamwe. A people living on both banks of the Giri River in northwestern Zaire.
MWENE BANGU	—	The title of the chief of the Niungu, a Pende people living east of the Kwilu River.
NATIVE DISTRICT	—	A term ("circonscription" in French) in use in the colonial era, and designating a recognized chiefdom or other traditional grouping or groupings.
NDOLO	—	An ethnic group located north of the Zaire River, midway between Mbandaka and Lisala.
NGALA	—	Usually known as the Bangala to Europeans. The Ngala were originally a people from Iboko and Mabale, near present-day Makanza, 200 km (120 mi) northeast of Mbandaka. The Ngombe people also became part of the Ngala grouping. The Ngala engage in fishing and in river trade, as well as in argiculture. As early recruits to the Force Publique, they spread their language and influence throughout the Zaire river region.
NGOMBE	—	*See NGALA.*
NGOYO	—	A small coastal kingdom which, in former times, existed north of the mouth of the Zaire River, in the region of Cabinda.

NGUII	—	A people living along the Kasai River, north of Kikwit. Their paramount chief is called the Vui.
NKUBA	—	Paramount chief of the Shila, a people of the Luapula River region.
N'KUM OKARE	—	Queen mother among the Nunu of Bandundu. The title is derived from ''N'kum'' (chief) and ''okare'' (wife).
NKUMU	—	The moneyed aristocracy among the Bobangi.
NKUNDO	—	A Mongo ethnic group located southeast of Mbandaka.
NOUVELLE-ANVERS	—	*See MAKANZA.*
NTOMB	—	A wine made from the bamboo plant by the Lunda (*q.v.*).
NTOMBA	—	A grouping of the Mongo (*q.v.*).
NUNU	—	A northwestern Bantu people, associated with the Tio (*q.v.*), or Teke.
NYAMPARA	—	Plural: Banyampara. A lieutenant among the Swahili (''Arabs'') in the regions subdued by them during the 19th century.
NYAMWEZI	—	*See YEKE.*
NYIM	—	The paramount chief of the Kuba (*q.v.*).
NZAMBI	—	The Supreme Being, closely linked to Africans, in Kimbanguist belief. (*See KIMBANGUISM*).
ORIENTALE PROVINCE	—	*See HAUT-ZAIRE.*
OTETELA	—	The language of the Tetela (*q.v.*).
PENDE	—	Also Bapende. A group located in southwest Zaire, in the Kwilu region, near the Angola border. Sub-groups include the Akwa Mushinga and the Yongo.
PORT FRANCQUI	—	*See ILEBO.*
REGA	—	*See LEGA.*
RUKAN	—	A sacred bracelet symbolizing royal power among the Lunda (*q.v.*).
RUWEJ	—	Title of the queen mother of the Lunda (*q.v.*).
SANKURU	—	Formerly Lusambo. It is on the right bank of the Sankuru River, about 880 km (550 mi) east of Kinshasa.
SAN SALVADOR	—	Now a town in northwest Angola, 112 km (70 mi) southeast of Matadi, San Salvador (or Sao Salvador), under the name of Mbanza Kongo, (*q.v.*), was formerly the capital of the kingdom of Kongo, which flourished from the 14th to the 17th centuries.
SHABA	—	Formerly the province of Katanga (*q.v.*). It is the southeasternmost of the

(SHABA)	—	eight Regions of Zaire. (See map on page 330). Its capital is Lubumbashi (q.v.).
SHI	—	A people living southwest of Lake Kivu. The name for their homeland is "Bushi."
SHILA	—	A people of the Luapula River region, in the southeasternmost part of Zaire.
SHIMUNA	—	A chiefdom of the Pende (q.v.), on the left bank of the Kwilu River.
SIMBA	—	An armed partisan supporting the 1964 rebellion in eastern Zaire.
SONGYE	—	A people of the Kasai Oriental (Eastern Kasai) Region, living between the Lomami and Lualaba rivers.
STANLEY FALLS	—	See WAGENIA.
STANLEY POOL	—	See MALEBO POOL.
STANLEYVILLE	—	See KISANGANI.
STUDY COMMITTEE FOR THE UPPER CONGO	—	In French, the Comité d'Etudes du Haut Congo. This committee was established by the A.I.A. (q.v.) in November 1878, to find ways to open easy communication between the Lower and the Upper Congo. The committee was superseded by the International Association of the Congo (q.v.) in 1883.
SWAHILI	—	(1) One of the four national languages of Zaire. It originated on the coast of East Africa, and is used as a lingua franca throughout eastern Africa. See also: KIKONGO, LINGALA, TSHILUBA: (2) A cultural, rather than an ethnic, group, the Swahili peoples consist of detribalized and "Arabized" peoples of the Muslim faith. In the 19th century, the Swahili established a loosely linked trading empire—dealing, among other things, in ivory and slaves—based in East Africa. In consequence, the Swahili became economically and militarily dominant in parts of what is now Zaire. The military power of the Swahili traders—often called "Arabs"—was broken by the Congo Free State in an "Arab" campaign which was concluded in 1894.
TEKE	—	See TIO.
TETELA	—	A Mongo (q.v.) group, speaking the Otetela language. The Tetela of the forest are called the Ekonda, while those of the savanna are called the Eswe.
THYSVILLE	—	See MBANZA-NGUNGU.
TIO	—	Also called Teke. A people who originally lived north and west of Malebo Pool. Their nominal capital was Mbe, north of the Pool.
TSHILUBA	—	Also called Kiluba, it is the language of the Luba, and one of the four national languages of Zaire. See also: LINGALA, KIKONGO, SWAHILI.
ULUUND	—	The name given by the Lunda (q.v.) to Lunda country.
U.N.E.L.M.A.	—	The Union of Former Students of the Marist Brothers (Union des anciens élèves des Frères maristes), a group founded after World War II that helped foster political self-consciousness among the African élite.

VUI	—	The title of the paramount chief of the Nguii (*q.v.*) people living on the Kasai River north of Kikwit.
WAGENIA FALLS	—	Formerly known as Stanley Falls. Seven cataracts on the Lualaba River, between Kisangani (*q.v.*) and Ubundu (former Ponthierville), stretching for over 100 km (60 mi), along the curve of the river. Below the seventh and largest cataract, the Lualaba becomes the Zaire River.
WATHEN STATION	—	*See NGOMBE LUTETE.*
YAKA	—	Also Bayaka. A people located about 250 km (155 mi) southeast of Kikwit, on the Kwango River, near the Angola border. In earlier times the Yaka had a powerful military state.
YEKE	—	The Yeke state was established in the 19th century in the Shaba region by Nyamwezi conquerors from what is now Tanzania. The name "Yeke" means "hunter."
YONGO	—	A Pende sub-group.
ZAIRE	—	In 1971 the name of the Republic of Congo was changed to the Republic of Zaire. For the origin of the name, see *"ZAIRE RIVER."*
ZAIRE RIVER	—	The name given in the Republic of Zaire to the Congo River. (Being an international waterway, the Zaire is still known as the Congo in international legal terminology). The name Zaire was first given to the river by Europeans in the later 15th century, being derived from the word *nzari* or *nzali* in local African dialects, meaning "river." In the 17th century the river, by association with the kingdom of Kongo, became known as the Congo. Being 4,700 km (2,900 mi) in length, the Zaire is the second longest river in Africa, being surpassed only by the Nile. It rises in Zambia, but for the greater part of its length flows through the territory of Zaire before emptying into the Atlantic Ocean at Banana. Kinshasa, (*q.v.*), the capital of Zaire, stands on its left bank at Malebo Pool (*q.v.*).
ZANDE	—	Also Azande. A Sudanic-speaking people living in both the southern Sudan and northern Zaire, and numbering about 750,000 in the 1970s. In Zaire they live between the Uele and Bomou rivers.

ZAIRIAN GEOGRAPHIC NAMES

The names of several major cities were changed in 1966. In 1971, the name of the Republic of Congo was changed to the Republic of Zaire. At this same time, other place names throughout the country were changed, with African names being used in place of those used during the colonial period (1885-1960), and after. Major name changes are listed below in alphabetical order.

Zairian Names

Bandundu - formerly Banningville.
Bukavu - formerly Costermansville.
Haut-Zaire Region - formerly Oriental Province.
Ilebo - formerly Port Francqui.
Kalemie - formerly Albertville.
Kananga -formerly Luluabourg.
Kinshasa - formerly Léopoldville.
Kisangani - formerly Stanleyville.
Lake Mai-Ndombe - formerly Lake Léopold II.
Likasi - formerly Jadotville.
Lubumbashi - formerly Elisabethville.
Makanza - formerly Nouvelle-Anvers.
Malebo Pool - formerly Stanley Pool.
Mapongu - formerly Brabanta.
Mbandaka - formerly Coquilhatville.
Mbanza-Ngungu - formerly Thysville.
Mbuji-Mayi - formerly Bakwanga.
Moba - formerly Baudouinville.
Ngombe-Lutete - formerly Wathen Station.
Shaba - formerly Katanga.
Ubundu - formerly Ponthierville.

Colonial Names

Albertville - now Kalemie.
Bakwanga - now Mbuji-Mayi.
Banningville - now Bandundu.
Boudouinville - now Moba.
Brabanta - now Mapongu.
Coquilhatville - now Mbandaka.
Costermansville - now Bukavu.
Elisabethville - now Lubumbashi.
Jadotville - now Likasi.
Katanga - now Shaba.
Lake Léopoldville - now Lake Mai-Ndombe.
Léopoldville - now Kinshasa.
Luluabourg - now Kananga.
Nouvelle-Anvers - now Makanza.
Oriental Province - now Haut-Zaire Region.
Ponthierville - now Ubandu.
Port Francqui - now Ilebo.
Stanley Pool - now Malebo Pool.
Stanleyville - now Kisangani.
Thysville - now Mbanza-Ngungu.
Wathen Station - now Ngombe Lutete.

CHRONOLOGIES OF THE KINGS OF THE KONGO AND THE ANT YAV (RULERS) OF THE LUNDA

KINGS OF THE KONGO

Wene........................14th century
. . . .
Nzinga Nkuwu (Joao I).........?-1506
Mvemba Nzinga (Afonso I)......1506-circa 1543
Pedro II.....................circa 1545
Nzinga Mpudi.................circa 1545-1561
Afonso II....................1561
Bernardo I...................1561-1566
Henrique I...................1566-1567
Alvere I.....................1567-circa 1586 (?)
Alvere II....................1586-1614
Alvere III...................1614-1622
Pedro II.....................1622-1624
Garcia I.....................1624-1626
Ambrosio I...................1626-1631
Alvere IV....................1631-1636
Alvere V.....................1636
Alvere VI....................1636-1641
Nkanga Lukeni (Garcia II).......1641-1661
Antonio I....................1661-1665

After this, further rulers are recorded, but the kingdom had declined.

RULERS OF THE LUNDA

Mwant Yav*	Dates of rule
Chibind Yirung	circa 1600-circa 1630
Yav a Yirung (Mwant Luseng)	circa 1630-circa 1660
Mwant Yav Nawej I (Yav a Yirung?)	circa 1660-circa 1690
Muteb a Kat	circa 1690-circa 1720
Mukaz Waranankong	circa 1720-circa 1740
Mulaji	circa 1740-circa 1750
Mbala	circa 1750-circa 1760
Yaav yaMbany	circa 1760-circa 1810
Chikomb	circa 1810 (ruled two months)
Nawej a Ditend	circa 1810 (1820?)-1852.
Mulaji a Namwan	1852-1857
Muteb a Chikomb	1857-1873
Mbal a Kamong Isot	1873-1874
Mbumb Muteb a Kat	1874-1883
Chimbundu a Kasang	1883-1884
Kangapu Nawej	1884
Mudib	1884-1885
Mutand Mukay	1886-1887
Mabl a Kalong	1887
Mishid a Nambing	1887-1907
Muteb a Kasangi	1907-1920
Kaumb	1920-1951
Ditend Yavu a Nawej III	1951-1963
Mushid II Lumanga Kawel (Mushidi Gaston)	1963-1965
Muteb II Mushid (Yav "Tshombe" David)	1965-1975
Mbumb II Muteb (Tshombe Daniel Muteb Dipang)	1975-

*The second or third ruler—Yav a Yirung, or Nawej I—appears to have been the first to be designated as the Mwant Yav, a title that was passed down to his successors.

> **Note on Rulers of the Lunda:** The data in the list of Ant Yav (the plural form of "Mwant Yav," meaning ruler of the Lunda) is tentative, since existing sources are in disagreement about a number of dates and forms of names, especially in the 18th and earlier 19th centuries. The following list, therefore, should be treated as a rough study guide, rather than as a definitive chronology.

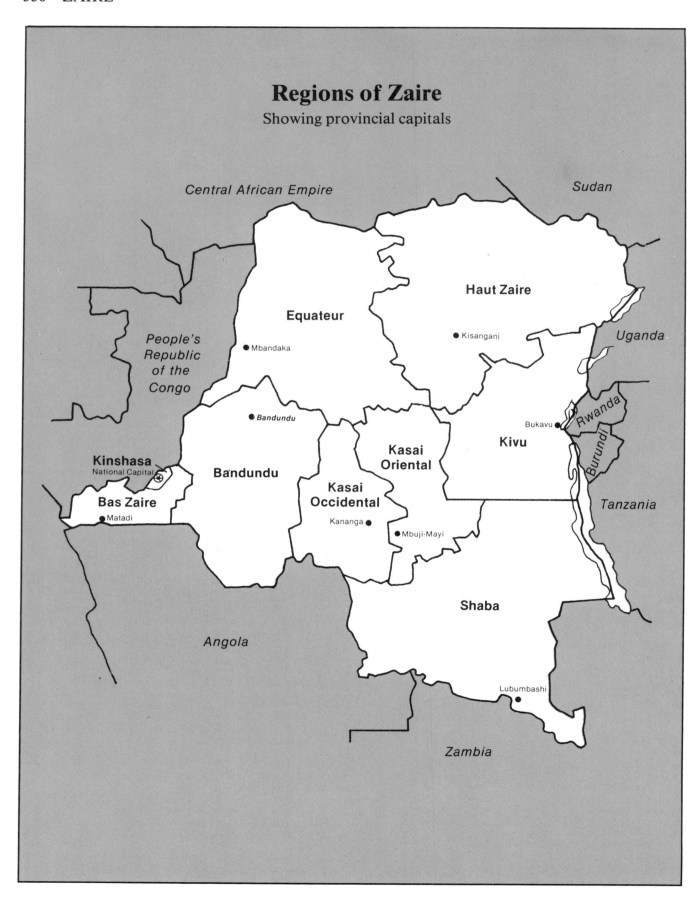

Regions of Zaire
Showing provincial capitals

Central African Empire

Sudan

Haut Zaire

● Kisangani

Equateur

Uganda

People's Republic of the Congo

● Mbandaka

● *Bandundu*

Bukavu ●

Rwanda

Kivu

Burundi

Kasai Oriental

Kinshasa
National Capital

Bandundu

Kasai Occidental

Tanzania

Bas Zaire

● Matadi

Kananga ●

● Mbuji-Mayi

Shaba

Angola

Lubumbashi ●

Zambia

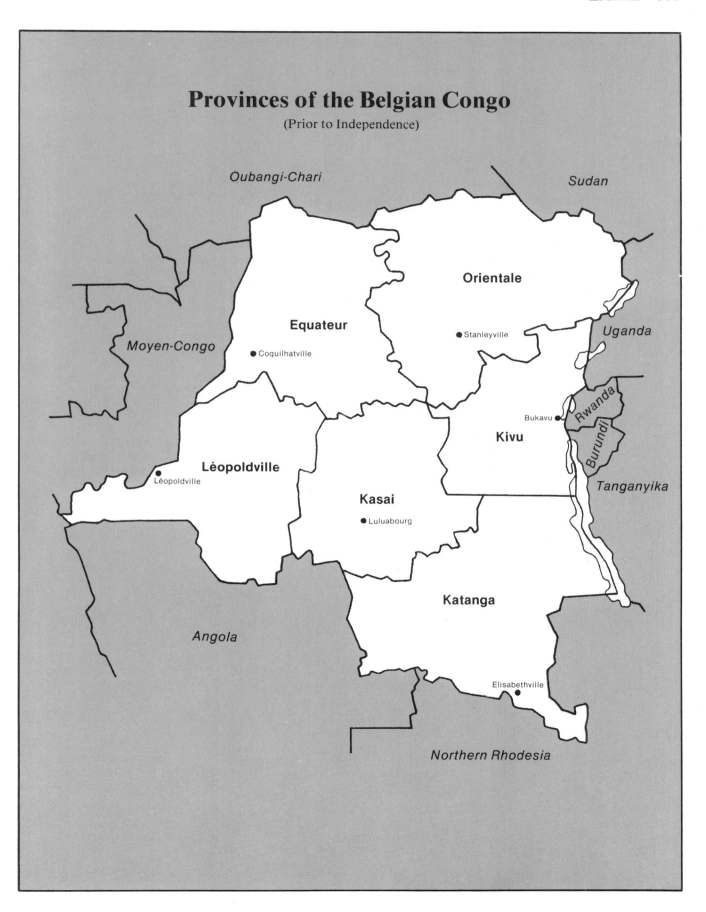

Provinces of the Belgian Congo
(Prior to Independence)

Oubangi-Chari

Sudan

Orientale

● Stanleyville

Equateur

Moyen-Congo

● Coquilhatville

Uganda

Rwanda

Bukavu ●

Kivu

Léopoldville

● Léopoldville

Kasai

Burundi

Tanganyika

● Luluabourg

Katanga

Angola

Elisabethville ●

Northern Rhodesia

ZAIRE: principal rivers and towns

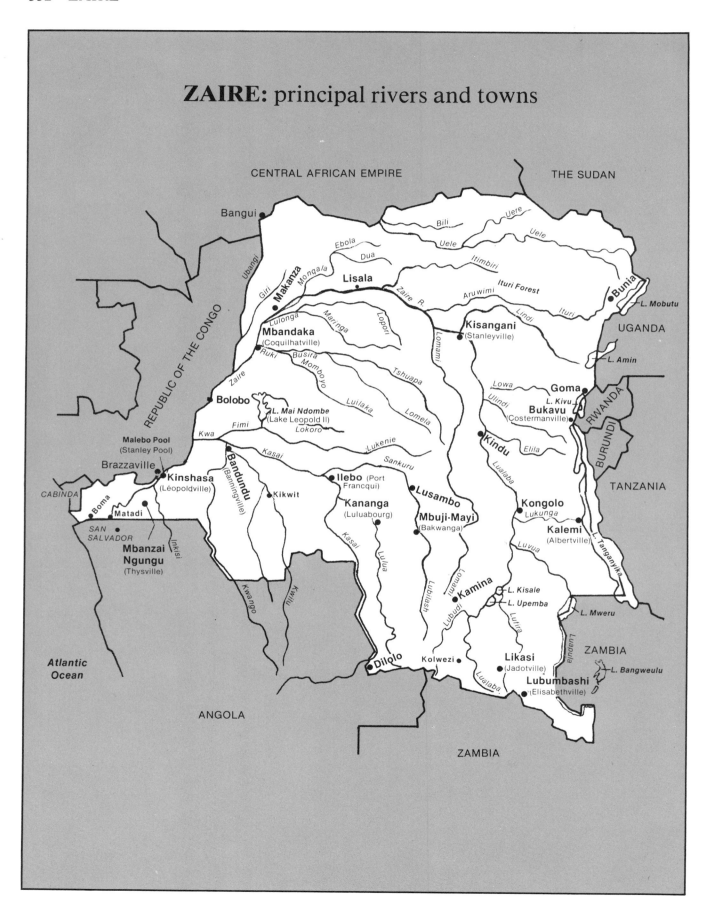

CENTRAL AFRICAN EMPIRE

THE SUDAN

Bangui

Bili

Uere

Ebola

Uele

Uele

Dua

Ubangi

Giri

Makanza

Mongala

Lisala

Itimbiri

Zaire R.

Aruwimi

Ituri Forest

Bunia

REPUBLIC OF THE CONGO

Lufonga

Maringa

Lopori

Lindi

Ituri

L. Mobutu

Mbandaka
(Coquilhatville)

Ruki

Busira

Momboyo

Tshuapa

Kisangani
(Stanleyville)

UGANDA

Zaire

Luilaka

Lomela

Lowa

L. Amin

Bolobo

L. Mai Ndombe
(Lake Leopold II)

Lokoro

Goma

Ulindi

L. Kivu

Fimi

Kwa

Bukavu
(Costermanville)

RWANDA

Malebo Pool
(Stanley Pool)

Kasai

Lukenie

Sankuru

Kindu

Elila

BURUNDI

Brazzaville

Bandundu
(Banningville)

Ilebo (Port
Francqui)

Lusambo

Lualaba

TANZANIA

Kinshasa
(Léopoldville)

Kikwit

Kananga
(Luluabourg)

Kongolo

CABINDA

Boma

Matadi

Inkisi

Kasai

Mbuji-Mayi
(Bakwanga)

Lukunga

Kalemi
(Albertville)

*SAN
SALVADOR*

**Mbanzai
Ngungu**
(Thysville)

Kwilu

Lulua

Luvua

L. Tanganyika

Kwango

Lubilash

Lomani

Lubudi

L. Kisale

Kamina

L. Upemba

L. Mweru

Lufira

Luapula

*Atlantic
Ocean*

Dilolo

Kolwezi

Lualaba

Likasi
(Jadotville)

ZAMBIA

L. Bangweulu

Lubumbashi
(Elisabethville)

ANGOLA

ZAMBIA

PEOPLES OF ZAIRE

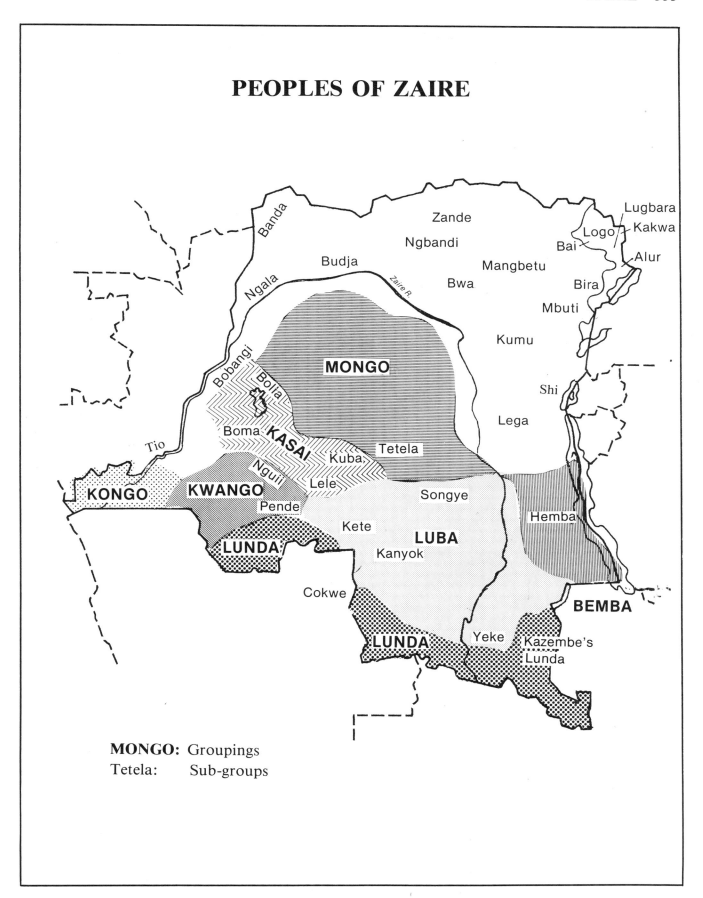

MONGO: Groupings
Tetela: Sub-groups

INDEX

Aachen, West Germany, 219

Aanza, 239

Abako, 186, 217, 218, 219, 244, 245, 315
    blamed for 1959 riots, 244
    declares independence for the Lower Congo, 218
    founding of, 217
    in 1957 elections, 218
    in May 1960 elections, 245
    A. Kinzonzi joins, 232
    meeting banned (1959), 187, 218

Abayomi Cole, John Augustus, 35, 36, 146, 154

Abeokuta, Nigeria, 44, 78

Aberdeen, Scotland, 69

A.B.F.M.S. See American Baptist Foreign Mission Society.

Abidjan, Ivory Coast, 312

Abolitionists, and *Amistad,* 142, 143

Abolition Bill, (in British Parliament), 21

Aborigines Department, (later the Department of Native Affairs), 24, 25, 101, 102, 129

Abwid, 214

Academy of Liège, 232

Accra, 36, 41, 44, 62, 63, 76
    All African Peoples' Conference held in, 187, 218, 243, 245
    Kpana Lewis deported to, 98

Acheulean (Chellean) Culture, 179

Ackeys. See Currency.

A.C.M.A.F., 310

Acts of the Apostles. See Holy Bible.

Adams, U.S. President John Quincy, 143

Adams, Henrietta (Mrs. Henrietta Fuduma), 65, 66

A.D.A.P.E.S. See Association des Anciens Elèves des Pères de Scheut.

Administrative Transport Company. See Société de Transport de l'Administration (S.T.A.).

Admiralty Court (of Royal Navy), 21

Adoula, Cyrille, 219, 225, 243, 312
    chosen prime minister, 273
    dismissed from office, 226
    1964 uprising against, 273

Advance, 138

Advisory Council on African Ethnology, World's Exposition, Chicago, 66

Aerts, Alfred, 213

"Afiwa," opera, 39

Afonso I. See Mvemba Nzinga.

Africa, Abdul Mohamed. See Wallace-Johnson, I.T.A.

Africa, decolonization of, 302

Africa and the World, 160

African Chamber of Commerce, Elisabethville, 309

African Civil Service Association, 118

African Interpreter and Advocate, The, 134

Africanization, 44, 145
    of Christianity, 229

African Methodist Episcopal (A.M.E.) Church, 65

African Morning Post, 159

African oak, 115

African Prince, The, 125, 126

African Sentinel, 160

African Standard, 160

African Steamship Company, 75

African Vanguard, 84

African Squadron. See Royal Navy, British.

African Times, The, 134

African Workers' Union, 159

Afro-Americans
    Thomas Peters, 131, 132
    Mr. and Mrs. Wilson, 135

A.G.E.L. See Association Générale des Etudiants de Lovanium.

Agricultural Society, founded in 1922, 36

Agriculture
    In Sierra Leone, 30, 31, 54, 89, 90, 91, 115, 146, 154
    In Zaire, 182, 183

Agriculture and Natural Resources, Ministry of, 54

Agricultural college. See Njala.

Agricultural Department, 90

AGRIFOR, 216

Ahinas, The, 295

Ahmadu, Alimamy, 134

A.I.A., 315, 326

A.I.C. See International Association of the Congo.

Air Congo, 255

Akar, John Joseph, 36, 37

Akar, Joseph Philip, 36

Ako. See Kosa.

Aku, 50, 96 168
    John Macaulay as king of, 105, 106
    Recaptives, 105, 106

Akwa Hago, 279

Akwa Kisenzele, 233

Akwa Mbangu, 223

Akwa Mishinga, 254, 259, 260, 261, 325

Akwa Mvubi, 233

Akwa Ndala, 231, 279

Akwa Samba, 233

Akwonkwo, 190

Alabama, 83, 138

Alabitaya, 168

A l'autre bout du monde, 303

"Alavear," See Alaver, Raphael.

Alaver, Raphael, 189, 190, 214

Albert Academy, Freetown, 36, 55, 72, 83, 111, 144

Albert I, 191, 228, 260

Albertville, (later Kalemie), 232, 320

Alfa, 111, 168

Algeria, government of, arrests Tshombe, 312

Algiers, 312

Alhaja, 168

Alhaji, 168

Alikali, (also Alkali), 116, 168
    dispute over, 116
    Fatima Birma Kamara as, 123
    Kunia Banna as, 123
    Moriba Kindo Bangura recognized as, 122
    of Port Loko, supports Suluku, 151

Ali Kongo, 127

Alimamy. See Almamy.

Alima River, 205, 290, 323

Alkali. See Alikali.

All-African People's Conference, Accra, (December 1958), 187, 218

Alldridge, T.J., 27, 67, 79, 86, 117
    at coronation of Gbatekaka, 117
    meets with Sherbro chiefs, 98
    signs treaty with Kai Londo, 88
    signs treaty with Mendegla, 117
    signs treaty with Nyagua, 128

Alleluya, 194, 195

Alley, the Rev. John Alfred, 109

Alliance des Bakongo. See Abako.

Alliance Française, 296

Allo, Congo, 302

All People's Congress (A.P.C.), 32, 33
    and 1962 elections, 49
    and 1967 elections, 33, 48, 49, 69, 101, 137, 152
    clashes with A.P.C., 33
    founded, (1960), 49
    government formed, (1968), 33, 49, 69
    wins 1973 elections, 33
    wins 1978 elections, 33, 152

Almamy, (also Alimamy), 73, 129, 168

Alpha Lalugba Kalei Samba. See Kai Samba I.

Alungu, 189

Alvare VI, 296

Amara Modu, 60

Ambriz, 229, 284

Ambuila, battle of, (1665), 313

Ambuila, province, 313

Ambundu, 297

Ambwela, 278

American Baptist Foreign Mission Society, (A.B.F.M.S.), 305, 306

American Civil War
    Amistad case and outbreak of, 143

American Indians, 181

American Methodist missionaries, 314

American Missionary Association, 65, 136, 137, 138, 143, 157, 158, 161, 172
    influence of, 143, 144

American Negro Academy, New York, 66

American War of Independence, 21, 56, 131, 173

American Wesleyan Methodist Church, 35

American Wesleyan Mission, 61

American Wesleyan Methodist School, Rogbane, 40

Americas, the discovery of the, 181

Amherst College, Massachusetts, 135

Amicale des Postiers Indigènes (A.P.I.C.), 243
Amicalism, 228
Amistad, 135, 138, 141, 142, 143, 144, 172
Amistad Committee, 135, 136, 142
Amukundo. See Lunda Amukundo.
Anany, Jerome, 226
A.N.C. See Armée Nationale Congolaise.
Anglican Church, 133, 153, 154, 157
Anglican Day School, 153
Angola, 182, 196, 202, 203, 209, 213, 215, 221, 227, 238, 249, 256, 269, 270, 283, 294, 300, 301, 325
    attempt to establish link with Mozambique, 240
    and the Bakongo, 321
    border with Zaire, 238
    and the Cokwe (Chokwe), 209, 221, 222, 270, 277, 283
    and the Kwilu River, 322
    mercenaries in, 311, 312
    merchants (pombeiros) from, 271, 284
    Mbanza Kongo in, 323
    Niungu people migrate from, 213
    relations of Angolan people with the Lunda, 286
    slave traders from, in gun trade, 212
    trade route from, 269
    trade route to Kasai, 270
Annapolis, Nova Scotia, 131
Annie Walsh Memorial School, 25
Annville, Pennsylvania, 55
Anamabu, Ghana, 76
Ansuma, 90
Anti-Slavery
    British treaty with Morea, 75
    and Sattan Lahai, 140
Anti-Slavery Conference, Paris, (1867), 133, 134
Anti-Slavery Society, (London), 99
    Sierra Leone branch established, 134
Anti-Syrian riots, (1919), 29
Antonians, The, 229
Antonio I. See Vita Nkanga.
Antwerp, Belgium, 217, 292, 301
Antwerp Exhibition, (1894), 292
Antwerp Geographical Society, 308
Antwerp Institut Universitaire des Territoires d'Outre Mer, 217
Antwerp Trading Company of the Congo. See Société Anversoise de Commerce au Congo.
Ant Yav, (plural of Mwant Yav), 278, 315, 324
A.P.C. See All People's Congress.
A.P.I.C. See Amicale des Postiers Indigènes.
Arab campaign, 315, 326
Arabic, 77, 78, 95, 129, 158, 168
"Arabs." See Swahili.
Armée Nationale Congolaise (A.N.C.), 198, 225, 307, 312, 319
    in Katanga, 225
        Evariste Kimba arrested by, 225
        and Kwilu rebellion, (1964), 312
        Lumumba's residence surrounded by, 246
        Second Division of, 198

Third Division of, 198
Thirteenth Infantry Battalion, 198
Tshombe arrested by, 225
Armée Populaire de Libèration (A.P.L.). See Simbas, The.
Arnot, Frederick, 270
Aro. See Sierra Leone Aro (Cooperative) Society.
Art, Kongolese, destroyed by Mvemba Nzinga, 281
Asambala, 295
Asan Yira. See Sori Wuleng.
Asante (Ashanti), 71
    British victory over (1874), 78
    Fante fear attack by, 78
    origin of Maroons, 21, 172
    and death of Sir Charles MacCarthy, 104
    war of 1823, 104
    war of 1863-64, 76
    war of 1874, (Sagrenti war), 71, 76, 78
Ashanti. See Asante.
"Ashantis of the Livingstone River," 291
Ashby, 135
Asia, decolonization in, 302
Asians, as traders in the eastern Congo, 231
Assanef, (Association d'Anciens Elèves des Frères des Ecoles Chrétiennes), 186, 315
Assessor's Ordinance, 41
Association des Anciens Elèves des Pères de Scheut, (Adapes), 217, 242
Association des Baluba du Katanga. See Balubakat.
Association du Personnel Indigène, (A.P.I.C.), 243
Association Générale des Etudiants de Lovanium, (A.G.E.L.), 250
Association Internationale Africaine. See A.I.A.
Association Internationale du Congo, (A.I.C.). See International Association of the Congo.
Association of African Middle Classes. See A.C.M.A.F.
Association of Colonial Writers and Artists, 302
Association of Former Students of the Brothers of the Christian Schools. See Assanef.
Association of Former Students of the Scheut Fathers, (Adapes). See Association des Anciens Elèves des Pères de Scheut.
Association of Universities, 302
Atene mission, 307
Athène of Kalina, 197
Athène of Nqiri Nqiri, 197
Atlanta, Georgia, 66. (See also Cotton States Exhibition).
"Atlanta Compromise," 66
Atlanta University, 144
Atlantic Ocean, 104, 179, 182, 184, 238, 327
Atomic Energy Commission. See United Nations Atomic Energy Commission.
Atrocities, in collection of rubber in the Congo Free State, 186
Augouard, Father, 290

Augustin, Capt. G., 314
Aurora, The, 40
Aushi, 214, 239, 268
    northern, 239
    southern, 239
Australia, W. Rainy emigrates to, 134
"Authenticity." See "Return to Authenticity."
Auto-da-fés, (burning of heretic), 267
Avenir Colonial Belge, 228
Avitaminosis, 162
Awoonor Renner, Bankole, 159
Awujoh, 50, 168
Azande. See Zande.
Ba-, prefix 316
Baba, 81
Baboma. See Boma, people.
Baboma North, 267
"Back to Africa" movement
    Nova Scotia's, 56, 57
Badagry, Nigeria, 105
Badjoko, Jean, 191
Badjoko, Joseph, 190, 191
Badjoko, Victor, 191
Bafodaya. See Bafodea.
Ba Foday Mansaray, 37, 38, 152
Bafodea, (Bafodaya), 37, 152
Bafwa-Sende, 193
Baga, 17, 92, 168
Bagbema, 26, 132
Bagi, 54
Bagru, 157, 168
    British expedition to, 23, 24
    invaded by Gbanya's mercenaries, 71
Bagru River, 157, 161
Bagruwa, 168
Bahr-al-Ghazal, 265
Bai, 168
Bai Banta, 119
Bai Bureh. See Bureh, Bai.
Bai Farima. See Bai Farma.
Bai Farima Tass, 84
Bai Farma, (Bai Farima), 18, 101, 140, 141, 155, 168, 172, 173
Bai Foki, 119, 122
Baiima, 101
Bai Inga, 73
Bai Kamara, 119
Bai Kompa, 47, 148, 168
Bai Sheka Bundu, 163, 164
Bai Sherbro, 22, 141, 168
    Lahai Young recognized as, 141
Bakalebwe, 221
Bakandi, 298
Bakisi, 262, 263, 264
    1960 plebiscite in, 263
Bakongo. See Kongo.
Bakongo Alliance. See Abako.
Bakoshi, 221
Bakuba. See Kuba.
Bakutu, 290
Bakwanga. See Mbuji-Mayi.
Bala, 221, 240
Balakata, 191
Balansama Mara, 38
Balearic Islands, 312
Balima, railway reaches, (1906), 29

Ballanta-Taylor, Nicholas Julius George, 38, 39
Ballot, Maximilien, 203, 258, 260
Balobo. See Lobo.
Balobo, sector, 253
Baloi, 192, 254, 275, 317
Baltimore, Maryland, 158
Baluba. See Luba.
Balubakat, (Association des Baluba du Katanga), 224, 225, 226, 310
Bamaku, 287
Bamba, Emmanuel, 226
Bambafara of Nieni, 39
    seeks British protection from the Sofa, 27
Bambara, 38, 127
Baminia, 191
Bamwe. See Mwe.
Bamwe sector, 266
Banabanga clan, 262, 264
Banana, 307, 323, 327
Banana Islands, 17, 169
Bananas, 183, 199, 236, 281
Banda Karifa, 39
Bandajuma, 121, 122
    district commissioner seizes cattle, 121
    as a division of the Protectorate (1896), 28
    and Hut Tax War, 122
    Momo Kai Kai as chief of, 121, 122
    taxation in, 121
Bandasuma, 107
    attacked by Ndawa, 107, 124
    treaty signed at, (1889), 107, 117
Bando Bodjoko, 191
Bandundu, (formerly Banningville), 260, 316
Bandundu Region, (formerly Léopoldville Province), 179, 189, 261, 316, 320, 325
Bangala. See Ngala.
Bangala district, 200, 202
Bangala, (place). 200. See also Bangala Station, Nouvelle-Anvers, and Makanza.
Bangalapumba, 233
Bangala River, 191
Bangala Station
    Early days of, 291, 292
    See also Nouvelle-Anvers, Makanza.
Bangele, 192, 200, 317
Bangi, 258. See also Bobangi.
Bangoma clan, 264
Bangura clan, 119
Bangura, John Amadu, 40
    attempts coup, 33
    executed, 33
    heads army, 33
    returns Sierra Leone to civilian rule, 33
Bangweolu. See Lake Bangweolu.
Banjul. See Bathurst.
Bank of Sierra Leone, 63
Bankole-Bright, Herbert Christian, 40, 41, 42, 43, 84, 85
Banner Church, 146
Banning, Emile, 308
Banningville. See Bandundu.
Bansongo. See Likoka.
Banta, language, 126

Banta, state, 111, 126, 165, 168, 169
Banta Gbangbatoke, 169. See also Banta.
Banta Mokele, 93, 94, 169. See also Banta.
Bantote, 289, 290, 316
Bantu, 179, 180, 182, 183, 316, 325
"Banta Africa," 210
Bantu languages, 317, 321, 322
Banyampara, 316, 325
Bapende. See Pende.
Baptist, free-will, (Church of God), 116
Baptist Missionary Society (B.M.S.), 197 206, 227, 252, 256, 266, 306
Baptists, 197
Barabara, 303
Barawa, 38, 113, 144, 168, 169
Barcelona, Spain, 311
Barlatt, C.J.G., 190
Barlatt, Samuel Josiah Sigismund, 42, 43
Barmoi, 140, 141
Baron Liebrechts, M.S., (later M.S. Ebeya), 199
Barreira, Balthazar, Father, 19
Barri district, 95, 117
Barrie Potoru, 158
Barston scholarship, 48
Baru, 157
Barungu, 238
Basanga, 241
Ba Shia, 99
Bashilange, 249
Basile, chiefdom, 236, 237
Basoko, 190, 200
Basongo, 250
Bassi Conteh, Pa, 134
Bas-Zaire Region, 179, 184, 189, 316, 317, 323
Bateke. See Tio.
Batetela. See Tetela.
Batetela revolts, 316. See also Tetela.
Bath, England, 145, 146
Bathurst, (later Banjul), 43, 75
    foundation of, 104
Bathurst, village, (Sierra Leone), 21
    amalgamated with village of Léopold, 21
Bathurst, Lord Henry, 104
Batsikama, R., 268
Batubenge, 294
Baudouin I, 218, 232, 243, 245, 303, 311
    1955 visit to the Congo, 232, 243
    1959 statement on the Congo's future, 244
Baudouinville, (Moba), 232, 233
Bauya, 100, 149, 165
    branch line from, built (1915), 29
Bayaka. See Yaka.
Bayeke. See Yeke.
Bayembi, 212, 213
Bayon, 165
Bayo Seri, 139
Bayo Yembe, 61
Bazombo, 287, 288
Beads, 293
Beatriz, Dona. See Kimpa Vita.
Beaufort, A. de, 248
Beernaert, Belgian prime minister, 308
Bee's wax, 184, 209

Beethoven, 232
Beh Sherbro. See Bai Sherbro.
Baei, 275
Beidhwai, 68
Beimba I, 166
Beka, 199
Bekalebwe, 240, 241
Belande, 241
Belgian Army, 301
Belgian Congo, The, 185, 186, 187, 193, 199, 301, 317, 318, 319
    King Baudouin's visit to, 232, 243
    Boma as capital of, 317
    governor-general of, 301, 302
    mission work in, 305, 306
    nationalist movement in, 302
    non-political organizations, 217
    religious sects in, 193, 194
    Service de Finances of, 216
    Ten-Year Development Plan, 302
    in World War II, 302
Belgian Minister for the Colonies, 186
Belgian Minister of African Affairs, 311
Belgian Parliament
    annexes the Congo, 185, 317, 318
    and the Congo Railway Company, 308, 309
    and the Pende revolt, 260
Belgians, 133, 162, 184
    found Bobangi chiefdom, 192
    creation of artificial chiefdoms by, 263
    send troops to the Congo, (1960), 245
    intervention of troops in the Congo, (1960), 245
    departure from the Congo, 237
    and Edjumbu, 200
    and Gandanda Gibanda, 203
    and steps to Congolese independence, 218, 244, 245
    relations with Kimbamba, 226, 227
    relations with Lumpungu, 241, 242
    relations with Patrice Lumumba, 219, 244, 245, 246
    relations with Mopoie Bangezegino, 265
    and Mungembe, 276, 277
    regain control after 1931 Pende revolt, 213
    oppose certain religious sects, 237
    rivalry with other colonial powers, 265
Belgian Society of Engineers and Industrialists, 308
Belgium, 133, 162, 185, 301, 302, 308
    African leaders flown to, (1959), 218
    Badjoko visits, 191
    Boike visits, 292
    aid for the Congo, 302
    Congolese visit, (1958), 187
    E.A. Disengomoka visits, 197
    government of, in exile, 302
    and Congolese independence, 243, 244
    J. Kapend visits, 216

(Belgium-Continued)
    Kasavubu and Bolikango sent to, 244
    aids secessionist Katanga, 311
    and Kimbanguism, 228
    J. Kiwele visits, 233
    P. Lumumba visits, 243
    P. Lumumba flown to, 244
    Ngonso sent to, 295
    Nkoy Kashama visits, 220
    backing for Congo railway from, 308
    Tshombe visits, 310
Belgo-Congolese cultural group, 243
Belle, (formerly Gbele), chiefdom, 86
Belle, people, 88
Bemba, 194, 239, 317
Bemeki Kabongo, 241
Bena Budia, 241
Bena Kalambayi, 241
Bena Kashyye, 270
Bena Kibeshi, 241
Bena Kizubu, 241
Bena Lukashiyi, 241
Bena Lulua, 271, 294
Bena Mabala, 240
Bena-Mbeba groups, 239
Bena Milembwe, 241
Bena Mitumba, 269
Bena Tshofwe, 241
Bence Island, (now Bunce Island), 71, 72
Bendajuma, 120
Bendeh, 87
Bendu, 55, 71, 75
Benduma, 88
Beneki Babenga, 241
Bengal Native Infantry, 52
Bengaro, 265
Beni, battle of, 300
Benin, Republic of. See Dahomey.
Benka-Coker, Ambrose, 43
Benka-Coker, Sir Salako Ambrosius, 43
Benna Soso, 92, 93
Bentley, Mrs. W.H., 257
Bentley, William H., 256
Benya of Blama, 87, 124
Beoku-Betts, Ernest Samuel, 40, 43, 44, 45
Bereira, 59
Bereira River, 26
Berghe-Sainte-Marie Station, 290
Berlin Conference (1884-85), 133, 184, 288, 318
Berlin West African Conference. See Berlin
    Conference (1884-85).
Bethanie, 234
Bethlehem, at San Salvador, 229
Betts, C.W., 43
"Beulah Hills," 35
Bia, 222
Bibete, 281
Bible. See Holy Bible.
Bicycles. See Nsu bicycles.
Bifuku, 317, 318
Bight of Benin, 77, 116
Bigomokaro Karhana, 252
Bihé, 222, 269
Bikiunga, 263
Bilali, of Tonko Limba, 45, 46, 93, 97, 140
    and conflict with Sattan Lahai, 24

Bili River, 233
Billaud, Jean, 64
Billeh. See Gbile.
Bilolo, 200
Bilsen, A.J. van, 186, 217
Binkolo, 40
Binti, 37
Bintumane, 17
Birhenjira, 252
Biriwa. See Biriwa Limba.
Biriwa Limba, 19, 22, 23, 60, 144, 169, 170,
    171, 172
    Fomgboe seeks help of, 69
    struggle with the Koranko of Nieni, 39
    conquered by Samori's Sofa, 26, 151
    ruled by Almamy Suluku, 150, 151
Birkenhead, England, 43
Birmingham, England, 58, 162
Bisa, 215, 239
Bishop, Adda, 40
Bishop, the Hon. Theopilus Colenso, 40
Bismarck, Otto von, 184
    at Berlin Conference (1884-85), 184
Biwaku, 276
Black Africa, 210
Black Americans
    music, 38
"Black Englishmen," 146
Blacksmiths, traveling, 23
Black Pioneers, 131
"Black Prince." See Nemgbana, J.F.
Black water fever, 62
Blakeney, Capt. J.E.C., 86, 128
Blama, 87
Blanco, Pedro, 108
Blouin, 272
Blyden, Edward, 78, 103, 145, 146
    and Dress Reform Society, 65
    visits Falaba (1872), 24
    visits Gbile, 68
    meets with J.A.B. Horton, 76
    founds *The Negro*, 77
    contributes to *Sierra Leone Weekly
    News*, 115
    visits Timbo (1873), 24
"Blue Helmets." See United Nations Emer-
    gency Force, (U.N.E.F.).
B.M.S. See Baptist Missionary Society.
Bo, 87, 91, 150. See also Bo district.
    government school, secondary school,
    40, 69, 89, 90
    school for sons of chiefs at, 29, 129,
    164
    Sierra Leone Observer published in,
    112
    surgery and clinic opened at, 112
Boakei Gomma, 117
Boakei Kai Samba, 89
Boakei Kekura, 81
Boakei Kpundeh, 90
Boakei Mina, 68
Bobandana, 210
Bobangi, chiefdom, 192, 200, 275
    founded (1906), 192, 317
Bobangi, people, 184, 191, 192, 200, 201,
    204, 205, 206, 274, 275, 282, 286, 287,
    288, 317, 325

    language, 206, 266
    merchants, 207, 251, 286, 288, 290
Bobeka, 235, 290, 291
Bobena, 274
Bobitu, 191
Bobole, 275
Bobolo (later Buburu), 234, 235
Bodenan, 312
Bo district, 124, 126, 127
    diamond mining in, 31
    and 1978 elections, 33
Bodjimba, 191
Bodjinga, 253, 298
Bodjinga division, 253
Bodjoko. See Badjoko.
Bodson, O.P., 270
Bogandu, 324
Bogboabu, 110
Bogbanga, 303
Boike, 190, 291, 292
"Boima," opera, 39
Boima Kahunla, 89
Bokala, 199, 200, 253
Bokambo, chiefdom, 298
Bokari, Almamy Kandeh, 46, 50, 141
    ruler of Morea, 46
Bokari, Alimamy, of Timbo, 59
Bokari Bombolai, ("William Rowe Bokari
    Bombolai"), 47
Bokari, Marlay. See Marlay Bokari.
Bokeka, 281
Bokembe, 281
Bokene, 253
Bokoko, 289
Bokole, 324
Bokombe, 281
Bokondo, 235, 299
Bokongo, 275, 317
Bokwala, 276
Bokwango, 200, 275
Bokwete, 275
Bokweye, 282
Bolanga, 299
Bolangbwa. See Bolangwa.
Bolangwa (or Bolangbwa), 191, 192, 200, 275
Bolebo. See Nkungu.
Bolero. See Dances, modern, in the Congo.
Bokongo, 192, 200
Bolebo, 299
Bolenge, 303
Bolia, 181, 317, 324
Bolikango, Jean, 217, 244
Bolinga, 274
Bolobo, 191, 192, 204, 266, 305
    Protestant mission at, 274
Boloki, 274, 290
Bolongo, 276
Boltamba, 23, 113
Bolukwansamba, 207
Boma (Baboma), people, 266, 267, 289
    history and oral traditions, 267
Boma, river port, 185, 216, 219, 238, 247, 288
    294, 317, 321
    capital of Congo Free State moved to,
    (1886), 185
    Nzamba exiled to, 276
Boma, thorn enclosure, 317

Bomalu, 85
Bomana, chiefdom, 253, 274, 275, 298, 303
Bomana, town, 277, 303, 304
Boma North, 289
Bomans, J.B., 261, 279
Bombali district, 71, 123, 134, 149, 150
Bombali Temne country
    Rassin mediates in, 134
Bomboh, Adama, 134
Bomboko, Justin, 225, 311
    and P. Mulele, 273
Bombo Lahai, of Tonko Limba, 45, 49, 69,
    93, 169
Bombolai Yusufu. See Yusufu, Bombo
    Lahai.
Bomboma, 274, 303
Bomejuri, 266, 267
Bomoko, 274
Bomolandi River, 285, 323
Bomole, 265, 266
Bomongo, 235, 274, 299
Bomou River, 233, 265, 327
Bompeh. See Bumpe.
Bondu, (also Bundu, or Sande), 94, 127,
    169, 173
    Soma (Yoko) enters, 127
Bondo Foyor, 87
Bondoko, 253
Bondongo, 281, 282
Bonebrake Theological Seminary, Dayton,
    Ohio, 55
Bongobong, 152
Bongombe, 281
Bongwande Lokekia, 200
Bonko, 69
Bonkombi, 274
Bonkula, 253
Bonney (Maaju Toray), 69
Bonny, Nigeria, 78
Bonsambi, 235
Bonsambo, 303
Bonsembe, 291
Bonsobo, 274
Bonthe, 55, 71, 75, 79, 96, 111, 160, 161,
    168, 169
    Governor Cardew visits, 52
    Evangelical United Brethren Church
      in, 111
    S.B.A. MacFor builds warehouses at,
      106
    Tongo Players brought to, 99
    trade through port of, 24
Bonthe Amalgamated Workers' Union, 160
Bonthe district, 111
Bonyange, 265, 276
Bonyoyi, 281
Bonzembo, 281
Booth, James, 74, 82
Bora, 54. See also Yogbo.
Borbowa, 158
Borough Road College, London, 114
Bosesera, 276, 277, 298
Bosilela, 276, 298
Bosira, 235
Bosoko, 281
Boston, Massachusetts, 142
Boston Conservatory, 38

Boston, Henry Josiah Lightfoot, 44, 48
Boston, Lauretta, 48
Boston, the Rev. H.H., 48
Botema, 88
Botshongo, 274
Boumedienne, Houari, 312
Bouré, 23
    visited by Winwood Reade, 24
Bowami, 193
Bowden, W.D., 80
Boya, Lake. See Lake Boya.
Boyeka, 275
Boyela, 324
Boyombo, 274
Boy Scouts, 43
Brabant, 302
Brabanta (now Mapongi), 248, 250
Bracongo brewery, 243
Bradshaw, Dr. Robert, 106, 133
Brass wire, Bobangi trade in, 205
Brazil, 64
Brazzaville, 187, 323
    C. de Gaulle visits, 187, 243
    Gbenye founds C.N.L. in, 312
    Katanga delegation visits, 311
    Pierre Mulele in, 273, 287
    Tshombe invited to, 311
Bressilac, Melchior de Marion, 48, 49
Brest, France, 48
Brima, 49, 50, 97
Brima Kondito, 68
Brima Konkori Sankoh, Alimamy, 118, 119
    122, 123
Brima Sanda of Sando Loko, 69, 93
Brisebois, Dieudonné, 304
Britain and the British
    and American Loyalists, 131
    and American War of Independence,
      131
    and Bokari Bombolai, 47
    recognize Bokari as ruler of Morea, 46
    and 1882 boundary convention with
      France, 27
    Congo railway, participation in fin-
      ancing of, 308
    Congo rubber collection, abuses,
      pressure to correct exerted by, 202
    agreement of 1895 with France, 27
    clash with French by mistake, 114,
      130, 132
    rivalry with France in West Africa, 26,
      46, 75, 95, 97, 141
    rivalry with France in northern Sierra
      Leone, 26, 27, 51, 92, 93, 141
    cooperation with France in Guinea,
      (1931), 74
    freed slaves, sponsors return to Africa
      of, 56
    Hut Tax uprising of 1898, suppression
      of by, 28
    relations with Isa of Kaliere, 27
    Islands of Los obtained by, 59
    oppose Karimu, 97
    support Konko Gbaku, 97
    and Maroons, 172
    and Momo Ja, 121
    and Momo Kai Kai, 121, 122

    Morea, gunboat sent to by, (1865-66),
      46
    and Nova Scotians, 173
    relations with Nyagua, 127, 128
    protection of British subjects in Sierra
      Leone, 24
    rivalry with other colonial powers, 265
    role in adjudicating Sierra Leone
      disputes, 24
    relations with Samori, 132
    and Sara Bayo, 140
    and Sattan Lahai, 140
    and the Sherbro, 54, 55, 56
    and Sierra Leone, 17, 20, 21, 24, 33,
      169, 170, 173
    founds Sierra Leone colony, 20, 173
    Sierra Leone settlement taken over by,
      (1808), 21, 169, 170
    and Charles Smart, 148
    and the Sofa, 27, 114, 130, 132
    H.M. Stanley tries to interest British
      in the Congo, 184
    and Suluku, 151
    and Suman, 152
    trading forts in Sierra Leone, built by,
      20
    attack Tambi, (1892), 51
    and treaties with African rulers, 27
    local treaties abandoned by, 27
    treaty, standard British, 27
    treaty with Futa Jallon, (1873), 24
    treaty with Kaloun Baga, 46
    treaty with Morea, 24
    treaty with Nemgbana, 124
    treaty with Port Loko, 24, 119
    treaty with Sherbro, 24
    treaty with Suman, 152
    and proposed British withdrawal from
      West Africa, 77, 78
    conflict with the Yoni, 149
    and Yoni expedition, (1886-87), 166
British Army Medical Service, 76, 77
British Council, 36
British Empire Exhibition, (1924), 63
British French Boundary Commission, (on
    the Sierra Leone-Guinea border), 93
British Guiana, 65
British Koya, 116
British Military Academy, Sandhurst. See
    Sandhurst.
British Secretary of State for the Colonies,
    41, 44, 62, 64, 67, 71, 104, 106, 130, 131,
    145
"British" Sherbro, 23
British Treasury, 56
British War Office, 70, 76, 77, 130
Britomert, H.M.S., 60
Brookfields, 50, 107
Bruges, 162
Brussels, Belgium, 62, 187, 191, 218, 219,
    224, 235, 243, 244, 272, 308, 309, 312
    Tshombe invited to, 310
    Tshombe visits royal palace in, 311
    Tshombe buried in, 312
Brussels Geographical Conference, 308, 315
Brussels Geographical Society, 308

Brussels International Exposition, (1958), 187, 235
Bubu, 151
Buburu, 235. See also Bobolo.
Bubuya, 73
Budge, William, visits Kpaa Mende, (1879), 24
Budi, 221
Budja, 201, 202, 317
Budjula, 199, 200
Buedu, 90, 91
Buganda, 181
Buisseret, Auguste, 186
Bukalenge Bua Nsala, 317
Bukama, 216, 224
Bukasa, Leon, 192, 193
Bukavu, 236, 237, 252, 262, 263, 264, 317
Bula, 229
Bula Matari, ("State"; also "Mbula Matari"), 194, 317
Bulanda, 211, 259, 297
Bulega, 318
Bull, Christiana, 115
Bullen, Capt. Charles, 155
Bullom, people, 17, 47, 155, 169, 171, 173. Also see Sherbro (southern Bullom). ivory carving among, 18
Bullom, country, 116, 119
Bullom Shore, the, 58, 59, 155
    British treaty with chiefs of, (1860), 116
Bulongo, 318
Bulopwe, 182, 211, 212, 318
Bumban, 144, 150, 151
    as capital of Biriwa Limba, 39, 140
Bumpe, (also Bumpeh), 17, 22, 54, 55, 148, 149, 168, 169
    British obtain rights in, 55
    chiefs sign treaties with British, 121
    conquered by Gbenjei, 165
    quarrels with Tikonko, 107
Bumpe River, 24, 71, 100, 126, 149
Bum River, 24, 107, 120, 121, 135
Bunce Islands, Sierra Leone, 17, 71, 115
Bundasuma, 124
Bundu. See Bondo.
Bundu, clan, 47
Bundu, Suleiman, 123
Bunduka, 123, 134, 164
    traditions of the, 164
Bungie, Alimamy, 50
Bungu, 297
Bunkeya, 220, 269, 270
Bunkula, 253
Bunumbu, 101
Burasira, 210
Bureh, Bai, 50, 51, 52
    association with Bokari Bombolai, 47
    fights for Bokari, 46
    arrested by the British, 28
    exiled to the Gold Coast, 28, 53, 128
    and the Hut Tax War (1898), 28, 79, 128, 135, 164
    joins coalition against Karimu, 69, 93, 97
Burema Yarri, 123
Burgomasters, election of, 218

Burnotte, 258, 260
Burundi, 181, 210, 301, 302
Bushangabuye, 252
Bushi, 252, 318, 326
Bushiri, Lungundu, 193, 194
Bushoong, 262, 304, 305, 318
Busimba Mikararagbe, Monsignor, 195, 196
Businga, 233
Busira River, 290
Buta, 222
Buylaert (Longo-Longo), 215
Bwami, semi-secret association, 182, 183, 237, 264, 318
    outlawed by Belgians, 237
Bwanda, 275
Bwele River, 231
Bwele-Lufuku sector, 230
Bwelo Milondo River, 279
Byaterana, 252
Cabbalism, 35, 146
Cabinda, 324
Cairo, Egypt, 272, 273, 312
Calabar, 153
    and recaptives, 105
Callewaert, 251
Cambier, Capt. E., 308
Cambier, Father, 212
Cambridge, England, 163
Cameroons, the, (Cameroun), 63, 210, 301
    World War I campaign in, 72, 159
Cameroun. See Cameroons, the.
Campacala. See Sampaio, Manuel Gomes.
Campbell, Henry Dundas, 59
    helps end Temne-Loko war, 59
Camp Hardy, 199, 246. Later Camp Lt. Colonel Ebeya (q.v.).
    P. Lumumba detained in, 246
Camp Lt. Colonel Ebeya, 199. Formerly Camp Hardy, (q.v.).
Camp Massart, 311
Canada, 104, 135, 172, 173
Cannibalism, allegations of, 89, 99, 100, 161, 203
Canoes
    used by Bobangi in trading, 205
    dug-out, 281
Cao, Diogo, 267, 280
Cape Coast, Ghana, 62, 63, 74, 76
Cape Mount, Liberia, 17, 18, 110
Cape Sierra Leone, 155, 171
"Capital of Copper." See Elisabethville.
Caps, L. 231, 254
Capuchin missionaries, 230, 296
Caravan routes, 184
Cardew, Sir Frederick, 51, 52, 53, 54, 79, 121
    and Bai Bureh, 51, 52
    and Bokari Bombolai, 47
    and R.C.B. Caulker, 55
    supported by Colonial Office, 53
    relations with F. Fawunda of Mano, 67, 68
    disciplines Frontier Force, 27
    tours of hinterland (1894, 1895), 28, 130
    and house tax, 28, 70
    agrees to arrest of Kabba Sei, 86
    visited by Kpana Lewis, 98

    relations with Krios, 53
    relations with Sir Samuel Lewis, 103, 104
    meets J. Mannah-Kpaka, 110
    and Momo Ja, 121
    and Momo Kai Kai, 121
    and Parkes, 130
    seeks establishment of Protectorate, 28
    proposes railway, 29
    visits Shenge, 56
    critical of Sierra Leone Weekly News, 115
Carr, Capt. C.E., 110, 121
Carven, J., 81
Casely Hayford, J.E. See Hayford, J.E. Casely.
Cassange, 240
Cassava, 36. See also Manioc.
CAST. See Consolidated African Selection Trust.
Cataract Railway, 308
Cataracts. See Zaire (Congo) River.
Cathedral Boys Primary School, Freetown, 48, 83
Catholic Church, 186
    probable first African bishop of the, 204
    school in Freetown, 62
    in the Kongo, under Portuguese protection, 296
    honors the Abbe Lankwan's memory, 234
    disagreement with liberals, 186
    rivalry with Protestants in the Congo, 306
    and trade union movement, 224
Catholicism, Roman, 48, 50, 104
Catholic, missions, 228, 231
    of Italian Capuchin Friars, 296
    P. Lumumba's education at, 242
    at Muhaku, 223
Catholics. See Christians, Catholic.
Catholic Writers Association, 302
Cattle, 23, 119, 235
Caulfield, Col. J.E., 98
Caulker family, 20, 54, 55, 56
    family feuds of the, 54, 55
    and Governor Rowe, 55
    and Turner Treaty (1825), 55
Caulker, Francis, 56
Caulker, George Augustus, 55
Caulker, George Stephen II, 54, 55
    grants British customs rights in Shenge, 55
    death of, (1881), 56
    dispute with his cousin John, 71
Caulker, James Canray Ba, 55
Caulker, John, 54, 71
    hanged, 55, 71
Caulker, Richard Canray Ba, 54, 55
    grants British customs rights in Bompeh, 55
Caulker, Solomon Brooks, 55, 56
Caulker, Theophilus, 54
Caulker, Thomas Kugba, 55, 56

Caulker, Thomas Neale, 55, 56
 murdered by his family, 28, 56
Caulker, William T.G., 55, 56, 103
C.C.F.C. See Compagnie du Chemin de Fer du Congo.
C.E.H.C. See Study Committee for the Upper Congo.
Centenary Tabernacle School, 159
Central Africa, 196
Central African Empire, 265
Central African Federation, 310
Central School and Union College, Burumbu, 101
Centre d'Etudes des Problèmes Economiques et Sociaux, 233
Centre-Extra-Coutumier. See Elisabethville. See Thysville.
Centre Pédagogique Ntu, 210
Cercle des Evolués, 243
C.F.L. See Chemins de Fer du Congo-Supérieur aux Grands Lacs Africains.
Chalmers, Sir David, 53
 and royal commission, 130
Chatlin, Louis, 190
Chamber of Commerce. See Sierra Leone Chamber of Commerce.
Chamberlain, Joseph, 53
Chambezi River, 239
Chambre de Commerce Indigène, 232
Charles II guinea. See Currency.
Charles Street, Freetown, 114
Charly, Pa, 59
Chatlin, 265
Chawala Makumba. See Myelemyele.
Chellian culture. See Acheulian culture.
Chemins de Fer du Congo-Supérieur aux Grands Lacs Africains (C.F.L.), 232
Chernor Abass, 123
Chester, England, 101
 Officers' Training School at, 101
Chibamb Kasokot, 238
Chibang Chelek Muswa Musapu, (Mai, or Mwana-Wut), 238. See also Chibang Kanyimbu.
Chibang Kanyimbu, previously Chibang Chelek, 240
Chibind Yirung, 196, 197, 278, 282, 283, 301, 324
Chicago, 65, 138
Chicago Theological Seminary, 138
Chicago University. See University of Chicago.
Chiefdoms
 pre-colonial states replaced by, 29
 introduction of new Native Administration, (1937), 31
 rotating chiefship at Port Loko, 123
 reorganization of, in Sierra Leone, 29
 reorganization of after World War I, in Zaire, 186
Chiefs
 relations with Sierra Leone Colony, 101
 gradual exclusion of, from government, proposed, 78
 represented in Sierra Leone House of Representatives, 32

and collection of house tax, 53
King's medal for, 89
represented on Sierra Leone Legislative Council, 31, 73
relations of Dr. M.A.S. Margai with, 111, 112
numbers of, in Sierra Leone, 29
participation in politics by, 89
anti-chief riots, (1955), 32
school for sons of, at Bo, 29
status of, 44
treaty relations of, with the British, 53
appointment of Yalunka chiefs, 61
Chige, battle of, (1892), 241
Chigud, 196, 300, 301
Chikomb, 286
Child Welfare Clinics, 162
China, 52
 support from, for 1964 Kwilu uprising, 273
 Pierre Mulele's visit to, 208, 234, 273
Chinyama, 239
Chinyat Munona, 268
Chipep (Kipepa), 239
Chisheng, 239
Chishinga, 215, 239
Chitend, 212, 238
Chitentam, 277, 279, 318
Chiyam, 196, 300, 301
Chot Kabamb, 215
Christ Church, Freetown, 106, 147
Christianity, 128, 181, 256
 Africanization of, 229
 and the African continent, 104
 J.A.B. Horton's advocacy of, 78
 and Islam, 116, 122
 and the kingdom of Kongo, 257, 258, 267, 268, 298
 and the Loko, 148
 Mabera Benoit converted to, 248
 Mani Kongo converted to, 181, 257, 280
 John Mankah converted to, 109
 promoted by Mvemba Nzinga, 181, 280
 at Port Loko, 119
 Prince Nemgbana educated as a Christian, 125, 126
 Nzinga Nkuwu abandons, 258
 Portuguese attempt to introduce to Sierra Leone, 19
 W. Raymond and, 135, 136, 137
 Sierra Leone Recaptives adopt, 21
 and Sengbe Pieh, (Joseph Cinque), 143
 and Charles Smart, 148
 and Sori Kessebeh, 149
 and the John Thomas family, 153
Christians, 253. See also Christians, Catholic; Christians, Protestant.
Christians, Catholic, 189, 229, 303
 and the Kongo kingdom, 267, 268
 Mani Kongo remains with, 296
 hostile to Protestants in the Congo, 306
 tensions with Protestants in Bobolo, 235

See also Kajinga Balihuta; Lankwan, A.; Semopa Bavon.
Christians, Protestant, 189, 197, 228, 229, 256, 257, 303, 305, 306
 mission at Bolobo, 274
 tensions and Catholics in Bobolo, 235
 Ibaka and, 206
 Mantanta Dundulu, first African Protestant in the Congo, 256, 257
 mission conferences, 306
Christ, Jesus, 189
Chromite, 30
Chungu, 215, 238
Church Missionary Society (C.M.S.), 76
 Opens Annie Walsh Memorial School, 25
 and policy of "decolonization," 64
 establishes Fourah Bay College, (1827), 25
 and Fourah Bay College, 84
 opens Grammar School, (1848), 25
 Grammar School, 35, 38, 42, 43, 48, 54, 62, 63, 76, 82, 83, 103, 110, 115, 128, 129, 145, 146, 147, 149, 156, 170
 Sir Charles MacCarthy obtains cooperation of, 104
 and John Mankah, 109
 Native Pastorate Church of, 43, 64, 65, 133, 153
 educates Charles Smart, 148
Church of Christ in Zaire, 306
Church of God,
 free-will Baptist Church, 116
 mission at Senehun, 71
Church of Jesus Christ on Earth by the Prophet Simon Kimbangu, 227, 228
 lifting of prohibition against, 228
Church of the Holy Spirit (Mpeve) of Esieme, 189, 190
Church Missionary Gleaner, 109
Cibwid, 279
Cifuku, 318
Cilol, 318
Cilundu, 212, 213
Cinene, 221
Cingue. See Sengbe Pieh.
Cinque, Joseph. See Sengbe Pieh.
Cinquez. See Sengbe Pieh.
Cinyat Mfemb, 214, 278, 279, 288, 289
 death of, 289
Clark Theological School, Shenge, 161
Clarkson, Lt. John, 56, 57
 appointed as governor, 21, 131
Clarkson's Prayer, 57
Clarkson, Thomas, 56
Cloth
 from Kono, 23
 from Sankaran, 23
 trade in, 205, 216
 weaving, 19
C.M.S. See Church Missionary Society.
C.N. Ki. See Comité National Kivu.
C.N.L. See National Council of Liberation.
Coby, Jack. See Kinia Banna.
Cocoa, 30, 36, 74
Coconuts, 249
Cod liver oil, 162

Coffee, 30
  plantations, 190
Coker, Sgt., 157
Cokwe, (Chokwe), 184, 196, 203, 209, 212, 215, 221, 271, 277, 283, 294, 300, 301, 310
  hostilities with Congo Free State, 271, 277
  join the Katanga Cartel, 310
  amongst the Lunda, 209, 277
  dominate the Lunda, 215, 277, 301
  Nawej a Ditend and, 286
  Ngongo Leteta and, 294
  as suppliers of rifles, 212, 221, 222, 270
Cole, C.E.O., 33
Cole, Julius Foday. See Gulama, Julius.
Collaert, J., 248
Collège des Commissaires, 219, 246
Collège Lankwan, 234
Collège Notre Dame, Dungu, 255
Collège Notre Dame of Idiofa, 234
College of Commissioners. See Collège des Commissaires.
Collège Saint Jean Beerkmans, 301
Collège Saint Michel, Brussels, 191
Collège Saint-Pierre, Ipamu, 234
Collignon, 258
Colonial Affairs secretariat. See Congo Free State.
Colonial Congress, 302
  Standing Committee of, 302
Colonial Defense Regulations, 160
Colonial Development and Welfare Acts, (1940-45), 32
Colonial Hospital, Freetown, 62
Colonial Minister, Belgian. See Hemelrijck, van.
Colonial Office, British, 53, 67, 102, 103, 106, 118, 133, 152
  advised against appointment of Africans to senior medical posts, 62
  and labor policies in chiefdoms, 72
  fails to ratify Turner treaty (1825), 55
Colonial Secretary (in Freetown administration), 116
Colonial Secretary, British
  and interior of Sierra Leone, 24
  and operation of 1863 constitution, 25
  supports Sierra Leone railway construction, 53
Colony, The. See Sierra Leone Colony.
Columbia University, New York City, 251
Comber, T., 289, 290
Combey manuscript, 91
Comité d'Etudes du Haut Congo. See Study Committee for the Upper Congo (C.E.H.C.).
Comité National de Kivu (C.N.Ki.), 193, 195
Comité Spécial du Katanga, (C.S.K.), 314
Commission for Educational Reform, Zaire, 210
Communism
  Belgians regard P. Lumumba as a communist, 245
  P. Mulele visits communist countries, 273

Compagnie Africaine Cooreman, 208
Compagnie de Chemin de Fer du Bas-Congo au Katanga, (B.C.K.), 224
Compagnie de Chemin de Fer du Congo, 308, 309
Compagnie du Kasai, 203, 213, 215, 258, 271
Compagnie du Sénégal, 153
Compagnie Française de l'Afrique Occidentale (C.F.A .O.), 129, 153
Compagnie Minière des Grands Lacs, (M.G.L.), 236
Company of African Merchants, Ltd., 153
Complot de la Pentecôte. See Pentecost Conspiracy.
Conaco (Convention Nationale Congolaise), 226, 313
Conakat, (Confédération des Associations Tribales du Katanga), 224, 226, 310
  and Moise Tshombe, 224, 310
  withdraws from 1960 negotiations, 245
Conakry, Guinea, 58, 59, 74
Cone shells, (conus), 278
Confédération des Associations Tribales du Katanga. See Conakat.
Confederation of Tribal Associations of Katanga. See Conakat.
Congo, 40, 50. See also Zaire.
  derivation of name, 318
  indentured labor for, 132, 133
Congo Afrique, 220
Congo Company of Commerce and Industry, 308
Congo Free State, 132, 133, 184, 185, 201, 202, 206, 207, 234, 271, 292, 293, 298, 313, 314, 318, 319
  administrator-general of, 251, 252
  and Arab campaign, 190, 314, 326
  army of, 247
  army of, and 1895 mutiny, 247, 313, 314
  atrocities in, 185, 186
  role of Bangala in modernization of, 290
  annexed by Belgian Parliament, 317
  agents penetrate Bobangi country, 192
  found post at Bobolo, 234
  Boma as capital of, 317
  and the chief of Bosilela, 276
  and Cokwe, 277
  hostilities with the Cokwe, 271
  commission of enquiry visits, 185
  expeditions sent by, 222, 314
  in the Giri River region, 276
  relations with Kasongo Nyembo I, 222
  establishes control in Kivu, 236
  hostilities with Lulua, 271
  relations with Lumpungu, 240, 241, 242
  and the Monia people, 266
  Mopipi Mutimana and, 264
  and Mopoie Bangezegino, 265
  and Mukenge a Tunsele, (Kalamba), 270, 271
  and Mumbendu, 274, 275
  and Mushid a Nambing, 277

  Ngongo Leteta and the, 241, 293, 294, 295
  northward expansion of, 265
  Nsungu kidnapped by soldiers of, 290
  A.T. Porter as consul of, in Freetown, 133
  precursor of, 315
  African revolt against rubber companies in, 201, 202
  introduces taxes and forced labor near Malebo Pool, 288
  and Tshisungu Kalamba, 271
  arrives in Uluund, 277
Congolese House of Representatives. See House of Representatives, Congolese.
Congolese, in Sierra Leone, 21
Congolese National Army. See Armée Nationale Congolaise.
Congolese National Assembly. See National Assembly, Congolese.
Congolese Trust Company, 255
Congolese University Center at Louvanium, (later Louvanium University), 302
Congo, My Country, 242
Congo Official University. See Elisabethville, State University of.
Congo Railway Company, 308
Congo (Brazzaville), Republic of, former French Congo, (now the People's Republic of the Congo), 208, 311
  P. Mulele visits, 273
  M. Tshombe visits, 311
Congo, People's Republic of, (formerly the French Congo), 187, 205, 282, 323
Congo, Republic of, (now Zaire), 216, 220, 309, 311, 312, 317, 318
  breaks relations with Belgium, 245, 311
  union with Ghana, 245
  independence for, 219, 310, 311
  post-independence crisis in, 242, 245, 246
  need for unity in, 220
  name changed to Zaire, (1971), 188
Congo River, 225, 247. See also Zaire River.
  correct nomenclature of, 188
Congregational Association of Illinois, 138
Congregational Mission, 138
Congregation of the Holy Ghost, 48
Congress of Congolese political parties, (1959), 244
Connecticut, 135, 142, 143
Conscience Africaine, 217
Conseil du Gouvernement Général, 197
Conseil National de Libération, 237
Consolidated African Selection Trust, (CAST). See also Sierra Leone Selection Trust.
  obtains diamond license, 30
Constantino, Gomes, 253
Constantino, Pedro, 229, 230
Constitution
  of Sierra Leone Colony, (1863), 25
  Slater Constitution, (1924), 31, 40, 44, 110

Stevenson Constitution, 41, 84, 85, 112; introduced, (1947), 32, 73; adopted, (1951), 32, 112
Constitution suspended, (1967), 101
Constitutional Commission of Luluabourg (Kananga), 197
Constitution, Congolese
   of 1960, 219
   of Luluabourg, (1964), 188, 218
   of 1967, 188
Conteh, Memuna, 134
Conteh, clan. See Konte.
Conus shells. See cone shells.
Convention Nationale Congolaise. See Conaco.
Cooperative Society, (British), 84
Cooreman African Company. See Compagnie Africaine Cooreman.
Copal, 201, 253, 277
Copper, 268, 269
   Bobangi trade in, 205
   bracelets, 278
   "capital of." See Lubumbashi (Elisabethville).
   copper crosses, 179
   ingots, 268
   from Katanga, 310
   role of, in Katanga secession attempt, 311
   Likasi as center for, 321
   mines, 279
   as tribute to the Mwant Yav, 239
Copperbelt, 225
Copper Cross. See Croix de Cuivre.
Colquilhat, Camille, 206, 207, 291, 292
Coquilhatville, (now Mbandaka), 200, 207, 219, 225, 311, 323. See also Mbandaka.
Corn, 36
   foods extracted from, 36
Corn, (maize), 182, 183, 249
Cornelis, Henri, 187
Corry, Joseph, 72
Corvée. See Forced labor.
Costermansville. See Bukavu.
Cotton, 23
Cotton States Exposition, Atlanta, Georgia, 66
Council of Legal Education, London, 48
Counter Manifesto, (1956), 218
Country cloths
   buried with Kai Londo, 88
Court of Mixed Commission, Freetown, 21
Court of Requests Ordinance, (1906), 156
Covey, James, 142
Cowrie shells, 179
Crawford, Capt. Coupland, 124
Creole. See Krios.
Creoles in the Kongo, 299
"Creoles, King of." See Johnson, Thomas.
Crocodiles, 284
Croix de Cuivre, 232
Crooks, J.J., 153
Crown, the British, 41, 42
Crown, the Massaquoi, 108, 109
Crowther, Bishop Adjai
   first student at Fourah Bay, 25
Cry Tamba, 36

C.S.K. See Comité Spécial du Katanga.
Cuba, 141
   importation of slaves banned, 141
Cults, Catholic, 189
Cummings, Emmanuel Henry, the Hon., 58
Cummings, Eustace Henry Taylor, Dr. 58
Currency
   ackeys as, 163
   Charles II guineas as, 163
   in Colony, 58
   iron bars as, 134, 135
   in Kissi-Mende areas, 23
   MacGregor Laird penny as, 163
   shells as, 296
   Sierra Leone dollar as, 163
   tobacco as, 136
Customary Chief, definition of, 318
Customs Department. See Sierra Leone Customs Department.
Cuvelier, J., 268
Dabia, 123
Dabo, 119
Dadi ben Ndoe. See Tshungu.
Dahomey, (now Benin), 49, 133
Daily Telegraph, (London), 287
Daily Telegraph, (Nigerian), 159, Dakar, Senegal, 48, 49, 56
Dakpara, 285,
Dalhem, Belgium, 308
Dalla Modu, 58. 59, 60, 116, 119
Dalo, Madam, 107
Dama, 89, 117, 124
Damatibolo, 38
Dambia, 69
Dan, village of, planned, 161
Dance. See Sierra Leone National Dance Troupe. Also see Kai's dancers.
Dances, modern, in the Congo
   bolero, 193
   rumba, 193
   tango, 193
Dangi, 200
Daniels, W. See Wallace-Johnson, I.T.A.
Dantili Samura. See Samura, Solimanga.
"Danville," 161, 162
Darfur, (Kordofan), The Sudan, 233
Daru, 91
da Silva, Daniel, 296
Darwinian theories, 156
d'Aspermont Lynden, Count, 311
Dauda, 166
Dauda, Almamy, 92, 93
Damuas and Co., 288
Davies, William Broughton, 25, 107
Davies, William James. See Faduma, O.
Davis, Darnell, 71
Dayton, Ohio, 35, 55, 161
de Boek, Father E., 303, 304
de Brazza, Savorgnan, 288
de Burgh, John Henry, 160
de Clercq, 277
de Gaulle, Charles, 187, 218, 243
   Tshombe visits, 312
de Lacerda e Almeida, Francisco José, 240
   expedition of, 240
   death of, 240
Delaere, Father Jacques, 223

Delcommune, A., 222, 290, 308
Delco. See Sierra Leone Development Company.
Deldugu, 144
Delobbe, J.B., 192, 200
de Macar, Oscar, 271
Dembelia country, (Yalunka), 61, 154
Dembelia-Musaia, chiefdom, 61
Dendale, Léopoldville commune, 218
Department of Native Affairs, Sierra Leone, 25, 129, 130, 132
Depression, The, (1931-34), 216, 232
   and the Pende, 258
   effects of in Sierra Leone, 73, 90
de Sagwea, Capt. J., 314
de Schryver, 194
de Sousberghe, Léon, 254
Dewagenière firm, 235
de Winton, Sir Francis, 70, 149, 251, 252, 290
Dhanis, Lt. (Baron), F., 241, 247, 314, 316
Dia, 86, 87
Dialungana Kiangani, Salmoh, 227
Diamonds, 30, 31
   "Diamond Rush" of the 1950s, 31
   illicit diamond ring, 30, 31
   mining, 30
   smuggling, 31
Diang, chiefdom, 38
Diangienda, Joseph, 227
Dia Mande, 222
Dibaya-Lubwe, 208
Dibwe, 295
"Dictionary and Grammar of the Kongo Language," 256
Dictionnaire Swahili-Français, Français-Swahili, 210
Diemba, 237
Digi Digi, 92
Diko, 61
Dikulwe River, 239
Dillard University, 144, 158. See also Straight College of New Orleans.
Dillett, Eugene, 60, 116, 119
Dilolo, 215, 216, 277, 278, 283, 286, 301
   founded, 277
Ding, 304
Diogo I. See Nzinga Mpudi.
Diogo Gomes, 299
Diomi, Gaston, 243
Disengomoka, E.A., 197, 198
Disho, clans, 212
Distilling, 36
District Councils, introduced in Sierra Leone, 32, 72, 89, 112
Disu, Pierre, 231
Ditend, 286
Ditend Yavu a Nawej III, 216, 309
Dixcove, Gold Coast, 76
Dixing, 68
Djala, 200
Djamba, 235, 299
Djando Maboko, 266
Djongo, 290
Djuma, 220, 307
Djund. See Ndjondo.
Documents pour l'Action, (later Congo Afrique), 220

Dodo, 79, 89, 96, 97, 127, 128, 157
Doherty, Governor Richard, 59
Dollar, Sierra Leone. See Currency.
Dolo-Bokala, chiefdom, 200
Dolo Botila, sub-chiefdom, 200
Dominer pour servir, 302
Dominica, 133
Dominican Fathers, 255
Domin-ya, 92
Dongo, 281
Dougan, Robert, 60
Douhet, 230, 231
Dove, the Rev. Thomas, 64
Dover, H.M.S., 60
Dowii Komei, 86
Dress Reform Society, 65, 145
Du Bois, William Edward Burghardt, 66
Duga, 144
Duke of Brabant. See Leopold III of Belgium.
Dukono, 86, 88
Dumagbe, 137
Dumba wa Kalala, 213
Dundusana, 201
Dungu, 255
Dura I, 60, 61
Dura II, Alimamy, 61
Duramani Kamara, 172
Durham University, 25, 42, 43, 44, 48, 58, 111
    awards honorary degree to Dr. M.A.S. Margai, 112
Dusu, 61
Dusu Sori, 61, 62
Dutch,
    Mani Kongo concludes alliance with, 296, 312
    conflict with Portuguese, 296, 312
Dutch Company, 252
Ealing Grammar School, London, 162
Earthquake. See Accra.
Easmon, Annette Kathleen, 63
Easmon family, 116, 117
Easmon, John Farrell, 62, 63
Easmon, McCormack Charles Farrell, 63, 64
Easmon, Walter Richard, 62
East Africa, 159
East Anglia, England, 57
East Balobo, chiefdom, 253
Eastern Kasai. See Kasai Oriental.
Eastern Province, 247
East Street. See Freetown.
Eat bread, to, (i.e. swear an oath), 154, 167, 169
Eaton Hall, Chester, England, 40, 101
Ebamba, 266
Ebamba, Maurice, 254
Ebamba Moboko Moi-Molanga, 277
Ebenezer Wesleyan Day School, Freetown, 74
Ebenga, 275
Ebeya, M.S., (formerly M.S. *Baron Liebrechts*), 199
Ebeya, Eugène, 198, 199
Ebiru, 199
Ebola River, 233
Ebondo. See Ebunda.

Ebunda, (Ebondo), 253
Ecole des Cadets, Luluabourg, 198
Ecole de Moniteurs, of Madzia, 197
Ecole Normale Moyenne, of Nivelles, 197
Economic Round Table, Brussels, 1960, 219
Edinburgh, Scotland, 40, 76, 82
"Editions Ngoma," 193
Edjumbu, 199, 200, 253
Education,
    in Sierra Leone, 25
    in Zaire, 210, 211
    inadequacy of higher education for Africans in Zaire, 218
Edwards, (colonial official, 1878), 108
Edwards-Loggie Mission, 156
"Effuah," opera, 38
Egba, Nigeria, 66, 103, 153, 156
Eglise de Jésus Christ sur la terre par le prophète Simon Kimbangu. See Church of Jesus Christ on Earth by the Prophet Simon Kimbangu.
Egypt, 285
    influence of in the Sudan, 265
E.I.C. See Congo Free State.
Eighth Line Regiment, Belgian, 308
Eisenhower, Dwight, U.S. President, 245
Ekango, 200
Ekita, 274
Ekonda, 274, 275, 300, 318, 324, 326
Ekongobololo, 275
Ekwakola, 265
Ekwalanga, 202
Ekwete, 275
Ekwong è Biar, 249
Eleanor, Queen of Portugal, 258
Eleanor, wife of the Mani Kongo, 258, 267
Elder Dempster Lines, 43
    seamen's strike in the, (1920), 43
Elections
    of December 1957 in Congolese urban centers, 218, 219, 243, 310
    national, in the Congo, December 1959, 244
    on May 21 and 22, 1960, in the Congo, 245, 272
    national, in 1965, in the Congo, 321
Eleke, 191
Elephants, 111
    Banta transformed into, 126
Eleusine, 183
Elisabethville, (later Lubumbashi), 186, 198, 216, 224, 225, 228, 232, 233, 246, 263, 309, 310, 311. See also Lubumbashi; State University of Elisabethville (formerly Congo Official University).
    1957 elections in, 224
    cathedral of, 232
    Centre Extra-Coutumier, 232, 233
    miners' strike in, 186
    controlled by U.N. troops, 225
Elizabeth II, Queen, 45, 48
Elliott Commission on Higher Education, 58
Elliott, Selina Beatrice, 76
Ellis, Capt. A.B., 132
Elmina, Gold Coast, 70
Eloa, (a Budja group), 201, 202
Emin Pasha, (Eduard Schnitzler), 306

England, 220
    Mantantu Dundulu visits three times, 256
    I.T.A. Wallace Johnson in, 160
England, John, 109
Engumba, chiefdom, 200
Engwangola. See Ngembe.
Ensala, 191, 200, 201
Enyamba, 300
E.P.I. See Evangelical Pedagogical Institute at Kimpese.
Epsom College, Surrey, England, 63
Epunga, 295
Equateur. See Mbandaka.
Equateur, Province and (later) Region, 179, 184, 191, 192, 198, 206, 275, 295, 305, 319, 323
Equateurville. See Mbandaka.
Equator Station, 207, 291, 305
Equator, The, 179, 207
Eseko, 201, 212
Esieme, 189, 190
    mission (Nazareth) at, 189, 190
Essor du Congo, 224
Eswe, 300, 314, 319, 326
Etapes et Jalons, 302
Etat Indépendant du Congo. See Congo Free State.
Ethiopia, 159
Etond, 221
Europeans, 183
    penetrate Central Africa, 183, 184
    economic interest in Congo Free State, 185
    arrival of in Sierra Leone, 19
Evangelical Pedagogical Institute, (E.P.I.) at Kimpese, 197
Evangelical Training Institute, at Mbanza-Ngungu, 197
Evangelical United Brethren Day School
    at Bonthe, 111
    at Moyamba, 69
    at Rotifunk, 36, 72
    at Shenge, 55
Evening Despatch, 40
Evolués, 186, 217, 220, 242
Ewango, 314
Executive Council of Sierra Leone, 89, 118
    enquiry by, 130
    established 1863, 25
    Finance Committee of, 89
    party representation in, 32
Eyeme, 189
Eylo, 193
Eyskens, Gaston, 303
Ezzidio, John, 64, 65, 96
    represented in Legislative Council, (1863), 25
Faagbandi, 87
    drowned by Kai Londo, 88
Faba Kpovowa of Dodo, 79, 89, 96, 97, 114, 127, 128
    death of, 128
Fabiola, Queen, 311
Fa Bundeh, 86
Fadugu, 139
Faduma, Du Bois, 66

Faduma, Mrs. Henrietta, (Henrietta Adams), 65
Faduma, John, 65
Faduma, Omojowu, 66
Faduma, Omolofi, 65
Faduma, Orishatukeh, 65, 66
Fairtlough, Major E.C., 86
Fakais, (farm settlements), 22, 169
Fakoi, 128
Falaba, 22, 61, 95, 132, 139, 144, 154, 169, 174
    visited by Edward Blyden, (1872), 24
    visited by Governor Cardew, 52
    Falaba-Bumban-Port Loko trade route, 23
    founding of, 154
    Fula prince killed in, 81
    visited by Gordon Laing, (1822), 24
    market in, 23
    seige and destruction of by Samori, 26, 61, 81, 144, 154
    rebuilt by Samori, 26
    and Sayo of Kaliere, 144
Falconbridge, Alexander, 125
Falconbridge, Anna Maria, 125, 126
Famine, after effects of, in Kissi Tongi, 90
"Fango Loli," 91
Fante, 78
    monarchy proposed, 78
"Farama" Tami. See Farma Tami.
Farma, "King," 66, 67
Farma Tami, 18, 66, 67, 168, 174
Farma Yani, 98, 99
Farmington, Connecticut, 135, 143
Fatima Fodi, 155
Fatimah Brimah Kamara, Alikali, 119, 122, 123, 149
Fatimah Brimah II, (previously Mohamadu Alikali), 119
Fato, 114
Fawosa, 94
Fawundu, Francis, 67, 68
Fawundu, Sengbe, of Mano, 67, 117
Feather, as power symbol, 317
Federal government, advocated for the Congo, 219, 310, 311
Fefegura, Ali, 150
Fenda Modu, 58
Ferensola, 113, 169
Fergusson, Governor William, 75, 116
Festing, Major Morton, 26, 27, 151
Fetishes and fetishism. See also Onema, Mama.
    of the Bantote clan, 289
    destruction of by the Kimbanguists, 227
    A. Sims combats, 306
Ficus plant, 214, 215, 324
    planted at Lunde, 215
Filo, (Hangah), 97
Fimi River, 322
Fina Bala. See Mori Musa.
Firia, 139
Fish, 239
    Lobala people seek, 281
Fishing
    among Bobangi, 205

in area north of Mbandaka, 265
and the Ngala, 324
Fisk University, 144
Flag, of Zaire, 188
Flament, 230
Flanders, 104
Flemish, 186
Flickinger, the Rev. Daniel K., 161
Florida, 157, 158
Fobaywulo, chief of Gbandi, 86, 88
Foday Tarawaly, nephew of Bokari, 46
Foday Tarawaly, Islamic scholar, 68
Foday Wise, Almamy, 46
Foloba, 90
Folosaba Yalunka, 61, 154
Folu, 158
Fomgboe, 68, 69, 93
    forms coalition against Karimu, 93
Fonnie, 160
Football, 91
Foray, chief, 108, 132
Foray Kallon. See Va Foray Sassabla.
Forced labor, (corvée), 193, 203, 249, 253, 261
    organized at Bobola by Leleka, 235
    Tiv chiefs reject, 288
Force Publique, (F.P.), 185, 198, 250, 276, 319
    establishment of, (1886), 198
    name changed to Armée Nationale Congolaise, (1960), 246
    and the Arab campaign, 185
    tortures Gandanda Gibanda, 203
    repression of Kitawala movement by, 195
    Makutu Mimboyo recruited by, 250
    Mumbendu's service in, 274
    mutiny of 1960, 187, 219, 245, 311
    and the Pende, 258, 260, 261
    and repression of Pende revolt, 223
    recruiting for, 264
    revolt of, (1944), 186
    P. Ryckmans joins, 301
    Tetela mutineers in, 222
    Joseph Kapend Tshomb serves in, 215
Forecaria, 45, 46, 62, 82, 92, 97
Foredugu, 47, 119, 123, 148
Foreka of Bomalu, 85
Fori Frigi, 139
Forna, Dr. Mohamed Sorie, 69, 70, 152
    and 1974 plot, 33, 101
    executed, 33, 101
Fortifications, around villages, 209
Forts. See also Accra, Anomabu, Cape Coast, Dixcove, Elmina, Keta.
    British forts on the Gold Coast, 76, 104
    Portuguese fort on the site of Freetown, 19
Fortress Monroe, 158
Fort Thornton, Freetown, 155
Forum, (Peoples), 84
Foulah. See Fula.
Fourah Bay College, 38, 42, 43, 44, 48, 55, 56, 58, 74, 76, 77, 82, 83, 118, 156, 169, 170
    College Council 43, 58. 157

Extra-Mural Department, 84
M.A.S. Margai at, 111
opened, (1848), 25
S.B. Thomas at, 154
science faculty at, 82
Fourah Bay Fund: The Alternative, 84
Fourah Bay Institute. See Fourah Bay College.
France, (and the French), 187
    agreement of 1895 with the British, 28
    recognize Bokari as ruler of Morea, 46
    boundary convention of 1882 with the British, 27
    cooperation with the British in Sierra Leone, (1931), 74
    clash with the British by mistake, 114, 130, 132
    rivalry with the British, 26, 27, 75, 76, 92, 93, 95, 97, 102, 141
    relations with British, 26, 46, 51
    territorial claims by right of conquest, 27
    Charles de Gaulle comes to power in, 187
    French explorers at Falaba, 144
    guns obtained from French territory, 274
    occupy Heremokono, 132
    relations with Issa of Kaliere, 27
    E. Kimba's visit to, 225
    Sir Charles MacCarthy's family exiled to, 104
    treaty with Maligi Gbele, 46
    Mopoie Bangezegino seeks refuge with, 265
    send a gunboat to Morea, 46
    gain port facilities in Morea, 46
    and Nemgbana, 125
    Pedro (Bartholomew) Nemgbana educated in, 125
    join with British to fight Porekere, 26
    award gold medal to W. Rainy, 134
    activities on Rio Nunez, 153
    rivalry with other colonial powers, 265
    and Samori, 132
    destroy Samori's empire, 140
    and Sattan Lahai, 140
    and Sierra Leone, 17, 128, 146
    and the Sofa, 27, 114, 132
    advance into Soso country, 62
    treaties with African rulers, 27
    traders from, in northern Zaire, 265
Franciscans, 299
Francqui, 222
Franquet, 235
Freemasonry, 35
Freetown, 35, 38, 40, 42, 43, 44, 47, 48, 49, 50, 51, 52, 53, 54, 55, 56, 58, 59, 60, 62, 63, 64, 65, 67, 68, 69, 72, 74, 75, 76, 77, 78, 80, 82, 83, 84, 91, 93, 95, 96, 97, 98, 99, 101, 102, 103, 104, 105, 106, 107, 108, 109, 110, 111, 114, 115, 116, 117, 118, 119, 120, 122, 125, 126, 128, 129, 132, 133, 134, 135, 136, 137, 140, 143, 144, 145, 146, 147, 148, 149, 150, 152, 153, 154, 155, 159, 160, 162, 165, 169, 170, 171, 172, 173

(Freetown-Continued)

Amistad Africans arrive in, 143
first bookshop opened in, 145
old buildings in, 63
arrival of Governor Cardew in, 52
first and second trials of William Caulker, 56
trial of Thomas Kugba Caulker, 56
Charles Street, 114
indentured labor from, for the Congo, 132, 133
relations with Dalla Modu, 58, 59
East Street, 153
educational institutions in, 25
visited by Fenda Modu, 58
founding of, 56, 57, 125
Fula community in, 128, 129
Gibraltar Wharf, 133
Howe Street, 163
and relations with the interior, 24
Jenkins Street, 129
trial of Kinigbo and others in, 55
Kissy Street, 50, 133, 153
Kpana Lewis visits, 98
Sir Charles MacCarthy's improvements to, 104
mail packets to, from Britain, 75
Maternity Hospital in, 162
Mende Mission arrives in, 143
named, (1792), 143
National Congress of British West Africa meets in, 36
as a naval base, 21
Nyagua brought to, 128
Peninsula, 173
Central Prison, Padembu Road, 160
Race Course at, 162
and Sierra Leone railway, 53
Recreation Grounds, 50
1955 riots in, 32
as source of arms for Samori, 95, 130
sanitary conditions in, 58
trades with Sankaran, 38
street names in, 63
trade routes to, 95
trade through the port of, 24
Victoria Park (Sewa Grounds), 129
troops sent to Waterloo, Sierra Leone, from, 105
Water Works Department, 155
Westmoreland Street, 153
Wilberforce Street, 133
in World War II, provisioning, 150
yellow fever epidemic, (1859), 49
Freetown Adult Education Committee, 84
Freetown City Council, 32, 44, 58, 84, 159
Freetown Municipal Council, 103
Freetown Town Council, 64
Free University of the Congo. See Université Libre du Congo.
French. See France.
French Catholics, 48
French Congo, 187, 197, 227, 235
French Equatorial Africa, 192, 275
French language, 243
as language of instruction in Zaire, 210
French Revolution, 104

Frontier Police. See Sierra Leone Frontier Police Force.
Frontier Road, (Kambia to Sulima), 27
Fuamba. See Kasongo Lwaba.
Fula, (Foulah, or Fulani), 47, 70, 92, 120, 121, 123, 125, 126, 128, 139, 149, 151, 152, 154, 155, 166, 170. See also Bunduka, Hubu, Jihad.
in Freetown, 128, 129
relations with Solimana, 81
Fulani. See Fula.
Fula Mansa, 70, 126, 148
Fulawahun, 127
Fumi River, 303
Fumu Vincent, 231
Funa, stream, 287
Futa Jallon, 17, 23, 38, 59, 81, 128, 129, 139, 144, 152, 154, 170, 171
Fula of, 37
possible origin of Limba in, 19
Futa Toro, 134
Fyfe, Christopher, 126
Gabon, 48, 210
Gabriel, Father Superior, 247
Galba-British, Jacob, 40
Galenga Mushingo, 213
Galesburg, Ohio, 138
Gallinas, 141, 170, 174
partial British protection of, 108
coast of, 107
disturbances in, in 1880s, 117, 134
food supply cut off, 108
visited by Governor Hay, 120
claimed by Liberia, 108
attacked by Liberian troops, 109
Mana Siaka as ruler of, 108, 109
and J. Mannah-Kpaka, 110
and Massaquoi family, 108, 109, 110, 137
origin of name, 19, 170. See also Vai.
pacification of, 117
raids on, 128
state regalia of, 108
Rogers family moves to, 137
state of, 22
Galumbu, 260
Gambia, The, 38, 43, 75, 76, 172
Boy Scouts of, 43
democratic king proposed for the, 78
Fomgboe exiled to, 69
J.C. May in, 114
Sir Charles MacCarthy in, 114
peanuts exported from, 85
Gambia Adventurers Company, 109, 137
Gambia Island
French granted land on, (1785), 125
French slavers on, 125
Gambia River, 114
Gambling, 72
Gamoni, 260
Gamparu, 307
Gandajika, 221, 294
Gandanda Gibanda, 202, 203, 214, 230
Gandu, 221
Garangaza, 269
Garcia II. See Nkanga Lukeni.
Garrett, George H., 27, 51, 99, 100

G.A.S.S.O.M.E.L., (Grouping of Mutual Ethnic Associations of the Lunda Empire), 310
Gatshinga, family, 254
Gaulle, Charles de. See de Gaulle, Charles.
Gavunji, 233
Gbaku, ("ruler"), 170
Gbambaia, 161
Hughes murdered at, 79
Gbana, 173
Gbana Bunje, 99
Gbandi, 18, 85, 86, 91, 96
conquered by Kai Londo, 88
link with Loko of Sierra Leone, 18
attacked by Mbawulomeh, 88
Gbangbai River, 94
Gbangbama, 93, 94, 99
Gbanga Koba-wa, 149
Gbangbatok, 94, 111, 126
Gbanka, 47, 70
Gbanna Bunjay, 161
Gbanya Lango, 70, 71, 164, 165
Gbanye, 128
Gbatekaka, 117
Gbele, (later Belle), Liberia, 86, 88
Gbendembu, 68
Gbendembu Gowahun, 51
Gbenjei, 54, 70, 100, 127, 165
Gbenjeh. See Gbenjei.
Gbenye, Christopher, 312
Gbe-say Kai Luseni, 110
Gbile, (Billeh), 68
Gbinti, 123, 163
French given port facilities at, 46
as timber port, 116
Gbo, chief, 164
Gbograma, 127, 164, 166
Gbo Kamagai, 126
Gboma, 233
Gbondou, 126, 127
Gbondu, 87, 90
Gbonjeima, 70
Gendama, 106, 108
Gentleman, The, 143
Geography of Sierra Leone, 147
George VI, King
coronation of, (1937), 45
Georgetown, Kentucky, 158
Germain, E., 248
Germans
participation by in financing of Congo Railway Company, 308
in East Africa, 241
Germany, 184
N.J.G. Ballanta studies in, 38
E. Kimba's visit to, 225
International Conference of Negro Workers in Hamburg, 159
I.B. Taqi studies in, 152
West, M. Tshombe visits, 312
Ghana, 40, 160, 187, 243, 245. See also Gold Coast.
ancient empire of, 92
union with the Congo, (1960), 245
gains independence, (1957), 302
Ghinti, 75
Gibbs, Prof. J.W., 142

Gibbs, Thomas Vann, 158
Giboba Gisenzele, 213
Gibraltar Methodist Church, 42
Ginger, (crop), 35
Gipende, language, 283
Giri marshes, 265
Giri, people, 276
Giri (Ngiri) River, and region, 192, 199, 200, 205, 234, 235, 254, 265, 266, 274, 275 276, 277, 281, 290, 298, 299, 303, 304, 317, 321, 324
Giri sector, 266
Gisaka, 252
Giuhun Tonagu, in Guma, 85
Gizenga, Antoine, 208, 245, 272, 273
    arrested, 273
Gleaner, Jamaica, 37
Gloucester, Sierra Leone, 76, 83, 96, 147
Goba, 127
Gobila, 290
Goi Mafula. See Lumpungu.
Gola, 17, 18, 86, 88, 158, 170
Gola Forest, 17
Golahun, 87
Golberry, 125
Gold
    boom ends, in Sierra Leone, 30
    mining boom of 1930s, in Sierra Leone, 30
    mining abandoned, (1940), 30
    discovered in Pampana River basin, 30
    Portuguese seek in south Kongo, 296
    trading in, in Sierra Leone, 19, 23, 24, 59, 119, 151
    mined in Wamuzimu, 236
Gold Coast, (now Ghana), 74, 302. See also Ghana.
    Bai Bureh, banished to, 52
    cocoa boycott in, 74
    Dr. J.F. Easmon as chief medical officer in, 62
    Gbanka exiled to, 70
    J.A.B. Horton on the, 76
    J.A.B. Horton seeks governorship of, 72
    Kpana Lewis exiled to, 128
    Sir Charles MacCarthy on, 104, 105
    National Congress of British West Africa founded in, 36, 44
    Nyagua banished to, 128
    Sierra Leone chiefs exiled to, (1899), 28, 53
    Sierra Leone contingent sent to Gold Coast, (1873), 71
    University College of, 58
    I.T.A. Wallace Johnson in, 159, 160
Gold Coast Chronicle, 62
Gold Coast Criminal Code, 160
Gold Coast Independent, 62
Gold Coast Spectator, 159
Gold Coast Supreme Court, 160
Golungo Alto, 286
Goma, 194, 195, 196, 210, 236
    diocese of, North Kivu, 210
Gombe (formerly Kalina) cemetery, Léopoldville, 198

Gombe-Matadi, 232
Gombla, 93
Gombu, Pa, 148
Gombu Smart, 71, 72, 148
Gomez, 231
Gondama, 107
    founded, 127
Gongoima, 127, 164, 165
Good Hope, 161
Gorama, 128
Gorama Mende, region, 126
Gospel Mission Hall, 35
Government Model School, Sierra Leone, 50, 146
Governor-General of the Congo, 218, 219
Governor-General of Sierra Leone, 43, 48
Governor's Council of Sierra Leone, 25, 75
    abolition of, (1863), 25
Grafton, 147
Grand Cordon of the Order of the Crown, (Belgian), 34
Grant, Marcus, 45
Grant, Willia, 106
Granville Town, 57, 170
Grassfields, 107
Gray's Inn, London, 42, 145, 146
Great Depression. See Depression, The, (1931-34).
Great Lakes Mining Company. See Compagnie Minère des Grands Lacs.
Great Lakes of East Africa, 179, 181
Great Lakes Railway, (C.F.L.). See Chemins de Fer du Congo-Supérieur aux Grands Lacs Africains.
Great Ngbandi. See Kola Ngbandi.
Great Scarcies River, 23, 24, 46, 52, 68, 116, 140, 141, 168, 173. See also Scarcies, The.
Greeks, as traders in the eastern Congo, 231
Greene, Graham, 50
Grenfell, R. George, 206, 256, 289, 290
Groundnuts. See Peanuts.
Guéroult, 104
Guggenheim award, 38
Guhulula, 203
Guinea, (coin). See Currency.
Guinea, 40, 110, 113, 138, 168, 170, 171, 172, 173, 174, 244. See also French Guinea.
    and the state of Morea, 46
    P. Mulele visits, 272
Guinea-Bissau, 172
Guinea, French, 28. See also Guinea.
    boundary with Sierra Leone, 52, 53
    and Haidara, 73, 74
Guinness, Henry and Fanny, 305, 306
Gulama, Julius, (Julius Foday Cole), 72, 73, 112
Gulama, Momoh, 72
Gulula, 206
Guma, 85, 86, 87
Gungu, 198, 199, 213, 214, 223, 226, 231, 261, 273, 279
Gunpowder
    Bobangi trade in, 205
    Cokwe trade in, 222
    Kasongo Kiniama seeks to buy, 221

    Swahili refuse to supply Misiri with, 269
Guns
    Bobangi trade in, 205
    Cokwe trade in, 212, 222, 270
    Kalala Kafumbe obtains, 212
    purchased by Kaninchin, 209
    Luba acquire, 270
    M'Siri obtains from the Swahili, 269
    Mumbendu trades slaves for, 274
    Ngaliema buys, 287
    Ngongo Leteta obtains, 293, 294
    Ovimbundu and Lwena traders supply, 269
    Tio obtain, 287
    traded for slaves, 220
Gurba River, 265
Guyana. See British Guiana.
Haidara, Kontorfilli, 73, 74, 166, 167
    supplies medicine to combat locust plague, 166
Haidara War, (1931), 73, 74
Hainaux, J., 253
Halifax, Nova Scotia, 56
Hallelujah Chorus, Handel's, 232
Hamadu, 61
Hamburg, Germany, 159
Hammocks, use of discouraged, 90
Hampton Institute, Virginia, 144
Handel, 232. See also Hallelujah Chorus.
Hanga, 80
Hangah. See Filo.
Hanssens, Capt. 206, 251
Harems, 236
Harford Girls' School, Moyambe, 72, 144
Harndon, Ann, 135
Harris, Elizabeth, 161
Hartford, Connecticut, 142
Hastings, Sierra Leone, 35, 50, 75, 82, 96, 105, 106, 125, 147, 152
Hatiba, 193
Hausa, 105
Haut-Zaire Region, formerly Orientale Province, 179, 193, 319, 321
Havana, Cuba, 141
Havelock, Governor Arthur Edward, 56, 102, 115, 165
Havu, 252
Hay, Governor Sir James Shaw, 27, 47
    policy towards interior, 120
    signs treaty with Makavoray, 107
    and Momo Kai Kai, 121
    at Tikonko, 121
Hayford, Joseph Ephraim Casely, 41
Hayford, Mrs. Casely, 63
Hazeley, Peter Philip, 74, 75, 83
Heard, Betsy, 59
Heddle, Charles, 75, 76
    as Krio representative on the Legislative Council, 25
    visits Port Loko, 119
Heddle and Co., 75
Heidelberg University, 152
Hemabu, 93, 94
Hemelrijck, van, 218
Hemp. See also Lubuku.
    administered by Mama Onema, 300

smoking of, 212, 270, 322
Henrique, Dom, 204, 280
   consecrated as bishop, 280
Henry, 155
Henry Reed, steamer, 306
Heremakono, 113, 132
Herico River, 155
Hewitt, Commander Sir William, 183
Hiam Kakoba, 221
Hides, trade in, 24, 119, 151
High Point, North Carolina, 65
Hill, Col. (later Sir) Stephen John, Governor,
   48, 71, 108, 116, 119, 133, 134
      sends gunboat, 108
      leads naval expedition to Kambia, 140
Hinde, 294
Hirst, Elizabeth, 164
Historians, of Zaire, 210
Historical Sketch of the Sierra Leone Gram-
   mar School, 1845-1935, 157
History of Sierra Leone, A, 147
History of Tropical Medicine, 162
Hodister, 190
Holmes, Capt. H.J., killed by Haidara, 73
Holo, 283
Holy Bible, 76, 138, 189, 227, 256, 257, 266
   Acts of the Apostles, 257
   translated into Kikongo, 256
   revised Kikongo version, 257
   translation into Mende begun, 138
   Proverbs, 257
   Psalms, 257
   St. Paul, 257
   parts of, translated into
      Temne, 109
Holy Spirit (Mpeve), 187
Holy Trinity Church, Freetown, 83, 153
Hood, Capt., 121
Hood, Dr. T., 70, 148, 166
Hoogstraeten, Belgium, 301
Horton's Collegiate High School, 78
Horton, Mrs. Fannie, (Fannie Marietta
   Pratt), 76
Horton Hall, 78
Horton, James, 76
Horton, James Africanus Beale, 76, 77, 78,
   79, 163
      one of the first Krio doctors, 25
Horton, Nancy, 76
Horton, Mrs. Selina Beatrice, (Selina Bea-
   trice Elliott), 76
Hote, Dr., 306
Hotel Relais, Kindu, 300
Hotobah-During, C.D., 84
Houphouet-Boigny, Félix, 243
House of Commons, British
   Select Committee of (1865), 77, 78
House of Representatives, Congolese, 245,
   246, 264
House of Representatives, Sierra Leone,
   (formerly Legislative Council), 32, 48,
   89, 137
House tax, (1896), 28, 47, 51, 52, 53, 55, 56,
   67, 70, 73, 79, 98, 120, 121, 130, 148,
   151, 161
      Momo Ja and, 120, 121
      Momo Kai Kai and, 121

      uprising against, 47, 52, 53, 56, 67,
      161, 164, 166
Housing, low cost loans for, 218
Howard University, 144
Howe Street. See Freetown.
Hubu, 152
Huggins, Judge Horatio, 134
Hughes, William, 79
Hum, 287, 288
Human Leopard Society. See Leopard
   Society.
Human sacrifice, renounced by Ngankabi,
   290
Humonya, Madam, 79, 80, 81
Humpa Rango, of Dodo, 157
Hungaan, 284
Hut Tax, (1896). See House tax.
Hut Tax War (1898), 28, 70, 79, 98, 130,
   151, 157, 161, 164, 166
      Bai Bureh and, 52, 135
      Fawundu during the, 67, 68
      Gbanka killed in the, 70
      Krios and, 104
Ikiko, 274
Ikobo, 298, 299
Ikwangbala, family, 281, 282
Ikwangbala, village in the People's Republic
   of the Congo, 282
Ikwangbala Bogondo fa Ikwango, 282
Ikwango, 282
Ilebo, 249, 250, 303, 319. See also Port
   Francqui.
Ileo, Joseph, 225, 243, 244, 246, 264, 311
Illinois, 138
Illinois Central Railroad, 138
Illustrated London News, 183
Ilobo, 262
Ilorin, Nigeria, 35
Ilunga, 283
Ilunga Kabale, 222
Ilunga Kalala, 182
Ilunga Kiluwe, 259
Ilunga Mbidi, (Kalala Mbidi). See Kalala
   Ilunga.
Ilunga Mbidi Kiluwe. See Mbidi Kiluwe.
Ilunga Mbili. See Mbidi Kiluwe.
Imam, 168
Imbangala, 182, 184, 203, 213, 249
Imbiada, 295
Imese, 282
Immatriculation, 242, 319
Impanga, 234
Imperi, 79, 98, 99, 106, 107, 133, 155, 161
      leopard murders in, 107
      Momo Ja and, 120, 121
      Momo Kai Kai and, 122
      in the Sherbro, 56
      Sierra Leone Frontier Police Force
      and, 28
      Sierra Leone Weekly News and, 115
Hyde, J.G., 157
"Hymn to Belgium," 232
Ibadan, 244
Ibadan University, Nigeria, 152
Ibadan University College, Nigeria, 58
Ibaka, (1820-89), 191, 204, 205, 206
Ibaka, founder of Bolobo, 205

Ibito, 282
Ibiza, Balearic Islands, 312
Ibo, 76
   independent state for, proposed, 78
   recaptives from, 95, 105
Iboko (Mpondo), 190, 205, 290, 291, 292,
   298, 319, 324
Ibond, ford, 278
Idara. See Haidara, Kontorfilli.
Idim a Kaumb. See Ngand a Bilond.
Idim Kaumb, 238
Idiofa, 198, 213. See also Collège Notre
   Dame, of Idiofa, (later the Collège
   Lankwan).
   in 1964 Kwilu uprising, 273
Idiofa territory, 189, 190, 234
Iesora, 141
Ifwanzondo, 234
Ijagbemi, E., 67
Ikelemba River, 200, 201, 207, 303
Ikembe, 281, 282
I.N.B.A.C. See National Institute for the
   Study of Agriculture in the Congo.
Independence, for the Belgian Congo, 224,
   244, 245, 311
      King Baudouin's announcement of
      progress towards, 187
      celebrated, 187, 219
      date of January 1, 1961 set for, 244
      demanded, 187
      role of Kimbanguism in the country
      after, 228
      Independence Day, June 30, 1960, 245
      preparations for, 219, 272
Independents, in 1967 Sierra Leone elections,
   101
India, 48, 162
Indian Army, 52
Indian Ocean, 179, 184, 278
Indonga, 298, 299
I.N.E.A.C. See Institut National pour
   l'Etude
Influenza epidemic, (1918), 42, 227
Ingende, 282
Ingham, E.G., 133
Inkisi River, 238, 296
Inner Temple, London, 133
Inongo, 267
Institute Colonial International, 302
Institute of Musical Art, 38
Institut Makanda Kabobi, 251
Institut national pour l'Etude Agronomique
   du Congo Belge, (I.N.E.A.C.), 191
Institut Polytechnique Congolais, 197
Institut Saint Boniface, Elisabethville, 224,
   232
Interim Municipal School, (later Regent
   Square Municipal School), Freetown, 58
International African Association, (A.I.A.),
   184, 308. See also A.I.A.
International African Service Bureau, 160
International Association of the Congo
   (A.I.C.), 184, 192, 206, 207, 319, 326
      and Hermann von Wissman, 270
International Conference of Negro Workers,
   Hamburg, Germany, 154

International Labor Exposition in Brussels, (1958), 218, 224, 243
International Labor Defense Congress, Moscow, 159
International Week in Nigeria, (1959), 244
Inter-Seminary Mission Alliance, Rochester, New York, 66
Investiture, 319
Ipamu, 234
Irebu, 191, 201, 207, 277, 303
Ireland, 62, 115, 137, 220
Irish Brigade, (of Louis XIV of France), 104
Iron. See also Wrought iron.
    smelting of, 278
    Yeke as iron-workers, 268
Iron bars. See Currency.
Iron ore, mining, 30
Isa, of Kaliere, 81, 144
    relations with the British, French, and Sofa, 27
    succeeds father as ruler, (1890), 27
    dispute with the Sofa, 95
    attacked by the Sofa, 27, 81
    changes last name to Toray, 81
Isambi, 207
Isangi, 191
Isindji, 286
Isirio, 265
Islam, 35, 49, 68, 122, 128, 129, 130, 134, 135, 166, 170, 172, 264, 265
    and Aku Muslims, 106
    advocated by E. Blyden, 78
    reform movement of Haidara, 73, 74
    one of Nemgbana's sons a Muslim, 125
    Alimamy Rassin and, 134, 135
    and Sesay family, 149
    and Sori Kessebeh, 149
    and the Soso Sankoh, 116, 118, 119, 122
    spread of, 116, 122
    and the Zande, 265
Israel, 56, 147
Itabwa, 268
Italy, 159
    E. Kimba's visit to, 225
Itanganika, 264
Iteno, 281
Iterbo, 195
Itongo, 282
Itsi. See Ngaliema.
Itumba, 281
Ivory, 184, 190, 191, 199, 209, 235, 238, 240, 241, 251, 252, 256, 264, 265, 269, 284, 287, 293, 295, 326
    Bobangi trade in, 205
    Congo trade in, 251, 252, 256
    price increases, 286
    Sierra Leone trade in, 19, 24, 110, 151
    sought by Swahili traders, 264
    Tio dealers in, 251
Ivory carving, (Bullom), 18
Ivory Coast, 172, 243, 312
Iwondo, 298, 299
Iyombo, 298
Iyonkum Marcel, (Nesfar), 208, 209

Jacksonville, Florida, 158
Jacobites, 104
Jadotville, 192, 225, 244. See also Likasi.
Jafua-Lue, 137
Jaiama, 113
Jaiama Nimikoro, chiefdom, 114
Jamaica, 20, 37
    Maroons from, 21, 172
Jamaica Point, 106
Jamba, 274
Jamburia, 128
Jando, 265
Jardine, Governor J.D., 150
Jawara, Yalunka clan, 61, 154
Jawe, chiefdom, 158, 159
Jaya, 109, 117
Jelaladdin, 68
Jemi Lenjeh, 124
Jenkins Street. See Freetown.
Jennings, M., 257
Jeremie, Sir John, Governor, 116
    visits Port Loko, 116, 119
Jesuits, 19, 220, 234, 307
    Jesuit Minor Seminary at Kinzambi, 234
    arrive in kingdom of Kongo, 299
    Jesuit Major Seminary at Mayidi, 234
    relations with Nzinga Mpudi, 299
Jesus Christ, 229
    allegedly born in San Salvador, 229
    allegedly baptized at Nzundi, 229
Jidaro, 137
Jihad, 37, 38, 154, 170
Jimgua. See Sengbe Pieh.
Jimmi, 87
Jimmy, King, 125, 155
Joao I, of the Kongo. See Nzinga Nkuwu.
Joao II, king of Portugal, 181, 257, 258
Joao III, king of Portugal, 280, 299
Jobo of Ngeihun, 87
    drowned by Kai Londo, 88
Jocelyn, S.S., 142
John, H.E.B., 112
John XXIII, Pope, 195
Johnson, the Rev. James, 106
Johnson, Obadiah Alexander, 82
Johnson, Philip, 74, 82, 83
Johnson, Bishop T.S., 83
Johnson, Thomas, ("King of the Creoles"), 24
Joint African and Malagasy Organization. See O.C.A.M.
Jolly, Col. Viscount, 308
Jones, Edward, 83
Jones, Ethelred Nathaniel, (Laminah Sankoh), 83, 84, 85, 112
Jones, Ransolina, 83
Jong, chiefdom, 156
Jong River, 108, 126, 156. See also Taia River.
    estuary of, 161
Joru, 22, 86, 117
"Joseph Kapend Tshombe et Fils," 309
Journey Without Maps, 50
Joya, 96, 97
Juba Kasai, 241
Judges, powers of, 53

Jumu, Amara, of Hanga, 80, 81
Jury rights, 53
Juxon-Smith, Col. Andrew, 33
Kaan Kabady, 262, 305
Kabagayi, 195
Kabala, 23, 144
    way station at destroyed, (1877), 23
Kabanda-Kalibu, 239
Kabare, 252
Kabba Sei, 85, 86
Kabebe, 269
Kabelia, 81
Kabemba, 279
Kabeya, 282, 283
Kabey a Mwanb, 209, 215
Kabila-wa-Katafu, 239
Kabinda, 216, 220, 221, 222, 240, 241, 247, 314
Kabinkolo, 61
Kabobola, 260
Kabobo Lukulu, 269
Kabongo, 216, 222
Kabubuya, 49, 166, 167
    Bombo Lahai Yusufu descended from ruling house of, 166
    and Haidara Kontorfilli, 167
    headquarters of Tonko Limba moved from, 49
Kabwe, 216
Kabw Muzemb, 221
Kafasia, 268
Kafirind, 278
Kafula of Wunde, 88
Kafumbe Bibau, 212
Kafunkumba, 216
Kagbana. See Kayamba.
Kagbo, 19, 110, 170
Kahunga, 223
Kahungula, state, 284
Kahungula, title, 284
Kai's dancers, 91
Kai Kai of Kissi Tongi, 88, 90
Kailahun, (formerly Sacambu), 85, 86, 87, 90, 91
    Governor Cardew visits, 52
    district of, 101, 124, 128, 159
    and the "Kailahun Salient," 28
    rebuilt, named for Kai Londo, 88
    allocated to Liberia, 28
    Liberian customs officer in, 28
Kai Londo, Gbandi chief, 86
Kai Londo, (circa 1845-circa 1896), 22, 85, 86, 87, 88, 117
    elected chief, 90
    named for Gbandi chief, 86
    defeats Kabba Sei, 85
    and Ndawa, 124
    attacked by Porekere and his Sofa, 26
    territory of, divided between Sierra Leone and Liberia, 28
Kai Samba I, (Alpha Lalugba Samba), 88, 89, 90
Kai Tongi, 90, 91, 92
Kaiwa, 97
Kaiyamba, in Moyamba district, 72
Kaiyamba, name of Kpaa-Mende state, 94
Kajiga Balihuta, 210, 211

Kakinga Mutombo, 282
Kakobola, 203, 223
Kakongo, kingdom of, 181, 238
Kakongo, people, 319
Kakrima, 152
Kakua, chiefdom, 127, 166
Kalaba, 214
Kalala Iluga, (first known as Ilunga Mbidi,
    then as Kalala Mbidi), 211, 259, 297
Kalala Kafumbe, 212, 213
Kalala Kamangwa, 213
Kalamba. See Mukenge a Tunsele.
Kalambaie, 221
Kalambakatshak, 277
Kalandala, 239, 319
Kalangba, 40, 71
Kalantuba, 61
Kalasa Mazuri, 268
Kalau, Louis, 213, 214
Kalemie, (formerly Albertville), 320
Kalenga Kitoga, 236, 237
Kalenga Kyalumba, 236
Kalenga Lwango, 236
Kaliang country, 39
Kaliere, 81, 95, 152
    demands Falaba's submission, 144
    becomes subject to Samori, 81
Kalima, 263
Kalina, 197
Kalina (now Gombe) cemetery, Léopold-
    ville, 199
Kalkoya, 111
Kallon, 158, 159
Kalombo, 256
Kalonji, Albert. 244. Also see M.N.C./Ka-
    lonji.
    put under house arrest, 244
Kalota, 139
Kaloun Baga
    British sign treaty with, 46
    treaty disavowed, 46
Kalu, 38
Kalulu, 220
Kalundwa, 239
Kalundwe, 209
Kalunguishi River, 239
Kamadugu, 110, 111, 113
Kamagai, 127
Kamaie, 220, 221
Kama, Mansa. See Mansa Kama.
Kamakuya, 69
Kamande, 166
Kamara, 37, 119, 122, 167. Also see Yalunka.
Kamarow, 38
Kamasele, 61
Kambakamba, 283
Kambala, 239
Kambama, 158
Kambayenge, 126
Kambia, 19, 23, 45, 68, 73, 94, 140, 141,
    149, 166, 174
    allied against Bilali, 45
    Bokari seeks exile in, 46
    bombarded by British, 140
    Governor Cardew visits, 52
    disturbances at, in 1850s, 24
    as terminus of frontier road, 27

Haidara in, 73
Krio traders at, 24
participates in attack on Port Loko,
    119
burned by Soso, 140, 141
Soso-Temne dispute over, 116
Kambol Maur, 215
Kamiliki, 139
Kamina, 216, 222, 311
Kamitatu, Cléophas, 208
Kamong Lwaz, 196
Kamuke, 37
Kananga, (formerly Luluabourg), 212, 216,
    221, 222, 242, 247, 248, 263, 270, 294,
    295, 300, 320. See also Luluabourg.
Kandale, 203, 223, 258, 260
Kande Bureh, 84
Kanene, 216, 309
Kanfori, Domin Konteh, 92, 170
Kangadio, 264
Kangu, 213, 216, 261, 320
Kangu Kumbi Lumbombo, 261
Kaninchin, 209, 215, 320
Kaniok. See Kanyok.
Kankan, Guinea, 38
Kanongish, 239
Kantapala, 238
Kanu, Almamy, 149
Kanumeya, 49
    becomes headquarters of Tonko
    Limba, 49
Kanyimbu Mpembe a Nkind. See Kanyimbu
    Newej Mpemb.
Kanyimbu Newej Mpemb, 214, 215, 238,
    239, 269
Kanyimbu Ntemana, 269
Kanyinda, clan, 212
Kanyok, 182, 209, 212, 221, 320
    founding of state of, 196
    opposition to Kasongo Kiniama, 221
    northern, 221
Kanza, Daniel, 218, 219
Kaoleh, 126, 127
Kaolin, clay, 267
Kaonde, people, 214, 289
Kapala, 98
Kapanga, 215, 216, 277
Kapata, 283
Kapata Fungi, 283
Kapema, 239, 269
Kapend, Joseph, 309
Kapenda Mukwa Ambungo, 249, 282
Kapenda Tshibidi, 283
Kapend, Moise. See Tshombe, Moise.
Kapend Tshomb, J., 215, 216
Kapita, Jean, 231
Kapolowe, 269
Kapondo, 214
Kaponto, 239
Karefa-Smart, Dr. John, 33
Karene
    established as a division of the Pro-
    tectorate, (1896), 28
    outbreak of Hut Tax War at, 28, 70
Kargbo, See Kagbo.
Kariko, 158
Karimu, of Samaya, 51, 69, 92, 93

Kasai, 181, 184, 198, 212, 216, 221, 224, 233,
    240, 242, 244, 245, 246, 247, 248, 250,
    258, 270, 271, 293, 294, 300, 301, 302,
    310, 317, 318, 320, 321, 322, 323, 324,
    325
    trade route from Angola to, 270
    Luba gain hegemony in, 270
Kasai Company. See Compagnie du Kasai.
Kasai Occidental, Region, (Western Kasai),
    223, 320, 321
Kasai Oriental, (Eastern Kasai), 320, 323,
    324, 325, 326
Kasai River, 189, 191, 208, 248, 249, 250,
    262, 271, 282, 283, 289, 290, 304, 316,
    319, 322, 327
    exploration of, 256
Kasangi, 233
Kasanje, Imbangala kingdom, 182, 249
    founding of state of, 196, 282, 283
Kasanje ka Imba, 282
Kasanji, clan, 260
Kasanji, village, 254
Kasanza Mbawvu, 254
Kasa-Vubu, Joseph, 188, 216, 217, 218, 219,
    220, 224, 226, 244, 245, 246
    lodges complaint against Belgium at
    the U.N., 245
    "federalist" position of, 244
    approached to form a government,
    245
    relations with Katanga, 311
    split with P. Lumumba, 245, 246, 272
    and responsibility for Lumumba's
    death, 246
    elected as Congo's first president, 245
    at 1960 Round Table Conference in
    Brussels, 244
    relations with M. Tshombe, 311, 312
    obtains United Nations support, 311,
    312
Kasa-Vubu zone, 218
Kasese, 195
Kashama, Dominique, 220
Kashama, Nkoy, (Stephane), 220
Kashib, 215, 239, 269
Kashing, 239
Kashinga, clan, 260
Kasidishi River, 196, 277
Kasongo, 294
    as headquarters of Tippu Tib, 293
Kasongo, region, 256
Kasongo Kalombo, 220, 221
Kasongo Kiniama, 220, 221, 294
Kasongo-Lunda, 189, 284. See also Kiamfu.
"Kasongo Lunda passage," 284
Kasongo Lwaba, (Fuamba), 212, 221, 241
Kasongo Nyembo I, 222
Kasseh, 47, 50, 56
Kasump. See Kaswup.
Kaswup, 239
Kasunko, chiefdom, 37, 139, 170
Kat, 216
Katako-Kombe, 247, 248, 295
Katana, 195, 252
Katanga, 193, 216, 224, 225, 226, 232, 233,
    244, 245, 309, 310, 311, 312, 314, 320,
    325. See also Shaba.

(Katanga-Continued)
    Armée Nationale Congolaise expedition to, (1962), 198
    copper from, 239
    expeditions to, 314
    independence of proclaimed, (July 11, 1960), 311
    Kitawala movement in, 194
    Luba of, 224, 226
    Lumumba taken to, 246
    national anthem, secessionist, 232
    provincial assembly of, 233
    attempted secession of, 187, 219, 224, 225, 245, 309, 311, 312
    secession ended, (1963), 311
    and the United Nations, 225, 245
    visit of Working Group to, 224
Katanga, chief, 268, 269
    death of, 269
    killing of his sons, 269
Katanga, chief of Lembe, 278, 279
Katanga, people, 214, 269
Katanga Cartel, 310
"Katangaise, La," 232
Katanga Union, 310
Katele, 215, 238
Ka Tegbe, 99, 106, 107
Katende Kafumbe, 212
Kathiri, 82
Katimbo
    market at, 23
    Sara Bayo ruler of, 139, 140
Katoko-Kombe, 242
Katola, 277
Katombe, 241
Katonda, 239
Katoto, 179, 182
Katshaka, 194
Kaumb, Mwant Yav, 216
Kavadilangombe River, 301
Kawama wa Luemba, 238
Kawaya, 283
Kawel, (Mulaj), 209, 215, 277, 278
    death of, 278
Kawend, 277
Kawend, battle of, 277
Kaweya, 126, 127
Kayako, Binti, 49
Kayamba, 93, 94
Kayaya, 250
Kayeye, 241
Kayinbow, 37
Kayumba, 269
Kazembe, kingdom, 268, 284, 288
Kazembe, (title of governor), 214, 215, 238, 239, 240, 268, 269, 270, 278, 320, 324
    Kazembe IV, (Chibang Kanyimbu), 240
    of the Luapula, 269
    Mutand a Yembiyemb as, 278
Kebbi Smith, Tom. See Tom Kebbie Smith.
Kebelai. See Bureh, Bai
Keboke, 290
Kecila, 289
Kecila salt pans, 214, 279
Keeya River, 88
Kefuegunde, 158

Keifa, 88
Kel, 262, 304
Keleha Hori, 97
Kele Mansa, 170
"Kembe," military title, 241
Kemoko Bilali, 94, 95, 132
    captures Marlay Bokari, 113
Kendo, 96
Kenema, town, 89
    modernized, 89
    secondary school at, 164
Kenema, district, 79, 87, 89, 96, 97, 117, 126, 127, 128
    administered by W.D. Bowden, 80
    diamond mining in, 31
    Governor Wilkinson visits, 80
Kenge, 307
Kengi-Mbomeh, 94
Kennedy, Sir Arthur Edward, governor, 60, 106, 109, 110, 134
    sends gunboat, 109
Kent, village, 106, 133
Kentucky, 158
Kenya, 160, 210
Kenyatta, Jomo, of Kenya, 160
Keta, Gold Coast, 76
Kete, 209, 249, 262
Khay, 260
Khenda, 213
Kholifa, 110, 111
Khori, ("country"), 170
    Solimankhori, 139
    Yalunka Khoris, 22
Kiabaka-Ubaka, 297
Kiamfu, title, 239, 284, 320
Kibangu, 229, 230
Kibangu, Mani. See Mani Kibangu.
Kibetu, 221
Kibombo, 293, 300
Kibonge, 190
Kibumba-Bumba, 297
Kibundji, 221
Kibwe, Jean Baptiste, 224
Kifuza, 234
Kigudi, clan, 279
Kigulube, 263
Kihanji, clan, 260
Kiha of Gbendembu, 68
Ki Ka Ku, Mende script, 95
Kikila, 274
Kikondja, 269
Kikongo, language, 197, 217, 227, 256, 257, 299, 321
    W.H. Bentley and, 256
    first written document in, 299
Kokonke Island, 75
Kikoro, 274
Kikoso Gibanda Mafu, 223, 224
Kikwit, 189, 190, 198, 199, 202, 203, 208, 213, 220, 223, 226, 227, 230, 231, 234, 248, 249, 254, 258, 259, 260, 261, 272, 273, 279, 282, 283, 284, 295, 307, 322, 325, 327
Kilamba, 203, 254, 258, 259, 260
    battle of, 259
Kilondo, 239

Kilega, language, 263, 320
Kilembe, 226, 293
Kileo, 221
Kilolo, 193
Kiluba. See Tshiluba.
Kilwa, 240
Kilwa, island, 239
Kimba, Evariste, 219, 224, 225, 226, 311
Kimbai, clan, 203
Kimbamba, 226, 227
Kimbangu, Simon, 189, 227, 228, 229, 230, 320
Kimbangu, village, 287
Kimbanguism, 189, 228, 229, 320
Kimbanguist Church of Zaire, 320
Kimbanguists, 189, 228, 229
Kimberley, Lord, 71
Ki-Mpanza family, 229
Kimpa Vita, (Dona Beatriz), 229, 230
Kimpese, 197, 306
Kimpoko, 287
Kimungu, 239
Kindoki, 251, 252
Kindolo, 287
Kindu, 263, 300
Kinganda, 264
King, C.B.D., president of Liberia, 36
King, C.T.O., 36
Kingeli IV, 252
Kingemba, 197
King-Harman, Governor Charles Anthony, 80
King Jimmy, See Jimmy, King.
King Memorial Church, Freetown, 56
"King Pikin." See Prince of Wales.
Kings College, Durham, England, 111
Kings College, London, 76, 82
Kings Mount, North Carolina, 65
King Street United Brethren Church, Pennsylvania. See United Brethren Church.
King Tom. See Tom, King
King Tom Docks Workers' Union, 160
King Tom Point, 125
Kingu, 300
Kingufu, 260
Kingulu, 261
Kinguri, 182, 249, 282, 283, 320
Kingwana, language, 263
Kingwengwe Kifofo, 230, 231
Kinigbo, 54, 55, 71
    hanged, 55, 71
Kinigbo War, (1875), 54, 55, 71
Kinkuma-Dizi, 216
Ki-Nlaza family, 229
Kinsenzele, 258
Kinshasa, (formerly Léopoldville), 190, 193, 204, 216, 224, 226, 227, 232, 234, 250, 251, 280, 295, 300, 305, 306, 307, 309, 311, 321, 322, 323, 325, 327. See also Léopoldville.
    literary circle in, 296
    open air trial in, 226
    first Protestant chapel built in, 305, 306
    original village of, 287, 288
Kintambo, 287, 288, 290

Kintibalia, 39
    abandoned, (1895), 39
Kintwadi, 228
Kinyama, 268, 269
Kinyimbe, 239
Kinzamba, 226
Kinzamba-Lozo, 226
Kinzambi, 220, 234, 272, 307
Kinzembo, 227
Kinzenze, 237
Kinzonzi, Augustin, 231, 232
Kinzungu, 213
Kipepa. See Chipep.
Kipiko, 239
Kiri, 267
Korongozi, caravan chief, 268, 321
Kisanda Kameshi, 283
Kisangani, (formerly Stanleyville), 188, 190,
    191, 193, 194, 206, 219, 222, 242, 255,
    272, 273, 285, 291, 300, 305, 321, 323,
    327
Kisanji, 231
Kisantu, 216, 219
Kisenga, 239
Kisimi Kamara, 95
Kisolokole, Charles, 227
Kissi, 23, 86, 87, 90, 124, 171, 173
    Kissi Kama, 90
    Kissi Tengea, 88, 90
    Kissi Tongi, 86, 88, 90, 91, 92
Kissy, 58, 147, 156
    Normal School at, 147
Kissy Road Traders Association, 153
Kitangwa, 233
Kitate, 293
Kitawala movement, 193, 194, 195
    repression of by colonial administra-
    tion, 195
Kitenge, Adolphe, 217, 248
Kitenge Ngundu, 293, 294
Kitona, 225
Kitondo, 239
Kittam, district, 120, 121, 157
    raids on, 128
Kittam River, 67
Kitumba, 222
Kitutu, 237
Kivianga, 256
Kivu, Province, later Region, 179, 181, 193,
    194, 195, 196, 224, 236, 245, 263, 264,
    322
    Masisi revolt in, (1944), 193, 194, 195,
    317, 318, 321
    1964 rebellion in, 225
    Swahili attacks on, 236
Kivu, Lake. See Lake Kivu.
Kiwele, J., 232, 233
Kizambi, 295
Kizenzi, 321
Kizu Mission School, 216
Knight, Charles, 95, 96
Knives, Lega, 183
Knox College, Galesburg, Ohio, 138
Kobo, 230, 231
Kogbandi Vangahun, 96, 97, 128
Koi, 172

Koinadugu, 37, 61, 62, 94, 111, 113, 139,
    151, 154, 155
    exempted from 1896 house tax, 28,
    53
    established as division of Protector-
    ate, (1896), 28
Koindu, market at, 23
Kokelly, Pa. See Tom II, "King."
Koko. See Gombu Smart.
Kola, 265, 321
Kola Ngbandi, 233
Kola nuts, 129, 139, 140
Koli, 274
Kolunkoray, 171
    built by Bilali, 45
    burnt by Supt. Parkes, 93
Kolwezi, 214, 216, 225, 239, 289, 311
    end of Katanga secession announced
    at, 311
    occupied by United Nations, 225
Komalu, 86, 87, 88
Kombana Lunda, 282, 283
Kombana Mutombo, 249
Kombili, 113
Kombo, 249
Kombo Kiboko, 233
Komende, 135, 143
Komo, people, 194
Kona, 149
Konde, 295
Konde Brima, 154
Kong, 54. See also Bagi.
Kongbora, 54
Kong Gbanya, 71
Kong Kuba, Bai Sherbro, signs 1825 treaty,
    98
King Kuba, (Herbert Lewis), son of Kpana
    Lewis, 99
Kongo Dia Ngunga, 217
Kongo, kingdom of, 181, 182, 204, 229, 230,
    256, 257, 267, 268, 280, 281, 296, 297,
    298, 299, 312, 313, 318, 319, 321, 322,
    323, 325, 327
    art of, destroyed by Mvemba Nzinga,
    281
    authority partly restored, 296
    period of decline after 1665, 313
    founding of, 237, 297
    army defeated by the Portuguese,
    (1665), 229, 313
    and the Portuguese, 257, 258, 280,
    281, 299
    non-Portuguese missionaries arrive in,
    296
    provinces of, 257
    brief restoration of, in the early 1700s,
    230
    succession dispute in, 268
    Vita Nkanga and, 312, 313
Kongo (Bakongo), people, 217, 288, 319, 321
Kongolo, 293, 300, 314
Konike, 150
    British drive Sofa from, 114
Konike Barina, 149, 150
Konike Temne, 39, 114, 132, 150
    threatened by Porekere, 26, 132
Konko Gbaku, 49, 97, 98

Konkori Sankoh, Alimamy. See Brima
    Konkori Sankoh, Alimamy.
Kono, people, 113, 114, 171, 172, 173, 174
    cloth from, 23
    Governor Cardew visits, 52
    diamonds, at, 30, 31
    entry into Sierra Leone, 19
    and the French, 132
    language, 19
    and Matturi, 113
    conflict with Ndawa, 114
    attacked by Nyagua, 113
    war with Nyagua, 127
    origin of name, 19
    Porekere in, 26
    of Sando, 39
    invaded by the Sofa, 113, 114
    link with the Vai, 19
Kono, place, 87, 88, 108, 113, 114, 124, 150,
    168
    British drive Sofa from, 114
Konte, 19, 37, 151, 169, 171
"Kontorfilli," 73
Konya Nallo, 93, 94
Konzo Ikulu. See Mount Ngaliema.
Koran, 68, 74
Koranic learning, 139
Koranko, 19, 22, 39, 45, 61, 94, 110, 111,
    113, 132, 140, 144, 158, 168, 169, 170,
    171, 172, 173
    traveling blacksmiths of the, 23
    seeks British protection from the Sofa,
    27
    Governor Cardew visits, 52
    enter the country, 110, 111
    Kono flee to, 113
    language, 171
    Marlay Bokari and, 113
    of Nieni, 39
    Porekere allies with southern, 132
    sections of country conquered by
    Samori, 26
    Samori's forces in, 134
Koranko Mara, clan, 38
Korba, 69
Kordofan. See Darfur.
Koroma, clan, 19, 38, 39, 171
Kosa, (Ako), people, 278, 288, 289. See also
    Ndembu-Kosa.
Kosh, 262
Kossoh, 47, 111, 171
Kota-Koli, 307
Kotoi, 283
Kowa, 126
Koya, 17, 47, 71, 101, 110, 116, 119, 120,
    124, 148, 158, 168, 171
    wars against Sierra Leone Company,
    72
Koya Temne, 148, 149, 155, 168
Koyeima Central School, 40, 164
Kpa, town, 127
    meaning of name, 127
Kpaa-Mende, (the western branch of the
    Mende), 18, 54, 70, 71, 127, 168, 171,
    174
    send contingent to the Asante War
    (1873), 71

(Kpaa-Mende-Continued)
visited by William Budge, (1879), 24
invasions of, in the early 19th century, 168
called Kaiyamba, 94
in the Kinigbo War, 71
Lomboi as last ruler of, 100
founding of Lower Kpaa-Mende, 127
and Moigula-Vonjo conflict, 107, 108
Moyamba and, 93, 94
state of, 22
state expands 54
and the Tongo players, 99
Madam Yoko as ruler of, 164, 165, 166
"Kpaka," (chair), 137
Kpaka, chiefdom, 109
Kpaka family, 110. See also Rogers family.
Kpana Farley, 85
Kpana Lewis, 98, 99
Kpanga district, 324
Kpaweh of Mende, 87
Kpawi Bundu, 87
killed, 88
Kpebe, 151
Kpeima, 96
Kpeje, 128
Kpejena, 124
Kpombai, 86
Kpo-veh, 85, 87, 97, 124, 171
Kpowamo-ei-Nepo, 99, 100
Kpowno-ei-Nepo. See Leopard Society.
Kpungu Kangaju, 100
Krim, 171
Krios, (Creoles), 35, 42, 50, 52, 53, 58, 79, 83, 84, 111, 112, 118, 119, 129, 130, 140, 141, 145, 146, 147, 152, 157, 160, 168, 171
agriculture and, 154
as "Black Englishmen," 146
relations with the British, 24, 129, 130
relations with Governor Cardew, 53
progressively excluded from office, 53, 146
growing influence of, 140
in Lagos, Nigeria, 147
language, 171
Sir Samuel Lewis as community leader, 102, 103, 104
massacred in Mende uprising, 53
interests represented in National Council of Sierra Leone, 32
origin of, 21
as a professional class, 25
and administration of the Protectorate, 104
relations with the people of the Protectorate, 112, 140, 160
and Port Loko property losses, 119
forced out of Rio Nunez area, 153
at Senehun, 71
status of, 25, 26, 53
at Tonko Limba, 74
as traders, 23, 24, 27
Krobo campaign of 1862, Gold Coast, 76
Kru, in campaign against Kpaa-Mende, 71
Kru Bay, 19

Krugba. See Kurugba.
Kruto, 39
Kuba, kingdom, 181, 261, 262, 304, 305, 321, 322, 325
Kubasa, 195
Kukuna, 45, 140
Bilali and, 45
Karimu's forces at, 93
Kukuna Soso, 93
Kulakonka, 38
Kulanjinga, 283
Kulu-Mantandu, 272
Kumase, Gold Coast (now Ghana), 62, 105
Kumbasa, 139
Kumba Wulen Lai, 113
Kumi, 222
Kumrabai, 107
Kumu, 321
Kunde Lungu, The, 289
Kundu, people, 207, 321
Kungba, 282
Kungulu, 207
Kunia Banna, 123
Kunjo, 86
Kuntebe, 236
Ku Ntwala, ("The Future"), 197
Kurugba, 171
Kuruwa, 132
Kutumpuku, 205
Kwa River, 190
Kwango district, 279, 284, 322
Kwango River, and region, 184, 189, 202, 213, 238, 239, 249, 261, 262, 282, 283, 284, 304, 316, 320, 327
Kwanza River, 238, 322
Kwelu, 47, 55, 70, 157
Kwenge Falls, 284
Kwenge River, 284
Kwenkwenda, ("Where Shall I Go"), 197
Kwese, 281
Kwilu, 273, 322, 324
1959 elections in, 208
1960 national elections in, 208
1964 rebellion in, 187, 189, 198, 208, 219, 225, 234, 237, 272, 273, 283, 300, 306, 307, 311, 322, 324, 326
Kwilu River, and region, 182, 202, 203, 213, 223, 226, 258, 260, 261, 262, 282, 284, 304, 322, 324, 325, 326
Kyaba, 239
Kyabunda, place, 262
Kyabunda. See Mopipi Mulongeki, Paul.
Kyalala Andre, 263
Kyana, 239
Kyana Kyamu, chief, 269
Kyembe, 214
Kyoli. See Shabunda.
Laba, 250
Lablama, 96
Laborde, William Melville, 165
Labor Department. See Sierra Leone Labour Department.
Labor, obligatory, 72, 91
Labour Party, British, 1945 election victory, 32

Lacerda e Almeida, De Francisco Jose de. See De Lacerda e Almeida, Francisco Jose.
Ladywood Dispensary, Birmingham, 162
Lagao Lamboi, 100
Lagos, Nigeria, 76, 82
Krios in, 147
Lahai Booth, James, 74
Lahai Golay, 156
Lahai Kaloko, Abdul, 69
Lahai Sheriff, 155, 156
Lahai Young, 141
Laia, 123
Laing, Alexander Gordon,
visits Falaba, (1822), 24
visits Kulakonka, (1922), 24
Lake Bangweolu, 214, 215, 239
Lake Boya, 211, 220, 222, 297
Lake Kasseh, 67
Lake Kisale, 179, 269
Lake Kivu, 182, 236, 252, 262, 264, 317, 318, 326
Lake Leopold II. See Lake Mai Ndombe.
Lake Mai Ndombe, (formerly Lake Leopold II), 181, 182, 208, 266, 267, 274, 289, 290, 303, 317, 322
Lake Mweru, 182, 214, 215, 238, 239, 259, 268, 269, 288, 289
Lake Nyasa, 240
Lake Samba, 222
island, 222
Lake Tanganyika, 232, 238, 268, 320
shells from, 239
Lamba, 214, 268, 269, 289
Lamboi, 100, 127
Lamin Abdul Lahai, 110
Lamina, 140, 141
Lamina Barmoi, 116, 140
Laminah Sankoh. See Jones, Ethelred Nathaniel.
Lamina Suntu, 61
Laminaya, 69, 93
occupied by Karimu, 93
attacked twice in 1890, 93
Langa, 93
Language
common national language for Zaire, 210
Lankanfali, 139, 140
Lankwan, Abbe Adolphe, 234
Lansana, David, 33, 48, 100, 101
La Politique Coloniale, 302
Largo, 61, 62, 124
Lashyaang Latot Landoon, 262
"Latent Riches of Sierra Leone, The," 147
Latin, 195
Latin script, 95
Lawson, Thomas George, 24, 101, 102, 116, 120
and British relations with the interior, 24
visits interior, 24
and J.C.E. Parkes, 129
and Port Loko rulership, 119
retires, 47
Lawson, William, 47

League of Nations Mandates, 302

Leavitt, Joshua, 142

Lebanese
  in Sierra Leone as businessmen, 26, 29, 44
  target of anti-Syrian riots, 29, 42
  as truck owners, 30

Lebanon Valley College, Annville, Pennsylvania, 55

Lega, people, 182, 183, 236, 237, 262, 264, 318, 321, 322

Legislative Council of Lagos, Nigeria, 82

Legislative Council of Sierra Leone, 36, 40, 41, 43, 44, 50, 53, 89, 118, 132, 145, 146, 147, 150, 153
  1951 elections to, 84, 85, 89
  established 1863, 25, 64
  J. Ezzidio first African on, 64, 65
  C. Heddle on, 75
  renamed House of Representatives, 32
  Sir Samuel Lewis as member of, 102, 103
  majority given to elected members, 32, 112
  J. Mannah Kpaka on, 110
  membership increased, (1924), 31
  parties represented in, 32
  powers of, 25
  Protectorate participation in, 32, 73, 112
  and administration of Protectorate, 98
  representation in, 41
  A.J. Shorunkeh-Sawyerr and, 145, 146, 147
  Toboku-Metzger and, 157
  I.T.A. Wallace Johnson and, 160

Leicester, near Freetown, 35

Leigh, Ann, 60

Lele, 250, 262, 322

Leleka, 234, 235

Le Marinel, Paul, 271

Lemba, 214, 216, 278, 287

Lembwe, 239

Lemvo, 256

Lendy, Capt. E.A.W., 39, 130, 132
  death of, 130, 132

Leo X, Pope, 204

Leopards, attacks by, 298

Leopard murders, 74, 79, 99, 100, 107, 161

Leopard skins, 293

Leopard Society, (Kpowno-ei-Nepo), 74, 79

Leopold II, Lake. See Lake Mai Ndombe.

Leopold Educational Institute, (secondary school), 44

Leopold II of the Belgians, 133, 184, 185, 186, 191, 201, 205, 207, 251, 256, 271, 288, 291, 308, 315, 318, 319
  hostile to Protestant missions in the Congo, 306
  Order of, 232

Leopold III of Belgium, (formerly the Duke of Brabant), 302

Léopoldville, (now Kinshasa), 185, 186, 187, 190, 193, 197, 198, 199, 216, 217, 218, 219, 224, 225, 226, 227, 228, 232, 234, 243, 244, 245, 246, 248, 250, 255, 272, 273, 295, 305, 311, 312, 321, 323
  African communes of, 218
  Kinshasa commune of, 244
  becomes capital of the Belgian Congo, 317
  Lingala-speaking population of, 217
  P. Lumumba leaves, 246
  music of, 193
  proposed pan-African conference in, 245
  radio, 219
  1959 riots in, 218, 243
  H.M. Stanley establishes station at, 305

Léopoldville province, (now Bandundu Region), 189, 232
  provincial council of, 197, 232

Leteta, chief, 251, 252

Leteta station, (at Mbanza Ngombe), 251

Lever Brothers, 258

Leverville, 272

Levi, John, 25, 64

Levuma, 114, 132

Lewis, the Rev. Alonzo, 143

Lewis, Herbert. See Kong Kuba.

Lewis, Sir Samuel, 102, 103, 104, 115, 134, 145, 146
  first African to be knighted, 25
  relations with Governor Cardew, 53
  retained by S.B.A. MacFoy, 107

Lewis, William, 103

Liange, 127

Libanda, 304

Libele. See Libiri.

Libenge, 295

Liberated Africans, 47, 140, 153. See also Krios, (Creoles); Recaptives.

Liberated African Department Yard, Freetown, 105, 106

Liberia, 36, 76, 85, 86, 87, 88, 91, 108, 110, 170, 171, 172, 174
  1911 boundary agreed with Sierra Leone, 28
  1917 boundary dispute with Sierra Leone, 36
  frontier with Sierra Leone, 52, 53
  raids across frontier, 85, 86
  attacks towns in Gallinas, 109
  claims Gallinas state, 108, 109
  signs treaties on Gallinas coast, 108
  allocated Kailahun, 28
  D. Lansana extradited from, 101
  seizes ships, 108, 109
  and Sierra Leone, 17
  example to Sierra Leone, 78
  claims South Sherbro, 108
  and events of 1898 uprising, 110
  D.F. Wilberforce banished to, 161

Liberian Commissioner for the Interior, (Native Affairs), 36

Liberian Order of Diplomatic Redemption, 36

Libinza, 254, 265, 266, 276, 277, 298

Libiri, (Libele), 253

Liboko family, 234

Liège, Belgium, 219, 232, 308

Lienart, 271

Likasi, (formerly Jadotville), 192, 214, 220, 225, 239, 268, 269, 278, 319, 322

Likoka, chiefdom, 298

Likoka, (Basongo), people, 276, 277, 298, 299. See also Ntanda.

Likoka. See Lobala-Likoka sector.

Likoka-Ntanda, 281

Likouala-Aux-Herbes River, 205

Likouala River, 205, 290

Likumbelo, 265

Lilamba, 266

Lilanga, 200

Likeko, 191

L.I.M. See Livingstone Inland Mission.

Limania. See Musoma.

Limba, 18, 22, 23, 28, 37, 45, 51, 61, 92, 123, 150, 152, 166, 169, 170, 171, 172, 174. See also Sela Limba; Tonko Limba.
  "Apostle to the Limba," (P.P. Hazeley), 74
  support Bilali, 140
  Governor Cardew visits, 52
  catechism, 74, 75, 83
  possible origin in Futa Jallon, 19
  language, 83
  Literature Committee, 75
  migrations of, 19
  Samori's forces in, 134
  country conquered by Samori, 26
  wars with Soso, 51, 74, 82, 83, 92, 93, 97
  war with Temne, 82
  associated with Wara-Wara hills, 19

Limpanya. See Somelier.

Limpoko, 265

Lincoln Academy, Kings Mount, North Carolina, 65

Lincoln's Inn, London, 48

Lincoln University, Pennsylvania, 83

Lindi River, 193

Lingala, 215, 217, 266, 292, 322
  Lingala-speaking population of Léopoldville, 217
  P. Lumumba fluent in, 244
  proposed as common national language for Zaire, 210

Lingenji, 205

Linguists, of Zaire, 210

Lion, Order of the, 264

Lisala, 199, 235, 324

Lisbon, Portugal, 296

Lisombo, chiefdom, 200

Liston medal for surgery, 62

Little Popo, 101, 116

Little Scarcies River, 149, 173

Liverpool, England, 107, 146, 162. See also University of Liverpool.

Livingstone, David, 287

Livingstone Inland Mission, (L.I.M.), 305

Livingstone River, 291

Locusts, plague of, 166

Loange River, 249, 282, 284

Loango, state, 181, 238, 322

Lobala, chiefdom, 282
Lobala, people, 235, 281, 282, 299
Lobala-Likoko sector, 235, 298, 299
Lobala Mpoko, 282
Lobo, (Balobo), people, 253, 298, 322
Lodja, 295, 300, 314
Lofoi Falls, 239
Loggie, 108
Logo-Ogambi, 255
Loi, 274
Loja county, Liberia, 86
Loka, 200
Lokele, 190
Loko, 18, 19, 40, 47, 50, 68, 69, 71, 93,
    94, 123, 148, 149, 171, 172
    "liberated" Africans released by, 60
    Governor Cardew visits, 52
    Dispersal of, 148, 149
    link with Gbande of Liberia, 18
    slaves bought by Gombu Smart, 71
    attacked by Karimu, 93, 97
    relation with Karimu, 93, 97
    language, 18
    origin of, 18
    wars with Temne, 59, 116, 148, 149
Lokole, 290
Lokolela, 277
Loko Massama, 58, 59
Loko Smart family, 148
Lolanga, 207, 277
Lomami River, 182, 190, 221, 222, 241, 247,
    293, 295, 313, 314, 326
Loma Mountains, 39
Lomba, 268
Lomboko, 141
Lomotwa, 214, 239, 268, 289
London, England, 48, 64, 130, 131, 133, 134,
    146, 147, 162
    Belgian government-in-exile in, 302
    Thomas Peters visits, 131
    World Trade Union Congress in, 160
London School of Economics, 36
London School of Tropical Medicine, 63
London University. See University of Lon-
    don.
Longangi, 236, 237
Longele River, 231
Longi, ("Lunge"), 94
Long Island, New York, 142
Longo-Longo. See Buylaert.
Lorge, A., 193
Los, Islands of, 59
    annexed by Britain, (1818), 59, 104
    claimed by Dalla Modu, 59
Losala-Djouma, 207
Losengo, 291
Lotembo River, 314
Lothaire, Commander H., 202, 314
Louisiana, 158
Louis XVI of France, 104
Louvain University, 301
Louvanium University, 250, 251
    Medical School, 216
    Congolese Parliament convened at,
    273
    1964 strike at, 250, 255, 295, 296, 302
Lovua River, 282, 283, 284

Lowama, 87
Lower Congo Region, (now Lower Zaire),
    216, 218, 219, 228, 251
Lower Congo to Katanga Railroad, B.C.K.
    See Compagnie du Chemin de Fer du
    Bas-Congo au Katanga.
Lower Loko country, 68, 69
Lower Zaire Region, (formerly Lower Con-
    go), 216, 229, 231
Loweya, 266
Loyalists, (in American War of Indepen-
    dence), 131
Lozelles General Dispensary, Birmingham,
    England, 58
Lozi, 279
Lozo, people, 226
Luajimu, 283
Lualaba River, 182, 211, 214, 215, 222, 239,
    240, 247, 259, 269, 270, 279, 288, 289,
    293, 294, 295, 297, 300, 326, 327
    Kalala Ilunga crosses, 211
Lunda, 184, 240, 283, 297, 312, 313
    occupied by the Dutch, 296, 312
    recaptured by the Portuguese, 296,
    313
Luapula, 238, 239, 268, 269
Luapula River, 214, 215, 238, 239, 268, 269,
    279, 289, 325, 326
Luawa, 90, 111
    Kabba Sei expelled from, 85
    ruled by Kai Londo, 22, 86, 87, 88, 90
    Kai Londo extends boundaries of, 86,
    87, 88, 90
    threatened by Ndawa, 124
    raids on, 86
Luba, (Baluba), 194, 196, 211, 212, 214, 220,
    221, 222, 224, 226, 259, 270, 282, 283,
    294, 297, 301, 310, 318, 320, 324, 326.

    See also Sanga.
    clan groupings among, 317
    founding of the state of, 196, 211
    of Kasai, 212, 224, 244, 310, 317, 318
    gain hegemony in Kasai, 270
    of Katanga, 224, 226, 310
    support the Lomotwa, 289
    and Lubuku cult, 322
    tensions with the Lunda of Katanga,
    310
    defeated by the Lunda, 214
    M'Siri fights the, 269
    oral tradition of, 259
    paramount chief of, 318
    Ngongo Leteta and, 294
    Ngongo Luhaka and, 295
    Nkongolo and, 297
    migrate from Shaba to Kasai, 270
Luba-Hemba, 239
Luba-Lubilangi, 212
Luba Samba, 289
Lubefu, 313, 314
Lubembi River, 221
Lubi River, 212
Lubilash River, 212, 221, 241, 259, 277, 294,
    295, 320, 324
Lubudi River, 214, 215, 239, 278, 289
Lubue River, 213
Lubuku, cult, 212, 270, 322

Lubumbashi, (formerly Elisabethville), 214,
    215, 216, 224, 228, 239, 322, 326. See
    also Elisabethville.
Lubunda lands, 239
Lubunda, Lozo chief, 239
Lubunda, Lunda blacksmith. See Rubund.
Lubutu, 193, 194
Lucas, Sir Keith, 32
Lueta, 248
Lufira River, 289
Lufuku River. See Upper Lufuku River.
Lufu-Ntoto, 232
Lugbu, 107
Luhaka, 247, 248
    death of, 248
Luhaka. See Shinga I.
Lui River, 283
Luilu River, 221
Luke, Hannah, 43
Lukeni, 237, 238, 297
Lukenie River, 290, 300, 314
Lukeni lua Nimi, 237
Lukoshi, people, 278
Lukoshi River, 278
Lukuga, 320. See also Kalemie.
Lukundo Sango, 283
Lukunga, 306
Lukwesa Ilunga, 238, 239, 240, 269
Lulaba, 189
Lulonga, 303
Lulonga River, 192, 201, 303
Lulua, 244, 270, 271
    chiefs of, 270
    resistance to Congo Free State, 271
    recognized as a distinct group, 270
    social upheaval among, 270
    Lulua River, 270, 301
    Mushid a Nambing drowned in, 278
Luluabourg, (now Kananga), 186, 197, 198,
    216, 219, 222, 242, 244, 247, 271, 294,
    314, 320
    1895 soldiers revolt in, 247, 271, 313,
    314, 316
    1944 revolt in, 317
Luluabourg Constitution. See Constitution.
Luluabourg-Malandji, (now Kananga), 270
Lumbuli, 248
Lumpkin, the Hon. Henry, 50
Lumpkin, William Rainy. See Bungie, Ali-
    mamy.
Lumpungu, Goi Mafula, (also chief Mui-
    kalebwe), 221, 240, 241, 242, 247
Lumumba, Patrice, 187, 219, 237, 242, 243,
    244, 245, 246, 247, 272, 302, 310
    visits Accra, 218
    proclaimed as an African martyr, 246
    confined to his residence, 219
    death of, 246
    followers of, in eastern Congo, 237
    relations with Kasa-Vubu, 219
    and P. Mulele, 272
    murder of, 187, trial of Tshombe
    sought for, 312
    relations with Kwame Nkrumah of
    Ghana, 244, 245
    forms political party, 218
    relations with M. Tshombe, 311

Lunda, (Aarund state), 181, 182, 196, 202, 203, 209, 213, 215, 216, 221, 238, 239, 240, 249, 250, 269, 277, 278, 279, 282, 283, 284, 286, 288, 289, 300, 301, 318, 320, 322, 324, 325, 326
 relations with Angola, 286
 expansion into Angola and Kasai, 301
 founding of, by Chibind Yirung, 196, 323
 land occupied by Cokwe, 277
 council of, 318
 influence expanded by Kanyimbu Newej Mpemb, 214, 238
 Kasongo Kiniama flees to, 221
 acquires some Luba customs, 182
 land chiefs, 301
 recover lands, 277
 influence extended by Lukwesa Ilunga, 238, 239
 origin of Mai Munene chiefdom, 250
 Mutand Yembiyemb and expansion of, 278, 279
 expansion under Mwene Putu Kasongo, 283, 284
 Ngand a Bilond extends power of, 288, 289
 Lunda Pende chiefdom of Kangu, 261
 Ruwej a Nkond and, 300, 301
 conflict with Shila, 239
 traditions, 300, 301
 tribal association of, 310
Lunda Amakundo, 284
Lundaland, 282
Lunde, 215
Lunga, 283
Lunga River, 295, 314
"Lunge." See Longi.
Lungu, 239
Lungumbila, 205
Lunkinda, 239
Lunya. See Monghere.
Luozi, 307
Lupambulu sect, 214
 1944-45 revolt of, 214, 261, 323
Lupembian (Lupemben) tradition. See Middle Stone Age.
Lupungu, 247, 248, 294
Lurgan, County Armagh, Ireland, 115
Lusaka, Zambia, 232
Lusambo, 216, 241, 263, 271, 293, 295, 313, 314
Lusambo province, (later Kasai), 248, 320, 323, 325
Lusanga, 279
Luseng, 301
Lusengo, 253, 254
Luso-African. See Portuguese-African.
Lusuna, 314
Lutipuka, stream, 268
Lutshiko, 284
Lutshiko River, 249, 282, 284
Lutshima, 258, 261,
Lutshima River, 226, 258
Lutundula Kilinda, 248
Luvua River, 269
Luvuvamu mu Nzo, ("Peace in the House"), 197

Lwena, 196, 209
 traders, 269
Lwena-Lwa-Ntipa, 239
Lynchburg, Virginia, 65
Lyons, France, 48
Maaju Turay. See Bonney.
Mabale, 205, 276, 290, 291, 298, 323, 324
Mabang, 154
Mabanta, 123
Mabanta Temne, 126
Mabaya, Albert, 231
Mabela, 211, 297
Mabella Coaling Company Workers' Union, 160
Mabenzo, 281
Mabera Benoit, 248, 249
Maboi Manga, 127
Mabole River, 149, 151
Macar. See de Macar, Oscar.
Macaulay and Babington, 59, 60, 75
Macaulay Brothers, 106
Macaulay, George, 106
Macaulay, "King" John, 104, 105, 106
Macaulay, Kenneth, 59, 60
Macaulay, Thomas, 153
MacCarthy Island, 114
MacCarthy, Sir Charles, 104, 105, 106
MacFoy, Solomon Benjamin Augustus, 99, 106, 107, 114
MacGregor Laird, 75
MacGregor Laird penny. See Currency.
Madagascar, 219, 225, 311
Madimba region, 231
Madina, 69, 97, 116
Madras, India, 48
Madrasi Islami, 129
Madrid, Spain, 311, 312
Madzia, 197
Mafessa River, 88
Mafonda, 123, 134
Mafute Benjamin, 233
Magbalu, 88
Magbele, 59, 109, 123
Magburaka, 149
Magistrate's Court Ordinance, Sierra Leone, (1905), 156
Magulu, 268
Mahamba, Alexander, 226
Mahdists, 265
Mahdist uprising, 265, 306
Mahenge, battle of, 301
Mahomed, 241
Mai. See Chibang Chelek Muswa Musapu.
Mail packet service, (Britain to Freetown, Sierra Leone), 75
Mai Munene, 239, 249, 250, 271, 283, 284
Mai Ndombe, region, 184. See also Lake Mai Ndombe.
Maize. See Corn.
Majaan cemetery, Lunde, 215
Majei, chiefdom, 127
Majoe, 94
Makala prison, 190
Makali, 150
Makanda Kabobi, 250, 251

Makanza, (formerly Nouvelle-Anvers, or Bangala Station), 190, 192, 199, 200, 201, 202, 205, 253, 254, 276, 290, 291, 298, 299, 303, 304, 322, 323, 324. See also Nouvelle-Anvers.
Makavoray, of Tikonko, 22, 85, 87, 107, 108, 121, 166
Makaya, 107, 124, 127, 128
Makeni
 Lamina Suntu banished to, 61, 150
 terminus of branch railway, 29
Makitu, 251, 252
Makoko, 287, 323
Makombe, 252
Makonde, 240
Makonga, 224
Makulu, 215
Makutu, 192, 200, 235, 317
Makutu Mimboyo, 250
Malamah, 153
"Malamah baft," 153
"Malamah House," Freetown, 153
Malal, 149
Malandje, 212
Malanga, 253, 254
Malange, (of Angola), 212
Malangi a Phumba, 254, 255
Malebo Pool, (formerly Stanley Pool), 180, 184, 205, 251, 252, 256, 266, 271, 286, 287, 288, 290, 305, 306, 307, 308, 321, 323, 327
 steamer Stanley transported to, 252
Malela, 314
Malema, 85
Malene, 122
Malfeyt, 190, 222
Mali, 172
Mali empire, 17, 92, 172
Maligia, 60, 119, 122
 British attack on, (1855), 60
 fighting at, (1880), 46
Maligi Gbele, 46, 51
Malinke. See Mandinka.
Malo, 124
Malu Malu, 314
Malumba, Lt. Col., 198
Malundja, chiefdom, 200
Malvoz, 279
Mambo, 55
Mambolo, 140, 141
Mambwe, people, 238
Mambwe, place, 238
Mampoko, people, 192, 200, 266, 275, 317
Mampoko, sub-chiefdom, 275
Mana Siaka, 108, 109, 110, 117
Manchester, England, 84, 106, 160, 308
 Pan-Africanist Congress in, (1945), 160
Manda, clan, 223
 of Kahunga, 223
 of the Lozo, 226
Mande, 139, 171, 172, 174
Mande language, 17, 19, 66, 73, 108, 172, 174
Mandingo. See Mandinka.
Mandika, 202
Mandinka, 17, 18, 19, 92, 94, 122, 125, 151, 170, 171, 172, 174

(Mandinka-Continued)
of Biriwa Limba, 151
blacksmiths among the, 49
attempts to mediate between King Tom II and the Colony, 155
immigration into Sierra Leone, 118
support the Nova Scotian uprising, 59
in alliance against the Sankoh, 119
Mandjumba, 202
Mando, 85, 86
Mandongo, 235
Mandradele Tanzi, 255, 256
Mandu, 101, 127, 166
Manena Lyabanza, 268
"Manes" people, 66, 67
Manga, Sierra Leone village, 205
Manga, Yalunka title, 22, 38, 139, 144, 172
Mangai, 189, 190, 208, 249
Manga Kombeh Balla, 92
Mangba, 192, 200, 317
Mangbetu, people, 183, 323
Mangbetu, state, 285
Mange Bure, chiefdom, 73
Mangowai, (Poro name of Kayamba), 93
Mangulu, 205
Mangwa, 235
Mangwaba, 235
Mani, Mandinka group, 17, 18, 141, 143, 172, 173
Mani, place, 141
Mani, title, 323
Manianga, 232
Maniema, 247, 295, 318
Manifesto, (1956), 217
Mani Kabunda. See Nsau ne Vunda.
Mani Kibangu, 229
Mani Kongo, 181, 204, 257, 258, 280, 281, 296, 297, 299, 300, 321, 323
Dom Henrique, 204
investiture of, 298
blessed by Mani Kabunda, 297
defeated by Mani Soyo, 296
Mvemba Nzinga, (Afonso I), 181, 280, 281
Nkanga Lukeni, (Garcia II), 312
Nzinga Mpudi, 299, 300
Nzinga Nkuwu, (Joao II), 181, 257, 258
Vita Nkanga, 312, 313
Mani Nsundi, 204
Manioc, (cassava), 182, 183, 205, 232, 236, 287
Mani Soyo, 323
Daniel de Silva, 296
becomes virtually independent, 296
defeats Mani Kongo, 296
Manuel, Dom, 257, 258
Mani-Vandu, 268, 323
Mani Vunda. See Nsaka ne Vunda.
Manjakewai, 87
drowned by Kai Londo, 88
Manjolu, 124
Mankah, John, 109
Mankika, 201
Mannah, John Rogers. See Mannah-Kpaka, John.
Mannah-Kpaka, John, (John Rogers Mannah), 109, 110

Mano-Dasse, 165
Mano Gbonjeima, 67
"Man of the Crossroads." See Mwin Pand.
Mano River, 109, 110
Mano Sakrim, 68
Mano Salija, 110
Mano Sewalu, 86
Mansa, title, 108, 170, 172
Mansa Kama, title, 111
Mansa Kama, warrior, 110, 111
Mansa Morifing, 111, 113
Mansaray, 19, 37, 152, 154, 172
Mansaray, Dankay, 36
Mansa Sewa. See Sewa, Mansa.
Mansfield judgement, (1772), 20
Mantantu Dundulu, 256, 257
Mantele, 281
Manua Sera, 268
Manuel I of Portugal, 204, 280
Manuel, Dom, (Mani Soyo), 257, 258
Manyaka, 235
Manzika, 285
Manpaki, 151
"Mapendo," 194
Mapongu. See Brabanta.
Mara, 19, 113, 172
Marampa, iron discovered at, 30
Mardulier, 202
Margai, Albert, 32, 33, 101
succeeds Sir Milton Margai as chief minister, 32, 164
calls elections, 33
Margai, Sir Milton Augustus Striery, 32, 33, 41, 42, 45, 84, 111, 112
and chiefs, 72, 73
death of, 32
Margaret Wrong prize, 197
Marinel. See Le Marinel, Paul.
Maritime and Waterfront Wages Board, 63
Maritz, Lt. Gaston-Maxime, 132
death of, 132
Marke, the Rev. Charles, 115
Marlay Bokari, 22, 113
Maro Bai, 59
Maroon Chapel, 35
Maroons, 63, 133, 172
and Farma Tami, 66
build houses and shops in Freetown, 104
arrive from Jamaica, 21
help suppress Nova Scotian revolt, 21
Marseilles, France, 48
Marxism, 273
Masama, Treaty of, (1879), 102
Masarico, queen of the Mani, 17, 18
Masimera, state, 71, 72, 148
Masingbe, 150
Masisi, 193, 194, 195, 263
Masisi revolt, (in Kivu province), 193, 194, 195
Masks, Lega, 183
Massa, 87
Massachusetts, 135
Massamah treaties, 141
disavowed, 141
Massa Paki, 151
Massaquoi, 108, 117, 172

Massaquoi crown, 108, 109
Zachary Rogers marries into Massaquoi family, 109, 110, 137
Massari, 290
Matabakemba, 276
Mata-Boike. See Ngemba.
Matacong, island,
ceded to the British, 59
occupied by the French, 46
Matadi, 185, 231, 232, 238, 280, 305, 306, 307, 308, 309, 323, 325
Matamba, state, 181
Matambakemba, 298
Matamumbete, 291
Matand, 239
Matantoko, 253
Mateko, 208
Matemu a Kelenge, (Mundele Funji), 258, 260
Maternity Hospital. See Freetown.
Matolo, Madam, 79, 89
Matoon, clan, 262, 304
Matotoka, 150
Matturi, 113, 114
Matundu, clan. See Matuum.
Matuum (Ntuun), clan, (also called Matundu), 262
Matwua, André, 228
Mauka, 247
Mavulo Gbembo Golei. See "Primer of Midwifery, A."
Mawaw, Paul, 215, 216
Mawoka, 209
Mayidi, 234, 250, 307
Mayiamene, M., 189
"Mayi Mulele." See "Mulele Water."
Mayombe, 216, 238
Maxwell, Sir William, Governor, 62
May, Cornelius, 115
May, Joseph, 114
May, Joseph Claudius, 96, 114, 115
Mayopeh, 149
Mayors of Freetown:
Barlatt, C.J.G., 42
Barlatt, S.J.S., 42, 43
Beoku-Betts, E.S., 44
Bishop, T.C., 40
Cummings, E.H., 58
Ezzidio, J., 64
Lewis, Sir S., 103
Thomas, J.H., 153
Thomas, T.J., 153
Mbaanc, 262, 304, 305
Mbaji a Ngoi, 283
Mbakam Mashiing, 262, 304
Mbaku Ditend, Mwat Yav. See Ditend Yavu a Nawej III.
Mbala, 284
Mbal a Kalong, Mwat Yav, 277
Mbamba, 257, 321
Mbandaka, (Coquilhatville), 184, 191, 199, 200, 201, 207, 208, 219, 225, 234, 235, 253, 274, 275, 276, 277, 281, 282, 290, 303, 318, 322, 323, 324, 325. See also Coquilhatville.
early history of, 206, 207, 208, 265
Mbanda a Nenga, 213

Mbangi, 254
Mbangom, 209
Mbangu, 233
Mbansa-Manteke, 306
Mbanza Kongo, (San Salvador), 204, 238, 267, 268, 280, 297, 299, 321, 323, 325. See also San Salvador.
Mbanza Ngombe, 251
Mbanza-Ngungu, (Thysville), 197, 199, 227, 228, 231, 238, 256, 323. See Also Thysville.
Mbanza-Nsundi, 280
Mbapa of Sandyalu, 87
Mbata, 257, 321
Mbata Kiela Minor Seminary, 216
Mbatas, 238
Mbawulomeh, 85, 86, 88
    defeated by Kai Londo, 88
Mbeba, 279
Mbidi Kiluwe, (Ilunga Mbili; also Ilunga Mbidi Kiluwe), 196, 211, 259, 297
Mboka, clan, 223
Mbole, 324
Mboloyamato, 281
Mbongo, 233
Mbonzi, 274, 276
Mboong a Iyool, 262
Mboshi, people, 205, 323
Mbowa, 87
Mboyawa, 100
Mbuji Mayi, (Bakwanga), 209, 211, 212, 216, 220, 221, 320, 324. See also Bakwanga.
Mbuji Mayi region, 301. See also Nkalanyi Mayi.
Mbuji Mayi River, 294
"Mbula Matari," (the State). See Bula Matari.
Mbul aNgoong, 304
Mbumb, Muteb a Kat, Mwant Yav, 209, 277
Mbunda, 254, 272, 273
Mbunda Kwese, 254
Mbundu a Gomoni, 259, 260, 261
Mbuun, people, 213, 234, 284, 304
McCormack, John, 62, 75, 101, 115, 116, 117, 119
    visits Port Loko, 119
    signs treaty with Sattan Lahai, (1861), 140
McCormack, Mary Ann, 62
MacDonald, Governor Norman William, 76
    petition to remove, 64
Mecca, 49, 129, 150, 164
Medals, 232
    Ekwakola receives, 266
    first Congo medal given to Makitu, 252
    Mopipi receives, 264
    Motengo receives, 266
Medekelema, 87
Medical Service, 62, 63, 76, 77, 82, 162.
    See also British Army Medical Service.
Medicine, herbal, 35
Medicinal plants, 35, 147
Medina, on the Bullom Shore, 59
Mel, language group, 171, 173, 174
Melacourie River, 17, 24, 26, 27, 46, 75, 92, 119, 163

closed to European traders, 60
region disrupted by raids, 141
and the timber trade, 116
Memorial Hall, Freetown, 84
Mende, 18, 22, 47, 72, 97, 120, 121, 124, 126, 127, 141, 143, 149, 158, 164, 169, 170, 171, 172, 173, 174
    send contingent to Asante war, (1873), 71
    British agreement with, 24
    British conclude treaties with, 121
    fined by British, 24
    Governor Cardew visits, 52
    warriors brought in by the Caulkers, 54, 55, 56
    Western education among, 144
    and Hut Tax War uprising (1898), 28, 53, 67, 86; suppressed by the British, 28, 29, 53
    in Kinigbo war, 54, 55, 71
    war with Kono, (1870), 127
    and the Kpo-veh wars, 85, 87
    land dispute between chiefs, 132
    advised by Sir Samuel Lewis, 104
    mission schools, 67
    institutions at Moyamba, 94
    railway construction through Mende country, 53
    incidents on the Temne frontier, 107
    and the Tongo Players, 98
    war waged by, (1875), 23
    possible war with Yarvai, 158
Mende country, 87, 124, 172
Mende dictionary, 138
Mende grammar, 35
Mende language, 18, 126, 142
Mende Mission, 135, 136, 137, 138, 143, 144, 157, 161, 172
Mende script, (Ki Ka Ku), 95
Mendegla, of Joru, 22, 85, 117
    quarrels with Kai Londo, 86
"Mendigrah." See Mendegla.
Mendor, 85
Mercantile Association, 75
Mercenaries, foreign, 225, 226, 311, 312
Mes opinions sur les problémes congolais ("My Opinions on Congolese Problems"), 226
Messages de guerre ("Wartime Messages"), 302
Messiah, second coming of predicted, 194
Metalworking, 19
    Kuba, 305
    Luba, 182
Methodist (formerly Wesleyan) Boys School, 40, 65
Methodist Church, 58, 118. See also Sierra Leone Methodist Mission.
Methodist Herald and West African Educational Times, 115
Methodist missions, 309, 314
Metzger, 156
Mfimi River, 289, 290
Mfua, 287, 288
Mfwatu, 232
M.G.L. See Compagnie Minière des Grands Lacs.

Miao River, 271
Michaux, Oscar, 271, 277
Middle East, 159
Middle Temple, Bar of, 43, 44, 103
Migeod, 127
Migwa Kasanza, Kangu, 261
Mikalayi, 212
Mikolo, 299
Mikondo, 307
Miliki, 134
Milambu, Emery, 248
Military Academy, Belgian, 308
Miller, the Rev. Albert, 143
Miller, Frederic Adolphus, 117, 118
Millet, 183
Milner, Lord, 41
Minerals, prospecting for, 30
Mineral rights, in the Kongo, Portuguese obtain, 296
Mine Workers' Wage Board, 63, 164,
Mining
    contribution to colonial revenue, 30
    in Sierra Leone, 30
Minkoto, 207
Mirabong Sesay, 150
Mirambo, 268
Misha mi Shyaang Matuum, 261, 262, 304, 305
Misongo, 290
"Missa Katanga," 232
Mission of Blacks, 228
Mission of Two Guineas, 48
Mkoli, 207
Mmame Yeri, 139
M.N.C. See Mouvement National Congolais.
M.N.C./Kalonji. See Mouvement National Congolais.
M.N.C./Lumumba. See Mouvement National Congolais.
Moanda, 307
Moanda River, 276, 277
Moa River, 86, 87, 88, 107, 117, 124
Mobagi, 54. See also Senehun.
Moba Georgine, 304
Mobele, 275, 281
Mobena, 274, 275
Mobayi Mbongo, 233
Mobeka, 253, 254
Mobele, 281
Mobusi, 298
Mobusi-Bomwanga, 298
Mobutu Sese Soko, (Joseph Mobutu), 188, 198, 199, 220, 224, 226, 246, 255, 264, 273, 311, 312
    administration of, 193
    appoints College of Commissioners, 219
    role in the 1960 constitutional crisis, 246
    deposes J. Kasa-Vubu, 219, 226, 312
Model School, the, 65, 118
Modjoka, 274
Moeko, port, 199
Moeko River, 199
Mofindoh, 87
Mofwe, Krio traders at, 24
Mofwe Lagoon, 238

Mohanadu Alikali, (later Fatimah Brima II), 119

Mohammedan Board of Education, 129

Mohila, Salomon, 276, 298

Mohua, 275

Moigula, 107, 108, 166

Mokabo, 207

Mokala, 208

Mokame, 235, 281, 299

Mokassi, 53

Mokoli, 207

Mokolo, 281

Mokolovesi, 235

Mokoma, 282

Mokondo, 274

Mokondola, 274

Mokoto, 275

Molanga, 276

Molasses, 36

Molei, 265, 266

Moli, 200

Molifo, 88

Molila, 207

Molonga, 266, 276, 298

Molongo, 276

Momaligi, 149

Mombeh, Kefue, 86

Momo Fula, 121

Momoh, A.J., 84

Momoh Gbow of Njaluahun, 89

Momoh Gete, 126, 127

Momoh Gulama, 100

Momoh Kukuwa, 107, 108

Momoh Sankoh, 118, 119, 120

Momoh Vangahun, deposed, 89

Momo Ja, 120, 121

Momo Kai Kai, 67, 120, 121, 122

Momori Kalko, 111

Momo Rogers, 110

Momo Tibo Rogers, 110

Mompena, 275

Mondjamboli, 202

Monga, daughter of Abwid, (18th century), 214

Monga, father of E. Kimba, (20th century), 224

Mongala River, 199, 201, 233, 290, 291

Monghere, (Lunya), 99, 127

Mongo, people, 182, 200, 300, 324, 325, 326
    name of the ancestor of the people, 182

Mongo, Sierra Leone chiefdom, 113

Mongo, Zaire place name, 205

Mongo Sunkutu, 269

Mongray, 155, 156

Mongwandi, 233

Monia, 253, 265, 266, 276
    and the Belgians, 266

Moniongo, chiefdom, 200

Monkton Coombe College, 145, 146

Monoki na Taba, 253

Monoko mwa Nkoi, 291

Monoko na Ntaba, 266

Monono, 275

Monrovia, 53, 76

Mons Officers Cadet School, Eaton Hall, Chester, England, 40

Montapala, 240

Montez, Pedro, 141, 142

Montgomery, Alabama, 138

Monuments and Relics Commission, 63

Monya, 276

Moore, Governor Henry Monck-Mason, 157

Moore, Capt. Samuel, 47, 70

Mopipi, family, 262

Mopipi Bitingo François, 263, 264

Mopipi Mulongeki, Paul, (Kabunda), 262, 263, 264

Mopipi Mutimana, 262, 264

Mopoie Bangezegino, 265

Morea, 46, 51, 68, 92, 93, 140, 141
    Bokari as ruler of, 46
    British send gunboat, (1865-66), 46
    British treaty with rulers of, 24
    French gunboat arrives, 46
    French given port facilities, 46
    Heddle's mission to, 75
    alliance with Kukuna against Bilali, 45

Morel, Belgian administrator, 228

Morel, E.D., 185

More Mina Lahai, 60

Mori, 168, 172

Moriba Kindo Bangura, 122, 123

Moriba Kindo Kamara, Alikali, 120

Mori Bundu of Foredugu, 119

Morifindugu, 22, 111, 113

Morifing, Mansa, 19

Mori Lamina. See Bilali.

Moriman, 22, 158, 172

Mori Musa, (Fina Bala), 113

Mori Shaka, 45

Morlai Limba, Pa, 123, 124

Morobe, 212

Morocco, 273

Mosaka River, 290

Mosangi, chiefdom, 200

Moscow, U.S.S.R., 159

Mossaka River, 205

Mosubi, 276

Motappan, 143

Motatshinga, 283

Motengo, 253, 265

Motombo Kola, 278

Motorists Union, 160

Mount Aureol, 25, 170

Mount Cameroon, 170

Mount Leopold. See Mount Ngaliema.

Mount Ngaliema, (Konzo Ikulu, formerly Mount Stanley, Mount Leopold), 287, 288, 321

Mount Stanley. See Mount Ngaliema.

Moustier, M., 144

Mouvement National Congolais (M.N.C.), 243, 244, 245, 246
    in May 1960 elections, 245
    M.N.C./Kalonji, 244
    M.N.C./Lumumba, 244
    split in, 244

Mouvement Populaire de la Révolution, (M.P.R.), 250, 251, 255; 273

Mouvement Populaire d'Union Africaine, (M.P.A.), 226

Movee, 165

Movement for the United States of Europe, 310

Mowoto, 165

Moyamba, 69, 70, 71, 72, 90, 93, 94, 100, 112, 144

Moyenne Giri, (Middle Giri), 253

Mozambique, 239, 240
    attempt to establish link with Angola, 240

Mozart, 232

M.P.A. See Mouvement Populaire d'Union Africaine.

Mpadi, Simon, 228

Mpaga Munyantangoy, 236

Mpagni Bobuanabongwe, 266, 267

Mpangu a Nzinga, 267, 268

Mpaka, Albert, 231

Mpala, 232

Mpangu, 248

Mpangu province, 267, 312

Mpanzu a Nzinga, 258, 267, 268

Mpanzu Mvemba, (Pedro IV), (the Mani Kibangu), 229, 230

Mpasa, 209

Mpata, 221

Mpelu Baboma, chiefdom, 266, 267

Mpemba Kazi, region, 238

Mpenbe, 257, 321

Mpeve. See Holy Spirit. See also Church of the Holy Spirit (Mpeve) of Esieme.

Mpeve uprising, 189, 190, 214

Mpinda, 257, 296, 299

Mpoko, 267

Mpokola, 198

Mpolo, Maurice, 246

Mpombo, 232

Mpondo, (Iboko), 190

M.P.R. See Mouvement Populaire de la Révolution.

Mpuka, people, 212

Mpungu, 257, 321

"Mpungwilu," 257

Mputu, 270

M'Siri Ngelengwa, (Mushidi Ngelengwa), 220, 222, 239, 268, 269, 270

Msuata, 290

Muandj, 209

Mubimbi, 248

Mudib, Mwant Yav, 277

Muekuana, 205

Muekuanga, 205

"Mufalme," (king), 194

Mufondu, 281

Mufunga, 214, 289

Mugeri-Katana, 210

Muhaku, Catholic mission at, 223

Muhanji, 213

Muhulu, 193

Muikalebwe. See Lumpungu.

Muin Cibalak, 278

Mujila River, 212

Mujinga, 249, 282

Mukabua, 271

Mukachilund, 196

Mukambu, 239

Mukaz Waranankong, 214, 215

Mukebu, 239

Mukej, 215

Mukelenge Mutombo, 283, 284. See also Mwatha Kombana.

Mukenge a Tunsele, (Kalamba), 270, 271, 272

Mukenge Kalamba, 212, 294

"Mukombozi," (Redeemer), 194

Mukulunzambi, (Shimuna Mukimba Mugamba), 223

Mukulweji River, 279

Mukut, Jebula, 216

Mukwakeza, 279

Mulaj, (earlier 19th century), 286

Mulaj, (later 19th century). See Kawel.

Mulaj, Jacques, 216

Mulamba Lowa, 295

Muland, 239

Mulele, Pierre, 198, 208, 234, 237, 254, 272, 273, 274, 306, 307, 311, 324
    returns from China, 234

Mulele uprising. See Kwilu, 1964 rebellion.

Mulelists, the, 198, 208, 234, 254, 272, 273, 306, 307

"Mulele Water," ("Mayi Mulele"), 237

Mulenga, 239

Mulenge, 212, 213, 324

Muli Kalunga, 220

Mulowe, sect, 237, 321

Mulopwe, 182, 211, 212, 221, 222, 318, 324
    Ilunga Kabale, 222
    Kabongo proclaims himself as, 222
    Kasongo Kalombo, 220, 221, 222
Kasongo Nyembo I, 222

Mkongolo, 297

Muloshi, 283

Mulumbwa, 239

Mumbendu, 274, 275

Mumford, Gold Coast, 76

Mumpema, 275

Mundala, 248

Mundele Funji. See Matemu a Kelenge.

Mundele Funji War, (1931). See Pende Revolt.

Mundjokola, 234, 235

Mengembe, 266, 274, 276, 277, 298

Mungombe-Kamituga, 210

Munkata, 239, 281, 282

Munongo, Godefroid, 224

Munsasa, 298, 299

Muntu, (African Man), 210

Mununga, 239

Murray Town, 103

Musa, 266, 274, 303

Musaia, 61, 62

Musakatshi, 294

Musamba Mputu, 212

Musand, 239

Musanga, 202, 203, 230, 231

Musanga Gafugusa, 231

Musanga-Kifwameson, 230

Musareka. See Musekula.

Musekula, (Musareka), 236

Museum. See Sierra Leone National Museum.

Mushenge. See Nsheeng.

Mushid a Nambing, Mwant Yav, 209, 215, 277, 278

Mushie, 289, 290

Mushigo. See Gallenga Mushigo.

Mushima Kainda, 214, 289

Mushinga, chiefdom, 254, 258. See also Akwa Mushinga.

Music
    African, 38, 39, 232, 233
    Black American, 38
    Congolese, 193
    of Léopoldville, 193
    Luba, 182
    Pende, 254
    of Shaba, 232
    Yeke, 232

Muslims, in the Sudan and northern Zaire, 265. See also Islam.

Musokantanda, 239, 278, 279

Musokatshi, 221

Musoko, 221

Musoma, (Limania), 275

Musos Shagindungu, 203, 258, 260

Mussolini, Benito, 159

Musumba, Lunda capital, 182, 214, 215, 216, 238, 240, 249, 269, 278, 279, 282, 283, 284, 286, 301, 309, 323

Musuna, 89

Mutambwe, Léon, 248

Mutand Mukay, Mwant Yav, 277

Mutand Yembiyemb, 239, 278, 279, 289

Mutara II, 252

Muteb a Kasang, Mwant Yav, 215, 277

Muteb a Kat, (late 17th century), 278. See also Mbumb Muteb a Kat, (19th century).

Muteba Tshibindu, 283

Mutimbi, 269

Mutohembe, 295

Mutondo, 214

Mutshatsha, 278, 289

Mutuelle des Tetela, ("Tetela Mutual"), 243

Mutundu, 223

Muyangala, 279, 280

Muyombu, 324. See also Ficus plant.

Mvemba Nzinga, (Afonso I, Mani Kongo), 181, 182, 204, 258, 267, 268, 280, 281, 298, 299, 313

Mwabidima, 214

Mwa Buniagu, 252

Mwadi a Ngoya, 282

Mwaket of Tumba, 300

Mwaku, 284

Mwamba Ciluu, 196

Mwami, (ruler), 252, 324

Mwamolanga, 266

Mwa Murhwa, 252

Mwanana, 259

Mwana Kankenza, 241

Mwana-Katenda, 239

Mwanandungu, 281, 282

Mwana Uta, 282

Mwant-Wut. See Chibang Chelek Muswa Musapu.

Mwant Yav, 182, 196, 209, 214, 215, 216, 238, 239, 269, 277, 278, 279, 283, 289, 301, 309, 315, 318, 324. See also Chikomb; Kaumb; Mbaku Ditend; Mbala Nawej; Mbumb; Mukaz Waranankong; Mishid a Nambing; Mutand; Muteb; Muteb a Kasang; Muteb a Kat; Nawej I; Nawej a Ditend.

Mwanza Kasongo. See Ngongo Leteta.

Mwasamotoko, 298

Mwata Yamvo. See Mwant Yav.

Mwatha Kombana, (Mukelenge Mutombo; fl. 17th century), 282, 283, 284

Mwatha Kombana, polity, 284, meaning of name, 282

Mwatha Kombana, (also Mwatha Yamvu), title, 283, chronological list of title holders, 283

Mwatha Muhega, 203

Mwatha Yamvu. See Mwatha Kombana, title.

Mwe, people, 199, 265, 266, 276, 324

Mwe, region, uprising in, 266

Mwema River, 277

Mwembe, 250

Mwe Nzila, (Shakatwala), 283

Mwene Bangu, 324

Mwene Kalunga, 284

Mwene Kongo, 279, 284

Mwene Mbangu, 213

Mwene Putu, Lunda title for the king of Portugal, 284. See also Kiamfu.

Mwene Putu Kasongo, 249, 282, 283, 284, 285

Mwenga zone, 236, 318

Mweni Lukanda, 283

Mweni Mavu, family, 283

Mwene River, 215

Mweru, Lake. See Lake Mweru.

Mwibele, 297

Mwilambongo, 234

Mwilu, 239

Mwilu, Marie, 227

Mwin Kanithshin, 301

Mwin Mpand, 215

Mwin Muandj, 209

Mwin Pand, ("Man of the Crossroads"), 239

Myelemyele, (Chawala Makumba), 214

Nabiembali, 285, 286

N.A.H.V., (Dutch Company), 288

Naimbana. See Nemgbana.

Naimbana, John Frederick. See Nemgbana, John Frederick.

Na-Kituti, 238, 239

Nalo. See Malo.

Nalou, 17

Nambing, 277

Names, of places, changed in Zaire, (1971), 188

Namina Lahi Sankoh, 119

Namina Modu Bangura, 119

Nashville, Tennessee, 55

Nasoko, 191

Nasser, Gamal Abdel, 272

National Assembly, Congolese, 187, 219, 245

National Association of Medical Herbalists in Great Britain, 35

National Bank (of the Congo), 255

"National Congolese Convention." See Conaco.

National Congress of British West Africa, (N.C.B.W.A.), 31, 36, 41, 42, 44, 50, 118, 147, 154, 156
    formed, 31
    meets in Freetown, 66
    sends delegation to London, (1920), 41
National Council of Liberation, (C.N.L.), 312
National Council of the Colony of Sierra Leone, (N.C.), 32, 41, 84, 85, 112, 160
National Institute for Agronomic Research, 255
National Institute for the Study of Agriculture in the Congo, (I.N.B.A.C.), 302
National Institute of the Belgian Congo for Agronomic Studies. See Institut National pour l'Etude Agronomique du Congo Belge.
National Interim Council, 40
National Liberation Council. See Conseil National de Libération.
National Office of Research and Development, (O.N.R.D.), 251
National Reformation Council, (N.R.C.), 33, 40, 69, 101, 152
National Society of the Liberated Africans and their Descendants, 64
Native Administration, system, (1937). See Chiefdoms.
Native Association, (later the Sierra Leone Association), 145
"Native Districts," 186, 324
Native Law Ordinance. See Protectorate.
Native Pastorate Church. See Church Missionary Society.
Native Postal Workers Brotherhood. See Amicale des Postiers Indigènes.
Nawej I, Mwant Yav, 301
Nawej a Ditend, Mwant Yav, 277, 286
"Nazareth," 189, 190. See also Esieme, mission at.
    at Nzundi, 229
Nazis, invasion of Belgium by, 302
N.C. See National Council of Sierra Leone.
N.C.B.W.A. See National Council of British West Africa.
Nchakal Makal, 196
Nchuvila, 287
Ndala, chiefdom, 230, 231
Ndala, son of Ilunga Kiluwe, 159
Ndawa the Great, 85, 87, 97, 107, 124
    killed at Dama, 117
    raids Dodo, 114
    attacks Mendegla, 117
    and Nyagua, 127, 128
Ndayin, Papay, 37
Ndembu-Kosa, people, 278
Ndengese, 324
Ndjondo, (Djundu), 192, 275, 317
Ndobo, 276
Ndola, Zambia, 311
Ndolo, 199, 200, 309, 324
    water dwellers of, 200
Ndolo-Bokala, 200
Ndondo, 275
Ndongela, clan, 231

Ndongo, 297, 299
Ndorwa, 252
Negro, The, 77
Negro Worker, The, 159
Nemgbana, (circa 1775-1793), 125
Nemgbana, title, 173
Nemgbana, Bartholomew. See Nemgbana, Pedro.
Nemgbana, John Frederick, 125, 126
Nemgbana, Pa, 148
Nemgbana, Pedro, (Bartholomew), 125, 126
Nendeka, Victor, 245
Nesfar. See Iyonkum Marcel.
New Era, 25
New Haven, Connecticut, 142
New Orleans, 138, 158
New Orleans Weekly, 144
New Testament, translated into Kikongo, 256
New World. See Americas, The.
New York, 66, 101
New York Herald, 287
New York World's Fair, (1964), 37
Neya, chiefdom, 144
Nfa Ali, 144, 151
Ngabu, Monsignor, 196
Ngako, 287
Ngala, (Bangala), people, 190, 198, 290, 291, 292, 319, 324. See also Iboko, Mabele.
    role in the modernization of the Congo, 290
    origin of the name, 29
Ngaliema, (Itsi), 251, 286, 287, 288, 290. See also Mount Ngaliema.
Ngalula, Joseph, 218, 243
Ngambi, 254, 324
Ngand a Bilond, (Idim a Kaumb), 288, 289
Ngandu, 247, 295, 313, 314
Ngangbe, of Medekelema, 87
Ngankabi, 289, 290
Nganzulu, 289
Nga Shiim, plain, 262
Ngbandi, people, 233, 276
Ngele ya Ntando, 201
Ngemba, (Mata-Boike, also Engwangola), 190, 290, 291, 292
Ngevau, 85
Ngiamba, clan, 260, 261
Ngiehun, 87, 88, 124
Ngiema, 87
Ngiri River. See Giri River.
Ngiri-Ngiri commune, Léopoldville, 218
Ngiri sector, 254, 305
Ngola, kingdom of, 181
Ngola, title, 199
Ngoma Masunda, Hortense, 216
Ngombe, 200, 265, 290, 324
Ngombe, village, 298
Ngombe Lutete, (formerly Wathen Station), 197, 256
    Baptist Missionary Society at, 227
    Central School at, 197
Ngombe Matadi, 252
Ngongo, 293
Ngongo Leteta, (Mwanza Kasongo), 221, 241, 247, 248, 292, 293, 294, 295, 313
    defeated by Dhanis, 241
    youngest son of, 248

Ngongo L'okole, 293
Ngongo Luhaka, 293, 294, 295
Ngonso, Sebastien, 295, 296
Ngoo, Congo na biso, 193
Ngoo, Zaire na biso, 193
Ngoso, mission at, 234
Ngoyi Kaumbu, (Yankaumbu), 241
Ngoyo, kingdom of, 181, 238, 324
Nguii, 189, 208, 248, 249, 325
Nguvulu, Alphonse, 243
Niabongonga, 298
Niangara, 285
Nicol, the Rev. George, 163
Nieni, chiefdom, 27, 39, 113, 173
    conquered by Suluku, 39
Nigeria, 35, 40, 43, 44, 74, 76, 78, 147, 153, 159, 170, 210, 244
Nigerians, in Sierra Leone, 21, 22, 64, 65, 76, 82, 95, 96, 103, 114, 115, 147, 168
Niger River, 38
    sources of, 52, search for, 144
    Upper, 95
Nikagboiyei River, 158
Nile Expedition, 316
Nile River, 184, 327
Nilis, Lt., 251
Nimi a Nzinga, 238
Nimi Hills, 113
Nimikoro, 113
    taken from Nyagua's control, 114
Ninth Line Regiment, (Belgian), 301
Nioki, 303
Nioko, 221
Niongwe, 254
Niungu, people, 213, 324
Nivelles, Belgium, 197
Nivelles Ecole de Régence, 197
Njala, agricultural college at, 90
Njalawa Kebiwa, 94
Njaluahun, 87, 89
Njia Kundohun, 126, 127, 164
Njila Gamoni, 260
Njili, stream, 287
Njondo, 200
Nkalanyi, 196, 301
Nkamba, 227, 228
Nkanga Lukeni, (Garcia II, Mai Kongo), 296, 297, 312, 313
Nkeni River, 205, 290
Nkieme, 290
Nkodi, 167
Nkombe, 281
Nkond a Matit, 300, 301
Nkongolo, 182, 211, 259, 297
Nkoto, 265
Nkrumah, Kwame, 160
    signs union of Ghana with the Congo, 245
    relations with P. Lumumba, 243, 245, 246
Nkuba, (ruler of the Shila), 215, 238, 239, 325
Nkumba a Ngundi, (later Mbanza Kongo), 238
"N'kum," (chief), 325
Nkum'okare, 289, 325
Nkumu, 325

Nkundo, 191, 324, 325

Nkungu, (now Bolebo), 281, 299

Nkuriam, 248, 249

Nkutu, 324

Nlemvo, meaning of, 256. See also Mantantu Dundulu.

Noa Nallo, 94

Nongowa, chiefdom, 79, 87, 88, 89, 96, 97, 128, 158
 allegations of cannibalism in, 89

Nordenfeld cannon, 271

Norfolk, England, 57

Normal School, Kissy. See Kissy Normal School.

North Carolina, 65, 131

Northern Province, Sierra Leone, 72, 164, 166
 1955 riots in, 32, 49

Northern Rhodesia, (now Zambia), 194, 311

Northern Rivers, in Guinea, (Bereira, Melacourie, Rio Nunez, Rio Pongas), 26, 60, 62, 68, 155

North Kivu, diocese of, 195, 196

North West Frontier campaign, (1868), 52

Nouvelle-Anvers, (now Makanza, earlier Bangala Station), 190, 198, 199, 200, 235, 253, 254, 266, 276, 292, 303, 304, 323, 325

Nova Scotia, 21, 56, 57, 131, 172, 173

Nova Scotian and Maroons Descendants' Association, 63

Nova Scotians, 21, 56, 57, 59, 60, 62, 129, 172, 173
 build houses and shops in Freetown, 104
 Thomas Peters as leader of, 131, 132
 rebellion of 1799/1800, 21, 59, 155

Novelists, Disengomoka the first in Zaire, 197

Nqiri Nqiri, 197

N.R.C. See National Reformation Council.

Nsaka, 224

Nsaku, clan, 298

Nsaku ne Vunda, (Mani Vunda, or Mani Kabunda), 297, 298

Nsala, 296

Nsanda, 228

Nsanga-Londe, 231

Nseke, 281

Nsele, 251

Nsheeng, (Mushenge), 262

Nshind, 239

Nsona, 221

Nsu bicycles, 231

Nsundi, 204, 238, 257, 280, 321

Nsungu, 290

Ntanda, 299

Ntenke, 239

Ntimansi collectivity, 197

Ntini Lukeni, 237

Ntinu Wene, 297. See also Lukeni.

Ntomb, 325

Ntomba, state, 181, 325

Ntomena a Mukulu, 221

Ntondo, 239

Ntu, (African genius), 210

Ntu Pedagogical Center. See Centre Pédagogique Ntu.

Ntuun, clan. See Matuum.

Nubians, 183

Nunu, 289, 290, 325

Nupe, Nigeria, 64, 115

Nyabaronge, 252

Nyagua, of Panguma, 22, 79, 85, 86, 96, 97, 113, 114, 127, 128, 132
 signs Bandasuma treaty, 107
 arrested by the British, 28
 exiled to the Gold Coast, 28, 53
 fights Porekere, 26, 132
 towns of, captured by Porekere, 26
 attacks Kono, 113
 seeks help of Kono, 114
 claims Tecuyama and Levuma, 132

Nyainyongwa, 298, 299

Nyakibanda, 195, 210

Nyambaka, 282

Nyamongwalanga, 253

Nyampara, 236, 264, 325

Nyamwezi, 268, 269, 325, 327

Nyangezi, 195

Nyangwe, 247, 270, 294, 314

Nyasaland, 194

Nyawa, 126, 127

Nyawa-Lenge, chiefdom, 127

Nyeeng mask, 262, 305

Nyim, (ruler of the Kuba), 262, 304, 305, 325

Nyonyo, 281, 282

Nzali, 327

Nzamba, 266, 276

Nzambi, (the Supreme Being), 227, 325

Nzambi Mapapu, 228

Nzari, 327

Nzemba Munene, clan, 231

Nzemba Munene, village, 279

Nzeza-Landu, Simon, 217, 218

Nzinga Mpudi, (Diogo I, Mani Kongo), 299

Nzinga Nkuwu, (Joao I, Mani Kongo), 181, 257, 258, 267, 268, 280
 converted to Christianity, 280
 abandons Christianity, 258, 280
 death of, 204, 268, 280

Nzofu Lukunda, 284

Nzundi, 229, 267

O.A.U. See Organization of African Unity.

O.B.B.A. See Old Bo Boys' Association.

Oberlin College, Ohio, 157, 158

Oberlin Collegiate Institute, Ohio, 135

Oblate Fathers of Mary Immaculate, (O.M.-I.), 250

Oblate minor seminary, Laba, 250

Observations, 72

O.C.A.M. (Joint African and Malagasy Organization), 312

Ofei, Wuta, 159

Ogambi. See Logo Ogambi.

Ohio, 135, 138, 157, 161

"Okare," (wife), 325

Okito, Joseph, 246

Okrika, 40

Old Bo Boys' Association, (O.B.B.A.), 164

Oldowan culture, 179

Olenga, Nicolas, 300

Olomo-Pese, 208

Omana, 248

Omaru, Al Haji, 128, 129

Omaru, Alimamy, 60

Omeonga, 248

O.M.I. See Oblate Fathers of Mary Immaculate.

Onalua, 242

Onema, Mama, 300

O.N.R.D. See Natural Office of Research and Development.

Orangeburg State College, South Carolina, 83

Orban, Lt. 206

Orkney Islands, 75

Organization of African Unity, (O.A.U.), 210, 312

Orientale province, (now Haut-Zaire Region), 193, 242, 243, 245, 325

Orth, John, 38

Oshwe, 189

Otetela, language, 293, 325, 326

Otterbein College, Ohio, 36

Ottoman Turks, administration of, in the Sudan, 306

Overe, 208, 249

Ovimbundu, 182, 184, 209
 traders, 269

Owong, 249

Oxford, 83

Oxford University, England, 220

Pacheco, Francisco, 286

Pacifists, in Sierra Leone administration, 132

Pademba Road, Freetown, 147
 prisons, 40, 69, 101, 152, see also Freetown Central Prison, Pademba Road.

Padmore, George, 160

Padwa, 256

Palabala, 305, 306

Palabala Range, 309

Palm kernels
 exported, 75
 industry, 29
 trade in, 24

Palm nuts, 251, 253, 299
 fall in price of, 203
 strike of Pende suppliers of, 258

Palm oil, 136, 199, 236, 253, 264, 299
 fall in the price of, 203
 industry, 29
 supplied by the Mangwa, 235
 trade in, 36
 low wages in the palm oil industry, 186

Palm plantations, 190

Palm trees, 183

Palm wine, 199, 299

Pampana River basin,
 gold discovered in, 30

Panabouro. See Nemgbana.

Pan African Congress, 244

Pan-African Federation, 160

Pan-Africanism, 65, 160, 243, 245. See also National Congress of British West Africa.

Pan-Africanist Congress, Manchester, England, (1945), 160

Pan-African People's Conference, Accra, (1958), 218, 243
Panda Yokina, of Panderu, 96
Pande, 278, 279
   origin and meaning of the name, 278
Pande a Muvomb, 279
Pande Mutaba, 268, 269
Panderu, 96, 97
Pangi, 318
Panguma, 86
   Governor Cardew visits, 52
   founded, 127
   exempted from 1896 house tax, 28, 53, 128
   Nyagua arrested at, 128
   ruled by Nyagua, 22, 79, 127, 128
   established as a division of the Protectorate, (1896), 28
Panya Mutumbo, 212, 241
Papalahun, 88
Paracommandos, Belgian, 311
Paris, France, 76, 133, 134, 160, 219, 255, 308, 311, 312
Parkes, James Charles Ernest, 25, 47, 67, 93, 102, 129, 130, 131, 132
Parkes, W.A., murdered, 108
Parliament, British, 99, 134, 147
Parliament, Congolese, 219, 226, 272
   in 1960 constitutional crisis, 246
   convened at Lovanium University, (1961), 273
   confirms Lumumba government, 245
   suspended, (1965), 219
Parodi Commission, 43
Parrots, 293
   Tippu Tib trades in, 293
Parti Solidaire Africain, (P.S.A.), 208, 234, 245
   in May 1960 elections, 245
   P. Mulele and, 272, 273
   split in, 208
Party of African Solidarity. See Parti Solidaire Africain.
Paterson, Zochanis and Co., 72
Pax Britannica, 29, 86
Peabody Academy, Troy, North Carolina, 65, 66
Peabody, George, 38
"Peace Poro," 117
Peanuts, (ground nuts), 75, 236, 249
   exported, 75, 85
Pearls, Bobangi trade in, 205
Pedro IV. See Mpanzu Mvemba.
Pedro V, King Don, of the Kongo, 256
"Peep of Day," 257
Peigneux, 279
Pellegrin, J.P., 75
Pena Mwiba, 293
Pende, 182, 202, 203, 213, 214, 220, 223, 226, 230, 231, 233, 249, 250, 254, 258, 259, 260, 261, 272, 273, 279, 282, 283, 284, 320, 323, 324, 325, 326, 327
   revolving chiefship among, 233
   and the Depression, 258
   Lunda-Pende chiefdom of Kangu, 261
   language. See Gipende. See also de Sousberghe, Léon.

Mai Munene's attempt to conquer, 249, 250
   and Muyangala, 279
   oral tradition, 254
   Pende revolt, or Mundele Funji war, (1931) and its suppression, 186, 202, 203, 213, 223, 226, 230, 258, 259, 260, 261, 279
   sorcerers, 220
Pendembu, railway reaches, (1908), 29, 53
Pene Luhaka. See Senga Raphael.
Pennsylvania, 83, 161
"Penny Bank," 84
Pensacola, 158
Pentecost Conspiracy, ("Complot de la Pentecôte"), 226
Penya Mutombo, 294
"People of the River," (clans among the Mpuka), 212
"People's Church," 84
People's University, Moscow, 159
P.E.P.U. See Protectorate Education Progress Union.
People's National Party (P.N.P.), 32
People's Party, 83, 84
Pepel and Marampa Miners Workers' Union, 160
Pequenino, 173
Pereira, Manuel Gaetano, 239, 240
Peterborough, Bishop of, 83
Peters, Patience, 133
Peters, Sally, 131
Peters, Thomas, 131, 132
Pétillon, Leon, 243
Petits Chanteurs, 232
Peuhl. See Fula.
Philosophy, African, 210
Phumba, 254
"Picaninny," 173
Pickering and Berthoud, 110
Pierre du feu, La, 267
Pike, Adolphus, 133
Pikin, 173
"Pikin Daddy," 162
Pine, Governor Benjamin, 105, 106
Pine, Governor Richard, 76, 77
Pineapples, 249
Pinto, Fr. Francisco Joao, 240
Pinto, Lourenzo Bezzera Corraia, 286
Pinzi, Arthur, 243
Pitman, Isaac, 114
Pittsburgh. See University of Pittsburgh.
Plantain Islands, 28, 54, 56, 71
Platinum, 30
P.N.P. See People's National Party.
Poetry, Luba, 182
Pogge, Paul, 212, 270
Poison, ordeal (trial) by, 305, 306
   renounced by Ngankabi, 290
Polar beer, 243
Polar Clubs, 243
Political Economy of British Western Africa, 77
Poll tax, proposed, 130
Polygamy
   prohibition of, by S. Kimbangu, 227
   Motengo and, 265, 266

and Mungembe, 277
Nabiembali and, 285
and Nzinga Nkuwu, 267, 280
A. Sims combats, 306
Pombeiros, (Angolan merchants), 284
Pompoli, of Biriwa Limba, 61
Ponthier, 290
Ponthierville, 327
Pope. See John XXIII; Julius II; Leo X.
Popo, 133
Porekere Foray Benia, 132, 133
   fights with British and French, 26, 132
   death, 26, 132
   attacks eastern Sierra Leone hinterland, (1893), 26
   and Kai Londo, 26
   in Kono, 26
   takes Nyagua's towns, 26
Poro, secret society, 93, 94, 98, 127, 165, 173, 174
   peace Poro of 1886, 107, 117
   Shorunkeh-Sawyerrs belong to, 146
   forces a trade embargo, 98
   Yoko (Soma) enters, 127
Porter, Arthur Thomas, 132, 133
Porter's Royal Hotel, Freetown, 133
Port Francqui, (Ilebo), 189, 208, 246, 319, 325
Port Loko, 19, 59, 70, 72, 73, 95, 109, 115, 116, 132, 140, 149, 168
   Bai Bureh and Governor Cardew at, 51
   British treaty with the Alikali of, 119
   C.M.S. mission at, suspended, (1850), 109; reopened (1878), 109
   Colony intervenes in succession dispute, 119
   district, 164
   district council, 164
   Krio traders at, 24
   dispute over rulership, 116, 118, 119, 120
   ruled by Sankoh, 118, 122
   attacked and burned by Soso, 116, 119, 140
   Soso hegemony overthrown in, (1815), 122, 123, 149
   Temne of, and Suluku, 151
   Temne rule over, 24, 122, 123, 149
   Temne Loko wars, 116, 149
   as a timber port, 116
   and Falaba-Bumban-Port Loko trade route, 23
   Governor Turner concludes treaty at, 123
Port Loko Creek, 24, 118, 151
Port Loko East constituency, 137
Porto Principe, Cuba, 141
Portugal
   Dom Henrique sent to study in, 204, 280
   Augustin Kinzonzi visits, 231
   Kongolese hostages taken to, 181
   Kongolese students sent to, 181, 280
   exploitation of the Kongo kingdom, 280, 281

Portuguese, 181. See also Forts.
arrival of, 181, 257, 280, 296, 321
attempt to introduce Christianity, 19
in the western Congo, 231
conflict with the Dutch, 296
and origin of the name "Gallinas," 170
Mani Kongo asks for artisans from the, 181, 280
seek to monopolize mission work in the Kongo, 296
invade southern Kongo, 296
defeat Kongo army (1665), 229, 312, 313
language, 231
at Luanda, 283
recapture Luanda (1648), 296
in Mozambique, 239
expedition from Mozambique to Angola, 240
and Mpangu a Nzinga, 268, 280
and Mvemba Nzinga, 268, 280
Nzinga Nkuwu and, 267, 280
in Sao Tome, 281
in Sierra Leone, 17, 19
and the name "Sierra Leone," 17
contact Soso, 92
Portuguese-African trade, 212, 270, 283, 286
at Tete, 239
traders, 199, 231, 253, 303
and Vita Nkanga, 312, 313
Potolu, 85, 86
Pottery, Luba, 182
Potts, "King" Abraham, 105
Poyo, chief, see Powpow.
Poyo, people, 214, 221
Powpwo, (Poyo), 265
Pratt, Fannie Marietta, (Mrs. Fannie Horton), 76
Pratt, William, 76
"Primer of Midwifery, A.", (Mavilo Gbembo golei), 112
Prince of Wales, 50
visit to Freetown (1925), 50, 82
Prince of Wales School, Freetown, 118, 152
Privy Council, British, 134, 160
Judicial Committee of, 160
Prometheus, H.M., sloop, 60
Protectorate, Sierra Leone, 62, 63, 72, 98, 129
early administration of, 104
divided into five administrative districts, (1896), 28, 53
relations with the Colony, 72, 73, 84, 85
alliance between rulers of, and educated elite in the Colony, 111
tour of, by E.H.T. Cummings, 58
aspirations of educated elite of, 73
first person from, at Fourah Bay College, 111
suspicion of Krios in, 104
Krios excluded from administration of, 104
relations with Krios, 112

interests represented in the Legislative Council, 31, 32, 73
status of Dr. M.A.S. Margai in, 112
first person from to obtain medical degree, 111
mining employment in, 30
National Protectorate newspaper, 112
Native Law Ordinance in, 72, 150
political influence of, 41
preparations for proclamation of, 130
proclaimed, (1896), 51, 52, 53, 54, 55, 61, 67, 69, 74, 79, 86, 97, 107, 108, 110, 114, 117, 121, 128, 129, 130, 148, 151, 152, 169
legal status of, 52
Protectorate Assembly, 32, 72, 89, 91
abolished, 32
instituted, 112
Protectorate Education Progress Union, (P.E.P.U.), 72, 73, 112, 164
Protectorate Ordinance of 1896, 28, 79, 98, 121, 157, 161, 166
Protestant Council of the Congo, (P.C.C.), (later the Church of Christ in Zaire), 306
Protestants. See Christians, Protestant.
Proverbs. See Holy Bible.
Province of Freedom, (1787-1808)
established, 19, 56, 125
abandoned in 1789, 21; re-established, 19
taken over by British government, 169
relations with nearby chiefs, 58, 59
Provinces, Congolese, 1966 reorganization of, 188
P.S.A. See Parti Solidaire Africain.
Psalms. See Holy Bible.
Public Committee Against the Introduction of the Criminal Code, (1918), 36
Public Records Office, London, 36
Public Works Workers' Union, 160
Pujehun district, 95, 112, 117, 120
Punch, 186
Punga, sect, 237
Pweto, region, 214, 239
Pyaang, 262
Pygmies, 179
Quakers, 96, 114
Quartey Papafio, Dr. B.W., 62
Queen of England, as Sierra Leone head of state, 33
Queen's Bench, London, 134
Queens College, Taunton, England. See Wesleyan College.
"Queen of the Ouaboume," 289
Race Course. See Freetown.
Rachid, 190
Radical Democratic Party, 160
Radio. See Léopoldville.
Railroad, Léopoldville to Matadi, 185
construction of, 185, 307, 308, 309, 317
opening of, (1898), 309
Railway. See Sierra Leone Railway.
Rainbow, the, 297
Rainy, William, 133, 134
name given to Alimamy Bungie, (William Rainy Lumpkin), 50

"Rakam," 196
Ramanakoto, Mrs. See Wright, Dr. Sophie.
Randle, Dr. John, 82
Rapp, M., 189
Rassin, Alimamy, 134, 135, 164
Raymond, Jane, 135
Raymond, Mrs., 135, 136
Raymond, William, 135, 136, 137
Reade. William Winwood,
visits Bouré, (1870), 24
visits Sewa, (1869), 144
Rebellions. See Kwilu, 1964 rebellion.
Rébellions au Congo, 273
Receptives, 21, 103, 105, 106, 152, 171, 173
Aku, 21
Mende, 143
settlement of, in villages, 21
A.B.C. Sibthorpe, 147
Recreation, 84
Redemption Fathers, 228
Rega, 325
Regent Square Municipal School, Freetown. See Interim Municipal School.
R.E.G.I.D.E.S.O. See Water and Power Distribution Authority, Léopoldville, 255.
Régie de Distribution d'Eau et d'Electricité—R.E.G.I.D.E.S.O. See Water and Power Distribution Authority, Léopoldville.
Rehovoth, Israel, 56
Renaissance, European, 181
Resin, 201
"Return to Authenticity," slogan, 188
Revelation of the Secret Orders of Western Africa: Including an Explanation of the Beliefs and Customs of African Heathenism, 35
Review of Reviews, 184
Ribbi, 149
Ribi River, 154
Rice, 136, 236, 264
cultivation of, 61
fine payable in rice imposed by British on the Mende, 24
produced by Konike Barawa, 149
quota imposed, 150
Richards, E., pseudonym, See Wallace Johnson, I.T.A.
Richmond College, Cape Coast, Gold Coast, 74
Rickets, tropical, 162
Rifles. See guns.
Right Thinking and Right Living, 197
Rio Nunez, 26, 60, 153
Rio Pongas, 26
Ripon, Lord, 130
Robaga, 18, 67
Robana, 125
Robari, 70
Robis, 155
Rochereau. See Tobu Ley.
Rochester, New York, 66
Rodrigues, Antonio Bonifacio, 286
Rogbane, 40
Rogers, Charles, 137
Rogers, James Western, 137

Rogers (Kpaka) family, 20, 109, 110, 137
and slave trade, 137
Rogers, Samuel Siaka, 137
Rogers-Wright, Cyril Banting, 32, 137
Rogers Zachary, (Sr.), (16?-1681), 109, 137
Rogers, Zachary, (Jr.), 137
Rokel River, (Sierra Leone River; also Seli
River), 17, 19, 39, 47, 52, 59, 71, 75, 109
111, 115, 116, 119, 120, 122, 123, 148,
151, 152, 155, 169, 170
estuary of, 115, 170
Rokel Temne, civil war among, 71
Rokon, chiefdom, 58, 71, 148
Rokrifie, 69
Rollings, Christiana, 153
Rollings, T.J., 153
Romangi, 47
Romani, 52
Romao, 286
Rome, 48, 195, 204
Dom Henrique visits, 204
Kongolese delegation to, 204
and missionaries to the Kongo, 296
Ronietta, 70, 80, 100, 166
hut tax to be levied at, 47, 148
established as a division of the Pro-
tectorate, (1896), 28
in Yoni campaign, 70
Root, Barnabas, 138
Root Cause of the Dissension Between the
Peoples of the Colony and the Pro-
tectorate, A, 84
Ropolo, 152
Rossi, Commander, 228
Rothkeni, 51
Rotifunk, 64, 72, 147, 149
birthplace of J.J. Akar, 36
Yoni attack on, 149
Round Table Conference, (Brussels, 1960),
187, 219, 224, 244, 245, 272, 310, 311
Economic Round Table Conference,
(Brussels, April-May, 1960), 272
Round Table discussions
in Coquilhatville, 225
in Léopoldville, 225
in Tananarive, Madagascar, 225
Rowala, 19
Mansa Kama establishes base at, 111
Rowe, Sir Samuel, Governor, 23, 46, 47, 54,
55, 71, 102, 141, 165
visits Bokari, 46
tours hinterland, (late 1970s), 47
signs treaty with Kaloun Baga, 46
in campaign against Kpaa-Mende, 71
visits Mambolo, 141
signs Massamah treaties, 141
leads punitive expedition against the
Mende, (1875), 54, 55
and Ndawa, 124
policies of, 103
revives and confirms Turner Treaty,
55
and Madam Yoko, 165
Rowula, "King." See Sattan Lahai.
Royal Academy of Sciences Overseas, (Belgian), 302

Royal Adventures of England Trading to
Africa, 20
Royal African Company, 20, 137
Royal African Corps, 104
Royal College of Physicians, 162
Royal College of Surgeons, London, 76, 162
Royal Colonial Institute, 41
Royal Garrison Artillery, 42
Royal Gazette and Sierra Leone Advertiser,
The, Freetown, founded 1808, 24
Royal Navy, British, 21, 56, 64, 142, 170, 173
African Squadron of the, 64, 173
Royal Niger Company, 40
Royal Order of the Lion, 257
Royal Sierra Leone Military Forces, 40, 100,
101
Royal Sierra Leone Regiment, 40
Royal Society for Tropical Medicine and
Hygiene, 63
Royal West African Frontier Force
cricket and football teams, 90
and Haidara War, 73
Ruanda, 181
Ruanda-Urundi, 301, 302
Rubber, 184, 253, 265
abuses connected with reduced, 202
atrocities in collection of, in Congo
Free State, and campaign against, 185,
186
Bushiri orders halt to harvesting of,
194
collection in Kangu chiefdom, 261
collection by the Lega, 264
obligatory harvesting of, 203
plantations, 190
production quotas, 192, 201
taxes collected in the form of, 201, 241
wild, 190
Rubund, (Lubunda), 278, 279
Rufisque, Senegal, 36
Rugari, 195
Rugu, 210
Ruiz, Jose, 141, 142
Rukan, 301, 325
Ruki River, 207, 290, 323
Rukombu, 300
Rumba. See Dances, modern, in the Congo.
Rutshuru, 195, 236
Ruwaz, 196
Ruwej a Nkond, Lunda queen, 182, 196, 282,
283, 300, 301, 325
Rwanda, 195, 210, 252, 301
Busimba in, 195
Ryckmans, André, 303
Rykmans, Pierre, 248, 301, 302, 303
S.A.B. See Société Anonyme Belge pour le
Commerce du Haut-Congo.
Sacambu, 87, 88
Sacré Coeur Mission, Stanleyville, 247
Saffa Kebi of Dama, 89
Sofroko Limba, 60, 61, 123, 151
Safroko Temne, 134
Sagba, 87
Said bin Ali, 269
Sain Bugu, 123
Saindugu, 119
Saint Anthony, 229

Saint Francis, 229
Saint Francis Xavier College, Bruges, Bel-
gium, 162
Saint John's Maroon School, 50
Saint Mary's Hospital Medical School, Lon-
don, 63, 162
Saint Paul, life of, 256
Saint Paul's Preparatory School, Colet
Court, London, 63
Sako, 274
Sakona, 88
Sala, 209
Salambongo, 193
Salt, 214, 216, 239, 279, 289, 293
Mutand Yembiyemb witholds infor-
mation on, 239
Samadiamb, 277
Samaria Church, 133
Samaya, 69, 92, 93, 97
Samba, 134
Samba, Lake. See Lake Samba.
Sambaia, 39
Samba Jombor, 134
Sambala, 247, 248
Samoa, 303
Samori Touré, 73, 88, 92, 93, 94, 95, 113,
114, 132, 134, 139, 140, 144, 151, 152,
154, 174
registered by Bambafara, 39
E. Blyden supports association with,
103
alleged agreement with the British,
(1885), 95
relations with the British, 26, 95, 130
fights with the British and French, 26
relations with the French, 95
Isa of Kaliere joins, 81
S. Lewis supports association with,
103
relations with Nyagua, 128
revolt in his empire, (1890), 26
relations with Sierra Leone, 95
attacks Sierra Leone hinterland,
(1884), 26, 113
renews attack on Sierra Leone, (1890),
26
receives arms from Sierra Leone, 26
destroys Solimana, 26
Sampaio, Manuel Gomes, (Campacala), 286
Sampwe, chief, 268, 269
Sampwe Mwanshya, 239
Samu, 46, 141
Samura, clan, 81, 139, 144
Samura, name, 81
Samura, Solimanga, (Dantili Samura), 138,
139
Samura, Alimamy, of Bonko, 69
Sanda country, 51, 69
Sanda Loko, 69, 93
Sanda Mogbolonto, 123, 134
Sanda Tenraran, 134
Rassin mediates in, 134
Sande, (Bondo), 94, 164, 165, 169, 173
midwifery and babycare in, 112
Sande bush, 165, 173
Sandhurst, British military academy, 40
Sandi, 108

Sando, 39
Sandoa, 216, 309
San Domingo, 20
Sandyalu, 87
Sanga, 179, 182, 214, 268, 269, 278, 289
    rebellion against M'Siri, 269
Sangara. See Sankaran.
Sangatile, 269
Sangu, 260, 261
Sankaily, 151
Sankaran, (Sangara), 19, 23, 38, 144, 151, 154
    seeks British protection from the Sofa, 27
    Koranko migrants leave, 113
    trade with Freetown, 38
Sankoh, 116, 118, 119, 120
    and Momoh Sankoh, 118, 119, 120
    rulership of Port Loko, 116, 118, 119, 120
Sankuru River, 182, 184, 216, 221, 241, 262, 293, 304, 319, 321, 323, 324, 325
    district, 248
    P. Lumumba apprehended at, 246
San Salvador, (Mbanza Kongo), 204, 229, 238, 256, 280, 296, 297, 299, 312, 313, 323, 325
Sa-Ntambw, 239
Santigi Bundu, 149
Santigie Bokari Kamara, Pa, 134
Sao Tomé, 281, 299
Sapi Confederacy, 18
Sara Bayo, 139, 140
Sasa, 265
Sasaposo, 223
Sassabla, Va Foray. See Va Foray Sassabla.
Sattan Lahai, (King Rowula), 23, 45, 140, 141
    conflict with Bilali in 1850s, 24
Saturday Ho, 35, 146
Savanna Zone, 179, 182, 183
Saw, 199, 200
Sawyerr's Advertising Medium, 146
Sawyerr, T.J., 145, 146
Sa Yere, 139
Sayers, E.F., 150
Sayo, 81, 95, 144, 152
Sayo Demba, 39
S.B. Thomas Agricultural Academy, 154
Scarcies, The, 17, 27, 46, 51, 52, 75, 102, 119, 141, 153, 173
    proposed canal to, 116
Scheut Fathers, 216
Scheut Mission, 212, 216, 248, 290
Schlenker, the Rev. C.F., 66, 109
Schnitzler, Eduard. See Emin Pasha.
Schryver, De. See De Schryver.
Scotland, 40, 69, 305
Scott, Henry H., 162
"Scramble for Africa," 26
Sculpture, wood, by the Kuba, 305
Seafarer, The, 159
Secessions, from the Republic of the Congo, 187
Second Division. See Armée Nationale Congolaise.

Secretary of State for the Colonies. See Colonial Secretary, British.
Secret societies, 35, 180
    secret society bush (country), 150
Sefu, 294
Sei, 126, 127
Seilenga, 127
Sei Molay, 93
Sekondi, Gold Coast, (Ghana), 76
Sela Kimba, 92
Sela Limba, 19, 93
    British chase Fomgboe in, 69
Selby, Olive, 55
Self-determination, 31
Seli River. See Rokel River.
Selma, Alabama, 138
Sembehun, 120, 157
Semba-Kamara, 107, 108
Semopa Brown, 303, 304
Senanaya, 93
Sena province, Mozambique, 240
Senate, Congolese, 246
Sendwe, Jason, 224, 310
Senegal, 26, 36, 75, 77, 104, 123, 134, 170, 172
Senehun, 54, 165
    Church of God mission at, 71
    founding of, 126, 127, 149, 157
    Gbanga moves capital to, 71
    Krio traders at, 24, 71
    Lamboi sees witch-gown at, 100
    Governor Rowe meets with chiefs at, 55, 71
    Madam Yoko as ruler of, 100, 164, 165
Senehun Ngieya, 127
Senga, Raphael, 248, 295
Sengbe, 38, 113
    part of, founded by Mansa Kama, 110
Sengbe Pieh, (Joseph Cinque), 135, 138, 141, 144
Sengele, people, 267, 324
Sengo, 199
Sengula Lumanda, 231
Serra Bundu, 148
"Serra Lyoa," (Lion Mountains), 173
Service des Finances. See Belgian Congo, Service des Finances.
Sesame, 183
Sesay Bety, of North Rokel, 59
Sesay, clan, 111, 149
"Settlers," in Sierra Leone, 21, 104
"Seventeen Nations," 105, 106
Seventh Line Regiment, Belgian, 308
Sewa Grounds. See Freetown, Victoria Park.
Sewa, Manga, 144
Sewa, Mansa, of Barawa, 38
Sewa River, 18, 26
    diamonds discovered in basin of, 30
Sewa Sayo, 144
Shaa Kempinu, clan, 266
Shaba Region, (formerly Katanga province), 179, 181, 193, 211, 212, 215, 216, 220, 232, 268, 269, 270, 278, 283, 288, 320, 322, 324, 325, 326, 327
    Upper Shaba, 239

Shabunda, (formerly Kyli), 262, 263, 264, 318
Shakatwala, chiefdom. See Mwe Nzila.
Shakatwala, clan, 282, 283
Shakatwala, Lunda leader, 283
Sharp, Granville, 20, 21, 56
    and J.F. Nemgbana, 125
Sharpe, Capt. Wilfred S., 28, 70
    deposes Bai Bureh, 51
Shaw, Tillotson, 50
Shekpendeh, 137
Shells
    as currency, 296, 313
    from Lake Tanganyika, 239
Shenge, 28, 35, 54, 56, 161
    British obtain customs rights in, 55
    W. and T.K. Caulker hanged at, 56
    Clark Theological School at, 161
    chiefdom devastated by the Mende, 54
    again attacked by the Mende, 55, 56
Sherabola, 173
    Mani king on Sherbro Island, 18
Sherbro area, 79, 82, 98, 128, 129, 137, 138, 153, 155, 157, 160, 165, 168, 172
    cession to the British, 17
    "British" Sherbro, 23
    British expedition to Bagru in, 23, 24
    Caulker family and, 54, 56
    civil wars in, 136
    Fawundu exiled from northern, 68
    Gambia Adventurers Company in, 137
    leopard murders, 99
    southern, claimed by Liberia, 108
    dominated by S.B.A. MacFoy, 106, 107
    and Mende Mission, 135
    Mende Mission schools, in, 67, 161
    Rivers, 106
    state of, 22
Sherbro, people, 18, 94, 96, 98, 108, 135, 136, 138, 168, 169, 171, 173
    chiefs sign anti-slavery treaties, 108
    and the Banta, 126
    British treaty with rulers of, 24
    rulers embargo trade with Freetown, (1897), 79
    language, 18, 138
Sherbro, Bai, (Beh), 59, 98
    arrested by the British (1898), 28, 70
    exiled to the Gold Coast, 28, 53
Sherbro estuary, 161
Sherbro Island, 18, 22, 55, 79, 98, 106, 107, 143, 168, 169, 173
Sherbro Monarch, 106
Shi, of Kivu, 181, 252, 318, 324, 326
Shila, 215, 238, 239, 325, 326
Shimba, 221
Shimbundu Makata, 183
Shimuna, 223, 326
Shimuna Mukimba Mugamba. See Mukulunzambi.
Shinga I, (Luhaka), 295
Shinje, state, 249, 282
Shinkasa Fort, 294
Shorthand, 114, 115

Shorunkeh-Sawyerr, Alfred Jones, 35, 145, 146, 147
Shorunkeh-Sawyerr, John C., 35, 36, 146, 147, 154
Shyaam aMbul aNgoong, 262, 304, 305
Shyaang aMbul, 262
Siaka, king, 108
Sibthorpe, Aaron Belisarius Cosimo, 35, 60, 147, 148
Sierra Leone, 173
    Attorney-General of, 43
    boundaries of, 17, 28, 36, 52, 53
    Chief Justice of, 43
    climate of, 17
    expansion of Colony of, 17
    economy of, 29, 30, 31
    geography and relief, 17
    independence negotiations, 32, 112
    independence date, 32, 112
    border dispute with Liberia, 36
    boundary with Liberia agreed upon, (1917), 109
    and state of Morea, 46
    migrations into and settlement of, 17, 18, 19
    national anthem, 36
    named by the Portuguese, 17, 173
    becomes Republic, (April 1971), 33
    Solicitor-General of, 43
    vegetation of, 17
Sierra Leone Aborigines Society, 118
Sierra Leone Aro (Cooperative) Society, 84
Sierra Leone Association, 103, 145
Sierra Leone Broadcasting Service, 36
Sierra Leone Chamber of Commerce, 118
Sierra Leone Church, 157
Sierra Leone City Council, 43
Sierra Leone Colony, 169, 173
    administration of, in mid-19th century, 25
    trade protected by Bilali, 46
    instability on its borders, 47
    1863 constitution of, 25
    relations with Dalla Modu, 59, 60
    establishment of, 19, 20, 173
    first exports from, 75
    Fomgboe arrives in, 68
    conquers lands west of Freetown, 155
    seeks aid of Gbanya Lango, 165
    relations with the hinterland, (later the Protectorate), 22, 59, 60, 72, 73, 84, 85, 101, 129, 145, 149, 151
    and Imperi, 79
    inland expansion of, 102, 103, 141
    and Nemgbana, 125
    intervenes in Port Loko dispute, 119, 122, 123
    Sherbro as part of, 106
    Sherbro ceded to, 55
    and Suluku, 151
    war with Temne, 155
    burns Temne towns, 148
    treaty with Temne, 155
    Temperance movement in, 115
    Turner Treaty confirmed by Governor Rowe, 55

Sierra Leone Company, 21, 56, 71, 125, 155, 170
    accepts J. Clarkson's services, 56
    founds Freetown, 125
    sends J.F. Nemgbana to England, 125
    in war against Koya Temne, 72
    contacted by T. Peters, 131
    finances Province of Freedom, 21
Sierra Leone People's Party, (S.L.P.P.), 32, 33, 49, 85, 101, 164
    wins 1962 elections, 32
    and 1967 elections, 33, 48, 101, 152
    withdraws from 1973 elections, 33
    and 1978 elections, 33
    formation of, 84, 111, 112
    Julius Gulama and, 72
    becomes official opposition, 33
    split in, (1958), 32
Sierra Leone Produce Marketing Board, 31
Sierra Leone Railroad Workers' Union, 159
Sierra Leone Railway, 29, 52, 54
    reaches Balima, (1906), 29
    construction begins, (1896), 29, 53
    branch line built, (1915), 29
    declared liability, (1940s), 29
    Magburaka as terminus of, 149
    reaches Pendemba, (1908), 29
    phased out, (1960s), 29
    strike of 1926, 44
Sierra Leone Ram, The, 146
Sierra Leone River. See Rokel River.
Sierra Leone Selection Trust, (S.L.S.T.), 30
    nationalization of, 31
Sierra Leone Society, 63, 163
Sierra Leone Sports Council, 43
Sierra Leone Studies, 63, 164
Sierra Leone Supreme Court, 48, 137
Sierra Leone Technical School, 78
Sierra Leone Times, 25
Sierra Leone Weekly News, 35
    founded, 114, 115, 154, 157
Sikandja, 274
Sikasso, Ivory Coast, 94
Sikolo, 274
Sikoro, 235
Sierra Leone Country Cloths, 63
Sierra Leone Cricket Association, 45
Sierra Leone Customs Department, 159
Sierra Leone Development Company, (Delco)
    bankrupt, 30
    granted mining concession, 30
Sierra Leone estuary. See Rokel River estuary.
Sierra Leone Exhibition, (1865), 147
Sierra Leone Farmers Association, 36
Sierra Leone Football Association, 43, 45
Sierra Leone Frontier Police Force, 28, 39. See also West African Frontier Force.
    search for Bokari Bombolai, 47
    disciplined, (1895), 27
    duties, 27
    collect House Tax, 28, 53, 56, 69, 79, 121, 148, 157, 166
    and Hut Tax War, 28
    inaugurated, (1890), 27, 130
    advance against Kabba Sei, 86
    seek refuge in Liberia, 110

    prevent disturbances after Mendegla's death, 117
    sent to end fighting in the north, 47
    fights against the Sofa, 86
    petty tyranny by, 27
Sierra Leone House of Representatives, 160
Sierra Leone Labour Department, 163
Sierra Leone Methodist Mission, 75
Sierra Leone National Dance Troupe, 37
Sierra Leone National Defence Fund, (1908), 36
Sierra Leone National Museum, 63
Sierra Leone Native Defence Fund, 43
Sierra Leone Observer, 112, 134
Sierra Leone Organization Society, (S.O.S.), 73, 84, 112
Sierra Leone Parliament, 152, 163
Sile, 236
Sili, station, 265
Silver
    manacles, gift of, 281, 313
    mines, Portuguese seek, 281
    Nkanga Lukeni refuses to cede silver mines, 313
    Portuguese seek silver mines in southern Kongo, 296
Simbas, (Armée Populaire de Libération, A.P.L.), 274, 300, 326
Simpson, D., 81
Sims, Aaron, 305, 306
Singer Sewing Machine Company, 44
Siniaki, 274
Sinko. See Shengbe Pieh.
Sinkunia, 154
Slater, Sir Ransford, Governor, 31, 44, 50
Slater Constitution. See Constitution.
Slavery, 204. See also Anti-slavery.
    institution of, and *Amistad* case, 143
    complaints of interference with, 60
    Kalombo freed from, 256
    Mende Mission frees slaves, 136
    Monia and Mwe enslaved by Libinza, 266
    Motengo reduced to, 265
    allegations of, in the Protectorate, 53
    among the Tio, 287
Slaves, 184, 200, 269
    active in trade, 205
    of *Amistad,* gain freedom, 135
    beheaded, 140
    sought by the Cokwe (Chokwe), 209
    as commodities, 284
    of Dalla Modu, 59
    escaped, 97, 102
    freed in Freetown, 21
    "Free Slave State," 45, 46, 140
    in the Gallinas, 108
    traded for guns, 220
    instability promoted to obtain, 269
    possibly buried with Kai Londo, 88
    search for in Kivu, 235
    freed at Largo, 124
    Loko, bought by Gombu Smart, 71
    Monia and Mwe, 266
    M'Siri captures, 269
    Mumbendu trades slaves for rifles, 274

(Slaves-Continued)
> Mungembe obtains, 277
> Muslims seek, in northern Zaire, 265
> Ngaliema enslaved and freed, 286, 287
> Ngaliema buys, 287
> Ngankabi acquires, 290
> Ngongo Leteta trades in, 293, 294
> Ngongo Luhaka and raids for, 295
> price of, declines, 286
> used as porters, 252
> presented to the Sofa, 139
> sought by the Swahili, 241, 264, 326
> Tippu Tib trades in, 293

Slave trade, 19, 70
> abolition of, 20, 21, 133, 173
> Bobangi involvement in, 191
> and the Congo Free State, 303
> Dalla Modu charged with slave trading, 59
> from Egypt and the Sudan, 285
> and indentured labor, 133
> in the Upper Kwango River region, 202
> participation in, by Kasongo Kiniama, 220
> Mwene Putu Kasongo and, 284
> renounced by Ngankabi, 290
> Ngongo Leteta and, 292, 293, 294
> Ovimbundu in, 209
> inception of the slave trade by the Portuguese, 281
> Sierra Leone as a base for the naval campaign against, 104
> Spanish and, 135, 141
> suppression of, on the Lulonga River, 192
> Swahili and the, 295
> transatlantic slave trade, 181, 182
> Tulante Mbidi and, 256

Slave Trade Abolition Act. (British), 147

Slave traders
> Bunduka as, 123
> from Egypt and the Sudan, 285
> French, 123
> expelled from Gallinas, 108
> Kamara Limba clan as, 167
> Loko as, 149
> criticize Mende Mission, 136
> raids by, 241, 277
> Spanish, 135, 141

Sleeping sickness, 203, 253, 274
> epidemics of the 1920s and 1930s, 277
> Mumpema and his brother die of, 274, 275

S.L.P.P. See Sierra Leone People's Party.
S.L.S.T. See Sierra Leone Selection Trust.
Small Bo, 87
Small Bum River, 156
Smallpox, 76, 268
Small Scarcies River, 58, 92, 140
S.M.A. See Society of African Missions.
Smart, Charles, of Mahera, 47, 148
Smeathman, Dr. Henry, 20, 21
Smith, Emma, 63
Smith, Dr. Robert, 153
Smith, Tom Kebbie. See Tom Kebbie Smith.
Soap, manufacture of, 36

Social Darwinism, 26
Société Anonyme Belge pour le Commerce du Haut-Congo, (S.A.B.), 190, 207, 288
Société Anversoise de Commerce au Congo, 201, 202
Société de l'Uélé, 255
Société des Linguistes du Zaire, 210
Société de Transport de l'Administration, (S.T.A.), 237
Society for the Promotion of Universal Peace, 57
Society of African Missions, (S.M.A.), 48, 49
Soden, C.W., 99
Sofa, 26, 132, 174
> attack Biriwa Limba, 151
> leave Biriwa Limba, 151
> British and French reactions to, 27, 132
> attack Falaba, 144
> capture Falaba, 81
> expelled from Sierra Leone-Guinea border area by the French, 27
> attack Isa of Kaliere, 27, 81
> beaten by Kai Londo, 88
> invade Kono, 114
> capture Marlay Bokari, 113
> repelled by Matturi, 113, 114
> attack Nieni, 39
> conflict with Nyagua, 128
> led by Porekere, 132
> destroy Samaya, 92
> relations with Sara Bayo, 139, 140
> fight against Sierra Leone Frontier Police, 86
> opposition to, in Sierra Leone, 27, 132
> capture Solima state, 61
> and Almamy Suluku, 151
> relations with Almamy Suman, 152
> and Wara Wara Limba, 152

Soka Toungi, 207
Sokong, of Imperi, 79
Solima, 38, 61, 81, 139, 154, 174
Solimana, 23, 81, 94, 144, 152, 169, 174
> seeks British protection from the Sofa, 27
> destruction of, (1884), 22, 26, 61
> founding of, 19, 22, 139
> oppose Fula of Futa Jallon, 38, 81
> history of, 22
> relations with Isa of Kaliere, 81

Solimankhori, 139
Soloni, 94
Solonto of Gbangbama, 93, 94
Soma, 127, 164. See also Yoko, Madam.
Sommelier, (Limpanya), 266, 276, 298
Sonde, 254
Songo Davies, J.A., 154
Songo Town, 53
Songye, people, 221, 240, 241, 247, 293, 295, 326
Sorgho, (sweet sorghum), 183
Sorghum, sweet. See Sorgho.
Sori Bangura, 49
Sori Bunki, 51
Sorie Limba, 60, 61
Sori Gbay, 92
Sori Kanu. See Sori Kessebeh.

Sori Kessebeh, (Sori Kanu), 148, 149
Sori Kutu, 149
Sori Sesay, Alimamy, 149, 150
Sori Wuleng, (Asan Yira), 38, 144
S.O.S. See Sierra Leone Organization Society.
Soso, 45, 51, 59, 68, 73, 75, 92, 93, 94, 97, 125, 140, 141, 149, 170, 171, 172, 174
> conflict with Bilali in the 1850s, 24
> entered Sierra Leone, 92
> support Foday Tarawaly of Morea, 46
> aid in attack on Fort Thornton, 155
> resist French advance, 62
> wars with the Limba, 51, 74, 92, 93, 97
> support Nova Scotian uprising, 59
> emigrants at Port Loko, 149
> rule Port Loko, 122, rule ended, 122, 123, 149
> dispute with Temne, (1861), 116
> conflict with Temne, 102, 122, 123, 149
> conflict with Tonko Limba, 69, 92, 93, 97

Soso Sankoh, family, 68, 116
Soumaliot, Emile, 311
Sousberghe, Léon de. See de Sousberghe, Léon.
South Africa, 52
> alleged recruiting in Freetown for mines of, 133
South Carolina, 56, 57, 83
Southern Leader, 158
Southern Province, 164
South Kivu, 263, 264, 318
Southeast Asia, 179
Soviet Union
> and British colonies, 31, 32
> in the Congo, 187
> P. Lumumba makes overtures to, 245
Soyo, 257, 258, 296, 321, 323
Spain, 141
> bans importation of slaves, 141
> consul of, in Boston, 142
> U.S. relations with, re- the *Amistad* incident, 142
Spaine, Postmaster J.H., 103
Speaker, of the Sierra Leone House of Representatives, 48
Spectator, 83
Springer, Mr. and Mrs. John M., 216
Stairs, Capt. William, 270
Stakler, 257
S.T.A. See Société de Transport de l'Administration.
Stanley Falls station, at Kisangani, 190, 291, 306, 326, 327
Stanley, Henry Morton, 184, 205, 206, 207, 251, 287, 288, 289, 290, 291, 292, 305, 306, 308, 321, 323
> named "Bula Matari," 317
> plans for a railroad, 308
> traces the course of the Zaire (Congo) River, 308
Stanley Pool. See Malebo Pool.
Stanley, steamer, 252

Stanleyville, (now Kisangani), 198, 219, 242, 243, 244, 245, 246, 247, 248, 262, 321, 326. See also Kisangani.
    Lupungu sent to, 247
    1959 riots in, 243
State Normal College, Tallahassee, Florida, (Florida A. and M.), 157, 158
State University of Elisabethville, (formerly the Congo Official University), 233
Statues, Lega, 183
Steamers, river. See Zaire River.
Steele, the Rev. James, 135
Stevens, Siaka, 32
    chancellor of the University of Sierra Leone, 33
    attempted coup against, (1967), 101
    and 1978 elections, 32
    as Minister of Labour, 45
    becomes prime minister, 33, 48, 152
    as prime minister of national government, (1968), 33, 40, 69, 101, 152
    becomes executive president, (1971), 33
    target of student demonstrations, 33
Stevenson, Governor Hubert, 32, 73, 112
Stevenson Constitution. See Constitution.
Stone Age, Earlier, Middle, and Recent, 179
Stools, Lega, 183
Storme, Father, 289, 290
Straight College of New Orleans, 158
Strauch, Col., 308
Study Committee for the Upper Congo, (Comité d'Etudes du Haut-Congo, or C.E.H.C.), 184, 251, 288, 308, 315, 319, 326
    Makitu and Leteta associated with, 251
Sudan, region, 122, 174
Sudan, the, state, 265, 285, 327
    Emin Pasha in, 306
Sudanese, migration of, 233
Sugarcane, 249
Sugar, West Indian, manufactured from molasses, 36
Suku, 283, 284
Sulima, 124, 128
    British customs post raided, 124
    terminus of frontier road, 27
Suluku, Almamy, of Bumban, 22, 23, 60, 140, 144, 150, 151, 152
    becomes ruler of Biriwa Limba, 39
    signs treaty with the British, (1888), 27
    his state subdued by Samori, 26
    Sofa forces expelled from, by the British, 26
    conflict with Yirimusukeli of Nieni, 39
Suman, Almamy, 152
    treats with British, 152
Sumanguru, 19, 174
Summary Convictions Ordinance, (1906), 156
Summer, A.T., 41
Sundiata, Keita, 92, 110
Sundi-Lutete, 232

Supreme Court. See Gold Coast Supreme Court; Sierra Leone Supreme Court; United States Supreme Court.
Surakata, 51
Susa, 69
Sus. See Soso.
Swahili, language, 210, 236, 264, 326
    as medium of science, culture, and commerce, 210, 236
    P. Lumumba fluent in, 244
    terms from, in general use, "boma," 317, "kirongozi," 321
Swahili, people, 183, 184, 247, 269, 270, 315
    Congo Free State campaign against merchants, 314
    customs of ruler's court, 237
    troops and Lumpungu, 221, 240, 241
    merchants, (traders), 190, 220, 221, 235, 262, 264, 268, 269, 270, 293, 294, 306, 315, 325, 326
    Ngongo Luteta's relations with, 294
    slave raids by, 241, 295
"Swahili-French, French-Swahili Dictionary," 210
Swanamurund, 301
Sweet potatoes, 249
Sweifel, J., 144
Syrians. See Lebanese.
Tabia, 88
    set ablaze, 88
Tabu Ley, (Rochereau), 220
Tabura, 239
Tabwa, people, 238, 239
Tabwa, place, 238
Taia River, (Jong River), 26, 71, 93, 108, 165. See also Jong.
Taiama, 71, 99, 127, 165, 166
Tananarive, Madagascar, 219, 225
    accords, 311
    Tshombe visits, 311
Takoyo, 94
Tallahassee, Florida, 157, 158
Tamangana, 22, 174
Tambi, 51
    British expeditions attack, 93, 97
    destroyed, 93, 97
    Karimu's forces at, 93
Tandu, chiefdom, 200
Tane, 152
Tanganyika, 241, 301
Tanganyika, Lake. See Lake Tanganyika.
Tango. See Dances, modern, in the Congo.
Tangolawa, 93, 94
Tansa Lamina, 141
Tanzania, 210, 269, 327
Tappan, Lewis, 138, 142, 143
Taqi, Ibrahim Bash, 152
Tara Placide, Abbe, 306, 307
Tasso Islands, 17, 115, 169
Taxes
    levied by Badjoko, 190
    and the Bakisi chiefdom, 263
    and the Boma people, 267
    in the Congo during World War II, 193
    in the Giri Region, 277
    and the Kangu chiefdom, 261

    women given to Motengo in place of, 266
    Mumbendu and tax collection, 274
    Mwene Putu Kasongo imposes, 284
    payment of, contested, 189
    among the Pende during the Depression, 203
    Tio chiefs reject, 288
Taylor, Sub-Inspector Charles, 108, 132
Teazer, H.M.S., 60
Tecuyama, 114, 132
"Te Deum bantou," 232
Teke, language, 306. Also see Tio.
Tellu, 132
Tembu, 68, 69, 93
Temeta, 37
Temne, 17, 18, 19, 39, 47, 72, 73, 83, 109, 111, 123, 125, 126, 134, 140, 141, 148, 149, 155, 157, 166, 168, 169, 170, 171, 172, 173, 174. See also Koya Temne; Mabanta Temne; Rokel Temne; Yoni Temne.
    "liberated" Africans released by, 60
    as mercenaries for Bokari, 46
    Brima Kondito travels to the, 68
    Governor Cardew visits, 52
    and Christianity, 116
    attack Colony traders, 71
    war with Colony, 155
    towns burnt by Colony, 148
    treaty with Colony, 155
    Farma Tami and, 66, 67
    and Fomgboe, 69
    attack Gbile, 68
    in Hut Tax War against the British, (1898), 28, 51, 148
    join coalition against Karimu, 97
    take over Kholifa, 111
    language, 109, Banta a dialect of, 126
    advised by Sir Samuel Lewis, 104
    wars with the Loko, 59, 116, 148, 149
    of Masimera, 148
    J. McCormack's relations with, 101, 115, 116
    incidents at frontier with the Mende, 107
    war with the Mende, 116
    oral traditions of, 66
    at Port Loko, 122, 123
    of Port Loko, British treaty with, 24
    Samori's forces in, 134
    in alliance against Sankoh, 119
    scriptures translated into, 109
    land for Sierra Leone Colony obtained from, 21
    dispute with the Soso, (1861), 116
    and the Soso, 122, 123, 149
    and Suluku, 151
    and the Treaty of Massama, (1879), 102
    wars among, in the 18th and 19th centuries, 23
Temne Marampa, 47
Temperance, 115
Temple, Octavius, Lt. Governor, 59
Tendele, 275
Tendwala, 284

Tengea Kissi. See Kissi.

Ten-Year-Development Plan for the Congo, 302

Tete, 239, 240

Tete La-Kusu, 324

Tete Ngombu, 248

Tetela, 219, 222, 241, 242, 243, 247, 248, 271, 292, 293, 294, 295, 300, 313, 314, 318, 319, 326. See also Ekonda; Eswe.

    revolt of soldiers at Boma, (1900), 294

    chiefdoms, 248

    homeland occupied by Congo Free State, 313, 314

    conflicts with Congo Free State troops, 314

    mutineers in the Force Publique, 222

    revolt of soldiers at Luluabourg, (1895), 241, 271, 294, 313, 314

    P. Lumumba's Tetela origins, 242

    agents of the Swahili and the Arabs among, 315

Thai, 220

Theological and Educational Institution. See Wesleyan Theological and Educational Institution.

Third Division. See Armée National Congolaise.

Third World countries, 187

Thirteenth (13th) Infantry Battalion. See Armée National Congolaise.

"Thirty Year Plan," 186

Thomas, Betty, 153

Thomas, Christiana, 153

Thomas, John, 153

Thomas, John Henry, "Malamah," 152, 153, 154

Thomas, Samuel Benjamin, (Abuke), 154

Thonist philosophy, 301

Thompson, George, 136

Thomson, C.M.A., 84

Thornton, Henry, 21

Thoronka Koranko, 39

Three Bills, The, of 1939, 41

Thys, Albert, 307, 308, 309

Thysville, (now Mbanza-Ngungu), 197, 228, 231, 232, 246, 309, 323. See also Mbanza-Ngungu.

    Centre Extra-Coutumier at, 232

Tikonko

    quarrels with Bumpeh, 107

    ruled by Makavoray, 22, 107, 166

    treaties signed at, 121

Tilkens, Lt. Gen. A.C., 302

Timber

    exported from Sierra Leone, 75, 115

    trading posts for established on the Lomami River, 190

    trade declines, 116

    used for fuel on the Ubangi River, 235

Timbo, 139, 166

    visited by E. Blyden, 24

    Alimamy Bokari of, 59

Timbuktu. See Tombouctou.

Tinalei, 113

Tio, (Teke), 184, 205, 286, 287, 288, 306, 323, 325, 326, 327

    as traders in ivory, 251

Tippu Tib, 241, 293

Tobacco. See Currency.

Tobback, Commander Nicholas, 190, 252

Toboku-Metzger, Albert Emerick, 65, 156, 157

Togo, 101

Tokba Asana Samura, 154, 155

Toko Simao Gonzalves, 228

Tom, "King," 114, 125

Tom II, "King," 155

    supports Nova Scotian uprising, 155

    wars against the Sierra Leone Company, 72

Tombo Island, 115

Tom Kebbie Smith, 155, 156

Tombouctou, (Timbuktu), 38

Tongi. See Kissi Tongi.

Tongo Players, Mende witch detectors, 99, 100, 161, 174

Tongovila, 126, 127

Tonkapa, 69

Tonkolili, 110, 149, 150, 152

Tonko Limba, 19, 49, 92, 93, 97, 134, 169, 174

    administrative center moved, 49

    Bilali, 24, 45, 46

    Bombo Lahai Yusufu as ruler of, 166, 167

    Fomgboe captured in, 69

    conflict with Karimu, 69, 92, 93, 97

    Methodist Mission at, 74, 82, 83

    Rassin mediates in, 134

Tonnoir, R., 267

Topoke, 190

Torong, 94

Totshi, 214, 307

Touré, Samori. See Samori Touré.

Touré, Sékou, 243

Towai, 87

Trade

    boycott of, with Krios, and Europeans, 98

    from the Sierra Leone interior, 23, 24

Trade route, Falaba / Bumban / Port Loko, 23

Trade unions, 31, 159, 160

    Catholic, 224

Training Institution, Wesleyan, 114

Transvaal campaign, 52

Travel, restrictions on, 186

Treaties

    British, with African rulers, 27

    standard British treaty, 27

    British abandon local treaties, 27, 28

    French, with African rulers, 27

    Franco-British agreement of January 1895, 28

    increase in treaty-making, 120

    British treaty with Kaliere, (1890), 27

    Leopold's agents conclude, with chiefs, 184

    between the Kongo and the Portuguese, (1517), 299

    Massamah treaties, 102

    between Mushid a Nambing and the Congo Free State, 277

    between Nkanga Lukeni and the Portuguese, (1649), 296

British treaty with Nemgbana, 125

British treaty with Nyagua, 128

J.C.E. Parkes and, 129

Alikali of Port Loko and, 119

Sierra Leone-Liberia boundary agreement (1911); ratified, (1917), 28

British treaty with Suman, 152

British-Temne treaty of 1807, 155

Turner treaty (1825), 55, 56, 98

Tregaskis, the Rev. Benjamin, 64, 65, 96, 115

Trinidad, 160

Troy, North Carolina, 65

Tsatshi, 307

Tshela, 216

Tshikapa, 233

Tshikapa River, 249, 282, 283

Tshiluba, (Kiluba), 322, 326

Tshinkeke, 270

Tshisungu Kalamba, 271

Tshitolian tradition. See Recent Stone Age.

Tshitolo, 221

Tshofa, 314

Tshofa, people, 221

Tshombe, Moise, 216, 219, 224, 225, 244, 245, 246, 309, 310, 311, 312

    "federalist" position, 244

    forms government, 226

    relations with Kasa-Vubu, 219

    and Katanga secession, 225, 245

    and P. Lumumba's death, 246

    at 1960 Round Table Conference, 244

Tshopo, 193

Tshumbiri, 266

Tshungu, (Dadi ben Ndoe), 293

Tuba, 285

Tucker family, 20

Tucker, Harry, 135, 157

Tucker, Nancy, 157

    during Hut Tax War (1898), 28, 56

Tucker, Thomas DeSaliere, 138, 157, 158

Tufia, 249, 282

Tufu River, 284

"Tukpe" Society, 85

Tulante Mbidi, 256

Tumba, 300, 309

Tungea, near Panguma, 26, 132

Tungula Falls, 283

Tunka, 110

Tunsele, 270

Tupelepele, 258, 260

Tupokoto, 249

Tupulu, 96

Turay, name, 81

Turner, Sir Charles, Governor, 55, 98, 116, 123

    takes troops to Port Loko, 123

Turner Treaty, (September 24, 1825), 55, 56, 98

Tuskegee Institute, Alabama, 83

Two Ps or Politics for the People, 84, 85

Two Voyages to Sierra Leone during the Years 1791-2-3, 125, 126

U.A.C. See United Africa Company.

Ubangi, 191, 233, 299

Ubangi River, 192, 200, 201, 205, 233, 234, 235, 266, 274, 281, 282, 290, 298, 317, 321

U.B.C. See United Brethren Church.

Ubundu. (Ponthierville), 327

U.D.P. See United Democratic Party.

Uélé Company. See Société de l'Uélé.

Uele River, 183, 265, 285, 294, 323, 327

Uganda, 210

Ululu, 205

Uluund, 277

U.M.H.K. See Union Minière du Haut-Katanga.

U.N.E.F. See United Nations Emergency Force.

Unelma, (Union des anciens élèves des Frères maristes), 186, 326

Unemployment
in the Belgian Congo, 194
in Léopoldville, (1959), 218, 243

Union des anciens élèves des Frères maristes. See Unelma.

Union des Intérêts Sociaux Congolais, (U.N.I.S.C.O.), 217

Union Minière du Haut-Katanga, (U.M.-H.K.), 193, 311

Union of Former Students of the Marist Brothers. See Unelma.

Union of Ghana with the Congo, (1960), 245

Union Royale Coloniale Belge, 302

U.N.I.S.C.O. See Union des Intérêts Sociaux Congolais.

United Africa Company, (U.A.C.), 159

United Brethren Church, (U.B.C.)
at King Street, Pennsylvania, 161
at Shenge, 161

United Brethren in Christ Mission, 162

United Brethren Publishing House, Dayton, Ohio, 35

United Democratic Party, (U.D.P.), 33, 69, 152
clashes with the A.P.C., 33
proscribed, 33

United Front coalition government, 137

United Methodist Collegiate School, Freetown, 65

United Nations Emergency Force in the Congo, (U.N.E.F.), ("the Blue Helmets"), 187, 311

United Nations, 40, 225, 245, 246
Atomic Energy Commission, 302
in the Congo, 40
Congo intervention requested, 187, 245
sends troops to the Congo, 219, 245
Charter, 243
controls Elisabethville, 225
supports Kasa-Vubu, 219, 246
in Katanga, 225
occupies Kolwezi, 225
Lumumba lodges complaint against Belgium with, 245
Lumumba visits U.N., in New York, 245
troops surround Lumumba's residence, 246
Security Council, 225
Trusteeship Council, 302

United Nations Emergency Force, (U.N.-E.F.), 40

United People's Party, (U.P.P.), 32, 160

United Progressive Party, 137

United States, 35, 55, 65, 83, 135, 138, 157, 161, 220
African missionary to the United States, B. Root, 138
and the *Amistad,* 142, 143, 144, 172
and the British Colonies, 31, 32
and the Congo, 245, 319
in the Congo, 187
Makari Kabobi's studies in, 250, 251
missionaries from, 197
W. Raymond, missionary from the, 135, 136, 137
U.S. Ambassador in London, 133
D.F. Wilberforce's status as a naturalized U.S. citizen, 161

United States Supreme Court, 135, 141, 143, 172

Universal Declaration of the Rights of Man, 243

Université Libre du Congo, (Free University of the Congo), 197

Universities. See Columbia University; Louvain University; Lovanium University; State University of Elisabethville; Université Libre du Congo; University of Aberdeen; University of California, Berkeley; University of Chicago; University of Edinburgh; University of Liverpool; University of London; University of Pittsburgh; University of Sierra Leone.

University College Hospital, London, 62

University of Aberdeen, Scotland, 305

University of California, Berkeley, 36, 37

University of Chicago, 55

University of Edinburgh, Scotland, 40, 76, 82

University of Liverpool, 58, 162

University of London, 44, 48, 63, 65, 162

University of West Africa, proposed, 31, 77, 78

Upemba, 196

U.P.P. See United People's Party.

Upper Congo region, 308

Upper Congo station
first established, 288

Upper Lufuku River, 231

Upper Mongala River. See Mongala River.

Upper Shaba. See Shaba.

Usman dan Fodio, 74

U.S.S.R. See Soviet Union.

Usumbwa, 268, 269, 270

Utanda, 194

Utica, (Tunisia,), 204
bishop of, 204

Uulund, 326

Vaana, 95

Vacca, Manuel, 183
destruction of his town by the British, 183

Va Foray Sassabla, (also Foray Kallon), 158, 159

Vahun, 88

Vai, (Gallinas), 171, 172, 173
reach the Atlantic coast, 19

called "Gallinas," 170
link with the Kono, 19
language, 19
"Manes" as possible ancestors of, 67
Mana Siaka as ruler of, 108, 109
origin of the name, 19
meet with the Portuguese, 19
entry into Sierra Leone, 19

Vallaeys, E., 233, 248

Valley Without Echo, 36

Vana, 54, 55, 71
hanged, 55, 71

Van Bilsen, A.J. See Bilsen, A.J. van.

Van Buren, U.S. President Martin, 142

Van der Hallen, 223, 261

Van der Meersch, Ganshof, 224, 225

Vandevenne, 213, 230, 235, 279, 281

Vandewelde, 216

Van Gele, 190, 207, 252

Van Hemelrijck. See Hemelrijck, van.

Van Hombeek, 258

Vanja Lekpeh, 126

Vanjelu. See Mandu.

Van Wayemberg, Monsignor, 302

Varhenyen, Charles, 304

Varma, 132

Vassama, 88

Vassama Gbandi. See Gbandi.

Vatican, 48, 296
Tshombe visits, 312

Vei. See Vai.

Vele River, 265

Venn, the Rev. Henry, 76

Verdick, 277

Verdussen, 202

Vernacular Studies, Board of Examiners for, 75

Vice-Admiralty Court, Sierra Leone, 134

Victoria Park (Sewa Grounds). See Freetown.

Virginia, 56, 138, 158

Virginia Theological Seminary, Lynchburg, Virginia, 65

Virgin Mary, the, 229

Verhaegen, Benoit, 273

Vers l'avenir, 302

Vise, Belgium, 308

Vita Nkanga, (Antonio I), 296, 312, 313

Vivi, 185, 308

Vohsen, Ernest, 153

Voix du Congolais, La, 197, 242

Vonjo, 107, 108, 126, 127, 132, 166

Vui, 248, 249, 325, 327

Vunda, 197

Vungu, kingdom, 238

Wagenia, 180

Wagenia Falls, 327

Waima, 52
Franco-British clash at, 52, 130, 132

Waku, 265

"Wali," (gems), 127

Walihun, 127

Wallace-Johnson, Isaac Theophilus Akuna, (also Abdul Mohamed Afric, W. Daniels, and E. Richards), 32, 41, 118, 159, 160, 161

Walloons, 186

Wambala, 276, 290

Wambe River, 283

Wamuzimu, chiefdom, 236, 237

Wandu, 313

Wangata, 207

as part of Mbandaka, 207

Wangata-Libongas, (the Riverbank Wangatas), 207

Wangatas, Riverbank. See Wangata-Libongas.

Wangwana. See Swahili.

Wanje River, 120, 121

Wansey, Nathaniel, 59

Wara Wara, 19, 28, 37, 61, 152, 171, 174

Wara Wara district, 37, 168

Wara Wara hills, 19, 113, 171

Wara Wara Yagala, 37

War College, Belgian, 308

War Department Amalgamated Workers Union, 160

Warren, H.G.

district commissioner of Kenema, 81

assistant inspector at Kwelu, 47

Washington, Martha, 289

W.A.S.U. See West African Student Union.

W.A.S.U. journal, 84

Washington, Booker T., 66

Washington D.C., Sierra Leone Embassy in, 40

Wasp, H.M.S., 155

Watch Tower Bible and Tract Society, 194. See also Kitwala movement.

Water and Power Distribution Authority, Léopoldville, (Régie de Distribution d'Eau et d'Electricité, R.E.G.I.D.E.-S.O.), 255

Water Dwellers of the Ndolo. See Ndolo.

Waterloo, 71, 75, 105

recaptive conflict at, 105

Water Works Department. See Freetown Water Works Department.

Wathen station, 252, 256, 327. See also Ngombe-Lutete.

Watsa, 255

Weaving, Kuba, 305

Weights and measurers in the Sierra Leone Colony, 58

Welensky, Sir Roy, 310

Wellington, village, Sierra Leone, 42, 114, 154

Wembo Nyama, 313, 314

Wembo Nyamba, village, 314

Wende, 124, 128

Wenner, F. 248

Wesleyan Boys School, Freetown, 58, 74, 114. See also Methodist Boys School, Freetown.

Wesleyan City Mission School, Freetown, 75

Wesleyan Day School, 153

Wesleyan (now Queens) College, Taunton, England, 65, 114

Wesleyan Methodist Church, 103

Wesleyan Methodist Society, 64, 74, 75, 82, 96

Wesleyan Mission, 64, 74, 75, 82, 83, 96, 97, 115, 135

Wesleyan Theological and Educational Institution, Freetown, 74, 96

Wesley Church, 64, 96

West African Civil Liberties and National Defense League, 160

West African Countries and Peoples, 78

West African Court of Appeal, 41, 45

West African Liberator, 134

West African Review, 36

West African Students Union, (W.A.S.A.), 83

West African Youth League, 41, 118, 160

West Atlantic groups in Sierra Leone, 18

West Balobo, 253

West Coast Youth League, 159

Western Area, 171

Western Kasai. See Kasai Occidental. West Germany. See Germany.

"West India Interest, The," 20

West Indian regiments, 60

West Indians, 129, 132, 133

West Indies, 56, 60, 104, 106, 143

Westminster Normal Training School, London, 114

Westmoreland Street. See Freetown.

We Yone, 152

W.F.T.U. See World Federation of Trade Unions.

"White Brochure," 308

Whipple, the Rev. George, 136, 138

White, John, 138

Whobay of Imperi, 133

Wilberforce, 114, 137, 159

Wilberforce and York, electoral seat, 160

Wilberforce, Daniel Flickinger, 99, 161, 162

Wilberforce, Elizabeth, (née Elizabeth Harris), 161

Wilberforce Street, Freetown, 84

Wilberforce, William, 20

Wilkinson, Governor Richard James, 80, 110

Will, Thomas, "king" of the Aku, 105

Wilmington, A.C., 131

Wilson, Tom, 141

Wilson, Mr. and Mrs., 135

Winstedt, O.R., 197

Winton, Sir Francis de. See de Winton, Sir Francis.

Wise, Commodore Charles, 140

Wissmann, Herman von, 212, 241, 270, 271

"Witch gown," 100

Wives

of Edjumbu, 200

wealth measured in numbers of, 199

Wolseley, Sir Garnet Joseph, 71

Women's Missionary Association, 149

Wonde, 184

Wonkafong, 58

Working Group, Belgian, (to assess the situation in the Congo), 218, 224, 243, 244, 303

World Council of Churches, 320

World's Exposition, Chicago, 66

World Federation of Trade Unions, (W.F.T.U.), 160

Congress of, 160

World Jamboree of Scouts, Birkenhead, England, (1929), 43

World Trade Union Congress, London, 160

World War I, 42, 63, 72, 186, 250

Cameroun campaign, 301

East African campaign, 241, 301

economic depression after, 166

Pierre Ryckmans in, 301

World War II, 31, 32, 72, 150, 186, 198, 253

and the Bakisi chiefdom, 263

organizations formed after, in the Congo, 217, 315, 326

pressures of colonialism during, 193, 194

religious sects in the Congo during, 193, 321, 323

religious sects in the Congo after, 237

harrassment of West African Youth League during, 160

Wovo, 284

Wright, C.E., 162

Wright, Charlotte, 163

Wright, the Hon. Claude, 163

Wright, Ernest Jenner, 162, 163

Wright, Dr. Sophie, (Mrs. Ramanakoto), 162

Wrought iron, 239

Wulade, battle of, 88

Wuli, (in Nieni), 39

Wunde, country, 86, 88, 164

Wunde Society, (Kpaa-Mende secret society), 71, 127, 174

Wurie, Alhaju Ahmadu, 135, 163, 164

Wycliffe College, Oxford, 83

Ya Bomporro Folah, 163

Yacehia, 38

Ya Dankay, 134

Yagala, Limba of, 23

Yaka, people, 283, 284, 320, 327

conquered by Mwene Putu Kasongo, 284

control of trade, 284

Yaka, state, 249, 282, 284

Ya Kaumbu, 221

Yakitenge, (paramount Bakalebwe chief), 241

Yakoma, 233

Yakombo, 201

Yale, 66

Yale Divinity School, 65, 142

Yalunka, 19, 22, 61, 81, 138, 152, 154, 155, 169, 170, 172, 174

traveling blacksmiths, 23

oppose Fula of Futa Jallon, 38

Yalunka Kamara, 139, 154

Yalunka Samura, clan, 138

Solimanga Samura as founder of, 138

Yambaisuk River, (Sherbro name for the Yambatui River), 94

Yambata, 202

Yambatui River, (Mende name for the Yambaisuk River), 94

Yams, 36, 199

Yamu Mwene Lunde Putu Kasongo, (Kiamfum or Yamwu), title, 284

Yamwu. See Yamu Mwene Lunde Putu Kasongo.

Yamutumbo Kaumbu, 241

Yana Tagesa, 139

Yandu, 93

Yangambi, 191, 242

Yania, 93
Yankaumbu. See Ngoyi Kaumbu.
Yan Kobah, 119, 120
Yanonge, 190, 191
Yarvai, 159
Yav a Yirung, 196
Yav, David, 216
Yavi Wuja, 94
Yeke, (Bayeke, Nyamweze), people, 232, 239, 268, 269, 270, 325
    army defeated, 269
Yeke, state, 327
Yele, 108
Yella Dansa, 154
Yellow fever, 1859 epidemic in Freetown, 49
Yenkain Kamara, 123
Yeri Pate, 139
Yifin, 39
Yima Yella, 154
Yindekuma, 113
Yira. See Mansa Kama.
Yirimusukali, 39
Yirisa Yella, 139
Yogbo, 54. See also Bora.
Yoko, Madam, (Soma), 70, 100, 107, 108, 157, 164, 165, 166
    fails to control sub-chiefs, 107, 108
    flees to Freetown, 108
    marries Gbanya Lango, 70
    during Hut Tax War, (1898), 28, 56

Yonge, Col., 120
Yongo, a Pende people, 254, 325, 327
Yoni Expedition of 1886-87, 166
Yoni, on Sherbro Island, 67, 98, 148, 166
    Rassin mediates in, 134
Yoni, clan, 120
    and disturbances of 1887-88, 24, 47, 70, 120, 126, 149, 168, 170
Yonso River, 284
York, Sierra Leone, 75, 96, 114, 135. See also Wilberforce and York electoral seat.
York Island, 169
Yoruba, 64
    allegedly descended from the Lost Tribes of Israel, 147
    in Sierra Leone, 21, 22, 65, 96, 103, 105, 114, 156, 168
    independent state for, proposed, 78
Youlou Fulbert, the Abbé, 311
Yser, battle of, 301
Yusufu, Bombo Lahai, (Bombolai), 49, 166, 167
Zaire, 40. See also Congo.
    ancient, 180, 181
    border with Angola, 238
    common national language proposed for, 210
    derivation of name, 327

Zaire River, (Congo River), 179, 180, 183, 185, 187, 191, 192, 198, 199, 200, 201, 204, 205, 207, 225, 238, 253, 257, 266, 267, 274, 275, 276, 277, 281, 286, 291, 292, 294, 296, 297, 299, 303, 305, 316, 317, 318, 319, 321, 322, 323, 324, 325
    cataracts on, 251, 308
    Diogo Cao at the mouth of, 267
    exploration of, 251
    Lukeni crosses, 238
    correct nomenclature of, 188, 327
    Portuguese on the, 280, 299
    H.M. Stanley establishes the course of, 184, 308
    steamers on the, 277, 288, 292
    trade on, 204, 205, 251, 280, 289, 291, 299
Zaire, Republic of, 179, 192, 196, 317, 318, 327
    name changed from the Republic of the Congo, 188
    place names changed in, (1971)
Zambezi River, 239
Zambia, 196, 214, 215, 300, 311, 317, 327
Zande, 183, 265, 285, 327
Zanzibar, 207
Zengo, 202
Zochonis, 145
Zulu campaign, 52
Zululand, 52